Y. Ben-Arieh

Jerusalem in the 19th Century
The Old City

YEHOSHUA BEN-ARIEH

Jerusalem in the 19th century

THE OLD CITY

Yad Izhak Ben Zvi Institute
Jerusalem 1984

St. Martin's Press, New York

© Copyright Yad Izhak Ben Zvi, POB 7660 Jerusalem, Israel, 1984
All rights reserved. For information, write:
St. Martin's Press, Inc., 175 Fifth Avenue, New York, NY 10010

Design: Pini, Jerusalem
Phototypesetting: Yad Izhak Ben Zvi; Plates: Tafsar; Printing: Daf-Chen
Printed in Israel
First published in the United States of America in 1984

ISBN 0-312-44187-8

LIBRARY OF CONGRESS CATALOGING IN PUBLICATION DATA
Ben-Arieh, Yehoshua.
    Jerusalem in the 19th century—the Old City.

    Translation of: Yerushalayim ba-me'ah ha-tesha'-'eśreh, ha-'Ir ha-'Atiḳah.
    "Sequel to... The rediscovery of the Holy Land in the nineteenth century"—Pref.
    Bibliography: p.
    Includes indexes.
    1. Jerusalem—History. 2. Jews—Jerusalem—History—19th century. I. Title.
DS109.925.B4713 1984   956.94'4   84-17769
ISBN 0-312-44187-8

Preface

Why a new book about Jerusalem? So much has been written about Jerusalem—the only city in the world holy to all three great monotheistic religions—that any new work runs the risk of merely summarizing or repeating previous material. The present book attempts to reconstruct a portrait of Jerusalem as it was in the nineteenth century, as reflected in contemporary writings. It is this, we believe, that gives it a unique flavor, both from the chronological point of view and—in particular—because of what we call its historical-geographical approach to the subject.

The nineteenth century marked a decisive turning point in the history of the city. In the early 1800's Jerusalem was still a small town in the heart of a rural district, with a population of 8,000-10,000 souls. By the end of the century, however, it had grown to become the capital of the Holy Land, extending far beyond the ancient city walls and boasting a population of over 70,000.

However, we are not interested merely in the study of nineteenth-century Jerusalem as an end in itself. The Jerusalem we know today is in many respects the product of developments which began in the nineteenth century. Conversely, many of the features of nineteenth-century Jerusalem that were modified or even swept away by those developments represent a situation which had not changed for centuries; they can therefore teach us a considerable amount about the city's past, including far-off periods concerning which our knowledge is sparse indeed.

The present book constitutes an attempt to implement the principle of synthesis customary in historical-geographical research, and to combine in one account the various components, passive as well as active, which, singly and in combination, have conditioned all facets of the city and its history. Geographical research aims at understanding the complex nature of places, regions and landscapes throughout the world, which are the products of various and sundry factors. A study, however thorough, of only one or a few of these factors may well miss its mark.

The above observations are certainly true when the object in question is a city, the sum result of the composite activity of those societies, communities, sects and so on that have inhabited it in the past and of those living in it today. For a historical-geographical study of a period in the history of a city, therefore, one must pinpoint and examine the actions and mutual relationships of the contemporary societies, as well as determine the influences brought to bear on them. And if this is the case for any city, all the more so for a city of such historical, cultural and spiritual value as Jerusalem — in a period that marked a dynamic turning-point in its history.

This work is actually a sequel to my earlier book, *The Rediscovery of the Holy Land in the Nineteenth Century*, which constituted the first phase in a historical-geographical study of the Land of Israel in modern times. Its aim was to evaluate the writings of travelers and explorers who visited the country in the nineteenth century, and to assess their contribution to the study of the land. We now proceed one step further, in an attempt to delve more deeply into the primary source material provided by these writers and indeed by all those who wrote about the development of Jerusalem in the period concerned.

Jerusalem in the Nineteenth Century is divided into two volumes: one dealing with the Old City, i.e., the area inside the ancient walls, and the other with the New City, outside the walls. In point of fact, this dichotomy is a consequence of our historical-geographical approach as outlined above, an approach which of necessity relates very differently to the two parts of the city. Thus, in Volume One our subject is an ancient, historical city, and we discuss the impress made upon it by the events of the nineteenth century; Volume Two, on the other hand, will be concerned with a new city growing up alongside the old, on ground formerly empty and uninhabited.

One result of this volume's concentration on the Old City alone is that events in Jerusalem at the end of the nineteenth century are treated only in brief, since the most significant developments at that time were taking place *outside* the walls. A more detailed account of those events must therefore be postponed to the second volume.

In our reconstruction of nineteenth-century Jerusalem we have made every attempt to capture the spirit of the times, for it is only through familiarity with contemporary historical-geographical conceptions and ideas that one can achieve a true understanding of the factors that have conditioned the development of a particular city or region. With this object in mind, we have incorporated in the text a considerable number of excerpts from contemporary sources. Moreover, most of our illustrations are original photographs or reproductions of original engravings.

There is a remarkable abundance of source material relating to nineteenth-century Jerusalem. A thorough understanding of such topics as demography, government and architecture would require going back to these aspects of earlier periods as well. However, we do not intend to cover the entire range of sources on Jerusalem — indeed this would be a practically impossible task for a single person. Our choice from this *embarras de richesse* has been governed by one consideration — the relevance of the material to our goal: to paint a historical-geographical portrait of Jerusalem in the specific period in question. Special attention has been paid to the early survey maps of Jerusalem; to the prolific writings of Western travelers, the Hebrew press and personal memoirs; as well as to sources which provide information about the structure of the city and other points of geographical interest.

The sources are listed at the end of the book in alphabetical order of the authors' names. Newspapers and archives referred to in the footnotes are not listed separately. Sources are cited by the author's name and an abbreviated form of the title (usually involving a few key words). If several editions of a specific item have appeared, with different pagination, the edition used is indicated in parentheses.

In preparing this study I have had recourse to several libraries, especially the Jewish National and University Library and its Judaic Studies Division, the Library of the Department of Antiquities at the Rockefeller Museum and the Yad Izhak Ben-Zvi Institute Library, all in Jerusalem. Most of the illustrations were reproduced from books in these libraries. I am indebted to these institutions and their staffs for their kind assistance.

In the course of my research, I have received financial assistance from the Central Research Fund and the Faculties of Humanities and the Social Sciences of the Hebrew University of Jerusalem, the Geography Department of the Hebrew University of Jerusalem, and the Research Division of the Yad Izhak Ben Zvi Institute.

I am indebted to my many students and colleagues at the Geography Department, who helped me both through the writing of reports and seminar papers on a variety of related subjects and through discussions of the many research problems associated with this important period in our national history.

Thanks are due to Mrs. Gila Brand for the devotion and talent she invested in translating this book from the Hebrew; to Mrs. Zfirah Rokeach, who ably edited the translation; to Mrs. Lucy Plitmann and Miss Sara Tsin, who prepared the index; and to Mr. David Louvish, who took considerable pains to prepare the book for the press. Finally, I wish to express my gratitude to the various people at Yad Izhak Ben-Zvi who have made the publication of this book possible, in particular: to former director Yehuda Ben-Porat and his successor, Zvi Zameret, who gave their support to the writing of the book and encouraged me to publish it in English as well; to Hananel Goldberg, who devotedly saw it through the press; and, last but not least, to Pini, who is responsible for its graphic design. My most sincere thanks to one and all!

Yehoshua Ben-Arieh
Jerusalem 1984

Table of Contents

Prologue

NINETEENTH-CENTURY JERUSALEM: THE SOURCES

Introduction

Before the nineteenth century, Jerusalem was rarely the subject of scientific research. It was portrayed in paintings and engravings of great artistic, and sometimes even of historical, value, but these were very far from being accurate cartographic descriptions of the city. Even after 1800, we find various maps which show extreme ignorance of the city's cartographic composition.[1] (See the Buckingham map below, p. 6).

Knowledge of Jerusalem's topographical and historical character before the nineteenth century was also exceedingly limited. Although travelers in previous centuries had recorded their theories about the location of various historical sites after investigating these matters, no attempt was then made to do methodical, scientific research. It was only in the nineteenth century that such inquiries and the first precise scientific mapping of the city were undertaken.

The Western travelers and researchers who began to probe Jerusalem at this time were primarily interested in historical Jerusalem — Jerusalem of the First and Second Temple, of the Muslim and the Crusader Periods. The city of their own day was of less interest to them. Nevertheless, their work contains valuable information about the nineteenth-century city. This may have been due to their desire to compare the Jerusalem of their time with the historical Jerusalem that had captured their interest. It may equally have resulted from their shock at the miserable conditions they encountered or, simply, from their wish to describe Jerusalem in its true colors. One way or another, the extensive Western travel and research literature of the nineteenth century offers us an abundance of material about Jerusalem's appearance, economy, inhabitants, sights and general development. The value of this material varies, of course, from writer to writer. The aims of these works, like the length of their authors' visits and their knowledge of the city, were not identical. Some visited the city for an extended period of time and carried out scientific research; others wrote their accounts after a hasty trip, on the basis of minimal knowledge of Jerusalem.

All of these sources, however, are of some value, especially for the first half of the century. So little other material is available for that period that the least morsel of information we can glean from them is significant for a reconstruction of the city's character and life-style. Obviously, the most reliable of these sources are the writings of scientific researchers and of those

_1_

---

1   Ben-Arieh, *Rediscovery,* pp. 11-17.

who spent long periods in Jerusalem, such as consuls, missionaries, doctors and other permanent residents of the city.

Before we proceed, let us consider Jerusalem's first survey maps, drawn up and published during the nineteenth century.

Mapping the City

The first steps in the scientific mapping of Jerusalem were taken by the German physician and botanist, F.W. Sieber, when he visited Jerusalem in 1818. Upon finding the existing maps of the city full of inaccuracies, he decided to draw up a new map based on precise geographical and topographical data. Taking some two hundred geometric bearings, he ascertained the precise position of the city walls, the various mosques, the Kidron Valley, and other topographically significant features. Sieber's map was highly praised because it was clear and a great deal more accurate than its predecessors. It too, however, contained many errors, particularly with regard to the network of valleys outside the city and the street system within it. Moreover, many important buildings seem not to have attracted Sieber's notice, while some of the structures he did indicate were wholly imaginary.[2]

Sieber's work spurred other researchers to map the city. Pioneer attempts in the 1820's and 1830's were carried out at the risk of reprisals by Muslim inhabitants, who frowned upon such activities of foreigners. Depicting the holy places in paintings and maps was considered sacrilegious by them. Several researchers working on the city wall were pelted with stones; others had to hide the nature of their work from local residents.[3]

The Egyptian occupation in 1831 led to a considerable improvement in security and many more researchers arrived in the country. Great progress in the study of Jerusalem was made during the 1830's. The first important contribution in this field was the mapping activity of the architect F. Catherwood and his colleagues in 1833. Their work was carried out in three parts: taking measurements, later used in drawing a general map of the city; preparing a "Jerusalem panorama"; and creating a detailed map of the Temple Mount. Catherwood took his equipment up to the roof of the tall building north of the Temple Mount known as Pontius Pilate's Palace.[4] It afforded him a view of the whole city, and enabled him, using a "camera lucida" composed of a series of prisms, to project an image of the city's panorama and of its important buildings onto paper.[5]

Catherwood's detailed map of the Temple Mount and, particularly, of the Dome of the Rock and of the Al-Aqṣa Mosque located there, included sketches of the outside of various buildings. Catherwood also sought to investigate and measure them from within, an act of great daring, since "infidels" who tried to enter Muslim holy places were then punishable by death. Before Catherwood's

2

2   For a facsimile of Sieber's map (1823) with brief explanations, see Meyer.
3   Ben-Arieh, *Pioneer*, pp. 95-100.
4   The home of the Turkish governor was so called because of the tradition that Pontius Pilate condemned Jesus on this spot. The building, on the Via Dolorosa, now houses the 'Omariyya School.
5   For more details about Catherwood's life and work, see Ben-Arieh, *Catherwood*, pp. 150-160.

time, no Western scholar had surveyed or mapped these sites from the outside, let alone from within. Two European travelers had, indeed, entered the holy places in the early nineteenth century, but their information was of limited value. In 1806, the Spanish nobleman known as El-Abbassi (Ali Bey) first disguised himself as a Muslim and then became a convert to Islam to facilitate his travels. The atlas appended to his book contains sketches and cross-sections of the Dome of the Rock and of other buildings on the Temple Mount, but these were based on observations and estimates arrived at covertly and recorded only afterwards, rather than on precise measurements recorded on the spot. Considering this, their relative accuracy is surprising.[6] In 1818, a British doctor, R. Richardson, also gained access to buildings on the Temple Mount, but his recorded impressions were more of a descriptive nature.[7]

Catherwood's general map of Jerusalem was used as a reliable base map of the city for nearly twenty years. Many researchers, including the well-known cartographer, Kippert, and the famous geographer-historian, Edward Robinson, used it as a basis for their own maps. Catherwood's map contributes relatively little specific detail, since he did not investigate the city itself; its importance lies in its correct cartographic portrayal of the city.

A new survey of Jerusalem was made in 1841, leading to the drawing of the second detailed map of the city: the British Admiralty map. The Turks had regained control over Palestine with the aid of the British navy, which had bombarded Acre and forced Ibrahim Pasha to withdraw. The navy then sent out several surveying parties to conduct mapping activities in the country. One party was sent to map Jerusalem and its environs, under the leadership of the British officers Alderson, Aldrich and Simmonds. C.R. Alderson, the leader of the whole operation, was the first to publish its findings. His reports, *Notes on Acre,* was published by the British Corps of Royal Engineers in 1844, together with topographical plans and cross-sections of the main coastal cities of Palestine, and a map of Jerusalem with explanatory notes.[8]

This map reached the general public in 1849, when it appeared as a supplement to the second edition of G. Williams' *The Holy City.* Williams provides a detailed description of the making of the "Ordnance Survey Map," which was based on the drawings made by Aldrich and Simmonds in 1841, and makes several corrections of it, particularly in the region of the Temple Mount. Williams also adds names and explanations—some quite detailed—of sites indicated on the map.[9]

The aims of this British expedition were different from those of previous researchers. It was less concerned with historical and religious sites than with places of military significance. For example, the Citadel of David appears, in a

---

6   El-Abbassi (Ali Bey) was a Christian Spaniard whose real name was Domingo Badia Y Leblich. Searching for a reputed Christian colony in Mórocco, he converted to Islam and adopted Muslim garb, traveling throughout North Africa and the Middle East in this disguise. See Ben-Arieh, *Rediscovery,* pp. 45-47; Bliss, *Exploration,* pp. 175-176.
7   Richardson, II, pp. 285, 308.
8   Alderson. A comprehensive article on the mapping activities of the Corps of Royal Engineers in Syria and Palestine was published by Yolande Jones in the *Journal of the British Cartographic Society* in 1973 (see Bibliography).
9   Williams, I (appendix in book flap).

detailed map drawn up by Alderson himself, in the margins of the general map of the city. In his notes, Alderson dwells upon the strategic importance of this site. On the other hand, the surveying party did not even enter the Temple Mount, conducting its mapping activities from roof-top observation points and using a theodolite.[10]

Jerusalem cartography was further advanced in the 1840's and 1850's by the work of the Swiss physician, T. Tobler. During his sojourn in Jerusalem in 1845, he made many measurements and came to know the streets and alleys of the city intimately (see p. 7). Tobler devoted much attention to topographic data, both inside and outside the city walls. He was less precise concerning the specific orientation of streets, giving only a general description of their plan. Nonetheless, his description provided far more detail than any previous map. He himself visited nearly all the city streets, asking the local inhabitants the names of streets and sites. Frequently, however, he was given a variety of answers and did not know which name to choose. He took particular pains to include all dead-end streets, because he regarded these as one of the characteristics of an Eastern city. Tobler's map of Jerusalem served as the basis of several others. When visiting the country for the second time, Robinson tried to coordinate the map of the Royal Engineers with that of Tobler, but found inaccuracies in the British map as well.

The Dutch cartographer, C.W.M. Van de Velde, arrived in 1851. Initially, he adopted the map of the Royal Engineers and made several corrections in it — particularly of its incorrect location of the corner of the Temple Mount and inaccurate depiction of the street network in the western part of the city. Eventually he found other errors and decided to prepare a new map instead. He used the British map, but made more use of the data provided by Tobler. Thus, the third detailed survey map of Jerusalem was born: the Tobler — Van de Velde map.[11]

This map was an important stride forward for Jerusalem cartography, but it too left something to be desired. While both Tobler and Van de Velde were careful to include all the new construction in the city, such as the Austrian Hospice or the Anglican cemetery on Mount Zion, they omitted some of the ancient names which had appeared on earlier maps. They hoped to provide a map which would serve the growing number of scholars studying Jerusalem, as well as help Christian pilgrims find their way to places of interest in and around the city.[12]

Two additional maps were published before the appearance of the detailed survey and map of Charles Wilson and his expedition: that of the Italian engineer, E. Pierotti,[13] and that of the American missionary-doctor, James Thomas Barclay.[14] Neither of them was wholly accurate, but these maps did contribute something to the development of Jerusalem cartography.

10   Williams, I, Supplement, pp. 9-13, 22, 31-34.
11   Tobler, *Planographie* (first edition, 1857; second edition, 1858).
12   Some of these maps also appeared in various guidebooks of Jerusalem published at the time.
13   Pierotti, Plan No. 2, *Jérusalem moderne*. In 1870, Pierotti published another, more detailed map of the city (see Bibliography).
14   Barclay, *Jerusalem and Environs*.

The most detailed and accurate scientific-mapping project carried out in nineteenth-century Jerusalem was that of Charles Wilson. In an effort to improve the city's water-supply system, Lady Burdett-Coutts, a British philanthropist, contributed £500 toward a survey of the city; a similar amount was collected from other contributors. A group sent by the Corps of Royal Engineers, led by a young officer named Charles Wilson, undertook the mission. Wilson and six other members of the corps arrived in Jerusalem in 1864. Eleven months later, in May of 1865, the survey was complete.

Wilson used this new material about Jerusalem to prepare the three-volume *Ordnance Survey of Jerusalem,* complete with plans and photographs, which was published by the British War Office a year later. The report contains, among other things, an extremely accurate survey of the changes in altitude between Jaffa and Jerusalem, and between Jerusalem and the Dead Sea and Solomon's Pools; its data were obtained by means of a theodolite and measuring rods. It includes an accurate map of Jerusalem (on a scale of 1:2,500), and one of the surrounding area (1:10,000), as well as plans of the Citadel of David, the Temple Mount and the Church of the Holy Sepulchre. Forty-three photographs of Jerusalem's walls, gates and buildings also appear.[15] (See Wilson's map, reproduced on p. 15 below.)

Later, Wilson served as one of the heads of the Palestine Exploration Fund together with his friend, Charles Warren. Their joint publications provide us with fascinating information about the city of Jerusalem in the nineteenth century.

Wilson's map seems to have brought the scientific mapping of Jerusalem to a close. Other maps of Jerusalem appeared throughout the nineteenth century; their importance lies in their providing us with a picture of the city's development in the second half of the century. The most notable of them is the map published by Conrad Schick in 1894-1895 in the German periodical *ZDPV.* In the thirty years between the publication of Wilson's map and that of Schick, great changes had occurred in the built-up areas of Jerusalem, especially outside the walls. Schick's map was the first to include all of the extensive New City. A comparison of these two maps illustrates just how great the change had been.[16] (A revised edition of Wilson's map appeared in 1876, incorporating new buildings constructed in the city since 1864-1865.)

Foremost among the maps that appeared between those of Wilson and Schick was the one presented by D. Guthe in *Palästina in Bild und Worte.* This map showed only the Old City and the area immediately around it, but gave special emphasis to public institutions; its portrayal of the city's built-up area was accurate for the early 1880's.[17] Another important map of the Old City, dating from 1883, was that of Dr. Sanderezki. Published in the *ZDPV,* it offered a program for touring the city, noting the names of different places, streets and neighborhoods.[18]

15   Ch. Wilson, *Survey.*
16   Schick, *ZDPV,* 1894-1895; a second edition, revised by Benzinger, appeared in *ZDPV,* 1904-1905.
17   Ebers — Guthe; this book is largely an adaptation of the English *Picturesque Palestine* (ed. Ch. Wilson), but the map is original and appears at the end of Vol. I, p. 505.
18   *ZDPV,* 1883, 1:2,500 map at beginning of volume, and explanatory article, pp. 43-80.

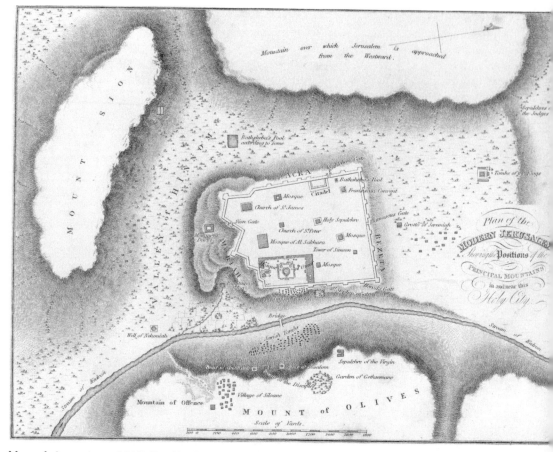

Map of Jerusalem, 1816 (Buckingham, p. 278)

A. Kümmel produced a noteworthy map of the Old City in the early twentieth century.[19] A number of other maps, mostly unrevised, appeared between 1894-1895 and World War I. The most significant of these was Dr. Benzinger's 1905 revision of Schick's map, and the map presented by L.H. Vincent in his book *Jérusalem: Recherches de Topographie, d'Archéologie et d'Histoire*. The latter shows Jerusalem's built-up area as of 1911 and, although many of its details are inaccurate, gives a reasonably correct over-all picture.[20] There are aerial photographs and other maps of Jerusalem dating from World War I and the beginning of the British Mandate, but these are outside the limits of our period.

Nineteenth-Century Researchers

The most important of all the Western students of early nineteenth-century Jerusalem was U.J. Seetzen. He was not a great expert on the ancient history of Jerusalem, but his scientific approach and sharp eye enabled him to make a

6

19   Kümmel (1904), Map of Old Jerusalem (1:2,500).
20   Vincent, end of Vol. I.

significant contribution to the study of Jerusalem as it was in his own time.[21] Only after his visit did other travelers begin to take an interest in the city's historical topography.

The other researcher who laid the foundations of the scientific study of Jerusalem was Edward Robinson. His *Biblical Researches in Palestine* shows how much attention he paid to a thorough historical familiarity with the city. Robinson was extremely interested in the work of Catherwood, and appended to his book a map adapted from Catherwood by Kippert. Robinson explored the Siloam Tunnel, which he describes very much as Warren was to do at a later date; the "protrusion" in the Wailing Wall known subsequently as Robinson's Arch; the remains of the Third City Wall, and other sites. Not satisfied with studying only historical Jerusalem, he described the contemporary city, dwelling upon the state of its various sites, population, economy, houses and water supply, among other subjects.[22] The publication of Robinson's book sparked a fierce battle among scholars over Jerusalem's topography and the location of its holy places. One of Robinson's most extreme opponents was George Williams, who also published a comprehensive work about Jerusalem.[23] David Roberts and William Henry Bartlett, both of them artists, visited Jerusalem at about the same time as Robinson, and prepared many paintings of the Jerusalem landscape.[24]

Tobler was another visitor who did much to enhance our understanding of nineteenth-century Jerusalem. Following his first visit (in 1835), he published a book in which he declared it a pity that there was no scientific investigation of Jerusalem. He believed that neither religious nor secular considerations should prevent archaeological excavations and other research. In 1845, Tobler returned to Palestine, spending some twenty weeks in and around Jerusalem. He made two other visits in 1857 and 1865, publishing his impressions and findings each time.[25]

Among the travelers who wrote about Jerusalem in the 1830's, 1840's and 1850's were A.S. Norov, V. Monro, J. Wilson, F.A. Strauss, E.W. Schulz, R.W. Stewart and W.H. Dixon.[26] The diary of the Greek monk Neophytus is a special source of information for the period 1821-1841.[27] Christian missionaries too, who had many opportunities to study the sites and ruins of

21 Seetzen, 4 volumes. See Ben-Arieh, *Rediscovery,* pp. 31-43; *Pioneer,* pp. 95-110.
22 There is a considerable literature on Robinson. See Ben-Arieh, *Rediscovery,* pp. 85-91; Bliss, *Exploration,* pp. 184-223; Benzinger, in Hilprecht, pp. 585-588.
23 As stated above, this book contains the British Admiralty Map as an appendix. The relations between Williams and Robinson seem to have been quite strained. In the introduction to the first edition of his book, Williams attacks Robinson for his heretical views about the location of the Church of the Holy Sepulchre. Robinson denounces Williams for the inaccuracy of the British Admiralty Map.
24 For information about Roberts and Bartlett, see Ben-Arieh, *Rediscovery,* pp. 80-83; 92-99; 142-143.
25 On Tobler, see *ibid.,* pp. 133-139, 165-168; Benzinger, in Hilprecht, pp. 588-591. The list of Tobler's works in Röhricht's bibliography extends over three pages, comprising 51 publications. As stated, Tobler also made a major contribution to Jerusalem cartography.
26 For the books of these travelers and others, see Bibliography.
27 This 70-page diary was translated into English by Spyridon and published in 1938 (see Bibliography: Spyridon).

Jerusalem, wrote about the city. For example, Barclay's *The City of the Great King* was published in 1857, with a wealth of information. Barclay also produced a map of Jerusalem; one of the ancient gates of the Temple Mount was named in his honor. Another missionary, W.M. Thomson, also provides us with insights into nineteenth-century Jerusalem,[28] while the writings of the British consul James Finn and those of his wife are important sources.[29] Carl Ritter's work provides a summary of the first half of the century; the writings of A.P. Stanley, H.B. Tristram and V. Guérin contain descriptive accounts of the 1850's and 1860's.[30]

A great deal of valuable material about Jerusalem appears in travel guides of the second half of the century, such as that written by the Franciscan friar, Liévin de Hamme, which appeared in French in 1869, 1875, 1887 and 1897. An English edition appeared in 1876, the year in which the famous *Baedeker Guide* was published. By 1912, six editions of Baedeker had been printed, in German, English and French.[31]

The first archaeological investigations of Jerusalem began in the mid-nineteenth century. When the French archaeologist F. de Saulcy visited the city in 1850-1851, he began to excavate the Tomb of the Kings. Although this was not a scientific dig, it is generally considered to be the first archaeological excavation in Palestine. De Saulcy published several volumes about Jerusalem in later years.[32]

Pierotti was an Italian engineer employed by the Ottoman authorities from 1854-1866. He too was interested in investigating the Holy City, and enjoyed access to many places in connection with his duties. In 1864, he published his *Jerusalem Explored,* with many plans and drawings.[33]

As we noted above, Charles Wilson conducted a cartographic survey of Jerusalem in the mid-1860's. Following the completion of this survey, the Palestine Exploration Fund (PEF) was established in London; one of its express aims was to further archaeological and historical research concerning Jerusalem. Just as Charles Wilson's work had marked the end of the scientific-experimental stage of Jerusalem cartography, the excavations carried out by his colleague, Warren, marked the beginning of scientific archaeological research in the city. Exploration of the city in the first half of the century had been characterized by a series of pioneering scientific maps; exploration in its second half was characterized by pioneering archaeological enterprises.

The first proper archaeological expedition in Jerusalem was that of Warren,

28 See Bibliography; Ben-Arieh, *Rediscovery,* pp. 163-167.
29 Much has been written about Consul and Mrs. Finn and their aid to the Jewish community. Opinions are divided over whether this aid was purely philanthropic or motivated by missionary intentions.
30 Ritter's resumé was adapted and edited by W.L. Gage. For more details about these explorers and their writings, see Bibliography and Ben-Arieh, *Rediscovery,* Index of Persons. Aside from these famous guidebooks, there are others relating to Palestine and Jerusalem.
31 In *Rediscovery,* I cited the guidebooks of Conder (1825), J. Murray (first edition—1858, second edition—1868, third edition—1875) and others.
32 See Bibliography and Ben-Arieh, *Rediscovery,* Index of Persons.
33 Pierotti's scientific opinions were much criticized in his day; see Ben-Arieh, *Rediscovery,* pp. 173-174. Nevertheless, his maps and illustrations are of great importance for understanding nineteenth-century Jerusalem.

dispatched by the PEF in 1867. Warren and his men spent three years digging at different sites in the city, particularly around the Temple Mount, in the Ophel region and in the "City of David." Their numerous findings appeared in various publications. Charles Wilson, of course, had begun to probe Jerusalem's past during his mapping mission. He had explored various hidden, underground structures, such as the famous arch north of the Wailing Wall, still known as "Wilson's Arch" although Tobler had discovered it before him. In 1871, after the Warren expedition had terminated its activities, Warren and Wilson published a joint account of their work, *The Recovery of Jerusalem.* In 1876, Warren published another book, *Underground Jerusalem.* The two books contain a great deal of interesting information about ancient, and about nineteenth-century, Jerusalem.[34]

The PEF published material about Palestine from its very inception. In 1869, the organization began to issue a regular journal, whose cover featured an illustration of the excavations around the wall of the Temple Mount. This journal contained a considerable amount of information about historical and contemporary Jerusalem.[35] In 1884, the PEF published a collection of maps, plans and sketches of Jerusalem and of its antiquities which summarized the state of archaeological knowledge of the city at that time. It also devoted a special volume of *The Survey of Western Palestine* to Jerusalem, correcting the findings of Warren and Wilson, and providing additional material about Jerusalem in the nineteenth century.[36]

Another scholar who contributed greatly to research about Jerusalem was the Swiss-born Conrad Schick. Schick, who settled in Jerusalem in the mid-nineteenth century, witnessed the discovery of its ancient sites and the broadening of knowledge about them. Many of his articles about Jerusalem appeared in the PEF journal. He also prepared models of the Temple and of the Church of the Holy Sepulchre. Schick built himself a house called "Thabor" on the Street of the Prophets (it houses the Swedish Theological Seminary today), and took an active part in the planning of many important neighborhoods and buildings in the city.[37]

In 1877, a special society for the exploration of Palestine was set up in Germany. The *Deutscher Palästina-Verein* (DPV) sponsored an archaeological dig in the City of David in 1881, under the direction of the German, Hermann Guthe. Conrad Schick helped him, and was a frequent contributor to the society's journal, the *ZDPV.* Some of the articles written by Schick and by others appeared simultaneously in the journals of the DPV and PEF, in German and in English.[38]

Other archaeological excavations were carried out at the end of the nineteenth century. For our purposes, these are much less important than the

---

34   See Bibliography: Wilson, Warren; Ben-Arieh, *Rediscovery*; Watson, pp. 41-53.

35   The numerous volumes of the *PEF QSt* offer a virtual treasure trove of information about Palestine in the nineteenth century (and other periods, too).

36   Warren—Conder, *Jerusalem;* see Bibliography.

37   Schick's models of Jerusalem are located in the St. Paulus Hospice (Schmidt School) opposite the Damascus Gate. Also see *NNADO,* 1902, pp. 2-12.

38   *PEF QSt* and *ZDPV;* see Bibliography.

earlier ones, since their reports concentrated on scientific findings and dealt less with the contemporary city and its residents. In addition, the many other sources at our disposal offer a nearly complete account of the period. Nevertheless, we will describe a few of the excavations in order to round out our survey of historical-archaeological research prior to World War I.

One of the sites of important archaeological digs at the end of the nineteenth century was Mount Zion. In 1874, when the English Mission was digging the foundations for its school, the remnants of an ancient wall of hewn stone were discovered. These remnants were studied by the British engineer, Maudsley, who found there a tall boulder bearing ancient chisel marks, subsequently known as the Pillar of Zion or Maudsley's Pillar. In 1894, a PEF expedition led by F.S. Bliss, the American archaeologist, arrived in Jerusalem to explore Mount Zion and the area east of it. On the grounds of the Protestant school, Bliss discovered the foundations of the First Wall, which had encircled the Upper City in the days of the Second Temple. He also excavated around the Siloam Pool and unearthed an ancient church dating from about 450 C.E., built by Eudocia, the wife of the Byzantine emperor Theodosius. Bliss returned to England after three years of work, and published the results of his explorations in a special volume.[39]

Another archaeological expedition to Jerusalem was the British one led by M. Parker from 1909-1911. This expedition created an uproar in the Muslim community because it was rumored that Parker had infiltrated the hidden underground chambers beneath the Temple site through secret passageways, and had stolen precious treasures belonging to King David. The Parker expedition was chiefly involved in exploring the City of David. Its findings, important for an understanding of Biblical Jerusalem, were published in 1911 by Père Vincent of the Dominican monastery in Jerusalem, in both English and French.[40]

There was also an expedition financed by the famous philanthropist, Baron Rothschild, that excavated in the City of David in 1913 under the leadership of the French Jew, Raymond Weill. This expedition discovered vaulted tunnels and rock-niches, apparently graves, which had been plundered in ancient times. Weill was certain that he had found the tombs of the kings of the House of David, and received the support of some scholars for his hypothesis. He also unearthed an interesting Greek inscription testifying to the existence of an ancient synagogue and hospice. Excavation was halted when World War I broke out, but continued after the war.[41]

The reports of the various archaeological expeditions are a source of fascinating information, both descriptive and cartographic, about progress made in nineteenth-century Jerusalem. At the end of the nineteenth century and in the beginning of the twentieth, various archaeological research

39 Bliss, *Excavations.*
40 As did many French historians of his time, Vincent included in his book, which was essentially an archeological and historical work, an extensive physical introduction to the city with geological and physical maps. He also provided a map of modern Jerusalem (as pointed out previously).
41 Weill, *La Cité de David,* 1920; see Bibliography.

institutions were established in Jerusalem, and tourism began to expand. Both these subjects will be dealt with in the second volume of this work.

Community Records and Consular Archives

Important data about nineteenth-century Jerusalem may also be retrieved from another kind of source: the records of the various communities and the consular archives of such countries as England, Germany and the United States. These, however, deal mainly with the second half of the century, and do not always serve us in our attempt to recreate historical and geographical Jerusalem. British and German consular records, the publications of the English missionary societies that were very active in Jerusalem during the nineteenth century, and the writings of permanent residents, however, have provided an important source for our study.

Very few Arabic works or Ottoman documents pertaining to the nineteenth century are now available. The only material published as of now deals with the end of the Ottoman period, that is, with the beginning of the twentieth century. It is possible that Ottoman records from earlier times may be discovered in archives in Turkey at some future date, but no such records are now known. The fact that the archives of many consulates, missionary societies and research associations which operated in nineteenth-century Jerusalem are now located in their home countries has not made research any easier.

It is also very likely that there is a wealth of information hidden away in the archives of various community groups and institutions, such as the Muslim *waqf, majlis* and *maḥkame*; the monasteries and different Christian sects; or the numerous Jewish organizations and *kolelim.* However, our primary goal is the reconstruction of Jerusalem's urban geography. For this purpose, those sources we have already noted are the most valuable: the first maps of Jerusalem, the prolific writings of Western explorers, and the Jewish sources (about which I will have more to say presently). Of course, I have used other sources as much as possible; they are listed in the bibliography at the end of the book.

Jewish Sources .

There is relatively little Jewish source material for the first half of the nineteenth century. From the 1860's onward, however, more is available, including Hebrew newspapers which mirror the city's development. The Jewish sources concentrate on the affairs of the Jewish community, providing very little information about other communities or general developments in Jerusalem. There is almost no cartographic material in them.

A certain amount of information about events in early nineteenth-century Palestine may be gleaned from the letters of the Gaon of Vilna's disciples, who immigrated at this time, and from the memoirs of Jewish community leaders. An unusual travel book written in the beginning of the century is that of Rabbi David de-Beth Hillel. For more important data about this early period, however, we must turn to Jewish sources of somewhat later date.

The most significant Jewish source for the beginning of the nineteenth century is Rabbi Joseph Schwarz's *Tevuot Ha-aretz*. Another source is *Korot Ha'ittim* by Rabbi Menaḥem Mendel of Kamieniec (1839) which, apart from describing the author's own experiences, was intended as a guide for new immigrants.

Influenced by Rabbi Menaḥem Mendel, Rabbi Moses Reicher wrote *Sha'arei Yerushalayim,* a Hebrew guide book for the benefit of newcomers to Palestine. It appeared in 1874, but seems to have been written in 1866-1867. Despite its late date, the book contains valuable information about the early part of the century. Reicher reports on the country's holy places, contemporary Jewish community, local foods and customs, government, coins, weights and measures, and much more. Reicher states that his book was written to encourage the Jews of the Diaspora to come and live in Palestine. This work is valuable for those interested in learning about daily life in nineteenth-century Palestine, but it is not wholly accurate and must be used with care. Another important book about Jerusalem, written slightly earlier (1858), is Dr. Ludwig August Frankl's *Nach Jerusalem.*

Other Jewish sources include the letters of Eliezer Halevi; the travel diaries of Sir Moses and Lady Judith Montefiore; the letters of Rabbi M.N. Cahanyu; the writings of Dr. Neumann, who served as chief physician of the Rothschild Hospital in Jerusalem from 1847, for fifteen years; the correspondence of the Jewish dignitaries of Jerusalem; and the Jewish press abroad, which reported on events in the Holy City.

The memoirs of long-time Jerusalem residents are yet another source of information. Most of these were published later, but contain a wealth of important data on the nineteenth century. Among them are the works of Joshua Yellin, Ephraim Cohen-Reiss, Mordechai Solomon, Joseph Rivlin and Isaac Schirion.

Following in the footsteps of Rabbi Joseph Schwarz, Rabbi Abraham Moshe Luncz established a regular forum for the study of Palestine and for general Judaic studies. His chief works include the thirteen-volume *Yerushalayim*, twenty-one Eretz-Yisrael almanacs and guidebooks in Hebrew, German and Yiddish. Much has been written about Luncz and it would be impossible here to evaluate his contribution. Suffice it to say that no study of nineteenth-century Jerusalem would be possible without a thorough examination of his many works.

P. Grayevsky is the most prominent of authors of compendia about the Jewish community of Jerusalem and the Old Yishuv in Palestine, but many other scholars have written similar summaries.

Conclusion

There is no doubt that the source material available today for the reconstruction of nineteenth-century Jerusalem is rich and varied. Many types of sources can be employed for this purpose. Yet it must be stressed that no single source or group of sources can provide us with complete, authoritative, and reliable information on its own. Only the simultaneous use of all these sources will enable us to create an accurate geographical-historical portrait of nineteenth-century Jerusalem.

Part One

The Old City: Its Appearance, Sources of Livelihood, Water Supply and Sanitation

Chapter One:
THE CITY PLAN; THE BUILT-UP AREA

The City Layout

The main geographical features of the Old City of Jerusalem, the layout of its built-up area, its city wall, its gates and streets, its markets and various quarters, originated not in the nineteenth century but in much earlier times. Accordingly, we will deal not with origins, but with Jerusalem as it was in the nineteenth century.

In the first half of that century, Jerusalem was confined to the Old City, whose total area, including the spacious Temple compound, was no more than some 0.85 sq. km. Charles Wilson, the famous nineteenth-century explorer, describes the Old City as follows:

> The form of the city may be described as that of an irregular rhomb or lozenge, the longest diagonal of which runs from N.E. to S.W., and is 4,795 feet or less than a mile long. The northern side is 3,390 feet long, the eastern 2,754 feet, the southern 3,245 feet, and the western 2,086 feet long, as measured straight from point to point.
> The total area of the city within the walls is 209.5 acres — or one-third of a square mile; but in addition to the large area of the Haram-es-Sherif, which is 35 acres, there are many open places about the city walls which are not built upon.[1]

In the nineteenth century, as in earlier periods, the Old City was divided into several quarters. However, it was only in the early nineteenth century that these quarters began to be called by the names familiar to us today. The names "Armenian Quarter" and "Christian Quarter," for instance, do not appear in European travelers' writings before 1806.[2]

In the nineteenth century, the Old City was customarily divided into four or five quarters: The Muslim, Christian, Armenian and Jewish quarters; the Mughrabi neighborhood was often cited as a fifth. None of the so-called quarters covered one-fourth of the city's area: the Jewish Quarter was said to have encompassed only one-twelfth of it.[3] The Armenian Quarter was also less than one-fourth of the Old City.

While these quarters were not entirely homogeneous in the composition of their populations, most Jerusalemites preferred to live near members of their own community in distinct neighborhoods. There were no Jews in the Christian Quarter, although Christians of various denominations and even a few Muslims lived there together. On the other hand, there were Muslims living in the Jewish Quarter and Jews living in the Muslim Quarter. Many Jews

14

1   Wilson, *Survey*, I. p. 8.
2   Tobler, *Denkblätter*, pp. 121-126.
3   *Ibid.*; see also Bovet, pp. 147-148.

Map of Jerusalem, 1864-65 (Ch. Wilson, *Survey*)

moved to the Muslim Quarter towards the end of the nineteenth century, because of Jewish population growth and the resultant overcrowding in the Jewish Quarter (see below, pp. 315-317). The larger quarters of the city were further subdivided according to the residence patterns of various religious denominations and topographical conditions. In the Christian Quarter, for example, Latin, Greek, Coptic, Ethiopian and other districts were sometimes distinguished. The Sephardi and Ashkenazi neighborhoods of the Jewish Quarter were more or less distinct. As time went on, Jewish immigrants tended to concentrate in groups according to their countries of origin and mother tongues. The Muslim Quarter was divided topographically into three sectors: the area west of the Tyropoeon Valley, the region east of it, and the valley itself (see below).

The City Wall and "The Citadel of David"

Nineteenth-century travelers found the Old City wall most impressive. Their numerous descriptions mention its stability, towers and gates, as well as the

Citadel of David
(Wilson, *Picturesque Palestine,* I, p. 5)

adjacent fosses and valleys, which were important for defense purposes.[4]

These descriptions note the existence of a path around the outside of the wall, from which the landscape could be viewed from various angles. Seetzen (1806) says it took about an hour to follow this interesting and varied route, which was an attraction for visitors. Norov (1835) says that the path was about four kilometers long, and that there was a much longer one at the foot of the hills around the city.[5]

The most frequently described site in nineteenth-century Jerusalem was the Phasael Tower, known to travelers as "The Citadel of David," "The Tower of David," or by some similar name. Seetzen (1806) writes that the "Citadel of Jerusalem" near the Hebron Gate (Bab al-Khalil, the Jaffa Gate) was a small fortress whose external wall was the city wall. Within the city walls, a stone-paved fosse separated this citadel from the alley running alongside it; there was a drawbridge over the fosse which could be raised. Several cannons were stationed at the entrance, with a Turkish officer and a few soldiers doing guard-duty inside.[6]

Turner (1815) says that Christian pilgrims were forbidden to enter the Citadel and that only a few of the thirteen cannons at the site seemed to be in working order. Tobler reports the presence of about one hundred Albanian soldiers there in the early 1820's. A decade later, Skinner says, only one or two

16

4   Wilson, *Survey,* I, p. 9: Strauss, p. 202.
5   Seetzen, II, p. 202; Norov, I, pp. 281-289.
6   Seetzen, II, pp. 23-24.

Citadel of David (Roberts)

cannons could be seen within the Citadel's walls. In 1835, Norov reports that the strong Citadel walls contained six towers and a weak military force, protected by dry moats. The small number of cannons there would suffice only for short-term defensive purposes. Ever since the Crusades, the two main towers had been called the towers of the Pisans, in honor of their rebuilders. Aside from a few old weapons, the fortress held nothing of note. Ewald says that in 1842 there were benches along both sides of the wooden bridge leading into the Citadel, and that the pashas of Jerusalem would sit on them and smoke with their officers.[7]

The margins of the British Admiralty map dating from the early 1840's contain a detailed plan of the Citadel of David drawn up by Colonel Alderson. Alderson emphasizes the Citadel's importance for defending the city; he states that it was equipped with artillery and vulnerable only to the heaviest of artillery attacks. In his opinion, this was demonstrated during the Peasants' Rebellion in the days of Ibrahim Pasha, when the rebels took over the whole city but failed to take the Citadel; the Egyptian forces at the site were able to maintain their positions, thereby facilitating Egypt's recapture of the city.[8]

Tobler relates that two large military camps were located in Jerusalem in the mid-1840's: the "Saraya" on the site of Pilate's Palace on the Via Dolorosa,

17

7   Turner, II, p. 168; Tobler, *Topographie,* I (relates to the years 1818 and 1821), p. 195; Skinner, I, p. 200; Norov, I, pp. 195-197; Ewald, I, pp. 52-53.
8   Williams, I, Supplement, pp. 22-23.

Jaffa Gate, mid-19th century (Bartlett, *Jerusalem Revisited*, title page)

and a new one at the Citadel, which was rebuilt by Ibrahim Pasha in 1838 and which had a modern army camp alongside it.[9]

The Citadel of David continued to serve as a military base throughout the nineteenth century. Charles Wilson, who surveyed and mapped Jerusalem in 1864-1865, provides us with a detailed plan of the Citadel and of the nearby Turkish army camp (the "Kishleh"), as well as with photographs of the surrounding area.[10]

The PEF volume devoted to Jerusalem states that Liévin drew a plan of the Citadel, as did Charles Wilson after him. Conder visited and described the site in 1872; it was mapped again in 1877, by Kitchener. All of these men indicate the ruins present there. In 1877 much of the rubble was removed. According to the PEF volume, the water in the Citadel cisterns was obtained from the Pool of Mamilla by means of an aqueduct. A market near the Citadel had apparently been built above a series of "trenches" whose entrance was located on a slope southeast of the Citadel.[11]

An 1876 issue of the newspaper *Ha-Levanon* reports that distinguished guests were welcomed to the city by salvoes fired from the cannon in the Citadel of David.[12] Liévin's guidebook notes in the early 1870's that one still needed a special permit from the Pasha to enter the Citadel.[13] According to a later edition, the entire Citadel was in a very bad state, except for the towers. It was

9   Tobler, *Denkblätter*, pp. 632-656.
10 Wilson, *Survey*, vols. of maps and photos. "Kishleh" is derived from the Turkish for "winter barracks"; see also below, p. 111.
11 Warren—Conder, *Jerusalem*, pp. 267-270. For a detailed account of the Citadel, including a plan, see *ZDPV*, I, 1878, 227-243.
12 *Ha-Levanon*, 28 Shevat, 1876, vol. XII, no. 18, p. 222.
13 Liévin (English), p. 105.

Damascus Gate, mid-19th century (Bartlett, *Jerusalem Revisited,* p. 187)

then occupied by several soldiers and served as an arsenal.[14] A detailed account of the Citadel in the 1870's is presented by Orelli: its interior was extremely ill-kept and the stairs, half ruined, had been replaced in some areas by ladders. The tower, which dominated the city, contained several extremely unattractive prison cells.[15] During early Mandatory times, there was free access to the Citadel. The courtyard was cleaned of its filth, but the inner buildings were still in ruins.[16]

The City Gates

According to nineteenth-century travelers, only four gates of the Old City were open during the first half of the century, one in each direction. All of them had L-shaped passages through which one entered, in order to prevent invading forces from bursting into the city.

Most frequently described was the Jaffa Gate, known also as the Bethlehem Gate, the Hebron Gate (Bab al-Khalil) or the Pilgrims' Gate. Physically impressive due to its proximity to the Citadel of David, this gate was the busiest of them all, constantly bustling with activity. All those entering the city through it were subject to thorough inspection by the military sentry. Apparently, special troops were garrisoned nearby in the Citadel in order to guard the gates, maintain order in the city, greet new pashas and important guests, and so on.[17]

In the 1850's, Wortabet mentions the existence of a customs house inside the

19

14   Liévin (1897), p. 297.
15   Orelli, pp. 186-187.
16   Zuta—Sukenik (1920), p. 80.
17   Ewald, pp. 52-53.

walls, near the Jaffa Gate. A small raised area outside the gate, near the north-western corner of the wall, served as Jerusalem's promenade; it was called the Jaffa Plain, because it was located on the high road to Jaffa. It was here that Jerusalemites would come at night for a breath of fresh air. A small café surrounded by grapevines was there as well, for their refreshment.[18]

The second most important gate was the Damascus or Shechem (Nablus) Gate—also known as the Gate of the Pillar, the Valley Gate or the Gate of Ephraim—in the northern wall of the Old City.[19] This was considered the most beautiful of all the gates, but it was less busy in the nineteenth century than the Jaffa Gate, even though all east- and north-bound traffic had to pass through it.

The eastern wall of the city contained a gate known today as the Lions' Gate because of the supposed lions carved on the Wall—two on each side. European travelers of the nineteenth century usually referred to it as St. Stephen's Gate, as St. Stephen was believed to have been stoned to death several hundred meters from this gate; many people went to that site in the nineteenth century to atone for their sins.[20] Other names for this gate included the Gate of the Tribes[21] and Mary's Gate. The latter name was used often by Christian travelers, who passed through it on their way to the tomb of the Virgin Mary, east of the Kidron stream. This gate also led towards the Mount of Olives, Bethany, Jericho and the Jordan River.[22]

The gate we know as the Zion Gate was often called the Gate of David, because of the nearby tomb associated with King David, on Mount Zion. Some travelers, however, point out that the Arabic inscription on the gate calls it the Zion Gate.[23]

In the first half of the nineteenth century, the Dung Gate (also known as the Gate of the Mughrabis, the Tyropoeon Gate and the Silwan Gate) was used infrequently. Stewart (1854) writes that the gate had been closed until a year before his visit to Jerusalem. It had then been reopened to allow water to be brought more easily from Ein Rogel. According to Stewart, the opening of the gate was exploited mainly by Arab villagers, who used it to reach the market-place.[24] Barclay (1857) indicates that the Gate of the Mughrabis in the Tyropoeon Valley was closed except in times of drought, when it was opened for a few hours each day to enable water carriers to bring water to the city from Bir Ayyub (Ein Rogel).[25]

Charles Wilson (1864-1865) reports that five gates were then open: the Jaffa Gate, the Damascus Gate, St. Stephen's Gate, the Zion Gate and the Dung Gate. Five others not in use were Herod's Gate (=Bab al-Zahira, mistakenly translated as the Flower Gate) in the northern wall, the Golden Gate in the

18   Wortabet, II, pp. 203-205. See also below, pp. 34-37.
19   See, e.g., Petermann, I, pp. 200-201.
20   Scherer, pp. 184-189.
21   Luncz, *Guide,* pp. 100-101.
22   J. Wilson, pp. 416-417.
23   Norov, I. p. 198; Vincent—Lee—Bain, p. 159.
24   Stewart, p. 262.
25   Barclay, pp. 431-432.

eastern wall of the Temple Mount, and the Single, Double and Triple Gates in the southern wall of the Temple Mount.[26]

Tobler, on his fourth visit to Palestine (1865), notes that the Dung Gate, which formerly had been closed, was now open.[27] Much later (1891), Luncz mentions that this exceedingly small gate had been open for the previous forty years,[28] which accords with our knowledge that the gate had been reopened in the 1850's.

The gate called Herod's Gate by the Christians and Bab al-Zahira by the Muslims was also closed during most of the century, being reopened to traffic only in 1875. According to the 1876 edition of the Baedeker Guide, Herod's Gate had been closed for twenty-five years but had recently been opened for several months each year to facilitate troop exchanges.[29] Luncz (1891) says that the stones that had blocked it until 1875 were removed at the request of the residents of the Bab Huta neighborhood of the Old City.[30]

In 1889-1890, the city wall near the northwestern corner of the Old City was breached and the New Gate built, so as to provide easy access from the Christian Quarter to the new monasteries and hospices for pilgrims built outside the walls. Liévin stresses that this gate, the eighth in the city walls, was simple and unadorned.[31] Luncz (1891) notes that the New Gate was located opposite the French Hospice and had been opened to allow hospice guests direct access to the Old City.[32]

Another change in the city wall was made in 1898: the wall between the Jaffa Gate and the Citadel was torn down and the fosse filled in so as to enable Kaiser Wilhelm II and his entourage to enter the city on horseback.

Apparently, the Golden Gate, also called the Gate of Mercy (Bab al-Rahma), the Gate of Eternity (Bab al-Dahiriya), and the Gate of Repentence (Bab al-Tauba), was blocked by stones because of an Arab superstition that Muslim control of Jerusalem would be lost if a foreigner came through it. Roberts (1839) notes that the Golden Gate had been opened once a year during the Crusader Period—on Palm Sunday—in keeping with the belief that the Messiah would pass through it on his way to the Temple Mount. He claims that the gate had been closed permanently since the Muslims returned to rule.[33] According to Lynch (1848), the name "Golden Gate" was given because the gate was richly ornamented.[34] Press reports in his 1921 guidebook that the Golden Gate had been repaired in 1892.[35]

The Locking of the Gates

For most of the nineteenth century, the gates of the Old City were locked at sundown and reopened in the morning—lest Bedouin marauders intrude during the night. According to a mid-century source, the keys were handed

26 Wilson, *Survey,* p. 80.
27 Tobler, *Nazareth,* pp. 329-330.
28 Luncz, *Guide,* pp. 100-102.
32 Luncz, *Guide,* pp. 100-102.
29 Baedeker (1876), p. 160; (1973), p. 34.
30 Luncz, *Guide,* pp. 100-102.
31 Liévin (1897), I, p. 183.
33 Monro, I, p. 182; Damer (Dawson), I, p. 291; Roberts, I, in text referring to the Golden Gate.
34 Lynch p. 407; Robinson, *Biblical Researches,* I, pp. 263, 322; J. Wilson, I, pp. 418-419.
35 Press, *Travel Handbook,* p. 160.

Zion Gate (Geikie, p. 477)

Lions' Gate (St. Stephen's Gate) (Geikie, p. 537)

over to the pasha each night.[36] In 1854, one traveler reports that caravans scheduled to reach the city in the evening or night hours were required to send word of their arrival in advance, so the guards would keep the gate open. It was necessary, of course, to reward the guards for this service. Refusal to do so meant having to spend the night outside the gate.[37]

In 1864, Dixon writes that four of the five city gates (including the Dung Gate) were locked and bolted at sunset. Only the Jaffa Gate, used by merchants and travelers returning from the coast or from Egypt, was left open for a half hour longer. After that time, this gate would also be locked; no one would be allowed into the city until dawn. Entry at night was possible only with a permit from the pasha. The local residents, Dixon says, accepted this arrangement, but the European Christians were bitterly opposed to it. Only bribes might occasionally be of help.[38]

Jewish sources also note that the gates of Jerusalem were locked and guarded all night long. Referring, it seems, to the middle of the century, Luncz writes as follows:

> The five gates of the period... were closed each night from sundown to sunrise.... Guards roamed the streets to prevent thefts... and from two hours after the closing of the gates, no one was allowed to walk the streets. In this way the inhabitants were protected from robbers and thieves (only Jews on their way to synagogue to recite midnight prayers were permitted to be outside at night in their Quarter).[39]

22

36   Mrs. Finn, *Home*, pp. 31-32.
37   Stewart, p. 250.
38   Dixon, II, pp. 10-11.
39   Luncz—Kressel, pp. 161-162 (translated from Hebrew).

As the neighborhoods outside the walls grew in size, determined opposition arose to the locking of the gates at night. Liévin (1869) says that the Jaffa Gate was sometimes opened before sunrise and closed an hour after sunset. Neil, however, says that current practice in 1873 was to leave the Jaffa Gate open all night long, at the request of the European population.[40] An 1871-1872 issue of *Havatzelet* also reports that the pasha of Jerusalem, Ali Bey, allowed the gates to be left open during the night for the convenience of those living outside the walls.[41] In the early 1870's, the opening and closing of the gates at night seems to have been in keeping with residents' requests. It was only later that locking them at night was ended officially. The first two gates regularly open at night were the Jaffa and Damascus Gates. The others were left open only at a later date.[42]

Throughout the nineteenth century, the city gates were also closed in the Friday noon hours. According to Skinner (1833), the guards would lock the gates and hurry to the mosque when the muezzin called Muslims to prayer. Several other sources also note this practice.[43]

Liévin writes in his guidebook that all the gates were closed on Friday between eleven-thirty in the morning and one o'clock in the afternoon. Warren and Mrs. Damer-Dawson both say that this was due to the popular belief that Jerusalem would be taken from the Muslims on a Friday afternoon.[44]

The following account was written by Reicher in the 1860's:

> The doors are locked from the second hour after sunset until the break of dawn. Armed guards stand at the gates night and day. At noon on Friday, all the gates are closed because Friday is the (Muslim) day of rest and they all go to the house of prayer on the Temple Mount. Even the Pasha and his soldiers go. This is why they close the gates. Fools believe that this is so as to prevent the Messiah of Israel from entering Jerusalem; they allege that the Jewish Messiah will enter Jerusalem on a Friday at noon. This, of course, is sheer nonsense, as the Sages said that the son of David would not arrive on a Sabbath eve....[In any case,] the gates are reopened two hours later.[45]

The Built-up Area and Its Street Network

Maps of the Old City of Jerusalem from the early part of the nineteenth century show broad stretches of land in the northeast and northwest which were cultivated plots or empty lots. The undeveloped area in the northeast was quite large, and surrounded part of the residential neighborhood near the Church of St. Anne. In the northwest, it included part of the Muristan district inside the Christian Quarter, and large stretches of land outside it, near the city walls. There was also a considerable amount of unoccupied land in the southern part of the city, between the Zion and Dung Gates.[46] Most of these

40   Liévin (English), pp. 6-7; Neil, p. 27.
41   *Havatzelet*, 3 Av, 1871, vol. I, no. 22, p. 85.
42   Luncz, *Guide*, p. 100.
43   Skinner, I, p. 213; Barclay, pp. 431-432.
44   Liévin (English), pp. 6-7; Warren, *Underground Jerusalem*, p. 493; Damer (Dawson), I, pp. 291-292.
45   Reicher, p. 56 (translated from Hebrew).
46   See the various maps discussed in the Prologue (in particular: Catherwood, Admiralty, Tobler—Van de Velde, Wilson).

areas were developed during the second half of the century, but even today there are small tracts of vacant land within the walls, mainly in the northeastern part of the city.

An outstanding feature of the built-up area of Jerusalem was its unusual street network, particularly its principal thoroughfares. Even in the nineteenth century, there were two main streets which bisected the city, one from north to south, from the Damascus Gate to the Zion Gate, and one from west to east, from the Jaffa Gate to the Chain Gate at the entrance to the Temple Mount. (It continued along the northern border of the Temple Mount to the Lions' Gate.)[47] These thoroughfares apparently followed the *Cardo* and the *Decumanus* of the Aelia Capitolina town plan; nineteenth-century Jerusalem had retained a city plan similar to that of the Roman city, at least insofar as its main streets were concerned.

Western travel literature of the period contains interesting descriptions of the city's built-up areas and streets. It stresses Jerusalem's lack of suburbs and the fact that the city was contained wholly within its walls. Several main streets followed a straight, unwinding course, but most of the side streets were meandering, narrow and dirty. Streets were usually between five and ten feet wide; some were broader, but many were even narrower. In the rare cases where there was paving, it was in bad condition. Some of the small streets were arched or vaulted, making them dark, and many were cul-de-sacs leading indifferently to clusters of houses or to ruins and desolate areas. The major thoroughfares were paved unevenly, with stones of different sizes as a rule; there was often a narrow channel running down the center which served horses and camels, sewage and rubbish. Pedestrians used the upper level of the street, on either side of the sunken channel. The channels were sometimes two feet deep; animal drivers often quarreled over the right-of-way because only one animal could pass at a time. The streets cited as major thoroughfares in the nineteenth century, usually those which serve in the same capacity today, often were known by several names. As a rule, the side streets had no names at all.[48]

According to Tobler, street names were much disputed. The confusion was compounded by the fact that different sources offered a variety of names for the same street. Tobler himself devotes an entire chapter of his book to examining the names of all the important streets and markets. He concludes that there were 170 streets in Jerusalem, though he notes that this number might be subject to change. Streets were, he says, between two and one-half and six feet wide, and few of them followed a straight course. Even those with a clear destination were tortuous. Most were very narrow and seemed to have been built with only people and animals in mind. Tobler adds that, even in his day, most loads were transported by pack animals.[49]

The sad state of Jerusalem's streets made a very dismal impression upon visitors, and was often used as an indicator of the poverty and backwardness of the city's various population groups.[50]

24

47 Wilson. *Survey*, I, p. 9.
48 Seetzen, II, p. 24; Turner, II, p. 266; Norov, I, pp. 282-289; Thomson, II, p. 474; Barclay, p. 433.
49 Tobler, *Denkblätter*, p. 133; Neumann, pp. 124-125; Luncz, *Guide*, pp. 97-99.
50 Olin, II, pp. 132-136; Taylor, pp. 345-346.

Dixon (1864) presents us with a particularly graphic account of the situation:

> Streets in the European sense of words have no existence in Jerusalem. No Oriental city has them, even in name. An Arab who has a thousand words to express a camel, a sword, a mare, has scarcely one word which suggests a street. A Hebrew had the same poverty of speech; for such a thoroughfare as the Broadway, the Corso, or the Strand, is quite unknown to the East. Solomon never saw a Boulevard. Saladin never dreamt of a Pall Mall. An Arab city must have sooks in which people trade, quarters in which people live; for such a city, even when it has grown into the greatness of a capital like Cairo or Stamboul, is still but an intricate camp in wood and stone. It must have quarters; but it need not have the series of open ways, cutting and crossing each other, which we call streets. Its houses are built in groups; a family, a tribe, a profession occupying each group of houses. A group is a quarter of itself, having its own sheikh, its own police, its own public law, and being separated from the contiguous quarters by gates which a stranger has no right to pass. Free communication from one to another is not desired; and such alleys as connect one quarter with another, being considered no man's land, are rarely honoured with a public name.[51]

Houses and Domes in the Old City

The crowded clusters of domes so typical of the Old City skyline were a constant source of wonderment to Western travelers. Every house had at least one dome over it and many had two or three, depending upon the number of their rooms. Travelers felt this bestowed a special beauty on the city and made all its houses appear as parts of one mass.

Travelers approaching Jerusalem from the south could see only the Old City wall, the Citadel of David and one tall, white building—the Armenian Monastery—from afar. From the north, however, particularly from the Mount of Olives, one could see a mass of domed roofs, nearly all of them of uniform height. The level Temple Mount stood out, with the contrasting cupolas of the Dome of the Rock and al-Aqṣa Mosque jutting up from it. Towards the west, one could also see the domed roof of the Church of the Holy Sepulchre and mosque minarets, as well as cypress trees and a few palms.[52]

Paxton believes these domed roofs were built because they afforded greater protection from the rain. Robinson, on the other hand, correctly attributes this type of construction to a shortage of the beams needed for flat roofs.[53]

In the 1870's, Orelli writes that it was the enormous number of domes topping the cube-like upper stories of the houses that lent Jerusalem its eastern character. He attributes this manner of building to the scarcity of wood and to the need to prevent rain-water from collecting on the roof-tops. Slanted roofs and chimneys were nowhere to be seen in Jerusalem—not on aesthetic grounds, but because there was a shortage of wood for building and heating purposes. Orelli adds that these domes also insured coolness in summer.[54]

Another phenomenon noted by travelers was that these arched roofs were nonetheless level enough to walk on. There were stairways leading up to them,

51   Dixon, II, pp. 10-19.
52   Light, p. 178; Stewart, p. 249.
53   Paxton, p. 134; Robinson, *Biblical Researches,* I, pp. 327-329: *PEF QSt,* I, 1869, pp. 145-147 (Warren report between pp. 260-280).
54   Orelli, pp. 111-126.

and most of them afforded panoramic views of the city. It was here that the inhabitants would sit on cool summer evenings and sunny winter days. At night, the sounds of singing and drumming could be heard from roof-tops all over the city.[55] These roofs were parapeted to prevent accidents, and partitions between them gave a sense of privacy. Small, hollow pottery tubes were inserted into the parapets for ventilation purposes, and so as to allow the women of the household, who often sat on the roof, a good view without it being possible to see them from the outside.[56]

We have already noted that many of the narrow streets had arches or vaults over them. These linked nearly all the roofs in the Old City and made it possible to walk from roof to roof over large distances. Homes more than one story high often had various "living levels," with the roofs of the first story serving as the courtyards of the second, and so on. Travelers say the houses in the Old City gave the impression of being heavy square blocks, since neither windows nor chimneys protruded from them.[57]

Olin (1840) records the fact that walls facing the street were usually windowless; if there were any windows at all, they were on the second floor and provided with wooden or iron gratings. Living quarters were generally on the second floor, the ground floor being used as a storeroom, kitchen or similar room. Houses were built of stone, very little wood being used. Many were in bad condition and on the verge of collapse. Repairing them was not customary: when one room deteriorated, the inhabitants would move to another, the old one becoming a garbage dump.[58]

Neumann also mentions the fact that many of the old houses in Jerusalem were in ruins. When unable to rent their homes to Jews or Christians, the Muslims would leave them to deteriorate. Thus the construction of any new building involved the removal of ancient ruins, and might result in numerous archaeological finds. Important buildings (especially Muslim *madrasas* or colleges), whose walls were made of marble blocks joined by lead strips, were often used as stables and warehouses rather than as homes.[59]

In his first book about Jerusalem (1876), Luncz describes Jerusalem's homes and their domed roofs:

> All the houses in the city are made of white limestone blocks. No wood is used; even the domes are supported by means of stone arches protruding from the walls. For this reason men do not fear fire. All of the large rooms are domed, the bigger homes having two or more domes.... Windows are very small and, in Muslim homes, are covered with wooden lattice-work on the outside. Doorways too are small... and open onto the courtyards.... Houses are not built uniformly with two or three stories, each atop another. One has a single story, another—two or three. One house is high and another low. One recedes, another protrudes. Houses stand facing each other, with so many short and narrow paths in between that a stranger may easily go astray. The roofs are also used, and stairs lead up to them. Most roofs are paved with stone to facilitate water collection. Around them are low walls built of hollow cylindrical tiles which serve two purposes: a) to allow refreshing hill breezes to pass through them in the early morning; b) to prevent strangers from looking inside....

55 Strauss, p. 203.
56 Stewart, p. 269.
57 See, e.g., Chateaubriand, p. 184.

58 Olin, II, pp. 132-136.
59 Neumann, pp. 126-131.

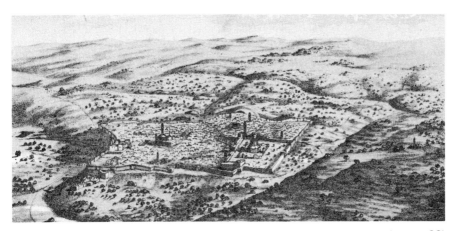

Jerusalem—view from south (Barclay, p. 88)

Luncz goes on to describe the many doorways of Muslims who had been to Mecca, which were engraved or colorfully inscribed with Arabic poetry, aphorisms and sayings.[60]

Courtyards and Home Interiors

Houses consisted of a series of rooms built around a spacious inner courtyard or *hatzer*. In the center of this courtyard was a cistern for collecting rain-water, which had been hewn beneath the whole of the courtyard and possibly beneath the house itself (see p. 74 below for more information about cisterns). Alongside one of the walls of the courtyard was a steep and narrow flight of stairs leading to the upper floor. In many cases, the original layout of these courtyards was altered at a later date when additional rooms were built within the courtyard area. Sometimes the entire courtyard would be filled by such "appendages," which were even built occasionally on different levels, completely obscuring the original plan of the house. The courtyard was usually reached through a corridor or narrow winding alley which had stairways leading to the various apartments. Eventually, toilet facilities were constructed in one corner of the courtyard for the use of all the tenants. Another corner was set aside for rubbish, which was usually collected once a week and taken through the Dung Gate to the Tyropoeon Valley with the aid of donkeys. The cramped living quarters and oriental life-style of Jerusalem contributed to making the courtyard the focus of daily life. Cooking, washing, hanging out the laundry, airing bedding and socializing all took place there. Towards evening, the whole family would gather in the courtyard to eat its main meal, seated on low stools. During the hot summer months, family members would sleep either in the courtyard or on the roof. The most comfortable apartments were to be found on the sunny and airy upper stories. In some cases, these tenants had access to a *hakura*—an unpaved area above ancient ruins. In the center of this *hakura* there would sometimes be an olive, mulberry, fig or palm tree in whose shade the courtyard residents might sit.[61]

27

60   Luncz, *Ways of Zion,* 1876, pp. 17-18 (translated from Hebrew).
61   Mrs. Finn, *Home,* pp. 43-49; Norov, I, pp. 282-289; *PEF QSt,* I, 1869, pp. 145-147 (Warren report between pp. 260-280); Press, *Hundred Years,* pp. 15-17.

In the middle of the century, Reicher notes that the city abounded in three-and four-story houses—a reference, apparently, to the various "living levels" of the city. He also writes that courtyards might provide access to as many as twenty or thirty homes. These courtyards had gates which were locked each night, and their own cisterns.[62]

European travelers attempted to explain why homes and courtyards were built in this unusual style. They attributed it to the oriental custom which compelled women—especially Muslim women—to isolate themselves from the outside world. The courtyard, then, was an architectural solution for the Muslim woman, enabling her to live her daily life in closed inner courtyards, hidden from the eyes of passers-by.

According to Neumann, the two most important factors considered when a house was built in the Old City were the water supply and the preservation of feminine modesty. These stone homes were closed to the street, and had courtyards and terraces to insure good ventilation. A large house would consist of a group of cube-like rooms of various heights, each of which had its own entrance from the courtyard.[63] Because the foundations, atop ruins, were insufficiently deep, house walls tended to crack and admit the elements.[64]

In the first half of the century, the interiors of Jerusalem homes were extremely simple, and typical of those found in other oriental cities. Floors were covered with straw mats and, sometimes, wool carpets. Pillow-covered divans lined the walls; sizable tables were conspicuously absent. Small round ones which were easily moved were used instead. (Cafés also provided low stools.) Clothing was kept in a trunk or suitcase, or in a small closet built into a wall recess only occasionally supplied with a door. Woollen mattresses were laid out on the floor at night, and rolled up and kept in the corner during the day. Tobler (1846) writes that in his day Christians and Jews had begun to use regular beds which did not have to be made up each night.[65]

Luncz (1876) describes how various household articles were stored:

> The inside walls are hollowed-out and used to store cotton- or rag-stuffed pillows and quilts during the day. At night these are spread out on the floor for sleeping. Other household items such as leather chests and glass vessels are also kept in these alcoves. Wooden chairs, tables, beds, boxes and chests are non-existent, but iron beds and other household items used in Europe can now be found in the homes of wealthy and distinguished persons.[66]

Heating

In the winter, homes were heated by burning charcoal in small stoves or stone fireplaces. Skinner (1833) stresses that the only fuel used in Jerusalem was charcoal brought from the Hebron district. Tobler (1846) writes that firewood was scarce in the Jerusalem vicinity and was usually brought from the Ḥalḥul region near Hebron. Various types of wood—not only for heating purposes—

28

62   Reicher, p. 57.
63   Neumann, pp. 126-131; Tobler, *Denkblätter,* p. 153.
64   Petermann, I, p. 205.
65   Tobler, *Denkblätter,* p. 182.
66   Luncz, *Ways of Zion,* pp. 17-18 (translated from Hebrew).

In a Jerusalem home (Barclay, p. 436)

were obtained there. Fine wood for furniture, however, was imported from Constantinople or Izmir. Wood and charcoal were transported to the city by camel and carried home by the women on their heads. Since wood was expensive, charcoal was preferred. Tobler found it odd that many of the heating stoves could burn anything from twigs to roots, as well as many other types of fuel. Neumann also states that firewood had to be brought from Hebron, wood for building from overseas, and olive-wood for carpentry from the mount of Olives. A special charcoal-burning stove was used for cooking. Schirion notes that homes were heated at the end of the century by burning charcoal in an open copper brazier called a "manjal." This method was introduced by Jerusalem's wealthy families.[67]

Lighting

At the beginning of the nineteenth century, European sources report that neither the Via Dolorosa nor any other street in Jerusalem was illuminated at night. According to Tobler (1846), the situation had changed little by the 1840's, when it was considered wise to equip oneself with a lantern before venturing out at night. Schulz (1851) says this was essential if one did not wish to be arrested by the soldiers.[68]

Homes were illuminated by burning sesame or olive oil or, infrequently, wax candles. A lamp was suspended at the height desired by a chain from a ring in

29

67   Mrs. Finn, *Home,* p. 36; Skinner, pp. 223-224; Paxton, pp. 112-135; Tobler, *Denkblätter,* p. 179: Neumann, pp. 8, 126-131; Schirion, p. 96.
68   W.R. Wilson, I, p. 252; Tobler, *Denkblätter,* p. 179; Schulz, p. 131.

the center of the ceiling vault. This gave sufficient light for conversation or coffee-drinking but for nothing else.[69]

Kerosene reached Jerusalem in the second half of the nineteenth century. A local source reports that, at the end of the century, most of the local residents, including the poorer Jews, burned wicks dipped in oil to light their homes. They used either any handy metal receptacle for this purpose, or a small pear-shaped utensil called a "gasikel," which was filled with kerosene. Its exposed wick protruded from the narrow opening and efficiently covered the room — more dark than light — with soot. The wealthy, by contrast, owned proper kerosene lamps with glass chimneys. These lamps were numbered according to the width of their wicks and the size of their chimneys. Another source notes that homes were illuminated by small, simple kerosene lamps. The "Blitz" lamps, which gave better light, reached Jerusalem only in 1890, when the larger synagogues acquired them.[70]

Towards the end of the nineteenth century, street-lighting began to be installed in the city. In 1896, the municipal council approved kerosene lighting in neighborhoods outside the walls as well. Such lighting was expanded and improved in anticipation of the visit of the Kaiser in 1898.[71] As the first decade of the twentieth century drew to a close, these kerosene lamps were replaced by "Lux" lamps. Private citizens also began to use them to light hotels and shops.[72] The introduction of this type of lamp constituted the most important advance in public lighting facilities prior to World War I. A number of private institutions in Jerusalem also began to install electric lighting, using their own generators; the first to do so was the Hospice of Nôtre Dame de France, which imported its equipment from France.[73]

Public Squares and Buildings

Very few of the numerous public buildings, churches, mosques and synagogues found in the Old City today existed in the early 1800's: most of them were built during the remainder of the century. The Dome of the Rock and the al-Aqsa Mosque, however, were prominent features of the Jerusalem landscape even then. Aside from certain repairs, such as the leveling of its courtyard and the building of a few structures, the Temple Mount was much as it is today. Next in importance was the Church of the Holy Sepulchre with its various wings. Some changes were made during the nineteenth century, but most of the building complex was of earlier construction. The third largest network of public buildings in the Old City was that of the Armenian Monastery and Church, and the surrounding structures. All of these will be dealt with in later chapters.

Apart from these three extensive compounds, there were no extremely large structures in the Old City. Large synagogues were non-existent, except for the inconspicuous Sephardi synagogues in the Jewish Quarter. The first new

69   Tobler, *Denkblätter*, p. 179.
70   G. Frumkin, pp. 23-24; Schirion, p. 96.
71   D. Yellin, *Writings*, I, p. 224 (1898); p. 278 (1897); Luncz, *Almanac*, XI, 1906, p. 223; Avitzur, *Daily Life*, pp. 69-73.
72   Luncz, *Almanac*, XVI, 1911, p. 153; XII, 1908, pp. 122-123; *Jerusalem*, IX, 1911, p. 180.
73   *Ha-Or* (Supplement to *Ha-Tzevi*), 26 Iyyar, 1892, vol. IX, no. 32, p. 1.

synagogue to be built in the nineteenth century was "Menaḥem Zion," in 1837, which was the first wing of the future Ḥurva Synagogue. The other large synagogues were built in the latter half of the century.

One of the most prominent buildings in the Muslim Quarter at the beginning of the century was the home of the Turkish governor. It was called Pilate's Palace, and encompassed a Turkish army camp.

It should be noted that most of the large Christian monasteries and churches date from the nineteenth century. The Church of St. Anne was still in Muslim hands in the early part of the century. The Church of the Flagellation and that of the Sisters of Zion, as well as other churches and Christian-owned buildings along the Via Dolorosa, were also built during the nineteenth century. There were several churches and monasteries in the Christian Quarter at the beginning of this period, but they were located in small buildings. The Franciscan Monastery of St. Savior, much described in western travel literature, was the most important of these. A Hospice called Casa Nova was erected alongside it in the 1840's. Also prominent was the large Greek Monastery next to the Church of the Holy Sepulchre.

All the sources mention the minimal number of public squares in the Old City. The most important open area was the one on the Temple Mount, but it was not a public place. The plaza at the entrance to the Church of the Holy Sepulchre and the courtyard near the Citadel of David did, however, serve in this capacity. The open area opposite the gate of the Citadel was also used on occasion as a fruit and vegetable market by farmers from the surrounding villages.[74]

Signs of Change during the Nineteenth Century

During the nineteenth century, the appearance of the Old City of Jerusalem began to change. For example, the newspaper *Ha-Levanon* reports the following improvements in 1865:

> From the Jaffa Gate... to the end of the Upper Market, all the ledges outside the shops and the stairs outside the courtyards were torn down, and the excess earth and stones thrown into the valley beyond the gate in order to broaden the entrance to the city. The market's paving stones, which were a hindrance to all passers-by, who used to stumble over them—some even breaking their legs, were now removed and replaced by others. All the ragged and patched straw awnings hanging from the wooden-slatted roofs, which dropped dirt and dust on all those walking beneath them, were pulled down and discarded....[75]

In February 1868, this newspaper complains that Jerusalem was filthy because of a lack of toilet facilities for the farmers and agricultural workers who came to the city.[76] By spring, however, it reported that market-places and streets had been widened, public toilets had been provided and gas lamps had been installed in the streets.[77]

In 1889, Luncz reports an improvement in the general appearance of the city.

31

74 Ewald, pp. 52-53; Tobler, *Denkblätter,* p. 126; Munk, pp. 117-118; Liévin (English), p. 50.
75 *Ha-Levanon,* 8 Tevet, 1865, vol. I, no. 1, p. 6 (translated from Hebrew).
76 *Ha-Levanon,* 12 Shevat, 1868, vol. V, no. 1, p. 92.
77 *Ha-Levanon,* 5 Sivan, 1868, vol. V, no. 21, p. 332.

Jaffa Gate — view from inside walls (Harper, p. 23)

Many streets had been paved, and damaged sewage channels repaired and extended. This, Luncz stresses, did much to better sanitation and health conditions in the city.[78]

It seems that paving activities were begun in 1864 and continued until 1885.[79] Nevertheless, muddy streets continued to trouble pedestrians, and some streets had to be closed to camel-traffic. In 1894, the PEF Quarterly reports that the increased population and the introduction of railway services to Jerusalem had made the streets so crowded that a laden camel could barely get through. Iron barriers were therefore placed at street entrances to prevent camels from entering and to allow only riderless donkeys or horses to pass. These barriers were set up at various entrances to the city and to some quarters and important streets.[80]

The process of installing street-lights was as long and drawn-out as that of cleaning the city. It was only in 1904 that all the streets were illuminated — and cleaned — regularly.[81]

Tobler reports having seen several well-built new structures in 1865 in the Old City. The European influence on construction, he notes, was very strong.[82] Because of the increase in building activity in the city, white stone was brought in from new quarries in Bethlehem and Anatot.[83] Methods of roof construction improved towards the end of the century. Shingled roofs began to appear in both the Old City and the new neighborhoods — particularly on houses built by East-European immigrants. Glass windows and modern shutters were introduced relatively late.[84]

32

78 Luncz—Kressel, p. 255.
79 Hanauer (1926), pp. 6, 127 (first edition, 1885).
80 *PEF QSt,* 1894, p. 266; Munk, pp. 117-118.
81 *MNDPV*, II, 1905, p. 60.

82 Tobler, *Nazareth,* pp. 302-304.
83 Mrs. Finn, *Home,* pp. 31-32.
84 Amiran *(Atlas),* pp. 26-28.

Jaffa Gate from the outside (National Library, photo album GR/2)

Other changes in the city are described in the PEF Quarterly of 1880. The slaughterhouses and tanneries were moved outside the city walls; clocks were installed on several large buildings; a German architect undertook to organize the municipal building (and sanitation) department. The use of European-style furnishings spread, while agricultural lands around Jerusalem were now cultivated by modern methods.[85]

In his article in the *ZDPV*, Schick examines the development of the city from 1831 to 1892, listing the new churches, schools, hospitals, hospices and hotels in and around Jerusalem.[86]

David Yellin offers an account of the reconstruction of the Cotton Market in honor of the visit of Wilhelm II at the end of the century:

> The long, roofed street leading to the site of our Temple, known as the Cotton Market (Suq al-Katanin), which was bounded on either side by rows of open, dirt-filled rooms known to our brethren as "the shops," is no longer the ravaged site it once was. By order of the Pasha, the whole street was given a coat of new white plaster from ceiling to floor and a level new road paved. The dust and dirt which had accumulated in "the shops" for hundreds of years were removed, and new doors built for each of them. Now it is a beautiful new street, through which carriages entering the city via the Damascus Gate may reach the gate of the Temple Mount. The government building was also completely renovated.[87]

Gad Frumkin also describes the Cotton Market, with its bath-houses and Arab blacksmiths' forges, in which cradles and other iron products were made. Later, he says, these shops were deserted and became a place to discard trash, until the Mandatory governor of Jerusalem, Sir Ronald Storrs, had them

33

85 *PEF QSt,* 1880, pp. 187-188.
86 *ZDPV*, XVI, 1893, pp. 237-246; XVII, 1894, pp. 1-24, 75-88, 165-179, 251-276.
87 Yellin, *Writings,* I, pp. 266-267.

New entrance near Jaffa Gate (*PEF QSt,* 1901, p. 10)

cleaned and reopened. They then became pottery shops run by the Pro-Jerusalem Society.[88]

In 1900, the PEF Quarterly reports significant changes in the city's topography as a result of the removal of artificial hills and other mounds of earth. An artificial terrace in the Muristan, which had been tilled annually in the past, was leveled; the earth removed from it was said to have nearly filled the wadi west of the Jaffa Gate. Another hill near the Austrian Hospice was removed, and its earth dumped outside the Damascus Gate. The ruins of the Church of St. Anne were moved outside St. Stephen's Gate, where they created an artificial hillock. Many other urban development activities were undertaken then as well.[89]

Changes in the Jaffa Gate and Its Adjacent Plaza

During the second half of the nineteenth century, the area of the Jaffa Gate and the plaza in front of it were considerably altered. Bertha Spafford Vester notes the accelerated rate of construction in the city in the 1880's. Upon their arrival in Jerusalem, she and her family had moved into the Mediterranean Hotel, located just inside the Jaffa Gate. During the 1880's the Grand New Hotel was built alongside it.[90]

One source says that, at the end of this decade, a municipal sand clock was placed near the Jaffa Gate where the old post-office had been. The English pharmacy previously situated in this building was replaced by a position, manned by a dozen soldiers who guarded the entrance to the Old City.[91]

34

88   G. Frumkin, p. 37.
89   *PEF QSt,* 1900, p. 194.

90   Spafford Vester, pp. 81-82.
91   Weiss, pp. 27-38.

Jaffa Gate Square, 1898 (*Kaiserpaar,* p. 194)

Schirion's memoirs contain an account of the building in the Jaffa Gate area:

> When commerce began to expand in Jerusalem, from about 1890 on, property-owning monasteries began to erect small buildings on the Jaffa Road; these comprised shops, offices and spacious, high-ceilinged warehouses. Old City merchants proceeded to move their businesses there. In the course of time, the monasteries used their income from these buildings to add more stories to them, and to build other large, modern buildings and hotels. The Howard or Fast Hotel on the Jaffa Road was built by the Armenian Monastery, and the beautiful Grand New Hotel inside the Jaffa Gate, with its attractive shopping arcade, by the Greek Monastery....[92]

Other structures were built inside the Jaffa Gate at this time, including the arcaded building where the American Colony shop was to be found for many years.

An 1899 issue of the PEF Quarterly contains a map and explanations of the changes made at the Jaffa Gate in anticipation of the visit of Kaiser Wilhelm in 1898. The commemorative plaque installed opposite the gate in his honor[93] was destroyed by the British after their conquest of Jerusalem.

David Yellin describes the plans for widening the main street of the Old City in 1899:

> Early in the secular year, the Pasha proposed to the council members and district leadership that many of the shops and houses from the Jaffa Gate in the west to entrance of the Temple Mount, the Gate of the Chain, in the east be torn down to allow the city's main street... to be broadened from twelve to sixteen cubits....

35

92 Schirion, pp. 111, 116.   93 *PEF QSt,* 1899, pp. 2-4.

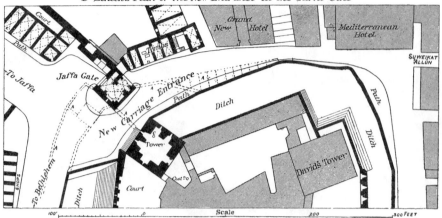

Dr. Schick's Plan of the New Entrance at the Jaffa Gate

Plan of new entrance near Jaffa Gate (*PEF QSt,* 1899, p. 7)

> The necessary budget for demolition, construction and compensation of shop-
> and home-owners came to 90,000 Turkish lira, i.e., over two million francs....[94]

Development of the area continued in the twentieth century. The newspaper
Hashkafa writes about construction opportunities in 1906:

> It has been decided to allow building over the fosses outside and inside the city
> wall near the Jaffa Gate, according to a set plan, and on condition that these
> buildings be financed by private citizens and that each builder enjoy the use of his
> building for a set period of time. All those interested in further information
> should enquire of Majlis Adarah in Jerusalem.[95]

In 1902, Luncz reports that a clock-tower and a fountain *(sabil)* were erected
at the Jaffa Gate to commemorate the twenty-fifth anniversary of the reign of
Abdul Ḥamid. This fountain was designed to provide wayfarers with drinking
water, which would be supplied by roofing over part of the Citadel trench to
trap rain water.[96]

In 1901, the PEF Quarterly published a photograph of the Jaffa Gate
showing the Citadel of David, the new carriage entrance and the new fountain,
and gave a description of the fountain.[97]

Hashkafa notes in 1904 that the pasha, Kazim Bey, had ordered the
municipality to beautify the city center near the Jaffa Gate and to build a tower
bearing a large municipal clock.[98] The thirteen-meter high tower was dedicated
in 1907; its timepiece had been imported from France.[99] The large clock could
be seen and heard from a distance. All Jerusalem residents donated money
towards the project, which cost over 20,000 francs (800 pounds sterling). The
beautiful white stone, Luncz notes, was quarried in the Cave of Zedekiah.[100]

At the beginning of the British Mandate, Zuta and Sukenik say that the
region inside the Jaffa Gate was the focal point of activity in Jerusalem. It was
here that the larger businesses and hotels were located, and transportation was

94 Yellin, *Writings,* I, p. 321.
95 *Hashkafa,* 28 Shevat, 1906, vol. VII, no. 36, p. 3; 8 Nisan, 1906, vol. VII, no. 47, p. 3.
96 Luncz, *Almanac,* VI, 1901, p. 165; Luncz, *Jerusalem,* V, no. 3, 1901, pp. 282-283.
97 *PEF QSt,* 1901, pp. 1-2.
98 *Hashkafa,* 17 Av, 1904, vol. V, no. 48, p. 441.
99 *Hashkafa,* 16 Av, 1907, vol. VIII, no. 84, p. 2; 20 Elul, 1907, vol. VIII, no. 93, p. 2.
100 Luncz, *Almanac,* XIII, 1908, pp. 122-123; Baedeker (1912), p. 33; Hanauer (1926), pp. 1-9.

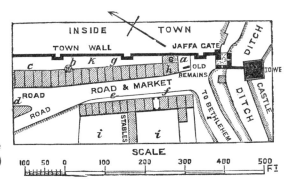

Plan of Jaffa Gate Square
(*PEF QSt*, 1887, p. 214)

made available to all parts of the city, Jaffa and Hebron. Railway passengers came here first, and all travelers arriving from the south—whether from Beersheba, Hebron or Bethlehem and its environs—entered the city through this gate. There was pulsing activity here from morning until late at night.[101]

Development of the Damascus Gate region also began toward the end of the nineteenth century. In 1911, the newspaper *Ha-Or* reports the opening of "new European-style warehouses" and the installation of "Lux" lamps near the gate. There were also an excellent pharmacy and a café to be found there.[102] Press notes that the plaza outside the Damascus Gate had begun to serve as a gathering place, while the field next to it became a grain market.[103] Thus began the competition between the Damascus and Jaffa Gate regions.

Summary

It should be noted that most of the physical changes in nineteenth-century Jerusalem took place towards the end of the century. Some were made earlier, in mid-century, but the pace accelerated in the 1880's and continued thereafter. It was mainly public areas which were changed: streets, markets, city squares, the as-yet-unoccupied land between the residential neighborhoods and the city walls, and that around the gates—especially around the Jaffa and Damascus Gates.

Although the changes in question did not affect the basic plan of the city, they did much to add variety and improve its appearance. It was in the nineteenth century that many public buildings of the greatest importance were erected in the Old City, and European elements were introduced in such areas as the Muristan, the Jaffa Gate, the New Gate, and so on. At the same time, the city's ancient historical features and oriental character were preserved. The sprouting of a New City outside the walls and a growing appreciation of the Old City as a center of cultural importance were the major changes in nineteenth-century Jerusalem.

37

101 Zuta—Sukenik, p. 79. The clock tower was removed after the British occupation.
102 *Ha-Or,* 6 Adar, 1911, vol. II, no. 101-286, p. 3.
103 Press, *Travel Handbook,* p. 179.

Chapter Two:

THE ECONOMY AND PURSUITS OF JERUSALEM'S POPULATION (ITS CRAFTS, COMMERCE, MARKETS AND RHYTHM OF LIFE)

Introduction

Early nineteenth-century Jerusalem was a small, impoverished city, but economic activity was not altogether absent from it. As the city developed, the economic picture changed; we will discuss it as it was for the greater part of the century, before major developments took place.

There is no doubt that the most important source of income for the majority of Jerusalem's inhabitants was contributions from abroad—the *halukka* money distributed among the Jews, and the donations sent to monasteries and various Christian sects.[1] Some of its Muslim inhabitants engaged in farming in and around the Old City.[2] This chapter, however, will deal with other types of livelihood: industry, craftsmanship and trade.

Industry and Crafts

The most important industries in Jerusalem at the beginning of the century seem to have been the production of soap and oil. Seetzen reports the existence of four large soap factories in 1806. Their products were of good quality, and were also marketed in distant places. The oil used came from the numerous olive orchards in the Judean Hills, and the soda from the Dead Sea.[3]

One Jewish source of the 1820's describes the soap industry as follows:

> There are many factories here which produce fine olive-oil soap with a pleasant fragrance. The best quality is called "al-maskh" in Arabic, and is exported to Egypt and all the surrounding countries. There are also many oil presses which extract sweet oil from sesame seeds.[4]

Robinson reports (in the 1830's) that there were nine soap factories serving this important industry in Jerusalem, and that factory wastes had formed several artificial mounds to the north of the city. (He also noted there were nine oil-extracting presses.) The first nineteenth-century maps of Jerusalem indicate

1   Many travelers note that religion was a major source of livelihood in Jerusalem, as each religious group received donations from overseas to help support its members.
2   For details about farming in the Old City, see Amiran *(Atlas)*, pp. 29-30.
3   Seetzen, II, pp. 21-22.
4   Rabbi David de-Beth Hillel; see Yaari, *Travels,* p. 503 (translated from Hebrew).

a whole series of such mounds,[5] and it is probably these which are referred to in the following description:

> Northwest of the city, not far from a place called the Tombs of the Kings, are two mounds or accumulations of ashes, one of them about forty feet high. Local inhabitants believe that these are the wastes from soap and washing soda made in ancient times. British researchers who visited the site think they are ashes from Temple sacrifices. Their presence makes it possible to determine the boundaries of the ancient wall, since ashes were disposed of outside it.[6]

Olin (1840) and Tobler (1846) also mention the soap factories of Jerusalem, most of which were owned by Muslims; only one, situated in the Jewish Quarter market, belonged to a Christian.[7] Neumann says there were nine or ten such factories. The soap made in them was cut into bricks or half-spheres, the best quality being infused with a blend of perfumes. According to Neumann, large amounts of sesame oil were produced in fifteen oil presses in the city.[8]

Warren (writing at the end of the 1860's) describes Jerusalem's soap industry in detail, saying that this was the only industry the city could boast. Local residents claimed it was declining, however, because locusts had damaged the olive trees and caused the quality and quantity of their oil to deteriorate. One manufacturer had even begun to import oil from southern Europe, but Arab residents did not like the soap produced from it because it was too soft.

Warren says Jerusalem had seven soap factories — five of them owned by Muslims, one by a Greek and one by a Protestant. Some seventy-six workers were employed. There were no manufacturing secrets or professional organizations of employees or employers. The soap contained olive oil, soda, lime and salt. Olive oil was supplied mainly by the surrounding villages; soda (alkali) was obtained from Damascus, Transjordan, the Jordan Valley, Gaza, Egypt and the Red Sea. Lime came from the limestone around Jerusalem, and salt from the shores of the Dead Sea, near Ein Gedi. There was no tax on soap unless it was exported. Some was exported to Egypt and Asia Minor, but less than had been in the past. Warren says he even encountered soap from Jerusalem in Europe.[9]

The second most important industry in Jerusalem was the manufacture and dyeing of cloth. In 1807, El Abbassi (Ali Bey) reports that some of the city's women engaged in weaving. According to Seetzen (1806), several people worked in the production of white cotton fabric. A textile-dyeing factory in the city employed twenty Christians; only blue dye was used by them. Strauss says there were several small looms in the city in 1845.[10] A detailed description of the indigo dye-houses is provided by Warren, who writes that this industry was located in the Muristan. The open space there was convenient for spreading out

5   Robinson, *Biblical Researches,* II, pp. 95-96; see also British Admiralty and Tobler — Van de Velde maps, cited in Prologue.
6   *Ha-Maggid,* 28 Elul, 1857, vol. I, no. 40, pp. 158-159 (translated from Hebrew).
7   Olin, II, pp. 137-138; Tobler, *Denkblätter,* pp. 228-229. Below, in our account of the Muslim Quarter, we shall see that some of these factories were located in the Bezetha area, not far from the Damascus Gate (see p. 177).
8   Neumann, p. 222; see also Strauss, pp. 278-280.
9   Warren, *Underground Jerusalem,* pp. 500-509.
10 El-Abbassi, II, pp. 240-245; Seetzen, II, p. 17; Strauss, pp. 278-280.

Weaving
equipment
(Lortet, p. 241)

the dyed material; in good weather, one could see broad stretches of ground covered with blue fabric. There were approximately ten such dye-houses, each one employing ten workers and apprentices. Though this trade was usually passed down from father to son, it was also open to others. Factory owners had no obligations to their apprentices and could dismiss them with only a few days' notice. If one of them left, no other dye-house in the city would hire him without the previous employer's consent. Most of the work was done for the *fellaḥin* and Bedouin, especially for their womenfolk. Warren adds that blue was the dominant color, but that others, such as different shades of green, were also in use. The dye was prepared by mixing indigo, imported from Europe by Jewish merchants, with soda and lime. The indigo was tax-free if used for local consumption. An inferior type of indigo was also grown in the Jordan Valley, but it was not used much.[11]

Another local industry was leather-processing. Seetzen writes that there was a factory which processed leather of all colors for export. About twenty skilled workers and twenty assistants, all Muslim, were employed there. It was located opposite the Church of the Holy Sepulchre and gave off bad odors, because there was not enough water for the proper removal of wastes and blood. This factory greatly annoyed the Christians, who believed the Muslims had placed it there deliberately. Turner adds that the Turkish-owned ruins of St. Peter's Monastery, a hundred paces southeast of the Church of the Holy Sepulchre, were used in 1815 as a tannery.[12]

Robinson mentions this large tannery too, adding that, like the soap and oil factories, it was owned by Muslims.[13] Strauss tells of a leather factory housed in the old buildings of the Knights Hospitallers, south of the Church of the Holy Sepulchre, and notes an enormous heap of waste in the building there.[14] Like the slaughterhouses, these tanneries were moved outside the city walls in the late 1870's.[15]

An important Christian industry was the production of souvenirs and religious articles. Seetzen says some Christian craftsmen made rosaries, while others fashioned crosses from shells, bones and similar materials. Candles, too, were produced in Jerusalem, mainly for use in monasteries and churches.[16] Robinson writes in 1838 that the major Christian enterprises, both in Jerusalem and in Bethlehem, were those that produced various kinds of souvenirs for sale to Christian pilgrims.[17]

According to Seetzen, the city had fifty gold- and silversmiths, all of them Christian. Some of them worked in the areas around Jerusalem and, for several months of the year, they would cross the Jordan to Kerak and Salt. There were also twenty Christian blacksmiths and two Christian watchmakers. In the oldest religious house in the city, the Franciscan Saint Savior's, there were

11   Warren, *Underground Jerusalem,* pp. 509-512; on the craft of dyeing, see Meyuḥas (in Luncz, *Almanac,* XII, 1907, pp. 49-53).
12   Seetzen, II, p. 22; Turner, II, pp. 268-269.
13   Robinson, *Biblical Researches,* II, pp. 95-96.
14   Strauss, p. 221; Neumann (p. 222) also mentions the existence of a tannery in the city.
15   *PEF QSt,* 1880, p. 188.
16   Seetzen, II, pp. 22-23.
17   Robinson, *Biblical Researches,* II, pp. 95-96; see also Olin, II, p. 137-138.

workshops for carpentry and blacksmithery, as well as a flour mill and baking ovens to supply its needs. Nevertheless, says Seetzen, Jerusalem's main source of income was the tourist trade.[18]

Strauss notes that Jerusalem's industries were of the simplest kind in the 1840's. The production of souvenirs and crosses from olive wood, shells and black stone from the Dead Sea was widespread.[19] Dixon (1864) writes that pilgrim souvenirs were on sale alongside every holy place: "torches" near the Greek churches, prayer beads near the mosques, candles and roses near the Roman Catholic churches.[20] Olin tells us that some women made a living from picking grass in the valleys around Jerusalem and selling it to Christian pilgrims for their horses.[21]

According to Seetzen, there was an important pottery and clay pipe-bowl industry in Jerusalem at the beginning of the century. Better quality pipe-bowls were made from Beirut clay, inferior ones from clay brought in from the village of Qastel (near the road to Ramleh). In order to strengthen the clay, various materials were added; these gave the pottery a coppery or reddish tint. The pottery was polished with a special substance. Neumann too mentions the city's pottery works.[22]

Warren says there were five ceramics plants, and that they employed mostly Muslims. Work was done in them only during the summer because the owners were poor and could not afford drying ovens. These factories produced jugs, pipes, pots, bowls, tiles and bricks. Warren notes that this industry was an ancient one in Palestine, and was mentioned in the Bible and in many historical records.[23]

The city's flour mills provided the basis for yet another "industry." Consul Finn writes that there were twenty public flour mills operating regularly in the city in 1854.[24] Later in the century, apparently in the 1870's, some of them went over to the use of steam, which greatly increased their output. Unable to stand the competition, the others were forced to close.

In the 1840's, printing presses began to appear in Jerusalem. Strauss says there were already three of them in use in the mid-1840's: one belonging to the Jews, one to the Latin Monastery and one to the Armenian Monastery. Bartlett claims that the Jewish press had printed mainly anti-missionary propaganda, and had closed down by 1853.[25] He was probably referring to Rabbi Israel Bak's printing press, which had been moved to Jerusalem after the Safed earthquake of 1837. The establishment of this and other Jewish presses in the city will be dealt with below, in our discussion of the Jewish community in the second half of the century. Printing would be one of the first branches of employment to herald new developments in Jerusalem; at this point however, its negative aspect interests us: until 1830, there were no printing presses or printers in the city at all.

The great changes in Jerusalem during the nineteenth century also led to the development of a construction industry. In the 1830's and 1840's, when the first

18 Seetzen, II, pp. 22-23.

19 Strauss, pp. 278-280.

20 Dixon, II, pp. 45-46.

21 Olin, II, p. 163.

22 Seetzen, II, p. 22; Neumann, p. 222.

23 Warren, *Underground Jerusalem*, pp. 513-519.

24 Finn, *Stirring Times*, II, pp. 63-64.

25 Strauss, pp. 278-280; Bartlett, *Revisited*, p. 42. Also see below, Part Four.

new buildings began to go up, Jerusalem had neither construction laborers nor skilled building workers, and they had to be brought from abroad. Little by little, progress was made. Warren writes that most of the stone-cutters were *fellaḥin* from Bethlehem, who spent between six months and two years learning their trade. They preferred not to work with hard stone, and were incapable of carving stones like those used in the Second Temple period, such as those of the Wailing Wall.[26]

Thus, industry was in a dismal state in Jerusalem during the first half of the nineteenth century. The main enterprises were soap and oil factories, coarse-cloth workshops, a tannery and a souvenir industry. Significant development took place only towards the end of the nineteenth and in the early twentieth century, prior to World War I.

Commerce

Commerce was also in a backward state at the beginning of the nineteenth century. Turner (1815) says that commercial traffic to and from the city was very limited: wheat was brought from Nablus and the villages of Samaria, and a small amount of soap was exported to the surrounding regions.[27] According to Tobler (1846), the location of the city was inconvenient for trade. The Cairo-Damascus road passed through Ramleh, several hours' travel from Jerusalem, and Jerusalem was therefore unable to benefit from the traffic it bore. Only wool was imported to Jerusalem from Egypt, while exports to Egypt consisted mainly of religious articles, such as crosses, holy icons, "stones of Moses" (bitumen from the Nebi Musa region), olive-wood furniture and soap. The souvenir trade aimed at Christian pilgrims was extensive; wholesale purchases were also made by European dealers, who sold these items overseas. The situation was such that merchants from Venice would bring their wares to Jerusalem and Jaffa, hoping to sell them there to European pilgrims.[28]

Neumann dwells on the fact that Jerusalem was cut off from the main commercial highway through Ramleh, and adds that Muslims too participated in the souvenir and religious-goods export trade. The busiest season, he says, was during the Easter pilgrimage, at which time merchants would arrive with their wares from Alexandria, Damascus and elsewhere.[29]

Summarizing the situation on the eve of the British Mandate, Zuta and Sukenik noted the workshops established by several monasteries, where young Christians learned trades under the guidance of expert craftsmen. Foreign trade was also more developed among the Christians: many of the more important merchants of Jerusalem were Christians. This, together with the charity they received from their fellow Christians overseas, put the Christians of Jerusalem in a better financial position than their Muslim neighbors.[30]

Frankl writes that goods from Great Britain, France, Switzerland, Austria and Bosnia were displayed in the markets during his visit in 1856. Silk and wool carpets from Damascus were available there too, but most Jerusalem

26 Warren, *Underground Jerusalem*, pp. 512-513.
27 Turner, II, pp. 268-269.
28 Tobler, *Denkblätter*, pp. 288-289.
29 Neumann, pp. 220-222.
30 Zuta—Sukenik (1920), pp. 65-66.

trade was with the rest of Palestine. Glassware, mirrors and rings, for example, were brought from Hebron. The Bedouin, too, brought their wares each day to the market places.[31]

Warren relates that most imports hailed from the ports of Marseilles and Trieste. Marseilles offered woollen goods, silk, metal utensils and alcoholic beverages, while from Trieste came glass, lumber and furniture. Great Britain supplied cotton and wool, as well as metal utensils. Fruit and vegetables were grown in the Jerusalem district. Exports included wheat, olive-oil and sesame seeds. Olive-oil was used in the soap industry, and was also mixed with clay and lime to produce an extremely strong cement. The souvenir industry was concentrated in Bethlehem, but the goods were also brought to Jerusalem and sold in large quantities in the entrance-plaza of the Church of the Holy Sepulchre.[32]

Neumann relates that most of the manufactured items in the city were products of England, France and Switzerland. Needlework was imported from Austria; matches, from Bohemia; glass, mirrors and rings, from Hebron; silks and woollen fabrics, from Damascus. On the whole, however, the markets were not well-stocked.[33]

Bovet dwells upon Jerusalem's limited amount of foreign trade. The only foreign representatives in the city were three or four Greeks. The British consul, Finn, stresses that commerce was much less brisk in Jerusalem than it was in Jaffa, the main source of income being from Christian pilgrims.[34]

Internal commerce in Jerusalem centered mainly on the supplying of fruit and vegetables by local villagers and Bedouin. Mrs. Finn writes that vegetables were grown in the valleys around Jerusalem and brought to the city in large baskets by the women. Grapes from the vineyards which covered the hillsides around the city were transported by donkey, and watermelons from the Nablus and Ramleh areas, by camel.[35]

Ritter says, in the mid-nineteenth century, that olives, figs, grapes and nuts (especially pistachios) grew abundantly near Jerusalem, and were sold in the city markets.[36]

In the early part of the century, Seetzen reports, the Bedouin brought cucumbers to the city from the Jordan Valley and Ein Gedi, sulphur from the Dead Sea region, and roses, fruit and the seeds of various kinds of trees from Jericho.[37] Lortet says later on that the Bedouin often came to the city to buy clothing, fire-arms and jewelry made of glass and silver.[38] A source from the 1850's notes that Jerusalem's markets were dirty and sparsely stocked, their wares intended primarily for the Bedouin who came there in large groups.[39] Since it was forbidden to enter Jerusalem with arms, the Bedouin had to deposit their weapons with the guards at the city gates until they left.[40]

31   Frankl, pp. 244-246. Reicher (p. 58) also speaks of the numerous stores in Jerusalem market places, which offered a variety of goods.
32   Warren, *Underground Jerusalem,* pp. 499-500.
33   Neumann, pp. 223-224.
34   Bóvet, pp. 144-148; Finn, *Stirring Times,* I, pp. 173-174.
35   Mrs. Finn, *Home,* pp. 321-322.
36   Ritter, IV, p. 182.
37   Seetzen, II, pp. 26, 206.
38   Lortet, pp. 237-242.
39   Ritchie, p. 221.
40   Pardieu, p. 281.

Turkish barber (Saulcy, *Jerusalem,* p. 41)

According to Strauss, writing in the mid-nineteenth century, the level of craftsmanship and trade in the city was extremely low. The bazaars were greatly inferior to those in the large cities of Syria, and only offered the few basic items required by Jerusalem residents and the Bedouin. Cucumbers, watermelons and onions were supplied by the local villagers, but many of the usual vegetables of Europe were unobtainable. Prices were low when there were successful harvests.[41]

Foodstuffs and Services

Tobler provides us with a picture of the food supply of Jerusalem during the 1840's:

> Milk is in short supply for most of the year. Most common is goat's milk, which is sold in jugs. Cow's milk is unavailable, and camel's milk is used only by Muslims, who make cheese and sour-milk products from it. Butter is only available in the winter. The oil is usually good — both sesame and olive-oil are available. Sesame butter and tehina are extremely popular foods. Both the Arab and the European-

44

41   Strauss, pp. 278-280.

Turkish musician (Lortet, p. 242)

style bread is good. White bread is usually baked by Jews, who apparently use an English missionary recipe. Meat is consumed in very large amounts; a huge number of goats and sheep is slaughtered each morning.... There are also many oriental foods made from different plants and grains. Aside from water, the Muslims drink coffee and various other beverages. The Christians and Jews also drink wine.[42]

Strauss gives us the prices of various commodities in the markets.[43]

According to Seetzen, there were twenty-five cafés and twenty-five bakeries in Jerusalem in the early nineteenth century. They were probably simple, extremely primitive establishments, similar to some we see in the Old City today, but they were certainly widespread. Schulz writes that most of the cafés were located (in 1851) in shabby, street-level rooms; some were on street corners under a vault or awning. They provided only coffee to drink and hookahs to smoke. People sat on the floor or on low stone benches draped with fabric. Glasses and hookahs were lined up on wooden shelves along the wall

45

---

42 Tobler, *Denkblätter*, p. 212 (translated from German).
43 Strauss, pp. 211-212, 278-280. Prices are cited in many other sources, including Jewish ones such as Cahanyu, pp. 76-77.

Musician (Thomson, 1860 edition, II, p. 577)

and a charcoal stove stood in the corner. The Turks and Arabs were very fond of these cafés; one could see them there all day long, sitting quietly, immersed in thought. Schulz notes in their favor that they behaved in a more civilized manner than café-goers in Germany, who were often rowdy. The price of coffee was five pence, and that of a hookah one penny.[44]

Shops and Markets

A detailed survey of shops and trade in the market-places of Jerusalem was carried out in the late 1860's by Warren, who felt that information about them would be of great interest to anyone wishing to understand Jerusalem of that time. He drew up a list of shops and warehouses located inside the markets; excluding the factories and businesses in monasteries and other institutions and the few factories near the outskirts of the city, he reached a total of 1,320 enterprises. He then classified them according to the type of business and the number and religion of the employees.[44*] Warren found that 1,932 persons were working in the markets at this time, or about 10 per cent of the 20,000 persons he estimated lived in the city. He considered this percentage applicable to all community groups except the Jews, many of whom subsisted on *halukka* funds. Of the 1,320 shops Warren inspected, 278 were vacant and in use only during the Easter season, when merchants from Damascus and other cities arrived. There were many ancient market places, particularly near the Temple Mount, which were deserted. Warren predicted these too would return to life and provide a livelihood for about one hundred more tradesmen, if commerce

44   Seetzen, II, p. 17; Schulz, pp. 123-124.
44* See table in Warren, *Underground Jerusalem*, pp. 490-497.

Musicians (Thomson, 1860 edition, II, p. 578)

continued to develop at the rate of the previous ten years. Some of the occupations cited were characteristic of certain community groups, while others were engaged in by a variety of groups. There were many shoemakers — 230. Though divided among the various communities, the proportion of Jews among them was high. Grocery shops came next: there were 189. They too belonged to members of various communities, but the Muslims seem to have been most prominent.[45]

Nineteenth-century sources indicate that the market places of Jerusalem seem to have been located on the same sites since the time of the crusaders, possibly even the Romans.[46] Some writers claim there was an organic link between the markets and the holy places. Dixon and J. Wilson stress that most of the markets were in the center of the city, close to the Temple Mount and the Church of the Holy Sepulchre.[47]

There is also an attempt to discuss the functional division of markets and shops in Jerusalem. Williams, writing in the 1840's, says that the three main bazaar-streets probably dated from ancient times, when each of them was set aside for a different branch of trade. In his day, however, each contained a variety of trades. Williams quotes Mujir al-Din as saying that in the fifteenth century, the western row was intended for the sale of spices, with the income

47

45 Warren, *Underground Jerusalem,* pp. 490-497. On the various shops and trades in the markets, see Meyuḥas, in Luncz, *Almanac,* XII, 1907, pp. 12-47; on shoemaking as a common Jewish occupation, see *ibid.,* pp. 46-47.
46 Warren, *Underground Jerusalem,* pp. 520-521.
47 Dixon, II, pp. 45-46; J. Wilson, I, p. 453.

being donated to the school established by Ṣalaḥ al-Din (Saladin). The center row was the "Green Market," where various vegetables were sold, and the eastern one was for textiles. Williams tries to establish other divisions as well, using additional sources.[48]

J. Wilson (in the early 1840's) notes that most shopkeepers in the Old City were either Christians or Jews, and cites the report by Palmerston stating that Muslims rarely joined commercial organizations. At the end of the 1860's, Warren relates, shops were usually arranged as in earlier centuries, according to the type of business and the religion of the owner, though less rigidly so. There were Jewish shops in the Street of the Jews, with only an occasional Muslim one; the Street of the Christians was nearly all Christian. The meat market was mostly Muslim, while other markets were usually made up of members of various religions; clusters of shops of the same kind, of greengrocers, of tailors, of shoemakers or of other tradesmen, were to be found.[49]

Other contemporary sources make no mention of a functional division of markets and workshops, only noting their proximity to the holy places. Joseph Meyuhas, who made a study of the Arabs of Palestine, stresses that Jerusalem and Jaffa were unlike other eastern cities, in which craftsmen usually formed unions and worked together on the same street.[50]

Nevertheless, markets were named for the main wares sold there, either in the past or the present. This is brought out in Reicher's description:

> All the markets are crowded with shops from one end to the other, and... are named for the merchandise sold in them. For example, one market is full of shops selling cotton and silk clothing and fabrics of all kinds... Others feature luxury goods; yet others, all kinds of scents which perfume the air from afar, not to mention from nearby. There is a market selling food-stuffs, a market for shoemakers, for gold- and silversmiths, for coppersmiths, for blacksmiths, for cotton-merchants, for grain and pulse-sellers, and apothecaries.[50*]

Nineteenth-century travelers' works abound in descriptions of the general appearance of these markets. Forbin, who visited in 1817-1818, says they had vaulted roofs, and that caravans of camels resting in the corners of the market were a common sight. W.R. Wilson tells of the shops he saw a few years later in the Suq al-Kabir quarter, which were small, dark and dirty.[51]

Luncz offers the following description of the markets at the beginning of the nineteenth century:

> On both sides of the street from the Jaffa Gate to the vaulted street (which the Jews call the "dark shops" today), there were narrow sidewalks for pedestrians which made the main street even narrower. The vaulted street was full of stones and mounds of dirt, and all the shops on either side of the main road, which today is the main market (the "Batrak Market")... were full of dirt and dung. Only recently, powerful men have moved in and cleared them out...

48 Williams, II, Supplement, pp. 26-27.
49 J. Wilson, I, p. 453; Warren, *Underground Jerusalem,* pp. 490-497.
50 Meyuhas, in Luncz, *Almanac,* XII, 1907, p. 10; see also Meyuhas' entire article, *ibid.,* pp. 3-74, and Baldensperger in *PEF QSt,* 1904, 1905, 1906.
50* Reicher, p. 58 (translated from Hebrew).
51 Forbin, p. 152; W.R. Wilson, pp. 127-130.

He also writes that the two ancient markets—the scent market and the meat market—were closed with wooden doors at nightfall, and that the shops in the other markets also shut down at sunset.[52]

Wortabet claims that the busiest street during the mid-nineteenth century was the one leading from the Jaffa Gate towards the Mosque of Omar. There were all kinds of shops located along this street in no special order, most of them belonging to Jews and Muslims. Near the bottom of the street was a vaulted section where the better shops were situated, especially fabric stores.[53]

Neumann tells of the wooden structures, some three feet high, on either side of the street, which merchants and craftsmen used as seats. Peasant women sat on the ground, displaying their wares around them. These women painted the corners of their eyes and their lips blue, and their fingers and palms yellow. They also had blue tattoos on their foreheads and chins.[54]

Luncz relates the following:

> The three main markets have not changed in character for hundreds of years. They may be described now just as they were in Jewish travel literature of the thirteenth century, giving us a picture of the goods and crafts of the East. The first is the jewelers' market wherein the filigree workers sit.... On either side of the street there are wide shelves on which the shopkeepers display their wares and the craftsmen place their workbenches.... Near its middle, this market merges with another, called in Arabic Suq al-Aṭṭarin (market of scents and unguents). This market is very narrow and passage is made even more difficult by the shopkeepers, who place part of their wares outside, making it impossible for three people to walk down it side by side. The shops are very small and look like wooden closets attached to the wall. The third market is called Suq al-Laḥam (meat market). It is slightly wider than the previous one and its shops are somewhat larger. The butchers are near its entrance; the coppersmiths are beyond them; near its end one finds the shoemakers who make the red shoes worn by villagers. These two markets had always been closed by wooden doors immediately after sunset, but the doors rotted away and were broken in recent years, ending this ancient custom.[55]

Barclay (1857) mentions the Jewish market, in the Jewish neighborhood; the Turkish market, on David Street and the Street of the Chain, and in the adjacent alleys; the Christian market, mainly on the Street of the Patriarch, with religious articles being sold near the Church of the Holy Sepulchre; the Arab market in the lower part of the Via Dolorosa and the adjoining streets, al-Wad and Khan al-Zeit; the corner market in the open area around the Citadel of David; and the cotton market on the stretch of road leading to the Temple Mount, characterized by its simple limestone buildings and their barred windows.[56]

David Yellin describes the main commercial streets of Jerusalem at the end of the century:

> One runs from west to east, in a straight line from the Jaffa Gate to the Grain Market (al-Bizar) and branches off to the north, into Batrak Street in the

52 Luncz—Kressel, pp. 161-162 (translated from Hebrew).
53 Wortabet, II, p. 177.
54 Neumann, pp. 222-224.
55 Luncz, *Guide,* pp. 156-157; on the three markets, see also Hanauer (1926), pp. 122-126.
56 Barclay, pp. 434-435.

Khan—café near Jaffa Gate (Wilson, *Biblical Lands*, p. 183)

Christian Quarter; the other also proceeds in a straight line, from the Grain Market to the Gate of the Chain.... It has two branches, one going north to the Damascus Gate, and the other—the Street of the Jews—south to the Zion Gate.[57]

Another interesting description of the two main streets is offered by Grayevsky:

There are only two commercial markets which cross the entire city, one through its length, one through its width, with four or five smaller markets branching off from them.... Some areas have vaulted stone roofs so that daylight comes only through smoke holes.... The market which crosses the city lengthwise from the Jaffa Gate to the western gate of the Temple Mount... is vaulted only in part and is wider than the other markets. Trade there is brisk and it is always crowded.... In the middle of this market, near the place where it is bisected by the other market which crosses the city through its breadth, there is an... assembly hall (according to Turkish law, all grain merchants must sell their wheat here and pay a small sales tax; anyone who does not do so is punishable by law). Village women sit around it with some of their harvest. The crowds here are so great that people are pressed one against another and make their way through with difficulty....

Grayevsky goes on to describe the other markets in the city, noting the large number of Jews who worked in some of them.[58]

Gad Frumkin says most of the shops along Khan al-Zeit Street were owned

50

57   Yellin, *Writings*, I, p. 15 (translated from Hebrew).
58   Grayevsky, *Hidden Treasures*, XI (translated from Hebrew). On the markets, see also Avitzur, *Daily Life*, pp. 99-106.

Street café in Jerusalem (Wilson, *Picturesque Palestine*, I, p. 33)

by Arabs, some of them tinsmiths and blacksmiths. The largest oil-press in the city, the sesame press, was also located there. This market was not particularly long. The shops were crowded together, most of them selling fruit and vegetables, and a few Arab-style cakes and sweets.[59]

The markets began to change towards the end of the century. The newspaper *Ha-Tzevi* reports the opening of a new market in Jerusalem in July 1885. Two Jews had taken out a long-term lease on it, and four Jewish shops had already been opened there. In 1908, *Hashkafa* notes that a new vegetable market had opened, reaching from the bridge of the "army tower" opposite the Jewish-owned Anglo-Palestine Bank to the Jaffa Gate.[60] Important markets and commercial zones were also being established outside the walls, but this will be left for the second volume of this work.

In 1894, the PEF Quarterly mentions a special cattle market open on Fridays in the square east of the Nebi Da'ud Gate (Zion Gate). To prevent possible damage by frenzied animals, it was decided to shift this market outside the

59   G. Frumkin, pp. 24-25.
60   *Ha-Tzevi,* 2 Av, 1885, vol. I, no. 38, p. 2; *Hashkafa,* 15 Adar, 1908, vol. IV, no. 26, p. 2.

52   Central market of Khan al-Zeit (Wilson, *Picturesque Palestine*, I, p. 71)

walls, to the Sultan's Pool.[61] This report is of relatively late date. However, it implies that the market had existed near the Zion Gate for some time; if not from the first part of the century, then quite possibly from the early second half on.

The Rhythm of Daily Life

The backward state of craftsmanship and trade in the first half of the nineteenth century contrasts sharply with the situation to be found later in the century. Western travelers' descriptions of life in the city at this time — or, to be more precise, of the absence of activity — serve to heighten our perception of Jerusalem's stagnation in these early years.

Robinson, for instance, writes of conditions in 1838 as follows:

> The glory of Jerusalem has indeed departed. From her ancient estate as the splendid metropolis of the Jewish commonwealth and of the whole Christian world, the beloved of nations and the "joy of the whole earth," she has sunk into the neglected capital of a petty Turkish province; and where of old many hundreds of thousands thronged her streets and temple, we now find a population of scarcely as many single thousands dwelling sparsely within her walls. The cup of wrath and desolation from the Almighty has been poured out upon her to the dregs; and she sits sad and solitary in darkness and dust.[62]

Bartlett, the famous British painter who visited Jerusalem in 1842, writes:

> Nothing can be more void of interest than her gloomy half-ruinous streets and poverty-stricken bazaars, which, except at the period of the pilgrimage at Easter, present no signs of life or study of character to the observer.[63]

Norov, a Russian writer of the 1830's, claims the city was deserted when none of the three religions was celebrating a holiday. During Christian festivals, when the Christian Quarter came to life, silence continued to reign in the Muslim and Jewish quarters as if nothing were happening.[64]

In the 1840's, Strauss writes, Jerusalem was desolate most of the year. Only in April did the city begin to come to life, with everything turning green and the city filling up with pilgrims. In May, however, the city would settle down again and the oppressive heat begin to return. Then the water supply would diminish and living conditions would become extremely difficult. Only a few of Jerusalem's very richest residents could afford the luxury of leaving the city to live in tents in the countryside around it.[65]

Summarizing the mid-1850's, Wortabet says there was no sign of commercial life in Jerusalem, aside from one or two main streets. All was so quiet that the area might have been believed to be unpopulated. The Street of the Christians and David Street were the only ones exhibiting any signs of life.[66]

After visiting the city in 1854, Stewart writes:

> Except the slumbering watchman who lies at the corner of the street, and the growling dogs who are scared by the light of your lantern, scarce a living being is to be seen abroad after nightfall. During the day you look in vain for any signs of

61   *PEF QSt*, 1894, pp. 265-266.
62   Robinson, *Biblical Researches*, II, p. 81.
63   Bartlett, *Walks*, p. 133.
64   Norov, I, pp. 282-289.
65   Strauss, pp. 200-201; pp. 273-278.
66   Wortabet, II, pp. 176-178.

commerce. A camel or two loaded with corn, and a handful of peasant women with baskets of vegetables on their heads, are all who now bear traffic to her markets....[67]

Reicher also describes how the city was guarded. Soldiers were posted in every market, changing guard every hour. Guards patrolled the city at night and, sometimes, were even joined by the pasha. From two a.m. until dawn, it was forbidden to go out without a lamp. Anyone caught without one was fined. Reicher adds that the guards in the market places also kept watch over the scales to prevent short weight.[68]

Neumann notes that adulterated foodstuffs were not to be found in the markets, despite the laxity of the market police. Sanitation, however, was completely neglected and filth was abundant. Numerous troublesome beggars, of all religions except the Jewish, roamed the streets. There had been cases of violence and blackmail directed against Jews in the past, but nothing of the kind had occurred recently. According to Neumann, security had improved lately due to the addition of an armed group under the supervision of a chief *kawass* to patrol the city streets day and night.[69]

Orelli describes the beggars of Jerusalem in the 1870's. Hordes of them would congregate near all of the gates to the city, standing on both sides of the road. They were pitiful creatures, clothed in rags, many of them sick or crippled. Holding out metal bowls, they would cry out to passers-by in the most heart-rending manner.

Orelli writes elsewhere that there were always idle men loitering near the Jaffa Gate, watching those entering and leaving, and especially observing foreigners. The place was a paradise for beggars. Sometimes a farmer from a nearby village would toss them a piece of fruit—a fig or an orange.[70]

In the summary of his account of the city, Orelli claims Jerusalem was no longer what it had once been. Nevertheless, it had a unique atmosphere which constantly evoked the past. This was the difference, for example, between Jerusalem and Cairo. Many people would come here and stay because of what the city symbolized, that is, because of its past. Aside from this, the city had nothing special to offer. Jerusalem, Orelli says, was a city of religion; even if a railroad were to be built, Jerusalem would not become a commercial city. Such attempts had always failed. Jerusalem's beauty lay solely in its religious institutions, in its houses of worship and holy places.[71]

Dixon provides us with very vivid descriptions of Jerusalem as it was in the 1860's. He portrays its houses and dwellings in this way:

> The rows of houses being interrupted at every turn by public buildings, now in ruins—old convents, hospitals, churches, mosques—and rents being high and custom lax, the vaults of these crumbling piles have been seized by Arab and Hebrew traders, partly cleared out, partly propped up, and converted into stables, baths and mills. The fallen hospice of the Knights Templars, on land adjoining the Holy Sepulchre, affords shelter in its vaults and corridors to a great many braziers, barbers, and corn-chandlers; one room in the great ruin being used for a bazaar, another for a tannery, a third for a public bath; the Syrian burrowing in

54

67 Stewart, p. 308.   69 Neumann, p. 225.   71 *Ibid.*, pp. 102-110.
68 Reicher, pp. 60-61.   70 Orelli, pp. 86-88; 94-95.

the foundations of the old hospice, just as an Egyptian herdsman cowers into a tomb, and a Roman smith finds lodging in a palace wall.

Enter this coffee-house, where the old sheikh is smoking near the door; call the cafigeh, the waiter, commonly a negro slave; command a cup of black comfort, a narghiley, and a morsel of live charcoal. Then look round the vault. A dozen men, all bearded, all bronzed except yourself, some in rich robes and shawls, some naked to the waist, some dressed in sacks and sandals only, squat about the chamber, each with his hookah and his cup, dozing by himself, chatting with his neighbour, listening to a story-teller's endless adventures of love and war. A fountain bubbles in the centre. Mules are feeding in the rear....

A public thoroughfare is often the poor Arab's only house, where he must eat and drink, and buy and sell. When he wishes to wash, to rest, and to pray, he repairs to the court of his mosque and at stated times to the mosque itself; for the mosque is the true Moslem's home, which he has a right to enter, and from which no official can drive him away. In the court of his mosque he is sure to find water, in the sacred edifice he is sure to find shade. After finishing his devotions, he may throw himself on the mats and sleep. No verger has the pretension to expel him from the house of God. But the offices for which the solemnity of his mosque would be unsuitable, must be done in the public places; where he may have to load his camel, to feed his ass, and to dine and smoke. Humble cooks and cafigehs wait for him at the street corners. On three or four broken stones, the cook lights a bunch of sticks, throws a few olives and lentils, a piece of fat, a handful of parched corn into a pan; and holding this pan over his embers, stirs and simmers these edibles into a mess, the very smell of which ravishes an Arab's soul. A twist of coarse bread, a mug of fresh water, and a pipe of Lebanon tobacco, make up the remainder of his meal; after which the tired wayfarer will wrap his mantle about his face, lie down among the stones, and pass the soft summer night in dreaming of that happier heaven of his creed in which the heat is never fire and the cold never frost, in which the wells are always full, the dates always ripe, and the virgins ever young.[72]

He goes on to tell us that

The streets of the Holy City should be trod by day; not only because noon is everywhere warmer in colour than evening, but because Jerusalem is a Moslem and Oriental town, in which the business of life suspends itself from sunset to sunrise.

No gas, no oil, no torch, no wax lights up the streets and archways of Jerusalem by night. Half an hour after gun-fire, the bazaar is cleared, the shops and baths are closed, the camels stalled, the narrow ways deserted. An Arab has no particular love for lamps and lights. A flicker satisfies him in his room, and he never thinks of casting a ray from his candle into the public street. Darkness comes down like a pall, and by the time that Paris would become brilliant with lamps and gas, Jerusalem is like a City of the Dead. For a little while about the edge of dark, a white figure may be seen stealing from house to house; at a later hour you may catch the beam of a lantern carried by a slave; a Frank has been out to see his friend; a cavash is going to the consul's house; a bey is visiting his posts. These men have lanterns borne before them; for in Jerusalem, as in Cairo and Stamboul, a man going home without a light may be arrested as a thief.

What should tempt the inhabitants into their sombre streets? In a Moslem town, there are no plays, no concerts, no casinos, none of the impure public revelries which help to seduce the young in London, Paris, and New York. Bad men, and worse women, may exist in Zion, as in any other populous place; but here they have to hide their shameful trades, having no balls, no theatres, no taverns, in

55

72 Dixon, II, pp. 16-18.

which they can meet and decoy the unwary youth. Gaieties of any kind are rare. The nuptial processions which enliven the night in Cairo with lamps and drums have no existence in the Holy Land, where the bridegroom fetches home his bride by day. No one gives dinners, scarcely any one plays whist. A Moslem loves his home, his hareem, and his offspring, but his house is seldom the place in which he chooses to see his friends. A Frank may invite his neighbours to come and sip acids and repeat to each other that there is still no news; a mollah may call some sheikhs to his roof, where they will squat on clean carpets and recite their evening prayers. Refreshed with lemon-juice, inspired by devotion, these sober revellers, each with his servant and his lantern, seek their homes and beds about the hour at which men in London are sitting down to dine.[73]

Another picturesque description appears in Dixon's account of daily affairs in the square outside the Bethlehem (Jaffa) Gate:

A camel is lying down under its load, a swarm of dogs fighting for a bone, a knot of peasants waiting to be hired. [In] their gabardines, and their gaudy shawls, squat the barbers and cooks, the pipe-cutters, donkey-boys, money-changers, dealers in pottery and in fruit, all busy with their work or chaffering about their wares.

In the Jerusalem of Suraya Pasha, this court in front of the Bethlehem gate — the chief entrance for trade and pilgrimage into the Holy City, just as the Damascus gate is the chief entrance for pomp and honour — is the market, the exchange, the club, the law-court, the playhouse, the parliament of a people who despise a roof, and prefer to eat and drink, to buy and sell, to wash and pray, in the open air. Here everybody may be seen, everything may be bought, excepting those articles of luxury found in the bazaar. Yon negro dozing near his mule is a slave from the Upper Nile, and belongs to an Arab bey who lets him out on hire. These husbandmen are waiting for a job; their wage is a penny a day. Last week they were shaking olives for the Armenians; next week they will be carrying water for the Copts; but their chief employers are the Greek monks, who own nearly all the best vineyards and olive-grounds lying within a dozen miles of this Bethlehem gate. They are a hardy and patient race; Moslem in creed, Canaanite in blood.[74]

The famous author, Mark Twain, who visited Palestine in the 1860's, included a literary portrait of the country and of Jerusalem in his book *The Innocents Abroad.* Neglect made a strong impression on him, and led him to paint a gloomy picture indeed:

The Holy Land truly *is* "monotonous" and "uninviting" and there is no sufficient reason for describing it as being otherwise.

Of all the lands there are for dismal scenery, I think Palestine must be the prince. The hills are barren, they are dull of color, they are unpicturesque in shape. The valleys are unsightly deserts fringed with a feeble vegetation that has an expression about it of being sorrowful and despondent.... It is a hopeless, dreary, heartbroken land.... Palestine sits in sackcloth and ashes. Over it broods the spell of a curse that has withered its fields and fettered its energies.... Renowned Jerusalem itself, the stateliest name in history, has lost its ancient grandeur and is become a pauper village; the riches of Solomon are no longer there to compel the admiration of visiting Oriental queens, the wonderful temple which was the pride and the glory of Israel is gone.... Palestine is desolate and unlovely. And why should it be otherwise? Can the *curse* of the Deity beautify a land?

Palestine is no more of the work-day world. It is sacred to poetry and tradition — it is dream-land.[75]

56

73   *Ibid.,* pp. 11-14.
74   *Ibid.,* II, pp. 1-2.
75   Twain, vol. II (Harper and Brothers, New York, 1911), pp. 357-359.

Jerusalem! Perched on its eternal hills, white and domed and solid, massed together and hooped with high gray walls, the venerable city gleamed in the sun. So small!.... The thoughts Jerusalem suggests are full of poetry, sublimity, and more than all, dignity. Such thoughts do not find their appropriate expression in the emotions of the nursery.

Just after noon we entered these narrow, crooked streets, by the ancient and the famed Damascus Gate, and now for several hours I have been trying to comprehend that I am actually in the illustrious old city where Solomon dwelt, where Abraham held converse with the Deity, and where walls still stand that witnessed the spectacle of the Crucifixion.

A fast walker could go outside the walls of Jerusalem and walk entirely around the city in an hour. I do not know how else to make one understand how small it is. The appearance of the city is peculiar. It is as knobby with countless little domes as a prison door is with bolt-heads. Every house has from one to half a dozen of these white plastered domes of stone, broad and low, sitting in the center of, or in a cluster upon, the flat roof. Wherefore, when one looks down from an eminence, upon the compact mass of houses... he sees the knobbiest town in the world, except Constantinople. It looks as if it might be roofed, from center to circumference, with inverted saucers. The monotony of the view is interrupted only by the great Mosque of Omar, the Tower of Hippicus, and one or two other buildings that rise into commanding prominence.

The houses are generally two stories high, built strongly of masonry, whitewashed or plastered outside, and have a cage of wooden latticework projecting in front of every window. To reproduce a Jerusalem street, it would only be necessary to up-end a chicken-coop and hang it before each window in an alley of American houses.

The streets are roughly and badly paved with stone, and are intolerably crooked—enough so as to make each street appear to close together constantly and come to an end about a hundred yards ahead of a pilgrim as long as he chooses to walk in it. Projecting from the top of the lower story of many of the houses is a very narrow porch-roof or shed, without supports from below; and I have several times seen cats jump across the street from one shed to the other when they were out calling. The cats could have jumped double the distance without extraordinary exertion. I mention these things to give an idea of how narrow the streets are.

The population of Jerusalem is composed of Moslems, Jews, Greeks, Latins, Armenians, Syrians, Copts, Abyssinians, Greek Catholics, and a handful of Protestants.... The nice shades of nationality comprised in the above list, and the languages spoken by them, are altogether too numerous to mention. It seems to me that all the races and colors and tongues of the earth must be represented among the... souls that dwell in Jerusalem. Rags, wretchedness, poverty, and dirt, those signs and symbols that indicate the presence of Moslem rule more surely than the crescent flag itself, abound. Lepers, cripples, the blind, and the idiots, assail you on every hand, and they know but one word of but one language apparently—the eternal "bucksheesh"....

Jerusalem is mournful and dreary, and lifeless. I would not desire to live here.[76]

A Summary; Herzl's Vision of the Old City

The descriptions of Twain, like those of other Western travelers, show nineteenth-century Jerusalem as a small, typically Eastern city; the buds of renascence were emerging here and there amid the ruins of this city, whose

57

---

76 *Ibid.,* p. 295

majestic past hovered over it and whose sanctity emanated from every crevice, whose present was sorrowful and filled with desolation and stagnation.

We might be critical of these descriptions and say they reflect the opinions of their Western authors and nothing more, whereas conditions were actually not as described. Perhaps their great disappointment at finding Jerusalem so different from their expectations, so far from the splendor of which they had dreamed, led these travelers to exaggerate the city's dismal state. Such criticism, however, seems unwarranted. The passages cited here may be colorful and picturesque but, beneath their literary wraps, they tell us about the state of the city, with its poor and varied populace and very backward life-style. How could such things be deemed fitting for a city with such a rich historical, religious and cultural past? Jerusalem of the nineteenth century was far from dignified. It was a small, miserable city, and the disappointment of its Western visitors was valid and sincere.

Equally profound was the disappointment of Theodor Herzl, the prophet of the State of Israel, upon his visit to Jerusalem in 1898. He, however, was able to channel his disappointment into a prophetic vision of the city:

> When I remember thee in days to come, O Jerusalem, it will not be with pleasure. The musty deposits of two thousand years of inhumanity, intolerance and uncleanliness lie in the foul-smelling alleys.... If Jerusalem is ever ours and if I am still able to do anything actively at that time, I would begin by cleaning it up. I would clear out everything that is not something sacred, set up workers' homes outside the city, empty the nests of filth and tear them down, burn the secular ruins, and transfer the bazaars elsewhere. Then, retaining the old architectural style as much as possible, I would build around the Holy Places a comfortable, airy new city with proper sanitation.... I am quite firmly convinced that a magnificent New Jerusalem could be built outside the old city walls. The old Jerusalem would still remain Lourdes and Mecca and Yerusholayim...[77]
> I would isolate the old city with its relics and pull out all the regular traffic; only houses of worship and philanthropic institutions would be allowed to remain inside the old walls. And the wide ring of hillsides all around, which would turn green under our hands, would be the location of a glorious New Jerusalem.... Tender care can turn Jerusalem into a jewel. Include everything sacred within the old walls, spread everything new around it.[78]

58

77 Herzl, II, pp. 745-747.
78 *Ibid.,* p. 753.

Chapter Three:
WATER SUPPLY: SPRINGS, POOLS, CISTERNS
AND THE AQUEDUCT

Introduction

Throughout the ages, Jerusalem's water supply has been one of the central factors in the city's growth and development. This was true of the nineteenth century as well. Following the British conquest of Palestine in 1917, there began the rapid modernization of the country that changed it almost beyond recognition. Thus, the years 1800-1917 may be considered as the last "historical" period. The importance of studying the nineteenth century is twofold. We are provided by it with a picture of life in Palestine just before the vast changes brought by modernization, and are also given a glimpse of conditions existing hundreds of years earlier, in times when changes in the country's appearance were few and far between. This is equally true of Jerusalem's water-supply system. Thus, by examining the state of affairs in the nineteenth century, we will see how antiquated methods of water supply were prior to the British Mandate and gain a general understanding of how the system functioned in earlier historical periods.

Jerusalem, wrote Tobler in the 1840's, was once said to be rich in water and yet wanting for water. In his opinion, the city really was well-supplied.[1] Here he appears to be in error. His impressions were probably based on the fact that many methods of supplying water were employed in the city. The opposite, however, seems to have been true: it was the shortage of water that forced Jerusalem inhabitants to resort to so many ways of assuring a continuous supply.

Tobler classifies Jerusalem's water sources as follows: spring or well water; rain water; water brought to the city by canals or pipelines; water brought to the city by water carriers.[2] Our discussion will follow a slightly different classification: spring or well water, particularly in the Kidron Valley; rain water collected in artificial pools; rain water collected in cisterns; and water brought from distant sources.

Sources of the Kidron; the Giḥon Spring

The Giḥon spring has been the city's most important water source throughout the history of Jerusalem, and was a prime factor in the establishment of a settlement in the area. Much has been written about this spring, about its

59

---

1   Tobler, *Denkblätter,* p. 53.
2   *Loc. cit.*; for a comprehensive historical account of the various water sources in Jerusalem, see
     Ritter, IV, pp. 29-158.

formation, discharge and long history. We will deal only with its state and importance in the nineteenth century.

Nineteenth-century travelers called the Gihon by many different names. Some Christians referred to it as "Mary's Spring" or "The Virgin's Spring." Others used the Biblical name "Gihon." Most common, however, was the local Arabic name, "Umm al-Daraj" (Mother of the Steps), because of the steps leading down to the spring. These travelers note between twenty-six and twenty-eight steps, including the fifteen or sixteen upper ones that led to an arched, cave-like structure, and eleven or twelve leading from it to the water. The water, they say, flowed from a broadened cleft in the rock. Each step was some ten inches high; the entire descent measured about twenty-five feet. The spring-cave itself was fifteen feet long and five to six feet wide, while its height was no more than six to eight feet.[3]

Nineteenth-century writers state that the water of the Gihon was brackish and was therefore used for drinking only in emergencies.[4] El-Abbassi (Ali Bey) writes in 1807 that the spring was usually used for irrigation and for watering sheep, but that, when the cisterns in the city were dry, it served also for domestic purposes.[5] According to Charles Wilson, the Gihon supplied a steady but small amount of water of inferior quality in the 1860's.[6]

These sources also comment that the water level in the Gihon changed from time to time.[7] The flow would suddenly strengthen and then, a little later, return to normal, in a sort of high and low tide. This would occur several times a day during the rainy season, but only once every few days in the dry season.[8]

According to the PEF Survey, the discharge of the Gihon spring increased two to three times a day in the spring, while the spring flowed only once in every two or three days in the autumn.[9] The PEF Quarterly reports a drastic reduction in the water level of the Gihon in 1900-1901, which was particularly evident in its outlet in the Pool of Siloam. The municipal team sent to investigate remedied the matter by removing accumulated silt from the tunnel.[10] Investigations during a later period revealed that the water supply of the spring ranged from 1,140 cubic meters per day at its peak to only 225 cubic meters at its lowest point.[11]

During the nineteenth century, the Gihon spring, particularly the Siloam tunnel, was the subject of much study. We shall discuss some of the research and its findings, which included the "Siloam Inscription." Robinson examined the tunnel in 1838 and found the water only a foot deep at most, with the usual depth being only four or five inches. He mistakenly identified the place as the

3 Seetzen, II, pp. 31-32; Norov, I, pp. 253-254; Robinson, *Biblical Researches,* I, pp. 499-503; J. Wilson, I, pp. 497-499; Stewart, p. 319; Vincent—Lee—Bain, illustration on p. 197.
4 Lynch, p. 407; Petermann, I, p. 206; Neumann, pp. 179-190.
5 El-Abbassi, II, p. 241.
6 Wilson—Warren, *Recovery,* pp. 25-26.
7 Monro, I, pp. 199-201; Schulz, p. 152; Paxton, pp. 112-135.
8 Geramb, I, p. 387; Orelli, pp. 172-173; Ch. Wilson, *Survey,* p. 84.
9 Warren—Conder, *Jerusalem,* pp. 365-371.
10 *PEF QSt,* 1902, pp. 29-35, including map and cross-section.
11 Amiran *(Atlas),* pp. 34-35, including statistics and sources relevant to water supply to Jerusalem.

Giḥon Spring (Geikie, p. 505)

Pool of Bethesda.[12] In the 1860's, Wilson and Warren investigated the Giḥon spring, the Siloam tunnel, and the Pool of Siloam. Warren walked the whole length of the tunnel in December 1867 (his findings are presented in detail in his letters dating from 1867 to 1869).[13] Liévin writes that when he visited the Siloam tunnel (apparently in the early 1860's), the water level was very high and investigation was difficult. At the end of the decade, Warren carried out excavations there, and the canal was cleaned and examined.[14] Some children trying to go through the tunnel in 1880 discovered the "Siloam Inscription," an ancient inscription consisting of six lines in Hebrew; it was cleaned by Conrad Schick and deciphered by Prof. A.H. Sayce, who visited the site at the beginning of 1881.[15] In 1891, someone attempted to remove the inscription (perhaps in order to sell it to a European museum). The Ottoman authorities finally detached it, breaking it in two in the process, and sent it to the museum

12   Robinson, *Biblical Researches,* I, pp. 499-503. Subsequent visitors to Jerusalem repeat Robinson's descriptions and data of the tunnel; see, e.g., J. Wilson, I, pp. 499-501.
13   Wilson—Warren, *Recovery,* pp. 239-267; their letters of Sept. 12, Oct. 11, Oct. 28, and Nov. 2, 1867. The considerable flow of water in the Kidron Valley is described in their letters of Dec. 18 and Dec. 21, 1869.
14   Liévin (English), p. 178.
15   Warren—Conder, *Jerusalem,* p. 345-365.

in Constantinople (now Istanbul), where it is still to be found.[16] In November of 1881, the PEF people again carried out investigations in the tunnel. This time the water level was much lower than when Warren had worked there (it had been up to his neck), making exploration much simpler. In 1891, Schick discovered an ancient canal which had carried water from the Gihon spring to the Pool of Siloam before the hewing of the tunnel.[17]

The Pool of Siloam

In their descriptions of the Pool of Siloam, the travelers of the nineteenth century distinguished between its two parts: a large, rectangular pool, and a smaller pool, hollowed in the rock, a few meters above it. The small, hewn pool received its water from the long Siloam tunnel and was at the tunnel's end.[18] According to these travelers, only traces were left of the Pool of Siloam's former splendor. Marble tiles and the bases of several pillars were discernible on its floor.[19]

Nineteenth-century explorers claim that the pool existing in their time was not the original one. Guthe, for example, writes that it had once been much larger, and that part of it had been hewn from stone. He estimates that the original width from east to west had been ninety-five feet.[20] Other travelers raise the possibility of another pool having existed nearby, south of the present-day pool. They say that below the present pool there were clear indications of a broader one, that also must have received its water supply from the Gihon. That broader pool was now almost completely filled with earth, and an orchard had been planted in it. Some believe that this was the pool mentioned in Nehemiah III, 15 as "the pool of Shelah by the king's garden," because of its proximity to the cultivated "Kings' Garden" region of the Kidron Valley.[21]

Nineteenth-century sources mention the special taste of the water in the Pool of Siloam. It was said to be relatively tastier than the water of the Gihon or the insipid water in the city's cisterns. This pool was used mainly for drinking purposes, especially by the residents of the village of Silwan, whose womenfolk came there to draw water. Silwan residents would also carry water to the city in large goatskin water bags to sell to the wealthy.[22] Mrs. Finn writes that Jerusalem inhabitants obtained most of their water from cisterns and that, towards the autumn when their water was depleted, water was brought by donkey from Ein Rogel and the Pool of Siloam and sold for a considerable price.[23] Consul Finn describes the situation as follows:

> ... the water supply of Jerusalem... is always scarce, first because of the crowded state of the houses, in each of which several families live; secondly because the

16 Luncz, *Guide,* pp. 136-137; Press, *Travel Handbook,* p. 84.
17 Baedeker (1912), p. 83.
18 Chateaubriand, p. 323; Strauss, p. 220.
19 Lynch, p. 407; J. Wilson, I, pp. 499-500; Norov, I, pp. 255-256; Vincent — Lee — Bain, photo, p. 227.
20 Warren — Conder, *Jerusalem,* pp. 345-346.
21 Stewart, pp. 315-321; Orelli, p. 173; Ch. Wilson, *Survey,* p. 79.
22 Lamartine, I, p. 370; Scherer, p. 212.
23 Mrs. Finn, *A Third Year,* pp. 123-130.

ater seller (Manning, p. 11)   Water carrier (Saulcy, *Jerusalem,* p. 200)

Moslem landlords have allowed the cisterns to fall into disrepair, so that the great number of them hold little or no water. Hence the poor Jews have always to buy water, which they obtain from the peasantry, who bring it into the city in skins on their asses from the springs at Siloam, Lifta, and elsewhere. When the rain has been abundant, the Jews have to pay less....[24]

Charles Wilson writes in the 1860's that peasants from the Pool of Siloam region sold water in the city, but this water had a bad taste and was quite expensive. In addition, the peasants would cheat their customers by filling the water pouches only partly. Warren claims the residents of Jerusalem did not like the water of the Pool of Siloam, and that only soldiers used it.[25]

The main source of the Pool of Siloam is the Giḥon, whose unpleasant-tasting water we mentioned earlier. The Pool of Siloam was located in the Tyropoeon Valley, and served as a kind of "reservoir-dam" as well, collecting the overflow waters of this valley, which were channeled towards it. Some writers believe that the Pool of Siloam also absorbed some of the city's underground drainage water and sewage.[26] It was this variety of sources that seems to have been responsible for the occasional changes in the taste of the water.

24 Finn, *Stirring Times,* II, p. 60.
25 Wilson—Warren, *Recovery,* p. 20; Warren, *Underground Jerusalem,* pp. 440-445.
26 Pierotti, I, p. 256.

The direct link between the Gihon and the Pool of Siloam caused the water level in the Pool of Siloam to fluctuate according to the flow of the Gihon. In 1896, according to the PEF Quarterly, the Pool of Siloam had dried up completely. Local residents suggested that this was because the water of the Gihon had found a new route, apparently an underground riverbed. This proved to be the case.[27]

Aside from the villagers' use of the Pool of Siloam for drinking purposes, and its use by Jerusalem inhabitants in times of emergency, the pool's main use seems to have been the irrigation of the gardens in the Kidron Valley. Alongside the pool there were only a few trees, mainly pomegranate, and bushes. The remaining water flowed through a narrow canal, partly hewn in the rock, into a trough at the edge of the Kidrom Valley. From there it was distributed to irrigate the green, flowering gardens. Women also did their laundry in the canal waters, turning the area into a meeting place for local residents.[28]

The waters of the Gihon and the Pool of Siloam were thought to have healing powers. One nineteenth-century traveler relates that the Arab residents bathed in the spring for this reason.[29] Another writes that the water was considered beneficial for eye afflictions.[30] A third notes that, near the entrance to the spring, there was a raised stone platform on which the Muslims prayed.[31] Others say it was the Jews of Jerusalem who thought the spring waters had special healing powers, and that the Jews went there in groups to bathe fully clothed.[32]

The Pool of Siloam was held sacred by the Christians. Various sources insist that this was the place where Jesus restored the sight of a blind man.[33] The water was thought to provide good protection against eye disease, just as it had in Jesus' time.[34] Christian traditions concerning the miracles worked there by Jesus led to the establishment of a church near the pool in both Byzantine and Crusader times. Archaeological excavations at the end of the nineteenth century disclosed an ancient bath-house and the remains of a church, apparently dating from the sixth century. Paving stones, steps carved in the hillside, and the remains of an ancient wall were also found.[35]

Christian researchers became active again at this site at the end of the nineteenth century. The PEF Quarterly reports that the lower pool, which had been used until then as a cesspool, was cleaned out almost completely by the Greek Church authorities, who intended to build a monastery in the area. A wall had also been built around the pool.[36] Early in the Mandate period, the presence of a lower pool southeast of the Pool of Siloam, apparently the "King's

27   *PEF QSt*, 1896, p. 132.
28   Lamartine, I, p. 370; Scherer, p. 212; Stewart, pp. 315-321; Carne, *Letters*, pp. 330-332.
29   Norov, I, pp. 253-254.
30   Petermann, I, p. 206.
31   Seetzen, I, pp. 31-32.
32   Orelli, pp. 172-173; Conder, *Tent Work*, I, pp. 313-314. See also Yellin, *Writings*, II, p. 31.
33   Seetzen, II, p. 31; Lynch, p. 407.
34   Scherer, p. 212.
35   Zuta—Sukenik (1920), pp. 184-185.
36   *PEF QSt*, 1904, p. 4.

Ein Rogel—Bir Ayyub (Vincent—Lee—Bain, p. 196)

Pool," which now belonged to the Greeks, was noted. The Greeks had filled it in with earth and planned to turn it into a vegetable garden. At about the same time, the Muslims built a mosque beside the Pool of Siloam.[37]

Ein Rogel—Bir Ayyub

The third source of water in the Kidron Valley described in detail by nineteenth-century travelers was Ein Rogel. Local inhabitants usually called it "Bir Ayyub,"[38] but some sources refer to it as "Nehemiah's Well." The sources point out that "Bir Ayyub" was the name of the structure located above the well, at the meeting place of three valleys: the Valley of the Kings (the Kidron Valley), the Tyropoeon Valley, and the Valley of Hinnom. Robinson (1838) writes about Bir Ayyub as follows:

> It is a very deep well, of an irregular quadrilateral form, walled up with large, squared stones, terminating above in an arch on one side, and apparently of great antiquity. There is a small rude building over it, furnished with one or two large troughs or reservoirs of stone.... The well measures 125 feet in depth, fifty feet of which was now full of water.[39]

According to Tobler, the well was shaped like an inverted pyramid with large, ancient stones composing its floor. South of it, there was a ruined

65

37 Zuta—Sukenik (1920), pp. 184-185.
38 Opinions differ as to whether Bir Ayyub was named after Job or after Joab.
39 Robinson, *Biblical Researches,* I, p. 332.

mosque, which Tobler dates to the first quarter of the eighteenth century.[40] Other sources repeat the information about the ruins of a mosque and of other buildings at the site, and about the existence of stone troughs there for watering cattle.[41]

Hewing marks in the rock led to the discovery of various water canals near this well (and near the Pool of Siloam and the Giḥon as well) in the nineteenth century. These were said to be part of an irrigation system watering the many gardens in the area.[42] The PEF volume on Jerusalem also cites the existence of several underground canals and aqueducts near the Pool of Siloam and Bir Ayyub. About 560 yards south of Bir Ayyub, there was another well; it was called the "Well of the Steps" because the Arab inhabitants believed there were steps leading to it from Bir Ayyub.[43]

The most characteristic feature of Bir Ayyub was its changing water level. During the rainy season, especially when rain was abundant, the well would fill up and its waters overflow.[44] During his visit to Jerusalem in 1806, Seetzen wrote that the winter weather had been extremely cold, and that snow had fallen. He noted that the large amounts of rain and snow affected the water supply at Bir Ayyub and, together with the Giḥon and the Pool of Siloam, had turned the Kidron into a swiftly rushing stream.[45] According to Ritter, the water level in the well was indicative of the amount of precipitation in each year. In 1814, 1815, 1817 and 1819, the well had overflowed three times, and twice in 1821. In 1815 and 1821, there had been large amounts of excess water, whereas in 1816 and 1820 the water level had not risen at all.[46] Williams (1849) writes that Schulz had examined the well and found that the water flowing from it in winter did not come from the well-head but from two side openings in the valley. The flow of water was similar to that of a spring and was of short duration. The longest period of flow remembered had lasted two months.[47] Mrs. Rogers (1856) also tells of the seasonal flooding at Bir Ayyub when, after a heavy storm at the end of March, all the water sources in the city had been replenished. There was a strong current in the Giḥon and Bir Ayyub, and even Solomon's Pools had filled within four hours.[48]

Pierotti writes that when he visited the well in October 1858, it was completely dry. But after strong rains in 1861, water flowed from the well to the Kidron for fifteen days.[49] The PEF Quarterly reports a flood at Bir Ayyub in January of 1874, as a result of heavy rain, noting that it was a rare occurrence for that time of the year.[50] The water in Bir Ayyub was apparently pure rain water, and of better quality than the waters of the Giḥon or the Pool of Siloam. Petermann (1853) writes that this water was the best available to the

40   Tobler, *Topographie,* II, p. 50.
41   Geramb, I, pp. 385-386; J. Wilson, I, p. 492; Luncz, *Guide,* p. 135.
42   Masterman, *Hygiene,* p. 58.
43   Warren—Conder, *Jerusalem,* pp. 371-375.
44   Geramb, I, pp. 385-386; Robinson, *Biblical Researches,* I, pp. 490-492; J. Wilson, I, p. 497; Stewart, pp. 315-316; Scherer, p. 213.
45   Seetzen, II, p. 385.   48   Rogers, pp. 292-293.
46   Ritter, IV, p. 148.   49   Pierotti, I, p. 253.
47   Williams, I, Supplement, p. 27.   50   *PEF QSt,* 1874, p. 75.

city. Thus, when this water was plentiful, many Arabs would fill goatskin bags with it and transport them to the city by donkey.[51]

It seems there were two ways of exploiting the water of Bir Ayyub: making use of the floodwaters in the winter, and drawing water from the well itself during the dry summer months when there was a water shortage in the city.[52] The PEF volume on Jerusalem states that Bir Ayyub was the only well which supplied the city with water during the summer. The volume also notes that the well was deep, with a large rock-hewn chamber for collecting the water that drained from the Kidron and the Valley of Hinnom. It belonged to the peasants of Silwan, who sold its waters in the city.[53]

A steady flow of water in Bir Ayyub was cause for celebration among the residents of Jerusalem. Tobler says that after heavy rains in the city, Bir Ayyub began to overflow. The inhabitants of Silwan quickly informed the head of the Jewish community of this, for a fee, of course. The event became the talk of the day, and great crowds went there to celebrate.[54] Seetzen (1806) adds that Jerusalem residents made use of the opportunity to clean their carpets and do their laundry in the swiftly flowing waters.[55]

Others writing during the century recorded that the flooding of Bir Ayyub was a joyful occasion for the people of Jerusalem, lending a festive atmosphere to the city and its environs.[56] The Jewish newspaper *Havatzelet* reports that residents of Jerusalem sang and danced at the sight of the overflowing water.[57] This is repeated by Luncz in 1891.[58]

At the beginning of the British Mandate, Masterman makes these comments:

> In the spring, after a very heavy rainfall, the water bursts up and for a few days runs down the valley as a little stream. The immense appreciation of the Oriental for "living water" is then very apparent, for hundreds of people come out of the city at such a time to sit or wander beside the "flowing Kidron."[59]

Thus, we may conclude that the Kidron valley served as one of Jerusalem's major water sources during the nineteenth century. The Pool of Siloam was fed mainly by the Gihon, but it also seems to have absorbed rain water and other water draining from the city. This drainage water, which penetrated the Gihon and, to a lesser extent, Ein Rogel, gave the water its brackish taste.[60] Ein Rogel was less affected, particularly when flooding occurred, because it held mainly rain water. In times of drought, at the end of the summer, and even during years of normal rainfall, water from the Kidron was sold in the city. Water from these sources was extremely important to the residents of Jerusalem and it is no wonder that the sight of rushing streams aroused such joy.

---

51 Tobler, *Denkblätter,* p. 35; Petermann, I, p. 206-207; on Bir Ayyub see also Ch. Wilson, *Survey,* p. 84.
52 Seetzen, II, p. 25; Neumann, pp. 7-8.
53 Warren—Conder, *Jerusalem,* p. 371; see also Wilson—Warren, *Recovery,* pp. 19-20.
54 Tobler, *Topographie,* II, p. 50.
55 Seetzen, II, pp. 17-18; 386-387.
56 Stewart, pp. 315-316; Scherer, p. 213; Orelli, p. 173. For a detailed description see Mrs. Finn, *A Third Year,* pp. 123-130.
57 *Havatzelet,* 26 Adar, 1871, vol. I, no. 13, p. 50.
58 Luncz, *Guide,* p. 135.
59 Masterman, *Hygiene,* p. 58.
60 *Loc. cit.*

Unfortunately, the sources in the Kidron Valley were far from the city and provided relatively small quantities of water.

Pools

A second type of water source was a prominent feature of nineteenth century Jerusalem: the open pool. Constructed in earlier centuries, these pools were now in poor condition, and were quite unimportant as water sources. Nineteenth-century writers offer numerous descriptions of the dismal state of these pools, occasionally lamenting the loss of their former glory and importance. The pools are called by a variety of names, some of them historical, others local. Let us examine several descriptions of each pool.

Birket Isra'il. One of the pools most frequently referred to in nineteenth-century writings is Birket Isra'il, which no longer exists. Until the end of the century, it was frequently called the Bethesda Pool. According to various sources, the pool was dry, and half-clogged by rock slides, rubbish and waste materials. The residents of surrounding buildings disposed of their sewage there. A few olive, pomegranate and fig trees grew inside the pool, amidst weeds and wild shrubs.[61]

Travelers state that the pool was about 150 feet long and 40 feet wide. There were two arches along its western side, for whose presence different explanations were offered. On its southern side, Birket Isra'il was adjacent to the wall of the Temple Mount.[62] Robinson (1838) claims the pool was larger: 360 feet long, 130 feet wide and 75 feet deep. This, of course, was without the accumulated rubbish. He believes that the arches in the southwestern corner continue under the nearby houses, making the full length of the pool 460 feet. In his opinion, the pool was part of the Antonia fortress (the Acropolis), but had been used as a reservoir, as shown by the plaster and silt still visible on its sides.[63]

Schulz (1851) writes that Birket Isra'il had been dry for 200 years;[64] Charles Wilson says there was no point in repairing it since it was not watertight.[65] The PEF volume on Jerusalem still identifies it in the early 1880's as the Bethesda Pool, and suggests that the arched passages were intended to support the houses built over them. Archaeological excavations inside these houses revealed pipes which may have been connected to the pool, as well as reservoirs, passages, doorways and steps somewhat similar to those found south of the Temple Mount wall, near the Single Gate.[66] At the end of the 1880's, it was proved that the Bethesda and Birket Isra'il pools were not identical. The correct site of the Bethesda Pool was discovered in 1888, and

---

61 Seetzen, II, pp. 24-25; Turner, II, p. 192; W.R. Wilson, p. 251; Skinner, II, p. 208; Baedeker (1876), p. 183; Neumann, pp. 179-190; Manning, pp. 115-116.
62 Monro, I, pp. 184-186; Norov, I, p. 218.
63 Robinson, *Biblical Researches*, I, p. 489; see also J. Wilson, I, pp. 415-416, who repeats Robinson's statements.
64 Schulz, p. 130.
65 Wilson—Warren, *Recovery*, pp. 22-23.   66 Warren—Conder, *Jerusalem*, pp. 122-126.

Birket Isra'il (Roberts)

Schick published a detailed article about it in the German periodical *ZDPV*.[67]

Birket Isra'il remained a prominent landmark in the Old City until the British authorities decided to do away with this "eyesore" in the 1930's, filling it in with earth. Although various buildings stand on it, the filled-in pool is still conspicuous today.[68]

Hezekiah's Pool. The next most impressive pool in the Old City during the nineteenth century was Hezekiah's Pool. Christian travelers called it the "Pool of the Patriarch" or the "Pool of the Holy Sepulchre" because it was in the Christian Quarter, not far from the Church of the Holy Sepulchre. Local inhabitants referred to it as Birket al-Ḥammam (Pool of the Baths), since it supplied water to the nearby public bath-house throughout most of the year.[69] Unlike Birket Isra'il, this pool did contain water in the nineteenth century. In addition to collecting rain water, it was fed by the Mamilla Pool outside the city by means of a small, open aqueduct that entered Jerusalem through the wall near the Jaffa Gate. Even in the rainy season, the amount of water collected was too small to fill the pool. Travelers note that in the spring it was

67   *ZDPV*, IX, pp. 178-183.
68   Just inside the Lions' Gate, alongside the northern wall of the Temple Mount.
69   Seetzen, II, pp. 24-25; Thomson (1860), II, pp. 522-529. The name "Hezekiah's Pool," though commonly used in the nineteenth century, is of course a misnomer, since King Hezekiah built the Siloam Pool.

Hezekiah's Pool (Lortet, p. 243)

only half full, and its water looked undrinkable.[70] One source says that its water was used by Jerusalem residents; others claim it supplied the Patriarch's Bath, at the southwestern end of the Street of the Christians.[71] According to Robinson (1838) and others, its breadth at the northern end was 144 feet, its length on the eastern side about 240 feet.[72]

According to Williams writing in the late 1840's, "it doubtless represents the Amygdalon, or Almond-Pool, mentioned by Josephus in his account of the siege by Titus." He also says "there is a descent to it by steps at the northwest angle, and the water, which in the rainy season runs in from the rude aqueduct at the southwest corner, occupies only a small part of the pool in the southeast angle."[73]

Many travelers noted that the houses were built up against the pool, their

70 Robinson, *Biblical Researches,* I, pp. 487-488; Olin, II, p. 174; J. Wilson, I, p. 437; Mrs. Finn, *Home,* p. 502; Thomson (1860), II, pp. 522-523; Wilson—Warren, *Recovery,* pp. 22-23.

71 Monro, I, p. 208; see also Williams, I, Supplement, p. 18.

72 Robinson, *Biblical Researches,* I, pp. 487-488; J. Wilson, I, p. 437; Baedeker (1876), p. 218; Vincent—Lee—Bain, p. 232.

73 Williams, I, Supplement, pp. 18-19. Williams was not aware of the error, which had already become common in his time; the word "amygdalon" was assumed to be Greek and translated accordingly as "almonds."

Hezekiah's Pool (Saulcy, *Jerusalem,* p. 187)

balconies actually jutting out over the water. On its north side, the pool was bounded by the Coptic inn built in the time of Ibrahim Pasha.[74]

Neumann (1887) relates that Hezekiah's Pool received water from the Mamilla Pool in the rainy season by means of a small aqueduct. The water, which was muddy and not very plentiful, especially in dry years, was used only by the nearby bath-house. Neumann claims the ancient walls of the pool were revealed when the new Coptic monastery was being built.[75]

Mamilla Pool. As we have noted, Hezekiah's Pool was linked to the Mamilla Pool. Nineteenth-century sources say the latter was a rain-water reservoir at the entrance to the Valley of Hinnom. It only filled with water in the winter, the quantity depending upon the amount of rain. It was not fed by any spring. Robinson writes that he found it empty.[76] On the other hand, it was filled to the top throughout Stewart's visit. The walls of the pool were made of hewn stone joined with a cementing material, and there were steps in the corners leading down to the bottom. The pool was some 300 feet long, 200 feet wide, and 20 feet deep.[77]

As for the aqueduct leading to Hezekiah's Pool, Tobler says it began as a canal one foot and four inches wide and nine to ten inches high, and narrowed down to only one foot wide and eight inches high after a few yards. Its bottom was completely lined with plaster. The aqueduct led into an underground pipe. Tobler progressed through it for a considerable distance, stopping at the place

74   Paxton, p. 134; Vincent—Lee—Bain, p. 237.
75   Neumann, pp. 179-190.
76   Robinson, *Biblical Researches,* I, pp. 352-354, 483-484; Seetzen, II, pp. 24-25; Tobler, *Topographie,* II, p. 50.
77   Stewart, pp. 309-311.

where a stick and a rag were usually inserted to plug the narrow pipe in order to fill the Mamilla Pool.[78] Ritter writes that traces of this aqueduct could be seen a meter and a half above the base of the northwestern corner of the Old City wall.[79] PEF sources report that the opening from the canal was located in the lower end of the Mamilla Pool.[80] Thirty-three meters from the head of the canal, there was a device for regulating the flow of water to the city.[81]

The sources also note that the area around the Mamilla reservoir, especially that northeast of it, held the largest Muslim cemetery in the city. The surrounding region was strewn with rubbish; as a result flood waters reaching the pool were unclean.[82]

With regard to the name of the pool, a church named for (an alleged) saint, Mamilla, is said to have been located nearby at one time.[83] Some of the nineteenth-century travelers mistakenly identify the Mamilla Pool as the upper pool of the Gihon, and the Sultan's Pool (see below) as its lower pool.[84]

The Sultan's Pool. Located outside the Old City in the Valley of Hinnom, the Sultan's Pool was a prominent feature of the Jerusalem landscape. According to PEF sources, it had been referred to as the Gihon in the fourteenth century. The Sultan's Pool was originally built by German knights in 1170 and repaired later by Suleiman the Magnificent (Abu Salim) between 1520 and 1566.[85]

The dimensions of the pool vary according to the different accounts. Robinson says it was the largest of the local pools, being 592 feet long. Its northern wall was 245 feet wide, its southern wall, 275 feet wide; the depth of the northern end was 35 feet, including nine feet of rubbish, while that in the south was 42 feet, including three feet of rubbish.[86] According to Luncz (1891), the length of the pool from north to south was 169 meters, and its width 61 meters; its depth in the northern corner (with the accumulated silt) was 10.90 meters and, in the southern corner, 13 meters.[87]

Some Jerusalem visitors claim there were two separate pools in the area: the Sultan's Pool in the north, and Suleiman's Pool in the south.[88] Others note that travelers to Bethlehem and Hebron used a strong, wide causeway which served as the pool's southern wall. Here, there was a Muslim watering fountain with an inscription in Arabic; it had formerly received water from the nearby aqueduct leading from Solomon's Pools. At the time they wrote, however, the fountain was dry.[89]

78   Tobler, *Topographie,* II, pp. 50.
79   Ritter, IV, pp. 59-77.
80   Warren—Conder, *Jerusalem,* p. 375.
81   Wilson—Warren, *Recovery,* p. 21.
82   Robinson, *Biblical Researches,* I, pp. 352-354; Wilson—Warren, *Recovery,* p. 21.
83   Stewart, pp. 309-311; Ritter, IV, p. 71.
84   Robinson, *Biblical Researches,* I, pp. 483-484; see also Norov, I, p. 267; Tobler, *Topographie,* pp. 5-6.
85   Warren—Conder, *Jerusalem,* pp. 376-377; see *PEF QSt,* 1898, pp. 224-229, for a detailed description of the Sultan's Pool. including a longitudinal section and a cross-section.
86   Robinson, *Biblical Researches,* I, pp. 485-486.
87   Luncz, *Guide,* p. 139; Norov, I, p. 269, gives slightly different measurements.
88   Tobler, *Topographie,* II, p. 5.
89   Robinson, *Biblical Researches,* I, pp. 485-486.

Sultan's Pool (National Library, photo album GR/2)

Opinions vary as to the source of the water in the Sultan's Pool. Some thought it was Solomon's Pools, by means of an aqueduct branch no longer in use. Others believed that, like the Mamilla Pool, this one was intended to collect rain water. According to Robinson, its water came from the Mamilla Pool, which was situated above it.[90] In any case, all the writers agree that the Sultan's Pool was dry at the time of their visits to Jerusalem. At most, small amounts of rain water collected near the causeway, and were used to water gardens on the slopes of Mount Zion.[91] The pool was almost wholly filled with refuse and dirt; there was a vegetable garden in its upper part, on the north side.[92]

Yellin writes that, at the end of the nineteenth century, the Sultan's Pool was used as a threshing ground for the nearby wheat fields. In the summer, farmers' wives also came there to crush potsherds so as to produce building material from them.[93]

Mary's Pool. In addition to the Birket Isra'il and Hezekiah pools inside the city, the Mamilla and Sultan's pools outside it and the Siloam Pool in the Kidron Valley, all of them prominent features of the nineteenth-century Jerusalem landscape, let us mention the Pool of Sitt Mariam. This pool was located outside the walls of the Old City, about 100 paces north of the Lion's

73

90   Seetzen, II, pp. 24-25; Robinson, *Biblical Researches,* I, pp. 485-486.
91   Wilson—Warren, *Recovery,* pp. 21-22.
92   Baedeker (1876), p. 231; Zuta—Sukenik (1930), p. 150.
93   Yellin, *Writings.* I, p. 15.

Gate and slightly higher than it. It was smaller than the others, and had openings in its southwestern, southeastern and northeastern corners. Tobler claims the structure was not an ancient one, and states that he found no mention of it in the sources prior to 1821. There had once been steps in all four corners of the pool, but only a few steps in the southeastern corner still remained.[94]

In addition to the pools we have noted here, a number of cisterns and of small reservoirs formed by dams and walls ringed the city.[95] None of these was topographically prominent or important as far as Jerusalem's water supply was concerned. Thus, we may conclude that the pools of Jerusalem, however much they attracted the attention of nineteenth-century spectators, were of little practical significance to the city's contemporary inhabitants.

Privately Owned Cisterns

The most important source of water during the nineteenth century was undoubtedly the city's cisterns, both private and public.

Contemporary sources relate that the residents of Jerusalem drank rain water collected in cisterns situated alongside their homes. Robinson (1838) says that all homes in the city had at least one cistern; the house he stayed at had four. These cisterns were usually rock-hewn and were between twelve and twenty feet deep. Most had circular openings at the top; some had stone tops and a device for hanging a pail. During the rainy season, these cisterns collected rain water from the rooftops.[96]

Tobler (1845) notes that the water collected in these cisterns was tasty, even after five months had passed. During this interval, he says, it would lose its aftertaste and could be used without being mixed with other water (although the inhabitants did so mix it). The water in the cisterns, which served as the city's major water source, had to suffice until the next rainy season. This had been the case for hundreds of years. Houses were designed so as to facilitate the collection of rain water. Roofs and courtyard pavements, for instance, were made extremely smooth, so that the greatest possible amount of water could be collected and led into cisterns through a network of pipes and gutters. These had to be kept spotlessly clean if the water was to be fit to drink. It was no wonder, then, that the Eastern peoples tried so hard to keep animals such as cats and dogs away from their homes, and thereby to prevent contamination of the courtyard or roof. Cisterns sometimes occupied the entire space beneath the house or the inner courtyard. There was scarcely a house in the city without a cistern; many had more than one. The homes of the poor, Tobler notes, had small, simpler cisterns that could supply water for only a few months after the rains ended. The cistern openings were round, small and usually covered; although some had a special apparatus with a wheel to help draw the water,

94 Tobler, *Denkblätter*, pp. 433-437; Wilson—Warren, *Recovery*, pp. 21-22.
95 For descriptions of remains of pools and cisterns see Robinson, *Biblical Researches*, I, pp. 345-346; Tobler, *Topographie*, II, p. 50; Wilson—Warren, *Recovery*, pp. 22-23; Olin, II, pp. 139-140; Pierotti, I, p. 148.
96 Seetzen, II, pp. 12, 25; Robinson, *Biblical Researches*, I, pp. 480-482; Wilson, *Survey*, p. 86.

most did not. For the most part, water was drawn by hand in jugs and buckets.[97]

Public Cisterns

In addition to its private cisterns, Jerusalem also boasted many public cisterns located near churches, monasteries, mosques and other public places, especially on the Temple Mount. At the beginning of the century, Seetzen writes that the cisterns on the Temple Mount were of large capacity and contained water even during times of drought. However, since both Jews and Christians were forbidden to enter the Temple Mount, only Muslims could use this water. They watered their livestock with it and used it for laundry, but did not use it for drinking.[98] Paxton (1830's), on the other hand, claims the water from the Mosque of Omar was taken home by the public.[99] Tobler (1840's) says that the Temple Mount cisterns were extremely important, and contained water from outside sources in addition to rain water. This water was saved for emergencies, when the regular water supply was cut off.[100] Documents from 1897 in the British Consular Archives show that Jerusalem residents were permitted to use this water in accordance with the number of family members, the amount of water in the cisterns and the season in question. This water was supplied free of charge, but non-Muslims were unable to take advantage of the arrangement since they could neither enter the compound themselves nor afford to pay a Muslim water-carrier.[101] Large quantities of water from these cisterns were also used by the mosques on the Temple Mount.[102]

The cisterns on the Temple Mount dated from earlier historical periods, and only a few of them were still in use during the nineteenth century. Explorations at this time, however, resulted in the discovery of many of them, and the renewed use of some.[103] These cisterns obtained their water from two sources: rain water collected from the Temple Mount and its environs, and water from Solomon's Pools, via the aqueduct (see p. 79 below). The latter seems to have been their principal source.

Another group of large public cisterns mentioned by nineteenth-century travelers was located in the Latin Monastery of St. Savior. Seetzen (1806) says there were twenty-four cisterns there, and that similar ones existed in other monasteries.[104] According to Robinson (1838), the twenty-eight cisterns then in the monastery could supply the needs of the entire Christian community in times of drought. Other sources say the water was sufficient for half a year, and was distributed free of charge to Catholics by the Catholic priesthood.[105]

---

97   Tobler, *Denkblätter,* p. 35; Neumann, pp. 7-8, 129; see also Olin, II. p. 178; Scherer, p. 187.
98   Seetzen, II, p. 12.
99   Paxton, p. 134; Olin, II, p. 178.
100 Tobler, *Denkblätter,* p. 35.
101 Hyamson, II, p. 410 (Nov. 12, 1897).
102 Vincent—Lee—Bain, pp. 121-122.
103 On the cisterns on the Temple Mount, see Warren—Conder, *Jerusalem*, pp. 217-225; Ḥavatzelet (16 Kislev, 1871, vol. I, no. 6, p. 21) also reports the discovery and cleaning of these cisterns and mentions their possible use for domestic purposes.
104 Seetzen, II, pp. 24-25.
105 Robinson, *Biblical Researches,* I, pp. 480-482; Ritter, IV, p. 143; Neumann, p. 129.

75

Qayit Bey Fountain (sabil) on Temple Mount (Wilson, *Picturesque Palestine*, I, p. 53)

Ancient Cisterns

European travelers mention a cistern called Helena's Cistern. Charles Wilson's account reads:

A little to the east of the Church of the Holy Sepulchre is a large cistern known as that of Helena, to which there is an entrance from the street leading up to the Coptic Convent... being estimated as 60 feet long by 30 feet broad.... There is only one shaft to this cistern which is used by both Moslems and Christians.... The depth of the cistern measured from the mouth of the shaft... is 66 feet; there is always a good supply of water, except in seasons of great drought... the supply must be derived entirely from rain collected on the roofs and terraces above....[106]

The extensive building activity and archaeological excavation undertaken in the nineteenth century led to the discovery of cisterns and ancient pools all over the city, some no longer in use. Examples of these were the cisterns found in the Muristan and in the vicinity of Christian buildings along the Via Dolorosa.[107] The construction of the Sisters of Zion Convent on the Via Dolorosa resulted in the discovery of the Twin Pools, cisterns which had once been fed by an aqueduct.[108] The PEF volume on Jerusalem describes this find, as well as the unearthing of the aqueduct in 1871. This aqueduct began in the northern part of the city, outside the Damascus Gate, and was destroyed during the construction of the Turkish city wall. It may also have supplied water to the cisterns on the Temple Mount.[109]

Another water source, which was something between a spring and a well, or a cistern and a pool, was Ein al-Shifa. It served the bath-house built next to it, and aroused the curiosity of nineteenth-century visitors to Jerusalem, who wondered where its water came from. In the 1830's and 1840's, it was investigated by several explorers. Wolcott, an American missionary, investigated the well in 1841-1842, and even descended into it. He found that although the well itself was 82.5 feet deep, the water in it was only about four feet deep. Its lower portion was a rock-hewn, arched chamber leading to a winding, eighty-foot channel that ended in a basin or well of unknown depth. Beyond this he could not go.[110]

According to Robinson, Tobler visited the well on March 16, 1846, at which time there was only an inch of water. In 1853, Barclay also descended into the well. After his first visit to Jerusalem, Robinson writes that the water stopped flowing forth in the dry season and had to be drawn by hand.[111] The PEF Quarterly of 1871 reports as follows:

> From the bottom of the shaft a channel, cut in the rock, and vaulted with masonry, leads down in a southerly direction to a small cave or basin, from which the water is obtained in summer by a man who descends for the purpose.[112]

Nineteenth-century writers make various guesses as to the origin of the water. Stewart (1854), for example, says the flow was intermittent, as in the Gihon. He therefore tries to connect the two.[113] Other travelers see a link between the water of Ein al-Shifa and that of the Siloam Pool, because they had a similar taste.[114] PEF sources attribute this similarity of taste to the fact that most of the water reaching both flowed first through ruins and garbage.[115] Pierotti (early 1860's) tries to find a connection between the underground

106 Wilson, *Survey,* p. 54, including additional details; Murray, pp. 177-181.
107 Spyridon, p. 126; Warren—Conder, *Jerusalem,* p. 290; Masterman, *Hygiene,* p. 60.
108 Wilson, *Survey,* p. 85; Masterman, *Hygiene,* p. 60.
109 Warren—Conder, *Jerusalem,* pp. 209-216, 263-264. The same source provides plans of the pools and adds details about their excavation and clearing. Information is also supplied about the aqueduct, including a contour map.
110 Williams, I, pp. 457-459.
111 Robinson, *Biblical Researches,* I, pp. 508-509; *Later Biblical Researches,* pp. 245-246.
112 *PEF QSt,* 1871, p. 103.   113 Stewart, pp. 275-276.   114 Petermann, I, p. 206.
115 Warren—Conder, *Jerusalem,* pp. 261-263; *PEF QSt,* 1871, p. 103.

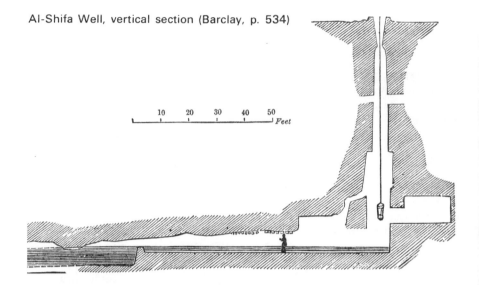

Al-Shifa Well, vertical section (Barclay, p. 534)

stream he saw near the convent of the Sisters of Zion and the water of Ein al-Shifa.[116] Such a connection is doubtful, it being much more likely that the well was fed by rain water flowing underground along the Tyropoeon Valley from the Damascus Gate. The PEF volume on Jerusalem describes the excavations carried out south of the Austrian Hospice at the corner of the Via Dolorosa:

> A shaft was commenced on the 19th May, 1869, where the Via Dolorosa joins it immediately... south of the Austrian Hospice.... A gallery was driven west through hard soil and large stones, and after 5½ feet, the old sewer from the Damascus Gate was found, which is 2 feet wide and 4 feet, 9 inches high; the floor is of rock... the roof is of flat stones laid across: this was examined for 130 feet southwards, and three shafts leading down into it were explored....[116*]

It seems that, at certain periods, water also reached the nearby bath-house by means of the aqueduct and pipeline from Solomon's Pools.[117]

The Increase in the Number of Cisterns

Pierotti estimates that there were 992 cisterns in Jerusalem by the end of the 1850's, most of them ancient and hewn in stone.[118] It is difficult to know whether this number is correct, but it certainly seems a reasonable estimate. Thomson says the great number of cisterns and the fact that each house had one meant that the city might have to surrender because of hunger, but never because of thirst.[119] In the course of the nineteenth century, construction activities both in the Old City and outside it increased and, along with them, the number of cisterns grew. The excavation of new cisterns was especially marked among western institutions and organizations, which sought to increase the amount of water they could offer to those under their patronage.

78

116 Pierotti, I, pp. 63, 257.
116* Warren—Conder, *Jerusalem*, p. 236.
117 Apparently, the water from this source also reached the water fountains on al-Wad Street; see pp. 166-167.
118 Pierotti, I, pp. 260-261.   119 Thomson (1860), II, p. 525.

Many cisterns were hewn outside the city walls too. A central cistern was one of the first facilities provided in every new Jewish neighborhood. It was also a chief concern of the builders of public institutions and private houses. Smith (who visited Jerusalem in 1901) quotes the owner of his hotel in the new city as teling him that the hotel had so many cisterns it could supply its own needs for three years.[120]

The growth in the number of cisterns continued throughout the nineteenth century. The importance of the cisterns is demonstrated by Ottoman law, which allowed the issuing of building permits for Jerusalem only on condition that a cistern be provided in the courtyard.[121] At the beginning of the Mandate period, the city engineering surveyors found 7,300 cisterns in the city, with an over-all capacity of 445,000 cubic meters (about 98 million gallons). The largest network of cisterns was that located beneath the Temple Compound, which held 15,900 cubic meters of water (or some 3.5 million gallons).[122] Masterman, however, says that British engineers had estimated the total capacity of all Jerusalem's cisterns at 360 million gallons.[123]

Rain-water cisterns were the major water source for Jerusalem residents for hundreds of years prior to, as well as during, the nineteenth century. The modest water-consumption habits of Jerusalemites were a contributory factor; as long as they remained modest, properly maintained cisterns could supply local needs, at least as far as quantity was concerned. There was difficulty mainly towards the end of the summer, when the cisterns ran dry, and even earlier if rainfall had been minimal. At such times water was brought from other sources, primarily from the Kidron Valley but also from those at greater distances, by aqueducts or by other means.

Aqueducts (until the 1870's)

The chronic water shortage in the Jerusalem region prompted the construction of an aqueduct to bring water from Solomon's Pools in the Hebron hills. Two aqueducts conveyed water to Jerusalem in ancient times: the low-level aqueduct and the high-level aqueduct.[124] In the nineteenth century, only the low-level aqueduct was in use, and that only in part. (Some contemporary explorers were even unaware that another one existed.) The low-level aqueduct appears on maps of nineteenth-century Jerusalem.[125] We have already mentioned the pipe which led from this aqueduct to the watering-fountain on the causeway above the Sultan's Pool. According to our sources, the aqueduct ran west of the Sultan's Pool and then across the valley to its north over a nine-arched bridge; it then circled Mount Zion's western and southern slopes

---

120 Amiran *(Atlas)*, p. 35; Smith, *Jerusalem*, I, p. 121.
121 Masterman, *Hygiene*, p. 58.
122 Amiran *(Atlas)*, p. 34; Rosenan—Wilinsky, p. 689; Avitzur, *Daily Life*, p. 44 (based on Hamburger, I, p. 213) says that, by the end of the Turkish regime, the Old and New City had 6,600 cisterns, with a capacity of half a million cu.m.
123 Masterman, *Hygiene*, pp. 8-9, 58.
124 See Masterman, *Hygiene*, pp. 8-9, 58-60.
125 See the maps of Catherwood, British Admiralty, Van de Velde and Wilson. For details on these maps, see Prologue.

—where traces of it were discovered in the nineteenth century—and brought water to the mosques on the Temple Mount.[126]

During the nineteenth century, the low-level aqueduct was used irregularly as a water source for the cisterns on the Temple Mount. Various sources tell of repairs undertaken to restore it to proper working order, and of damage to it that stopped the flow of water completely. A Jewish source dating from 1834, for example, notes that the pipes were blocked by peasants during their uprising, so that no water could reach the Maḥkame, the Muslim Court adjacent to the Temple Mount.[127] On the other hand, sources dating from the 1840's report that the aqueduct was functioning as usual. Tobler writes that this water was a blessing to Jerusalem, because it was abundant and reached the city when conditions were most difficult. In 1844, the pasha of Jerusalem had the aqueduct repaired; one year later, it was reported to have delivered large quantities of water to the city. Tobler says it was easy to distinguish between the ancient structure and later additions to it, especially in the section between Ṣur Bahir and Abu Tor. From time to time the aqueduct was damaged, but it was always repaired.[128] Rabbi Joseph Schwarz mentions the benefits derived from this aqueduct while discussing Jerusalem's water problem in a letter sent to his brother in 1837.[129] At the end of the 1850's, Scherer describes the suffering caused by the lack of water in Jerusalem. The splendid aqueducts which had formerly supplied large quantities of water from Solomon's Pools were in ruins, and the little water that still flowed in them was used for the Dome of the Rock.[130] Guérin writes that the flow of water from the Etam stream had been renewed, but the aqueduct was then blocked again and water reached only as far as Bethlehem in 1863.[131] Another attempt was made to repair the aqueduct in 1866.[132]

Luncz (1891) describes the repairs to the aqueduct in 1866:

> Not far from the Cotton Market there... is a canal which brings water from Solomon's Pools. The canal was repaired in 1866; Montefiore, who was then in Jerusalem, contributed 300 pounds sterling for this purpose. However, the inhabitants of our city did not benefit from this project for long. Water carriers and residents of Bethlehem sabotaged the pipes soon thereafter, because they wanted the water from Solomon's Pools for themselves.[133]

It is worth remembering that Charles Wilson's entire mapping and surveying project in Jerusalem in 1864-1865 was designed to examine the possibilities for improving the city's water supply by bringing water from Solomon's Pools.[134]

---

126 J. Wilson, I, pp. 494-495; Stewart, pp. 309-311; Wilson—Warren, *Recovery*, pp. 233-234; Warren—Conder, *Jerusalem*, pp. 376-377.

127 Cahanyu, pp. 90-91.

128 Tobler, *Denkblätter*, p. 35; idem, *Topographie*, II, p. 84; see also Lady Egerton, p. 25.

129 Yaari, *Letters*, p. 374.

130 Scherer, p. 187.

131 Guérin, *Judée*, III, p. 309.

132 Cahanyu, pp. 90-91, *Ha-Levanon*, 8 Ḥeshvan, 1866, vol. II, no. 20, p. 308.

133 Luncz, *Guide*, p. 131 (translated from Hebrew). On Montefiore's contribution to the repair of the Jerusalem aqueduct, see Gat, p. 56, based on Montefiore's diary.

134 Wilson—Warren, *Recovery*, pp. 236-237. The survey was made possible by the contribution of Lady Burdett-Coutts. In 1870 she intended, according to Warren, to make another donation toward the organization of Jerusalem's water supply, but the authorities were opposed. Wilson tries to explain this opposition. See also Hyamson, II, p. 393.

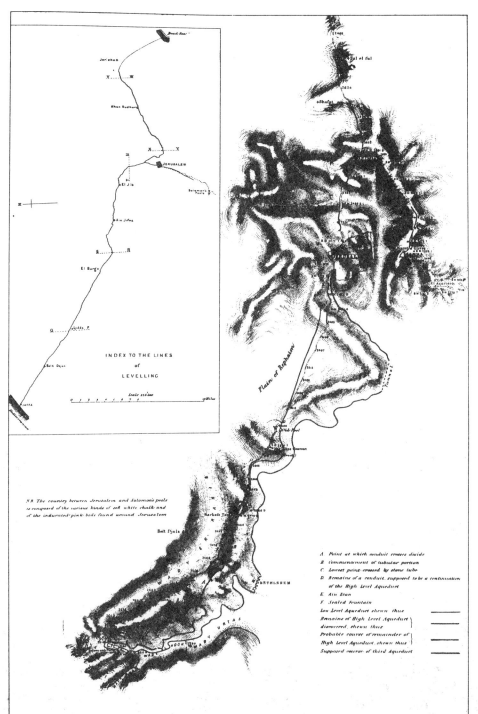

Map showing altitudes from Solomon's Pools to Jerusalem, 1865 (Wilson, *Survey,* 1:2500 map)

Warren (late 1860's) gives the following account of the city's water-supply situation and the operation of the aqueduct:

> Three years ago the low-level aqueduct from Solomon's Pools was repaired by the Turkish Government at the expense of the people... the unfortunate fellahin had had to bring their own stones and lime... water only runs to Jerusalem for a few weeks in each year, though to Bethlehem it runs constantly. At the present time, the water is running to waste about one mile north of Bethlehem. When the water does get a chance of running into Jerusalem, it is allowed to go to the Serai and the Mahkama (Judgement Hall) and then the surplus is turned off into the great sea at the southern end of the Noble Sanctuary.... This low-level aqueduct gives at Bethlehem a supply of about 500 gallons per minute. Allowing 1/3 of this for the population of 5,000 in that town, and 2/3 for the 10,000 quartered about the lower portion of Jerusalem, we have a rate of 45 gallons a head per diem... it would, however, be necessary to construct receiving tanks, as half this quantity would be running in during the night and would otherwise run to waste... it is probable that the low-level aqueduct would require new pipes before it could be put into good repair. At present, the pipes as far as Bethlehem appear to be uniformly of about 10 inches diameter, but from thence to Jerusalem they vary very much. This aqueduct is fed from Ain Etam, and the surplus water from the Pools of Solomon. Finding that this low-level aqueduct will only supply the lower portion of Jerusalem, it is necessary to see what can be done for the upper portion.... The inhabitants of this portion are principally Jews and Christians, the former being poverty-stricken and quite unable to buy water.... It is apparent that they must be supplied at a higher level, not lower than the Jaffa Gate, in order that water may replenish fountains in their streets. For this purpose, the Sealed Fountain above the Pools of Solomon can be taken advantage of, and [water] brought down in closed pipes.[135]

Warren goes on to calculate how much water could be brought from this fountain to the higher parts of the city.

The aqueduct underwent additional repairs in the 1870's. The newspaper *Ha-Maggid* reports in 1873 that Nazif Pasha had repaired the pipes and placed guards in many places to prevent the peasants from doing any damage.[136] Other sources say repairs were ordered by Izzat Pasha in the early 1870's, but the flow of water to the Temple Mount lasted only a short time.[137] *Ha-Maggid* also relates that a benefactress from Britain had donated 25,000 pounds sterling tò insure the supply of water from "the River Arub" to all residents of Jerusalem, regardless of religion, requesting that guards be placed all along the line to deter would-be vandals. Kamil Pasha notified the heads of the various communities as well as all the European consuls in the city that the rest of the expenses would be divided among the city's residents.[138]

Acts of vandalism and repairs to the aqueduct continued in the following years. In 1879, the newspaper *Ha-Tzefira* writes that the water pipes running from Ein Etam to Jerusalem were undergoing repairs after having been blocked by the inhabitants of nearby villages.[139]

In the course of the century, the aqueduct became an increasingly important

135 Warren, *Underground Jerusalem,* pp. 441-443.
136 *Ha-Maggid,* 6 Av, 1873, vol. XVII, no. 30, p. 276.
137 Murray (1875), pp. 173-181; Liévin (1897), I, pp. 426-427; Neumann, p. 190.
138 *Ha-Maggid,* 21 Adar, 1874, vol. XVIII, no. 11, p. 93 (copied from *Ḥavatzelet*); see also *Ha-Levanon,* 16 Adar, 1874, vol. X, no. 29, p. 231.
139 *Ha-Tzefira,* 29 Nisan, 1879, vol. VI, no. 14, p. 108.

component of the city's water supply, particularly in late summer and during droughts. Furthermore, since the aqueduct was repaired by the authorities with the assistance of foreign contributions, the water on the Temple Mount gradually became available to the non-Muslim population, in particular to the Jews. Thus, for example, Hamburger writes in his memoirs that a faucet was installed near the *Maḥkame* and water was distributed from there to city residents:

> In the summer, when water in the cisterns ran dry, the attendant at the *Maḥkame* would distribute water to the local inhabitants, one free container of water a day per woman. Many Jews and Arabs would stand on line every day, for two or three hours before noon. When the *Talmud Torah* cistern was empty, two pupils from each *ḥeder* in rotation were sent out with a container to fetch water from the *Maḥkame*. The attendant immediately placed these pupils at the head of the line, saying that he did this so they would not miss their classes. We also lived in peace and affection with the other Arab residents, both young and old.[140]

Interesting references to the sale of water from sources in the Kidron Valley may be found in various memoirs of the period. Weiss, for example, tells of the "water market" near the Dung Gate, to which the Arabs of Silwan would bring tins and skins of water on donkeys. The Jews would buy water, take it home and empty it into special clay barrels designed for this purpose.[141]

Warren gives a detailed description of water-supply conditions during the 1870's:

> Jerusalem is for the most part supplied with water attached to, and, generally, under the houses; it is only towards the end of the dry season that water in any quantity is required from other sources; and the amount varies very much each year according to the rainfall.... The Christians this year... appear to have required very little extra water; those who had small tanks borrowed from those who had larger. The Mahometans drew the little extra they required from the tanks under the Noble Sanctuary. What was brought up from Bir Eyub was sold principally to the Jews. Towards the end of the season, on an average, 35-40 donkeys were employed bringing up water from Bir Eyub: ten trips each day, two skins or kibies each load, each skin containing about six gallons. This gives a supply per diem of from 4,200 to 4,800 gallons.[142]

Barclay, on the other hand, says that 25,000 gallons of water were brought from Bir Ayyub on September 12, 1853, or five times as much as the amount indicated by Warren.[143] Obviously, Warren is offering an average figure, while Barclay is describing an extreme case. Warren goes on to say this:

> In very dry seasons, however, water is brought from Siloam, Lifta, Ain Karem, and elsewhere, and the people have to buy what they can get, or do without, as it best suits their pockets.... The water from Bir Eyub and from the Noble Sanctuary is sold at the same rate....[144]

The *Jewish Chronicle* also abounds in descriptions of Jerusalem's water problems. An issue from 1872 reports that the city depended principally upon

140 Hamburger, II, p. 58.
141 Weiss, pp. 30-32.
142 Warren, *Underground Jerusalem*, pp. 440-441.
143 Barclay, *City,* p. 515.
144 Warren, *Underground Jerusalem*, p. 441.

cisterns and rain-water reservoirs. These cisterns were nearly empty in the fall, at which time there was a shortage of water in the city. The newspaper comments that the water from the Pool of Hezekiah was used for the Turkish baths, and that the water remaining was covered with algae. The writer proposes to turn the city's pools into gardens, to build new cisterns, to prevent water loss due to seepage from existing cisterns and to maintain the purity of the water. He claims that water seeping from the cisterns could be observed in the deep caves beneath the city. He notes current plans to convey water from Solomon's Pools by means of the ancient aqueducts, which were to be repaired, and to fill the city's pools with water from springs in the vicinity. The foundations of these aqueducts were still strong and usable; in his view, it would be necessary to provide new conduits.[145]

In the German periodical ZDPV, Schick offers a summary of the Jerusalem water situation, and describes the city's water sources from ancient times until the mid-1870's. He also provides a topographical map of the city and a diagram of the water conduits leading to it.[146]

Conveying Water from a Distance (1880-1914)

At the end of the nineteenth century, Jerusalem's water-supply situation worsened considerably. The population had grown markedly and there had been a succession of droughts. The Ottoman authorities were forced to take vigorous measures to restore the ancient aqueducts at this time.

In 1891, the newspaper Ha-Or assesses the city's water needs and discusses the possibilities of satisfying them for a population numbering 45,000. There were neither parks nor factories in Jerusalem, and 50 liters of water a day per person would be sufficient, considering current living habits. If the number of inhabitants were to rise to 65,000, it would be possible to make do with 42 liters a day per person. Cisterns could supply 20 liters a day per person, an amount sufficient for domestic consumption. The additional 20 to 25 liters a day per person could be furnished by spring water, to be piped to the city. The springs cited by the newspaper include, among others, Ein Yalu near Malha and Ein Hanniyye beyond the village of Walaja; they could supply annually eight kilograms of water a day per person, but they belonged to the villages near which they were located. Other springs in the Jerusalem area were in Ein Karem, Lifta, Koloniya and Ein Fara. The problem was that all of them were located lower than Jerusalem. Solomon's Pools supplied three liters of water per second, but were also below most of Jerusalem. Only the al-'Arub spring could serve the entire city, since its water could reach all of it by gravitation. Located nine kilometers southwest of Solomon's Pools, the al-'Arub spring produced nine liters of water per second, which reached the pools by a Roman aqueduct. It was proposed to build a pool with a capacity of 2,000 cubic meters

145 *Jewish Chronicle*, Feb. 16, 1872, no. 151, p. 12.
146 *ZDPV*, I, 1878, pp. 132-176. In addition to the main map, there are several smaller maps and cross-sections connected with the Jerusalem water supply. The article also discusses cisterns, wells, the various pools, aqueducts and water conduits, Solomon's Pools and their environs (the four springs), distant springs and how water was conveyed from them to Jerusalem.

of water — the amount the city needed for twenty-four hours — on a high site in Jerusalem, with pipes leading to all parts of the city.[147]

In 1894, the PEF Quarterly reports that the Turkish Ministry of Public Works had decided to repair the ancient aqueduct leading to Jerusalem. This would provide the city with 2,500 cubic meters of water daily, 1,000 cubic meters of which would be distributed to the poor free of charge at the Dome of the Rock, the Church of the Holy Sepulchre and other places where pilgrims congregated. The renovated aqueduct would be joined to the old 'Arub conduits; the water would be directed through a tunnel 3,570 meters long. This would call for an investment of some two million francs.[148]

In 1898, the newspaper *Ha-Maggid* states that, in honor of the visit of Kaiser Wilhelm II, the conduits leading from Solomon's Pools and Ein Etam had been repaired and water now flowed to the receptacle in the *Maḥkame,* near the Chain Gate at the entrance to the Temple Mount. This water was insufficient at present for all the inhabitants of the city; it served only those who lived nearby. Thus, it would be necessary to bring in water from the abundant springs of Wadi 'Arub.[149]

David Yellin also describes repairs to the aqueduct in 1898:

> One of the important repairs which have been carried out in our city is the repair of the conduits from Solomon's Pool and Ein Etam to our parched city; the very sight of water flowing within its walls refreshes the spirit of the inhabitants.

These pipes, he adds, had been broken by the peasants of Bethlehem and had been unusable for twenty years.[150]

The early twentieth century brought with it important developments concerning the restoration of the Jerusalem aqueduct. The matter took on special urgency in view of the series of dry years that befell the city at this time and affected the water supply of the springs in and around Jerusalem. In 1901, the PEF Quarterly, for example, says that Ein al-Hod, behind Bethany on the road to Jericho, now gave very little water. This little was used by passers-by; as a result, the women of Abu Dis did not have enough to meet their needs. The anticipated rains did not fall and water had to be brought to Jerusalem by rail. Despite this, its price was quite reasonable.[151]

The water shortage of 1901 prompted the Ottoman government to take measures concerning the water supply of Jerusalem. According to the PEF Quarterly, precipitation in the entire country was below average in that year. By March 10th, less than fifteen inches of rain had fallen in Jerusalem. The amount of drinking water was decreasing rapidly, and severe crop damage was foreseen if rain did not fall towards the end of the normal rainy season. The municipality received permission from the Ottoman authorities to bring water from Wadi 'Arub and its vicinity, and an attempt was made to interest foreign investors.[152] That year, the journal reports that peasants were bringing full leather water bags from distant springs such as Lifta, Ein Karem, Ein Yalu and Ein Ḥanniyye in the west, and Ein Fara and al-Bira in the north, by donkey.

147 *Ha-Or/Ha-Tzevi,* 7 Shevat, 1891, vol. VII, no. 13, p. 51.
148 *PEF QSt,* 1894, p. 234.
149 *Ha-Maggid,* 5 Av, 1898, vol. VII, no. 28, p. 230. 151 *PEF QSt,* 1901, pp. 210-211.
150 Yellin, *Writings,* I, p. 242 (19 Sivan, 1898). 152 *Ibid.,* p. 101.

Since the carriage road to al-Bira was now complete, water was also brought to Jerusalem by carriage in large, sealed and well-packed containers. The authorities built a reservoir thirteen feet wide and forty feet long southwest of the Sultan's Pool, in the upper part of the Valley of Hinnom. This pool was filled with water brought in large containers by rail from the village of Battir and the spring of Walaja. The authorities also planned to replace the clay pipes of the aqueduct from Solomon's Pools with iron pipes four or more inches in diameter.[153]

The PEF Quarterly of 1902 summarizes the development of the Jerusalem waterworks as follows: the construction of a pipeline and aqueduct from the Sealed Fountain near Solomon's Pools and from Ein Etam; the dedication of the waterworks on November 27, 1901; the construction and renovation of the reservoir in Abu Tor. At a later date, this journal relays further details of the conduit and reservoir in Abu Tor, which had become the chief reservoir of the Jerusalem water system.[154]

There are many descriptions of these waterworks in Jewish sources as well.[155] In 1902, the newspaper *Hashkafa* writes that the original intention had been to bring in water from other springs, but because of insufficient funds only temporary repairs could be made to the conduit from Solomon's Pools and nearby sources. The new pipes supplied five liters of water a day per person, or 400 cubic meters per day; this water sufficed for the domestic needs of 3,000 families. At the moment, there was an overabundance of water in the new pool, and so one of the pipes had been disconnected.[156]

Masterman writes in early Mandatory times that, in the course of the nineteenth century, the Turkish authorities had made many attempts to repair the low-level aqueduct, but Bethlehem residents, who wanted the water for themselves, repeatedly sabotaged the pipes. In 1901, following a year of severe drought, the Turks decided to remedy the situation once and for all. First, they brought water from Battir by train. Four months later, they installed four-inch iron pipes which conveyed water directly from Wadi Artas to Jerusalem. The tunnel of the ancient aqueduct served as a reservoir; water was collected there at night for use the next day. In this way, Jerusalem was supplied with 40,000 gallons of water per day. The water flowed into the Hinnom Valley, and from there to the Temple Mount, where surplus water was directed to the cisterns. Residents of Jerusalem could fill their containers from two taps near the entrance to the Temple compound for a certain fee. This was certainly progress of a sort, but it was late in coming. Many years earlier, on at least three occasions, the British had offered to renovate the old aqueducts as an act of philanthropy; the Turks had rejected their offers.[157]

The pipes laid in 1901 did not hold up well either, and required periodic repairs. In 1907, the newspaper *Hashkafa* reports that they were no longer

153 *Ibid.,* pp. 319-320.
154 *Loc. cit.; ibid.,* 1902, pp. 4-5.
155 *Ha-Maggid le-Yisrael,* 21 Elul, 1901, vol. X, no. 32, p. 357; *ibid.,* 8 Shevat, 1902, vol. XI, no. 3, p. 33.
156 *Hashkafa,* 23 Shevat, 1903, vol. III, no. 3, p. 18.
157 Masterman, *Hygiene,* pp. 60-61.

usable. The current pasha (Akram Bey) attempted to restore the flow of water from Solomon's Pools.[158]

The water shortage seems to have been severe in 1905 and 1907. In 1905, *Hashkafa* writes that most of the cisterns in the city were dry and that Jerusalem's poor Jews, who usually lacked money even to buy bread, now had to pay for water too.[159] Two years later, we are told, the Jewish communal leaders of Jerusalem had decided to transport water by train from the spring near Battir. From the railway station it would be piped into the pool near the houses built under the sponsorship of Montefiore, and then transported by carts to all the neighborhoods inside and outside the city walls.[160] One month later, the newspaper says that the pool and pipeline were almost ready for use.[161]

By 1908, there were new plans for supplying water to Jerusalem. Two of the proposals presented were to drill inside the city until underground water sources were reached, and to generate electricity by using water from the Jordan River, transmitting the electricity to Ein Fara where it would power water pumps to drive water to Jerusalem. (The latter proposal could not be implemented as funds were lacking.)[162]

In 1909, a newspaper report claims that a German firm had been granted a concession to provide Jerusalem with water for the next thirty years. Private consumers would pay for their water; the government would receive seventy cubic meters per day free of charge. After thirty years, the concession would revert to the municipality.[163]

Two more proposals for bringing water to Jerusalem were discussed in 1910. A French firm was reportedly granted a licence to provide water to the city, using two pumps at Ein 'Arub. At first it was planned to bring water from the Hebron area, where the water was close to the surface, but doctors claimed it was not fit for use. The advantage in using the water from Ein 'Arub lay in its flowing only twenty meters below the level of Jerusalem; it would not be difficult to elevate it. It was proposed to pipe the water into two pools in the city, one at the foot of the Russian tower on the Mount of Olives, which would supply water to the Old City, and another atop a hill near the Schneller Orphanage for the neighborhoods outside the walls. The second proposal was that of a German company to bring in water from Ein Fara in Wadi Qelt. Because this water would be very expensive, this proposal too was dropped.[164]

The severe water shortage also led to the first attempts at drilling wells in the city. Neumann (1877) says that drills imported from England for this purpose had been used on many sites, but no water had been discovered.[165] The PEF

---

158 *Hashkafa,* 27 Elul, 1907, vol. VIII, no. 95, p. 3.
159 *Ibid.,* 10 Kislev, 1905, vol. VII, no. 14, p. 3.
160 *Ibid.,* 13 Tammuz, 1907, vol. VIII, no. 75, p. 3.
161 *Ibid.,* 29 Av, 1907, vol. VIII, no. 88, p. 2.
162 *Ibid.,* 7 Shevat, 1908, vol. IX, no. 33, p. I. At this time the idea of bringing water from Ein Farah and the Yarkon was first raised; see Zionist Archives, Z 2/320.
163 *Ha-Tzevi,* 26 Elul, 1909, vol. XXV, no. 246, p. 3.
164 *Ha-Or,* 4 Tammuz, 1910, vol. I, no. 104, p. 3; *Ha-Tzevi,* 26 Ḥeshvan, 1909, vol. XXVI, no. 36, p. 1. See also Luncz, *Jerusalem,* IX, 1911, p. 390; *Almanac,* XVIII, 1913, p. 175.
165 Tobler, *Topographie,* II, p. 50; Neumann, p. 176.

Quarterly describes the drilling project carried out in a garden south of the German Colony in 1904, which led to the discovery of water at a depth of over 100 feet. The journal gives an account of the various strata through which the drilling was done, and says the water was twenty feet deep. However, the pit would fill with rocks and soil when the water was pumped in the dry season, and had to be cleaned periodically.[166] The municipal authorities dug a well on the street leading to the railroad station, above the valley bridge, for the use of Mishkenot Sha'ananim and Yemin Moshe residents. Arab ruffians used to harass the Jews who came to draw water there every day.[167]

These drilling projects were part of the over-all attempt to solve Jerusalem's chronic water problem, but they do not seem to have provided much of a solution. They did not penetrate to any great depth, and provided only small amounts of water. It became clear that the solution lay in bringing water from afar. This was achieved in full only after the British conquest; within six months after General Allenby took Jerusalem, water began flowing to the city from Wadi 'Arub. Reservoirs were built in the wadi itself as well as in Jerusalem. Pumping stations were established, and pipes laid. The southern aqueduct was equipped with new six-inch iron pipes through which 1,360 cubic meters of water could flow each day. The water was pumped to a point some seventy to eighty meters above the rest of Jerusalem. The cisterns in the city were also cleaned, and modern, systematic methods employed to insure a steady supply of water. Thus began a new era in the history of Jerusalem's water supply.[168]

Summary

If we grade the various water sources of nineteenth-century Jerusalem by importance, the private and public cisterns take considerable precedence over all the others. After these would come the supplementary sources in the Kidron Valley, which were especially important in the summer and in drought or near-drought conditions. The aqueduct was helpful to some extent, serving to increase the quantities of public water available on the Temple Mount at first, and supplementing the city's general water supply at the end of the century, when the population had increased and several years of drought had occurred in quick succession.

The pools were of very limited value, in contrast to ancient times, when pools and aqueducts played a central role in Jerusalem's water supply. This may be explained by the change in the status of nineteenth-century Jerusalem as compared with its status during other periods, in particular, by the change in the central government's interest in the city's development. Supplying water via pools and aqueducts required a strong, progressive central government prepared to build and maintain them, and to supervise their operation, Cisterns, on the other hand, were simple facilities which every institution, family or home-owner could provide independently, with government aid and

166 *PEF QSt,* 1904, pp. 296-297.
167 *Ha-Or,* 21 Av, 1910, vol. I, no. 153, p. 3.
168 Masterman, *Hygiene,* pp. 60-62.

at no great expense. Jerusalem in the nineteenth century did not have a strong central government capable of handling the development of aqueducts and pools. Thus, cisterns were the most suitable water-supply device available to the city's inhabitants. This also seems to have been the case in other historical periods, when the authorities were incapable of dealing with the problem.

The cisterns and the other limited sources were able to meet Jerusalem's water needs primarily because consumption was low. There is no other explanation for the ability of these conventional sources to supply enough water at a time when the population expanded from fewer than 10,000 souls at the beginning of the nineteenth century to about 70,000 by the eve of World War I. While there was no increase in the actual water supply, the sources in the Kidron Valley seem to have been exploited more fully as time went on. The capacity of the pools remained constant and they remained negligible water-supply sources throughout. The major growth was in the number of cisterns. If we adopt the figures cited earlier, the thousand cisterns of the early 1860's had multiplied sevenfold by the end of World War I. The quantities of water brought from remote areas also increased somewhat, owing in part to the attempts to transport water by rail and carriage, but mainly because of the renewed use of the formerly ruinous aqueduct and pipeline from Solomon's Pools and other sources in the Mount Hebron district.

The end of the period we are discussing was characterized by attempts to find new solutions for the city's water problems, but those actually implemented depended on traditional sources and methods of supply. As occurred in other fields, the modernization of Jerusalem's water supply centered at first on improving and developing old techniques; it was only later that any revolutionary techniques and sources were employed. As Ottoman rule drew to a close, Jerusalem was in its first phase of modernization. A sweeping revolution was to arrive only under the British.

Chapter Four:
SANITATION AND HEALTH

Introduction: The Drainage System

The highly unsanitary conditions prevailing in Jerusalem during the nineteenth century had four main sources: the absence of sewers and drainage canals; the failure to remove refuse for disposal outside the city limits; the poor and unhygienic living conditions; the shortage of water and the use of contaminated water, especially that drawn from neglected and infected cisterns.

We have already mentioned the total absence of sanitary facilities in nineteenth-century Jerusalem, and the fact that sewage flowed through most of its streets in open channels. Charles Wilson, who investigated the city's ancient sewer system, writes as follows:

> Intimately connected with the water supply is drainage of the city, of which it is hardly too much to say that there is none. Those drains which exist are little more than cess-pits, and, except after heavy rain, there is no discharge from the mouth of the present main... in the Valley of the Kedron.... This old drain is still perfect for more than 700 feet, and might be made use of in any new system of drainage. The great difficulty in the way of any improvement is the enormous quantity of sewage which is now collected in the rubbish beneath the town, and which, if opened, or disturbed, would probably give rise to an epidemic.[1]

At least some of the city's residents were aware of the existence of ancient drainage channels and knew their routes. This we learn from the fact that, during the Peasants' Revolt against Ibrahim Pasha in 1834 (see p. 109 below), the rebels infiltrated into Jerusalem through the sewers leading to the village of Silwan.[2] These sewers did not function properly in the first half of the nineteenth century, and it was only in its second half that the city authorities began to have them cleaned and to establish an urban sewage system.

In 1864 a British physician, Dr. Chaplin (one of Jerusalem's best-known doctors), published an article entitled "The Fevers of Jerusalem" in which he gave a detailed description of the city's utter lack of sanitary facilities:

> Jerusalem is one of the most unhealthy of cities, and fever is its principal disease. Orientals, Europeans, immigrants and natives, alike suffer; and during the sickly period of the year almost one fourth of the population become ill... it is shamefully and abominably dirty. Some ancient drains are still in existence; but they are imperfect, and not one house in fifty has its cesspools connected with them.... All kinds of animals and vegetable matter are allowed to lie and rot in the streets. If a dog or cat dies, it putrefies in the roadway, or is eaten by one of its companions. In a walk through the city during the cold weather, a dozen of these

1   Wilson—Warren, *Recovery,* pp. 27-28; Amiran, "Development," pp. 28-29.
2   Yaari, *Memoirs,* I, pp. 109-110; Schwarz, *Produce* (Luncz edition, 1900), p. 483.

animals may be seen lying dead. The remains of horses, donkeys and camels are usually dragged outside the city, and left just under the walls to be devoured by dogs and jackals.... For seven months of the year there is no rain, and the air during this long dry season becomes filled with the loathsome dust and odour which result from so much impurity.... Almost the whole of the water drunk in Jerusalem is collected from the rains and preserved for use in underground tanks or cisterns.... With proper care in cleaning cisterns, water may in this way be kept sweet and good for many months; but if such care be not taken, it becomes loaded with organic matter, and acquires a bad smell and taste. The water of the best wells, indeed, usually contains [an] abundance of animalculae towards the end of the summer.... Rats and mice also fall in and still further contaminate it. On the whole, it may be safely affirmed that after the month of July no water in the city is fit to be drunk without being previously filtered or boiled.... Of all the causes of disease in operation in the Holy City, this factitious kind of malaria is undoubtedly the most influential.[3]

Much of this information is quoted by Luncz in his *Ways of Zion and Jerusalem,* published in 1876, twelve years after the publication of Chaplin's work. Luncz claims that there had been no improvement in the city's sanitary conditions over the last decade. Chaplin, in fact, does mention certain improvements being made in the second half of the century, but these were apparently not very significant.[4]

As time went on, progress was more evident. In 1880, the PEF Quarterly reports the establishment of a sanitation department headed by a German doctor.[5] In 1887, it reports that drainage work had begun in the area south of the Damascus Gate and around the gate itself. An ancient sewer was discovered beneath the street leading north from the market; it was cleaned and included in the new network.[6]

In 1894, the Quarterly writes about the drainage system in the neighborhoods outside the Old City:

A few years ago the Russians made, under the inspection of the local authorities, a new drain from all the buildings on their property west of the city, by which all used water and dirty fluid was conducted down into the city drain, and so down to Siloah.... In the course of the last 20 years several colonies or settlements of Jews have been built north-west of the city, and as no sewers were provided, the retention of the dirty water had made the settlements more and more unhealthy. The leaders of the settlements, therefore, resolved to make a drain, leading into the Russian one....[7]

Garbage Disposal and Poor Living Conditions

Another reason for the unhealthiness of nineteenth-century Jerusalem was accumulated filth and garbage. It should be remembered that the city had been built over the ruins of thousands of years. Both inside the walls and just beyond them, the area was covered with piles of rocks, earth, ashes, bones, rotted trees and so forth, and these mounds sometimes reached a height of many meters.

91

3 Schmelz, *Studies,* pp. 121-126.
4 *Ibid.,* p. 123.
5 *PEF QSt,* 1880, p. 188.
6 *Ibid.,* 1887, p. 216.
7 *Ibid.,* 1894, p. 264; see also *ibid.,* 1905, pp. 13-14 (in obituary of Chaplin).

As in previous centuries, garbage was not disposed of outside the city walls but was thrown into ruined chambers beneath its houses or strewn over all the empty lots in the city.

Wilson's survey of 1864-1865 includes details on the amount of garbage in Jerusalem. He says:

> Over the whole of the ground occupied by the present city of Jerusalem there is a large accumulation of rubbish, which attains its maximum in the valley running down from the Damascus to the Dung Gate, where it is not less than from 50 to 70 feet deep, and in places perhaps more than this. Where the Armenian gardens are situated, near the Citadel, there is from 25 to 30 feet of rubbish and in other places more or less.[8]

Wilson also describes the large piles of garbage just outside the city walls:

> To the south of the city the ground is deeply covered with rubbish.... Along the western side of the city the rubbish is very deep, and no remains of buildings could be found. Except in the immediate vicinity of the Damascus Gate there does not appear to be much rubbish to the north of the city.... On the east of the city... the rubbish covering everything....[9]

Paxton also says that, in 1839, the area outside the southern wall was

> ...the depository of rubbish and filth of all sorts. The whole face of the hill, both on the Gihon and the Kidron side, is evidently much enlarged, and made to project into the valley, from the quantity of rubbish thrown over it. Once it must have been a high and almost, if not altogether, perpendicular bank, but now the rubbish has almost wholly hidden the face of the rock... thus forming a steep but sloping bank of rich, soft earth. Some parts of it are planted with trees, and portions are used for cultivating vegetables of various kinds.[10]

Zuta and Sukenik repeat this information in early Mandatory times, claiming that the entire area from the Zion Gate to the Dung Gate was an enormous rubbish heap on which trees and vegetable gardens had been planted.[11]

These unsanitary conditions continued to exist in the second half of the nineteenth century. Orelli writes in the 1870's that the police had once required every citizen to bring in a certain amount of garbage each day, or be fined instead. This practice was soon abandoned, leaving the dogs to take care of the garbage. Despite their annoying barking, no one chased the dogs away because they eliminated at least part of the problem. Dogs were destroyed only when there were too many of them.[12]

Sanitation services improved at the end of the century. A street-cleaning machine was reportedly purchased in 1896, to sweep the lanes and sprinkle water on them to keep down the dust.[13] It was used mainly in the neighborhoods outside the walls; conditions inside the Old City remained difficult. Hurlbut says that, although modern homes were being built in 1897, garbage was still being thrown into the streets, which were seldom cleaned.[14]

Conditions were especially bad in the Jewish Quarter; it was much more

92

8   Wilson, *Survey,* p. 56.

9   *Ibid.,* pp. 61-62.

10 Paxton, pp. 112-135.

11 Zuta—Sukenik (1930), p. 120.

12 Orelli, p. 101.

13 Schirion, p. 162.

14 Hurlbut, pp. 45-86.

crowded than the Muslim Quarter, and there were no vacant rooms available for garbage disposal. Barclay (1857) says that the Jewish Quarter lacked all sanitary facilities, and was the poorest and dirtiest quarter in the Old City.[15] Gadsby attributes the many illnesses of the Jews to bad nutrition, overcrowding, poor living conditions (many of the homes were dirty and on the verge of collapse), and the lack of clean water in their wells and cisterns.[16] Porter (1869) says the houses were half-ruined, and the streets and courtyards full of garbage and animal bones.[17] Merrill (1883) writes that the alleys of the Jewish Quarter were full of dirt and decay. A local rabbi told him that the residents' pleas to remedy the situation had been ignored by the authorities.[18]

The slaughterhouse located in the Jewish Quarter made things even worse, as we shall see later on; no less a nuisance was the tannery in the Christian Quarter. Both were subsequently moved outside the Old City walls (see p. 235).

The Contamination of Cisterns

The lack of sanitation, the defective drainage system and the accumulation of refuse led to the contamination of the water in the city's cisterns. That these cisterns were improperly maintained and cleaned exacerbated the situation. Charles Wilson writes as follows:

> The principal dependence of the inhabitants is on the cisterns, which receive the water collected on the roofs and terraces of their houses. Those cisterns which have lately been built by Europeans in convents and dwelling houses are good, and, being carefully cleaned out once a year, always keeping the water sweet, but it is far otherwise in the native houses. When rain commences to fall, every effort is made to collect as much as possible, all the channels are thrown open, and through these the summer's accumulation of rubbish is carried into the cisterns below; water is even collected from the streets, and the state they are in at the end of the dry season is almost too filthy for description. During early summer little evil arises from using the water of these cisterns... towards autumn, however, the water gets low... and the mixture which thousands then have to use as their daily beverage is too horrible to think of. It is at this time... that the fever season commences.[19]

Several Jewish sources also say the cisterns were one of the chief reasons for illness in the city. In a letter to Joel Salomon, Cahanyu writes:

> Water is always lacking here in the Holy City. Many people, whose cisterns go dry, have to buy water all summer long, and it is quite usual for all the inhabitants of the Holy City to remain without water, being obliged to spend large sums for it. Last year, for example, there was no rain and the cisterns did not fill until January, making water expensive.... God knows what will happen at the end of this year, since the cisterns did not fill up properly last winter and there was no heavy, final spring rain at all.... In times like this, many poor people drink muddy water, salt water, stagnant water and... contract all kinds of illnesses, may God save us. What are the thirsty poor to do?[20]

According to Zuta and Sukenik, diseases of several kinds were brought on

15   Barclay, *City,* pp. 437-454.
16   Gadsby, p. 80.
17   Porter, *Giant Cities,* p. 124.
18   Merrill, *East,* p. 414.
19   Wilson—Warren, *Recovery,* pp. 26-27.
20   Cahanyu, p. 28 (translated from Hebrew); see also Schirion, p. 99.

by the authorities' lack of action and the residents' negligence. Malaria, for example, was spread because cisterns were not covered. Neighborhoods built in high places were better off in this respect than those in low-lying sectors, where many impoverished people lived in extremely overcrowded conditions. Eye diseases and intestinal ailments were also common.[21]

It is worth emphasizing that cisterns could furnish good water, providing that cleanliness were maintained and only clean water allowed to reach them. Wise householders cleaned the roof and catchment areas draining into their cisterns before the rains came. They diverted the quickly-contaminated water from the first rainfall and prevented it from entering the cisterns. The tanks themselves had to be replastered within and cleaned from time to time. Water from such cisterns was clean and sweet. Theoretically, the cisterns were safer than a public water network, because cisterns were isolated from each other and could not spread contamination. In practice, however, Jerusalem's cisterns were one of the chief causes of disease, since most of them were unclean. Very often, cracked walls allowed sewage to seep in. Even the rain water they collected was dirty and disease-bearing. Dr. Masterman, a British doctor who worked in Jerusalem for the twenty years before World War I, declared that virtually no progress had been made in this respect under Ottoman rule.[22]

In the early twentieth century, Jewish and other groups apparently began demand that something be done about the cisterns. In September of 1910, the newspaper Ha-Or appealed to Jerusalem residents to repair their cisterns and remove the dirt accumulated in them before the rainy season.[23] On the eve of the war, two medical delegation were dispatched to Jerusalem to investigate the situation and suggest means of improvement. According to their findings, between 25 and 60 percent of the inhabitants suffered from endemic malaria. Matters improved only after the British conquest, when the British army emptied all the cisterns in the city (using the water for its cavalry horses!), laid a pipe from Solomon's Pools, and permitted the reuse of cisterns only when they had been properly cleaned and equipped with a good cover and pump. The Mandatory authorities were strict about their use, and about proper disinfection measures.[24]

Diseases and Epidemics

Wholly inadequate sanitation, overcrowded housing and bad nutrition led to the frequent illnesses and epidemics of nineteenth-century Jerusalem. Various types of malaria and dysentery were very common, while there was an epidemic of cholera, plague or similar maladies every few years.[25]

Nineteenth-century travelers had a great deal to say on this subject. H. Light, who visited Jerusalem in 1814, says that he had to leave the city in a hurry when an epidemic of plague began. In order to avoid the disease, the monasteries closed their gates and avoided all contact with the city.[26]

Paxton reports an attack of plague in the spring of 1838:

21 Zuta—Sukenik (1920), pp. 70-71.
22 Masterman, Hygiene, p. 9.
23 Ha-Or, 13 Tishrei, 1910, vol. II, no. 181, p. 2.
24 Amiran, Atlas, Jerusalem, p. 29.
25 Schmelz, pp. 130-132.
26 Light, pp. 188-189.

The plague made its appearance shortly after our arrival (end of April and beginning of May 1838). The monks from some of the religious houses left the city, and took refuge in other places. We found the monks at Bethlehem keeping quarantine, and there was plague in some of the convents in the country. A health officer from Jaffa visited the city on the 16th, and declared his intention to shut up the gates, and prevent egress or ingress, until the plague abated.[27]

Robinson says of the same period that all stores in Jerusalem closed down because of the plague; by April 30, all the pilgrims and merchants had left the city. The gates were shut in order to isolate the city from May 18th until the beginning of July.[28]

British Consul Young believed the epidemic resulted from poverty and hunger, as Moses Montefiore and his wife were informed when they visited Palestine for the second time.[29] The well-known artist, Roberts, who had planned a trip to Jerusalem at this time, was forced to postpone his visit until the quarantine ended.[30]

Another epidemic erupted in 1847. G. Fisk says that a quarantine sector was established for fear of the plague, and travelers were not allowed to enter the city itself until they had been examined by a medical officer.[31]

A severe epidemic, which took a heavy toll in lives, occurred in 1865-1866. According to Tobler, cholera spread throughout the city at this time, causing the closure of the new southern gate (apparently the Dung Gate).[32] A Jewish source says the epidemic began on the first day of the Sukkot holiday in 1865 and lasted for two months.[33] It had spread from Egypt through Jaffa to Hebron and thence to Jerusalem. The newspaper *Ha-Levanon* reports that the Bikkur Ḥolim Hospital was already open when the epidemic broke out, and provided considerable assistance to those in need.[34] Some observers believe the low population figures recorded in Montefiore's 1866 census of the Jewish community reflect the terrible cholera epidemic of the time.[35]

Isaiah Press, born and bred in the Old City, also describes its numerous diseases:

> The poor sanitary conditions and the shortage of food, water, medical specialists and beneficial drugs led to the outbreak of diseases which spread from house to house and courtyard to courtyard, assuming epidemic proportions and causing many deaths. Burial-society lists from those days reveal a dreadful situation. Mortality rates were especially high among young children. My mother told me about a diphtheria epidemic which struck half the children in the city....[36]

Towards the end of the century, sanitation and cleanliness improved somewhat, but the diseases and epidemics continued. The educator Ephraim Cohen-Reiss tells of a severe cholera epidemic early in the winter of 1900. The

27 Paxton, p. 228.
28 Robinson, *Biblical Researches,* I, pp. 368-369; II, pp. 320-321.
29 Yaari, *Travels,* p. 566.
30 Roberts, I, Preface.
31 G. Fisk, p. 257.
32 Tobler, *Nazareth,* p. 302.
33 J.I. Yellin, *Our Forefathers,* pp. 27-32.
34 *Ha-Levanon,* 8 Ḥeshvan, 1865, vol. II, no. 20, pp. 309-310.
35 Schmelz, pp. 132-134.
36 Press, *Hundred Years,* p. 21.

isolation of the city forced a number of pupils at the Laemel School, whose homes were in Jaffa and the Jewish settlements, to postpone their return to school for two months. When the quarantine was lifted, many people left the country.[37]

The PEF Quarterly reports in 1905 that a very severe fever epidemic had claimed the lives of many children, especially among the Jewish population. At the same time, malaria spread with unusual rapidity through the city. The Quarterly commends the inhabitants' readiness to take precautionary measures.[38]

The Establishment of Health Facilities

There was noteworthy progress in sanitation and health in Jerusalem during the second half of the nineteenth century. The establishment of medical institutions will be dealt with at length when we discuss the various community groups below. Here, we will summarize their development in the first seventy years of the century.

At the beginning of the nineteenth century, there were very few hospitals in Jerusalem. The building known as the *Takiyya* (see p. 160) housed poor, sick Muslims but could hardly be called a hospital.[39] Seetzen (1806) says that the pharmacy in the Franciscan monastery was the largest he had ever seen in a Levantine country. The monastery's Spanish doctor, Brother Francisco, had been serving it for several years. Most of the pharmacy's drugs were received as gifts from Europe, but some of them were compounded on the spot. There was also a special medicinal-herb garden. The monastery produced Jerusalem's famed friar's balsam, whose formula was secret; two other, cheaper drugs similar to it were produced to meet the demand. Both drugs and medical treatment were provided free of charge, but one might leave a gift for the doctor or monastery.[40]

The Jews had no hospitals at the beginning of the century. Health conditions improved only during the reign of Ibrahim Pasha, when western elements began penetrating into the city. The first delegation of the London Missionary Society arrived in 1838, and began to offer medical services. Before this, there seems to have been no medical institution worthy of the name (see p. 255).

The painter, W.H. Bartlett, writes that when an English family and some American missionaries fell ill in 1834, there were no doctors in the city to treat them. Providentially, the officers and surgeon of an English ship at Jaffa visited Jerusalem and assisted the sufferers.[41]

A physician who visited Jerusalem in November of 1834, J. Roser, says his services were constantly in demand because the city, despite its 22,000 inhabitants, had not a single doctor to its name, not even in the army. He was warmly welcomed by the residents of Jerusalem, who were just recovering from a plague epidemic. Roser adds that he served as pharmacist at the only

37   Cohen-Reiss, p. 180; see also Luncz, *Jerusalem*, VI, 1903, pp. 167-172.
38   *PEF QSt*, 1905, p. 376.   40   Seetzen, II, p. 205.
39   Whaley, p. 121.   41   Bartlett, *Revisited*, p. 41.

dispensary in the city, in the monastery at which he was staying, since the monk in charge had died of plague.[42]

There were important developments in the health field in the early 1840's. In 1842, Montefiore appointed Dr. Simon Fraenkel to establish a clinic and pharmacy in Jerusalem (see p. 336). At the same time, the London Missionary Society expanded the medical service it had begun in 1838, and set up a medical center headed by Dr. Macgowan. In his first report, Dr. Macgowan comments that "the want of attendance, of cleanliness, of suitable nourishment, and of ordinary precautions, is quite appalling. The absence of these destroys more lives than the disease itself."[43] In the wake of this report, the English Missionary Hospital was founded in December of 1844.

Throughout the 1840's, these two enterprises were the major health institutions of Jerusalem. According to Bartlett, "the Medical Mission (of the Society for Promoting Christianity amongst the Jews) has been perhaps one of the most beneficial efforts made for the good of Jerusalem... and was for several years the only source of medical aid for the whole city."[44]

Other medical institutions established at this time were the Prussian hospital in the Deaconesses' House (see p. 258), the clinics in the Franciscan and Greek monasteries, the Latin Patriarchate hospital and the American semi-medical center of Dr. Barclay.[45]

In the 1850's, important strides forward were made by the Jewish community, which opened its first two hospitals: the Rothschild Hospital in 1854, and the Bikkur Holim Hospital in 1857. Both will be discussed below, in the chapter on the Jewish community.

Unfortunately, the city's hospitals and clinics were incapable of handling the severe epidemic of 1866.

Reicher describes the hospitals of Jerusalem in the 1860's as being:

> a) The English Hospital, which owns a very large courtyard surrounded by beautiful, luxurious buildings several floors high. Its doctors are from London; all the patients, Jews, Muslims, and Christians, receive free medication and hospitalization. b) The French Hospital, which is also free. c) The Jewish Hospital established by Moses Montefiore in a large, attractive courtyard....[46]

With regard to the last-named, Reicher's account is not accurate: it was a clinic, not a hospital. He also omits the clinics and hospitals of various community groups in Jerusalem.

Dr. Neumann, who served as a doctor in Jerusalem, lists the non-Jewish hospitals in the city at about the same time: the English Missionary Hospital; the free Latin Hospital, which treated some 200 patients of all religions each year (this is the "French" hospital mentioned by Reicher); the Prussian Deaconesses' House; the Russian Hospital, located in the Russian Compound outside the Old City, which was a modern, thirty-bed facility intended for Russians but accepting patients of other religions as well; a children's hospital, also located outside the Old City, which was a new institution donated by the

42 Roser, pp. 428-429.
43 Bartlett, *Revisited*, p. 61.
44 *Ibid.*, p. 41.
45 *Loc. cit.*
46 Reicher, pp. 58-59 (translated from Hebrew).

Duke of Mecklenburg-Schwerin. Neumann also notes the existence of a hospital for the Muslim poor in the *Takiyya* building, known to Europeans as the Helena Hospital. It was quite large and occupied two-thirds of al-Takiyya Street. Nearby was a hospital for the blind. There was also an Indian Hospital.[47]

The 1876 Baedeker Guide provides a list of Jerusalem doctors: Dr. Chaplin, the physician of the London Mission; Dr. Sandreczki, the physician of the German institutions; Dr. Schwarz, an Austrian, of the Rothschild Hospital; Dr. Mazaraki, of the newly-established Greek Hospital. The pharmacists included Damiani, on the Via Dolorosa, and others, at the various hospitals.[48]

When Schirion first came to Jerusalem, he says, there were only five physicians, all of them general practitioners; there were no specialists. The first Jewish doctor was Dr. Shraga Feivel Popeles, who accepted poor patients at the expense of the Frankfurt Committee for Charities in the Holy Land. The other physicians were European Christians. The Greek doctor, Dr. Mazaraki, was also the chief physician of the Misgav Ladach Hospital, and treated poor patients at the hospital free of charge or for a token fee.[49]

Before 1870, in spite of considerable attention devoted to health care, treatment and facilities were limited. A revolution in public health began only at the end of the century.

Leprosy

One phenomenon that indicates the gravity of sanitary and health conditions was the existence of a lepers' neighborhood in nineteenth-century Jerusalem; it made a deep impression on visitors to the city.

Of 1838, Robinson writes that "within the (Zion) Gate, a little towards the right, are some miserable hovels, inhabited by persons called leprous... they are pitiable objects, and miserable outcasts from society. They all live here together, and intermarry only with each other."[50] According to Strauss (1845), the lepers, who numbered about thirty, were the most conspicuous beggars in the city.[51] Ritter says that the authorities ignored the lepers' terrible plight, and offered them no assistance.[52] After visiting them in 1851, Schulz reports that these lepers lived in ten or twelve miserable clay huts whose doors faced the wall near the Zion Gate. There were then about forty lepers. They married only among themselves, and sometimes lived to be fifty years old. From time to time, they collected alms within the city walls.[53]

The lepers' huts were marked on the British Admiralty Map drawn up by Williams in 1849. He says these unfortunate people were to be found only in Jerusalem and Nablus.[54] Van de Velde also includes the lepers' houses in his map of Jerusalem in the 1850's.[55] Stewart, who visited Jerusalem in 1854, offers this description:

47 Neumann, pp. 273-275.
48 Baedeker, 1876, pp. 145-146 (1973, pp. 36-37).
49 Schirion, pp. 146-157; Press, *Hundred Years,* pp. 21-24.
50 Robinson, *Biblical Researches,* I, pp. 359-360.   53 Schulz, p. 134.
51 Strauss, p. 205.   54 Williams, I, *Supplement,* p. 24.
52 Ritter, IV, pp. 41-54.   55 Tobler, *Planographie.*

The lepers' village (Thomson, 1860, I, p. 530)

Near the Zion Gate ... there is an open space, just where the hill begins to descend towards the east, a part of which is occupied by a small village of miserable huts, separated by a wall from the rest of the town.... It is the quarter of the lepers. More than a hundred of these miserable creatures live here in a community of their own, chased away from the society of their fellow-men, and propagate the malady from generation to generation.... It has all the appearance of elephantiasis, sometimes affecting the feet and legs, at other times the arms and other parts of the body.... These poor creatures are to be seen every day seated along the paths, near the gates, exhibiting their sores, and begging earnestly in the name of God for alms.[56]

Frankl (1856) says the lepers' huts were known as the "dwellings of the wretched." Although they were built of stone and clay, they looked like ruins. Their roofs were made of dry branches. They were inhabited by sixty or seventy lepers, none of them Jews, and very few of them Christians.[57] According to Swift, who visited Jerusalem in 1854, Montefiore had initiated the collection of

99

56 Stewart, p. 294.
57 Frankl, p. 231; see also Isaacs, p. 42; Thomson (1860), II, p. 516; Pierotti, p. 221.

funds for the establishment of a lepers' hospital.[58] The leper issue was faced at the end of the 1860's, and closed institutions began to be built for the lepers. One of the first of these was the German Protestant institution established on Mamilla Street. The Baedeker Guide of 1876 says that a German-run leper hospital was opened in 1867, but that not all the lepers had become inmates: some could still be seen begging on Jaffa Road. By 1873, there were thirteen lepers in the hospital.[59]

In 1876, Orelli writes:

> Father Tappe's leper house is located outside the Jaffa Gate and was founded by a German noblewoman. At the moment eighteen lepers reside there, twelve men and six women, all of them Arabs. This disease is gradually expected to disappear if the government assists in confining the sufferers to special institutions — not because the disease is so contagious, but because it is hereditary. Nevertheless, the disease is not as severe as it was in the past, and proper treatment can alleviate some of the patient's discomfort.[60]

At the end of the century, the rest of the lepers were moved outside the city. Liévin's guide states that a lepers' institution was established in 1875 near Bir Ayyub in the Kidron Valley. These lepers were protected by the local sheikh and lived on contributions from local residents. They managed their own affairs. The authorities provided them with 43 kilograms of bread per day; since they were forbidden to enter the city, their daily supply of bread and water was brought to them by a man of Silwan.[61] Neumann relates that the lepers had once lived in twenty small and shabby houses near the Zion Gate under absolutely shameful conditions, but were now housed in a large, four-room house outside the city, near Nehemiah's Spring (Bir Ayyub). A fifth room was added to this house by Montefiore.[62]

A later edition of Liévin's guide (1897) describes the establishment of a new lepers' home in Jerusalem, apparently referring to the transfer of the old institution on Mamilla Street to its new quarters in the Talbieh area.[63] Franklin, a visitor to Jerusalem at the beginning of the twentieth century, notes the existence of a new lepers' hospital on a hill near Emek Refa'im.[64] The 1912 Baedeker Guide says this hospital was not far from the German Colony, and housed some fifty or sixty of Jerusalem's seventy or eighty lepers. Other lepers were housed in the Turkish Lepers' Hospital (apparently the one in the Hinnom Valley), while still others collected alms on Jaffa Road.[65]

Luncz (1891) describes the establishment of lepers' homes near Nehemiah's Well and in Talbieh:

> The small houses... on the southern slope of the Mount of Olives are the homes of the unfortunate Muslims afflicted with leprosy, which many medical scholars believe is the same disease mentioned in our Holy Torah. This illness stays with a

58 Swift, pp. 250-252.
59 Baedeker, 1876, p. 234 (1973, p. 124).
60 Orelli, pp. 111-126.
61 Liévin (1887), I, p. 417.
62 Neumann, pp. 274-275.
63 Liévin (1897), I, p. 123.
64 Franklin, p. 25.
65 Baedeker, 1912, p. 70.

person until he goes to his grave; it is not contagious, but is inherited. A society of German monks has built a large hospital for persons with this disease in the western corner of the city, at the edge of Emek Refaim, and they see to it that the patients do nót leave the home or procreate. This hospital, however, is not large enough for all the lepers; therefore, many of them sit at the crossroads begging for alms, arousing horror and disgust.[66]

As for the pitiful hovels of the lepers near the Zion Gate, Joshua Yellin states that the municipality destroyed them after the leper institutions had been built outside the Old City.[67]

Summary

The fact that a group of lepers lived in Jerusalem until the middle of the nineteenth century is perhaps the best illustration of the neglect and primitive conditions characteristic of the city at this time. During the second half of the century, however, the confined and stagnant Old City of Jerusalem began to grow and to change completely.

66   Luncz, *Guide,* pp. 135-136 (translated from Hebrew).
67   Y. Yellin, *Memoirs,* p. 6.

Part of the Muslim quarter—al-Wad region, on Wilson's map—1865
(Ch. Wilson, *Survey*, 1:2,500 map)

Part Two

Ottoman Rule; the Muslim Population; the Temple Mount and the Muslim Quarter

Chapter One:
OTTOMAN RULE

The Status of Jerusalem in the Early Nineteenth Century

For hundreds of years after the end of the Crusader period, Jerusalem, like the Holy Land as a whole, was a backwater. There was some progress in the time of the Mamluks, when a large number of *madrasas* (religious schools) and important Muslim buildings were built, and at the beginning of Ottoman rule in the sixteenth century, when the city walls and towers and the Citadel of David were repaired by Suleiman the Magnificent. Generally speaking, however, progress during the entire Muslim period up to the Egyptian occupation of 1831 was very limited in scope, involving only partial renovation of religious, governmental and residential structures.

The influence of the central government was nominal in Jerusalem throughout the Ottoman period. Jerusalem residents found themselves at the mercy of the whims and ruthlessness of local rulers, pashas, who exploited the population and not only failed to provide protection from the violence, greed and capriciousness of the soldiers and their officers but, on the contrary, turned the city's agriculture, industry and commerce to their own personal advantage.[1]

The Ottomans valued Jerusalem mainly for its religious significance to Muslims and respected its holiness, though less, apparently, than their predecessors, the Mamluks. All the Muslim holy places in Jerusalem and its environs (the al-Aqṣa mosque, the Dome of the Rock, Nebi Musa and the Cave of the Patriarchs) continued to be the destinations of Muslim pilgrims, not only from the Holy Land but also from other Muslim countries. These pilgrims visited Jerusalem on their way to the holy cities of Mecca and Medina, or on their way back. As the ruler of the Muslim world, the Ottoman sultan considered it one of his obligations to protect these pilgrims. The Turkish authorities also maintained the Muslim *madrasas,* repaired mosques, and extended grants and other forms of financial aid to the 'ulema (Muslim religious scholars) in Jerusalem. All these actions, however, did not alter Jerusalem's plight. Throughout the nineteenth century, it remained a city neglected by its government.[2]

At the beginning of the nineteenth century, Jerusalem was still a small town in the Ottoman Empire, lacking all but religious significance. Its population was roughly equal to that of towns such as Acre, Gaza, Shechem (Nablus), amounting to between 8,000 and 10,000 persons. If we divide this population figure among the three major religious groups, we find that there were

104

1   Gibb—Bowen, p. 208.
2   Heyd, *Ottoman Documents,* p. 151.

Street of the Chain (Ch.
Wilson, *Picturesque Palestine*)

approximately 2,000 Jews, fewer than 3,000 Christians, and about 4,000 Muslims.[3] Jerusalem served as the district town for only its immediate area. It was far from the coastal road, the famous Via Maris, the main thoroughfare that connected Egypt, a flourishing province of the Ottoman Empire, with the imperial capital of Constantinople. The international and interregional commercial routes that linked the Mediterranean coast with the coasts of the Persian Gulf were also far away. Thus, it is not surprising that, when Napoleon invaded the country in 1799, he was not interested in capturing Jerusalem and apparently did not even visit it, whereas he besieged Acre for several months.[4]

In the early nineteenth century, the Holy Land was split between two administrative provinces or *pashaliks*: the mountainous region from the area north of Shechem to the area south of Hebron, together with Transjordan, belonged to the province of Damascus, while the Galilee and the coastal district belonged to the province of Sidon. In the eighteenth century, the capital of the Sidon province was moved to Acre. The center of local power also moved from Damascus to Acre; anyone who controlled Acre controlled the whole country. Thus, in the early nineteenth century, Jerusalem was theoretically a district town in the province of Damascus, to which most of the country belonged, with the exception of the Acre and Safed districts;

105

3   See below for population of other communities.
4   Temperly, p. 284.

practically speaking, however, it was under the control of the governors of Sidon. These governors, who resided in Acre, ruled over the central and southern sectors of the country by virtue of their military supremacy and the weakness of the central government and of the governor of Damascus.[5]

The Pashas of Acre and their Ties with Jerusalem in the First Thirty Years of the Nineteenth Century

At the end of the eighteenth century and in the first thirty years of the nineteenth, three governors ruled over the province of Sidon: Jezzar Pasha (1775-1804), Suleiman Pasha (1804-1818), and Abdullah Pasha (1818-1831).[6] Jezzar's position became stronger after the defeat of Napoleon, and it was then that he established his control over Jerusalem. The city was at the mercy of both Suleiman and Abdullah at certain times, though Jerusalem was not officially within their domain.[7] During their rule, however, there was a series of uprisings. The days of Abdullah Pasha were difficult ones for Jerusalem and especially for the protected communities in it, the Christians and the Jews, whom Abdullah sought to humiliate. Consul Finn writes that the pasha ordered Christian women to wear black garments, and Jewish women red ones. He also abused these communities in other ways, which naturally influenced Muslim inhabitants to take similar action.[8] As Muḥammad 'Ali's armies prepared to march into the Holy Land, Abdullah Pasha, now more powerful, was in control of nearly the whole country, at least in theory. Abdullah signed himself as the *"vali* of Sidon and Tripoli, and *mutaṣarrif* of Gaza, Jerusalem, Nablus (Shechem) and Jenin." He also changed his deputies (*mutesellims*) in Jerusalem and Jaffa from time to time.[9]

During the first three decades of the nineteenth century, Jerusalem was usually governed by a civil governor, the *mutesellim,* who was responsible for keeping the peace and collecting the taxes and customs duties imposed by the central government. Most of the *mutesellim*'s income seems to have come from the non-Muslim communities: from the feuding Christian churches, which competed over rights in the holy places; and from Christian pilgrims, who paid a tax upon entering the city and an additional sum for an escort to the Jordan river. All monasteries were in need of permits to hold processions, repair churches, and so on, and they sometimes made the authorities gifts of money. The Jews, too, paid taxes and made gifts to the authorities.[10] The *mutesellim* resided in a building on the Via Dolorosa; this building, which now houses the 'Omariyya school, overlooks the Temple Mount and the whole of the Old City.[11] There was also a garrison of soldiers in the Citadel of David.[12]

Until the Egyptian occupation, juridical power in Jerusalem was mainly in

5   Ma'oz, "Jerusalem," pp. 261-264.
6   *Loc. cit.*
7   Ben-Zvi, *Eretz-Israel,* p. 339.
8   J. Finn, *Stirring Times,* I, p. 201; II, pp. 17-18.

9   Ben-Zvi, *Eretz-Israel,* p. 345; and see sources cited there.
10   Assaf, *History,* II, pp. 288-289; and see sources cited there.
11   Western visitors to Jerusalem in those days often mention this building, usually calling it "Pilate's Palace," as it was the traditional site of Jesus's trial; see also below, p. 169.
12   See also sections on the Citadel, p. 15 above, and the Ottoman garrison, p. 135 below.

the hands of the *mullah* (the Turkish *qadi*), who was appointed once a year by the sultan on the recommendation of the Sheikh al-Islam in Constantinople. The *mullah* would appoint a *qadi* or *naqib* from amongst the inhabitants to serve the entire city. This *qadi* was obliged by law to pay for his appointment according to the status of the region under his jurisdiction. Since the *mullah* served a single term that lasted only a year, he tried to earn as much as possible so that he could live a life of ease in Constantinople afterwards, until his next appointment. An important source of income for him was legal wrangling between monasteries. The *qadi* received percentages of business transactions, inherited estates, the certification of documents and so on. All officials made a practice of evading the law and of heaping tax upon tax.[13]

On the whole, the Turkish government caused the local inhabitants much suffering; the residents of Jerusalem were no exception—Muslims, Christians and Jews alike. Still, the Muslim population seems to have fared somewhat better than the others in the early nineteenth century, because the Muslim leadership of *qadis* (judges), *muftis* (Muslim spiritual leaders) and *'ulema* (religious scholars) was extremely influential, and because they were patronized by the local rulers and the military to some extent. Compared with the Muslims, the Christian and Jewish inhabitants of the Ottoman state were second-class citizens. They were forbidden to carry arms, and had to pay a special poll-tax, called the *jizye,* which symbolized their inferiority and served as payment for the protection extended them by the state. Courts would not accept their testimony against Muslims, and senior government positions were beyond their reach, with very few exceptions. Aside from such political and legal restrictions, non-Muslims were also subject to social and religious constraints.[14]

Egyptian Rule in Jerusalem (1831-1839)

The first change in the status of Jerusalem took place in 1831, when the forces of Muhammad 'Ali and Ibrahim Pasha took the city. The Egyptian army advanced on two fronts: the infantry crossed the desert, while the navy sailed for Jaffa and captured it without a fight. When news of the invasion reached the Turkish soldiers in Jerusalem in December of 1831, they said that they would refuse to surrender unless given the back pay owed them by the pasha of Acre. Once the Egyptian troops arrived in Jerusalem, however, they gave in peacefully.[15] One source writes that Jerusalem fell to Ibrahim Pasha on December 7, 1831, when he marched into the city with an army of 40,000 soldiers.[16]

Egypt's nine-year occupation of the Holy Land and Syria brought about numerous changes. Ibrahim Pasha immediately abolished the former Ottoman administrative division of the country into two provinces, and appointed a general governor over all of Syria and Palestine, whose seat was in Damascus. The governors of all the cities in the area were subordinate to him. Now that

107

13   Basili, II, p. 157; Assaf, *History,* II, p. 290; Abir, pp. 291-294.
14   Ma'oz, "Jerusalem," pp. 263-264.
15   Spyridon, p. 84.
16   Liévin (1897), I, p. 176.

The Supreme Vizier (Wittman, p. 46)

Chief cook of the Janissary Corps (Wittman, p. 230)

Acre was no longer the seat of the pasha, it began to decline in importance. The status of Jerusalem, on the other hand, began to rise.

Ibrahim Pasha's central government diminished the power of feudal overlords and raised the status of the government officials, the *mutesellims*. A considerable administrative advance was the establishment of city councils *(majlis),* composed of representatives of the population, whose task it was to advise the administrative authority on matters of taxation, customs duties and commercial disputes. In particular, they made it their concern to improve the legal status of non-Muslims.[17] The Egyptian government also restricted the judicial power of the *mullah* and his assistants, leaving to their care only matters of inheritance and marital status. All other affairs were dealt with by the municipal councils. It was also arranged that the Jerusalem *mullah* would receive his salary from the treasury, so that he would not take bribes from the monasteries.[18]

The Muslim community of Jerusalem and of the country as a whole derived little satisfaction from the regime of Ibrahim Pasha. For the first time in centuries, Jerusalem was ruled by a strong, centralized government based in Damascus and Cairo. Order and security were maintained by force; Muslim citizens were subjected to compulsory draft and disarmament. The Muslim religious leadership was politically and economically weakened by the withdrawal of many of its judicial and other public duties, and the cessation in the flow of the large sums of money it had once received from the monasteries and the Christian and Jewish communities. Needless to say, all levels of the Muslim population felt that great harm had been done by the innovations of

17 Ben-Zvi, *Eretz-Israel,* p. 346. See also sources cited there, note 3. On the administration and establishment of the *majlis,* see Hofman, "Administration," pp. 330-333.
18 Basili, II, p. 157; Assaf, *History,* II, p. 290.

the Egyptian government: the leadership because of the blow to its supremacy and income, the other classes because of the draft and strict laws. Both were bitter about the equality of status granted to Christians and Jews.[19]

In contrast to the state of the Muslim community, that of the Christian community improved vastly under Egyptian rule. The government was much more liberal than the Turkish regime had been, and more open to the influence of the European powers. This eased the plight of the Christian and Jewish minorities in Jerusalem. Ibrahim Pasha abolished the arbitrary taxes and duties levied upon pilgrims; he tried to wean his subordinates from their habit of extracting money directly from citizens, by granting them a regular salary from the state treasury.[20] During the period of Egyptian rule, the Christians were permitted to repair churches and erect new buildings. They were granted freer access to the Church of the Holy Sepulchre and other shrines, and restrictions on missionary activity were eased. Christians and Muslims enjoyed a similar status in many spheres. For the first time in the city's history, Christians were represented in the municipal advisory council, along with Muslims. They were no longer oppressed by the authorities and by Muslim notables or maltreated by Muslim mobs. They even began to receive government and economic posts.[21]

The Jews were also treated much more liberally during the Egyptian occupation. They were now allowed to repair synagogues and to pray at the Wailing Wall without a special *firman*. In addition, their living conditions and settlement opportunities in Jerusalem were considerably improved.

The Egyptian government was much stronger than the preceding regime, and it enforced law and order in the country. The Bedouin were restrained, highway robbery ceased and general security reigned. Travelers on their way to Jerusalem were no longer required to pay a toll to the villagers of Abu Ghosh. The number of European visitors increased and immigration to the Holy Land gained momentum. This orderly, efficient government, however, began to irritate the local inhabitants. It was difficult to evade the payment of taxes, because fewer officials now accepted bribes. Muslim religious leaders who disapproved of Ibrahim Pasha's liberal attitude toward Christians; public notables who had lost their power; Bedouin who could no longer pillage the countryside; and, most of all, the peasants, who were subject to conscription — all joined forces against the Egyptian administration. The situation took a turn for the worse with the mass flight of peasants to the hills, to escape military service. Dozens of villages were deserted and flourishing areas turned barren, becoming hideouts for thieves and bandits. This led to riots and uprisings in the mountain districts. In 1834, a large-scale rebellion, known as the Peasants' Revolt, broke out, also reaching Jerusalem, where the city's Muslim residents joined the revolt along with peasants from the surrounding villages.[22] Within three weeks, the whole country was involved. The uprising spread quickly to both sides of the Jordan. The Arabs of Judea and Samaria also converged on

19   Ma'oz, "Jerusalem," p. 265; Assaf, *op. cit.,* p. 217; see also literature cited there.
20   Spyridon, pp. 87-88.
21   Ma'oz, *Ottoman Reforms,* pp. 17-20; see also sources cited there.
22   For a detailed description see Spyridon, pp. 89-120.

Muḥammad 'Ali
(Madox, II, frontispiece)

Jerusalem; Ibrahim Pasha was not in the city at the time, and the Egyptian garrison there numbered no more than 600 troops, while thousands of rebels had infiltrated the city through ancient underground sewage channels. They took control of all of Jerusalem except for the Citadel, which was held by the remaining Egyptian troops, equipped with cannons. All attempts to take the Citadel failed. Meanwhile, Ibrahim Pasha hurried back from Jaffa, bringing with him a thousand soldiers who helped him to restore order quickly. The rebels were severely punished, many of them being captured and put to death.[23] The rebellion of 1834 brought in its wake attacks on the Christians and Jews of Jerusalem, and the city was ransacked for five or six days. The Christians were able to save themselves by hiding in monasteries. The Jews, however, suffered terribly, for they had nowhere to go.[24]

It seems that Ibrahim Pasha's reign was also an extremely important turning point in building in Jerusalem. The architect Schick writes that, aside from their thorough repair of the city walls between 1536 and 1539, the Turks had neither built nor encouraged any building in the city. Christians were forbidden to erect new structures (although building permits could sometimes be obtained with great difficulty), and those structures that did exist were small and pitiful. The city itself abounded in vacant buildings, and the number of its inhabitants declined. Ruins were everywhere; even the areas around Jerusalem were barren. The flow of pilgrims slowed down as Western enthusiasm for the Holy Land subsided. The city remained desolate until the days of Ibrahim Pasha, who restored security and opened the way for renewed building activity. Settlers, pilgrims and missionaries began to arrive from Europe. This building

23 Robinson, *Biblical Researches,* III, p. 135; Macalister, *PEF QSt,* 1906, pp. 38-39; *PEF QSt,* 1918, pp. 142-144; Abir, pp. 302-303.
24 Macalister, *PEF QSt,* 1918, pp. 142-144.

activity persisted and even increased after the expulsion of Ibrahim Pasha.[25]

The local Egyptian governor lived in the Saraya building on the Via Dolorosa, and Egyptian soldiers were garrisoned in the Citadel of David. The government also constructed several buildings in the days of Ibrahim Pasha: the Kishleh army camp near the Citadel; a small fortress in Wadi Joz; another fortress between Wadi Joz and the al-Tur mountain ridge; and a ring of fortifications to guard the Jaffa-Jerusalem road. In addition, various buildings on Mount Zion around the Tomb of David were renovated for Ibrahim Pasha's use when he visited Jerusalem. (He probably chose to stay there so as to avoid the epidemics that occurred frequently in the city.) In 1839 the city's first two windmills were erected.[26]

The strong Egyptian government in Syria and the Holy Land required vast amounts of money. Hence a further rise in taxes and growing discontent among the inhabitants. By the end of the 1830's, animosity toward the rule of Muḥammad 'Ali had reached a peak. New uprisings broke out; the European powers, interested in ousting Egypt from Syria, helped the Turks to overthrow the government.[27]

The Renewed Ottoman Administration (1840-1856)

In 1840, the Ottomans again ruled the Holy Land, after having driven out the Egyptian army with the aid of Britain and other powers. The expulsion of the Egyptians was also helped by the rebellion of the Muslims and their sheikhs, who had opposed Egyptian rule and now welcomed the returning Turkish forces. The Egyptian troops in Jerusalem and Jaffa were alarmed by the prevailing spirit of rebellion and after many cities (including Acre) had fallen into Ottoman hands, they pulled back to Gaza. Armed peasants raided Jaffa, and Jerusalem was thought to be next in line. It appears that, each time there was a political crisis, the wealth of Jerusalem's monasteries aroused the greed of mountain dwellers from the surrounding area. The Muslims also sought revenge upon the Christians and Jews, whom they regarded as the allies of the Egyptians. This time, however, Jerusalem was saved by the British demand that the Ottoman government protect the Christians and Jews from harm, and by the courageous stance of the Jerusalem qadi.[28]

The return of Turkish rule in 1840 was extremely important for the status and development of Jerusalem. The new Turkish regime was quite different from the one prior to the Egyptian occupation, primarily because of its tendency towards centralization. One reason for this was the military reform of Sultan Maḥmud II, which had begun even before the Egyptian conquest. As a result, the Janissary Corps was replaced by a regular army, subject to the central government rather than to pashas and local emirs. A second reason was the institution of direct taxation, handled by a special branch of the central government. A third was the nine years of centralized Egyptian rule, which had

25   Schick, *ZDPV,* XVII, 1894/5, pp. 264-276.
26   *Loc. cit.*; Assaf, *History,* II, p. 129.
27   Ben-Zvi, *Eretz-Israel,* pp. 346-348
28   Assaf, *History,* II, pp. 218-222; see also sources cited there.

Abdul Majid (Damer-Dawson, I, p. 188)

weakened the power of feudal governors, so that the government could enforce its authority more easily than in the past.

This period is known as the Tanzimat, the period of Turkish law reforms. These reforms had already been approved in 1839, but were difficult to implement. Gradually, however, they began to have an increasing effect on the Ottoman Empire. The Tanzimat was intended, among other things, to appease the powers that had aided Turkey in driving out the Egyptians; it also included laws concerning the equal status of non-Muslims in the Ottoman Empire. These laws reinforced the special status of the foreign consulates and the Western powers in the Holy Land. Both elements subsequently enjoyed an inordinate amount of influence in Jerusalem.[29]

After the Ottomans regained power, the Holy Land east and west of the Jordan river continued to be divided into two administrative provinces, Damascus and Sidon. Now, however, all the western districts were annexed officially to the province of Sidon, with Beirut as its capital instead of Acre. The districts on the eastern bank of the Jordan remained part of the province of Damascus. An intermediate administrative category between a province and a district was also organized west of the Jordan: the *mutaṣarriflik*. Thus, the districts of Jerusalem, Shechem and Gaza were integrated into the *mutaṣarriflik* of Jerusalem. The governor of this enlarged unit, the *mutaṣarrif*, was subject to the government of Sidon or the central government in Constantinople.[30]

Still, the government seems to have held little sway in Jerusalem. The aim of the Sublime Porte to centralize rule resulted in the appointment of pashas for only one year at a time. The *mullah* (who henceforth also acted as *qadi*) was to

112

29   On the changes in Ottoman Law during 1840-1860, see Ma'oz, *Ottoman Reforms*.
30   Ma'oz, "Jerusalem," p. 272.

serve for three years. The pashas were deprived of their authority to inflict capital punishment, and they themselves might be tried and punished for abusing their office.[31] This, of course, weakened the power of the local governors and almost nullified their ability to influence the development of Jerusalem. The situation was wholly different for several European consulates and the branch offices of certain religious communities, whose permanent workers lived in Jerusalem for lengthy periods and left an indelible mark on it.

The government changes instituted after the return of the Ottomans also extended to the administrative structure of the provinces. The officials heading the Turkish administration began to be assisted by the city council or *majlis*, which represented the entire local population (the Muslim and Christian communities, and others). Such a council was also appointed in Jerusalem. One source writes that the order to establish the *majlis* was issued on November 11, 1840. The Jerusalem *majlis* was composed of fourteen members, among them Aaron, the *vekil* (official) of the Jewish community, and Joseph, the *vekil* of the Frankish community (probably the Roman Catholics).[32]

According to Neumann, who seems to be referring to the 1860's, the Turkish government in the city was both civil and military. Criminal and civil lawsuits were brought before the municipal judge or *qadi*. Military affairs were controlled by the *kim basha*, whose troops served both as a garrison and as a municipal police force. The civil governor was aided by the *majlis*, which consisted of eight notables (four Muslims, three Christians and one Jew), as well as by the *mufti*, the *qadi*, the director of the large mosques and the commander-in-chief of the army. The council was presided over by the pasha or, in his absence, by the *mufti* or *qadi*. The Muslims elected their delegates by casting lots among the distinguished families; the Christians, through the monasteries; the Jews, by appointment of the Hakham Bashi. The *majlis* met in full strength twice a week, and part of it four times a week. Special investigations were carried out by two delegates, who received thirty grush a day for their labors. The establishment of the *majlis* was an important step forward. However, the local population had been oppressed for so long that it lacked any political consciousness, and so the *majlis* could have no real impact. Theoretically, the pasha was supposed to consult the *majlis;* in fact, he was all-powerful.[33] It therefore seems that, despite the good intentions implicit in establishing municipal councils and the desire to grant citizens a say in local affairs as preparation for representative government, the councils themselves had little positive value. They quickly became instruments of tyranny in the hands of the Turkish government, particularly with regard to the city's minorities, since the councils consisted mainly of Muslims and the minority representatives dared not go against the will of the pasha. In this way, the pasha obtained public authorization for his exploitation.[34]

Nevertheless, it should be pointed out that non-Muslims fared much better under the new Ottoman government than under the previous one. They were

31   Assaf, *History,* II, p. 292.
32   Ben-Zvi, *Eretz-Israel,* p. 350; see also sources cited there.
33   Neumann, p. 225.
34   Gat, *The Jewish Community,* p. 81.

Muslim military judge (Wittman, p. 228)

Turkish minister of protocol (Wittman, p. 326)

no longer forbidden to ride horses, nor were they required to wear distinguishing clothing; yet they continued to be discriminated against to some degree. For example, the *kawass* of a consul still had to be a Muslim, and only a Muslim could take another Muslim to court or have him arrested for stealing. A Christian who dared to do so would provoke rioting and other kinds of trouble.

The Crimean War and the Continuation of Reforms (1856-1876)

The Crimean war led to yet another turn in the development of Jerusalem. The war affected economic conditions in the city to some degree, but the treaty signed at its end had an even greater effect. Among other things, the Paris Treaty, signed on May 30, 1856 determined the status of non-Muslims in the Ottoman Empire and the rights of priests and rabbis; it specified how the latter were to be elected, who would pay their salaries, and so on. To satisfy the wishes of the European powers, Turkey continued to develop its network of law reforms (the Tanzimat).[35] In 1856, the governor of Jerusalem issued, with great pomp and circumstance, the famous edict known as *Ḥatt-i Humayun*, which augmented the rights extended to non-Muslims in the *Ḥatt-i Sherif* of Gulhane in 1839. Non-Muslims were guaranteed proper representation in the *majlis*; the regulations were changed to allow foreign subjects to purchase land; all discrimination was eliminated from the administrative protocol; and official permission was granted to practice all forms of religion. Thus, the sultan prohibited all religious persecution and affirmed the equality of all Ottoman

114

---

35   Ben-Zvi, *Eretz-Israel,* p. 335; Ma'oz, *Ottoman Reforms,* pp. 27-29.

subjects before the law. However, in spite of all these declarations and other liberal reforms, such as paid release from military service, real discrimination was not rooted out.[36]

During the years of the Crimean war, there was great tension in Jerusalem between the Muslims and the other communities. Finn says the Muslim masses perceived the Crimean war as a war between Islam and Christianity, even though the Turks were aided by such Christian powers as Britain and France (the Russians were regarded as the defenders of Eastern Christianity). In Jerusalem, a clash was feared on Easter, involving the many Greek Orthodox pilgrims and the Muslims celebrating the holiday of Nebi Musa, who streamed to the city in greater numbers than usual from the surrounding villages and especially from the Nablus district.[37]

In 1854, in the midst of the Crimean war, the Jerusalem district became an independent province and its governor, a pasha, received his orders directly from Constantinople. At the end of the 1850's, the Nablus district was separated from the *mutaṣarriflik* of Jerusalem. Even then, however, the Jerusalem district was usually subject to the central government, particularly after 1873. These administrative changes prove that Jerusalem was rising in importance in the eyes of the Ottoman government, no doubt because of the increasing activity of the Christians and Jews and the expanding interest of the European powers.[38] The special independence granted to Jerusalem in those days did not go unnoticed by the Hebrew press.[39]

Until 1855, non-Muslims continued to pay the *jizye* or poll-tax. In that year, they were exempted from it, and were required instead to pay the *bedel,* or army exemption tax, as they were not permitted to serve in the army until 1908. The testimony of a Christian or Jew against a Muslim was still invalid in the Muslim courts; even in the newly established secular courts, such testimony was often rejected.[40]

In 1861, Abdul Aziz (1861-1876) rose to power. He differed in temperament from his predecessor and was less enthusiastic about the reforms. Only under pressure from France were the reforms resumed. In 1864, the Law of Vilayets was passed, reinstituting district administration and the incorporation of non-Muslims in the city councils. The Tanzimat Council, which included the Council of State and the Council of Justice, was reorganized in 1868. Educational institutions arose, too, and the Ottoman Citizenship Law was passed a year later in an effort to implement the *Ḥatt* of 1856. In the same year, the *Mejelle,* the collection of laws of justice (of the *Shari'a*), began to appear, its publication continuing until 1876.[41]

Despite the reforms, the Ottoman state continued to be Muslim by definition and by character, and only Muslim inhabitants were full-fledged members of its political community. Christians and Jews were still regarded by the

36   Ma'oz, "Changes," pp. 154-157.
37   J. Finn, *Stirring Times,* I, pp. 201-204, 300-301, 504.
38   Ma'oz, "Jerusalem," p. 272.
39   *Ha-Levanon,* 24 Av, 1872, vol. IX, no. 1, p. 8; *Ha-Tzefira,* 8 Tevet. 1879, vol. VI, no. 48, pp. 381-382.
40   Ma'oz, *Ottoman Reforms,* pp. 194-199.
41   Lewis, *Emergence,* pp. 120-124.

administration as second-class citizens, and a large proportion of government and local officials treated them with scorn if not hatred, taking every opportunity to oppress them and restrict their activities. Nevertheless, there seems to have been a difference in the treatment of Christians as opposed to Jews, and of Ottoman Jews as opposed to European Jews. Ottoman Jews were ridiculed and humiliated; Christians and Jews of foreign nationality were regarded with a mixture of anger, suspicion and hatred.[42]

Ostensibly, the reforms in Ottoman law should have led also to progress in the Turkish administration of Jerusalem after 1856. However, all attempts at change were quickly headed off by the governors themselves. The promised reforms never materialized, and corruption and deterioration increased.[43]

The Rule of the Jerusalem Pashas (1840-1876)

Throughout the nineteenth century, from the resumption of Ottoman rule until World War I, Jerusalem was governed by a pasha. When the Ottomans returned to Jerusalem, the city was run by a *mutaṣarrif,* or pasha of two horse-tails, who was appointed in Constantinople for one year and was subject to the *vali* of Sidon (or Beirut) instead of to that of Damascus. Such pashas gave first priority to amassing money and exploiting their power, while ignoring the needs of the local population. Western travelers visiting Jerusalem in the 1840's and 1850's complain time and again about the frequent change of pashas, their despotism and their exploitation of the inhabitants.[44]

Strauss (mid-century) writes that the activity of the local government was scarcely felt in the city. This was due largely to the constant change of pashas, who knew that their position was short-lived and had no thoughts of the city's future. The pasha's duties were to collect taxes and maintain order in the country. Concern for education, agriculture or commerce was far from his mind and from the interests of his administration. Peace and security were maintained mainly by the village notables, the sheikhs, who also elected the village councils; their primary ambition was to become as wealthy as possible, and this often led to disputes among them. The pasha, who served as "peacemaker," frequently employed whole army units for this purpose, thereby increasing his influence in the area. Actually, it was not peace the pasha desired, but his own enhanced status. Once, the pasha even jailed the leaders of rival factions—because they became reconciled without his intervention. In effect, there was no real government in the country. Foreigners, like permanent residents, fared well if they maintained good relations with the local bands and Bedouin tribes by making them gifts of money.[45] Another source says that the inhabitants of Abu Ghosh renewed their "taxation" of travelers on their way to Jerusalem, and that one of the village leaders, Mustafa Abu Ghosh, captured and murdered two government officials. He then sent a threat to the helpless pasha of Jerusalem that he would attack the city if anyone harassed his band.[46]

116

---

42 Ma'oz, *Ottoman Reforms,* pp. 202-205.
43 J. Finn, *Stirring Times,* II, p. 191; Assaf, *History,* II, p. 140 (see also sources cited there).
44 Schulz, p. 136.
45 Strauss, pp. 278-281.   46 Williams (1849), I, pp. 454-455.

An attempt was made to enforce order in Jerusalem and the mountain districts in 1846, when Kibrisli Pasha rose to power. This pasha took vigorous measures to strengthen the Turkish government and subdue the various sheikhs fighting in Judea and Samaria, but he was successful for only a short time.[47] According to Finn, Kibrisli Pasha was later raised to the rank of Turkish ambassador to England, then to commander-in-chief of the army, and finally to the rank of Grand Vizier.[48]

Several sources from the middle of the nineteenth century offer descriptions similar to our account of the early part of the century. The governor of Jerusalem paid a fee to the sultan for his post, and recovered his outlay by collecting all sorts of taxes: *miri*, customs and special duties, such as those extracted from the Christians. These sources estimate that more than 100,000 piastres went into the pasha's treasury. Furthermore, all pilgrims paid the governor for the privilege of entering the holy places; the fee was usually ten piastres plus an additional sum for the trip to the Jordan river. Any work carried out for the monasteries, such as repairs, renovations or the changing of locks, incurred payments to the governor. A fee was also charged for every religious ceremony, and the governor received a percentage from the export of all ceremonial objects. In addition, there were illegal taxes and numerous instances of robbery.[49]

Neumann writes that the fee paid for Jerusalem and Bethlehem came to 80,000 piastres a year. The butchers paid additional 10,000 piastres. He says that, on the whole, taxation was not as heavy as was believed in Europe, and that the tax burden was divided. It was unfortunate, however, that the Arab effendis demanded additional gifts; for the Jews alone, these came to 50,000 piastres a year. The *jizye* was collected from all men over the age of twenty, who were divided into three groups, paying fifteen, thirty, or sixty piastres a year according to their incomes. Christians paid this tax through the monasteries, with payment for poor Catholics coming from the monasteries themselves. Jews also paid through their community institutions, taking money for the poorest Jews from the communal treasury.[50] Neumann stresses that, for the Ottoman government, it was not the taxes sanctioned in writing that were of major importance, but the arbitrary ones not so sanctioned, which were dependent on local governors and tax-collectors.

The pashas who ruled Jerusalem up to 1876 were replaced so often that no figure of special importance to Jerusalem stands out among them, though several are mentioned in nineteenth-century literature.[51] It should be pointed out that, after the Crimean war, there was a change in the type of Ottoman official appointed as pasha. The new governors were more modern in outlook, had good manners, spoke French, had visited the European capitals, and were familiar with European culture.[52]

47   Basili, II, p. 54; Assaf, *History,* II, p. 61; Macalister, *PEF QSt,* 1906, pp. 46-48.
48   J. Finn, *Stirring Times,* I, p. 10.
49   Taylor, *La Syrie,* pp. 327-328; Damas, III, p. 67; Ritter, IV, p. 142.
50   Neumann, pp. 230-231.
51   Isaacs, p. 165; Pierotti, I, pp. 273-274.
52   Warren, *Underground Jerusalem,* pp. 10, 148, 297-298, 380-398. Eliav, *German Policy* (Hebrew volume), p. 324, lists the governors of Jerusalem from 1855 to 1914. However, comparison with the Hebrew press indicates that this list is incomplete and some of the dates inaccurate.

The Continuation of Ottoman Rule (1876-1908)

As far as the status of the Sublime Porte is concerned, it may be said with assurance that, throughout the days of Abdul Majid (1839-1860) and Abdul Aziz (1861-1876), there was no change in the general state of affairs in the Holy Land or in any other part of the Ottoman Empire, aside from the first stirrings of technology and modernization. With the fall of Abdul Aziz, whose reign saw the acceleration of the Empire's economic collapse, and especially after the rise of Abdul Ḥamid; more pronounced changes began to be felt in the Ottoman Empire and in the Holy Land. These were partly the product of political events in Europe following the Franco-Prussian war. After this war, Turkey became increasingly opposed to Western-style reforms and capitulation rights for foreigners and Christians; a sense of Ottoman patriotism took hold. Abdul Aziz was overthrown in May of 1876, to be followed by Murad V for a short term and then by Abdul Ḥamid II. During the last-named's reign, the post of Grand Vizier was assumed by Midḥat Pasha, the leader of the "Young Turks," who sought to establish a liberal, constitutional state along European lines. When the representatives of the Great Powers met in Constantinople in 1876 after the war between Serbia and Montenegro in order to decide the fate of the Balkans, the sultan proclaimed the adoption of a constitution that would grant equal rights and constitutional freedom to all Ottoman subjects. This was not just the result of Western pressure, but an attempt to meet the demands of a large group of intellectuals who sought to curtail the sultan's despotism.[53]

As for the ideology of the "Young Turks" movement, which had already begun to take root in 1860, its basic tenets were: war against foreigners; the independent revival of the Ottoman Empire; the establishment of a constitution and of parliamentary law; and the abolition of tyranny. In the course of time, the concept of *watan* (homeland) began to be valued above that of Islam. Finally, a movement called *Unity and Progress* was founded; this movement was to bring about a basic revolution in Turkey, but only at the relatively late date of 1908-1909.[54]

The last phase of Ottoman rule was colored largely by Abdul Ḥamid II, who remained in power for a long time (1876-1909). As we have said, he supported the reforms and even proclaimed the adoption of a constitution. It seems, however, that he had no intention of fulfilling his proclamations. In 1877, he dismissed the liberal Grand Vizier, Midḥat Pasha, and sent him into exile. A year later, he dissolved the parliament, which reconvened only thirty years later. At this time, considerable changes were taking place in Turkey's foreign relations. France and Britain, for many years the patrons of the reforms and Turkey's political and military backers, now despaired of the continued existence of the Ottoman Empire. After the Berlin Congress (1878), Britain and France began to annex parts of the Empire (Cyprus, Egypt and Tunisia). The Ottomans then gained a new friend, Germany, which sent officers to train the Turkish army and was granted various privileges in return.[55]

53 Ma'oz, "Changes," pp. 154-157.
54 Assaf, *History,* II, p. 142.
55 Lewis, *Emergence,* pp. 178-194.

During Abdul Ḥamid's thirty-year reign, no reforms were instituted in legislation or in political life. Yet progress was made in the spheres of economy, administration and education. Abdul Ḥamid maintained an imperial policy and did his best to exercise real control over the peripheral territories within his jurisdiction. Administrative centers were established in the mountain districts, and the outskirts of the desert became the focus of extensive settlement activities involving refugees, mostly Circassians and Turkomans, who were settled across the Jordan. The Bedouin were also "encouraged" to form permanent encampments. In the big cities, new public offices and new mosques arose as symbols of imperial authority and of the patronage of the sultan.[56]

The *majlis,* the most important government body established during the Tanzimat period, underwent change at the end of Ottoman rule. The 1864 Law of Vilayets, and the 1879 creation of secular courts as opposed to the *Shari'a* courts in the provinces subject to reform, led to the restriction of its authority. At this time, the *majlis* derived its authority principally from the Law of Vilayets, which gave it the power to decide matters pertaining to public works; agriculture; finance; tax collection; *zaptiya* (police); the land registry and external affairs. It was prohibited from becoming involved in any legal affairs. The *majlis* now had two types of members. There were members *ex officio* such as the *mutaṣarrif*; the *qadi*; the *mufti*; the *muhasbeci* (treasurer) and the representatives of four religious communities: the Greek Orthodox, the Roman Catholics, the Armenians and the Jews. In addition, there were four elected members, one of them apparently being a Christian. Socially, the minorities were poorly integrated in the council. This was particularly evident in the case of the Jews, who were often not represented in its sessions.[57]

At the end of the nineteenth century, Jerusalem was governed by a prominent leader, Rauf Pasha, who ruled for quite a considerable period (1876-1888), curbing local violence and restricting the power of certain Muslim families.[58] Rauf was a forceful ruler, and a zealous upholder of Islam. In the memoirs of the first Jewish colonies established in the 1880's, he is mentioned from time to time as an opponent of Jewish colonization. He also encouraged and developed the custom of Muslim pilgrimages to Jerusalem and Nebi Musa.

In the 1890's, particularly in their latter half, and in the first decade of the twentieth century, the constant rotation of pashas in Jerusalem is noted frequently. This phenomenon became even more pronounced on the eve of World War I. It seems that would-be pashas tried to win over members of different sects in Jerusalem in order to gain support for their appointment.[59] This incessant change of rulers had a deleterious effect on the city, and adversely affected the ability of the government to contribute to the city's development.[60]

---

56   *Loc. cit.*; Pollack, pp. 244-250; Assaf, *History,* III, pp. 9-21.
57   Gerber, pp. 16, 20-21.
58   *Ibid.,* p. 13; Assaf, *History,* III, pp. 12-14.
59   *Ha-Or,* 1 Sivan, 1911, vol. II, no. 173-348, p. 2.
60   Gerber, pp. 4-7. The constant turnover of pashas was a salient feature of the government of Jerusalem toward the end of Ottoman rule.

The Courts, Land Ownership and Taxes

An important part of public life in Jerusalem was the *Shari'a* court, headed by the *qadi*. In addition to his juridical duties, the *qadi* was considered the most important official after the pasha; in the pasha's absence, he would preside as chairman of the administrative council. Sometimes the *qadi* would even substitute for the district pasha, if this position were not filled temporarily by the military pasha. The *Shari'a* court met in a building known as the *Maḥkame* (the *Tankiziyya,* built in the Mamluk period, a spacious building near the Gate of the Chain, overlooking the clearing before the Wailing Wall). This court dealt with all matters of personal status involving Muslims, and quite often involving non-Muslims too, including the laws governing alimony, wills and inheritance. At the end of the Ottoman period, a single civil court of first instance was also opened in Jerusalem; it met in one of the large rooms in the back of the Saraya. There was no magistracy in the city, and appeals had to be brought before a higher court in Beirut or Damascus. Criminal cases were also dealt with there.

In addition to the secular and religious courts, Jerusalem had consular courts, which dealt with the personal status of their subjects and settled simple disputes between them. The judge was usually the consul, his deputy or his dragoman. Disputes between a foreign national and an Ottoman citizen, as well as certain criminal offenses committed by foreign nationals, were handled by the Ottoman civil court. In such cases, the foreign national came to court with the consulate dragoman, who sat on the bench along with the judges. If he did not, he was at least escorted by a *kawass*.[61]

Now the reforms also began to be applied to the Jews of Jerusalem, some of whom received administrative posts. Joseph Krieger, for example, was the pasha's dragoman, and held other positions in the service of the Turkish governors. He was later dismissed from his post as the pasha's secretary. Some say that this was the result of pressure from the Christian Mission since, as a Jew in a high-ranking position, he could stand in the way of its activities.[62]

Details of the workings of the courts in Jerusalem are supplied by Neumann. He says the Muslim court was hindered by the absence of a civil code of law. The judge acted in accordance with the Qur'an and legal statutes from the sixteenth to eighteenth centuries. The first instance, in both civil and criminal matters, was the *qadi,* who served a single term and was then replaced by someone sent from Constantinople. The office of *bash katib* (secretary) passed from father to son. The next-highest authority, to whom one could appeal, was the *mufti,* the spiritual leader of Jerusalem. The supreme court was the council of the *'ulema* in Constantinople, headed by Sheikh al-Islam. Application to this court, however, was prohibitively expensive, so that only very important issues reached it. The consulates served as courts for Jerusalem's non-Ottoman ("Frankish") residents. In addition, the Christians and Jews had courts of their own. The Jews had a rabbinic court headed by the Ḥakham Bashi, who was held in respect by the authorities. Sentences in the Turkish courts usually

120

61   G. Frumkin, pp. 108-109.
62   Malachi, p. 332 (1883); Gat, *The Jewish Community,* p. 82.

involved imprisonment, but sometimes a fine was imposed instead. Physical abuse was common in prison, either as a punishment or in order to extract a confession, but death sentences were almost unheard of. In one unusual case, four persons accused of a grave offense were put to death. If a foreign national and a Turkish citizen were tried together, a consular representative had to come to court and sign the verdict. Since lawsuits in the *Shari'a* court were quite costly, Muslims often brought their problems before a consul, so as to save money.[63]

Most of the built-up land in Jerusalem, including the sites of mosques, monasteries and public buildings, belonged to the *waqf* or pious foundations of the various community groups. Very little land was privately owned; if a landowner died without a male heir, his land became community property.[64] The *Ḥazaka* system of home ownership, practiced by the Jews of the Old City, will be discussed in the chapter on the Jews (see p. 327). *Inter alia*, the Ottoman reform movement involved the issuing of several land laws that made it easier for non-Muslims to buy land and houses. These laws, however, had a much greater effect outside the Old City than inside it, because more of the land inside was already developed and owned by pious foundations.[65]

The subject of taxes in the Ottoman Empire and the way they changed in the course of the nineteenth century is complex, and we shall deal with it only briefly, emphasizing the taxes connected with Jerusalem. One kind of tax frequently mentioned in Jewish sources is the army tax. Nuemann writes that the obligations of the Jews of Jerusalem towards the authorities were no different from those of Jews in other part of the Ottoman Empire. All males paid a head-tax commensurate with their financial ability.[66] According to a Jewish source from the end of the century, non-Muslims were exempt from military service; instead they paid a head-tax. The government did not collect taxes on an individual basis, but demanded payment of the total amount according to the number of males in the community. In Jerusalem, the *kolelim* paid the ransom for all their members, including the few who received no *Ḥalukka* money. Another Jewish source from the same period adds that foreign nationals residing permanently in the country were exempt from this tax.[67]

Aside from the army tax paid by non-Muslims, there were other taxes paid by all residents of Jerusalem. Luncz lists the taxes in 1891 as follows: army tax; land and building tax (on both cultivated and uncultivated land, and on buildings according to worth), from which residents of the Old City of Jerusalem, Mecca and Medina were exempt; export and import tax, from which charitable institutions were exempt; wine, liquor and tobacco tax; grape tax; wheat and livestock tax (*'ushr*), according to crop yields and the number of animals born each year.[68]

Neumann writes that, because of Jerusalem's holiness and the poverty of its inhabitants, there was no collection of direct taxes in the city. An indirect tax was collected at the city gates, partly in money and partly in merchandise.

63 Neumann, pp. 229-231.
64 Ritter, IV, pp. 191-192.
65 Sokhovolsky, pp. 79-90.

66 Neumann, p. 375.
67 G. Frumkin, p. 105; Schirion, pp. 130-133.
68 Luncz, *Guide*, pp. 23-24.

There was also a small export tax. Europeans were exempt from indirect tax on items imported for their institutions.[69] Robinson also says Jerusalem residents paid no property tax on land or buildings.[70] A Jewish source for the end of the century repeats the fact that homes in the Old City were exempt from property tax, in view of the sanctity of the city, but those built outside the walls were not. This source divides the taxes into three categories (excluding the army tax): property tax (*vergi*), customs duty, and tithes. The *vergi* was paid by all inhabitants regardless of nationality; it amounted to one percent of the value of the house or land, and one-half percent of the value of a house resided in by the owners themselves. The assessment of homes was carried out once every three years by special government and municipal officials.[71]

Our information concerning the payment of customs upon entry to Jerusalem is contradictory. Liévin (1896) writes that a customs duty of up to eight percent was paid on religious articles such as crosses and icons. On the other hand, the Baedeker guide for the 1870's says that all municipal taxes levied by the Turkish government were abolished in 1874, and that the luggage of those entering the city was no longer searched.[72] Schick (1896) mentions the abolition of the gate tax once collected from porters and from all those arriving at the city gates with pack animals.[73] At the same time, the authorities seem to have become stricter about general customs duties. According to one Jewish source, they levied a tax of one percent on all exports and of eight percent on all merchandise entering the country (even used articles). This tax was part of the Capitulations agreements, and any increases had to be approved by the foreign governments in question. These governments responded to the Turkish requests to raise the tax only in 1910, when it was increased to eleven percent.[74]

The newspaper *Ha-Levanon* complains in 1867 of the heavy tax burden imposed by the Turkish government in order to improve its financial condition. Among the new taxes was a meat tax in Jerusalem, which severely affected the city's poor. Later, the newspaper reports a heavy duty on raw materials, whereas no such tax was imposed on finished products. This led to a deceleration in the development and growth of the economy.[75]

At the end of the century, when the municipality became more active, we find mention of special taxes and duties intended to improve the city's appearance. One example was a stamp tax on bills, checks and assorted documents.[76]

The Jerusalem Municipality

In the 1860's, Jerusalem saw the formation of its first municipal institution: the *Baladiyyat al-Quds*. One of the veteran members of the Jerusalem Municipality writes that the first *baladiyya* was established in 1863 in a dark alley near the

69   Neumann, pp. 230-231.
70   Robinson, *Biblical Researches,* II, pp. 92-93.
71   Schirion, pp. 130-133.
72   Liévin (1869), p. 6; Baedeker (1876), p. 144.
73   Schick, *NNADO,* 1897, pp. 8-9; *PEF QSt,* 1880, pp. 187-188.
74   Schirion, pp. 130-133.
75   *Ha-Levanon,* 27 Tevet, 1867, vol. IV, no. 1, p. 13.
76   Schirion, pp. 130-133.

Saraya. It operated in two or three small rooms. From 1863 until the British occupation of Jerusalem, the municipality was headed by twenty-three Muslims and one Greek with Turkish citizenship.[77] The establishment of the Jerusalem Municipality should be seen in the context of the Ottoman reforms which followed the Crimean war. At this time, in 1855-1856, a royal proclamation was issued concerning the formation of municipalities. This was the first step towards the institution of self-rule under Ottoman administration. The municipality order proper appeared only twelve years later (1867-1868), and was revised in 1869-1870.[78]

Each municipality consisted of six members, a mayor and a deputy-mayor. The municipal physician and engineer also had the right to offer an advisory opinion. Members were elected by a majority vote of mukhtars and sheikhs, with the endorsement of the local government. Appointment of the mayor required the *mutaṣarrif's* approval. Neither the mayor nor the members of the municipality received a salary. The municipality's job was to grant the citizens a say in the administration of certain local affairs. Nevertheless, even after the reforms, Ottoman officials managed to swallow up these institutions and enforce their will upon them. In practice, therefore, municipal self-rule was no more than an idea for many years to come.[79]

The Jerusalem Municipality became more active in the latter half of the 1880's. Perhaps this was due to the new Ottoman laws issued in 1886 and 1890, permitting the establishment of a municipality in any city, large or small. The number of members ranged from six to twelve, according to the size of the city, and they were elected for four years by all Ottoman males over the age of twenty-five who owned a certain amount of property and paid an annual tax. The municipality's duties were: supervising building activities; maintaining the road and water systems; keeping the city clean; and providing such utilities as lighting. It had the right to expropriate land for the general good; to demolish dangerous buildings; to repair roads; to develop public bath-houses; to establish fire departments, parks, recreation areas and markets; to levy taxes on carriage-drivers; to supervise commercial weights and measures, public health, cafés and restaurants, charitable institutions, and so forth. The municipality was also charged with preparing an annual budget and financial report; supervising the city's account books; administering the city's lands and assets; allocating public works among the different quarters; endorsing bills of purchase and sale of the municipality's assets; approving the employment of city officials and overseeing the work of engineers. The city engineer, physician and veterinarian were advisory members of the *baladiyya*. The secretary, treasurer and police were subordinate to the *baladiyya* committee, which met at least twice a week. There was even a special office in charge of registering street names and house numbers; the amount and type of property belonging to each landowner; the number and names of city residents; all financial transactions; and births and deaths.[80]

77   Brinker, *Jerusalem Almanac*, X, pp. 274-277; Vilnay, *Jerusalem*, III, p. 52, lists all the
       Jerusalem mayors during the Ottoman period by name, without citing any source.
78   Assaf, *History*, II, p. 140; Gorion, pp. 54-57.
79   Assaf, *History*, II, p. 293; Ben-Gurion—Ben-Zvi, p. 103.
80   Gorion, pp. 54-57; *Ha-Omer*, Parshandata, 1907, pp. 11-13.

In the second part of the 1880's, we begin to find numerous accounts of improvements in Jerusalem initiated by the municipality: a population census was taken; a police force with fourteen policemen (one of them Jewish) was set up to keep the peace and supervise sanitation; a decision was taken to repair and pave the city streets, and to dig new sewers; a medical clinic run by a skilled physician received patients of all religions three times a week, free of charge.[81] Other sources tell of cultural progress in the city at this time. In 1888, it was decided to build a theater outside the Old City, where plays would be staged in Arabic, Turkish and French. Funds were set aside for the establishment of schools even in small towns and villages.[82]

The descriptions of municipal activity continue into the 1890's. For 1890-1891, Luncz writes of the general hospital, founded by the city council, which accepted patients regardless of religion or nationality. This hospital had thirty-two beds, and a house physician was on duty three times a week to examine villagers from the Jerusalem vicinity free of charge. The municipality also turned the large lot in front of the Russian compound, formerly a resting place for camels and donkeys strewn with garbage and dung, into a lovely public park. Twice a week, on Sundays and Fridays, a military band performed music there. Another idea of the municipality was to clean Jaffa Road, which was unpaved, several times a week. However, since water was expensive, this project was not carried out in full.[83] Other sources describe the activities of the municipality in 1891, in which year there was a rumor that the *baladiyya* intended to renovate the Sultan's Pool so it could supply the city with water. It was also said that many homes and shops would be built beside and above it. The municipal hospital was also founded that year; among the guests were dignitaries of the Jewish community. In 1892, a military hospital was established in the courtyard of the Kishleh.[84] By the mid-1890's, the municipality had set up a fire department and paved the city streets. (The square before the Wailing Wall was also paved.) Towards the end of the decade, an organized effort was made to assign numbers to all the houses in the city.[85]

The twentieth century brought with it further developments for Jerusalem. In 1900, Sultan Abdul Ḥamid celebrated the twenty-fifth anniversary of his reign, and a *sabil* was constructed in his honor near the Jaffa Gate. It was designed by the city engineer in the Arab style, and was the first public structure put up solely for decorative purposes. Now, the first cultural institutions also began operating in Jerusalem. In 1901, a museum of antiquities was opened at the initiative of the municipality, and a theater built beside the Jaffa gate.[86] According to Luncz, all the antiquities discovered in 1900, either by chance or in the course of excavations by the Palestine

81 Luncz, *Jerusalem Yearbook,* II, 1887, p. 168
82 *Ibid.,* III, 1889, p. 202.
83 *Ibid.,* IV, 1892, p. 223.
84 *Ha-Or,* 3 Av, 1891, vol. VII, no. 39, p. 1; *Ha-Or,* 24 Elul, 1892, vol. VIII, no. 41, p. 1; Liévin (1897), I, pp. 185-186.
85 Luncz, *Almanac,* III, p. 130; IV, p. 157.
86 *Ibid.,* VII, pp. 171-172; Luncz, *Jerusalem Yearbook,* V, 1901, p. 283; X, 1905, p. 166.

Exploration Fund, were placed in this museum.[87] In 1904 we are told that the pasha of Jerusalem, Kazim Bey, thought of establishing a special market to sell products of Bethlehem. The city's Turkish baths were repaired and reorganized in the same year.[88] In 1906, Rashid Bey decided to arrange a horse race in Jerusalem; a year later, a law was passed prohibiting the construction and enlarging of homes or the addition of stories without a permit.[89] A tower was also put up next to the Jaffa gate during that year (p. 36).[90]

At the end of the nineteenth century, elections were held for the Jerusalem Municipality, but few people participated in them. David Yellin writes that, in 1898, about 700 Muslims and 300 Christians took part in the voting.[91] The first real elections were held in 1908-1909 when the Young Ottoman revolution brought basic changes in the country.

All these facts clearly show that the Jerusalem Municipality became increasingly active in the last thirty years of Ottoman rule. This trend became apparent at the end of the 1880's, and from then on it continually gained strength. With such activity possible, the previous inactivity of the central and local governments becomes all the more glaring. For the greater part of the nineteenth century, the government exhibited no desire whatsoever to develop Jerusalem. The city was far from being its principal concern, and the question of its progress was hardly of interest to it.[92]

87 *Ibid.,* V, 1901, p. 283.
88 *Hashkafa,* 17 Av, 1904, vol. V, no. 48, p. 441; *Ha-Tzevi,* 27 Tishri, 1902, vol. XXV, no. 11, p. 1.
89 *Hashkafa,* 28 Shevat, 1906, vol. VII, no. 36, p. 3; *Hashkafa,* 27 Tamuz, 1907, vol. VIII, no. 49, p. 3.
90 Luncz, *Almanac,* XIII, pp. 122-123.
91 Yellin, *Writings,* I, p. 202.
92 Gerber, p. 32.

Chapter Two:
THE MUSLIM COMMUNITY

Introduction

One of the most problematic subjects connected with nineteenth-century Jerusalem is the size and composition of its population. Different sources offer a variety of estimates, some conflicting, for the population in general and for the Muslims in particular. It should be kept in mind that, until the British Mandate (1922), there was no official census that can be considered complete and trustworthy. All we have are partial censuses and a great many estimates. In fact, the main obstacle in sketching a true picture of the size and development of Jerusalem's population in the nineteenth century is not the *lack* of data, but a surfeit of contradictory data.

Travelers visiting Jerusalem during this period, and others as well, frequently present population figures. Although we have based ourselves of necessity on such sources in dealing with many aspects of the city, it seems that the demographic data they offer must be approached with great caution. Often, these figures were intended as nothing more than general approximations. Sometimes, the data are the product of personal impressions, of errors in calculation, or of reliance on a faulty source. The matter is especially complicated with regard to the Muslim community. While figures for the Jews and Christians may be based on data provided by the communities themselves, the only relatively reliable sources for the Muslims are based on official Ottoman data which, for most of the nineteenth century, are very partial indeed. In many cases, even the Ottoman data have come down to us indirectly, through the writings of Western travelers who obtained their information from the Jerusalem authorities. Such data usually related only to Ottoman males, and the age span they encompassed seems to have changed in the course of the century. Over-all figures were reached only through multiplying the official figures for males by some possibly arbitrary number; the result might or might not reflect the improved sanitary conditions that affected family size and life expectancy. It should be remembered that the Ottoman registries were kept for tax collection and draft purposes, and probably were not very accurate. Thus, it seems impossible to quote a precise figure for either the Muslim population or the over-all population of nineteenth-century Jerusalem; however, we can establish a numerical range that reflects general demographic developments within the Muslim community. This can be achieved by relying only on population estimates that appear in relatively trustworthy sources, correlating these estimates, and considering them in the light of all we know about the period and about

Jerusalem. In this manner, we will draw some general conclusions, noting principal changes rather than slight fluctuations from year to year. We must remain skeptical about the degree to which the yearly fluctuations in population recorded in nineteenth-century literature can teach us of actual demographic changes. Most of the data are so inaccurate as to exclude any possibility of using them in this way. Unsanitary conditions and epidemics took their toll, but the diverse and conflicting demographic material that reflects them does not permit specific conclusions.

Population at the Beginning of the Century

How many Muslims lived in Jerusalem in the early nineteenth century? The data that seem most reliable are those of Seetzen, who claims that his source was the Turkish government. When he visited the city in 1806, the Muslim population was 4,000, in an over-all population of 8,750.[1]

Another comparatively trustworthy source is Robinson, who toured Jerusalem in 1838 and devoted a special section of his book to the subject of population. Robinson views as excessive the estimates of various Western travelers who say that the population of Jerusalem was between 15,000 and 30,000 souls. He, too, believes that there were fluctuations in the growth rate, but emphasizes that no precise figures could be reached since, in those days, censuses were not conducted in oriental cities. The usual estimates then set the population at 15,000 souls, with Muslims in the majority. Robinson doubts both assertions. He points out that, after the Egyptian occupation, the authorities began registering all males subject to tax payment and to the draft. Although the minimal age for being registered was unknown, Robinson assumes that it was between eighteen and twenty. It was customary to regard such figures as being equal to one quarter of the entire population. Robinson admits that the demographic data of the Ottoman government were the most reliable source for population estimates but, even so, thinks that they should be accepted with reservations. The fear of being drafted and the desire to avoid taxes led many to avoid being listed, and this produced artificially low figures. Data for the foreign communities could be obtained from their leaders, in order to complete and revise the official statistics. Seven hundred and fifty adult Muslim males were registered with the authorities; Robinson believes that 1,100 would be a more accurate number. Multiplying this number by four and rounding off the result gives a total of 4,500 persons, a number which Robinson considers to be the actual size of the Muslim population at the time of his visit.[2]

Robinson's estimate is close to that of Seetzen. It is quite possible that, in the thirty-odd years between their accounts, there were considerable fluctuations in the number of Muslims. The peasant uprisings of 1826, the revolt against the Egyptian government in 1834, the iron rule of Ibrahim Pasha and, above all, the heavy tax burden and military conscription surely took their toll of the Muslim population. On the other hand, Jerusalem's development, particularly

---

1   Seetzen, II, p. 18.
2   Robinson, *Biblical Researches,* II, pp. 85-86.

in the 1830's, should have resulted in a certain amount of growth in this group, which made up the majority of those working in public utilities. We must also take into account the Muslim rural districts ringing the city, which made migration to and from villages quite likely. Chateaubriand (1806) points out that, when the pasha came to Jerusalem, most of the Muslims would flee to the hills outside the city.[3] Such migration could make a considerable difference in the population figures for Jerusalem in various years. Still, all the fluctuations we mention here seem to have been internal ones. The average Muslim population for the early nineteenth century was probably a stable 4,000.

The Population in 1840-1870

For the 1840's, we have the relatively reliable demographic data provided by Tobler and Schultz, who also seem to have based themselves on the estimates of the Ottoman authorities. Tobler says there were 4,500 Muslims in 1845 (excluding the Turkish troops, who numbered 1,600).[4] Consul Schultz's figure for the same year is 5,000.[5] These figures indicate that the estimates of Seetzen and of Robinson were not too low. We know that Jerusalem began to develop in the 1840's; it hardly seems reasonable, therefore, that the Muslim population would decline at this time. Quite the opposite: later figures back up the earlier estimates of Seetzen and Robinson, and even seem to hint that they may have been slightly too high. There is an implication that the growth of the Muslim community in the 1840's was still minimal.

From the early 1850's, we have additional assessments based on Ottoman data. One source even tells of the appointment in 1851 of a special census-taker (*nasir al-nufus*) who also handled travel permits and the registration of the deceased (the guards at the city gate were paid to count the number of deceased persons taken out for burial).[6] Government censuses during these years still incorporated only males. However, it is unclear from the literature exactly what age group was counted. Some travelers mistakenly assumed that the figures given related only to adult males, and subsequently multiplied them by four (as did Robinson). On the other hand, Stewart says of the 1851 census that its figures included Ottoman citizens of all ages and should therefore be multiplied only by two. He goes on to say that the figure customarily given for the city's over-all population was 25,000 to 30,000.

In Stewart's opinion, this was much too high. On the basis of the 1851 census, his data were: 2,820 Muslims and 400 African Muslim males in a total population of 5,721 Ottoman males. Following Stewart and multiplying the number of males by two, we find that there were 5,640 Muslims, 800 African Muslims and a total of 11,442 Ottoman citizens at that time.[7] An estimate close to that of Stewart is offered by Petermann (1853), who also counts only males. Petermann claims he obtained his data from the Prussian consul, but they correspond with the figures of the Turkish authorities. According to him, there

3   Chateaubriand, p. 341.
4   Tobler, *Denkblätter,* pp. 360-361.
5   Quoted by Williams (1849), II, pp. 613-614; Mrs. Finn, *Reminiscences,* p. 53, lowers the figure to 4,000.
6   Tobler, *Denkblätter,* p. 347.   7   Stewart, p. 299.

were 3,074 Muslim males in Jerusalem. This would suggest a population of 6,148 souls.[8]

As we said previously, some travelers thought the Ottoman data had to be multiplied by four, and thereby reached excessive figures, especially for Muslims and Christians. Munk, for instance, writes that there were 3,580 Jews in addition to 12,286 Muslims and 7,998 Christians, making a total of 23,454 persons. If we multiply Petermann's data by four, we obtain nearly the same figures as these.[9] Tobler's population estimates for 1853 are nearly identical to those of Petermann. They are the result of a new kind of census, but Tobler implies that the figures relate to taxable males and must be multiplied by four. However, he seems to have been mistaken (he may have assumed that the same census method used in the 1830's and 1840's was still used in the 1850's). As we showed above, these figures should be multiplied only by two.[10] It is interesting that, in 1859, F. Bremmer repeats the error, using the results of the 1851 census and multiplying them by four. Her figures are as follows: total population: 23,354; Muslims, including Turks: 12,286; Christians: 7,488; Jews: 3,580.[11]

The first estimates we quote for the 1860's are those of Pierotti (which relate to 1861). He says that there were then 7,598 Muslims, including 680 Turks and 64 lepers, in a total population of 20,453.[12] Pierotti, the municipal engineer during the reign of Suraya Pasha, seems to have derived these figures from the Turkish authorities. Thus they are relatively reliable, especially with regard to Ottoman subjects.

The 1860's were marked by the arrival of scientific expeditions in Jerusalem. Charles Warren, whose expedition spent the years 1867-1869 in exploring the city, quotes figures from Liévin's guidebook of 1869; total population: 20,850 (21,000); Muslims: 7,500 (7,565).[13] These estimates are very close to those of Pierotti. The PEF Survey also cites data for the 1860's or early 1870's, based largely on Liévin's figures. However, it also mentions the estimate of British consul Moore for 1873-1874, according to which the total population was 20,900, and included only 5,000 Muslims.[14] The British consulate's figures for the Muslims were low on other occasions, too. A report to the British Foreign Office in 1864 speaks of 4,500 Muslims, and a slightly later one (March 1865), of 5,000.[15]

In the 1850's and 1860's, it seems that the Muslim community of Jerusalem comprised between 4,500 and 7,500 souls. By way of compromise, let us say that there were 5,500 Muslims in 1850; 6,000 in 1860; and 6,500 in 1870. Later figures (for the 1870's) reinforce our assessment, because the growth of the Muslim population was relatively slow, not at all like that of the Jewish community. The latter was already absorbing considerable numbers of immigrants at this time, whereas growth in the Muslim community derived

---

8   Petermann, I, pp. 232-233.
9   Munk (1871), p. 118.
10 Tobler, *Denkblätter*, pp. 351-353.
11 Bremmer, II, p. 112.
12 Pierotti, II, pp. 10-13.
13 Warren, *Underground Jerusalem*, pp. 490-496; Liévin (1876), I, p. 137.
14 Conder—Kitchener, *Survey*, III, pp. 162-163.
15 Hyamson, II, p. 336.

from a limited amount of migration from the surrounding villages and from improved sanitary conditions.

The Population at the End of the Century

One of the best demonstrations of the slow growth of the Muslim community derives from the editions of the Liévin guidebook for 1869, 1887 and 1897. The demographic data for the Muslims in these three editions are relatively stable, whereas the figures for the Jewish population take enormous leaps.[16] The first English edition of the Baedeker guide (1876) offers the following figures, with Liévin's estimates in parentheses; total population: 24,000 (20,938); Muslims: 13,000 (7,565); Christians: 7,000 (5,373); Jews: 4,000 (8,000). Baedeker's estimates, particularly for the Jews, are obviously incorrect. The guide itself comments that the Turkish statistics of 1874 related to households or families, and would give smaller population figures than the above: 1,025 Muslims; 638 Jews; 738 Christians; and total of 2,393 families. Multiplying the number of Muslim and Christian families by five or six brings us closer to the correct figures for these communities. This is not so for the Jews, because of the large proportion of foreign citizens among them at this time, who do not appear in the Turkish records.[17]

For the end of the 1880's, Luncz says that the over-all population of Jerusalem was 41,375 souls, with 7,960 of them being Muslims.[18] This implies a Muslim population of close to 8,000 in 1890, which would reflect quite a reasonable growth rate. Later editions of the Baedeker guide contain demographic data which are quite different and much more correct both for the whole population of Jerusalem and for the Muslim community in particular. The fifth edition, an English one by Dr. Emanuel Benzinger dating from 1912, gives an over-all population of 70,000; a Jewish population of 45,000; a Muslim population of 10,000; and Christian population of 15,000.[19]

A summary of our findings shows that, by the end of the nineteenth century, the Muslim community did increase in size, but at a relatively slow rate. A discussion of population figures for the late nineteenth century and early twentieth century must take into account the statistics of the British census of 1922, the first reliable census of Jerusalem's inhabitants. The over-all population was then found to be 62,600 souls, including 34,300 Jews; 13,500 Muslims; and 14,700 Christians.[20] So we see that, in the early days of the British Mandate, the proportion of Muslims in the total population of Jerusalem was still relatively small. It is true that World War I severely affected population growth in the city, but this was so mainly for the Jews. Let us remember that the census relates to 1922, four years after the British occupation began. Thus, its findings also back up our conclusion that the size of the Muslim community of Jerusalem in the nineteenth century need not be overestimated.

16   Liévin, see Ben-Arieh, "Jewish Community," p. 100 n. 71 and p. 103 nn. 85, 86; see also
      Cuinet, pp. 626-628. These data do not seem very accurate.
17   Baedeker (1876), p. 161; (1973), p. 35.
18   Luncz, *Guide*, p. 103.
19   Baedeker (1912), p. 24; see also Ben-Arieh, "Jewish Community," p. 101 n. 77 and p. 103 nn.
      83, 84.   20   Barron, *Census.*

The following chart offers approximate figures for the Muslim population on the basis of our findings (adding statistics for the period of Mandatory rule to show growth in more recent times):

Muslim Population of Jerusalem in Modern Times

To 1860	1810: 4,000	1835: 4,500	1850: 5,400	1860: 6,000
To 1890	1870: 6,500	1880: 7,500	1890: 9,000	1890: 10,500
From 1910	1910: 12,000	1922: 13,500	1931: 20,000	1946: 33,700

The Muslim Community

Unlike the other religious communities of nineteenth-century Jerusalem, the Muslim community had no prominent minority groups, apart from the North African or Mughrabi Muslims, the Indian Muslims and the black Muslims. The North Africans had been living in Jerusalem for hundreds of years, concentrated in an area beside the Wailing Wall known as the Mughrabi Quarter. The Indian Muslims are described by J. Wilson (1843). They included a number of Indian pilgrims who had decided to stay in Jerusalem after visiting Mecca and Medina. Some had married local Muslims, but they lived in a separate part of town.[21] Ritter repeats this information in the middle of the nineteenth century, telling of a small colony of Indian Muslims in Jerusalem. They were welcomed by the Muslim community because of the gifts they brought, usually of rice. As British citizens, they were protected by the British consulate. Many of their sect lived in Damascus.[22]

Neumann, a long-time resident of Jerusalem, divides the Muslim population into Syrian Arabs; Ottoman immigrants; Berbers (North Africans); black Muslims; Ethiopians; and Indians. There was also a special sect of "holy men" who wandered the streets and subsisted on alms. If on some occasion they sat down at someone's table, no-one dared to throw them out. Neumann also claims that the Muslim community had an upper and a lower class. The upper class was made up of several families holding municipal and religious positions (members of these families completed their studies at the theological college in Cairo). The ancestors of the North African Muslims (Moors) had been expelled from Spain in 1491; their descendants lived in Ḥarat al-Mughrabiyya and had special privileges in return for guarding the mosques on the Temple Mount. The fact that there were several distinguished Muslim families in Jerusalem is also mentioned in other sources.[23]

131

21   J. Wilson, I, p. 445.
22   Ritter, IV, pp. 192-193.
23   J. Finn, *Stirring Times,* I, pp. 180-181; Y. Yellin, *Memoirs,* pp. 178-188; Porath, "Awakening," pp. 365-369.

Praying Muslim (Porter, *Jerusalem*, p. 52)

Ben-Zvi dwells upon Jerusalem's Muslim population in the early twentieth century. He says that most of the Muslims then in the city were native-born Arabs from the surrounding villages. Among them were a number of rich families descended from followers of 'Omar Khalif. Some were the offspring of intermarriages with Christians. There were also Arabs from Morocco, Algeria and Tunisia, that is, Mughrabis, who had come to Jerusalem as pilgrims. Other Muslim pilgrims living in the city included black Muslims, Ethiopians, Indians, Circassians and Tartars. Very few Muslims were ethnic Turks. The majority were simple day laborers. Muslim artisans, shopkeepers or café-owners were rare. Most of the pilgrims lived near the Temple Mount in apartments owned by the *waqf*.[24]

Various sources repeat the fact that the Muslims usually engaged in physical labor, either as day laborers, porters or mule-drivers. However, while Muslim artisans and craftsmen were few and far between, there were many small shopkeepers who sold groceries and spices.[25]

We are also told of ties between the Muslims of Jerusalem and the villagers and Bedouin from the surrounding area. Lortet's research expedition at the end of the 1870's reports that the Muslim Quarter was inhabited by artisans and farmers from the environs of Jerusalem. The expedition also stresses that the Bedouin came to town frequently to buy guns, clothing and jewelry fashioned of glass and silver.[26] The reverse phenomenon — Jerusalem residents fleeing the city for the outlying villages, especially in times of emergency — was also to be found (see above, p. 127).

132

24   Ben-Zvi, *Travels*, pp. 15-16; *idem, Travel Impressions*, pp. 120-121.
25   Zuta—Sukenik (1920), p. 65; Warren, *Underground Jerusalem*, pp. 490-497.
26   Lortet, p. 188.

Praying Muslim (Lortet, p. 277)

To celebrate holidays and special occasions, the Muslim inhabitants of Jerusalem often picnicked in the Kidron valley outside the city walls. As we said in the last chapter, such outings were also customary in the winter, when Ein Rogel overflowed. Skinner (1883) writes that the olive groves near Shiloaḥ (Silwan village) served as a gathering place for Muslims on Fridays.[27]

Muslim Pilgrimages and Processions

The Ottoman authorities and the Muslim inhabitants of Jerusalem sought an answer to the bustling activity of the Christian churches and European consulates in the city. Too weak to take direct action, especially against their encroachment on holy places and appropriation of large expanses of land outside the city walls, the Turkish government responded in an indirect manner. It set out to foster and encourage Muslim pilgrimages to the mosques on the Temple Mount, with the aim of strengthening Muslim ties to Jerusalem. It urged Muslims to undertake a *ziyara,* or visit to Jerusalem, upon returning from the *hadj* (pilgrimage to Mecca and Medina), and developed the Nebi Musa festivities that took place at Eastertime. In honor of this holiday, Arab villagers from the environs of Jerusalem and residents of Hebron and Nablus were encouraged to visit Jerusalem precisely when the city was filled with Christian pilgrims.

133

27 Skinner, I, p. 218; Seetzen, II, p. 204.

In the last chapter, we spoke of Jerusalem's religious status in the eyes of the Ottoman authorities. We should add that, though there may have been a standstill in religious activity and a drop in the importance attributed to it, Muslim religious sentiments had by no means disappeared. Pilgrimages to Mecca continued throughout the ages, nourishing and keeping alive religious fervor in limited circles. As non-Muslim activity increased in Jerusalem, the Ottoman government and Muslim leaders began to foster Muslim religious feelings. At first the results were disheartening but, in the course of time, they improved.

Western sources describe Muslim pilgrimages to Jerusalem and Nebi Musa in the nineteenth century. They write that pilgrims from all over the Muslim world visited Jerusalem: from India; the borders of China; all parts of central Asia; Nubia; Morocco; the eastern coast of Africa; Saudi Arabia; and all the districts of Turkey. These pilgrimages were intended to balance the pilgrimage of thousands of Christians, who came to Jerusalem for Easter.[28] Conder offers an account of the Muslim pilgrimage to Nebi Musa, which he witnessed when he visited Jerusalem:

> In 1875 the pilgrimage to Neby Musa was going on at the same time, and parties of wild fanatical Moslems paraded the streets of Jerusalem, bearing green banners surmounted with the crescent and inscribed with Arabic texts. A body-guard armed with battle-axes, spears, and long brass-bound guns accompanied each flag, and a couple of big drums with cymbals followed. It speaks well for the Turks, that with all the elements of a bloody riot thus ready to hand, with crowds of fanatics, Christian and Moslem, in direct contact, still no disturbances occurred.[29]

Jewish sources also contain descriptions of the Nebi Musa celebration. The newspaper *Havatzelet* writes that masses of Muslims gathered in Jerusalem from the neighboring towns and villages to celebrate the festival of the prophet Moses, which always coincided with the holiday of the Christians. The newspaper is pleased to report that the festivities were proceeding without incident "thanks to God and our esteemed government, which supervised the activities and maintained peace and tranquillity among the residents and guests of the city."[30] Another Jewish writer of the end of the century says that, in his childhood, when throngs of twenty or thirty thousand Russian Christians reached the city each year for Easter, an order was issued by Rauf Pasha to assemble some forty to fifty thousand peasants from all the villages for the Nebi Musa celebrations, in order to tip the scale in the Muslims' favor. He used every measure to lend special glory to this holiday and increase the number of celebrants.[31]

The pilgrimage to Nebi Musa was the largest *ziyara* in the Holy Land during the nineteenth century; no other boasted as many participants. The ceremonies began a week before the Greek Orthodox Good Friday, which heralded the approach of Easter. As the festival of Nebi Musa drew near, public announcements to that effect were made in Jerusalem. On that Friday, throngs

28 J. Finn, *Stirring Times,* I, pp. 85, 456; II, pp. 222-223.
29 Conder, *Tent Work,* I, pp. 334-335.
30 *Havatzelet,* 25 Nisan, 1889, vol. XIX, no. 30, p. 236.
31 Drori, pp. 203-208.

of Arabs from the nearby villages, and even from Hebron and Shechem, gathered in the city for a mass procession from the Ḥaram (Temple Mount) to Nebi Musa. The ceremony began with the bringing of the green flag of Nebi Musa, embroidered with threads of silk and gold, from its place of safe-keeping at the home of the Ḥusseinis (the Old-City street where they lived is still called the Street of the Flag). The flag was handed to the *mufti* on a platter. After reciting a prayer, he unfolded it and attached it to a pole. Raising the flag signified the beginning of the procession. In the time of the Turks, it was accompanied by a military band and an honor guard. From the Street of the Flag, the procession made its way to the Ḥaram, passed through one of its northern gates, and left the city through the Lions' Gate. This pilgrimage, coinciding with the period of Christian pilgrimage, sometimes led to bloody confrontations between Muslims and Christians. There were also arguments between Muslim celebrants from different towns, such as those from Shechem and Hebron.[32]

The Ottoman Garrison

On the whole, the number of Ottoman citizens in Jerusalem appears to have been quite small. Most of them were members of the Turkish garrison, whose size it is difficult to determine, especially since it probably changed from time to time. The various sources that offer population figures for Jerusalem usually include these Turkish soldiers as part of the Muslim community. There seem to have been a few hundred of them as a rule. Warburton (1843) writes that there were 800 Turkish soldiers in the city.[33] Tobler (1848) raises this to 1,600; Pierotti (early 1860's) lowers it to 680.[34] Scherer (late 1850's) offers information about the Turkish garrison which helps to explain the discrepancy in these figures. He mentions a home guard posted at the Dome of the Rock, and composed of several hundred recruits from Bedouin tribes. However, since these tended to be hot-headed and often attacked non-believers, the government needed a garrison of soldiers to restrain them, especially at festival times. Recently, some 1,500 men from regular units had been so deployed, but more would probably be required now, he adds, to make peace between the different Christian sects, whose members hated each other bitterly and often came to blows.[35]

Dr. Neumann sets the size of the Turkish garrison (in the 1860's, it seems) at some 1,500 or 1,600 soldiers. He says that two battalions resided at the camp beside the Citadel of David, under a high-ranking military commander who had very little real power.[36] The Turkish soldiers in Jerusalem were garrisoned in two places: the Turkish Saraya on the Via Dolorosa near the home of the governor (see p. 158), and the barracks next to the Citadel. This seems to have been the case until the end of the century. As the period under discussion drew to a close, the Citadel barracks rose in importance, as a result of the city's development outside the walls. A Jewish source relates that the large Turkish garrison in the Citadel and the small barracks on the Via Dolorosa held about

---

32 *Loc. cit.*; see also *ZDPV*, XXXII, 1909, pp. 207-221; Hartmann. *MNDPV*, 1910, pp. 65-75.
33 Warburton, II, p. 201.   35 Scherer, p. 188.
34 Tobler, *Denkblätter,* pp. 360-361; Pierotti, pp. 10-13.   36 Neumann, pp. 213-217, 225.

1,000 soldiers between them. The offices of the military commander of Jerusalem and its environs were located at the Citadel. Although he had few troops at his command, he held high military rank and the title of pasha.[37]

Languages and Education

The Turkish language seems to have had no real standing in Jerusalem. Robinson (1838) writes that, after three centuries of Turkish rule in Jerusalem, the influence of the language was undiscernable. Anyone who wished to deal with the inhabitants of the Holy Land, Muslim or otherwise, had to do so in Arabic.[38] Ignorance of Turkish in the Holy Land was such that, in 1840, the governors of Gaza, Jerusalem and Hebron could not even read the pasha's *firman* written in that language, but required a Turkish secretary for that purpose. Turkish was used only in the offices of the pashas; all other Ottoman government bureaus were run in Arabic.[39]

As far as the local Muslims were concerned, not much cultural progress was made in the nineteenth century. The educational level of Jerusalem's Arab inhabitants, both Muslim and Christian, seems to have been very low. Robinson (1838) estimates that no more than three percent knew how to read and write.[40] The Arabic language might have flourished during Egyptian rule (1831-1840), as it was then the language of the government, but there was evidently very little development in this sphere either.[41] For the period following the Egyptian occupation, Basili writes that there was not a single Muslim printing press in all of Syria. Arabic books were printed in Cairo, by order of Muhammad 'Ali. Basili adds that the number of Muslims who could read was very small. Education in Syria was limited to the study of Arabic and the reading of the Qur'an, which was taught in various city and village mosques by the Muslim clergy.[42]

Neumann (1860's) writes that Arabic was the main language of the local population; Turkish was used only by clerks and the military.[43] A source for 1868 relates that the Turkish government had decided to publish an Arabic periodical that would be mandatory reading for all sheikhs and city notables.[44] This plan was never carried out. A later source comments that the Arab residents of the Holy Land usually had to content themselves with the Arabic newspapers printed in Syria and Egypt, since there was no local Arabic newspaper. Even foreign newspapers were not in great demand, because the percentage of illiteracy was so high. Only in 1904 do we read of an official government newspaper in Turkish and Arabic being issued for the residents of Jerusalem and the Galilee. This paper was called *Quds al-Sherif.*[45] In 1910, two

37 G. Frumkin, p. 54.
38 Robinson, *Biblical Researches,* I, p. 422.
39 Assaf, *History,* II, p. 250; Basili, II, p. 323.
40 Assaf, *loc. cit.,* based on data cited by Robinson for 1838.
41 *Ibid.,* pp. 250-251; and see sources cited there.
42 *Ibid.,* p. 252; Basili, II, pp. 145-146.
43 Neumann, pp. 217-218.
44 *Ha-Levanon,* 11 Tamuz, 1868, vol. V, no. 26, p. 413.
45 Luncz, *Almanac,* XVIII, 1907, pp. 10-11; *Hashkafa,* Supplement, 9 Nisan, 1904, vol. V, no. 26, p. 221.

Professional letter-writer (Geikie, p. 452)

Arabic newspapers are mentioned: *Anṣaf,* which had been appearing in Jerusalem for a year or two; and *Iqdam,* which was closed down by the government.[46] In 1911, another source mentions an Arabic weekly called *Al-Nafir* in addition to the government paper *Quds al-Sherif.*[47]

Tobler (1846) offers a detailed report on Jerusalem's Muslim schools. There were seven traditional schools of the *Kutab* type, usually located alongside the city's mosques. Here, the Qur'an was taught by rote, the teacher reading a section and the pupils repeating it. With regard to the *madrasas* or high schools, Tobler notes six of them adjoining the Temple Mount, all of them actually forming a single institution. Three more were located in the city. Here, too, studies centered on the reading of the Qur'an.[48] In his survey of Jerusalem, Charles Wilson (1865) relays similar information.[49] Somewhat later, Neumann mentions eight or ten main elementary schools, a few smaller ones, and some high schools (*madrasas*). There was no Muslim school for girls. Basic schooling

137

46   *Ha-Or,* 9 Adar B, 1910, vol. I, no. 19, p. 2.
47   Luncz, *Almanac,* XVI, 1911, p. 65.
48   Tobler, *Denkblätter,* p. 449.
49   C.W. Wilson, *Survey,* p. 45.

included only a little reading and writing, and anyone who was literate was considered to be educated.[50] Hartmann (late 1870's) says that there were seven Muslim schools, with 341 pupils. In 1892, Luncz describes the city's first Turkish government school. The institution accepted pupils of all religions; it taught Arabic, Turkish, French and the basic sciences. At the same time, there were seven Muslim elementary schools for boys, and one for girls.[51] Another source for the end of the century (1897) says that the American colony took the Muslim girls' school under its wing at the request of the municipality.[52] In 1915, during World War I, the Ṣalaḥiyya high school and college was established in Jerusalem, as its first modern school stressing Islamic studies. It also served as a teacher's college. Studies were partly in Arabic, partly in Turkish.[53]

The first modern Christian schools to be set up in Jerusalem were also intended to serve the Muslim community, but it is difficult to ascertain to what extent they attracted Muslim children. We should also point out that the schools of the Anglican Protestants were first established with the Jews in mind; from the early 1850's onwards, they tried to attract Muslims as well. Muslim boys indeed did study at Christian schools, but only in limited numbers. Fear of the Mission was great in those days, and both Muslim community leaders and the Ottoman government were strongly opposed to such education.[54]

Gradually, Muslim education also began to assume a more modern guise, but the trend gained momentum only at the end of the nineteenth century and, particularly, on the eve of World War I.

Printing Presses; Building Activities; Summary

A factor of great importance in raising the educational level of Old City residents was the printing press. Here, too, the Christian Arabs played a key role. Even before the middle of the nineteenth century, the Armenians, the Latins (Franciscans) and the Greek Orthodox ran printing presses. At first, they published only religious literature and textbooks, but their contribution to the literacy of the Arab masses in the Old City was considerable.

As far as building activity was concerned, the Muslims of Jerusalem lagged far behind the other communities. Robinson writes that building in the Holy Land decreased greatly in the Ottoman period. In Jerusalem, the Turks built almost nothing after Suleiman had the city walls repaired. On the contrary: one *madrasa* became a jail, while other institutions were turned into homes or even left as ruins. Construction activities involved mainly the repair of collapsed buildings after catastrophes such as earthquakes and wars, and were probably carried out by inferior local builders. We have already said that an increase in building activity in Jerusalem began during Egyptian rule. Nevertheless, it seems that foreigners were responsible for much of the progress made.

50   Neumann, pp. 234-277.
51   Luncz, *Jerusalem Yearbook,* IV, 1892, pp. 222-223.
52   Spafford Vester, pp. 192-193.
53   Tibawi, *Islamic Education,* pp. 104-105; Grunwald, pp. 164-165.
54   Assaf, *History,* I, pp. 253-254.

According to Schick, when the Jews began to build large synagogues in Jerusalem, they brought over a special Greek builder from Constantinople to supervise the work until the Jews and Arabs learned the art of building. The Protestants' Christ Church was built by stonemasons and construction workers from Malta. European builders and the culture they brought with them also affected the arrangement of home interiors, and led to the first changes in the city's building conventions.[55]

In summary, then, one might say that, compared with other communities, the Muslims made the smallest contribution to the development of nineteenth-century Jerusalem. There is an explanation for this. In many ways, the Muslim community was the most backward and conservative in Jerusalem. Unlike other communities in the city, it enjoyed no Western backing. Its protector was the Ottoman government, which was itself "sick" and which, instead of showing concern for its subjects, exploited them to its own advantage. Muslim religious fanaticism prevented progressive ideas from infiltrating Muslim society. The strict prohibition against the conversion of Muslims was quite effective in keeping Christian elements at bay and, at first, prevented close social and cultural contacts of Muslims with the Europeans who began to settle in Jerusalem. Thus, the Muslim community and along with it the Ottoman government were the slowest elements in the modern development of the city and, initially, they tried to hold back development altogether. When they failed, they joined the progressive effort, but usually by way of a response or an afterthought.

Aside from the extensive pilgrimage movement, the Muslims did little to develop Jerusalem for most of the century. As Finn relates, the Muslims would have nothing to do with government proposals to spend money on repairing roads and ports:

> The actual state of things can hardly be better represented than in the reply once received after our deploring the condition of the seaports, without a pier or even a jetty along our whole Mediterranean seaboard, and we had also spoken of the need of a second gate to the busy port of Jaffa, and of the bad roads with the absence of any wheeled carriages throughout Syria. 'But', said Effendi—(not a Turk, but one of the Arab city notables), 'we do this on principle. When I have money to spare I lay it out on a house, a slave, a diamond, a fine mare, or a wife; but I do not make a road up to that object in order to invite strangers to come that way. Now Jerusalem is the Jewel after which all the Europeans are greedy; why should we facilitate access to the prize they aim at?'[56]

The Muslims may not have contributed much to the development of Jerusalem, but their standing in the Old City was very high. The most important region in the city, the Temple Mount, was in their hands, and the neighborhood in which they lived was the city's largest. The status of the Temple Mount and the structure of the Muslim Quarter are the topic of our next discussion.

139

55   Schick, *ZDPV*, XVII, 1894, pp. 266-268.
56   J. Finn, *Stirring Times*, II, p. 191.

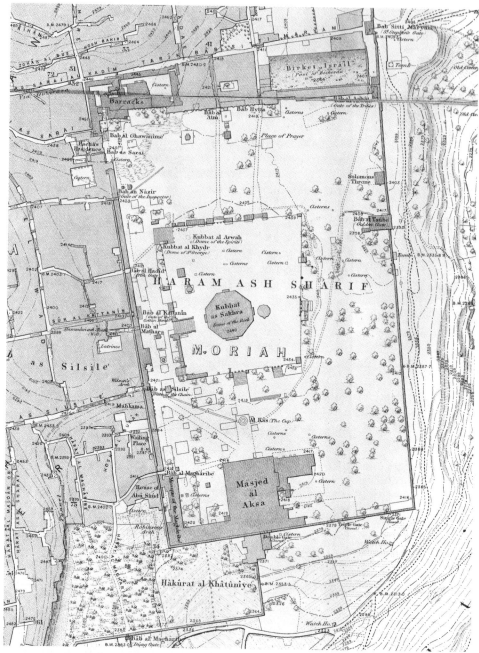

The Temple Mount on Wilson's map — 1865 (Ch. Wilson, *Survey*, 1:2,500 map)

140

Chapter Three:
THE TEMPLE MOUNT

Introduction; Non-Muslim Descriptions of the Area until 1840

Of all the regions in the Old City, the Temple Mount region is outstanding. In its appearance, plan and buildings, the Temple Mount antedates the nineteenth century. Our interest lies in those aspects of the Temple Mount that fall within our period of discussion. The main issues involved are: the status of the region and its accessibility to non-Muslim visitors in the nineteenth century; the physical state of the region and the area's use by Muslims in the period under discussion; and the first scientific explorations of the district at this time.

Seetzen (1806), who spent many years traveling around the Ottoman empire, calls the Temple Mount the most beautiful area in the whole region. However, he notes, it was not a public place, and was closed to Jews and Christians.[1] Seetzen did not enter the compound himself, but only circled it from the outside and observed it from nearby rooftops, as did other travelers. In 1807, Ali Bey (El Abbassi) arrived in Jerusalem; as we mentioned earlier, he succeeded in gaining entry to the Temple Mount. He left us two sketches of the place.[2] In 1815, another Western traveler, Turner, repeats that Christians were barred from the Temple Mount. He also stresses the fact that the Golden Gate had been blocked by the Muslims, so as to prevent infiltration into the area.[3] In the 1820's, Richardson managed to enter the Temple Mount.[4]

After the Egyptian occupation (1831), the Mount was still off-limits to non-Muslims, but the prohibition was observed much less strictly; sometimes, explorers were able to obtain special permits for a brief visit. This was the case with Catherwood, who ventured into the Temple enclosure in 1833 and prepared maps of it (see p. 2).[5] It appears that other travelers succeeded in entering the Temple Mount as well. From their relatively detailed accounts, it is unclear whether they were actually inside the area or merely surveyed it from the outside, basing their descriptions on other sources, especially that of Mujir al-Din, dating from the fifteenth century. In any case, their annals give us an idea of the extent of Western curiosity and knowledge about the Temple Mount at this time.

In the early 1830's, Monro relays certain details about the courtyard of the Temple Mount and the mosque interiors, which he seems to have seen with his own eyes. Among other things, he says, there were many trees under which the Muslims sat with their *nargilas* (pipes). The main mosque, in the center of a

---

1   Seetzen, II, p. 24.
2   On the mapping of the Temple Mount, see Prologue.
3   Turner, II, pp. 275-276.

4   See note 2.
5   See Prologue.

paved platform, was reached through a series of arched doorways with steps leading up to them. Inside the mosque, according to Monro, were the Gate of Paradise and the Stone of Paradise, a large black marble slab where believers prayed as they went in. This stone, no longer there, is said to have been removed by Jamal Pasha during World War I.[6] Monro goes on to describe various parts of the mosque: the two rows of pillars supporting the dome; an iron screen between the pillars, with three doors facing north, east and west; a low, wooden balustrade surrounding the rock upon which Muḥammad trod before ascending to heaven, and the canopy of red and blue cloth above it. On the southwestern side of the rock, he notes, was the footprint of Muḥammad. The inside of the dome was sheathed in gold, and each of the building's eight sides was decorated with window-shaped mosaics.

Monro also describes the al-Aqṣa mosque. Facing it was a fountain. The façade of the mosque had eight square columns and an entrance. Inside the building and opposite the main gate was a wooden partition. The two central rows of pillars were round; the others were square. Monro also writes that a staircase led to Solomon's Stables in the southeastern corner of the Temple Mount, and that this underground structure was very large and had numerous pillars.[7]

Norov seems to have penetrated into the Temple enclosure in 1835. He writes that the Dome of the Rock was as holy to Islam as were the mosques of Mecca and Medina. Christians were forbidden to enter it on pain of death. Norov succeeded in doing so with a special recommendation and *firman,* but he had to disguise himself in oriental dress and was inside for only a short time. He describes the rich decorations of the mosque, and the trees growing in the courtyard. The Golden Gate was closed for fear that a Christian conqueror might come through it some day. The Corinthian columns of this gate were still visible. Nearby, outside the walls, was a stone that the Muslims said came from Solomon's throne. The gate, therefore, was thought to be from the same period. Opposite the eastern entrance to the mosque was an octagonal marble structure similar to the mosque itself, and having a dome supported on slender Corinthian columns. This was called The Throne of David or David's Place of Judgment. In the center of the Dome of the Rock, there was the Holy Rock that had fallen from the sky and marked the place of Muḥammad's ascent to heaven. On the fence around this rock, several flags, the shield of Muḥammad, the large sword of 'Ali and the spear of David were to be found. The rock itself bore an inscription from the Qur'an; upon it lay the saddle of Muḥammad's noble steed, al-Burak, and the scales that the Prophet would use on Judgment Day.

Norov describes the al-Aqṣa mosque as being a red building with a dome. He repeats a view commonly held in those days — that the structure had once been a church, and discusses various Christian traditions associated with the place. He was unable to visit the underground portion of the building, he reports, because the key had been "lost."[8]

6   Vilnay, *Old City,* I, p. 61.
7   Monro, I, pp. 181-228 (April, 1833).
8   Norov, I, pp. 221-236 (May, 1835).

Curzon, who visited Jerusalem in 1834, writes that the roof of the Dome of the Rock was covered with green glazed tiles that shone in the sun. The walls were covered with beautifully worked marble in different colors, and the inside of the dome was decorated with passages from the Qur'an. Altogether, the edifice was extremely impressive. In the center of the mosque, a rock imprinted with the fingerprints of the Archangel Gabriel, as well as with the footprints of the Prophet Muḥammad and his "camel," were to be seen.[9] The great majority of Western explorers reaching Jerusalem in the 1830's were barred from entering the Temple Mount. Among those barred was Robinson, whose data about the site were taken chiefly from Catherwood.[10]

From the 1840's to the Crimean War

After the return of the Turks in the 1840's, foreigners continued to be denied access to the Temple Mount and, especially, to its mosques.[11] The painter, Bartlett, who visited Jerusalem in 1842, describes how his architect friend Catherwood infiltrated into the Temple enclosure, and relies on his data. Among other things, he says, there were several buildings between the Dome of the Rock and the al-Aqṣa mosque which served as dervish colleges, Turkish schools, and so on. The Golden Gate was sacred to the Muslims, who had placed a throne for Muḥammad on the eastern side of the wall, facing Mecca.[12] J. Wilson, who reached the city in 1843 and relies often on Robinson's data, quotes Catherwood on matters pertaining to the Temple Mount. Robinson and Wilson cite Catherwood's measurements for the Dome of the Rock, al-Aqṣa and other structures in the area.

J. Wilson correctly notes that the staircases leading up to the platform of the Dome of the Rock were surmounted by vaulted arches: three on the western side; two on the northern side; two on the southern side; one on the eastern side. There were underground rooms located between them at irregular intervals for destitute Muslim pilgrims, who ate and slept at the mosque's expense. Wilson also offers information about al-Aqṣa and the mosques nearby. He says that women, who were banned from the central mosque, had a special place here. Stone steps to the west of the main entrance led down to an ancient gate. In the southwestern corner of al-Aqṣa was the Abu-Bakr mosque. There was a row of eight pillars down its center, supporting arches. Perpendicular to this mosque, and to its west, was the Mosque of the Mughrabis. The buildings at the back of this mosque were offices. On the other side of al-Aqṣa, near the wall of the Ḥaram, was the small Mosque of 'Omar. Adjoining it was another, smaller mosque, known as the Mosque of the Forty Prophets.[13]

After visiting Jerusalem in the middle of the century, Strauss mentions a whole series of halls, constructed principally of ancient building blocks, in the western part of the Ḥaram. Some of these halls were used as schools, others as

9   Curzon, pp. 170-171 (Spring, 1834).
10 Robinson, *Biblical Researches*, I, pp. 361, 379, 423, 439, 447-450.
11 Olin, II, p. 262.
12 Bartlett, *Walks*, pp. 148-168.
13 J. Wilson, I, pp. 477-479; see also Tobler, *Planographie*.

The Temple Mount (Stebbing, p. 153)

dwellings for dervishes and guards. In the southeastern corner of the Mount were steps leading down to a hall 600 feet wide. Strauss mistakenly assumes that this was part of the great network of cisterns built beneath the Temple in the days of Solomon (the cisterns were so large that Jerusalem never suffered from a water shortage when under siege).[14]

In 1848, the research expedition of Lynch came to Jerusalem. One of the members of this expedition made the following entry in his diary:

> Next to Mecca, Jerusalem is the most holy place of Muhammedan pilgrimage, and throughout the year, the Mosque of Omar and its court are crowded with turbanned worshippers. This mosque, built upon the site of the Holy Temple, is the great shrine of their devotions. It is strictly guarded against all intruders, and there is a superstitious Muslim belief that if a Christian were to gain access to it, Allah would assent to whatever he might please to ask, and they take it for granted that his first prayer would be for the subversion of the religion of the Prophet.[15]

Tobler (1853) writes briefly of the few Christians and Jews who had managed to obtain entry permits to the Temple Mount and its mosques, especially in the days of Muḥammad 'Ali.[16] Ritter also tells of the Temple Mount, which had flowing water and beautiful shady trees. The western side of the Temple enclosure had five gates, and served as its main entrance. There was no gate on either the eastern side (apart from the Golden Gate, which was walled up) or the southern side.[17] Williams (1849) points out that the British

144

14 Strauss, pp. 214-215.
15 Lynch, p. 404.

16 Tobler, *Topographie,* I, pp. 456-512 (1853).
17 Ritter, IV, pp. 115-121.

Dome of the Rock, view from northwest (Pierotti, plate 26)

naval officers working in Jerusalem in 1841 had probably been barred from entering the Temple Mount, and made their sketches from the rooftops of nearby houses by using a theodolite. Williams himself made use of Catherwood's material and map, as well as of the sketches of El Abbassi (Ali Bey). He states that the foremost authority on the Temple Mount was the Arab historian, Mujir al-Din, selections from whose work he translates in his appendix. Williams also seems to have based his map and explanatory notes chiefly on this source, and added information of his own.[18] In his explanation of Muḥammad's Throne (no. 14 on the map), he comments that the tradition was probably a late one, as Mujir al-Din made no mention of it. To all appearances, the "throne" was only a piece of marble column protruding from the wall. Wilson says that the northern gate of the Dome of the Rock, the Gate of Paradise (no. 44 on the map), was so called because of the beautiful garden once located there, in Crusader times. He also cites Catherwood's contention that the well on the porch opposite the western gate of the Dome of the Rock was connected with the medicinal springs of Ḥammam al-Shifa.[19]

Travelers in the 1850's continue to describe the Temple Mount. De Saulcy, who visited Jerusalem in 1851, writes that foreigners were forbidden to enter the compound, but could observe it at close range from the governor's palace, one of the modern buildings near the Temple Mount.[20]

145

18   Williams (1849), I, Supplement, p. 37.
19   *Ibid.,* p. 38.
20   De Saulcy, II, p. 81.

Entry Permits after the Crimean War

It seems that, after De Saulcy's visit to Jerusalem, the Ottoman authorities changed their attitude toward foreigners who wished to visit the Temple Mount. Petermann, who came to Jerusalem in March of 1853, says that he and a few other European Christians were allowed in — on payment of a fee of one pound sterling. The "Mosque of 'Omar" was in the center of the Mount, he writes, apparently on the spot where the temples of Solomon and Herod once stood. The mosque had a large dome supported by numerous mosaic-covered pillars. The mosaics had become extremely worn with age, but were never repaired. Until recently, non-Muslims were forbidden to enter this area, known as Ḥaram al-Sherif. The Mosque of Omar was strictly guarded, and foreigners, except for those with a special permit from the sultan, were kept far away from it. Petermann calls the Temple Mount "Mount Moriah," and the Upper City, "Mount Zion." He also mentions the arch of the bridge that once connected the Temple Mount and the Upper City, identified by Robinson and named after him.[21] Other travelers, such as J. Wilson (1843) and Schulz (1851), also note the existence of Robinson's Arch.[22]

In July of 1855, Sir Moses Montefiore and his wife visited the Temple Mount and its mosques.[23] In the same year, the Duke of Brabant and his wife were also allowed to make such a visit. Mrs. Finn says that they were accompanied by the city's foreign consuls, as the sultan had granted them an entry permit in token of his appreciation of Christian military aid during the Crimean War. The North African guards posted at the mosques had to be locked up in one of the pasha's chambers until the end of the visit, so as to prevent rioting and violence.[24]

The final turning point in the matter of non-Muslim admission to the Temple Mount seems to have been reached at the end of the Crimean war (1856), as the European powers increased their say in Ottoman affairs and the law reforms began to take hold.[25] After visiting Jerusalem in 1857, Isaacs writes that the current governor, Kamil Pasha, allowed non-Muslims into the Dome of the Rock.[26] Foreign visits to the Temple Mount upon payment of an entrance fee continued in the 1860's. One source for 1864 writes that the fee was very high: one pound sterling per person.[27] In 1868, another writer sets the fee at five shillings per person.[28] According to a visitor of 1867, Christians had been permitted into the Temple compound for a large sum of money ever since 1857. They also needed a *firman* from the pasha, and one or two soldiers as escorts to protect them from the fanatical guards on the Temple Mount.[29] In 1869, Porter repeats that not every tourist could enter the area, and that it was necessary to have a special permit from the pasha, which could be obtained at his palace.[30]

21   Petermann, I, pp. 197-201.
22   J. Wilson, I, p. 475; Schulz, p. 134.
23   J. Finn, *Stirring Times*, II, pp. 331-337.
24   *Ibid.*, pp. 320-328; Mrs. Finn, *Reminiscences*, pp. 128-130.
25   See above, pp. 114 f.
26   Isaacs, p. 65.
27   Macleod, pp. 138-140.
28   Ashwort, p. 76.
29   Wallace, p. 234.
30   Porter, p. 121.

Interior of Dome of the Rock (Barclay, p. 495)

Local factors such as the situation in Jerusalem and the status of the reigning pasha seem to have played a role in the matter of admission to the Temple Mount. Even after the Crimean war, it was not something that could be taken for granted, but required a special permit from the pasha. Nevertheless, it should be pointed out that the Temple Mount and its mosques were among the first Islamic holy places opened to non-Muslims.[31]

In 1873, Conder relates that the courtyard of the Temple Mount was entered through a gate near the Cotton Market. Opposite it was a staircase leading to the platform, where one had to remove one's shoes. In the center of the Dome of the Rock, there was a rock covered with silk hangings and known as "the Rock" or the "Rock of Paradise." Conder finds the al-Aqṣa mosque a disappointment.[32] In 1876, Orelli writes that no Jews entered the Temple Mount; this was not because they were forbidden to do so, but because they were afraid of defiling the sanctity of the place or of treading on the site of the Holy of Holies. Christians often visited the site after paying a tax to the pasha. They were escorted by a Turkish *aga*. Orelli also points out that, beneath the al-Aqṣa mosque, one could see the remnants of an ancient gate (the Ḥulda Gate) through which the Temple courtyard might be entered from the south.[33] According to Liévin (1875), Europeans could visit the mosques by means of a permit that their consuls obtained from the district governor. Visits were forbidden on Fridays and during the month of Ramadan.[34]

Later on, obtaining a permit became merely a formality, and it was usually unnecessary. The newspaper *Ha-Or* reports in 1910 that special permits were no longer required, and that the courtyard was open to visitors in the mornings

31 Hodder, p. 169.
32 Conder, *Tent Work*, pp. 317-326.
33 Orelli, pp. 111-126.
34 Liévin (1875), p. 203.

Cave inside the Rock (Ch. Wilson, *Picturesque Palestine*, I, p. 60)

and afternoons. Order was maintained by policemen who, the paper states, were not to be paid.[35] At the beginning of the British Mandate (1921), Zuta and Sukenik also say that Jews and Christians might enter the Temple Mount all day long without a permit, except for Muslim holidays, Ramadan and so forth.[36] Press (1921), on the other hand, writes of the need for a permit, though he adds it was only a formality. He notes that visits were forbidden on Fridays after eleven o'clock because this was the time Muslims gathered for prayers. Foreigners were also barred from the area during the week of Passover, when the Muslims celebrated the festival of Nebi Musa.[37]

Renovations on the Temple Mount

The opening of the Temple Mount to Western visitors after the Crimean war, and the changes beginning to take place in the Old City, including archaeological activity around the Temple Mount walls, led the Turkish authorities to carry out renovations in the area. However, in the period we are discussing, these repairs were minimal. Charles Wilson (1864-1865) comments that pieces of marble falling from the Dome of the Rock and from other buildings were kept in the structures, east of the al-Aqsa mosque, used as storerooms.[38] There are reports of the restoration of the Minbar al-Saif in 1830

148

35 *Ha-Or,* 25 Adar B, 1910, vol. I, no. 30, p. 2.
36 Zuta—Sukenik (1930), p. 202.
37 Press, *Travel Handbook*, pp. 137, 141.
38 Ch. Wilson, *Survey*, p. 41.

by Maḥmud II,[39] but this seems to have been an exceptional case. The photographs of the Wilson expedition (1864-1865) show that at the time, the lower part of the Temple Mount courtyard, below the stairs leading to the upper platform, was unpaved land.[40] From 1873 to 1875, several repairs were made in the Dome of the Rock by order of the sultan.[41]

Discussing these repairs in the 1870's, Liévin writes that the Turks paid about 2.3 million francs to renovate the place.[42] The PEF Survey notes that Clermont-Ganneau, Conder, Drake and Schick investigated the Dome of the Rock while these activities were going on in 1873.[43] In 1881, when the eastern wall of the Temple Mount collapsed in part and the stones of the Arab period fell off, an order was given to repair the damage immediately.[44]

Thanks to the repairs and the admission of Western explorers who were interested in the mosque's history, the date of the construction of the Dome of the Rock was discovered in the mosaics around the dome: the 72nd year of the *Hejira* (691 C.E.). This proved the hypothesis that the mosque was built by 'Abd al-Malik, and renovated by Abdullah Mamun in 831 C.E. The latter had his predecessor's name removed and his own inscribed instead, but he forgot to change the date of construction.[45]

Reports of restoration work at the Dome of the Rock appear again in the 1890's.[46] In 1898, David Yellin, who held pro-Ottoman views, describes the participation of the Alliance school in these activities:

> Great preparations are being made at the Ḥaram al-Sherif, the site of our Temple, to repair every crack and repaint all the places where the paint has darkened through the years. Even the splendid ball at the top of the lead dome will be, repaired and reglorified at the crafts department of the Alliance school in our city.[47]

It should be pointed out, however, that all of these repairs were superficial, and made no major difference in the general design and plan of the buildings on the Temple Mount.

Archaeological Excavations Around the Temple Mount

Easing the restrictions on the entry of foreigners to the Temple Mount and the Dome of the Rock after 1856 did not affect the ban on scientific explorations and archaeological excavations in the area. Wilson and Warren, who headed research expeditions in the 1860's, were not permitted to work on the Temple Mount. Warren goes into great detail in describing the strenuous efforts he made to obtain such a permit, to no avail.[48] In 1869, the sultan even signed an

---

39   Warren—Conder, *Jerusalem*, pp. 82-83.
40   Ch. Wilson, *Survey*, Photographs, Plates, 2A, 8, 9.
41   Warren—Conder, *Jerusalem*, pp. 82-83.
42   Liévin (1897), I, p. 461.
43   Warren—Conder, *Jerusalem*, p. 246.
44   *Ibid.*, pp. 82-83.
45   Ben-Arieh, *Rediscovery*, p. 206.
46   Vincent—Lee—Bain, p. 233.
47   Yellin, *Writings*, I, p. 258 (translated from Hebrew).
48   Warren, *Underground Jerusalem*, pp. 1-15.

Facade of al-Aqṣa Mosque (Porter, *Jerusalem,* p. 53)

order prohibiting all excavation on the Temple Mount. Thus, all studies of the area were carried out on territory outside it.

Since much has been said here and elsewhere about the expeditions of Wilson and Warren (see p. 8), we will discuss only some of their findings, particularly those that are associated with other explorers and topics to be dealt with in this book.

One of the areas outside but connected with the Temple Mount, that was thoroughly studied by the PEF, was Robinson's Arch. The archaeologists provide numerous details of this arch and of the bridge of which it was thought to be a part.[49] In a shaft sunk opposite the arch, they found a cistern which, when cleaned, revealed a low passage leading to the wall of the Temple Mount. At the wall, it divided in two, running north and south. The passage was three feet wide and two feet high, and was paved at the top and sides. Near the Temple Mount wall, it was blocked by rockslides. The northern branch continued past Barclay's Gate, but a rockslide at that point prevented further exploration to the north. The total length of the northern passage as measured by the PEF was 165 feet. Above it, at Barclay's Gate, there was a wall or arch that had probably supported a bridge leading to the gate.[50]

Barclay's Gate, located below the gate of the Mughrabis, was named after its investigator, J.T. Barclay. The gate had already been mentioned by El Abbassi (Ali Bey), who saw it from the inside and says its lintel was made of a single, very large stone. Some travelers refer to it as the Burak Gate or Muḥammad's.

150

49 Wilson—Warren, *Recovery,* pp. 72-90.   50 Warren—Conder, *Jerusalem,* pp. 177-178.

Gate.[51] The PEF explorers relate how they reached the elevated area in the eastern part of the al-Burak mosque via an ancient passage in a cistern. The tunnel was over twenty meters long, led east from Barclay's Gate to a vaulted chamber, and then took a right turn to the south.[52]

The explorers note that Wilson's Arch, located to the north of the Wailing Wall, served as a roof for a large part of the al-Burak pool, first discovered by Tobler and De Vogüe. De Vogüe examined the stones of the Temple Mount wall in 1862 and described them in his book on Jerusalem, but Wilson was the first to realize the significance of the arch in the course of his work two years later.[53]

According to Tobler and others, the street running from the Damascus Gate to the Dung Gate passed beneath Wilson's Arch in the Middle Ages (today the level of the street has risen to that of the Street of the Chain, and actually passes over the arch). The 1876 Baedeker guide also points out that the Gate of the Chain stood upon a large arch discovered by Tobler and later named Wilson's Arch.[54] The PEF explorers say there is very little resemblance between Wilson's Arch and Robinson's Arch. In their opinion, the former was not built before the fifth or sixth century. Wilson suggests that it may have been rebuilt by Constantine or Justinian.[55]

The British surveyors write that, in January 1888, a series of arches was discovered to the west of Wilson's Arch. They believe it to be part of a street that once existed below the Street of the Chain. These arches are completely different from those of the Maḥkame, and seem to have been built in an earlier period. There were two rows of arches and a long "secret passage" beneath the street that may have run from the Gate of the Chain to the Citadel. Mujir al-Din mentions such a passage beneath the Street of the Chain. The vaults were found 150 feet from the Temple Mount wall. Some may have been used as sewers, and others, as reservoirs. The eastern side of the "secret passage" was ruined and full of rubbish.[56]

Underground tunnels were also discovered in the southern wall of the Temple Mount. The PEF Survey reports a tunnel found on October 18, 1867, some 108 feet from the southeastern corner of the wall beneath the Single Gate, nineteen feet below the floor of Solomon's Stables and sixty feet under the Temple Mount. It was 69 feet long, and three feet wide, and was perpendicular to the southern wall. The tunnel was full of rubbish. Its height ranged from six feet at the northern end to fourteen feet at the entrance. The function of the tunnel was uncertain, but it was probably meant to channel water or sewage.[57]

Other tunnels were discovered under the Triple Gate. This gate also faced Solomon's Stables but, below it, explorers found tunnels leading to the Temple courtyard and to various cisterns on the Temple Mount. These were built so that the water flowed at different levels, and were used not for draining blood from the altar but for cleaning the blood channel — perhaps the tunnel under

51   Murray (1875), p. 156.   53   Warren—Conder, *Jerusalem*, p. 195.
52   Wilson—Warren, *Recovery*, pp. 15, 332-334.   54   Baedeker (1876), p. 185; (1973), p. 66.
55   De Vogüe, pp. 2-8. Present-day scholars consider "Wilson's Arch" (or, at least, its foundations) to be a Herodian structure.
56   Warren—Conder, *Jerusalem*, pp. 199-204, 270-271.
57   *Ibid.*, pp. 161-163.

Arch beneath al-Aqṣa Mosque (Barclay, p. 507)

the Single Gate. When the large stones that blocked the northern passages were
removed, they were found to be connected to two cisterns (nos. 10 and 11) on
the Temple Mount. The explorers managed to clean sixty feet of the tunnel
leading north before work was halted by the pasha. The explorers add that
there were two series of tunnels, one upper and one lower. They provide
additional details, but note that various difficulties prevented them from
investigating the area thoroughly. At one spot they even found an entrance
branching off from another tunnel, which proves that it was a passage and not
a water conduit.[58]

As for the Single Gate itself, one source writes that it dated from a relatively
modern period. The ancient gateway was narrower and buried far beneath it. It
was built of large dressed stones, and was mostly full of debris.[59]

It is generally thought that the western part of the Double Gate is newer than
the eastern part. This gate leads into the subterranean structure known as the
Aqṣa al-Qadima, located beneath the present al-Aqṣa mosque. The vaulted
roof of the Aqṣa al-Qadima rests on a large pillar made of a single block and
topped by a skillfully carved capital.[60]

The PEF carried out excavations in the eastern and northern sections of the
Temple Mount, too. There are detailed descriptions of its southeastern and

152

58   *Ibid.*, pp. 165-166.
59   Munk (1875), p. 152.
60   Wilson—Warren, *Recovery*, p. 118.

Subterranean structures beneath al-Aqṣa (Barclay, p. 510)

northeastern corners, and of the Golden Gate area. There may also have been another wall to the east of the Temple Mount wall. Digging on the northern side, the explorers found and examined remnants which had also drawn the attention of such earlier investigators as Schulz, Williams and De Vogüe. In the vicinity of the Via Dolorosa, they studied the remains of columns, gates and a wall, which may be connected with the "Second Wall" of Jerusalem.[61]

The nearby Antonia fortress was also examined. Here, the explorers found the remnants of a tower; a conduit built of small stones and plaster, which had been reinforced with oil; and sections of a mosaic beneath the conduit. The 1876 Baedeker guide reports the discovery beneath the Convent of the Sisters of Zion of several rock-cut passages and vaults leading to the Temple Mount.[62]

Summary

The archaeological excavations around the Temple Mount in the nineteenth century attest the growing scientific interest in the city. The vast importance of the Temple Mount as the site of the Temple of the Jews and of prominent mosques, Christian structures and other historical sites, coupled with the patent inaccessibility of the place, served to broaden the scope of professional

153

61   *Ibid.*, pp. 135-186, 251-252.
62   Baedeker (1876), p. 209; (1973), p. 94.

interest and literature concerning the scientific exploration of Jerusalem. The fact that the Temple Mount was a center of attraction both as a place to visit and as a scientific phenomenon, induced us to devote a special chapter to it in this book. Neverthless, it is clear that the major significance of the Temple Mount in the nineteenth century was in its role as a sacred shrine for the Muslims of Jerusalem and the world. This aspect will be examined in our next chapter, which deals with the Muslim Quarter.

Muslim Quarter in the 1870's — aerial view (Illes)

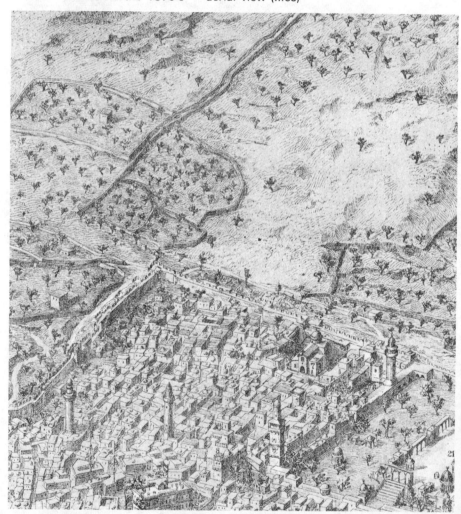

Chapter Four:
THE MUSLIM QUARTER AND ITS FUNCTIONAL STRUCTURES

The Plan of the Muslim Quarter

Today the Old City of Jerusalem is usually described as being divided into four quarters: the Muslim Quarter, the Christian Quarter, the Armenian Quarter and the Jewish Quarter. This division, however, was not in use at all before the beginning of the nineteenth century. Explorers and visitors of earlier days make no mention of a Christian or Armenian Quarter; the term "quarter" itself was probably imposed by Europeans, who employed it at home. In Jerusalem the term applies to groups of buildings or neighborhoods, each with a focal point around which the homes cluster; there are certainly more than four in the city.

The focal points of the various neighborhoods are the historical-religious sites which have always had powers of attraction, even in ancient times. The plan of the Old City at the beginning of the nineteenth century was very much a product of days gone by: the region closest to each specific focal point was the most densely populated one, and population gradually thinned further out, so that the territory between different focal points was vacant or nearly so.

The focal point for the Muslims of Jerusalem was the Temple Mount, where the al-Aqṣa mosque and the Dome of the Rock were located. Muslims did not live on the Temple Mount itself, because of its holiness, but they tried to stay as close to it as possible. This could only be accomplished in the north and west where the walls of the Temple Mount faced the center of the city. In the east and southeast, the Temple Mount wall was part of the city wall, and no one lived outside the walls. Hence, the Muslim population of the Old City inhabited a strip of land parallel to the northern and western walls of the Temple Mount, with the territory closest to the Temple Mount containing important Muslim structures (mosques, *madrasas,* religious colleges) and government buildings (the governor's house, barracks, prison, *majlis, maḥkame*). The majority of the Muslim population also lived in this area, in an apparent effort to reside as close as possible to the sacred site. The outer part of the strip, that most distant from the Temple Mount, was populated only sparsely.

The area north of the Temple Mount, between the crowded Muslim strip and the city wall, contained large tracts of unoccupied land. The northeastern corner of the strip near the Temple Mount was bounded by an enormous pit that had once been a pool, Birket Isra'il. Bordering its southeastern corner was the Wailing Wall, which was sacred to the Jews. Nevertheless, a large Muslim population settled there, eventually establishing a separate Muslim enclave

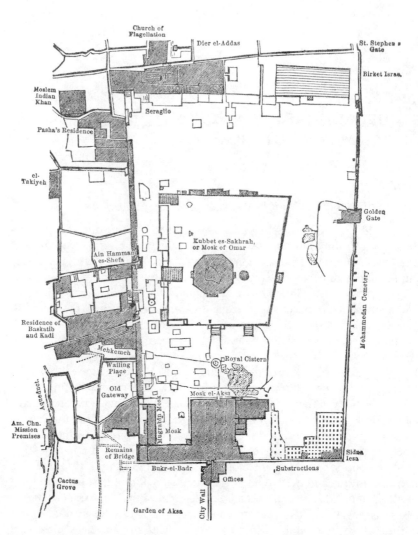

Muslim buildings adjoining the Temple Mount (Barclay, p. 239)

known as the Mughrabi (North African) neighborhood; it adjoined the Mughrabi mosque in the southwestern corner of the Temple Mount.

The borders of the Muslim Quarter in the nineteenth century are difficult to define. On the one hand, the Muslim Quarter was constantly expanding; on the other, it was being infiltrated by Christians and Jews, especially in the second half of the century. The most flexible part of the neighborhood, in which the most changes took place, was of course the less settled region located some distance from the Temple Mount.

Two neighborhoods in the Muslim Quarter receive special attention in nineteenth-century travel literature: the Mughrabi neighborhood near the Wailing Wall, and the Bezetha neighborhood, as the northeastern corner of the Old City was called. Early in the nineteenth century (1806), Chateaubriand writes that the Mughrabi neighborhood was inhabited by Moors (North Africans) who had been expelled from Spain in the days of Ferdinand and

Isabella. They were well received by the residents of Jerusalem, and had their own mosque. Their main task was guarding the holy places, in return for which they received bread, fruit and a small amount of money.[1] Special relations — on the whole, tense ones — developed between the Jews and the Mughrabis because of the proximity of the latter's homes to the Wailing Wall. The Mughrabis, like the rest of the Muslims, regarded the Jews as infidels and harassed them. The Jews had to pay the Mughrabis in order to keep them from disturbing prayer services.[2]

The Bezetha region was also described quite frequently. Various writers report that it was neglected, and developed only in part. Robinson (1838) writes that, on the top of this hill, there were small, ill-kept buildings. To the southeast there were homes and a church connected with the Convent of St. Anne. The entire northeastern slope of the neighborhood was covered with gardens, fields and olive groves, and had very few buildings.[3] According to other Western travelers, Bezetha was full of ruins. It was sparsely settled by Arabs, who lived in miserable homes. In the middle of the neighborhood, there was a mosque surrounded by gardens.[4]

This situation is clearly indicated in the various maps of nineteenth-century Jerusalem;[5] it seems to have persisted until the late nineteenth and early twentieth century. Zuta and Sukenik (1921) relate that the Bezetha region was covered with mounds of earth, and that gardens and wheat fields were planted there. In the northeastern corner, the earth reached the top of the city wall.[6] (The situation is still much the same today.)

The sparse settlement of the Bezetha region seems to have been responsible for the penetration of Europeans into the area. Jews came to settle, as early as the first half of the century, in the Bab Ḥuta neighborhood that was part of it. Christian buildings and foreign consulates were established in Bezetha, too, especially along the section of the Via Dolorosa north of the Temple Mount, and in the Damascus Gate region. A good description of the whole area, including the Temple Mount, is provided by Dixon (for 1864). He tells of two Muslim quarters located on the other side of the Tyropoeon valley, one of them secular and the other sacred. The secular quarter, Bezetha, was further north, and was relatively secluded. It had high walls around it, and green gardens. The sacred quarter, the Temple Mount, was set apart from the secular one by a high wall, and constituted a district unto itself: a district of mosques, arches, columns and gardens.[7]

Ewald (1842) also juxtaposes the neighborhoods of Bezetha and of the Temple Mount. Bezetha was the center of the soap, oil and leather industries, while the Temple Mount contained mosques, a pilgrim hospice, *madrasas,* several prayer sites and cypress trees.[8]

---

1   Chateaubriand, I, p. 334; Ritter, IV, pp. 50-51.
2   See also below, p. 308 ff.
3   Robinson, *Biblical Researches*, I, p. 392.
4   Ritchie, p. 217; Kean, p. 21; Barclay, pp. 450-454.
5   See the maps of Catherwood, British Admiralty, Tobler and Wilson, cited in Prologue.
6   Zuta—Sukenik (1920), p. 112.
7   Dixon, II, p. 6.
8   Ewald, pp. 43-52.

Obviously, the most important part of the Muslim Quarter was the section closest to the central mosques. The entrance gates to the Temple Mount were located on its western and northern sides and, as a consequence, important buildings were built there, both inside and outside the walls. These buildings held religious schools and dwellings for dervishes and guards.

The Seat of the Turkish Governor

It is interesting that the seat of the Turkish government also adjoined the Temple Mount. Nineteenth-century travelers say that the government was housed in a large building called "Pilate's Palace" on the Via Dolorosa (now the 'Omariyya school). Seetzen (1806) dismisses the possibility that this building was actually Pilate's palace, in view of the extensive destruction in Jerusalem from Roman times on. Nonetheless, one room was commonly assumed to be the place where Jesus's fate had been sealed. The entrance to this room was blocked up by a wall, but the marble door frame was still intact; pilgrims who visited the site were in the habit of kissing it. The building was used as the governor's residence; one could see the whole of the Temple Mount from the upper room, where Jesus was said to have been sentenced.[9]

In the days of Ibrahim Pasha, the local Egyptian ruler also lived in this building. It was from the rooftop of this building that Catherwood (1833) sketched his famous panorama of Jerusalem (see p. 2). His map marks the structure as Pilate's Palace; the same designation is to be found in other maps of the period.[10] Monro, who visited the site in the early 1830's, comments that it contained the ruins of buildings, including stables, a prison and barracks. Norov, who arrived in 1835, also describes Pilate's Palace on the Via Dolorosa, and reports the existence of an observation porch facing the Dome of the Rock. He says that an arch passed from this palace to the houses on the other side of the street and that a dervish, the pasha's servant, lived inside it.[11]

After the return of the Turks in 1840, this building on the Via Dolorosa continued to be the residence of the governor, who was now pasha of the whole country. The Turkish barracks seem to have grown in size. Maps dating from this period show that the Saraya (barracks) extended along the whole of the Temple Mount wall to the northeast.[12]

Many of the sources that call the seat of the Turkish governor "Pilate's Palace" associate the region with John Hyrcanus' fortress (the *Baris*) and with Herod's Antonia fortress, which lay close by. Some even call the place "Herod's Palace."[13] Williams (1840's) writes that the government headquarters were in the Antonia fortress, once the official residence of Pontius Pilate, and now a residence for soldiers.[14] Strauss repeats this information, adding that one could ascend to the flat roof of Pilate's Palace if one knew the right people. He himself was taken up by the army doctor posted there.[15] Certain writers suggest that Herod's palace was located further north, in

9   Seetzen, II, p. 35.   11   Norov, I, pp. 139-146.
10 See above, note 5.   12   See above, note 5.
13 Monro, I, p. 183; Norov, pp. 139-141, 216; Pfeiffer, pp. 112-113.
14 Williams, I, Supplement, p. 29.
15 Strauss, pp. 167-180; Tobler, *Topographie*, I, pp. 220-262; G. Fisk, pp. 268-269.

Pilate's Palace, seat of the Turkish governor (Lortet, p. 255)

Bezetha. It appears in that location in the map drawn up by Catherwood and in the British Admiralty Map, which shows it next to a mosque for dervishes.[16] This, of course, is a mistake: these maps confuse the Antonia fortress built by Herod with his private palace.

When Frankl visited Jerusalem in 1856, the pasha's residence was still in the same building. He writes as follows:

> ... we came to the home of the pasha, built on a site near the Sanctuary. Going down two steps, we reached an untidy courtyard full of debris. There were groups of soldiers, prisoners and servants sitting all around. From there, we walked up a flight of stairs to a large room — the courtroom. How very far removed from what I had imagined! The courtroom in a small town in Europe is more impressive and more dignified. The walls were whitewashed and, around the room, there were couches with shabby woollen covers. Aside from these, the room contained nothing at all. This was the room in which the pasha received his guests.[17]

Of approximately the same period, Finn relates that the pasha's house was extremely neglected, and was even used as a prison. The walls of its drawing

159

16 See above, note 5.
17 Frankl, p. 166.

room were hung with paper bags containing correspondence and receipts.[18] The governor's residence on the Via Dolorosa continued to be used as Turkish barracks until the end of the century, as we see from the guidebooks of Baedeker (mid-1870's) and Liévin (late nineteenth-century edition).[19]

It seems that, even before the middle of the century, the seat of government and pasha's residence expanded into the area outside the northwestern corner of the Temple Mount. This is where it appears in the British Admiralty Map of the 1840's and in subsequent maps, such as that of Van de Velde (1857) and Wilson (1865).[20] Later on, the home of the pasha and the military barracks were separated. The barracks remained in the same location until the end of the Ottoman period. They were extremely important for guarding the Temple Mount when Muslims gathered there on Fridays and holidays. The pasha's residence, however, moved from place to place: at first to the northwestern corner of the Temple Mount; then to the Muslim Quarter near the Damascus Gate; and finally, at the end of the Ottoman period, outside the city walls.[21] The move to the Damascus Gate region seems to have taken place in the 1880's. One contemporary source reports that at that time the Turkish pasha built a house there, with a terrace on its roof and many rooms. He moved and rented it out after tragedy had struck his family.[22] At a later date (1903), we find a report that the pasha of Jerusalem had settled outside the city walls in the large, new courtyard of the Ethiopian church, opposite the Russian compound.[23]

There is no doubt that the choice of the historical Antonia fortress as the seat of the Turkish government was influenced by topographical considerations: it facilitated control of the Temple Mount area. Like previous rulers, the Turks feared possible uprisings, expecting them to begin here after prayers, when large crowds were assembled. That topography continued to play an important role in nineteenth-century Jerusalem is borne out in the case of the Antonia fortress and also in the case of the Citadel.

The Saraya and Other Functional Muslim Structures

Another Ottoman administrative center in the Muslim Quarter during the second half of the nineteenth century was the large Saraya building, today located on 'Aqabat al-Takiyya street. In 1872, the newspaper *Havatzelet* reports that Nazif Pasha had ordered the renovation of the ruined "Queen Helena building" to fit it for use as a courthouse and splendid residence for the pasha of Jerusalem.[24] In the first half of the century, this building was known as al-Takiyya, or the hospital or hospice of Queen Helena. Seetzen (1806) writes that, not far from the governor's residence, a little beyond the hostel for Indian dervishes, there was a handsome building called al-Takiyya. It was a

18   J. Finn, *Stirring Times*, I, p. 161.
19   Baedeker (1876), p. 183; (1973), p. 94; Liévin (1897), I, p. 207.
20   See above, note 5.
21   Williams (1849), *British Admiralty map*.
22   Lagerlöf, p. 250.
23   *Hashkafa*, 11 Tishri, 1903, vol. V, no. 2, p. 11.
24   *Havatzelet*, 29 Tishri, 1872, vol. III, no. 2, p. 14.

philanthropic institution, and provided poor pilgrims and travelers with food. The outside walls were covered with smooth marble; the building itself was on the verge of collapse.[25] Turner (1815) relates that he visited "Helena's Kitchen," a large, impressive building of yellowish marble with unusual doors. It was a soup kitchen sponsored by the sultan for poor Muslims and pilgrims. The Turks divided the structure into several rooms; some served as stables, others contained ovens. They built a mosque and a bath-house over it. In the kitchen, which had a small dome supported by four shabby pillars, some of the original cauldrons might be seen. Sometimes an official was sent from Constantinople to act as host to an important guest. When this happened, the needy suffered, because the guests consumed all the food.[26]

Williams (mid-1840's) comments that the Khan al-Takiyya, usually known as Helena's hospital, was a conglomeration of ruined buildings with a series of richly decorated chambers in the Saracenic style. It must have been an important palace, he says, possibly the one mentioned by Mujir al-Din that was built by Sitt (Lady) Tunshuq in 1391. Williams notes that the hospital belonged to the *waqf,* which owned many buildings in the city and in Beit Jala. The street where it was located was called 'Aqabat al-Takiyya or 'Aqabat al-Sitt (the lady), but also retained the ancient name of 'Aqabat al-Suq (the market).[27]

Schulz (1851) offers a description of an almshouse in the city, that also seems to relate to the al-Takiyya building. He speaks of a hospice for the needy established by a Turkish philanthropist. The building was now in a state of neglect. Inside were five large cauldrons, some of them still usable. Everything else was covered with dirt, rocks and ashes. Schulz notes in this connection that, aside from a few private institutions, there were almost no Muslim charitable institutions. Even if money were collected for philanthropic purposes, the pasha probably took much of it for himself.[28] Reicher (1867) also describes the "Queen Helena" building:

> Inside the city is a beautiful, large, well-kept building known to all as Queen Helena's palace. It is entirely of marble, with lead joining its stones rather than mud and straw. It also has large windows with broad, very old iron frames and transparent, watertight windows like those once used in the Temple. The building is 100 cubits in length and in breadth. On both sides, there are very high gates carved with flowers and flower buds, and flanked by marble pillars. These gates are twenty cubits high and two cubits wide. Within, there are numerous uninhabited dwellings and ruins. I was inside several times, and saw three extremely large copper pots used in our Sanctuary.... Here they collect grain from the sultan's house all year long, and prepare food for needy Ishmaelites.... The place is called in Arabic "Maṭbakh al-Faqari," or the kitchen for the poor.[29]

As we mentioned earlier, the al-Takiyya building became the seat of the city and district government in the early 1870's. Various sources note that the Helena hospital was now in use as the palace of the Jerusalem pasha and as the center of Turkish district rule. They also say that the municipal civil court was

25 Seetzen, II, p. 36.
26 Turner, II, 267-268.
27 Williams (1849), I, Supplement, pp. 27-28 (no. 31).
28 Schulz, p. 135.
29 Reicher, p. 57 (translated from Hebrew).

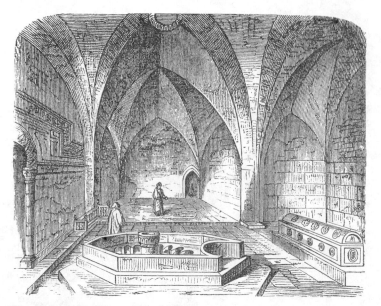

The Maḥkame (Sepp, I, p. 333)

located in one wing of the palace, and that it had a separate entrance.[30]

Another key structure in the Muslim Quarter in the Ottoman period was the Maḥkame, near the Gate of the Chain, which housed the Shari'a court. This building (the Tankiziyya) had been erected in the Mamluk period; it was located over Wilson's Arch. It was damaged during the years of Egyptian occupation, and its towers were razed at the order of Ibrahim Pasha, to prevent its use as a stronghold for rebels.[31] Tobler says that the city's Muslim court was located there and that it was also the residence of the *qadi* in the middle of the nineteenth century. Towards the middle of the 1870's, Liévin reports that a sarcophagus from the Tombs of the Kings was placed beside the Maḥkame. The French consul, de Bremmer, later transferred it to a museum in Paris.[32]

Mosques and Muslim Schools

Other functional structures in the Muslim Quarter that deserve mention are the various mosques. Seetzen (1806) writes that there were fifteen mosques in the Old City. The most important of them were the Dome of the Rock and al-Aqṣa on the Temple Mount, which were also the most ornate. Aside from these, there were five private Muslim prayer-houses. Another three mosques were located outside the city walls, with the most prominent of them being the Nebi Da'ud mosque on Mount Zion. Seetzen stresses that many of these mosques were not in use. According to Turner (1815), the city had only ten mosques.[33] Tobler writes in the middle of the century that the most important mosques were on the Temple Mount, but that there were seven others within the Old

30   G. Frumkin, pp. 8, 108-109.
31   Spyridon, p. 126, who states that the Maḥkame was outside the walls, probably meaning the walls of the Temple Mount.
32   Liévin (1875), p. 198.
33   Seetzen, II, pp. 18-19; Turner, II, p. 222.

City walls: two in the Christian Quarter, on either side of the Church of the Holy Sepulchre; one in the Jewish Quarter, near the Sephardi synagogues; two in the Bezetha region; one in the Mughrabi Quarter; and one in the Muslim Quarter. Tobler cites a number of other mosques that were not used in the first half of the century as well, among them one near the Zion Gate, two near the Damascus Gate and another two that were closed. He says that the number of mosques had once been much greater. According to Barclay (1857), there were then eleven mosques in Jerusalem and its vicinity.[34]

The variation in figures may be a product of the way in which different authors reckoned the mosques on the Temple Mount: some counted each one separately, others grouped them into a single unit. Especially prominent in this respect was the al-Aqṣa mosque, which included the Abu Bakr mosque, the Mughrabi mosque, the Little 'Omar mosque and the mosque of the Forty Prophets (see p. 143). (We will discuss some of the mosques situated in other neighborhoods later.)

Aside from mosques, Jerusalem and its environs also held sacred tombs of Muslim sheikhs. In his notes for the British Admiralty Map, Williams remarks that these tombs had no special features. He quotes Maundrell, who says that the Muslims had many more dead holy men than living ones, hence the great number of sacred tombs.[35]

We spoke of Muslim schools, the *kutabs* and *madrasas,* in our last chapter (see p. 137). Here, we will consider a few additional educational institutions found in the city in the first part of the nineteenth century. One of these was the college for blind dervishes, located not far south of the residence of the Turkish pasha on the street leading to al-Takiyya and the Temple Mount.[36] This college appears on the first survey maps of Jerusalem.[37] Williams says that the muezzin (who called Muslims to prayer from the minaret) was usually a blind dervish, so as to avoid invading the privacy of the surrounding inhabitants.[38] At the end of the Ottoman period, a Turkish jail was established in the region of the dervish college; hence, the nearby entrance to the Temple Mount was also called the Prison Gate. This jail was located on either side of the gate, although Pierotti's map (1861) showed it as being only on the north side.[39]

Another building located to the west of the northwestern angle of the Temple Mount, not far from the private residence of the pasha, was a college and hospice for Indian pilgrims. It is marked on nineteenth-century survey maps; Williams claims that 'Ali Bey stayed there when he visited Jerusalem. He calls it the Mosque Sidi 'Abd al-Khadr.[40] Seetzen (1806) also says there was a hospice for Indian dervishes and pilgrims near the Temple Mount.[41] According to Barclay (1857), it was a large *khan* for Muslim pilgrims.[42]

---

34 Tobler, *Topographie*, I, pp. 456-464; Barclay, pp. 437-454.
35 Williams (1849), I, Supplement, p. 14 (no. 1).
36 Barclay, p. 452.
37 See above, note 5.
38 Williams, I, Supplement, p. 29 (no. 34).
39 Pierotti, *Jerusalem*, Map; Barclay, p. 450.
40 Williams (1849), I, Supplement, p. 29 (no. 37); El-Abbassi, *L'Atlas*, Plan LXXI.
41 Seetzen, II, p. 36
42 Barclay, p. 452.

Al-Wad Street, arches and fountain (*sabil*) (Horne, II, plate 20)

Other functional structures cited in contemporary literature were hospitals. Van de Velde's map (1857) shows a military hospital outside the Temple Mount, on the northwest. Pierotti also says that the Muslims had a military hospital, while Barclay speaks of a Turkish hospital not far from the pasha's house, on the street leading to the Damascus Gate.[43]

Yet another important Muslim institution in the neighborhood was the al-Khalidiyya library on the Street of the Chain, at the end of the alley descending

43 Tobler, *Planographie*; Pierotti, pp. 277-279; Barclay, pp. 450-452.

Fountain (*sabil*) near Gate of the Chain (Ch. Wilson, *Picturesque Palestine*, I, p. 48)

to the Wailing Wall. (This library was named after its founders, the famous al-Khalidiyya family of Jerusalem.)[44]

Markets, Khans, Sabils and Bathhouses

Prominent in the Old City were the ancient markets and *khans* common to all oriental cities. We discussed various market places in our examination of the city's economy. Now, we will focus on the main *khan,* which, as Williams notes, was conveniently located next to the bazaars, as in other cities of the East. *Khans* served primarily as stables for camels and horses. Since travelers and their animals were often lodged together, the rooms were unfurnished, and each guest had to fend for himself. In Williams' opinion, the oriental inhabitants of Jerusalem were unfamiliar with hotels in the Western sense of the word.[45]

Tobler (1840's) describes Khan al-Sultan (which he calls Khan al-Suq) as follows: the *khan* was located to the north of Suq al-Kabir and to the east of the goldsmith's market. It was built around an inner courtyard, and had two stories. Soldiers guarded it, and one could see that it had once been a distinguished place, large and handsome. Few people stayed there while Tobler was in Jerusalem except at Eastertime, when caravans arrived from Damascus.[46] Barclay (1857) points out this *khan* as being the most important in the city.[47] There were *khans* in other places in Jerusalem, but they were not *khans* in the usual sense. Tobler (1846), for example, calls the new Coptic monastery north of the Pool of the Patriarch (which became a Turkish military academy after 1849) the *khan* of the Copts.

The Muslim Quarter also contained *sabils* (water fountains) and bathhouses. Barclay (1857) relates that, in addition to the *sabils* on the Temple Mount, there were several beautiful ones in other parts of the city: one near St. Stephen's Gate (the Lions' Gate); a second one opposite the entrance to the Maḥkame; and two in the western part of al-Wad Street, parallel to the Temple Mount.[48] The British Admiralty Map shows two *sabils* on al-Wad Street. Williams says they were both beautifully constructed, dry, and dated from the same period.[49]

According to Seetzen (early nineteenth century), there were five public baths in Jerusalem.[50] Tobler (1840's) repeats this information, adding that their use was very much dependent upon the amount of rain water collected in winter. He lists the bathhouses as follows: Ḥammam al-Batrak (the patriarch's bath), near the Greek church of John the Baptist; Ḥammam al-Shifa (the bath of healing), in the vicinity of Ein al-Shifa, very close to the cotton market; Ḥammam al-'Ayn (the bath of the spring), near Ḥammam al-Shifa, its water

---

44 Detailed consideration of this and other historical (Mamluk) buildings in the Muslim Quarter would be outside the scope of this volume.
45 Williams (1849), I, Supplement, p. 26.
46 Tobler, *Denkblätter*, p. 419.
47 Barclay, pp. 437-454.
48 *Ibid.*, pp. 452-453.
49 Williams (1849), I, Supplement, pp. 27-28 (nos. 30, 33).
50 Seetzen, II, p. 25.

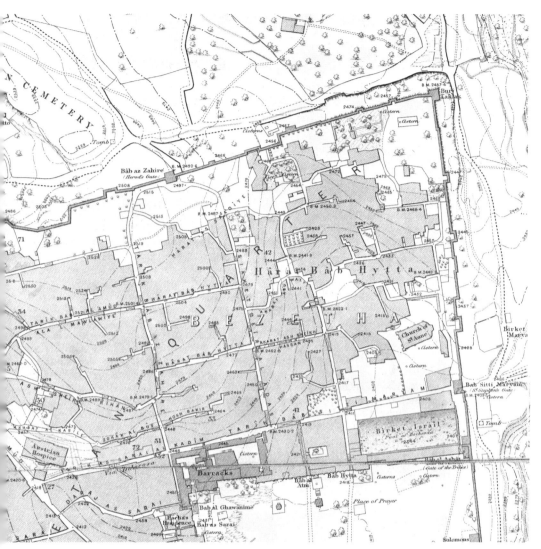

Part of the Muslim Quarter — Bezetha region, on Wilson's map — 1865
(Ch. Wilson, *Survey*, 1:2,500 map)

coming from Solomon's Pools by aqueduct. Prior to 1821, he adds, water was
brought on the backs of donkeys, camels and sometimes even men. He also
lists Ḥammam Maryam (Miriam's bath), very close to St. Stephen's Gate, to
the west, as being not very pleasant; and Ḥammam al-Sultan (the sultan's
bath), in the passage between the Via Dolorosa and al-Wad Street. He notes
that the building was not very large, and that it had two arches.[51] Williams
writes that Ḥammam al-Shifa was once known as the bath-house of 'Ala al-
Din. One entered it from the cotton market, a ruined bazaar once occupied by

167

51   Tobler, *Denkblätter*, pp. 433-437.

cotton merchants.[52] The water sources for the al-Shefa bath and well were discussed in Part One above (see p. 77).

Barclay points out that the bathhouse near St. Stephen's Gate received its water from a pool outside the Old City (Pool of Sitt Maryam) by means of a conduit, while the patriarch's bath (in the Christian Quarter) was fed by the Pool of Hezekiah. Barclay also says that Ḥammam al-Sultan was the largest and most attractive of them all, though it was already partially ruined in his day.[53] (He does not cite the water source for this bathhouse, but there was probably a conduit running from the direction of the Damascus Gate, similar to that leading to Ḥammam al-Shifa.) A typical description of the bathhouses in the Old City is provided by Press (1921):

> ... Bathrooms with tubs and showers were unknown in Jerusalem in those days. Mothers bathed their small children in basins and then used the bathwater for washing the floor. On Fridays, men took their older sons to the ritual bath in Ḥurvat Rabbi Judah He-Ḥassid or baths near other synagogues. Before holidays, they would go to one of the Old City's three bathhouses... al-'Ayn... al-Shifa... al-Batrak.... Upon reaching such a bathhouse, one enters a large hall with a round dome some twelve meters high. In the center is a pool, and lining the walls are many couches where the bathers may relax. Large towels hang in mid-air, four or five meters from the floor. The bathing rooms are windowless, with ventilation holes around the circular domes. Next to the walls are small pools, into which hot water flows from a hole in the wall. The bather sits on the stone floor beside the pool, draws water in a tin can, and pours it on his body, scrubbing himself with sponge and soap. If he can afford to pay another few *grushim* (piastres), he hires the bath attendant to lay him on the floor and scrub him with sponge and soap. After bathing, he enters the steam room, sits for a few moments on a stone shelf, and absorbs the invigorating vapor until the bath attendant arrives with a large towel to wrap him in. Escorted into the spacious hall, he lies down on a soft couch and enjoys total relaxation. If he wishes, he orders a cup of coffee and a *nargila* (a bottle for smoking tobacco). When he leaves the bath, he feels renewed and refreshed.[54]

Aside from the many functional structures we have already mentioned, new Christian buildings and other Western institutions began to appear in the Muslim Quarter during the nineteenth century. These will be dealt with briefly in our next chapter.

168

52   Williams (1849), II, pp. 454-461; I, Supplement, p. 27 (no. 30).
53   Barclay, p. 452.
54   Press, *Hundred Years*, pp. 20-21 (translated from Hebrew).

Chapter Five:

PENETRATION OF CHRISTIAN AND WESTERN ELEMENTS INTO THE MUSLIM QUARTER

The Via Dolorosa

One of the most interesting aspects of nineteenth-century settlement in the Old City is the rapid establishment of Christian institutions along the famous Via Dolorosa in the Muslim Quarter. The Christian traditions associated with the place served as the impetus, of course, but it was not until the rise of Ibrahim Pasha that Christians were allowed to build or settle there.

In the early nineteenth century, the Christians had almost no foothold in the Muslim Quarter. As we mentioned earlier, the most prominent building still intact on the Via Dolorosa was Pilate's Palace, which was located to its south, adjoining the wall of the Temple Mount. Inside it and further along the Via Dolorosa were various sites of religious and historical significance for Christians.

Turner (1815) describes the route taken by the Via Dolorosa, including a cross-section marking the sites of importance.[1] Horne (1834) provides an attractive drawing of the street as it looked in the early nineteenth century, noting that its paving was almost completely ruined, making passage difficult.[2] According to J. Wilson (1843), the Via Dolorosa was very narrow and paved with rough stones. Close to its middle was the ancient Ecce Homo arch.[3] Tobler (mid-century), however, says that most of the Via Dolorosa was well-paved, and built up along its length. Only beside the Ecce Homo arch were there ruins.[4] Williams (1840's) writes that the Ecce Homo arch was also called Pilate's arch. It had been mentioned by travelers ever since Crusader times, and was the subject of numerous drawings.[5] (According to tradition, this arch marks the spot where the governor uttered the words: "Behold the man!" when referring to Jesus.)[6] South of the arch, in the region of Pilate's Palace, was the Praetorium, the courtroom where Jesus was said to have been sentenced. Below it was the prison in which Jesus was kept. Further on, on the other side of the street, were the ruins of a monastery, with remnants of the entrance to the Praetorium beneath it. The staircase down which Jesus was taken after his sentence was transferred to Rome, and is now located in a church called the

---

1   Turner, II, p. 191.
2   Horne, in text to illustration of Via Dolorosa.
3   J. Wilson, I, pp. 413-414.
4   Tobler, *Topographie*, I, pp. 220-267.
5   William (1849), I, Supplement, p. 29 (no. 38).
6   See, e.g., Petermann, I, pp. 201-204.

Via Dolorosa (Stebbing, p. 148)

Scala Santa (holy stairs). Williams marks this spot on the British Admiralty Map, and says that there were two ancient arches there, built into the wall of the Saraya.[7]

7   Monro, I, p. 177; Williams (1849), I, Supplement, p. 30 (no. 39); Vincent—Lee—Bain, pp. 251-253.

The Church of the Flagellation, St. Anne's, and the Sisters of Zion

The first modern building erected on the Via Dolorosa in the nineteenth century was the Church of the Flagellation, at the second Station of the Cross, opposite the site of the Praetorium. According to Christian tradition, it was here that the Romans flogged Jesus. Williams, who visited the church in March of 1843, relates that it was built about a year and a half before his visit. The tradition associated with the site dated back to Crusader times but, until its renovation by the Franciscans, the site, like many others, served as a stable and as a weaving workshop.[8]

In the mid-1840's, Tobler writes of a chapel north of the street leading to St. Stephen's Gate (the Lions' Gate). It was entered through a door in the wall. The chapel, built in 1838 to commemorate the pilgrimage of Duke Maximilian of Bavaria, was opened for worship in 1839.[9] In 1851, Schulz says, a large, paved courtyard led to the tiny chapel that had been renovated only ten years earlier. There was a niche under the altar, where five beautiful lamps burned, interspersed with small plants. The bottom of the niche was a slab of marble inscribed in Latin.[10] (The guidebooks of Baedeker and Liévin, dating from the mid-1870's, say that the site was presented to the Franciscans in 1838 by Ibrahim Pasha, and that the new chapel above the ancient ruins had been paid for with funds from Duke Maximilian of Bavaria.)[11]

Another site restored in that vicinity was the Church of St. Anne. In 1806, Seetzen relates that, a little way from Pilate's Palace, in a deserted region full of ruins, there was a partially collapsed structure composed of a church and what seemed to be a monastery. Beneath the floor of the church there was a cave in which the Madonna was said to have been born.[12]

In 1833, Monro writes that the home of Mary's parents was located on the street leading the Antonia fortress. After Jesus's death, a church was built on the spot, probably the oldest church in the world. When Monro was there, nothing was left but grass-covered ruins. Once a nunnery had been located there, but Ṣalaḥ al-Din (Saladin) had turned it into a school.[13] Norov (1835) feels certain that the remains of an ancient church from the days of Constantine and St. Helena could be found at the site of the home of Mary's parents (her birth-place), but that the place was now in ruins. He also says that the church faced a narrow lane leading from the Via Dolorosa to Herod's Gate, which was sealed at that time.[14] According to Robinson (1838), beneath the ruined church of St. Anne there was a cave, in which the Virgin had been born. The arches in the church were probably the work of the Crusaders.[15] Williams (1840's) repeats the assumption that this was the birth-place of the Virgin. The nunnery once located here had been turned into a Muslim *madrasa*

8   Williams (1849), II, pp. 461-462.
9   Tobler, *Denkblätter*, p. 349.
10   Schulz, pp. 130-131.
11   Baedeker (1876), p. 208; (1973), p. 92; Liévin (1897), p. 211.
12   Seetzen, II, p. 36.   14   Norov, I, pp. 216-217.
13   Monro, I, pp. 184-186.   15   Robinson, I, p. 344.

Via Dolorosa — the road from Lions'
Gate to Governor's Palace (Lortet, p. 282)

and hospital by Saladin. The church lay in ruins for many years until the pasha of Jerusalem undertook to restore it in 1842.[16]

In the early 1860's, Pierotti writes that the Church of St. Anne, near "Mary's Gate" (the Lions' Gate), now belonged to the French. It served as a stable for the government's horses and as a resting place for camels and their drivers in 1854. On October 19, 1856, through the efforts of the French consul, the sultan presented the site to the French for the erection of a Catholic church, which began a year later.[17] In the 1870's, Liévin reports that the Franciscans had the right to perform mass at the Church of St. Anne. He adds that, in 1842, the pasha of Jerusalem had begun to turn the place into a mosque, building a minaret in place of the church's bell-tower. The work, however, was never completed; after the Crimean war, Sultan Abdul Majid presented the building to the French, who restored it.[18] The Baedeker guide (1876) adds that, in order to visit the Crusader Church of St. Anne, one needed a permit from the French consulate. References to this church go back to the seventh century. Alongside it was a nunnery that Saladin turned into a school. It remained in Muslim hands until it was presented to Napoleon III in 1856. When the Muslims repaired the dome of the church, some of its ancient frescoes were destroyed.

172

16   Williams (1849), I, Supplement, p. 30 (no. 41).
17   Pierotti, pp. 144-154.
18   Liévin (1875), p. 134.

St. Anne's Church (Sepp, I, p. 664)

De Vogüe found remnants of them when he visited the site. The French did not carry out extensive repairs, but only built a wall around the church.[19]

Later sources report the activity of the White Fathers in the Church of St. Anne. The king of France committed the building to the care of this monastic order in 1878.[20] The 1912 edition of the Baedeker guide says a monastery and seminary were built beside the church, at which time a rock-cut pool and parts of a medieval church were discovered there.[21] Early Mandatory sources add that the monastery of the "White Friars" ran a museum, and had an ancient pool in its courtyard, perhaps the Bethesda pool.[22]

A third site renovated in the area was the Church and Convent of the Sisters of Zion on the Via Dolorosa. Pierotti (early 1860's) writes that, in November 1857, the Sisters of Zion Society bought a tract of land several yards northeast of the Bethesda pool, near the Ecce Homo arch. Pierotti was asked to excavate there; he found another, smaller arch.[23]

According to Liévin's guide, the Convent and Church of the Sisters of Zion was founded by Père Ratisbonne. The extremely simple-looking building was begun in 1859 and finished in 1868. Later, it was enlarged and Corinthian-style columns were added for support. In 1891, twelve windows were opened up in its dome.[24] Other sources write that the land on which the convent of the Sisters of Zion stood was purchased by a converted Jew named Ratisbonne, in order to establish a workshop for Christianized Jewish children. In the 1860's, the convent provided between thirty and forty boys, and about twenty-six girls, with food, lodging and clothing.[25] Later sources relate that the Catholic convent of the Sisters of Zion housed sixteen nuns and 120 girls.[26] Thus, it

19   Baedeker (1876), pp. 207-208; (1973), pp. 91-92.
20   Vilnay, *Old City*, II, p. 91.
21   Baedeker (1912), p. 49.
22   Zuta—Sukenik (1920), p. 113; Press, *Travel Handbook*, p. 162.
23   Pierotti, I, p. 60.
24   Liévin (1897), I, pp. 329-330.
25   Herbert, pp. 81-82; Cowper, p. 40.
26   Fulton, p. 485; Baedeker (1876), p. 209; (1973), p. 94.

Arches in the Convent of the Sisters of Zion, before construction (Pierotti, p. 13)

seems that the institution grew larger towards the end of the nineteenth century. The PEF Survey reports that the convent of the Sisters of Zion had purchased a small Turkish structure north of its first building and demolished it in order to build another.[27] According to another source, the convent was built above the remains of the Antonia fortress. It contained a school and chapel, and one could buy souvenirs and bouquets of wild flowers there.[28]

Other Christian Buildings

In the early twentieth century, other Christian buildings rose alongside the Sisters of Zion and the Church of the Flagellation on the Via Dolorosa. We will discuss only two of them. In 1905, the PEF QSt writes of an old church discovered in the region held by the Franciscans south of the Church of the Flagellation, near the church of the Sisters of Zion. The Franciscans restored it, and built a small monastery there.[29] The same journal says that the Greeks were clearing away the ruins between the church of the Sisters of Zion and the Austrian hospice on the Via Dolorosa, in order to put up new buildings.[30] The Greeks then built the Praetorium, where they showed an ancient, rock-cut prison on three levels, in which Jesus was believed to have been held by the Romans. (In Arabic, the place was called Ḥabs al-Masiḥ or prison of Christ.)

Tracing the restoration of the Via Dolorosa in the nineteenth century, we find that none of the important Christian buildings on this street existed in the beginning of the century. Only the church known as Deir al-'Adas may have been there at that time. The existence of this church is mentioned by various travelers and it is marked on certain maps, but it was probably not used as a church in the nineteenth century. The PEF QSt of 1896 offers a detailed description of it, along with a general account and sketches of the Bab Ḥuta quarter in which it was found.[31]

Another building in the Muslim Quarter associated with Christianity was the house of Simon of Cyrene. Sources from the first half of the century say that this house was in Bezetha. According to Norov (1835), it was located at the end of the narrow lane running from the Via Dolorosa to the sealed Herod's Gate. An Arab family lived among its ruins, tending a small vegetable patch.[32] Williams marks the site on the British Admiralty Map. He says there was a ruined church there which, in Crusader times, had been called the convent of St. Mary Magdalene.[33]

Nineteenth-century sources also mention the House of Lazarus on the Via Dolorosa. Monro (1833) says it was situated at the point where the Via Dolorosa turned left, and that it was inhabited by monks. This was the place where Jesus fell for the first time beneath the weight of the Cross. The Christians commemorated the event by building a monastery, which the Turks later turned into a Turkish bath.[34] Norov (1835) also mentions a public bath on the foundations of a church built by St. Helena.[35] At a later date, we find a

27 *PEF QSt*, 1892, p. 16.
28 Kean, p. 45.
29 *PEF QSt*, 1905, p. 275.
30 *Ibid.*, pp. 275-276.
31 *Ibid.*, 1896, pp. 122-131.

32 Norov, I, p. 217.
33 Williams, I, Supplement, p. 30 (no. 31).
34 Monro, I, pp. 176-177.
35 Norov, I, pp. 129-146.

House of the Rich Man on al-Wad Street, north of Via Dolorosa (Lortet, p. 235)

report that the Armenian Catholics were building a church at the first turn of the Via Dolorosa. Remnants of an ancient church known as Notre Dame de Spasme could be seen in its crypt.[36]

The House of the Rich Man was another Christian site on the Via Dolorosa. It was near the third Station of the Cross and, according to travelers, was one of the most beautiful buildings in Jerusalem.[37] The Gate of Judgment is also mentioned. Monro (1833) says that it was located in the center of the city, and through it passed those sentenced to death, on their way to Golgotha. Opposite this gate, there was a pillar without a capital; it was inscribed with the names of the convicts.[38]

Various Christian travelers describe a small structure called the House of St. Veronica. The site contained marble columns; facing it was a pillar with a lamp on top. Inside the building, one might see a rock imprinted with Jesus's footprint.[39] (A description of the House of St. Veronica is to be found in the 1896 issue of the PEF QSt.)[40] The House of St. Veronica constituted the main foothold of Greek Catholicism in the Old City in the first half of the nineteenth century. Williams marks it on his map as belonging to those Greeks who had

36   *PEF QSt*, 1902, pp. 122-124.
37   Schulz, p. 132; Petermann, I, pp. 201-204.
38   Monro, I, pp. 174-175; Vilnay, *Old City*, II, pp. 88-89.
39   Monro, *loc. cit.*; Pfeiffer, pp. 112-113.
40   *PEF QSt*, 1896, pp. 214-218.

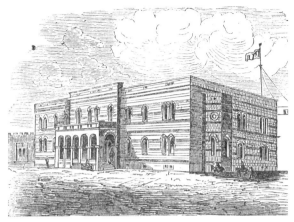

rian Hospice (Sepp, I, p. 881)

left the Orthodox Church and had accepted the sovereignty of the Pope.[41] The 1876 Baedeker guide says that there were thirty Greek Catholics in the city, led by a Father Elias.[42] In 1878, this sect established a high school and dormitory for boys on the Via Dolorosa, near the Church of St. Anne. This was part of the activity of the White Fathers, whom we mentioned earlier.[43] One source lists the early twentieth-century Greek Catholic strongholds in the Old City as follows: the Church of St. Veronica at the sixth Station of the Cross; the high school, church and museum at St. Anne's; and a shrine on the Mount of Olives.[44]

New Western Buildings: the Austrian Hospice

Before moving on to a general discussion of the Christian Quarter, we will consider a few Christian and Western sites established in the Muslim Quarter in the second half of the century. Christian penetration of the area was a direct consequence of its relative emptiness. Speaking of al-Wad Street in the 1840's, Tobler says that it was a deserted street on which it was very easy for "Franks" to settle.[45]

Undoubtedly, the most important Western structure in the Muslim Quarter was the Austrian hospice, a religious institution under the aegis of the Austrian consulate in Jerusalem. Construction of the hospice, which was located on the corner of the Via Dolorosa and al-Wad Street, was begun in 1856 with the active assistance of the Austrian cardinals and the Austrian consul in Jerusalem.[46] Building activities continued for four years, and cost 300,000 gulden. Among other things, it was necessary to remove debris thirteen meters deep, build new terraces and put up a high wall around the building. The façade of the monumental structure was covered in red and white marble, the national colors of Austria. It contained forty rooms, that could accommodate 140 pilgrims; two refectories; a hospital and a small church.[47]

41   Williams (1849), I, Supplement, p. 19 (no. 12).
42   Baedeker (1876), p. 163; (1973), p. 37.
43   Luncz, *Jerusalem Yearbook*, II, 1887, pp. 88-89.
44   Goodrich-Freer, p. 146.   46   Busch, p. 154.
45   Tobler, *Topographie*, I, pp. 196-220.   47 Neumann, p. 309; *ZDPV*, VII, 1884, pp. 288-289.

Finn describes the construction of the hospice. Every day for two months, 200 mules worked at clearing away the rubbish.[48] Neumann says that antiquities were discovered at the start of construction: a mosaic floor and, below that, a niche with five rock-hewn pillars. Since there was not enough money to continue the dig, extremely interesting material may have been lost.[49] Construction of the Austrian hospice ended in 1860. A special wing was set aside for the use of Emperor Franz Josef, who stayed there during his visit to Jerusalem in 1869. All of the consuls in Jerusalem, and other notables, were invited to the lavish dedication ceremony which took place in the garden of the hospice.[50] The Austrian hospice was instrumental in widening the scope of Austrian pilgrimages to Jerusalem. It should be remembered that, at this time, there were no hotels in the city, and it was customary to lodge at the hospices of various churches, usually according to one's country of origin. The Austrian hospice continued to be used until World War II, being periodically renovated and enlarged.

It should be emphasized that, when the hospice was built, the northeastern sector of the Old City was sparsely settled. The Austrian consulate, however, was located nearby. A source for the 1860's writes that the Austrian consul lived in a beautiful house in Bezetha, not far from the Damascus Gate. The house was richly furnished, apparently through contributions by wealthy European Jews who expressed their gratitude for the services rendered their brethren in Jerusalem in this way.[51] Reicher (1876) also tells of the Austrian consul's lovely residence in the Old City, near the Damascus Gate and the Austrian hospice.[52] In the early days of the British Mandate, Zuta and Sukenik write that the Austrian hospice was used as a shelter for orphans and as a guest-house.[53] Later, the place became a hospital; it still serves in this capacity today.

The Western Consulates

We have expanded upon the Austrian hospice because its establishment was indicative of important developments in the Old City in the second half of the nineteenth century, as well as of the penetration of non-Muslim institutions into certain parts of the Muslim Quarter. The consulates were another prominent element in non-Muslim settlement in this area.

The first consulate to rise in the Muslim Quarter was the Prussian-German Consulate established in 1842, the second of the Jerusalem-based consulates; the British consulate preceded it in 1838. In 1868, the German Consulate became the General Consulate of the North German Alliance; in 1871, it expanded into the General Consulate of the German Reich.[54] The Prussian consulate bought a large building in the Muslim Quarter, and turned it into an important German center. This building is described by Consul Rosen, who says that it had been registered under the name of a Muslim clergyman, since foreign subjects could not purchase real estate at that time. Only several years

48   J. Finn, *Stirring Times*, II, p. 385.
49   Neumann, p. 309.
50   J. Finn, *Stirring Times*, II, p. 385.
51   Busch, p. 318.
52   Reicher, p. 59.
53   Zuta—Sukenik (1920), p. 114.
54   Eliav, *German Consulate*, pp. 57, 71.

German Hospice (Sepp, I, p. 879)

later was it registered officially as being the property of the Prussian empire. The building was a spacious one, with several stories and an inner garden. It was located in the Muslim Quarter on the narrow lane called 'Aqabat al-Takiyya, descending from the Church of the Holy Sepulchre. The building cost 350,000 Turkish piastres. Rosen provides an illustration of it drawn by his mother.[55]

Another German institution near the consulate in the Muslim Quarter was the Johannitarian hospice. In 1842, the king of Prussia, Friedrich Wilhelm, ordered the establishment of a hospice for German pilgrims in the Holy Land. Some 46,000 talers were collected in the Protestant churches of Prussia in that year. These funds were used to rent a building near the Via Dolorosa in 1851. Christian travelers relate that one could stay at the hospice for fifteen days, and that needy pilgrims were exempt from payment.[56] In 1855, a house was purchased in the same region. Busch offers details of the transaction and notes that, in 1858, the Prussian section of the Johannitarian order undertook responsibility for maintaining the building. In 1863, the ownership of the contents of the house was transferred from the Prussian consulate to the Johannitarians. The house itself was small, and only three rooms were actually assigned to guests. Usually there were between 150 and 200 guests a year. In 1871, seventy-five paying guests stayed there for a total of 780 nights (about ten nights each), and thirty-three non-paying guests for a total of 372 (about eleven

179

55   Rosen, p. 5.
56   Hertzberg, p. 16.

nights per person).[57] In the 1860's, the value of Prussian real estate in Jerusalem (the consulate and the Johannitarian hospice) reached some 140,000 talers, or three times their purchase price. At this time, the consulate already had a scientific library with 400 books, open to visitors.[58]

The third consulate to be established in Jerusalem, the French consulate, was located at first in the Christian Quarter. On the British Admiralty Map (for the 1840's), Williams marks the home of the French consul in a spot overlooking the Pool of the Patriarch.[59] Later, however, the consulate moved to the Muslim Quarter. In 1857, Barclay says there were three consulates in the neighborhood: the Prussian consulate on 'Aqabat al-Takiyya, almost opposite the Takiyya; the French consulate, near the Damascus Gate; and the Austrian consulate, slightly south of the French consulate.[60] The British consulate joined them in the 1860's. Finn writes that, in 1863, Consul Moore moved near the Damascus Gate in the Muslim Quarter, not far from the Austrian consulate.[61]

The penetration of Western consulates and institutions into the region southeast of the Damascus Gate evidently raised the neighborhood's prestige. The region served in many respects as a springboard for various institutions that later moved outside the city walls. The region reached a developmental peak in the 1860's and 1870's. Dixon, who visited Jerusalem in 1864, says several Europeans of high rank resided there among the Muslims. To the east of the Damascus Gate lived the Turkish pasha, the Austrian consul and the British consul. Also located in this area were the school of Salaḥ al-Din, the Austrian hospice, a home for dervishes and a military hospital; in short, all the most important public buildings and the most aristocratic groups in the city.[62]

Later on, in the early 1880's, the first group of American Colony residents settled nearby before establishing their neighborhood outside the Old City. One source says that they bought a house at the top of the Bezetha hill, between the Damascus Gate and Herod's Gate. It was a large structure, with attractive balconies and many rooms and corridors, which had once belonged to a Turkish police officer. There was enough room in it for most of the Colony members; only a few families had to seek accommodation elsewhere.[63]

In our chapter on the Jews, we will see that many Jews began to settle in the Muslim Quarter in the second half of the century. Again, this was possible mainly because the neighborhood was sparsely populated (see pp. 376-388).

The Damascus Gate; Summary

The last part of our discussion of the Muslim Quarter will be devoted to the Damascus Gate. The Damascus Gate and the Jaffa Gate were the most important gates in Jerusalem; we spoke of the former's splendor in the chapter dealing with the city's appearance. Interesting archaeological finds were

57 Busch, p. 154; Strauss, p. 205.
58 Strauss, p. 205; *ZDPV*, VII, 1884, pp. 288-289.
59 Williams (1849), I, Supplement, p. 20 (no. 13).
60 Barclay, pp. 453-454.
61 J. Finn, *Stirring Times*, II, p. 384.
62 Dixon, II, pp. 6-7.
63 Spafford Vester, pp. 67-70.

discovered at its foot as early as the nineteenth century. In 1838, Robinson writes of a dark, square chamber found near the Damascus Gate, adjoining a wall of large, ancient stones. On the western side of the gate, there were stairs leading up to the city wall and another chamber with large ancient stones in it. Robinson associates these finds with the Second Wall of Jerusalem, dating from the days of the Second Temple. Tobler, too (in the 1840's), says that an ancient building was visible beside the Damascus Gate.[64] In 1876, the Baedeker guide reports the discovery of an ancient gate below the present one. A cistern and the remains of a wall were found, apparently dating back to Crusader times. Below the gates there were subterranean chambers made of large stones.[65]

When settlement began outside the Old City walls in the second half of the nineteenth century, the Damascus Gate again played an important role. Whole neighborhoods and important buildings were built facing it, and major thoroughfares began there, namely, the Street of the Prophets leading towards the Jaffa and Shechem roads, both of which will be discussed in the second volume (forthcoming).

The fact that non-Muslim institutions and population elements (Jews, Christians and Europeans) penetrated the Muslim Quarter on a large scale reinforces our earlier conclusion that the Ottoman government and Muslim community were the least active factors in the development of nineteenth-century Jerusalem. Sparse settlement and large empty spaces in the Muslim Quarter, coupled with relatively little population growth in the Arab sector and Muslim disinterest in building up the area, opened the way for ever-expanding settlement by Jews, Christians and Europeans. Infiltration of non-Muslim elements into this region was only a stage in the general trend towards expansion, an intermediate phase that preceded settlement outside the ancient walls. Later, when the settlement activities gathered momentum, the transitory stage came to an end, and non-Muslims ceased their expansion into Muslim territory.

---

64   Robinson, *Biblical Researches*, I, pp. 463-464.
65   Baedeker (1973), p. 134.

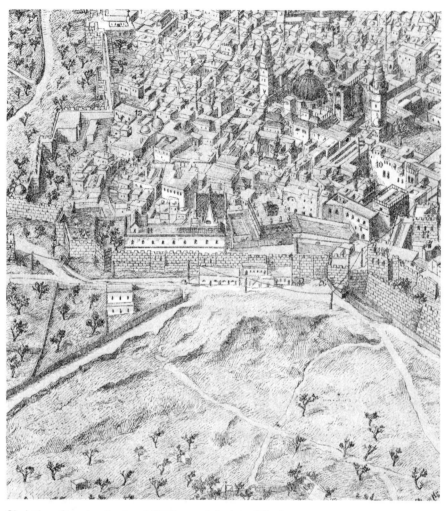

Christian Quarter in the 1870's, aerial view (Illes)

Part Three

The Christian Communities; The Christian Quarter; The Armenian Quarter

Chapter One:

WESTERN ACTIVITY; CHRISTIAN INHABITANTS AND PILGRIMS

The European Consulates

Before discussing the Christian population of nineteenth-century Jerusalem, let us devote a few general remarks to the European consulates which opened their doors in Jerusalem at this time.

While Ottoman influence on the development of Jerusalem was very limited for the greater part of the nineteenth century, the role of the European powers was quite important. This was largely due to the re-establishment of the Capitulations. These were treaties which exempted foreign subjects from the jurisdiction of the Ottoman state in which they lived; such rights were first extended to French citizens, in 1535, by Sultan Suleiman the Legislator. Eventually, they were granted to the subjects of other European powers, and became a factor of great importance in the relations of these powers with Turkey. In theory, the Capitulations freed foreign subjects from Ottoman jurisdiction, insured religious freedom to minorities, and put the holy places in Jerusalem under Western protection. In practice, however, they were rarely exploited, and may even be said to have been annulled until the Turkish law reforms of the Tanzimat period.[1]

The reforms of the Turkish Tanzimat, initiated in 1839, which granted equal rights to non-Muslims living in the Ottoman Empire (see p. 139), reinstituted the Capitulations in effect and strengthened the special status of Jerusalem's foreign consuls at the end of the period of Egyptian rule. After the closing of the French consulate at the beginning of the eighteenth century, Jerusalem was devoid of permanent foreign representation until Muḥammad 'Ali allowed the British to open a consulate in 1838. This was a deviation from standard practice: foreign consulates, more commercially than politically oriented at the time, were usually located in the coastal towns of Acre and Jaffa, or in Ramle (which was also near the sea). Thus, for example, a Russian consulate was opened in Jaffa in 1812 to serve Russian Orthodox pilgrims. In the days of Ibrahim Pasha, there were two British vice-consuls in Jaffa and Haifa; both

---

1   Ben-Zvi, *Eretz-Israel*, pp. 331-337, and see sources cited there; Colbi, pp. 65-77; Lewis, *Middle East*, pp. 34-46.

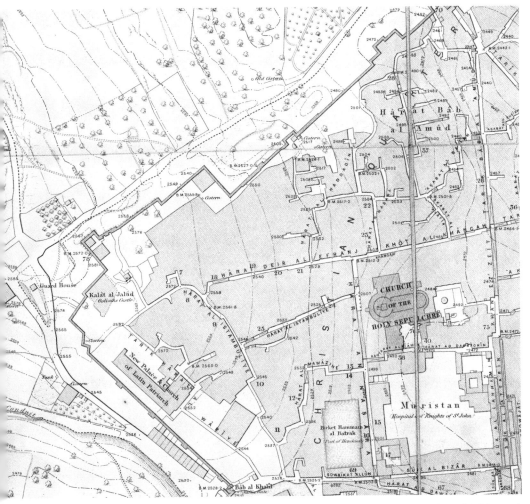

Christian Quarter on Wilson's map — 1865 (Ch. Wilson, *Survey*, 1:2,500 map)

were subordinate to the consul-general in Alexandria. After the establishment of a permanent consulate in Jerusalem, a vice-consul, later raised to the rank of consul, was appointed to run it.[2]

The other powers quick to follow. Within twenty years, all the important Western powers, including the United States of America, had set up permanent consular bases in Jerusalem. Prussia opened a consulate in 1842, France in 1843 and Austria in 1847. Russia also had consular representation in Jerusalem in the 1840's, but its official consulate was opened only in 1858. An attempt was made to establish an American consulate in 1844. Italy followed (as Sardinia, until 1860), as did Greece, Spain and Iran. In the course of time,

185

2   Ben-Zvi, *Eretz-Israel*, p. 332, and see sources cited there.

Holland, Belgium and Norway opened consulates. Denmark and Sweden had a joint consulate.[3]

As foreign consulates gradually increased in power, the standing of the non-Muslim minority groups of Jerusalem improved. They established themselves in neighborhoods of their own; each sought to live according to its religion and customs. As the Christian community was split into sects, the rivalry and competition among them was exploited by various European countries to advance their political aims and to expand their sphere of influence in the Ottoman Empire. Great Britain was followed by France in the attempt to exercise influence in Jerusalem. Just as Britain granted protection to the Jewish community, France resumed its long-standing guardianship of the Roman Catholic (Latin) community and shrines. Inter alia, Pope Pius IX was persuaded to restore the Latin patriarchate in Jerusalem, that had been abolished shortly after the conquest of Ṣalaḥ al-Din, in order to keep the Greek Orthodox and Protestant communities from gaining too much strength. France's status as "protector" of the Roman Catholic church was officially sanctionèd in Section 62 of the Berlin Treaty (1878), but its endeavors to win this recognition were long opposed by the other Catholic countries.[4]

Other Christian sects and European powers were equally active. In 1845, a new Greek Orthodox patriarch of Jerusalem was elected; a year later, the Russian archimandrite arrived. Russia invested a great deal of effort to enhance its prestige among the various denominations of the Eastern Church. It claimed to be the guardian of the Arabs belonging to the Greek Orthodox church, and extended its protection to the Greek Orthodox patriarchate in Jerusalem. Through the Russian Ecclesiastical Mission and, later, the Imperial Russian Pravoslav Society in Palestine, the Czarist government contributed funds towards the establishment and maintenance of churches, schools and hospices.[5]

This battle of interests among the Western countries served to increase the enmity among the Christian sects, which had originated in the religious fanaticism of the clergy. Any attempt, real or imagined, of one sect to infringe upon the established claim or ancient rights of another, such as altering a shrine in any way, trying to open another door in a church or instituting the slightest change in the long-standing status quo, was sufficient to arouse serious controversy and international repercussions. Many holy places, such as the Church of the Holy Sepulchre in Jerusalem and the Church of the Nativity in Bethlehem, had maps, plans and building models which explicitly showed the division of their ownership among various Christian sects.[6]

The relations among the sects became significantly worse in the 1850's. Both Russia and France intervened in their religious disputes, the former as protector of the Greek Orthodox community, and the latter as patron of the

3   On the first consulate in the city see, e.g., Neumann, p. 217; Baedeker (1876; 1973 reprint), pp. 18-19; Baedeker (1912), p. 19; Luncz, *Almanac,* I, 1896, pp. 17-18; Luncz, *Jerusalem Yearbook,* I, 1882, p. 18.
4   Ben-Zvi, *Eretz-Israel,* pp. 331-334; Colbi, pp. 77-107; Zander, pp. 25-54.
5   Hopwood, pp. 33-95.
6   See below, Chapter Two.

sul Finn
s. Finn, *Reminiscences*, p. 64)

Mrs. Finn
(Mrs. Finn, *Reminiscences*, frontispiece)

Roman Catholics. The current ruler of France, Louis Napoleon, was pushed into supporting the demands of the Roman Catholic clergy in the Holy Land by the clerical party, since the Capitulations entitled France to protect this community and its shrines. Czar Nicholas I saw it as his duty to guard the rights of the Orthodox church and the Orthodox subjects of the Sultan. France demanded the restoration of joint religious dominion over the Church of the Holy Sepulchre and the Church of the Nativity, which had been controlled by the Greek Orthodox church for about one hundred years. Russia insisted on upholding the terms stipulated in the days of the Arab conquest, when the Greek Orthodox church was the sole representative of Christianity in the Holy Land and Jerusalem. Any change in the status quo was fiercely opposed by the Czar; the Russian ambassador in Constantinople threatened to quit the Turkish capital within a day should changes be made. The French ambassador threatened a naval blockade of the Dardanelles. The Sublime Porte tried in vain to satisfy the demands of both sides, proposing the appointment of a negotiating committee or of other bodies in order to reach a compromise solution. Intermediaries were of no avail; the Crimean war erupted in 1853. For the third time since the invasion of Napoleon and the conquest of Muḥammad 'Ali, the Holy Land became the focal point of world interest and served as a pretext for the outbreak of a bloody conflict. The battles took place outside the Holy Land; the peace treaty signed at their end nullified Russia's claims and further augmented European influence in the Holy Land.[7]

In our discussion of Ottoman rule, we examined the constitutional changes that took place in the wake of this peace treaty. The more dependent the Ottoman government became upon the European powers and the more the Capitulations were enforced, the easier life became for Jerusalem's non-Muslim inhabitants. The European powers took advantage of their rights of jurisdiction and protection over their subjects in Turkey, and their consular representatives were quick to intervene if their subjects were mistreated in any way, each one being concerned for his own country's prestige. It was not surprising that consuls were so sought after, and that thousands of Christians belonging to different sects—as well as the ever-growing Jewish minority in the Holy Land—clamored for the protection of Britain, Austria, Germany, France, Russia and other countries. The consuls themselves took members of various nations and minorities under their wing with an eye to expanding their influence in internal Turkish affairs.[8]

Towards the end of the century, various sources note that the foreign consuls in Jerusalem lived in a world of their own, quarreling with each other over rights of precedence. They also enjoyed special privileges. The 1876 Baedeker guide, for instance, stresses the fact that consuls in the East had extraterritorial rights, and that the American and British consuls (in Jerusalem and Beirut only) had jurisdiction over any civil problems arising among their countrymen, even if these involved outsiders. Baedeker also states that permission to visit the mosques could only be obtained through the consulates.[9] Another source dealing with the consuls' judicial rights says that only foreign nationals were tried by the consuls and that trials involving a foreign subject and an Ottoman were held in an Ottoman court. The Ottoman court could only summon a foreign subject through his consul; during its deliberations, a consular representative was always present to guard his national's rights.[10]

Later, we will deal with the great influence of the consuls on the development of Jerusalem in general and that of the Jewish community in particular. At present, let us just say that Jerusalem's progress in the nineteenth century would have been impossible without the special status held by the consuls, a status that enabled them to preserve the interests of their nationals within the special framework of the Capitulations. Consular protection was very much responsible for the survival and development of the Jewish community, the most dynamic element in Jerusalem at the time. The consulates' power and influence grew steadily in the course of the century, with the consuls taking

7   Ben-Zvi, *Eretz-Israel*, pp. 334-336, and sources cited there.

8   The patronage extended by the consuls to various communities, especially the Jews, will be discussed below.

9   Baedeker (1876; 1973 reprint), pp. 18-19; see also note 3.

10 Schirion, pp. 115-116.

The Prince of Wales (later King Edward VII) on his visit to Palestine in 1862 (Mrs. Finn, *Reminiscences*, p. 236)

orders from no government except their own and their offices constituting a sort of miniature government. From their reports, it seems that the consuls thought of the Holy Land as annexed territory. Their presence in the city hastened the introduction of modern practices and ideas. It was they who launched and encouraged the first new construction projects both inside and outside the Old City. Without a doubt, they were the pioneers and pace-setters of the development of modern Jerusalem.

The Christian Population at the Beginning of the Century

At the beginning of the century, Jerusalem's Christian community was a small one. The population figures cited for the various sects in Western travelers' writings are generally similar, probably because they were derived from the same sources, the heads and representatives of the Christian sects. The Ottoman authorities may also have consulted these leaders for administrative purposes.

At the start of the century, the Christian community included one third of the city's population. There were three main sects: the Greek Orthodox, the Roman Catholics and the Armenians; the three smaller ones were the Copts, the Ethiopians and the Syrians. Seetzen (1806) gives the following figures: Greek Orthodox, 1,400; Roman Catholics, 800; Armenians, 500; Copts, 50; Ethiopians, 13; Syrians, 11; total, 2,774 Christians. He obtained this information from the Turkish governor and the various sects.[11] Until the 1840's, many other travelers present a similar figure for the Christian population of Jerusalem (about 3,000), but usually provide no details of the size of sects or of their sources, whether for the community as a whole or for different groups. The estimates of some travelers are obviously unacceptable. El-Abbassi (1807), for example, says there were 20,000 Christians in a total population of 30,000.[12] It seems that here we must exercise our discretion, ignoring the general and unfounded estimates of some sources in favor of those which appear relatively reliable.

Robinson seems to be a dependable source. We have already mentioned his sound approach to demographic data in our examination of the Muslim community (p. 127). Robinson says he received his information from the local authorities but, since only males above the age of eighteen or twenty were counted, he multiplied the figures given him by four. He suggests a slight revision of the official figures for the Greek Orthodox community, from 400 to 460. This would yield 1,840 Greek Orthodox Christians instead of 1,600. The figure of 260 registered Roman Catholics would then represent 1,040 Christians and the 130 Armenians, 520. After rounding off his figures, Robinson claims the total Christian population was 3,500.[13] Without rounding off and revising the number of the Greek Orthodox Christians the total would be 3,160; with the smaller sects not taken previously into account, it would reach about 3,250. This seems a quite reasonable figure as it is, without revising or rounding off. The lower figure corresponds with Seetzen's estimate, and shows a degree of growth that seems logical in view of the city's development, especially during the Egyptian occupation in the 1830's, when the Christian community was well treated by the authorities. The division into sects coincides with that of Seetzen, and shows a growth rate suited to the amount of time that had passed.

The Christian Population from 1840 to 1870

Consul Schultz provides us with a detailed population estimate for 1845 that seems to be based on Ottoman sources and on direct information from Christian community representatives. His figures are as follows: Greeks, 2,000; Roman Catholics, 900; Armenians, 350; Copts, 100; Ethiopians, 20; Syrians, 20; total Christians, 3,390.[14] A very similar estimate, also based on Ottoman sources and on direct information (possibly identical), is Tobler's figure for 1846. Tobler claims there were 2,000 Greek Orthodox, 900 Roman Catholic, 50 Greek Catholic, 400 Armenian, 100 Coptic, 50 Protestant, 38 Ethiopian and

190

11   Seetzen, II, p. 18.
12   El-Abbassi, II, p. 242.
13   Robinson, *Biblical Researches*, II, pp. 80-86.
14   Williams, II, pp. 613-614.

Nubian, and 20 Syrian Christians, for a total of 3,558 souls.[15] The data of Schultz and Tobler coincide with regard to the two largest sects. However, Tobler says there were more Armenians and Ethiopians, and he cites figures for two additional sects, the Greek Catholics and the Protestants. The Schultz and Tobler statistics seem an adequate basis for estimating the size of the various Christian groups in Jerusalem until the end of the 1840's. It is somewhat surprising that the Christians did not exploit the liberalization which took place with the return of the Turks to strengthen their foothold in the city. The Christians and the Jews differed greatly in this respect: the latter began streaming to Jerusalem in large numbers at this time. Tobler notes this, stating that while the Jews came to their ancestral land to live, die and be buried there, the Christians only made pilgrimages, after which they returned home.[16]

From the beginning of the 1850's, we have new figures at our disposal. The Turkish authorities in Jerusalem had appointed a special census-taker, whose task it was not only to count the residents but also to grant traveling permits and to register the dead (those guarding the city gates were paid to count the number of dead bodies removed for burial).[17] As we have noted, a Turkish census in those days included only males. However, the data from the 1850's seem to include the males of all ages, and should be multiplied only by two. Stewart offers the following figures on the basis of the 1851 Turkish census of the Christian population (including males of all ages): Greeks, 763; Roman Catholics, 482; Armenians, 208; Copts, 79; Greek Catholics, 28; Protestants, 21; Syrian Jacobites, 8; total, 3,062 Christians.[18] These figures are slightly lower than those of Schultz and Tobler for the 1840's. This is particularly true of the two large sects, the Greek Orthodox and the Roman Catholics. This results primarily from the fact that Stewart's information does not include non-Ottoman subjects. The Roman Catholic clergy, some Greek Orthodox priests and certain other members of these sects were affiliated with consulates and missions, and were not registered as Ottoman subjects. Stewart estimates that there were about 400 such persons. If we add this number to the total Christian population figure, we will obtain a figure much closer to that of Schultz and Tobler. The data for 1851 reinforce our earlier conclusion that the figures of these two writers may be accepted as being generally correct until the end of the 1840's.

Petermann offers an assessment close to that of Stewart for 1853. He says that, according to Ottoman data for 1852, there were 1,852 Christian males in Jerusalem. Multiplying this by two gives a total population of 3,704, excluding foreign subjects. Petermann estimates the number of Greek Orthodox at about 2,000 souls, that is, 400 families and 150 clergymen.[19] Pierotti quotes population estimates for 1861: total Christian population, 5,242; Greek Orthodox Christians, 2,700; Roman Catholics, 1,270; Armenians, 526; Anglicans, 206; Lutherans, 62; Copts, 130; Ethiopians, 80.[20] Pierotti (the city engineer during the rule of Suraya Pasha) probably derived these figures from Ottoman sources, but he seems to have adjusted them on the basis of personal

---

15   Tobler, *Denkblätter*, pp. 360-361.
16   *Loc. cit.*
17   *Ibid.*, p. 347.

18   Stewart, p. 299.
19   Petermann, I, pp. 218-219, 232-233.
20   Pierotti, I, pp. 12-13.

observation, especially the figure for the Greek Orthodox community; the actual figures were probably somewhat lower.

At the end of the 1860's, the first edition of Liévin's travel guide appeared in Jerusalem. Since Liévin was on close terms with the city's Christian community, his population estimates are likely to be accurate. Warren, who resided in Jerusalem at this time, relies on Liévin's figures, as does the PEF Survey. Liévin's data for 1869, which appear in Warren's *Underground Jerusalem* with slight modifications, are as follows: Greek Orthodox, 2,800; Roman Catholics, 1,500; Protestants, 300; Armenians, 510; Greek Catholics, 30; Armenian Catholics, 16; Copts, 130; Ethiopians, 75; Syrians, 12; all Christians, 5,373. Warren believes the number of Greek Orthodox should be raised to 3,500 but this seems unreasonable.[21] The PEF Survey uses Liévin's figures, but also notes British consul Moore's assessment of 5,300 Christians for 1873-1874.[22] The demographic information offered by the PEF and Liévin is usually quite accurate, but the period to which it refers should always be taken into consideration. The statistics Warren cites in Liévin's name are taken from the first edition of the latter's guide, published in 1869.[23] However, Warren's book appeared only in 1876. The PEF Survey appeared between 1881 and 1884, but its population data apply to the end of the 1860's and the early 1870's. A comparison of the figures of Liévin and Pierotti reinforces our previous conclusion that Pierotti's assessment is high for the beginning of the 1860's, being much more suited to the end of the decade.

Among the most prominent changes in the composition of the Christian community in the thirty-year interval between 1840 and 1870 was the establishment of an active Protestant congregation in Jerusalem. Consul Finn supplies detailed data for 1853 about the contribution of the Anglican Church, and these lend credibility to our own general estimates. His figures for the Protestants are: Anglicans, 52; Jewish Christians, 59; Jewish non-believers, 26; Christian Arabs, 42; Lutherans, 23; total, 202.[24]

The Christian Population at the End of the Century

Liévin continues to present population figures for the Christian community in subsequent editions of his book. In the second edition, published in 1876, we find: Greek Orthodox, 2,800; Roman Catholics, 1,000; Greek Catholics, 35; Armenian Catholics, 5; Armenians, 510; Copts, 130; Ethiopians, 75; Syrians, 15; Protestants, 300; total Christians, 5,470.[25] These numbers seem more appropriate for the early 1870's. In the third edition, published in 1887, Liévin raises his estimates for the larger sects: Greek Orthodox, 4,000, and Roman Catholics, 2,000. The others are as follows: Greek Catholics, 50; Armenian Catholics, 20; Armenians, 510; Copts, 100; Ethiopians, 75; Syrians, 15; Protestants, 300; total Christians, 7,070.[26] Here the figures are appropriate for the early 1880's, and are slightly high for the Greek Orthodox and Roman Catholic communities.

192

21   Warren, *Underground*, pp. 356-357, 490-496.
22   Conder—Kitchener, III, pp. 162-163.
23   Liévin (1876), I, p. 137.

24   J. Finn, *Stirring Times*, I, p. 155.
25   Liévin (1876), I, p. 137.
26   *Ibid.* (1887), I, p. 161.

Liévin hardly changes his data for the smaller sects from edition to edition (and this holds true for the Muslims too). On the other hand, his figures for the Jews and large Christian denominations (Greek Orthodox and Roman Catholic) show sizable increases. These do seem to have been the fastest-growing communities at this time, but Liévin's figures only indicate the direction and approximate scope of growth. The fourth edition, printed in 1897, relays the following data: Christians, 7,980; Greek Orthodox, 4,300; Roman Catholics, 2,300; Greek Catholics, 150; Armenian Catholics, 20; Armenians, 520; Copts, 100; Ethiopians, 75; Syrians, 25; Protestants, 400.[27] Here too the figures are more suited to the early 1890's, though the book appeared after the middle of the decade.

Another source from which we may obtain demographic information about the nineteenth-century Christian community of Jerusalem is the Baedeker guide in its various printings. However, as we pointed out in Part One of this volume (p. 130), the data in the first edition are inaccurate, apparently because an error was made in calculating the Ottoman-subjects population, and because foreign subjects were not taken into consideration. The initial printing (in 1876) cites an over-all Christian population of 7,000 persons. This hardly seems possible, especially since the figure refers to the beginning of the decade. The editor must have realized how unlikely it was, for he adds in parentheses Liévin's estimate of 5,373 for the same period.[28] The fourth English edition of the Baedeker guide (by Dr. Benzinger), published in 1900, changes its population figures entirely: total Christians, 13,000; Greek Orthodox, 6,000; Roman Catholics, 4,000; Greek Catholics, 200; Armenian Catholics, 50; Armenians, 800; Copts, 150; Ethiopians, 100; Syrians, 100; Protestants, 1,400. These statistics are probably excessive for the stated period, although the parallel German and French versions of the guide carry similar figures.[29] In the sixth edition, printed in 1912, these data appear: total Christians, 15,000; Greek Orthodox, 7,000; Roman Catholics, 4,000; Greek Catholics, 250; Armenian Catholics, 50; Armenians, 1,000; Copts, 150; Ethiopians, 100; Syrians, 100; Protestants, 1,600.[30] The statistics in the later printings of the Baedeker guide show an exceptionally rapid rise in the number of Christians in Jerusalem at the end of the nineteenth century and in the early twentieth century. The figures may not be wholly accurate, but they clearly indicate a pattern of accelerated growth for the three major Christian sects in Jerusalem at that time. A considerable increase in population is certainly reasonable, given the extensive urban development taking place during this period.

No discussion of demographic data for late nineteenth and early twentieth-century Jerusalem can ignore the data of the first British census, carried out in 1922. This census indicated there were 34,300 Jews, 13,500 Muslims and 14,700 Christians included in a total population of 62,500. The figures for the Christian sects are as follows: Greek Orthodox, 5,945; Syrian Orthodox, 371; Roman Catholics, 3,560; Greek Catholics, 278; Syrian Catholics, 45; Armenian Catholics, 103; Maronites, 45; Armenians, 2,367; Copts, 103; Ethiopians, 73; Anglicans, 1,279; Presbyterians, 52; Protestants, 348; Lutherans, 19; Templers,

193

---

27   *Ibid.* (1897), I, pp. 186-187.

28   Baedeker (1876; 1973 reprint), pp. 35-37.

29   *Ibid.* (1900), pp. 22-24.

30   *Ibid.* (1912), p. 24.

117; others, 24; total, 14,699.[31] The total number of Christians according to this census more or less corresponds with that for the eve of World War I. The war had a disastrous effect upon Jerusalem. The Christian community, however, decreased only slightly in size, and it revived again in the early days of the British Mandate.

Christian Sects in Jerusalem, 1800-1922[32]

Year	Greeks	Greek Catho- lics	Roman Catho- lics	Arme- nians	Armenian Catho- lics	Copts	Ethio- pians	Syrians	Protestants	Total Chris- tians
1800	1,400		800	500		50	13	11		2,774
1835	1,600		900	520					a few	3,020
1850	1,900	50	1,000	500		100	30	20	50	3,650
1860	2,230	50	1,200	600	10	100	50	10	200	4,450
1870	2,600	50	1,400	660	20	100	75	15	300	5,220
1880	3,300	100	1,750	710	20	100	75	15	430	6,500
1890	4,100	150	2,150	770	20	100	75	25	610	8,000
1900	5,000	200	2,850	850	50	130	100	70	1,000	10,250
1910	5,900	250	3,500	1,300	50	150	100	100	1,600	12,950
1922	5,945	278	3,560	2,367	103	103	73	371	1,851	14,615

An examination of the 1922 British census figures, and of the data for the end of the nineteenth century and the beginning of the twentieth, reveals that the city's Christian population was slightly larger than its Muslim population. This was probably due to the widespread activity of the churches at the end of the century, as they built monasteries, church buildings and various institutions, as well as residential neighborhoods outside the Old City in the German Colony, American Colony and elsewhere.

The Greek Orthodox Community

If we examine the population figures for the various Christian communities, we see that the Greek Orthodox community is the largest of them. It was composed largely of local Arabs, but there was also a small group of monks whose number, role and position are discussed by various nineteenth-century writers.[33]

In 1843, J. Wilson writes that there were 100 monks in Jerusalem, about thirty of whom lived in the Church of the Holy Sepulchre. Nearly all of them were foreigners, and most were from the Greek islands. Local Arabs were barred from joining their ranks; however, monks could not hold the secular church positions usually assigned to resident Christians.[34] Of more or less the same period, Strauss says that the Greek Christians constituted a majority

31   Barron, 1922.
32   The figures in the table (aside from those for 1922) were obtained by averaging the various data cited above.
33   Guthe, pp. 81-91; Maschopoulous, pp. 204-311; Colbi, pp. 77-85.
34   J. Wilson, I, p. 451.

among the Christian sects. Most were Arabs, some of them being priests. Prayers were conducted mainly in Arabic. According to Strauss, there were between 100 and 150 Greek clergymen in Jerusalem.[35]

Neumann stresses that the Greek Orthodox were local inhabitants who spoke Arabic and had Arab priests. Only the higher clergy and the monks in the community's twelve monasteries were Greek-born.[36] As for the status of these Greek monks, Seetzen writes that in his day (the beginning of the century) there was no Greek patriarch in the city, and that the Greek monks were subordinate to Patriarch Antimos of Constantinople.[37]

In 1845, the Greek patriarch, Cyril II, moved his seat to Jerusalem, thereby abolishing the ancient patriarchal custom of residing in Constantinople.[38] Strauss says that during his stay in Jerusalem, the head of the largest monastery in the city was elected patriarch in place of one who had died in Constantinople. This new patriarch decided to re-establish Jerusalem as the seat of the patriarchate for the first time in over a hundred years — a sign of the city's rising importance. The new patriarch was installed in an elaborate ceremony at the Church of the Holy Sepulchre. In the days that followed, he received high-ranking Turkish and Christian officials. (Strauss knew this because he resided at the Greek monastery while he was in Jerusalem, together with Prince Albert of Prussia.)[39] In the early 1860's, Pierotti writes, the Greek patriarchate in Jerusalem, which was responsible for all the Greek Orthodox Christians in the country, was located in the large Greek convent of St. Constantine.[40] The 1876 Baedeker guide also reports that Jerusalem's large Greek convent had been serving as the seat of the Greek patriarch since 1845.[41]

We will discuss the Greek Orthodox community and the buildings owned by it later when we discuss the Church of the Holy Sepulchre, the Greek convents, ·and this community's contribution to building Jerusalem at the end of the nineteenth century.

The Roman Catholic Community

The second largest Christian sect in Jerusalem throughout the nineteenth century was the Roman Catholic (Latin) community. Robinson claims that its members' ancestors were Arabs who converted to Christianity in the days of the Crusaders.[42] This is also the view of Strauss.[43] According to Petermann, a small number of them were "Frankish" or non-Arab foreigners, including Copts, Syrians and Greeks who had joined the Catholic church.[44] Ritter stresses that the Roman Catholics in Jerusalem all spoke Arabic, and were considered to be Arabs.[45]

There was no Roman Catholic (Latin) patriarchate in Jerusalem at the beginning of the nineteenth century. The community was led by the Franciscan convent of St. Savior (St. Salvador). Although St. Savior's had been placed in

35   Strauss, pp. 237-238.
36   Neumann, pp. 276-284.
37   Seetzen, II, p. 20.
38   Temperly, p. 229.
39   Strauss, p. 238.
40   Pierotti, I, p. 12.
41   Baedeker (1876; 1973 reprint), pp. 95-96.
42   Robinson, *Biblical Researches*, II, p. 88.
43   Strauss, pp. 241-243.
44   Petermann, I, pp. 217-218.
45   Ritter, IV, pp. 204-205.

charge of ecclesiastical functions in the Holy Land by the pope, the seat of the Roman Catholic patriarch was still in Italy at the beginning of the nineteenth century.[46]

Seetzen (1806) reports that there were twenty monks in the St. Savior convent—three of them Portuguese—and twenty-one local clergymen. The position of father superior was always held by an Italian, while the procurator, who managed the financial affairs of both the convent and the Roman Catholic community in the Holy Land, was a Spaniard. Up to that time, the vicar had always been French but, as no monks had arrived from France since the Revolution, the Spaniards and Italians took turns in this position every three years.[47] Taylor (1830's) writes that the St. Savior convent served as coordinator of all seventeen Roman Catholic missions in the Ottoman Empire. These missions were run by Franciscans from different countries, mostly Italians and Spaniards and some Frenchmen. Normally, the father superior of each was Italian, the procurator Spanish, and the vicar French. Each of these officers had an assistant. The *directoire* was composed of the heads of the convent and their assistants, plus one other person, usually of Portuguese origin. The convent of St. Savior was financed largely by grants from Catholic powers; some additional income came from pilgrimages and the sale of religious articles produced in the Jerusalem and Bethlehem monasteries.[48] Turner (1815) says that thirty-three monks lived at St. Savior, although there had once been sixty.[49] Robinson (1838) puts the figure at between forty and fifty.[50]

At the end of the century, Liévin writes that only fifty friars resided at St. Savior in 1876; this number had risen to seventy by 1887, and 100 by 1897. At this time, St. Savior also ran an orphanage and several vocational workshops.[51]

The activities of the Franciscans, and other matters concerning the Roman Catholics in Jerusalem, will be examined further when we deal with the Church of the Holy Sepulchre, the Christian Quarter and the various Christian sects below. Here, let us note only that the number of European clergymen in Jerusalem, Greek Orthodox and Roman Catholic alike, did not exceed a few dozen for each community. In both cases, communal ranks were swelled mainly by local Arabs.

Armenians, Protestants and Smaller Sects

Third in size among the Christian sects at the beginning of the nineteenth century was the Armenian community. Towards the end of the century, however, the Protestants began to catch up with the Armenians. Both these groups will be discussed more fully later on; here are several basic facts about them.

For most of the nineteenth century, the number of Armenians remained around 500. At the beginning of the twentieth century, as the city developed and Armenian refugees from the slaughter in Turkey began to arrive, the community grew rapidly, albeit for a short time.

There were no Protestants at all in Jerusalem at the start of the nineteenth

196

46   Strauss, pp. 241-243.
47   Seetzen, II, pp. 9-10.
48   Taylor, pp. 332-345.
49   Turner, II, p. 163.
50   Robinson, *Biblical Researches*, II, p. 88.
51   Liévin (1897), I, p. 197.

Orthodox pilgrims buying candles for the Holy Fire ceremony at the Church of the Holy Sepulchre (Ch. Wilson, *Picturesque Palestine*, I, p. 22)

century, and Protestant missionaries were even driven from the city at that time. The community began to grow after the 1830's, and flourished only towards the end of the century, when Europeans settled in Jerusalem in large numbers. By the close of the nineteenth century, there were at least 1,500 Protestants in the city.

Three other Christian sects were prominent in early nineteenth-century Jerusalem: the Copts, the Ethiopians and the Syrian Christians. These communities, however, remained small throughout the century, and will be dealt with later in this book. As time progressed, two more sects, the Greek Catholics and the Armenian Catholics, established themselves in Jerusalem. Their influence in the city was still extremely limited during the period under discussion. Their first appearance in demographic data pertaining to nineteenth-century Jerusalem was in the 1840's. Petermann (1853) relates that the Greek Catholic patriarch of Antioch, whose seat was in Damascus, also served as the patriarch of Jerusalem. He established a patriarchate and church there, and appointed a clergyman to lead the community.[52] The church of the Armenian Catholics, located on the corner of al-Wad street and the Via Dolorosa, was built in the second half of the century (see p. 176).

Christian Pilgrimages

Many Christian pilgrims visited Jerusalem in the nineteenth century. Contemporary sources consider the extent and changing character of such pilgrimages, which were not, of course, a nineteenth-century invention. They began hundreds of years earlier. Nevertheless, they had a character and pace of their own in the nineteenth century. Tobler (1845) points out that the number of pilgrims had once been much greater, but had declined over the previous two centuries. At the time of writing, he says, pilgrimages by members of the Greek Orthodox and Roman Catholic church had yet to resume their former proportions. Tobler offers estimates of the numbers of pilgrims arriving between 1666 and 1845, giving the names of important pilgrims and of the places they visited. He says there were approximately 10,000 pilgrims in 1831, 5,000 in 1845, and only 2,000 in 1846.[53]

Earlier, on April 20, 1806, Seetzen had noted that the holy places were constantly teeming with visitors. Overseas wars, however, had led to a shortage of certain supplies that previously had been available. For this reason, he says, new monks and pilgrims were no longer so warmly welcomed in Jerusalem. Elsewhere, Seetzen writes of the arrival of 100 Armenian and of 350 Greek pilgrims between November 29 and December 4, 1806. These pilgrims would, presumably, stay on until Easter. (Jewish and Muslim pilgrims were rarely counted, because they had no specific times for pilgrimages and were much less numerous.) Seetzen adds that 100 additional pilgrims were expected to arrive from Jaffa on December 5, 1806. On March 10, 1807, he states, there were reportedly 2,000 pilgrims in the city, half of them Greek Orthodox and the other half, Armenians; but he thought that this figure was exaggerated. Seetzen estimates that each visitor would spend 200 piastres on living expenses and gifts to his monastery. This would make a total income from pilgrims of 400,000 piastres; however, the amount was usually greater.[54]

At the beginning of the nineteenth century, most pilgrims reached Jaffa by boat, and then rode to Jerusalem. Nevertheless, quite a few reached the Holy Land by riding through the neighboring countries. The majority of pilgrims during this period were Greek Orthodox or Armenians from various districts within the Ottoman Empire. Others included Copts and Christian Arabs with Turkish citizenship. About 1,000 pilgrims passed through Jaffa Port annually at the beginning of the century.[55] Thus, the average number of Christians visiting Jerusalem at that time must have been between two and three thousand: 1,000 Greeks, 1,000 Armenians, and a mixture of Roman Catholics and members of other sects to complete their number. Sometimes there may have been as many as 5,000 or more pilgrims in one year.

198

52   Petermann, I, pp. 217-218. On the Greek Catholics see also above, p. 176 f.
53   Tobler, *Denkblätter*, pp. 469-504.
54   Seetzen, II, pp. 36-37, 199, 204-205, 400.
55   Avitzur, *Jaffa*, pp. 72-73.

Christian pilgrimages increased considerably during the period of Egyptian rule, after Ibrahim Pasha abolished the tax on pilgrims. There were great numbers of them to be found in Jerusalem, especially before Easter, as Skinner (1833) notes. Elsewhere, Skinner notes that European pilgrims were offered free accommodation at the convent of St. Savior. He also tells of a group of 300 Armenian pilgrims, many of them children, who came to stay at the Armenian monastery.[56]

According to the monk Neophitus, the number of Greek Orthodox pilgrims each year, from the Turkish occupation of Jerusalem until 1834, did not exceed 3,000, while Armenian pilgrims numbered over 4,000 a year (from 1825-1834). These, plus a small group of Roman Catholics and other Christians, brought the total to no more than 10,000 souls a year; often, there were many fewer than this. The situation improved greatly in 1834. Neophitus writes that the Church of the Holy Sepulchre was overflowing with pilgrims on Holy Saturday, with 4,500 Greek Orthodox; 6,000 Armenians, Copts and Syrians; and 2,000 Catholics, Maronites and other Christians. There were 14,000 souls inside the building, including the pasha and 300 soldiers (about 500 pilgrims had had to remain outside for lack of space), when the Great Fire broke out. In the ensuing panic, forty-three Greek Orthodox men, women and children, as well as more than 100 Armenians, all of whom had been standing near the exit, were crushed to death. More than 300 of those present were injured.[57] (The 1876 Baedeker guide relates, apparently in error, that 300 pilgrims had been killed at the Church of the Holy Sepulchre in 1834, when the authorities tried to suppress an uprising.)[58]

Taylor (for the 1830's) also writes about the pilgrimages to Jerusalem. He says there were very few Roman Catholic pilgrims, but that Greek Orthodox Christians and members of Eastern sects from Constantinople, the Aegean islands, Anatolia, Syria and Egypt flocked to the country in great numbers. They reached Jaffa in November, traveled to Jerusalem, and lodged at the city's various monasteries until after Easter. Taylor notes that there had been more pilgrims in the preceding century, and the city had derived a great deal of income from them. In his day, there were still many pilgrims, but a large part of the money went into the pockets of the city governors.[59] In some years, the number of pilgrims was very small. A case in point was 1839. Neophitus attributes this to the cholera epidemic in July and August, and to the news of war between the sultan and Muḥammad 'Ali. Greek Orthodox pilgrims numbered around 1,000, and Armenians about 1,300.[60] Roberts, just one year earlier, states that there were 20,000 pilgrims per year;[61] according to Stephens, there were between 10,000 and 20,000 pilgrims in the city at Easter of 1836.[62] These estimates seem rather high.

Christian pilgrim activity increased considerably during the Egyptian

---

56 Skinner, I, pp. 225, 249.
57 Spyridon, pp. 87-89.
58 Baedeker (1876), pp. 191-202; (1973), pp. 86-87.
59 Taylor, pp. 329-330.
60 Spyridon, p. 127.
61 Roberts, I, in text to illustration of David's Tower, p. 2.
62 Stephens, p. 109.

occupation, as we noted above. Some five to ten thousand pilgrims reached Jerusalem each year, thanks to the Egyptian government's liberal policies, which included the abolition of many taxes previously imposed on pilgrims. In addition, relative security reigned in the country, and maritime transportation in, the eastern part of the Mediterranean basin had improved.

A change occurred in the numbers and religious composition of the pilgrims in the mid-1840's. Strauss (1845) tells of an annual increase in the number of pilgrims from both East and West. In that year, the first steamships from Marseilles and Trieste set sail for the Holy Land, bringing pilgrims for the Easter celebrations. When Strauss was in Jerusalem, there were 5,000 pilgrims. This was quite a number, and, as each pilgrim contributed to the monasteries and holy places visited, for himself and for his relatives, a considerable income resulted. Strauss adds that it was necessary to direct pilgrims who came to pray at the Church of the Holy Sepulchre where to go, so as to maintain order among the thousands of visitors.[63]

Ewald writes that in 1843 the city's 7,500 pilgrims included some 2,500 Greek Orthodox; 2,000 Armenians; 300 Copts; 1,000 Roman Catholics; and 1,000 Christians of other sects.[64] Bovet, who undoubtedly gives inflated population figures, says it was impossible to establish the size of Jerusalem's population correctly because the number of pilgrims was so high, and encompassed some 15,000 Greeks and 10,000 Armenians (but very few Roman Catholics).[65] Pierotti, on the other hand, says there were many Roman Catholic pilgrims, and that the churches in Jerusalem provided housing and, if necessary, also hospitalization for them. Pierotti used information from the archives of the St. Savior convent when he compiled the following table.[66]

The Number of Pilgrims at the Convent of St. Savior, and the Length of their Stay

Year	number of pilgrims	number of days
1850	3,611	16,373
1851	3,797	28,580
1852	5,696	20,109
1853	5,574	21,364
1854	4,620	18,144
1855	6,874	23,522
1856	5,470	21,302
1857	7,196	26,280
1858	5,809	25,800
1859	7,116	27,792

(The data in the table do not reveal how many of the pilgrims were Roman Catholics. Nevertheless, from the over-all rise during the 1850's, it is reasonable to assume that number of Catholics rose too.)

200

63   Strauss, pp. 239-243, 281-282.

64   Ewald, p. 186

65   Bovet, pp. 137-138, 149.

66   Pierotti, I, p. 275.

The 1850's, especially the years following the Crimean war (1856), marked another change in the composition of the pilgrims reaching Jerusalem: At this time, the number of Russian pilgrims rose very rapidly. One source does report as many as 3,000 to 4,000 Russians in the city earlier, in 1839,[67] but the major increase took place after the Crimean war. According to F. Bremmer (1859), between ten and twenty thousand Christian pilgrims were arriving in Jerusalem each year, most of them from Russia or from countries ruled by Turkey.[68] Neumann says that the number of pilgrims sometimes rose to 20,000, but their average number was 10,000. Other tourists, too, visited the city. Most of the pilgrims arrived in the winter or close up to Easter. This lent much life and color to an otherwise drab, sparsely populated city.[69] In the second half of the century, we find many references to intensified Russian pilgrim activity. We will have more to say about this in our second volume, when we deal with the buildings of the Russian Compound, erected to serve the many pilgrims arriving at that time. Whereas Russian pilgrimages had been carried out on a relatively limited scale in the first half of the century, they assumed much greater proportions in the second half.

As Jerusalem, and the country as a whole, were exposed to more modern ideas in the 1860's, pilgrimages too assumed a new character. Little by little, they took on more of a "tourist" quality; by the 1870's, something resembling modern guidance for tourism had begun to appear.

Summary

Throughout the nineteenth century, the number of Christian pilgrims visiting Jerusalem rose from year to year. The peak season for pilgrimages was between Christmas and Easter, particularly close to the latter. A rough estimate shows that the average number of pilgrims was approximately equal to the resident Christian population, and sometimes even exceeded it. In certain years, Christian pilgrims even outnumbered the entire population of Jerusalem. During the first half of the century, most pilgrims were Greek Orthodox or Armenians, but there were also other Christian Arab pilgrims from different parts of the Ottoman Empire. In the second half of the century, these pilgrimages changed in composition and in magnitude, as more Russians and Roman Catholics came. Tourism of a European type began to penetrate the city, bringing with it some Protestant pilgrims.

The main object of all these pilgrimages was to visit the Church of the Holy Sepulchre, especially at Easter, when festive ceremonies were held. The Church of the Holy Sepulchre in the nineteenth century will therefore be our next subject.

201

---

67   Roberts, I, p. 290.
68   Bremmer, I, p. 173.
69   Neumann, pp. 213-217.

Chapter Two:

THE CHURCH OF THE HOLY SEPULCHRE

Introduction: The Structure of the Church

For most of the Christian sects in Jerusalem, as throughout the Christian world, the most important and sacred local shrine is the Church of the Holy Sepulchre. Neither the earlier history of the site nor that of the crucifixion and burial of Jesus Christ will be gone into here; it is this site in the nineteenth century that interests us. By studying the accounts of Western travelers and explorers who visited the church at this time, we can understand its status and importance, and its contribution to the development of Jerusalem in the nineteenth century. First, we will discuss various aspects of the church. Next, we will follow the descriptions and impressions recorded by travelers throughout the century.

No other site in nineteenth-century Jerusalem was described in such minute detail as the Church of the Holy Sepulchre. This, of course, is hardly surprising. Most of the travelers were Christians, for whom the site was of utmost importance. So fascinated were they by its history and holiness that they spent many hours studying it and recording their thoughts for posterity. In the first half of the century, many writers cite the belief that the Church of the Holy Sepulchre was established by Helena, the mother of Constantine. Composed of a number of parts, it was shaped like a cross.[1] Some point out that there were actually several different churches united under one roof: the chapel over the tomb of Jesus, completed by Constantine in 335 C.E.; the Golgotha chapel; and the church built above the spot where the cross was found. When the Crusaders conquered Jerusalem in 1099, they combined the three churches into one large one.[2] The inner part of the building was also a sanctuary and, being enclosed, formed a church within a church. The entire structure was topped by two domes, one black and one white, over the inner church and the Church of the Holy Sepulchre.[3]

1   Wittman, pp. 174-176; Turner, II, pp. 163-179.
2   Schulz, pp. 95-96; Norov, I, pp. 147-157.
3   Skinner, I, p. 212; Curtis, pp. 181-185.

The Division of the Interior Among the Sects

Travelers point out that the Church of the Holy Sepulchre was controlled largely by three sects: the Greek Orthodox, the Roman Catholics and the Armenians. The Copts, the Syrians and the Ethiopians, who were in the minority, had very limited rights there. The Greek Orthodox held precedence; it was this community that rebuilt the church after the fire of 1808.[4]

Strauss (1845) writes that ownership of the Church of the Holy Sepulchre had once been divided among eight sects, but that, since the recent fire, the Greek Orthodox had exercised complete control. They set aside special prayer sanctuaries: for the Roman Catholics, in the northern part of the church; for the Armenians, in the Chapel of St. Helena; for the Copts, in the small chapel on the western side of the Holy Sepulchre; for the Syrians, in a small chapel on the western side of the rotunda.[5] Some explorers provide detailed maps of the church, showing the division of control among the sects.[6]

The Great Fire of 1808, and Subsequent Repairs

We have already indicated that territorial rights in the Church of the Holy Sepulchre were crucial to the relations of various Christian sects and the European powers. The great fire of 1808 in the church, which destroyed the pillars supporting the dome and caused it to collapse, marked a turning point in these relations. Nineteenth-century travel literature abounds in references to this fire, some of them contradictory. Light, who visited Jerusalem in 1814, says that the Church of the Holy Sepulchre had burnt down several years earlier, and that some blamed the Armenians for the fire; it was alleged that the Armenians believed themselves to be the only ones wealthy enough to be able to renovate the church, and they hoped therefore to take their pick of holy sites. Thus the Armenians were despised by both Greeks and Roman Catholics.[7] Pierotti (1861) also claims that the Armenians were responsible for the fire on October 12, 1808.[8] Curzon (1834), however, an earlier visitor, attributes it to the carelessness of some drunken Greek Orthodox priests who accidentally set some wood on fire and tried to extinguish it by dousing it with brandy, thinking it was water.[9]

As for the repairs, all writers agree that they were carried out mainly by the Greek Orthodox,[10] apparently with the assistance of Russia, then the protector of the Greek Church.[11] However, before the repairs were begun, the Greek Orthodox, Roman Catholics and Armenians had fought over the right to

---

4 Norov, I, pp. 167-169; Olin, II, p. 296; J. Wilson, I, pp. 448-449; Curtis, pp. 181-183.
5 Strauss, pp. 210-221.
6 See, e.g., Williams, I, p. 447.
7 Light, p. 179; Sanjian, pp. 173-203.
8 Pierotti, I, p. 110.
9 Curzon, pp. 162-167.
10 Schulz, pp. 95-96; Forbin, p. 143; Warren—Conder, *Jerusalem*, p. 40; Pardieu, pp. 241-248.
11 Roberts, I, in text to illustration of the Greek Orthodox chapel in the Church of the Holy Sepulchre; Williams, II, pp. 118-119.

administer the holy task. The entire Christian world was asked to donate funds for the restoration of the church. The sultan granted a special *firman* allowing building activities to begin in May, 1809. As the Greek Orthodox had contributed most of the money, they supervised the work, thereby expanding the influence of their church in the Holy Land and strengthening it.[12]

Basili writes that the restoration of the Church of the Holy Sepulchre was important for intercommunal relations, both in principle, in that permission had been given to rebuild and enlarge a church, and in practice. The Greek Orthodox clergy, the party most involved in the repairs, had borrowed large sums of money from local Armenians, Muslims and Jews. This money was used to make payments to the Turkish governors, the Muslim courts, and even Muslim sheikhs and dignitaries; it also enabled the monasteries to expand their philanthropic activities. A serious setback occurred in 1821, when Greece and Turkey went to war and contributions from abroad ceased. The Jerusalem patriarchate could not repay its debts, even after selling all the gold and silver vessels belonging to the Church. Muslim and Jewish creditors demanded the immediate sale of the Greek Orthodox monasteries and the property of the Church of the Holy Sepulchre. After the war of 1829, which led to the Adrianople treaty, Sultan Maḥmud altered his attitude toward Christians and the Church, forcing the creditors to agree to repay the debt over a period of ten years, with ten percent of it to be paid each year, interest-free. He even offered to contribute some of his own treasury to the Church of the Holy Sepulchre. This offer was refused, but the condition of the Greek Orthodox Church improved steadily thereafter.[13]

In the course of the nineteenth century, other repairs and improvements made in the Church of the Holy Sepulchre served as a source of contention among the various Christian denominations. Taylor (1855) writes that the church had been renovated by a European architect at the expense of the Greek Orthodox, thereby putting them in a position of control. The condition of the building had deteriorated again recently and it needed further repairs.[14] Elsewhere, Taylor says the Greek Orthodox became increasingly influential between 1757 and 1812. After the great fire of 1808, he says, the Catholics lost control of the Church of the Holy Sepulchre once and for all and, despite the efforts of the French government, were unable to obtain what they wanted. It was only in 1852 that the sultan granted them some rights; the church thus became the joint property of the different Christian sects.[15]

The disagreements among the sects, especially between the Greek Orthodox and the Roman Catholics, over the repair of the dome are described in many sources. Petermann, for example, says the argument was still going on in 1853, after four years of deliberation. The Greeks sought to repair the dome because they would thereby attain full control of it. The Catholics obtained an injunction against them, but the Greeks would not allow the repairs to be carried out by the Catholics. Meanwhile the dome remained as it was, with each side blaming the other.[16]

---

12   J. Finn, *Stirring Times*, I, pp. 201-204, 300-301, 504.
13   Assaf, *History*, II, pp. 215-216; Basili, II, pp. 203-206.
14   Taylor, pp. 252, 282.   15   *Ibid.*, pp. 250-252.   16   Petermann, I, pp. 257-258.

Petermann says that the flat roof of the Church of the Holy Sepulchre was surmounted by a large dome, 100 paces in diameter. This dome was covered with stone tiles to prevent rain-water from seeping into the Chapel of the Sepulchre, which was located directly beneath it. The tiles had been damaged slightly; the Roman Catholics claimed the Greeks had done this intentionally, so as to be able to demonstrate their mastery over the church by repairing them. (This quarrel served as one of the pretexts for the war between Turkey and Russia.)[17] Bovet (probably for the same period) writes that one of the church domes was almost in ruins, and that the Greeks and Roman Catholics, who had enough money to repair it, were fighting over who should do the work. Eventually, the Turks decided to renovate the dome at their own expense.[18] The affair is also reported by Liévin and the Baedeker guide, reporting that the fire-gutted dome of 1808 was rebuilt immediately by the Greek Orthodox; it was again in ruins in 1858, and repaired in 1869 at the expense of France, Russia and the Ottoman government.[19]

Christian Supervision of the Church

In view of the disputes over the control of different parts of the Church of the Holy Sepulchre, each sect closely guarded those areas already under its control. The church as a whole was also subject to Christian supervision, although the keys and the responsibility for admitting visitors were in the hands of the Ottoman government and certain Muslim families.

On the matter of surveillance or supervision, Monro writes (during the Egyptian occupation) that the church administration was composed of twelve Catholic monks, twelve Armenians, fifteen Greeks and two Copts, all of whom lived in the church.[20] Curzon (1834) also says that there were monks who resided permanently in the church and accepted various items brought by pilgrims through an opening in its door.[21] Strauss reports that, in the 1840's, clerics and monks from the four major sects were always present to say mass at the proper times, and that overnight vigils by pilgrims were common. The church was open only on Sundays and holidays. Since its doors were usually locked, he says, food was handed in through a small opening. Order was maintained by Turkish guards in order to prevent quarreling among the sects.[22]

It seems that even prior to the period of Egyptian rule, there were monks living in the church, but they were fewer in number. Light (who visited Jerusalem in 1814) points out that twelve monks, three from each important sect, lived in the church and had their food supplied by the monasteries.[23]

Returning to the middle of the century, we find Pardieu (1851) stating that, although the Church of the Holy Sepulchre was owned jointly by all the Christian sects, its keys were kept by the Turks. The church was opened only for religious ceremonies. There were always six Roman Catholic priests living at the church, who were replaced every three months.[24] Taylor (1855) writes of

17 *Ibid.*, pp. 192-206.
18 Bovet, pp. 241-243.
19 Liévin (1897), I, pp. 253-254; Baedeker (1876), pp. 191-209; (1973), pp. 191-202.
20 Monro, I, p. 211.
21 Curzon, pp. 162-167.
23 Light, p. 182.
22 Strauss, pp. 210-211.
24 Pardieu, pp. 241-248.

Façade of the Church of the Holy Sepulchre (Ch. Wilson, *Picturesque Palestine*, I, p. 16)

thirteen priests who guarded the Franciscan chapel constantly. Food was sent in to them, and they never left the premises until others came to replace them.[25] It seems, therefore, that the number of monks living in the church changed from time to time, but that there were always some representatives of each major sect living there permanently.

In the 1860's, Damas complains that the Greek Orthodox had taken over the church, allowing the Catholics to hold services only three times a day. The Catholics even had to ask the Turks for the keys. Still, they had managed to obtain Turkish permission to establish a small monastery near the church; several Franciscans lived there, never leaving the building, and maintaining no ties with the outside world. Every three months, six monks would be sent to relieve them. Food was sent over daily from the convent of St. Savior.[26]

In the 1870's, Orelli repeats that monks and pilgrims lived in the church, which had many rooms, halls and hidden corners. One room contained a precise scale model of the church; it had been made for the Great Powers. The sections belonging to each denomination were marked off by different colors in the model. The monks who lived in the church did so in conditions of great hardship. Sometimes, the wall of a certain room belonged to one sect, and the floor to another. This situation led to many disputes. He adds that the main section of the church belonged to the Greek Orthodox, who enjoyed the firm support of the Russians.[27]

The Courtyard

Many travelers describe the courtyard at the entrance to the Church of the Holy Sepulchre. From here, one could see the church's great façade, flanked on its left by a half-ruined tower (damaged by an earthquake) and, on its right, by the living quarters of the Copts. The façade consisted of two-storied portals, topped by arches. On the ground floor, one of the doors was always closed. The decorated capitals above the windows and doors were damaged. On the lintels, there were carvings in bas-relief of New Testament scenes.[28]

According to Conder, the approach to the church was from the south, which had

> ... an open court in which according to the legend the Wandering Jew stays for a moment once in every century to beg admission, and hears a voice which bids him resume his endless journey. In front of us rise the beautiful Gothic doorways, the pillars scrawled over with the names of pilgrims and with dates from the fourteenth century downwards; beneath our feet lies old Philip D'Aubigny, close by the threshold, and over his head each year thousands of pilgrims press through the narrow portal.[29]

Seetzen (1806) writes that the small courtyard in front of the Church of the Holy Sepulchre was used regularly as a market place for souvenirs and gifts.

25 Taylor, p. 288.
26 Damas, I, pp. 131-133.
27 Orelli, pp. 127-134, 195-197.
28 Norov, I, pp. 147-154; Monro, I, p. 221; Schulz, pp. 95-96; Nugent, II, pp. 78-82; Petermann, I, p. 202; Orelli, pp. 127-134.
29 Conder, *Tent Work*, I, pp. 330-335.

These included crosses, models of the Holy Sepulchre, decorations, porcelain mugs, statuettes of saints, and so forth, all quite expensive. The area was also frequented by money changers, who provided the pilgrims with local currency. The Franciscan convent owned a large warehouse there, perhaps unique, stocked with religious articles and souvenirs made in Bethlehem for export to Italy, Spain and Portugal.[30] At prayer times, people swarmed into the courtyard, which resembled a market place. Women sold jewelry and crosses made of tortoise shell or olive wood from Gethsemane, and beggars were to be found in great numbers.[31] Wortabet (1855) adds that jars of bitumen from the shores of the Dead Sea were also sold there as souvenirs.[32] Lynch (1851) says the courtyard was thronged with pilgrims and armed Turkish soldiers in his time. Pedlars sat on the ground selling food, rosaries, crosses, icons, palm branches, models of the holy places, and so on. Despite the presence of soldiers, there was great disorder.[33]

Ottoman Supervision and Custody of the Keys

Nineteenth-century sources give differing accounts of the supervision of the Church of the Holy Sepulchre in the course of the century. Chateaubriand (1806) writes that the place was guarded by Muslims, who received money from visiting pilgrims.[34] In the same year, Seetzen says that every pilgrim paid a certain fee on his first visit to the church; he himself paid 33½ piastres.[35] Light (1814) says the church keys were kept by the Turks, and that the entrance fee was equivalent to fifteen shillings. A fee was charged for every ceremony, depending on its length.[36] In the early 1830's, Geramb relates that the church was still guarded by Muslims, who collected an entrance fee from every pilgrim.[37]

Later sources do not mention such a fee. Curzon writes that, in 1834, he waited for the Muslim guards to unlock the door, which was open only on certain days. However, he says nothing about paying.[38] According to Neophitus, the entrance fee was abolished on January 13, 1834, and a festive opening of the church was held on that day.[39] Stephens (1836) reports that the key was held by the governor of Jerusalem. A Muslim guard was posted at the door, which was opened only at fixed times. Three monasteries had to agree to such an opening, and their representatives had to be present.[40] Roberts (1838) writes that, as all pilgrims sought to visit the Church of the Holy Sepulchre, the flow of visitors was very heavy on the fixed days mentioned above. The door was opened late, as a rule.[41] In 1842, Mrs. Pfeiffer writes as follows:

> The open space before the church is neat enough.... Visitors to this church will do wisely to provide themselves with a sufficient number of para, as they may expect to be surrounded by a goodly tribe of beggary. The church is always

30   Seetzen, II, p. 15.
31   Skinner, I, p. 224; Curzon, pp. 162-167; J. Wilson, I, pp. 446-447; Martineau, p. 498.
32   Wortabet, II, p. 177.   35   Seetzen, II, p. 3.   38   Curzon, pp. 162-167.
33   Lynch, pp. 404-405.   36   Light, p. 182.   39   Spyridon, p. 86.
34   **Chateaubriand.**   37   Geramb, II, p. 108.   40   Stephens, p. 109.
41 _ Roberts, I, in text describing the Church of the Holy Sepulchre.

locked; the key is in the custody of some Turks, who open the sacred edifice when asked to do so.[42]

It is clear, therefore, that during the first half of the nineteenth century the Church of the Holy Sepulchre was open only at certain times, its keys were kept by the authorities, there was an entrance fee, and additional payments were required once one was inside. Under Egyptian rule and in later years, conditions improved gradually: the entrance fee was abolished and visiting hours were lengthened.

In 1851, Schulz writes that an entrance fee was no longer charged, but that the keys of the church were still in the hands of the Muslims.[43] In 1856, Dupuis relates that the massive iron doors of the church were usually locked in the evening and the keys taken to the pasha, who was responsible for appointing a gatekeeper.[44]

According to Charles Wilson's account of the 1860's, a certain Muslim family had the exclusive right to open the door, but could do so only upon instructions from church authorities. Prayers were conducted in the morning and afternoon. Sometimes one could enter at noontime if one bribed the porter or appealed to the church authorities.[45] Orelli (1876) points out that the church was not always open on schedule, and that, when it was open, it was very crowded.[46] According to the 1876 Baedeker guide, the church was usually closed between 10.30 a.m. and 3.00 p.m. but, if the porter were tipped, he might let one in nonetheless after 10.30.[47]

On the subject of guards, Norov (1835) notes that the cell of the Greek sacristan was at the right of the entrance, and that of the Turkish porter at the left.[48] Lynch (1848) writes of two old Muslims sitting on a raised bench near the church entrance, enjoying themselves over a cup of coffee.[49] Schulz (1851) adds that the Turkish soldiers stationed at the church were between ten and twelve in number. Another guard was posted near the chapel on the site of the crucifixion.[50] Petermann (1853) says that, opposite the church, there was a grassy area (probably the Muristan) that had once belonged to the Johannitarian convent. The Turkish soldiers who guarded the church pitched their tent there, and turned their horses out to graze.[51] Porter (1869) stresses that the permanent guard in the church was intended to prevent fighting among the Christian sects.[52]

Christian Disputes in the Church

Dixon (1864) provides a good description of the continuing rivalry of the various Christian sects at the Church of the Holy Sepulchre:

> Among the crowds who gather in this porch and worship under this dome, there are twenty rivals, and not two brothers. A pilgrim of one country believes the

42 Pfeiffer, pp. 113-114.
43 Schulz, pp. 95-96.
44 Dupuis, I, p. 65.
45 Ch. Wilson, *Survey*, p. 48.
46 Orelli, pp. 127-134.
47 Baedeker (1876), pp. 191-205; (1973), pp. 74-88.
48 Norov, I, pp. 147-157.
49 Lynch, pp. 404-405.
50 Schulz, pp. 96-97.
51 Petermann, I, p. 206.
52 Porter, p. 131.

pilgrim from another country to be a heretic and a scoundrel, a deserter from the true church, a denier of the true God.... Every friar in Jerusalem imagines that his Christian neighbour is already damned beyond hope of mercy; being worse, far worse than a benighted Moslem, an abandoned Jew. A Turk has no better light; a Jew has been cursed with a heart of stone; but what excuse can a Christian pastor imagine for a brother who has had his choice, and has wickedly selected an impure creed?[53]

Dixon goes on to express his distaste in colorful terms:

Each sect has a right to its turn of service before the shrine; a service of chants and candles, much clouding of incense, much blazing of flambeaux, much glamour of incantation in ancient and mystic tongues; making a scene as wild as the bronzed and picturesque men whom it appears to kindle into flame.

The Copts, say, are standing before the shrine: long before they have finished their service of sixty minutes, the Armenians have gathered in numbers round the choir; not to join in the prayers and genuflexions, but to hum profane airs, to hiss the Coptic priests, to jabber, and jest, and snarl at the morning prayer.... To steal one moment from the false church is held to be a victory for the true. Often these priests and worshippers come to blows; but on the very first cry of an attack — an affair of candles, crooks, and crucifixes — the Turkish guard is under arms and on the spot; and unless blood has been drawn, in which case the church is cleared and locked up, the ferocious rivals are allowed to complete their hymns and prayers under the protection of a line of Moslem matchlocks.

Dixon also finds fault with the dome:

Look at the great dome. It springs over the Sepulchre, the Holy of Holies, the very Shrine of Shrines. If there is one piece of man's work on earth that should be strong and perfect, built of marble and gold, and of all that is costly and durable, surely it is yon vault over the Tomb. Yet the dome of the Sepulchre is a wreck. The plaster is falling from the wall; the metal has been stolen from the roof; the paint is either washed away by the rain or scorched away by the sun; and the showers of winter come rattling through the rents. Any day, any hour this magnificent Tomb may be destroyed by its crumbling canopy of stone and lead.[54]

The Stone of Anointing and Golgotha

The first site described by nineteenth-century visitors to the church was the Stone of Anointing. Upon entering the church, one's attention was immediately drawn to a marble slab on the ground opposite the door. Lamps hung over it, and large wax candles stood at each corner. Pilgrims would kneel beside it and kiss it. This was the stone upon which Jesus' body was embalmed before burial. Behind it was a wall decorated with large paintings, the biggest of them showing Jesus being taken down from the cross. The Stone of Anointing was of imported marble. To its right were the tombs of the Christian kings and the steps leading up to Golgotha.[55] Each step leading up to Golgotha was carved out of a single stone.

The low-ceilinged chapel located at Golgotha contained two altars, one belonging to the Greek church and the other to the Roman Catholics. Below

210

53 Dixon, II, pp. 238-239.
54 *Ibid.*, pp. 238-240, 244.
55 Curzon, pp. 162-167; Norov, I, pp. 147-157; J. Wilson, pp. 446-447; Conder, *Tent Work*, I, pp. 324-326; Nugent, I, pp. 78-82.

the center of the Greek altar there was a gold cross and a hole where the original cross once stood. Some visitors say that there were three holes: one for the cross of Jesus, and two for those of the thieves crucified alongside him. To the right was a fissure in the rock, caused by the earthquake that occurred at the time of Jesu's death. The hole and fissure in the rock were adorned with gold and silver, and bore a Greek inscription. The face of the rock was covered with yellow marble. Above the Greek altar were gilt pictures and lamps donated by various Christian kings, as well as other religious articles, also made of gold. The ceiling was decorated with frescoes with a blue background. Behind the altar, separated from it by a thin partition, was a chapel with a stone in its center. This was said to be the place where Abraham had prepared to sacrifice Isaac. The Catholic altar was located to the right of the Greek altar, on a slightly lower level.[56]

Nineteenth-century travelers write about the Greek Chapel of Adam at the foot of Golgotha, the Chapel of St. John, and the tombs of the Crusader kings of Jerusalem. The Copts believed that Adam was buried at Golgotha, and kept a lamp burning there at all times. They also marked the place where Melchizedek, the founder of Jerusalem, was buried.[57] Godfrey of Bouillon and his brother Baldwin had been buried beneath the cross, but their tombs were destroyed by the Greeks. Godfrey's sword and spurs were kept by the Catholic monks.[58]

The Gallery, the Chapel of St. Helena and the Chapel of the Holy Cross

Descending the staircase from Golgotha, one reaches the gallery that encircles the church of the Greeks. The gallery occupies most of the central part of the building; the remainder is occupied by the rotunda. The gallery contains many small chapels commemorating different events of the Passion. These are designed to prepare the pilgrim for prayer at the Sepulchre itself.[59]

Further on is a flight of twenty-nine steps leading down to the Chapel of St. Helena, where the natural rock is visible. Another thirteen steps descend to the Grotto of the Finding of the Cross. The Chapel of St. Helena belongs to the Armenians. According to Christian tradition, it was built by St. Helena to commemorate the discovery of the cross upon which Jesus had been crucified. It was into this cave that the condemned and the crosses had been thrown. The Chapel of St. Helena contains two altars. The first, resting partly on Egyptian pillars, is dedicated to St. Helena, and the second one, on the left, to the Good Thief. Here, one is shown the rock-cut niche where St. Helena sat, and the small window, facing the cave, through which she saw the place where the cross was found. Orelli (1875) reports that there was a bronze statue of the pious empress. In the cave where the cross was discovered, there was a Greek altar;

---

56 Monro, I, p. 211; Norov, I, pp. 147-157; Curzon, pp. 162-167; Lynch, pp. 405-408; Conder, *Tent Work,* I, p. 330.
57 Monro, I, p. 211; Wittman, pp. 158-176; Norov, I, pp. 147-157.
58 Curzon, pp. 162-167; Lynch, pp. 404-405; Nugent, pp. 78-85.
59 Norov, I, pp. 147-157.

Grotto of the Finding of the Cross in the Church of the Holy Sepulchre (Stebbing, p. 138)

facing the steps, there was a Catholic chapel. All of these sites were shrouded in semi-darkness, which made them very **picturesque**.[60]

After emerging from the subterranean Grotto of the Cross and continuing along the gallery, one reaches other small chapels. One of them belongs to the Armenians; the other, dedicated to the Roman officer Longinus, belongs to the Greeks. If one makes a full circle of the Greek "Katholikon," one reaches a chapel where the cords used to bind Jesus' feet are kept. Another chapel is dedicated to the Virgin Mary. All of these places are owned by the Greek Orthodox.[61] If, however, one leaves the Katholikon and walks to the end of the gallery, one arrives at the church of the Franciscans. It is located to the right of the rotunda, and occupies a small wing of the central structure. It was renovated after the great fire in 1808, and contains the Column of the Flagellation. Seetzen (1806) says it was richly decorated with paintings, but Charles Wilson claims it was in poor condition in his time. When there were many pilgrims inside, he says, it was hard to breathe, and one could not stay there long.[62]

212

60 Wittman, pp. 158-176; Monro, I, p. 211; Norov, I, pp. 147-167; Curzon, pp. 162-167; J. Wilson, I, pp. 448-449; Orelli, pp. 127-134.

61 Norov, I, pp. 157-167; Wittman, pp. 174-176.

62 Seetzen, II, pp. 5-9; Norov, I, pp. 157-167; Curzon, pp. 162-167; Nugent, pp. 78-85; Ch. Wilson, *Survey*, p. 51.

Katholikon in the Church of the Holy Sepulchre (Roberts)

The Katholikon

Western travelers describe the Greek Orthodox Katholikon as being the central structure in the Church of the Holy Sepulchre. Here, among other things, are the spot that marks the center of the earth and the thrones of the patriarchs of Jerusalem. Two walls decorated with paintings of the saints separate this structure from the rotunda. These walls are connected by the Arch of the Kings, which forms the entrance from the rotunda to the Katholikon. The inside of the Katholikon is reminiscent of an ancient Russian church. It is topped by a dome borne on four connected pillars. Travelers say that this dome and that of the rotunda are visible above all the buildings in Jerusalem. The paintings on the walls are gifts from Russia, notable not for their artistic merit but for their gold and silver decorations. Above the Arch of the Kings is the double-eagle insignia of Czarist Russia. Lining the sanctuary of both sides are wooden benches for the monks, and, in the furthermost corner, chairs for the patriarchs. In the center of the structure is a marble bowl topped by a cross, attached to the floor. Travelers report that the Greek Orthodox say this signifies both the center of the church and the navel of the earth. Curzon (1835) describes it as a mounted black marble ball beneath which lies the head of Adam. (The belief that this is the center of the world was copied, apparently, from the temple of Apollo at Delphi.) A semi-circular altar is situated nearby, atop a low platform. Used for important ceremonies, it is surmounted by a

213

canopy borne on four gilded pillars. The pillars of the church are made of green marble, while the chapel itself is of yellow and white marble. A piece of the cross is kept in a special box on the altar. Opposite the entrance to the Holy Sepulchre is a platform used by the church choir. It is quite large, and ornamented with gold and holy icons. To the left of the altar is the church treasury; to the right is a door leading to Golgotha. Further on is the entrance to the cells of the Greek monks who live in the church.[63]

The Rotunda and the Holy Sepulchre

To the west of the Katholikon is the rotunda. Nineteenth-century travelers write that it was formed by two rows of square pillars, and contained the tomb of Jesus. The pillars, eighteen in number, were carved in the Corinthian style. They were built in three rows connected by arches, and supported the dome of the huge structure. The dome had a skylight in the center, so that the sun shone on the marble chamber containing the Holy Sepulchre. Some visitors say that, before the great fire, the dome was supported by white marble pillars, while the dome itself was of Lebanon cedar.[64]

The Edicule of the Holy Sepulchre is described in nineteenth-century sources as being a rectangular structure located directly beneath the cupola. One end of it was rounded, and contained an altar belonging to the Copts. The other end was square; outside it was a marble platform, with marble steps leading up to it, and handrails on either side. Large silver candelabra stood beside the door. The chapel itself consisted of two rooms. After taking off one's shoes, one passed through a narrow door and entered a room with a smooth piece of marble in the middle. It was on this stone, which once covered the Holy Sepulchre, that the angels sat when they told of the resurrection. Travelers add that a fragment of it is kept in a marble vase illuminated by fifteen costly lamps.

From the Chapel of the Angel, which had small round windows on either side, another small door led into the inner room. Here one found the Holy Sepulchre, but the original rock was hidden beneath a white marble slab. The sepulchre occupied the whole width of the room, and half of its entire area. Hanging from the ceiling were six rows of gold- and silver-plated lamps, with six in each row, making a total of thirty-six lamps. These burned day and night; the smoke rose to openings in the dome. The wall next to the sepulchre was decorated with a mosaic depicting the resurrection and, facing the doorway, there was a small picture of the Virgin Mary. Costly fresh flowers scented the air. The Sepulchre was usually wet with perfumed water and the "tears of sinners."[65] The lamps belonged to different Christian sects, each of which tried in this way to stake out its claim beside the Holy Sepulchre. Churches all over the world sent gifts to the Church of the Holy Sepulchre with a similar motive. Travelers point out that it was filled with splendid and costly gifts. Here and

63 Norov, I, pp. 167-169; Wittman, pp. 158-176; Seetzen, II, pp. 5-9; Lamartine, I, pp. 355-358; Curzon, pp. 162-167; Orelli, pp. 127-134.
64 Norov, I, pp. 157-167; Wittman, pp. 174-176; Curzon, pp. 162-167.
65 Norov, I, pp. 157-167; Nugent, pp. 78-85; Lynch, pp. 404-405; Schulz, pp. 100-108.

The Holy Sepulchre
(Porter, *Jerusalem*, p. 76)

there, one noticed a sorry-looking lamp or an unpretentious picture of Jesus—the gifts of poor churches—but these received the same devoted care given to items donated by wealthy churches.[66]

Burial Caves and the Canopy of the Virgin

Various nineteenth-century sources stress that there were many burial caves near the tomb of Jesus and that, ostensibly, even the Holy Sepulchre was inside a cave.[67] Some emphasize that the tombs of Nicodemus and of Joseph of Arimathea were near the Holy Sepulchre. Bordering the wall of the burial

215

66 Orelli, pp. 127-134.   67 Norov, I, pp. 157-167.

Chapel of the Holy Sepulchre (Manning, p. 103)

caves was the Chapel of the Armenians, which suffered no damage in the fire of 1808. Facing it were the entrances to the Chapel of the Syrians and the two tombs. The antiquity of these tombs was unquestionable, and strengthened the belief in the authenticity of the Holy Sepulchre, since it proved that the site had been used for burial even earlier.[68] The PEF Survey reports on the excavations at the tomb of Joseph of Arimathea, noting the discovery of a passageway that may have led to another burial chamber, now covered by the church. Other PEF explorers, such as Wilson and Conder, also investigated the site.[69]

Finally, we reach the Canopy of the Virgin. Nineteenth-century sources write that, between the southern part of the rotunda and Golgotha, there was a marble slab with a wrought-iron canopy over it. This marked the spot where the Virgin Mary had stood as the body of Jesus was lowered from the cross. Nearby were the steps leading to the Chapel of the Armenians, so that the site belonged to them.[70]

Religious Ceremonies

Many of the Christian pilgrims who visited Jerusalem in the nineteenth century

68 Wittman, pp. 174-176; Norov, I, pp. 157-167; Monro, I, p. 211; Curzon, pp. 162-167; J. Wilson, pp. 448-449; Nugent, II, p. 47.
69 Warren—Conder, *Jerusalem*, pp. 319-331.
70 Norov, I, pp. 157-167; Curzon, pp. 162-167.

participated in the festive ceremonies at the Church of the Holy Sepulchre. Seetzen's visit (1806) coincided with the Festival of the Holy Fire. On that day, the church and adjoining courtyard were thronged with people. In a tent near the door sat the Turkish governor, the *qadi* and other Muslim dignitaries. There was a barrier at the doorway to regulate the crowds. The larger part of the church was occupied by the Greek Orthodox. The Armenians sat quietly on the side, but the Greeks were very noisy and ill-mannered. There were even some young Muslims in the crowd. It was the Greeks' privilege to receive the Holy Fire in the Sepulchre. The event was preceded and followed by a grand procession.[71]

Norov (1835) describes the ceremonies and preparations for Easter. By the end of March, Jerusalem was already filling up with pilgrims, and preparations were under way at the Church of the Holy Sepulchre. When he visited on March 31, it was possible to enter the courtyard and even the church proper in the middle of the night. Both sections of the large gate were open, and innumerable lights flickered before the large paintings depicting Jesus being removed from the cross and being buried. At the mass held at dawn, the church was crowded with believers from all over the world. The hallowed silence customary in European churches was absent here. Candles were lit while the palm branches were being blessed. A procession from the Greek altar in the Katholikon made its way through the sacred gate of this church to the Holy Sepulchre on the other side of the building. Leading the procession was the Muslim gatekeeper, who cleared the way with shouts and cracks of his whip. During prayers, pilgrims touched the holy pictures and flags, and mothers held up their children to do likewise. All of this was in preparation for Easter. On the first day of Holy Week, it was customary to bathe in the waters of the Jordan, the waters of salvation, before receiving the holy sacrament. Afterwards, the pilgrims would remain at the Church of the Holy Sepulchre until the Day of Resurrection (Anastasis). Thus, there was a constant stream of travelers going back and forth between the Jordan River and Jerusalem. The city was already swarming with pilgrims a day before this, and had the look of a carnival. Row upon row of laden camels and horses made their way through the streets, and the bustle of new arrivals could be heard all night long. Sometimes, the pilgrims were accompanied to the Jordan by an interpreter from the Greek monastery. In the weeks before Easter, the road from the Greek monastery to the Church of the Holy Sepulchre and the courtyard in front of the church were full of pedlars selling crosses, holy icons, and other such items, mostly from Bethlehem. During the day, not only the courtyard but also the church itself became a market place. All kinds of food were sold there, and the crowds strolled around smoking and drinking coffee.

Religious rites were usually performed at night, as strangers were a source of disturbance during the day. Separate ceremonies were held by each community. Rites associated with the anointing, the bathing of the feet and so forth were performed before masses of spectators on different days of the week. On the sixth day, the Syrians and the Copts held relatively modest processions, followed by an elaborate Armenian procession. The Roman Catholic

217

71 Seetzen, II, pp. 5-9.

procession began in the Catholic church and passed through the entire building. Its participants were friars of the French order. When this was over, a procession re-enacting the crucifixion began.[72] Strauss (1845) adds that the Catholic procession stopped beside every chapel to sing hymns in Italian, Spanish, German, English, French, Greek and Arabic. After carrying the cross to Golgotha, the procession returned to the Holy Sepulchre, where people were kneeling and praying all the while. Before, during and after the Holy Fire ceremonies, the church rang with noise and confusion. The Turkish guards could barely restrain the enthusiastic pilgrims by using their rifle butts. Every year, the Turkish pasha was present at the ceremony; it began only when he arrived. The clerics were able to circle the Holy Sepulchre only twice, despite the strenuous efforts of the Turkish soldiers. Large sums of money were paid for the privilege of receiving the Holy Fire from the patriarch. The Armenians had long wanted to abolish this evil; the Greek Orthodox were opposed, because they did not wish to cast aspersions on their predecessors and because abolishing a practice that held so prominent a place in the popular faith might cause a decline in the number of pilgrims. Until the time of the ceremony, large numbers of men, women and children lived at the church, eating, drinking and sleeping there.[73]

Schulz (1851) writes that the rite of the Holy Fire attracted crowds of Jerusalemites, from Greeks to Muslims, whose behavior was hardly in keeping with the sanctity of the place. If they were not laughing and shouting, they were dancing and eating. The Armenians were the best-behaved, he notes, and occupied the right side of the church. Distinguished guests who wished to watch the ceremony were seated on the balcony. Of course, there were armed Turkish guards at hand: without them, there might have been bloodshed. The ceremony usually continued until two p.m., at which time the Armenian and Greek bishops received the Holy Fire (from the heavens) and relayed it to the Chapel of the Angel adjoining the Holy Sepulchre. At this point, the crowd would become ecstatic. People were often injured, and sometimes even crushed to death. This Holy Fire was used to light all their candles, either directly or from candle to candle. It was said to bring blessings on one's home, to protect one from illness, and so on. In view of the disorder caused by this ceremony, the Turkish authorities prohibited it from being held on Sunday evening, the first day of the holiday. Instead, it was held a day earlier. The evening before the ceremony, the Franciscans went in procession to the Stone of Anointing, where the anointing was performed by the leader of the Franciscans in the Middle East. They then proceeded to the Holy Sepulchre, praying and delivering sermons in different languages. Although there were some abuses of true Christianity, Schulz adds, these processions were as orderly and dignified as was possible with such a large, diverse crowd.[74]

Many other Christian travelers describe the ceremonies at the Church of the Holy Sepulchre, each stressing different aspects. However, we will content ourselves with these, and proceed to a discussion of the Christian Quarter as a whole.

72 Norov, I, pp. 73-78.   73 Strauss, pp. 239-243.
74 Schulz, pp. 94-99, 104-106; see also Dupuis, I, p. 65; Orelli,, pp. 127-134.

Chapter Three:

THE CHRISTIAN QUARTER; THE GREEK ORTHODOX
AND ROMAN CATHOLIC COMMUNITIES

The Plan of the Christian Quarter; the Dispersal of the Christian Sects

In the nineteenth century, the area known as the Christian Quarter consisted, as it does today, of the northwestern part of the Old City. Nineteenth-century travelers point out several characteristic features of the Christian Quarter in their day. It was inhabited by members of different Christian sects and a few Muslims (mainly around the Damascus Gate), but there were no Jews in it at all. The Greek Orthodox and Roman Catholic communities stood out in particular, but other sects lived there too. To some extent, separate neighborhoods were distinguishable within the Christian Quarter, especially those of the Greeks and the Roman Catholics. Other sects were generally too small to have neighborhoods of their own. Still, they had different life styles, and there was constant rivalry among them. The Christian Quarter also contained the large, uninhabited Muristan district; two mosques; the Pool of Hezekiah; and a Turkish bath, located east of the street of the Patriarch.[1]

As in other periods, the concentration of Christians in their own quarter, and the evolution of denominational neighborhoods, stemmed primarily from the desire of each sect to stay as close as it could to the place most holy to it.[2] The most important site for the Christians of Jerusalem was unquestionably the Church of the Holy Sepulchre. At the beginning of the nineteenth century, the largest and oldest Christian community in the city was the Greek Orthodox one, which controlled most of the Holy Sepulchre complex. Its members lived in close proximity to the church. Nearby was the city's largest Greek monastery, which was the seat of the Greek metropolitan in the Holy Land and which was, from the spring of 1845, the headquarters of the Greek patriarch of Jerusalem. In the early nineteenth century, many of the smaller Greek churches and monasteries were also to be found in the Christian Quarter, very close to the Church of the Holy Sepulchre.

The second largest Christian community in Jerusalem at the beginning of the

219

1   Tobler, *Denkblätter*, pp. 121-125; Barclay, *City*, pp. 437-454; Damas, II, p. 163.
2   On the attitude of the Christian sects to the holy places in Jerusalem see, e.g., Zander, pp. 35-36.

century, the Roman Catholics, also concentrated in the Christian Quarter; again, the magnetism of the Church of the Holy Sepulchre was responsible. There was a continuing battle between these groups over the possession of different parts of the building, as we have noted. Early in the century, the Roman Catholics had held several strategic points within the church, but the position of the Greek Orthodox community was much stronger. After the Crusades, the Franciscan order had assumed the leadership of the Roman Catholics of Jerusalem and the Holy Land. Until the sixteenth century, their headquarters in Jerusalem had been the Coenaculum, the site of the Last Supper, on Mount Zion. Expelled during that century, the Franciscans succeeded in acquiring the largely abandoned convent of St. Savior from the Georgian church. From then on, St. Savior has been the hub of Franciscan activity, and a secondary focus of Roman Catholic activity, in Jerusalem.

The Copts and the Ethiopians also remained close to the Church of the Holy sepulchre. As we have seen, neither of these sects then numbered more than a few dozen souls. Nevertheless, they did hold certain areas of the church, albeit limited in size. This, and their strong emotional ties to the site, led the community members to reside in the large courtyard and the dilapidated shacks beside the church and to its east.

The tiny Syrian Orthodox community also controlled a small portion of the Church of the Holy Sepulchre. In addition, however, it had an ancient church and monastery of its own, St. Mark's, which it held in great religious esteem. The community therefore concentrated around St. Mark's rather than the Church of the Holy Sepulchre.

The Armenians, the third largest Christian community in the city, claimed both the church and the monastery of St. James and several "strongholds" in the Church of the Holy Sepulchre. Along with the Greek Orthodox and the Roman Catholics, the Armenians were major contenders in the battle for ownership of the Church of the Holy Sepulchre in the nineteenth century. Nonetheless, they preferred to live near their own church and monastery. This neighborhood was, and still is, the most cohesive of all the Christian neighborhoods in the Old City. Enclosed by a wall, it constituted a separate society with institutions and customs of its own.

Thus, we see that the Christian sects concentrated around the city's holy places, primarily around the Church of the Holy Sepulchre, but also around the separate centers of the various communities.

We will now dwell on the two main denominations in the Christian Quarter, the Greek Orthodox and Roman Catholic communities, and leave our discussion of the others until later.

The Greek Orthodox Community and Its Large Convent

We have already discussed the fact that this community controlled most of the Church of the Holy Sepulchre, and that the large Greek convent located nearby was the seat of the Greek synod and the Greek patriarchate. Tobler writes that, in the early 1850's, the convent was inhabited by five bishops, ten archimandrites, dozens of other clerics, and a service staff.[3] Various sources

220

3   Tobler, *Topographie*, pp. 274-278.

relate that this Greek convent was large but irregularly shaped. There were some seventy or eighty rooms, inhabited by dozens of Greek monks of all ranks. It was the largest of the Greek monasteries, and was connected to the Church of the Holy Sepulchre by an arch over the Street of the Patriarchs. A balcony led to the domed roof of the church: the building also bordered on the Holy Sepulchre bell-tower, and there were steps leading from the convent to the church courtyard. The Greek convent contained several churches, the most important of them being the Church of St. Constantine. The property of the convent seems to have extended east and north of the main building, with the eastern section constituting a separate entity known as the Convent of Constantine. North of the main building, on the other side of the street, there was a comfortable hospice for pilgrims, with a courtyard and garden.[4]

An important part of the convent was its library. Travelers in the beginning of the nineteenth century record that it contained 2,000 books in various languages, including 500 Greek manuscripts on thin parchment. One of the most beautiful was a twelfth-century illuminated manuscript of the Book of Job, with large lettering and illustrations of Job's suffering.[5] The most precious volume was a New Testament, said to have belonged to St. James, the first bishop of Jerusalem. There was also a Bible received by the monastery as a gift from Byzantium.[6]

The Other Greek Monasteries

The Greeks also had a considerable number of other monasteries, dispersed throughout the city. They served mainly to accommodate Greek pilgrims. In 1806, Seetzen writes that there were nine Greek monasteries for men in Jerusalem, but that most of the monks lived in the main monastery. There were also five convents for women, two of them for widows.[7] According to Robinson (1838), the Greeks had eight monasteries for men, inhabited by a total of sixty monks. The smaller monasteries were located in different places, and served as hospices for pilgrims; only one or two monks lived in each. Robinson also says that there were five convents for women, inhabited by thirty nuns.[8] The data provided by Seetzen and Robinson are similar, indicating that, at the beginning of the nineteenth century, the Greeks had thirteen or fourteen religious houses in the Old City, five of which were for nuns. Some sources point out that they were actually in use only around Easter, when pilgrims lived in them. During the rest of the year, there were only watchmen and perhaps a monk or two in each.[9]

Williams (1840's) writes that Jerusalem had many Greek churches where prayers and rites were performed in two languages by the city's six priests.[10] These churches and monasteries appear on the British Admiralty Map together with explanatory footnotes.[11]

4   Norov, I, pp. 188-190.
5   Curzon, p. 172.
6   Norov, I, pp. 188-190.
7   Seetzen, II, p. 20.
8   Robinson, *Biblical Researches*, II, pp. 80-89; Millard, pp. 255-256; J. Wilson, I, p. 451.
9   Paxton, pp. 120-121; Taylor, pp. 329-330; Norov, I, p. 190; J. Wilson, I, p. 451.
10 Williams, I, Supplement, pp. 16-17; II, p. 529.
11 Williams, I, Supplement, pp. 15-20.

Greek Patriarch Damianos of Jerusalem
(Blyth, p. 308)

Wilson's map of Jerusalem (1864-1865) included the following Greek monasteries: "St. George (No. 3); St. Basil (No. 7); St. Theodore (No. 8); St. Demetrius (No. 10); the Virgin (for nuns) (No. 13); St. John the Baptist (No. 17); St. George (No. 19); St. Michael (No. 21); St. John Euthymius (No. 22); the Lady (No. 23); St. Nicholas (No. 25); Gethsemane (No. 39); Abraham (No. 40)." [12] Pierotti's map for the 1860's adds the monasteries of St. Catherine and St. Charalambos (Nos. 31 and 48 on the map), and points out the location of a proposed new monastery (No. 54). [13] Other Christian sources also dwell on the large number of Greek Orthodox monasteries. [14] The Convent of St. George was sometimes called the "Jewish convent," because it was on the edge of the Jewish Quarter; there was another Convent of St. George in the Christian Quarter. J. Wilson says the Convent of St. Demetrius was the largest of these institutions, and that it housed the bodies of deceased monks. [15]

During and after the Egyptian occupation, improvements were made in some of these monasteries, and the Greek Church began to acquire some new buildings and build others. According to Tobler, renovation of the Convent of St. John commenced in 1840. (Robinson reports that it was finished in 1852.) When the new foundations were being dug, a vaulted chamber was discovered; it turned out to be an ancient Greek chapel more than forty feet long. The height of its doors and windows proved that the street level had once been much lower. Tobler also writes that work began in 1848 on a Greek Orthodox church alongside the Casa Nova of the Franciscans. [16]

The 1840's were marked by additional progress for the Greek Orthodox community. Neophitus says, for example, that the Greek Church bought a

12 Ch. Wilson, *Survey*, 1:2,500 map.
13 Pierotti, Plan II, no. 54.
14 See, e.g., Norov, I, p. 190.
15 J. Wilson, I, p. 451; and see *PEF QSt*, 1900, pp. 253-257, for a description and sketch of the Greek Orthodox Church of St. Demetrius.
16 Robinson, *Later Biblical Researches*, p. 184; Tobler, *Topographie*, I, p. 344; and see *PEF QSt*, 1899, pp. 43-45, for a description and sketches of the underground church.

Greek monks in Jerusalem (Hedin, p. 173)

large building northeast of the Church of St. Euthymius for 15,000 piastres.[17] Strauss (1845) reports extensive purchases of land by the Greek Orthodox, who sought to provide additional accommodations for pilgrims at Eastertime.[18]

The 1876 Baedeker guide relays the following information:

> The Greeks possess... (the) Monastery of St. Helena and Constantine, 100 monks; Monastery of Abraham, 30 monks; Monastery of Gethsemane for pilgrims, 30 apartments; Convent of St.Basil, 10 deaconesses; St. Theodore, for 200 pilgrims; St. George, for 200 pilgrims; St. Michael, for 200 pilgrims; St. Catherine, for 200 pilgrims; Euthymius, 30 deaconesses; Seetnagia, 30 deaconesses; Spiridon, for 100 pilgrims; Caralombos, for 500 pilgrims; John the Baptist, for 500 pilgrims; Nativity of Mary, 40 deaconesses; St. George (a second of that name), for 50 pilgrims; Demetrius, for 200 pilgrims; Nicholas (containing a printing office), for 300 pilgrims; Spirito (near the Damascus Gate), for 150 pilgrims.[19]

This list includes two new monasteries built in the mid-nineteenth century: Spiridon and Spirito.

The PEF QSt of 1895 carries an article about the ancient churches in Jerusalem, along with a map showing their locations, and the plans of several of them.[20]

Schools and Health Institutions

The rivalry of the Christian sects, which increased in the 1840's, spurred developments in the sphere of education. In 1838, Robinson writes that the schools of the Greek Orthodox taught only ancient and modern Greek. Greek clergymen did not have a sound knowledge of Arabic, although this was the language in which the local Arab Christians prayed. For this reason, ties

223

17 Spyridon, p. 127.
18 Strauss, pp. 237-238.
19 Baedeker (1876), p. 162; (1973), p. 36.
20 *PEF QSt*, 1895 (article on ancient churches).

between the clergy and the community were weak.[21] In the 1840's, Tobler mentions the Greek school for boys located south of the new Roman Catholic religious house, opposite the Convent of Demetrius, which had opened in 1842 through the efforts of an American society. It had a department for Greek Orthodox students and a smaller one for Muslims. West European teaching methods were employed, and a greater range of subjects taught than at the Catholic school.[22]

In the explanatory notes to his map (No. 11), Williams writes that the main Greek convent ran a high school. There was also a primary school where children learned reading, writing and the elements of their faith.[23] Petermann (1853) also mentions the school in the Greek monastery and says it was established with the help of the Protestant bishop, Samuel Gobat.[24] The Greeks also opened a college in the Monastery of the Cross.[25]

Basili notes the vast amount of money invested by the Orthodox Church in schools during the mid-nineteenth century. The church did so rather reluctantly, as a reaction to the activities of the Protestants and the Catholics. Basically, however, it believed that education was not in the inhabitants' best interest. Greek Orthodox schools taught reading and writing in Arabic; prayers; and selections from the Old and New Testaments. The convent attached to the Church of the Holy Sepulchre ran a seminary for local clerics of low rank, where Greek, theology, the writings of the Church Fathers, geography and history were taught. An institution somewhat like a religious college was founded in 1852. Competition among the Christian missionaries, however uncultured their methods and intentions, produced a rash of schools in Jerusalem. The number of literate persons rose greatly as a result, but the education they received was quite superficial.[26]

Consul Finn writes that, in 1853, the Greek Orthodox boys' school had ninety pupils, and the college in the Monastery of the Cross had fifty.[27] Petermann says a printing press was opened at the Greek convent in the same year.[28] For the early 1860's, Pierotti lists a religious seminary; two schools for boys; a school for girls; eighteen monasteries to accommodate pilgrims; several hospices for pilgrims and the needy; and a printing press.[29] According to the 1876 Baedeker guide, the Greek Orthodox girls' school had two teachers and sixty pupils, and the boys' school, three teachers and 120 pupils.[30] Luncz notes that the latter was founded in 1848, the former in 1862. Both held classes every morning. A boarding school was opened in the Monastery of the Cross in 1855.[31]

21 Robinson, *Biblical Researches*, III, p. 465.
22 Tobler, *Denkblätter*, pp. 441-443.
23 Williams, I, Supplement, p. 19.
24 Petermann, I, pp. 218-219.
25 Strauss, pp. 237-238.
26 Assaf, *History*, II, pp. 252-253; Basili, pp. 220-223.
27 J. Finn, *Stirring Times*, II, pp. 101-105.
28 Petermann, I, pp. 192-200.
29 Pierotti, I, pp. 277-279.
30 Baedeker (1876), p. 162; (1973), p. 36.
31 Luncz, *Jerusalem*, II, 1887, pp. 88-89.

Developments in the Greek Orthodox community also extended to medical facilities. Petermann (1853) and Pierotti (1861) both emphasize the fact that the Greek convent had a dispensary. The Baedeker guide of 1876 mentions "a handsome new hospital." Built in the 1870's, this hospital appears on the western side of the Christian Quarter in the Ebers and Guthe map.[32]

The progress of the Greek Orthodox community of Jerusalem in the fields of education and health was very much a product of its new economic prosperity. Neumann writes that the once-poor community was now wealthy and influential, and it was thus able to establish many schools in the city.[33]

Greek Orthodox Building Activity in the Old City; Summary

The vast wealth accumulated by the Greek Orthodox community enabled it to undertake several impressive building projects in the Old City during the nineteenth century, particularly towards its end. Most of these were carried out near the Jaffa Gate, the New Gate and the Muristan. In 1887, the PEF QSt reports that the Greek convent was erecting a large building in the Old City near the Jaffa Gate, and intended to open some shops beside it.[34] Another source for the 1880's says that the Grand New Hotel was under construction opposite the Citadel of David, and that shops were being built beneath it by the Greek Orthodox priest who served as treasurer of the Church of the Holy Sepulchre. A row of shops with apartments over them was also being put up over the Crusader ruins in the Muristan.[35] Luncz (1889) writes that the "Greek Orthodox Church has built a large hotel above the Euthymius market inside the city (near the Jaffa Gate). This hotel has fifty rooms and is the largest and most beautiful in the city." Later, in his *Palestine Almanac,* Luncz reports that a third floor had been added to the Grand New Hotel, which could now accommodate 200 guests.[36]

In 1895, the PEF QSt reports that a large part of the northwestern corner of the city near the New Gate belonged to the Greek convent. One of the monks was building a row of shops along the street. Behind them were apartments, warehouses and stables; behind these were living quarters.[37] The newspaper *Ha-Tzevi* repeats the fact that the Greeks were building homes and shops near the New Gate, as does a later source (1910).[38]

The third region built up by the Greek Orthodox was the Muristan. The PEF QSt of 1899 writes that the Greek convent was preparing most of its property in the Muristan for the construction of a series of shops along the new road west of the Lutheran Church of the Redeemer.[39] We also find reports of the

---

32 Petermann, I, pp. 197-200; Pierotti, I, pp. 277-279; Baedeker (1876), p. 162; Ebers—Guthe map.

33 Neumann, pp. 306-308.

34 *PEF QSt,* 1887, p. 213.

35 Spafford Vester, pp. 87-88.

36 Luncz, *Jerusalem,* III, 1889, pp. 203-204 (translated from Hebrew); Luncz, *Almanac,* 1897, p. 155.

37 *PEF QSt,* 1895, p. 113.

38 *Ha-Or,* 1 Tevet, 1910, vol. II, no. 235, p. 2.

39 *PEF QSt,* 1899, p. 113.

building activity of the Greeks in the Hebrew press. In 1903, *Hashkafa* writes that the Greek Church had built a new street with a fountain in the middle, and seventy shops. The street began at the Batrak, and continued until the Saraya.[40] Luncz (1901) writes that the "Greek Church purchased the remainder of the property of the Johannitarians, or the Muristan... which was full of dirt and refuse, and cleared it all away to build large shops... and a magnificent *sabil*. Above the shops, they built living quarters...."[41]

In addition to their property inside the Old City, the Greeks also owned several sites outside the walls. They seem to have been the sole or principal owners of the Church of Mary (the Virgin's Tomb), part of the Garden of Gethsemane, and the Monastery of the Cross. They also had rights in the Church of the Ascension on the Mount of Olives, and owned the monasteries of Mar Elias, Mar Saba, and part of the monastery and church in Bethlehem.[42] In the second half of the nineteenth century, the Greeks engaged in agriculture, and put up buildings outside the Old City; this will be dealt with in our second volume.

The Greek Orthodox community at the beginning of the twentieth century was, therefore, quite well organized. It had large elementary schools for boys and girls; a well-equipped hospital; welfare organizations; and a large amount of property inside and outside the Old City.[43]

The Roman Catholics, the Franciscans and the St. Savior Convent

Unlike the Greek Orthodox community, the Roman Catholics had only one central religious house in Jerusalem at the beginning of the nineteenth century: that of the Franciscans. The Franciscans were the oldest Catholic group in the country. This mendicant order was established at the beginning of the thirteenth century by St. Francis of Assisi; its world center was in Rome. A special branch of the order had been awarded the task of guarding the Christian holy places, under the title of "Custodia Terrae Sanctae" (Custody of the Holy Land); its head was known as the "Custos Terrae Sanctae," or Custodian of the Holy Land. In the nineteenth century the Custody operated in the Ottoman Empire, from Constantinople to Cairo. However, it also had special representatives in countries all over the world, who engaged in propaganda and fund-raising on behalf of the Custody and the holy places. The headquarters of the Custody were in the St. Savior convent, where the Custos resided and administered affairs with the assistance of a council.[44] From the outset, Franciscan activity in Jerusalem centered on caring for pilgrims and obtaining a foothold in the holy places, then totally controlled by the Greek Orthodox.

After their expulsion from the Coenaculum, the Franciscans purchased the partly abandoned St. Savior convent, which had been a convent for elderly

40 *Hashkafa*, 6 Nisan, 1903, vol. IV, no. 25, p. 196.
41 Luncz, *Jerusalem*, V, 1901, p. 184 (translated from Hebrew).
42 Petermann, I, pp. 218-219.
43 Goodrich-Freer, p. 106.
44 Medebielle, pp. 62-63.

Georgian women, in the sixteenth century. One source says that the transfer of the convent was authorized by the sultan. The friars paid the women still residing there 1,000 dinars.[45] The original St. Savior, the cellar of the present-day building, was extremely small. Various additions to the building were made over the years. The carpentry and blacksmith shops still standing today date back to 1600. A boys' school, previously located in Bethlehem, was opened in 1615. Construction of all the workshops was completed in 1800. The first school for girls was established in 1830, and run by the Sisters of St. Joseph after their arrival in 1846. A printing press was opened in 1846-1847. An orphanage for boys was established inside the convent, and one for girls, outside it.[46]

In the early 1880's, extensive building activities at the convent ceased, at roughly the same time that the construction of the French Catholics' Notre Dame and St. Louis hospital outside the Old City began. One work of the time relates that the Franciscans were about to complete their expanded church and its clock-tower. It states that large buildings were constructed beside the church to accommodate priests and pilgrims, and that stores and workshops were established to furnish employment for members of the community.[47]

As for St. Savior itself, nineteenth-century sources claim it was built like a fortress, and was capable of withstanding attack.[48] Located in the northwestern sector of the Old City, its balconies provided a beautiful view of Jerusalem, the Mount of Olives and part of the Dead Sea.[49] Williams writes that the St. Savior convent occupied the highest spot in the city. Some local, Christian-hating, Turkish and Muslim residents persuaded the governor that it was even higher than the Citadel; as a result, the authorities ordered many of its buildings lowered. Williams goes on to say that the convent was large and covered several acres of land. It was a world unto itself, with its own blacksmiths, carpenters, shoemakers, tailors, millers, bakers and so on.[50] Other writers repeat that the convent was an independent unit, with a workshop for the various craftsmen who plied their trades there. Jerusalem had very few craftsmen aside from those at the St. Savior convent. During the holiday season, these craftsmen were busy with work at home; at other times, they traveled all over the country doing a variety of jobs.[51]

Turner (1815) writes that the convent supplied 800 Christians and a number of Muslims with bread each week. It also distributed fabric for clothing. This had been customary for a long time despite the poverty of the convent, which was now heavily in debt.[52] According to Taylor (1831), the St. Savior convent was in very bad condition and in need of extensive repairs. However, a permit from the authorities was prohibitively expensive. In 1831, the convent could accommodate 100 persons. It was inhabited by twenty-five friars, all of them

45 *Ibid.*, pp. 91-92.
46 Personal testimony of the local friars.
47 **Spafford Vester, pp. 87-88.**
48 Paxton, p. 120.
49 Seetzen, II, pp. 11-12.
50 Williams, I, Supplement, pp. 15-16.
51 Seetzen, II, p. 17; W.R. Wilson, I, p. 230.
52 Turner, I, p. 163.

Hospice of St. Savior Monastery
(Sepp, I, p. 855)

Italian or Spanish, each of whom had a furnished room.[53] Tobler says that, in 1846, there were fifty-four friars in the convent, who remained in the country for a period of three years. These friars were severely affected by the rebellion of 1826.

In 1829 and 1837, the pasha of Damascus raised property taxes for churches and monasteries in Jerusalem and its vicinity to a total of 7,000 piastres a year. Local Arab sheikhs, such as the Sheikh of Abu Ghosh, demanded large additional sums as "protection" money. In 1845, the new pasha, Muḥammad, increased the tax to 10,000 piastres. Tobler estimates the annual expenditure of the Catholic monasteries at 15,000 pounds sterling. He also notes that, like the other communities, the Franciscans sought to attract new members by offering financial aid; this resulted in a veritable traffic in souls.[54]

Neumann relates that the Roman Catholics, most of whom were natives of the country and spoke Arabic, lived in the vicinity of the Franciscan convent and were dependent upon it. They were extremely poor. Some of them earned a living from carving religious articles, others subsisted on the charity of the convent. The expenses of all the Roman Catholic convents in the country came to 100,000 Spanish talers. Elsewhere, Neumann comments that it was customary among Christians as well as Jews in Europe to support the poor of the Holy Land. Catholic countries sent money through the Franciscan convent to help their Catholic brethren in Jerusalem. He estimates that, from 1650 to 1850, some sixty million francs were collected for this purpose.[55]

Norov (1835) voices harsh criticism of the country's monks and friars. He says these were usually Franciscans or oriental Christians who, unlike the missionaries, spent only three years each in the country. They were sent here as a punishment, he adds; one might deduce their character from this. There were justifiable complaints made about them. Nevertheless, the religious orders were commendable for the hospitality they extended to pilgrims. Poor travelers received food throughout their stay in Jerusalem; a cutback was expected, however, because of decreased contributions from abroad. The central Roman

228

53 Taylor, pp. 332-345.
54 Tobler, *Topographie*, I, pp. 267-344.
55 Neumann, pp. 282-283, 299-301.

Catholic religious house was the Terra Sancta. Affiliated with it were twenty others, and a total of some 200 monks.[56]

During the first half of the century, the main role of the St. Savior convent was to accommodate pilgrims. Seetzen comments that this aim was barely realized because the number of European pilgrims was very small. The services provided by the house were not really at its own expense, because it was unthinkable that a pilgrim should leave without making a donation. It was true that the annual expenses were high, but there were other reasons for this. The house made payments to many monks all over the Middle East; it covered the cost of maintaining various religious houses; it paid protection money to the Muslims; it made substantial "gifts" to the pasha. When various houses were asked to pay sums of money to the local authorities, they were assisted in this by the central house. Large expenses were defrayed by the income from religious articles, exported to southern Europe or sold to visitors in Jerusalem.[57] Petermann (1853) also relates that the Franciscan religious house owned a large warehouse of olive-wood and shell souvenirs sold to tourists.[58]

At the beginning of the nineteenth century, the number of pilgrims staying at the St. Savior was small, but it increased gradually. Skinner (1833) relates that guests were lodged at the convent free of charge, as a rule. Still, it had not hosted a large group of pilgrims for a long time.[59] When Curzon visited Jerusalem in the spring of 1834, he expected to receive room and board at the Franciscan house, as was customary. He was disappointed when the friars accommodated him in a building outside the convent.[60]

In 1842, Bartlett notes that the Roman Catholic religious house had the best guest accommodations in the city. Next best was the Armenian one. In 1843, Warburton writes of the Roman Catholic house as being the wealthiest and most influential in the country.[61]

The Casa Nova; Knowledge of the Holy Land; The Printing Press; The Schools

In the first half of the nineteenth century, pilgrims arriving at St. Savior were lodged in the building itself. In the 1840's, the Casa Nova was built for this purpose. Ritter (late 1840's) writes that the Catholics had a beautiful hospice beside their religious house where European pilgrims stayed.[62] De Saulcy (1850) relates that the rooms there were small, with two beds in each. Accommodation was inexpensive, but the meals were meager.[63] Williams (late 1840's) marks the Casa Nova on his map, recording that pilgrims of all nationalities, regardless of religious affiliation, were entitled to stay there for a period of two weeks. Each person paid as he saw fit. The house supplied only good bread and bad wine, but it expected guests to pay generously.[64] Subsequent maps, such as that of Charles Wilson, also mark the location of the Casa Nova. Petermann (1853) relates that the Franciscans took in foreigners of

56 Norov, I, pp. 241-243.
57 Seetzen, II, pp. 207-211.
58 Petermann, I, pp. 217-218.
59 Skinner, pp. 201-202.
60 Curzon, p. 162.
61 Bartlett, *Walks*, pp. 14-15; Warburton, p. 148.
62 Ritter, IV, pp. 205-206.
63 De Saulcy, I, p. 554.
64 Williams, II, pp. 568-569; I, Supplement, pp. 15-16.

all Christian sects. As at all houses of the Terra Sancta group, pilgrims without means were granted room and board free of charge for three days.[65]

In April of 1859, Scherer writes of the great hospitality of the Franciscans. They put other monasteries to shame, he says, so unconcerned were they with remuneration. He says that the Casa Nova accommodated more than 1,400 pilgrims during Holy Week that year. The rooms were large and airy, but one had to share them with others; the few single rooms were reserved far in advance by important personages and noble ladies. Since guests were so numerous, one could not expect any special attention or service. Pilgrims had to comply with the instructions and regulations of their hosts.[66] In 1875, the Franciscan guide, Liévin, repeats that all pilgrims were welcome to stay at the Casa Nova for up to three days.[67]

The Franciscans possessed an excellent knowledge of the Holy Land, perhaps because they were so involved with pilgrims. Wittman (1800) relates that the friars at the Roman Catholic house gave him a special guidebook of the Holy Land which they themselves had written. Norov (1835) notes that the library of the Franciscans did not contain important works, as did that of the Greek convent, but the Catholic guidebooks displayed a more thorough knowledge of Jerusalem and of the Holy Land in general.[68]

The Franciscans further contributed to the study of the Holy Land by establishing their own printing press and publishing many books about the country. The Franciscan friar, Liévin, served as a tour guide for forty years, and published four editions of his famous guidebook.[69] The establishment of the Franciscan press was hindered by two major obstacles: the Turkish authorities' mistrust of Christians, especially with regard to culture and education; and a lack of capital. The first obstacle was removed when Muḥammad 'Ali came to power, but the lack of capital remained a problem. Help came from Austria. The cardinal of Vienna, Vincent Edward Milde, took affairs into his own hands, bringing Jerusalemites to Vienna to learn the printing and bookbinding trades. In July of 1846, all the requisite machinery reached Jerusalem, along with Arabic and Latin typefaces. The first page was set on January 27, 1847; the press began to operate the next day. By the end of the nineteenth century, the Franciscan press was publishing books on a variety of topics, from theology to mathematics.[70] The ties between Catholic Austria and the Franciscan house were notable. According to Neumann, the consul of Austro-Hungary had actually extended his aegis over this house.[71]

St. Savior was also active in the field of education. At the beginning of the nineteenth century, it ran a school for Catholic boys. A local resident taught them to read and write Arabic, and a friar taught them Italian and Latin so that they would understand the rituals. They learned no other subjects, not

65 Petermann, I, pp. 202, 217-218.
66 Scherer, pp. 176-184.
67 Liévin (1876), p. 5.
68 Wittman, pp. 173-184; Norov, I, pp. 181-190.
69 On Friar Liévin and his travel guide see Mertens, pp. 329-332.
70 On the Franciscan press see Petrozzi, pp. 64-69; Ritter, IV, pp. 204-205; Petermann, I, pp. 217-218; Lortet, p. 232.
71 Neumann, pp. 231-233.

even arithmetic. The boys assisted the friars during various religious ceremonies. When the boys reached the age of twelve, their parents would take them out of the school to learn a trade. There was no school at all for girls.[72] Taylor (1831) also mentions this school. He says the pupils ate at St. Savior but slept at home. In 1831, there were fifty-two of them.[73]

The Establishment of the Latin Patriarchate

The 1840's brought important changes in the Roman Catholic (Latin) community of Jerusalem. First of all was the renewal of the patriarchate. Originally established in the days of the Crusaders, this institution ceased to exist when the Crusader kingdom collapsed (1291) and the last patriarch, Nicholas, drowned in the sea while trying to escape. From that time on, Roman Catholic interests in the Holy Land, especially in the holy places, were represented by the Franciscan order (whose leader was officially recognized in 1342).

The appointment of Jerusalem's first Protestant bishop, Alexander, in 1841, sparked the interest of the Roman Catholics of Central Europe, who demanded a counterbalance to Western Protestant and Greek Orthodox activity in the city. On January 14, 1842, the decision was made to appoint a Roman Catholic bishop. This, however, was opposed by the Franciscans. The arguments of their delegate convinced the cardinals to postpone implementation of the decision, although it had already been agreed upon in principle. The arrival in 1846 of Samuel Gobat, the second Protestant bishop in Jerusalem, reawakened the issue of a Roman Catholic bishopric; on January 25, 1847, the decision to appoint a Latin patriarch was made. On July 23, an apostolic writ was issued, marking the establishment of the Latin patriarchate of Jerusalem.[74]

The Latin patriarchate was not welcomed by the other Christians of Jerusalem. We have already mentioned the opposition of the Franciscans, who regarded it as an affront to their 400-year reign as the sole representatives of the Roman Catholic Church in the country. The matter also aroused the suspicion of the Greek Orthodox and, as it turned out, not without cause. Catholic missionaries succeeded in winning over members of the Greek Orthodox community, thanks to their superior facilities for education, welfare and public health, and the support they enjoyed of the Great Powers. Also opposed were the autonomous Eastern Catholic communities, primarily the Greek Catholic Church, which had an Arab nationalist character, and which saw the renewal of the Latin patriarchate as an attempt to "Latinize" the Catholic Church in the East.

The establishment of the Latin patriarchate increased Catholic activity in Jerusalem. Williams (1849) writes that the Latin patriarch resided at first in St. Savior.[75] Later, he moved to another building, northeast ot the Jaffa Gate. Petermann (1853) says that the Latin patriarch, who lived in a new building

72   Seetzen, II, p. 12.
73   Taylor, pp. 332-345.
74   Medebielle, pp. 28-29.
75   Williams, I, Supplement, pp. 13-39; II, pp. 568-569.

The Latin Patriarchate in Jerusalem (Belloc, p. 120)

near the Jaffa Gate, had several Lazarite monks at his command. The Franciscans, fifty in number, sought to free themselves from his jurisdiction and to control Terra Sancta. Most of them, however, were uneducated Spanish and Italian friars who knew no Arabic despite their long residence in the country; they were therefore at a disadvantage.[76]

Strauss also relates that the relations between the new Latin patriarch and the Franciscans were far from good. He says the position of patriarch was filled by G. Valerga, a missionary well known for his travels in Persia and Armenia.[77] Scherer (1859) attributes the bad feeling to the fact that the Franciscans represented the policy of Rome, while the patriarch was an expression of France's desire for control. The Franciscans complained that the patriarch had reduced their income and assumed too much authority, disregarding their position as the representatives of Catholicism for hundreds of years.[78]

At the end of the 1850's, construction began on a new building for the Latin patriarchate. Pierotti (1859) writes that the old one, which belonged to the Franciscans, was to become a hospice. In that year, the foundations for the new building were laid in the northwestern sector of the city.[79] In the early 1860's, Damas reports that Patriarch Valerga, who had been appointed in 1846, was building a seminary in Beit Jala and a large building in Jerusalem.[80]

76   Petermann, I, pp. 217-218.
77   Strauss, pp. 241-243.
78   Scherer, pp. 177-179.
79   Pierotti, I, p. 162.
80   Damas, I, pp. 131-133.

Wilson's map of Jerusalem (1864-1865) shows no Latin patriarchate at all. On the other hand, Pierotti marks both the old building and the new one, under construction.[81] According to the 1876 Baedeker guide, the new quarters of the Latin patriarchate were built in 1864 by workers from Bethlehem, following a plan drawn up by the Patriarch Valerga. The building was said to contain an impressive library.[82]

Catholic Women's Orders; Education; The St. Louis Hospital

After the establishment of the Latin patriarchate, two women's societies began to function in the city: the Sisters of Zion, whom we mentioned briefly in our discussion of the Via Dolorosa in the Muslim Quarter, and the Sisters of St. Joseph. Both were active in education. French interest in the city also became stronger, culminating in the establishment of the St. Louis hospital.

Tobler mentions two Roman Catholic schools in 1846, one for girls and one for boys. According to reports from 1848, the girls' school was attended by Christian Arabs. Until 1845, the boys' school met in a dark room in the northern courtyard of St. Savior. In 1846, it moved to a building having a separate entrance.[83]

Dupuis writes that the Roman Catholics in Jerusalem ran two schools in the early 1850's: one for children, serving between two and three hundred pupils, and another, for Roman Catholic youths.[84] The former is, apparently, the school of the Franciscans, and the latter, the Roman Catholic seminary. Consul Finn says that, in 1853, the patriarch moved the Roman Catholic seminary from Jerusalem to Beit Jala.[85] According to Neumann, the Franciscans ran relatively good schools in all the Terra Sancta religious houses. The school in Jerusalem had 150 pupils who studied Arabic, arithmetic, geography and religion. The higher classes also studied Italian, French and literature. Particular emphasis was placed on Italian, which most of the local Roman Catholics knew well.[86]

Petermann (1853) writes that the Franciscan house also had a small hospital, run by four nurses.[87] Wortabet says there was a Catholic hospital in Jerusalem in the 1850's.[88] It seems that the two educational institutions of the Sisters of Zion and of the Sisters of St. Joseph, as well as the St. Louis hospital, were already in existence by 1855. At that time, Consul Finn says, the hospital received 12,000 francs a year (500 pounds sterling) from France, and the institutions of the Sisters of Zion and the Sisters of St. Joseph were given 3,000 francs (125 pounds sterling) each.[89]

Summarizing Catholic activity in the early 1860's, Pierotti says that this

81 Wilson, *Survey*, 1:2,500 map; Pierotti, plan 2.
82 Baedeker (1876), p. 216; (1973), p. 98.
83 Tobler, *Denkblätter*, pp. 438-441.
84 Dupuis, I, p. 120.
85 J. Finn, *Stirring Times*, II, p. 102.
86 Neumann, pp. 306-308.
87 Petermann, I, pp. 217-218.
88 Wortabet, II, p. 221.
89 J. Finn, *Stirring Times*, II, p. 397.

community had a boys' school; two girls' schools, run by the Sisters of St. Joseph and the Sisters of Zion; a seminary, which had moved to Beit Jala; the St. Louis hospital; three hospices (Casa Nova, the hospice of the Church of the flagellation, and the Austrian hospice); a printing press; a carpentry shop; a smithy and several almshouses.[90]

For a somewhat later period, probably the end of the 1860's, the Baedeker guide provides the following information:

> The most important Latin institution is the Franciscan Monastery of St. Salvator.... The building now contains an excellent printing-press, where even Arabic is printed (chiefly school-books). In the school attached to the monastery 170 boys are taught, the poorer being also boarded. The Latins also possess an Industrial School, a Hospital for both sexes (physician, Dr. Carpani), and two girls' schools, viz. that of the Sisters of Zion, for 120 pupils, and that of the Sisterhood of St. Joseph (12-14 in number), for 200 pupils, who are boarded, and some of them lodged also, in the institution.[91]

Catholic activity in Jerusalem continued into the second half of the nineteenth century, and became even more extensive. Additional orders began to operate in the city, and many Catholic institutions arose. This activity was especially noticeable outside the city walls, and thus will be dealt with in the second volume of this work.

The Mosques and the Muristan

In addition to the Greek Orthodox and Roman Catholics, the Christian Quarter also contained Copts and Ethiopians, with whom we shall deal later, when we discuss the Christian minority groups. Two other noteworthy features of the Christian Quarter were the mosques next to the Church of the Holy Sepulchre, and the large expanse of unoccupied land known as the Muristan.

Of the 'Omariyya mosque, Williams writes that it had once been part of the hospital of the Knights of St. John, and the site of the residence of Ṣalaḥ al-Din (Saladin) after he conquered Jerusalem. One of Ṣalaḥ al-Din's sons built the mosque in 1216. Williams indicates that the Christians found calls to prayer from its minaret particularly annoying, because of it close proximity to the Church of the Holy Sepulchre. It was destroyed in an earthquake in 1459 and rebuilt on the same foundations in 1465.[92] The second mosque, al-Khankeh, is also mentioned in the literature and maps of the nineteenth century, but without special note.

Another frequently mentioned region is the Muristan which, until the end of the 1860's, was full of ruins. Nineteenth-century literature abounds in descriptions of the various ruined churches in and around the area. In his explanatory notes to the British Admiralty Map, Williams provides details of the homes and churches in the Muristan.[93]

Mrs. Rogers writes in the 1850's that only three exterior walls were left of the Knights of St. John. Partitions now divided its interior into three sections, one of which was used as a tannery. In the others, one could see the skeletons of

90 Pierotti, I, pp. 227-279.
91 Baedeker (1876), p. 203; (1973), p. 37.
92 Williams, I, Supplement, p. 17.
93 *Loc. cit.*; Norov, I, p. 215.

donkeys and horses; the area was used as a garbage dump. Built in Norman style, probably in the eleventh century, it had been a resting place for pilgrims on their way to the Holy Sepulchre. Visiting the site again in 1859, Mrs. Rogers found its door locked. The property in front of it had been turned into a shop or warehouse for glass beads and bracelets made in Hebron.[94]

Scherer (late 1850's) describes the plans to build in the Muristan and the fighting over the acquisition of the land:

> The splendid hospice of the Johannitarians had collapsed and fallen into ruin. Until just a short while ago it was used as a slaughter-house and burial ground for animal carcasses. The whole area smelled as a result and it was quite unpleasant, especially since it was in the center of the city and the Church of the Holy Sepulchre was right nearby. At long last, however, the consulates saw to it that this nuisance was removed. The property itself is valuable, and different communities are battling over it. Some say it will go to the Russians because they do not yet have a central building suitable for their secular and ecclesiastical officials, and do not wish to be dependent upon the Greek patriarch.[95]

In the end, it was the Germans who acquired the place.

The German Center in the Muristan

In 1869, when the Prussian crown prince visited Jerusalem after participating in the festivities marking the opening of the Suez canal, the sultan made him a gift of the eastern half of the Muristan. (The western half belonged to the Greek patriarch.)[96] When the Germans dissolved their alliance with the Anglicans, they built a small church on this site. In the 1880's, they were already talking of establishing a Protestant center near the Church of the Holy Sepulchre. Money began to be collected for this purpose with the assistance of the German emperor, Wilhelm II, and the *Evangelische Jerusalems-Stiftung* (Jerusalem Fund) was established in his country. By 1889, a considerable sum had been amassed, and a German architect of repute was commissioned to design a new Protestant church and community center in the Muristan. The architect intended to incorporate remnants of the Crusader structures found in the area in the new building. The Gothic-style cruciform church was to have a dome and the highest tower in the Old City.[97] The cornerstone of the Church of the Redeemer, as it was called, was laid in 1893, and the church was consecrated on October 31, 1898 in a festive ceremony attended by Emperor Wilhelm and his wife, Augusta Victoria. According to one source, this church was established to serve as the nerve center of the German Protestant community throughout the Ottoman Empire.[98]

Many other sources discuss the German Church of the Redeemer, dwelling upon its unusual tower, embellishments, and ancient foundations, and the incorporation of elements from the church that had once stood there. Also stressed is the slow pace of construction, due to archaeological finds in the

94 Mrs. Rogers, pp. 26-27.
95 Scherer, pp. 185-186.
96 Baedeker (1912), p. 47.
97 Blyth, p. 116; Carmel, pp. 119-126; Luncz, *Jerusalem*, V, 1899, pp. 115-139.
98 Ilan, p. 18.

Johannitarian ruins in the Muristan (Wartensleben, p. 196)

course of the work, a factor which greatly increased building costs.[99] Some sources provide maps and sketches of the ancient churches in the Muristan before the construction of the new church.[100] They write that the street upon which the Church of the Redeemer stood was named for Prince Frederick Wilhelm, father of Emperor Wilhelm.[101]

The Muristan itself was square-shaped; it was surrounded by houses bordering David Street on the south, Christian Street on the west, the meat market on the east, and an alley leading to the Church of the Holy Sepulchre on the north. The houses within the Muristan also formed a square, with five alleys leading to the center, where there was an elegant fountain. Four of these alleys had gates which were locked at night, and whose keys were held by the clergy. The Prussian eagle was engraved on the lintels of the gates. The Muristan neighborhood was built in the German style, and served both residential and commerical purposes. Many gold and silversmiths opened shops there. Homes and shops alike there were larger, better appointed and more soundly built than those in the rest of the city.[102]

A few years after the church was completed, another building arose in the vacant lot. At first it was used as a hospice, then as a German Protestant archaeological institute and a Protestant school. The archaeological institute was founded in 1903 to provide a place for German Protestant theologians to pursue their study of the Holy Land and its antiquities.[103] The Protestant

99   *PEF QSt*, 1894, pp. 146, 261; 1898, p. 248; Kelman, photo, p. 22; Franklin, p. 161.
100 *PEF QSt*, 1901, pp. 51-53; 1902, pp. 42-56.
101 *Loc. cit.*
102 *Loc. cit.*
103 *PEF QSt*, 1904, p. 5.

Lutheran Church (*Deutsche Kaiserpaar*, frontispiece)

school was a branch of the Syrian orphanage; it consisted of three classes and a kindergarten, with a student population of between 160 and 240 children. In 1913-1914 the school was taken over by the *Evangelischer Verein für Jerusalem*.[104]

The Russian Church of Alexander

The Russians had owned property near the Church of the Holy Sepulchre even before the Germans did. Pierotti, who worked for the Ottoman authorities in Jerusalem, writes that the land was purchased in 1858 at his suggestion.[105] Russian sources confirm this, adding that the Russian consul bought it from a Coptic monk with the intention of building a consulate and a hospice large enough for a thousand pilgrims. The site was cleared in 1859; the excavations, in which Pierotti took part, revealed an important historical find: a corner of what was thought to be the Second Wall of Jerusalem. As a result, construction came to a halt. In 1860, the Russians abandoned the idea of building there altogether. Instead, as we shall see in our second volume, they began to build the Russian compound outside the Old City. When the French baron, De Vogüe, explored the site in 1862, he discovered an ancient gate and threshold. With the consent of the Russian consul, he continued excavating at his own expense, on the theory that this was the last gate through which Jesus had passed on his way to the crucifixion. In 1865, Charles Wilson arrived with the British expedition and found large, ancient paving stones on either side of the threshold. Other foreign explorers investigated the place, which was of great interest to Christians, but no activity was initiated by the Russian committee, ostensibly for lack of funds — to the chagrin of Russian intellectual and scientific circles.

237

104 Ilan, p. 44.
105 Pierotti, p. 33.

In the 1880's, the Imperial Pravoslav Society displayed an interest in the site, and began building on it in 1887. Archaeological finds were kept in a special museum on the northern side of the property. The threshold was encased in glass, and flanked by icons presented by the Czar. Above it a small church commemorating Alexander Nevsky was built. On the southern part of the property, there was a home for thirty persons who had devoted their lives to working in the Holy Land. The southwestern side was taken up by homes for employees of the Imperial Pravoslav Society: teachers, service staff and nurses, all of them sent specially from Russia. Construction terminated in 1890, after a hospice had also been built there, primarily for clergymen and high-ranking pilgrims.[106]

Zuta and Sukenik provide us with an apt summary of the Christian Quarter, although it dates from the beginning of the British Mandate:

> The quarter is full of old and new monasteries and churches belonging to the different Christian sects. The largest buildings are those of the Greeks and the Catholics, both French and Italian. The streets are narrow and uneven, but they are impressively clean.... To this very day, it is almost impossible for Jews to walk freely in the alley near the Church of the Holy Sepulchre. The church guards are Muslim. Inside the Christian Quarter is the Muristan, where the St. John hospital is located. The property was given to the government of Prussia by Sultan Abdul Aziz. When it was cleared, the remains of a church, houses, halls and stables were found. The church now on the site was built by the Germans on the foundations of the ancient one. Opposite this is a Russian hospice, where one can see the remains of ancient buildings from the time of Constantine, and the gates of an ancient wall extending from north to south. The continuation of these structures was discovered in the Coptic chapel near the Church of the Holy Sepulchre in 1907.[107]

106 Dmitrievskii, 1884, p. 12; Paleolog, pp. 12-20.
107 Zuta—Sukenik (1930), pp. 109-112 (translated from Hebrew).

Chapter Four:

THE EASTERN COMMUNITIES: COPTS, ETHIOPIANS, ARMENIANS AND SYRIANS; THE ARMENIAN QUARTER

The Copts

The third Christian group that settled near the Church of the Holy Sepulchre was the Coptic community, whose size we noted in our discussion of the Christian population. At the beginning of the century, Western travelers relate, the Copts had only one very poor monastery in Jerusalem, St. George. A little further away, in Deir al-Sultan, they owned a courtyard inhabited by priests and monks.[1] In addition, there was an extremely shabby Coptic chapel in the Church of the Holy Sepulchre.[2] Norov (1835) writes that the Coptic monastery was in a side building of the Church of the Holy Sepulchre, and was dedicated to the Patriarch Abraham. Elsewhere he mentions a small Coptic oratory, to the right of the courtyard before the church, which marked the spot where the Binding of Isaac took place, according to Coptic tradition. A rock on the floor decorated with various symbols was said to be the rock of sacrifice.[3]

Around the middle of the nineteenth century, Ritter says that the Copts, like their friends the Ethiopians who also opposed the Greek Church, were on good terms with the rich, socially prestigious Armenians. These last were the only ones who could afford to grant the Copts aid and protection. The Copts' major piece of property, he says, was the monastery on the eastern side of the Church of the Holy Sepulchre. It was headed by a married man, as were all other Egyptian monasteries. It was also used as a hospice for pilgrims, but these were few and far between.[4]

In 1843, J. Wilson repeats that the Copts owned the Deir al-Sultan monastery, which was an adjunct to the Church of the Holy Sepulchre, as well as another small monastery, St. George, near the Pool of Hezekiah. When Muḥammad 'Ali occupied the country, the Copts were allowed to erect a new building near St. George. They were forced to leave it, however, when Muḥammad's forces pulled out of Jerusalem. On the whole, the Copts were a tiny sect, and few of their co-religionists from abroad came to visit them. They

239

1   Seetzen, II, p. 20.
2   Skinner, I, p. 210.
3   Norov, I, pp. 147-153.
4   Ritter, IV, pp. 202-203.

also hosted Ethiopian pilgrims, who had ties with the Coptic Church.[5]

Robinson mentions the new building established by the Copts in the days of Muḥammad 'Ali. In 1838, Robinson says a Coptic structure was being built north of the Pool of Hezekiah. During another visit, in 1852, he writes as follows:

> The Copts have a smaller convent of St. George on the west of the pool of Hezekiah; adjacent to which, during the Egyptian rule, they began to build a larger convent or rather Khan, which was abandoned by them when Ibrahim Pasha withdrew from the country, and has since been used as barracks by the government.[6]

Williams provides a similar account of the Coptic house.[7] Petermann (1853) says that the northern side of the Pool of Hezekiah was the back wall of the Coptic monastery. (He adds that its eastern side served as the wall of the only decent guest-house in the region, while the other two sides formed the walls of private homes.)[8]

Williams (1849) claims that the Coptic community lived off the rent of six small houses.[9] According to Petermann (1853), there were very few Copts in the city, most of them clerics who lived in their monastery all year long. For the early 1860's, Pierotti writes that the Copts ran a hospice and had homes for members of their community.[10]

The 1876 Baedeker guide reports that there were several rooms for pilgrims in the Coptic monastery, and that the key of the cistern of St. Helena was kept there. The water in this cistern was inferior in quality, it adds, but was used nonetheless by poor Roman Catholics.[11] A later edition of the guide (1912) says that, in 1907, remains of the atrium of Constantine's basilica were found in the cellar of the Coptic hospice. Its gates and threshold were clearly visible.[12]

At the beginning of the British Mandate, Press notes that the Coptic community in Jerusalem numbered 100 souls, and that it owned two monasteries in the Old City.[13]

The Ethiopians

Seetzen writes that, in 1806, the Ethiopians shared Deir al-Sultan with the Copts and seemed quite poor. There were only ten Ethiopian monks and three nuns, all of whom dressed in shabby clothing. The rooms of Deir al-Sultan were built around a paved courtyard. In its center was the dome of the Chapel of the Holy Cross. The Ethiopians had their own chapel, small and unattractive. Their superior was an old man who was ill at the time of Seetzen's visit. The Ethiopians suffered greatly from the cold in Jerusalem, and some of them had died during their year-long journey from Ethiopia.[14] Strauss (1845)

5   J. Wilson, I, pp. 452-453.
6   Robinson, *Later Biblical Researches*, p. 198.
7   Williams, I, Supplement, p. 19.
11 Baedeker (1876), pp. 202-203; (1973), pp. 36-37.
12 Baedeker (1912), pp. 79-80.
13 Press, *Travel Handbook,* p. 133.
14 Seetzen, II, pp. 10, 274.

8   Petermann, I, pp. 204-206.
9   Williams, II, p. 564.
10 Pierotti, pp. 277-279.

states that the Ethiopians were influenced by other Christian sects. They were similar to their Coptic neighbors in religious outlook. The Ethiopian Church was subordinate to the Coptic patriarch in Cairo, but it had its own monastery in Jerusalem and suffered no lack of Ethiopian pilgrims. Because of the great distance from their homeland, Ethiopian pilgrims stayed in Jerusalem an entire year.[15] As we said above, the Ethiopians tried to win the favor of the Armenians in their battle against the Greek Orthodox, the strongest sect in the city.[16]

When the Protestants made their appearance in Jerusalem, they expressed interest in the Ethiopian community there. Strauss, a Protestant, says that the "Abuna" in Ethiopia had asked Bishop Gobat to take chief responsibility for the Ethiopian monastery. Bible classes were arranged and ties established with the Mission, making pilgrimages from Ethiopia beneficial to the Protestant Church as a whole.[17] Petermann (1853) also reports that the Ethiopians had placed themselves in the hands of Bishop Gobat. In the past, they had enjoyed many privileges in Jerusalem, such as having their own chapels in the Church of the Holy Sepulchre and running a large monastery. The plague, however, brought all this to an end. The Armenians burned all the Ethiopians' books for fear the plague had infected them, too, and then proceeded to occupy the Ethiopian holy places.[18]

Of the 1860's, Charles Wilson says that the Ethiopian community consisted of seven priests and seventy laymen who lived in the worst poverty imaginable. He lays most of the blame on the Copts, who stole everything from them, even their chapel near the western end of the Church of the Holy Sepulchre.[19] The Baedeker guide of 1876 notes that the Ethiopians of Jerusalem had a monastery and a community of seventy-five souls. Elsewhere, it reports that most of them lived in miserable shacks southeast of their church, which was connected by a passage to the Church of the Holy Sepulchre.[20] At the end of the century, important developments took place with regard to this community, but these will be discussed in the next volume.

The Syrians; the Maronites

The property of the Syrian Christians of early nineteenth-century Jerusalem was outside the Christian Quarter: namely, the Church of St. Mark, located between the Jewish and Armenian Quarters.[21]

J. Wilson (1843) points out that the Syrians had a very ancient monastery, allegedly the site of the home of St. Mark. He also says that the land upon which the new Anglican Christ Church was built had originally belonged to them.[21*] Williams (1840's) writes that the Syrians' ancient monastery on "Mount Zion" inside the Old City was the only monastery still in their

15   Strauss, p. 239.
16   Ritter, IV, pp. 202-203; Norov, I, p. 192.
17   Strauss, p. 239.
18   Petermann, I, p. 226; Marston, pp. 187-188.
19   Ch. Wilson, *Survey*, p. 53.
20   Baedeker (1876), pp. 203, 263; (1973), pp. 37, 87.
21   Norov, I, pp. 214-215.
21* J. Wilson, I, p. 452.

possession, of the several once owned by them.[22] In the explanations to his map, Williams writes that two places in Jerusalem were associated with the Syrians. The first was the Church of St. James (No. 17 on the map). The Turks and the *waqf* of the Haram had confiscated this land and built a mosque on it, and the Protestants had established Christ Church nearby. The second was the Syrian Convent of St. Mark (No. 20 on the map). Williams claims this was one of the oldest monasteries in Jerusalem, and was also held sacred by Christians of other denominations. St. Mark's was the seat of the Syrian bishopric, and had many traditions connected with it, such as its being the site of the Virgin Mary's baptism.[23]

Ritter writes that, in 1840's, the Syrian Christians or Jacobites of Jerusalem were left with only one small church and the Convent of St. Mark; since there were no longer members of this sect in the city, this property was transferred to the Ethiopian monastery.[24] Tobler says the Syrian religious house had only one monk living in it in 1846.[25] According to Petermann (1853), there were important Syriac manuscripts in the monastery. Some of the valuable ones had been sold to the former Prussian consul of Jerusalem by the Syrian bishop. However, when the consul found out that the bishop had joined the Maronite sect and had sold them illegally, he returned them to the Syrians. Ever since then, the Prussian consul had been held in esteem by the Syrian clergy. Petermann goes on to say that the Syrian community consisted of one family, two priests and a bishop, all of whom lived in the monastery. They claimed that their church, which had been renovated in 1848, was the oldest one in Jerusalem. It was dedicated to St. James (St. Jacob). Syrian monks wore a black tarbush with a white skull-cap underneath it and another black scarf over it, which was concealed by their cassock. They prayed seven times a day, four times between midnight and noon, and three times between noon and midnight. Four times a day, they prayed in their cells, and three times, in the church.[26] In 1856, another source reports that the Syrian monastery was able to accommodate 450 to 500 worshippers with ease. The remains of an ancient church had been discovered there some years before.[27] At the beginning of the British Mandate, Press relates that the Syrians in the Old City were Syrian Jacobites, who owned one church, and were twenty in number.[28]

Another small Christian sect, to which we will devote only a few words, was the Maronite community. It is difficult to ascertain from nineteenth-century literature whether this community actually existed in the city at that time. Stewart (1854) says that, like the Copts and Jacobites, the Maronites had several monasteries in Jerusalem. However, the sect was very small and had no influence on the surrounding population.[29] Stewart may have erred as to the existence of this community at the time of his visit, as other sources make no mention of it. At any rate, if there were such a community, it was extremely small.

22   Williams, II, pp. 561-562
23   Williams, I, Supplement, pp. 21-23.
24   Ritter, IV, p. 201.
25   Tobler, *Topographie*, I, pp. 267-279.

26   Petermann, I, p. 226.
27   Ritchie, p. 222.
28   Press, *Travel Handbook*, p. 133.
29   Stewart, p. 292.

The Armenian Quarter; its Church and Convent

The Armenians, whose neighborhood we will now consider, constituted the third largest Christian community in nineteenth-century Jerusalem.

The term "Armenian Quarter" can be interpreted in either a narrow or a broad sense. Tobler chooses the latter, dividing Jerusalem into four quarters: the Armenian and Christian Quarters in the west, and the Jewish and Muslim Quarters in the east. He says the Armenian Quarter was on "Mount Zion" within the Old City, in the southwestern part of town. It bordered David Street on the north, the city wall on the west and south, and the Jewish Quarter on the east. According to Tobler, the Armenian Quarter included the Citadel of David and the new barracks nearby. The neighborhood derived its name from the two Armenian churches within its limits and from the Armenian community which constituted the majority of its residents. Tobler emphasizes that the location of the Armenian Quarter was considered to be the most beautiful and salubrious in Jerusalem, and that its history was closely linked to that of the church and convent of St. James. The Armenians chose to settle in the vicinity of their church, and thus created the Armenian Quarter. Christian sources, however, said that the quarter received its present name only after 1806 and that even then, it was used only in connection with the street of the Armenian convent.[30]

In the more restricted sense, the term "Armenian Quarter" applies only to part of the area of which Tobler speaks: the walled-in area that constitutes a largely independent unit with its own network of public services. The inner wall has gates which can seal off the neighborhood from the rest of the city. These gates are locked at night even today, making the Armenian Quarter the most clearly defined and compact neighborhood in the Old City.

The most important structure in the Armenian Quarter was the Convent and Church of St. James. Nineteenth-century travelers and explorers are united in their praise of its richness and beauty.[31] In 1806, Seetzen writes that the Armenian convent and patriarchal church near the Citadel were situated in more open surroundings than the other churches and convents in the city. The spacious grounds surrounded rooms sufficient for a large number of pilgrims. Seetzen says that the religious house itself was irregular in shape, and the church, the most beautiful in Jerusalem. Its tiled floor was carpeted, and golden ornaments were abundant. Most of the lamps were made of silver, and paintings and decorations were everywhere. The ceremonial dress of the priests was elaborate and very costly, and the processions they held were extremely rich and varied. If one realized that all this wealth—the precious stones, the gold and the silver—came from members of the community, it became obvious that the Armenians were skillful and prosperous businessmen.[32]

Turner (1815) also mentions the fact that the Armenians engaged in commerce. Their convent was the richest and largest in Jerusalem, and was

---

30 Tobler, *Denkblätter*, pp. 121-126; *Topographie*, pp. 196-197. An important book about the Armenian community of Greater Syria, of which the Jerusalem community is a part, has been published by A.K. Sanjian (see Bibliography).

31 See, e.g., Whaley, p. 210.

32 Seetzen, II, pp. 13-14.

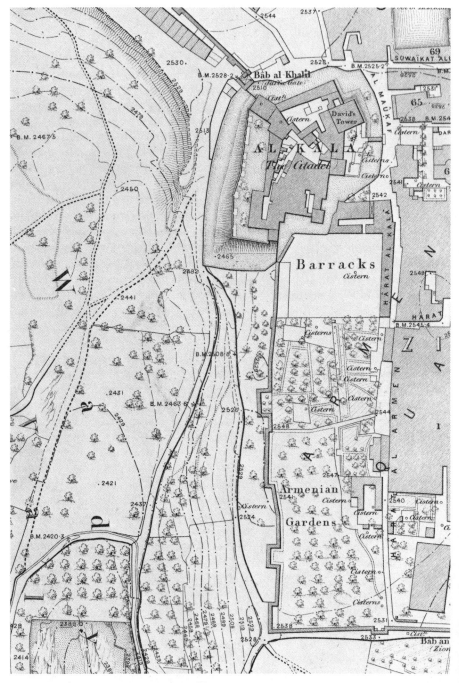

Armenian Quarter on Wilson's map — 1865 (Ch. Wilson, *Survey*, 1:2,500 map)

244

reported to contain 350 rooms. Pilgrims who were too poor to pay for lodgings crowded the alleyways. Turner describes the church interior in detail, praising its spaciousness and beauty.[33] Skinner (1830's) writes that the Armenian convent was then hosting 300 Armenian pilgrims, many of them children.[34] Paxton (also in the 1830's) says the Armenians' large, well-maintained convent was used to accommodate pilgrims but that, during their stay, they were exposed to all kinds of superstitions about the holy places, and this hindered the work of the missionaries.[35] Norov (mid-1830's) reports that the Armenian convent was built on the site where St. James had been tortured to death. One of the first churches in the Holy Land was located here. It was richly decorated in oriental style, with blue-tiled walls and carpeted floors. Gold and silver lamps shone everywhere. In one of the chapels, he says, one could see the place where St. James had died. The spacious courtyard of the convent was surrounded by arches, and there were 700 small rooms always available to pilgrims. The monastery also owned several minor buildings used to accommodate the large caravans that often came there.[36]

Bartlett has this to say about the Armenian convent in 1842:

> The only building in Jerusalem that presents any considerable appearance of comfort; the compactly-built façade, the neatly paved street in front, over-shadowed by noble trees, and the portly and highly respectable looking monks about its doorway, are all redolent of ease, and wealth, and cleanliness — rare in the city of Jerusalem.... The church of St. James, connected with this convent, is considered by travellers as one of the most sumptuous in the East, enriched by the liberality of wealthy Armenian pilgrims.[37]

J. Wilson (1843) writes that the monastery had room for 2,000 to 3,000 pilgrims.[38] Other sources from the 1840's and 1850's claim that the numerous buildings of the Armenian convent could house up to 4,000 persons at Eastertime. The convent had the most beautiful gardens in the city, full of shady trees. In its grounds was the Church of St. James, on the site where the saint had been put to death. The enormous dome of the church was supported by four massive, square pillars, and the church itself was the most ornate in the city. Part of its floor was covered with mosaics, and there were many gold-framed paintings and mother-of-pearl ornaments.[39]

Relating to 1846, Tobler writes that the convent of the Armenian patriarch was inhabited by more than one hundred clerics, including five bishops. It was a rich convent, perhaps the wealthiest in the Holy Land and the entire Levant.[40] In 1857, Barclay describes it as one of the largest institutions in the city. It extended over many acres of land, and could host 8,000 pilgrims.[41] According to Neumann, the Armenian patriarch was highly respected in Jerusalem. The convent had 120 monks, and about a thousand rooms where

33   Turner, II, pp. 163, 187-188.
34   Skinner, I, p. 249.
35   Paxton, p. 121.
39   Strauss, pp. 204-205; Schulz, pp. 134-135; Conder, *Tent Work*, p. 160; Scherer, p. 194.
40   Tobler, *Topographie*, I, pp. 267-279.
41   Barclay, p. 445; Sanjian, pp. 204-207.

36   Norov, I, pp. 191-192.
37   Bartlett, *Walks*, p. 77.
38   J. Wilson, I, p. 452.

Armenian monks in Jerusalem (Hedin, p. 179)

close to 4,000 pilgrims could stay. Most of the permanent residents engaged in commerce, or worked as clerks in the consulates.[42]

Such praise for the Armenians and the Armenian Quarter is also balanced by criticism. Of 1876, Orelli writes that the Armenian church was one of the strangest in the city. Instead of bells, it used a primitive instrument to call believers to prayer: a nine-foot board with a piece of metal on one end which produced a non-melodious but far-reaching sound when struck. The Armenian church, he says, was one of Jerusalem's wealthiest ecclesiastical institutions, and this contrasted sharply with the poverty of those who came to pray there.[43]

Williams (1849) writes that the Armenian monastery had a beautiful library, and had once belonged to the Georgians.[44] Another source, from the end of the century, also reports that the Armenians had bought their church from the Georgians, who could not afford to pay the taxes demanded by the Turkish authorities. The same source writes that the Armenian patriarch of the Holy Land and Cyprus lived in the church.[45]

The Armenian community seems to have taken root in the area in the Middle Ages. Petermann (1853) says one part of the church was established by Hethom II, the king of the Armenians, whose son was buried there. A pillar in the

246

42   Neumann, pp. 276-280, 303-306.
43   Orelli, pp. 109-110.
44   Williams, II, pp. 559-560; I, Supplement, I, pp. 23-24.
45   Vincent—Lee—Bain, p. 149.

Armenian Patriarchate and entrance to Convent of St. James (Barclay, p. 445)

entrance hall bore the burial inscription of an Armenian bishop who had died in 1238.[46]

New Developments; Building Activity and Education

From the 1840's onward, the Armenian community began to expand its building activities. Tobler (mid-1840's) writes that the convent had its own mill and bakery. The mill had been operated by animal power until 1843, when a windmill was built at the nunnery of Deir Zeituny. By 1846, however, it was no longer working, and only its tower was left.[47] Other sources report that two new enterprises were opened near the Zion Gate in the middle of the nineteenth century. One, a flour mill that appears opposite the Zion Gate on the 1857 Van de Velde map, did not operate for very long.[48] The second, a ceramics factory, was north of the lepers' colony. Williams marks it on the British Admiralty map (No. 24), noting that it was located well, because the valley of Hinnom just outside the Zion gate contained two layers of clay appropriate for ceramics.[49] Petermann (1853) makes explicit mention of a new patriarchate building, which seems to have been built in the Armenian Quarter in the 1840's.[50]

Progress was also made in the field of education. As early as 1846, Tobler mentions an Armenian school for boys and girls slightly north of the convent of St. James. The schooling it provided was not on a very high level but, at least, the Armenians, unlike other sects, educated their girls as well.[51] Charles Wilson (1860's) writes that a new boarding school had just been built in the Armenian neighborhood, and that it was also used to lodge pilgrims.[52]

46 Petermann, I, p. 221; Sanjian, pp. 11-13, 95-101.
47 Tobler, *Topographie*, I, p. 352.
48 Tobler, *Planographie*, map.
49 Williams, I, Supplement, p. 24.
50 Petermann, I, pp. 211-221.
51 J. Finn, *Stirring Times*, II, pp. 101-105.
52 Ch. Wilson, *Survey*, p. 59.

According to Luncz, the Armenians ran a school for boys and a school for girls, as well as a teachers' seminary (with boarding facilities) established in 1866.[53] Neumann writes that the Armenian school was attended by eighty boys, who studied in Armenian and Arabic. There was also a seminary there, he adds. Elsewhere, Neumann comments that the colloquial language of the Armenians was Arabic, while Armenian was spoken only by the educated.[54] The Armenians say that the theological seminary still located in the Armenian Quarter today was established in 1843, and that the priests ordained there are still sent to administer religious, social and cultural activities in Armenian communities all over the world.

Another important cultural institution in the Armenian Quarter was the printing press, still in existence today. Local residents say it was founded in 1833, and was the first printing press in Jerusalem. In 1853, Petermann relates that the Armenian religious house had a printing press that had already published outstanding works in Armenian and Turkish.[55]

Summing up the state of the community in the 1860's, Pierotti says that the Armenians had a seminary; a printing press; a girls' school; a boys' school; an excellent hospice for pilgrims; and almshouses for the poor.[56] In 1876, the Baedeker guide records that the large Armenian monastery was inhabited by 180 monks and had room for a thousand pilgrims. In it were a printing press; a seminary with forty students; a small museum; and a photographic studio.[57] In 1875, Liévin says that the Armenians also had a hospital for pilgrims.[58]

At the end of the nineteenth century, the Armenians began to build both inside and outside the Old City. The PEF QSt of 1887 relates that the new shops south of the Jewish Quarter and east of the Zion Gate were built by the Armenian convent as well as by Muslims.[59] In 1898, the periodical states that a guardhouse had been built forty years earlier in the wall near the Armenian Quarter, slightly east of the Zion Gate. Over the years, it had fallen into ruin, but was repaired recently and now used as it had been formerly.[60] In 1901, the PEF QSt reports that the Armenian convent had purchased land north of the northeast corner of the city at Burj Laqlaq, (the "Stork Tower") and intended to carry out excavations there.[61] In the second volume of this work, we will discuss the building activities of the Armenians outside the ancient walls, especially those outside the Jaffa Gate.

Other Armenian Sites; Summary

Aside from the central convent and large church of the Armenians, European visitors describe other sites belonging to the community. Seetzen (1806) mentions two convents: the large Convent of St. James for monks, and the smaller Deir Zeituny for nuns. (To this day, special olive trees grow in the courtyard of Deir Zeituny, giving the convent its name.)[62]

53 Luncz, *Jerusalem*, II, pp. 88-89.
54 Neumann, pp. 217-218
55 Petermann, I, pp. 219-233; Sanjian, pp. 78-87.
56 Pierotti, I, pp. 277-279.
57 Baedeker (1876), p. 162; (1973), p. 36.
58 Liévin (1875), p. 110.
59 *PEF QSt*, 1897, p. 241.
60 *Ibid.*, 1898, p. 82.
61 *Ibid.*, 1901, p. 3.
62 Seetzen, II, p. 20.

Turner (1815) writes that alongside the Armenian church was the site of the house of the high priest Annas, marked by an olive tree surrounded by a fence. Near it was another Armenian church, a small room which was painted blue and richly decorated.[63] According to Norov (1835), this church was called the Church of the Holy Angels. He, too, mentions an olive tree surrounded by a fence, which protruded from one of the walls. This was said to be the tree to which Jesus was tied when he was taken prisoner. The church was not very large, but was quite beautiful. As in the huge Church of St. James and other Armenian churches, he adds, the walls were covered with tiles.[64]

According to the Baedeker guide, Deir Zeituny was inhabited by thirty nuns.[65] The PEF QSt says that it was located east of the large Convent of St. James, about 100 meters north of the Zion Gate. Not many people visited it because the alley leading to it was hidden between buildings. The church was also known as the Church of the Olive Tree.[66] The Armenians also owned an ancient church on Mount Zion, outside the Old City walls, to which nineteenth-century sources refer as the House of Caiaphas. We will discuss this church in the second volume.

Apart from the three holy places controlled by the Armenians inside and around the Armenian Quarter, they also had a foothold in other parts of nineteenth-century Jerusalem. As we said before, they owned certain parts of the Church of the Holy Sepulchre. Contemporary sources also relate that the Armenians celebrated mass in the Church of Mary in Gethsemane and in the Church of the Ascension on the Mount of Olives. Important ceremonies were conducted by the patriarch himself, with the participation of the entire Armenian clergy in elaborate dress. Some sources also point out that the Syrian Jacobites, the Ethiopians and the Copts often took part in the Armenians' ceremonies.[67]

At the beginning of the British Mandate, Press and Zuta—Sukenik offer a detailed account of the contemporary Armenian community and its quarter. They point out that part of the wall around the Armenian Quarter was made of small square stones laid one on top of the other, without plaster. In the days of the Turks, the Armenians found it difficult to obtain a permit to build a wall, and circumvented the restrictions by using no binding material at all.[68]

The Armenians, the third largest Christian sect in Jerusalem during the first half of the nineteenth century, were very wealthy, with most of them being successful businessmen and socially prominent. They had the most beautiful monastery and the richest church in the city, which was no less important in their eyes than the Church of the Holy Sepulchre. The grounds of the Armenian religious house and the neighborhood as a whole were covered with lovely greenery, and the head of the community was an independent leader, reigning over his community in all of the Holy Land and Cyprus.[69]

63   Turner, II, pp. 187-188.
64   Norov, I, p. 198.
65   Baedeker (1876), p. 162; (1973), p. 36.
66   *PEF QSt*, 1895, pp. 249-252.

67   Petermann, I, pp. 219-223.
68   Zuta—Sukenik (1930), pp. 108-109.
69   Ritter, IV, p. 199.

Chapter Five:
THE PROTESTANT COMMUNITIES: INSTITUTIONS AND MISSIONARY ACTIVITIES

The Penetration of Protestants into Jerusalem

At the beginning of the nineteenth century, the Protestants had no foothold in Jerusalem at all. However, as years passed, they became very active; eventually, they became the most dynamic Christian group in Jerusalem.[1]

The Protestants first began to penetrate into Jerusalem in the early 1820's, but there was almost no missionary activity at that time. The Protestants in the Ottoman Empire were in a difficult position, because their faith was not recognized officially and they had no legal status. Their first planned activity in Jerusalem began only in the early 1830's under Egyptian rule, when the Protestant missionaries of the American Board of Commissioners for Foreign Missions and those of the London Society for Promoting Christianity amongst the Jews established themselves in the city.[2]

The Protestants in Jerusalem still faced obstacles in the 1830's, especially at the beginning of the decade. However, when Ibrahim Pasha assumed power, the Protestant Church succeeded in making considerable headway in the Holy Land. Its first attempts to obtain a permit for building permanent institutions in Jerusalem and elsewhere in the 1820's had failed, because of the opposition of the district governors and their representatives. Under Ibrahim Pasha, the Protestants were allowed not only to pursue intensive religious activities but also to build and run various educational institutions. As it was against the law to convert Muslims, their missionaries concentrated on other Christian sects and on the Jews. Thus, the first Protestant congregations in the Holy Land included former members of the Greek Orthodox and Jewish communities. Rather than diminishing Protestant activity, the return of the Turks in the 1840's intensified it. Basili writes that the expulsion of the Egyptians from the Holy Land unlocked the doors for the missionaries, who surged forth to conquer the country by religious, cultural and philanthropic means.[3] The

250

---

1   On Protestant activity in Jerusalem, see Halsted; Tibawi, *British Interests*, pp. 1-27; *American Interests*, pp. 8-30; Colbi, pp. 85-94; Vereté.
2   Murray, (1875), p. 123; Olin, II, pp. 313-315; Hyamson, II, p. 403.
3   Assaf, *History*, II, p. 252; Basili, pp. 220-221.

Ottoman regime had been assisted by Britain and Prussia, both of them leading Protestant powers, in its efforts to drive out Muḥammad ʿAli. Protestant activity in Jerusalem was facilitated by negotiations between the King Friedrich Wilhelm IV of Prussia, the Queen of England, and the Archbishop of Canterbury. These negotiations resulted in the establishment of a joint Protestant bishopric in Jerusalem. In order to avoid a conflict of authority with other Christian sects, this bishopric was headed by a "bishop *in* Jerusalem" rather than a "bishop *of* Jerusalem."

The Protestant Bishopric and the Activity of the American Protestants

Nineteenth-century travelers offer many accounts of the establishment of the Protestant bishopric in Jerusalem. They write that, after the American Presbyterians had become interested in the Holy Land and had founded an aid center in Jerusalem for eastern Christians, Protestant activity in the city expanded greatly. With the expulsion of Muḥammad ʿAli, a joint bishopric of the Anglican and the Prussian Protestant churches was established, in order to allay competition between them and to increase the prestige of the two Protestant powers.

The first Protestant bishop, appointed in 1841, was Dr. Alexander, who was a Prussian-Jewish convert. He died after four years in office, and was succeeded in 1846 by Samuel Gobat.[4] Gobat served as bishop for thirty-three years until his death in 1879. His activities made a considerable impression on life on Jerusalem.

The joint Protestant bishopric was maintained until 1887, although the different factions had begun to manifest conflicting interests. Arguments broke out between the Germans and the Anglicans, and the Americans decreased their activity, moving their center to Beirut.[5] During his second visit to the city in 1852, Robinson noticed that the American missionary community had almost ceased to exist. The missionaries who had hosted him in 1838 left Jerusalem in 1843; the only Americans left were Dr. Barclay and his family.[6] There is still an American Protestant cemetery on Mount Zion dating from that time; it should be distinguished from the general Protestant cemetery, established later on the western slope of Mount Zion. This site is marked on the British Admiralty Map.[7]

Disputes Between the German and Anglican Protestants; the Dissolution of the Joint Bishopric

The relations between German and Anglican Protestants are discussed by a number of nineteenth-century travelers. Schulz (1851) complains that the Anglican community had taken over the Protestant Church in Jerusalem

---

4   Bovet, pp. 248-252. On Gobat see *Samuel Gobat...*

5   On American missionary activity among the Arabs see Grabill, pp. 3-34.

6   Robinson, *Later Biblical Researches*, p. 164.

7   Williams, Admiralty Map, no. 56. On American missionaries and scholars living in Jerusalem, see also Grabill, pp. 38-39.

because there were more Anglicans than Germans. In his opinion, the Anglican element would eventually overshadow the German element, especially since increasing numbers of Protestants were speaking English. By way of example, he cites the Protestant Mission school, where German-speaking, Polish-Jewish converts were taught English and gradually forgot their German. Despite the fact that most of the missionary and teaching posts were suited to and filled by Germans, he adds, the German missionaries themselves were attracted to the Anglican Church and, as time went by, became Anglicans.[8]

Strauss also emphasizes the differences between the Anglicans and the Germans. Most of the active missionaries in Jerusalem were German, as were many of the Jewish converts. However, all of them belonged officially to the Anglican Church and to Anglican missionary societies, and had no intention of leaving them. While commending the fact that the German Evangelical Church had joined forces with the Anglican Church, Strauss insists on the importance of enhancing the status of the German institutions too. More than 50,000 taler had been collected in Germany to establish German institutions in Jerusalem, and a Prussian consul, Dr. Schultz, had been appointed. A German hospice had been founded so that German pilgrims would not be attracted by other churches. There were many Germans all over the country, most of them craftsmen in great demand because of their fine work. Nevertheless, Strauss claims the German Church did not exhibit enough concern for the spiritual and religious well-being of these people. He adds that use of the German language was quite widespread in the Holy Land and Jerusalem, not least because many Jews spoke German.[9]

Orelli praises the special standing of the Protestant Church in the 1870's, in relation to the other Christian churches. It did not participate in the interchurch feuding, and could act as a peacemaker. For example, the Protestant Church owned no part of the Church of the Holy Sepulchre. The resultant neutrality gained it the respect of the other sects, while the simplicity of the Protestant prayer service served as a protest against the excesses of the other churches. Orelli thought it was a good idea to unite the Protestants of Jerusalem under one bishop, as eastern peoples with an inclination towards Protestantism could appreciate having a single bishop and a single liturgy. Nevertheless, relations between the Germans and Anglicans could stand much improvement.[10] Orelli was not to see this wish fulfilled: the joint bishopric was dissolved in 1887, as we have noted.

The activity of the Protestants in Jerusalem may be divided into three periods: the interval up to the joint bishopric or, rather, up to the appointment of Samuel Gobat; the joint bishopric, mainly the period of Gobat's office; and the years that followed. Protestant activity was important largely because of the response it evoked from the other communities. In our discussion of the other Christian sects, we noted that many of their educational and medical enterprises were reactions to Protestant missionary activity. Our discussion later on of the Jewish community will also touch on its response to Protestant endeavors.

252

8   Schulz, pp. 119-121.   9   Strauss, pp. 255-273.   10   Orelli, pp. 197-198.

Christ Church; the Homes of the British Consul and the Protestant Bishop

The building that served as the first Protestant center in Jerusalem was Christ Church; it can be seen today opposite the entrance to the Citadel of David. Travelers write that the foundations of this church were laid in 1841, and that building was completed only in 1848; the consecration was held on January 21, 1849. Building materials had been brought from the quarry near the village of 'Anata. Although the church was not large, was simply designed and had no tower, it was quite attractive and well-built. It was close to Gothic in its style, and was built in the shape of a cross of white limestone.[11] The famous architect, Schick, writes that builders were brought over specially from Malta and Great Britain, and that they taught their trade to local residents.[12] In a certain sense this building may be seen as the first large, modern structure to be built in modern Jerusalem.

Construction of Christ Church extended over a long period of time, because antiquities were discovered while digging for the foundations was in progress. These included an ancient aqueduct found at a depth of twenty to forty feet. As a result, all building activities were brought to a halt by special Turkish decree. The aqueduct that was discovered might perhaps have been connected to the conduit or drainage canal in the courtyard of Barclay's home near the church; PEF explorers thought the latter might have been part of the aqueduct mentioned by Mujir al-Din, that ran from the Citadel to the Gate of the Chain.[13] Schulz says that the church was erected as the private chapel of the British consul, because that was the only way in which the Turks would allow it to be built. He also deplores the fact that the nearby home of the British consul, which was made of the same stone, tended to lessen the effect of the church.[14] Schulz informs us that the ceiling was paneled with smooth brown wood, and that the benches were made of the same material. The interior decoration, he says, was English in style. In front of the church, there was a spacious courtyard surrounded by a wall with two gates. The building was erected by the London Society for Promoting Christianity amongst the Jews (known briefly as the "London Jews Society"), at a cost of some 20,000 pounds sterling. Morning prayers were conducted in English, and afternoon prayers in German. More people took part in the English service, because the community had a large number of English-speakers.[15]

Williams, who marks the church on the British Admiralty Map (No. 18), describes it as the "church and courtyard of the London Jews Society." It was located on land that had once belonged to the Syrians, and was called both the Anglican Church of St. James and Christ Church.[16] Stewart (1854) also says that the Anglican church was the property of the London Jews Society and,

11 Strauss, pp. 244-255; Woodcook, pp. 123-124; Bovet, p. 221.
12 Schick, *ZDPV*, XVII (1894-95), p. 266.
13 Warren—Conder, *Jerusalem*, p. 271.
14 Schulz, pp. 93-94; Bovet, p. 221; Woodcook, pp. 123-124; Halsted (p. 163) cites a translation of the *firman* regarding the construction of Christ Church.
15 Schulz, pp. 93-94.
16 Williams, I, Supplement, p. 22.

253

Christ Church (Geikie, p. 489)

along with the nearby home of the British consul, operated under the British flag.

In 1898, the PEF QSt reports the following:

> The Rev. A.H. Kelk, Minister of Christ Church and leader of the London Mission to the Jews, has had a set of tubular bells put up on Christ Church, which hitherto had only one small bell, not on the church itself but on one of the neighbouring buildings. This bell was put up in the year 1854, when the Moslems were not prepared to hear the bells, and with a little one on the Church of the Holy Sepulchre, was the very first bell in Jerusalem. It has, however, been followed by many, some of them large. Last Christmas, a set of three bells was also put up on the tower of the new German Church of the Redeemer, and I heard their voice first on Easter Day. People are being taught to ring them, so that when the Emperor comes they may be able to do it well.[17]

Williams marks the home of the British consul on the British Admiralty Map (No. 16), and points out that part of it had been built by Consul Young. When he returned to England, he transferred the ownership rights to the Prussian government.[18] It seems that the British consul continued to reside there for a certain period of time, and then moved to the vicinity of the Damascus Gate (see the discussion of the Muslim Quarter, p. 180).

The residence of the Protestant bishop did not adjoin the church, but was on David Street, near the Pool of Hezekiah. The bishop was escorted from it to church by two *kawasses*.[19] His residence is marked on Williams' map, too (No.

254

17 *PEF QSt*, 1898, p. 141.
18 Williams, I, Supplement, p. 21.
19 Tobler, *Topographie*, I, p. 380.

Kawass of Bishop Blyth, 1887 (Blyth, p. 164)

14). Williams points out that the house was actually built for a wealthy Jew named Amzalag, a British subject who had recently passed away. The house was very comfortable to live in, but its neighborhood was rather noisy. In the days of the Crusaders, the area had been a grain market. Now, it was a vegetable market, and the loud cries of women and greengrocers were well-nigh deafening.[20]

The Mission Hospital

Another Protestant institution established in Jerusalem was the "English Hospital." Bartlett writes about it in this way:

> The first step towards the establishment of this valuable institution was the sending out, in 1838, of a medical missionary, Mr. Gerstmann, who, being himself a converted Jew, was certain to sympathise with the distressed condition of his countrymen.... "Our plan," wrote Mr. Nicolayson, "is to form something that may grow into a hospital. Be not alarmed at the name 'Hospital;' we are not going to erect a palace like the hospitals in London...." The arrival in 1842 of Dr. **Macgowan, the able physician appointed by the "London Society for Promoting** Christianity among the Jews," gave a still further impulse to the work.... The necessity for establishing an hospital was warmly urged by the doctor and generally responded to by the Society. A suitable house was soon found and fitted up. It was opened on the 12th Dec. 1844, and it has ever since been fully occupied.[21]

In 1849, Williams marks the hospital on his map (No. 19), indicating that it also had a pharmacy. This was the least satisfactory facility of the London Jews Society. The hospital's twenty beds were usually occupied by Jewish invalids, who obtained the best medical treatment available from Dr. Macgowan, the Mission's surgeon.[22]

Petermann (1953) relates that the hospital was founded by Mr. Nicolayson to

255

20 Williams, I, Supplement, p. 20.
21 Bartlett, *Revisited*, pp. 59-61.
22 Williams, I, Supplement, p. 23, map; Tobler, *Planographie*, map.

serve Jews and converts. The latter preferred to be treated at home in order to avoid abuse from their former co-religionists. The hospital was well run, he says, and located near the Jewish Quarter. The first floor had rooms for male patients, and the third, for women and children. The second floor held a small kitchen. There was a total of thirty beds; in times of emergency, forty could be provided. The doctors lived nearby. The hospital was directed by the economist, Mr. Kelman, who had held this position for the last twenty years. Near the hospital was a pharmacy as well as the quarters of Dr. Macgowan and his assistant, Mr. Simon, who also made house calls.[23] Frankl (1856) writes that the Protestant Mission had founded a thirty-six-bed hospital in Jerusalem for the members of all religions.[24] The 1875 edition of Liévin's guide says that the English hospital was well maintained, and conducted missionary activities aimed at converting Jews to Protestantism.[25]

The establishment of Christ Church and the English hospital was under way before the arrival of Bishop Gobat and, to a large extent, even before the establishment of the joint Protestant bishopric. These institutions were furthered particularly by the Anglican branch of the Protestant Church, with the active force behind its actions being the London Society for Promoting Christianity amongst the Jews. Another kind of Protestant institution that found its way into the city was the community school, with its prime movers again being the Anglicans.

Anglican-Protestant Schools and Work Centers

According to Tobler, Bishop Alexander opened an elementary school in Jerusalem as early as 1843. It was situated not far from the Armenian school, and slightly west of the English hospital. The program was not well organized, and there were few pupils. Only in 1849 did the student population increase; one of the reasons for this was the enrollment of several Jews recruited by the Mission. The Anglicans also founded a vocational school that taught carpentry. It closed for a year, and then re-opened in 1848, accepting converted Jews. Pupils received clothing, food, and other supplies throughout the school year.[26] Neumann also says that, aside from a hospital, the Mission had founded an elementary school and vocational school for carpentry. Due to financial difficulties, these institutions had very few pupils. At the end of 1849, the vocational school was attended by eight converts. A year later, some of these converts became Roman Catholics, one reverted to Judaism, and others left the school altogether. Only three pupils remained.[27] Halsted reports that a workshop was opened in 1843, coinciding with the establishment of the Anglican church and the English hospital. This institution aimed to prepare converted Jews for a productive life in a new occupation, as converts were ostracized by Jewish society and cut off from their former sources of income;

23   Petermann, I, pp. 214-215; Ish-Shalom, notes on pp. 515, 558, 673.
24   Frankl, p. 192.
25   Liévin (1875), p. 129.
26   Tobler, *Denkblätter*, pp. 444-450.
27   Neumann, pp. 284-294.

most of them had been in the service professions or had kept shops.[28]

Petermann relates that the Protestants had once run an institution near the Damascus Gate which had trained Jewish converts for missionary work. When the desired results were not achieved, the place closed down for a few years and was then re-opened as a vocational school for Jewish converts. Pupils were instructed in religious theory and taught a trade, eventually becoming Christian craftsmen. Each pupil chose the field that interested him, and worked under a Christian practicing that trade. The institution owned an olive-wood workshop, located near the school.[29] Schulz (1851) calls the institution the Protestant Converts' Home, pointing out that it owned a large workshop for various crafts and ran a "bazaar" where one could buy oriental souvenirs and articles produced at the workshop. Prices were fixed but high, with all proceeds going to the institution. The converts' home itself was large and well suited to its purpose. The building had cost 700 pounds sterling, and an equal amount had been spent on furnishings and equipment. The well-known British philanthropist, Lady Burdett-Coutts, had assisted in the purchase. The Converts' Home accepted unmarried Jews having an interest in Christianity, and gave them a religious and vocational education. They were required to undergo a trial period at the institution. The director of the converts' home was a converted Polish Jew named Herschon.[30]

The development of Protestant institutions in Jerusalem accelerated with the arrival of Bishop Gobat in 1846. Warren writes that Gobat's endeavors in the field of education led the Roman Catholics and Greeks to introduce improvements in their own schools.[31] Stewart (1854) says Gobat built two schools in Jerusalem: a girls' school with fifteen students, including Jews, converts and Arab Christians; and a boys' school with forty students. Gobat seems to have improved an existing boys' school in this case. The three teachers were of English, German and Arab origin.[32] Wortabet (1856) relates that the Gobat Boys' school, which accepted pupils of all religions, was about to move to Mount Zion. The present institution, which was located in the city and had both a regular and a boarding-school program, had fifty pupils and six teachers. Bishop Gobat also established a girls' school attended by some thirty or forty pupils. Consul Finn says it, too, was open to pupils of all religions.[33] Buchanan writes that, in 1859, the Anglican boys' school was outside the city walls, near the southern corner of Mount Zion. It was attended by thirty-two Syrian Christians, Jews and Muslims, who studied English, geography and the Scriptures. The girls' school was housed in a comfortable building inside the city. Its twenty-two pupils learned sewing and other subjects, including religious ones.[34] These schools continued to operate throughout the period under discussion, and are mentioned from time to time in the sources. One

---

28   Halsted, p. 164; Robinson, *Later Biblical Researches*, pp. 164-165.
29   Petermann, I, pp. 215-216.
30   Schulz, p. 136. On Herschon see Ish-Shalom, p. 594 n. 3; see also Isaacs, p. 79; Wortabet, II, pp. 219-221.
31   Warren, *Underground Jerusalem*, pp. 88-100.
32   Stewart, pp. 301-304.
33   Wortabet, II, pp. 207-209; J. Finn, *Stirring Times*, II, pp. 101-105.
34   Buchanan, pp. 206-207.

source, for example, writes that, in 1884, Bishop Gobat's school was located opposited Mishkenot Sha'ananim, above the valley of Hinnom. Pupils studied shoemaking under a German cobbler. The girls' school, run by a Mrs. Bailey under the direct patronage of the London Jews Society, was then being transferred to the home of the Baileys.[35]

In the early 1850's, an attempt was made to found an English college in Jerusalem. Consul Finn tells us about it:

> The college was opened in April, 1854. Pupils of the most diverse nations and habits of mind offered themselves — Jews, Syrians, a Maronite, a Greek deacon, Jewish Christians — speaking no one language well in common... but before the end of the first term... the English language alone was sufficient.... The Jerusalem English College was... suspended in 1855 after a brief but most interesting experiment....[36]

All the Protestant institutions we have mentioned were initiated and supported by the Anglican branch of the Protestant Church. By the second half of the nineteenth century, the German Protestants were also active in Jerusalem. As we said earlier, this community felt that it was being overshadowed by the Anglican Church, and it therefore sought to fortify its own position and institutions.

The Activity of the German Protestants

One German Protestant organization that was particularly active in Jerusalem was the Deaconess Sisters. The building it rented in the city served both as a medical center and as a hospice. A mission school was opened there, too.

Petermann relates that the German hospital, the Deaconesses' House, was founded in 1851. It served members of all religions, and also included a hospice for poor Germans, mainly Prussians, who received free room and board for fourteen days. Foreigners with means paid a small fee. Petermann paid eight piastres a day for himself, and six for his servant. The Deaconesses also ran a school for orphans. The physical and spiritual needs of patients and pilgrims alike were tended by four nuns, who also taught the orphans and took care of nine or ten of them in the afternoons. Subjects such as religious studies and prayer were taught in both English and German.[37]

According to Stewart (1854), there was a Prussian hospital in Jerusalem, attached to which there was a hospice for poor pilgrims. The hospital was run by three nuns, he states, and was open also to local Arabs who desired to be treated there.[38] Isaacs (1857) says the institution of the German Deaconesses was not far from Christ Church. It had a school for Protestant children, some of whom belonged to converted Jewish families. There was a hospital there, too.[39]

The German Protestant Mission in Jerusalem also established other institutions. One was the Brothers' or Craftsmens' House, initiated by Spietler, the secretary of the Christian Society in Basle. Spietler was a man who had romantic missionary visions, one of them being a dream of renewed Christian

35 Mott, pp. 72-73.
36 J. Finn, *Stirring Times*, II, p. 107.
37 Petermann, I, pp. 196, 215-216.
38 Stewart, I, pp. 301-304.
39 Isaacs, pp. 37-40; Dupuis, pp. 138-139.

bonds between Jerusalem and Ethiopia. He planned to establish twelve "apostolic stations" along the route taken by Jesus' apostles according to the New Testament. For this purpose, he needed traveling craftsmen who would work for a living and spread Christianity. Near Basle, Spietler founded a training center called the Brothers' House (*Brüderhaus*), and planned to set up the first of his stations in Jerusalem. In 1846, some of these craftsmen were sent to the Holy Land. They rented a building in the Old City, but ignorance of local conditions, financial difficulties and excessive demands on the part of Spietler led to their failure. Some of the Brothers returned to Basle; others stayed on, and joined the general missionary effort under Bishop Gobat. In 1854, Spietler tried again, but the project failed for similar reasons. As before, some of the Brothers remained in the country; a few of them became prominent figures in Jerusalem's Christian community. Of particular note were the architect, Conrad Schick, who became one of the city's most important scholars; Baldensperger, a tailor, who worked as a missionary in Bethlehem and sought to introduce modern agricultural methods; and Johann Ludwig Schneller who, in 1860, established the Syrian orphanage that bore his name, outside the city walls.[40]

Schulz writes of the Brothers' House after his visit in 1851. The institution was designed to accommodate unmarried Christians, but eventually disintegrated because of a manpower shortage and the illness of some of the Brothers. Three of them joined the ranks of Bishop Gobat, he notes, and the rest left the country. Only one remained there: one Miller, who was "waiting for God to show him the right path." Miller now taught only two youths, Schulz reports, whereas once there had been fifteen. Miller was a watchmaker, and on good terms with the Arabs. Sometimes, he hosted Christian pilgrims. He also tended the garden behind the house, with the help of an Arab. The upper floor of the building was rented to the Baptists, and the place was clean and orderly.[41]

The Jewesses' Institution

Another Protestant institution was a workshop for women run by a Miss Cooper and her assistants. Their objective was to teach Jewish women to sew, and then employ them. One source relates that the school was established in 1848, and had fifty pupils.[42] Of 1851, Schulz writes that the women's vocational school was attended by about twenty Jewish girls: three or four Sephardim, a few of North African origin, and one, of Italian.[43] In 1853, Finn also mentions a sewing and weaving school for Jewesses run by a Miss Cooper. It employed between sixty and eighty women. At a later date, he says ninety-five women worked and studied there, and that another eighty-five worked at home. Thus, employment was found for 180 women, who supported 350 souls in this manner.[44] Bartlett (1855) cites Miss Cooper's vocational school as one of the

40   Ilan, pp. 18-20.
41   Schulz, pp. 127-128.
42   Tobler, *Denkblätter,* pp. 444-450; Petermann, I, pp. 215-216.
43   Schulz, pp. 124-125.
44   J. Finn, *Stirring Times,* II, p. 70.

institutions not totally affiliated with the Mission, and states that fifty Jewesses studied sewing there.[45]

The Anglicans also introduced the "Industrial Plantation" project, which hired needy Jews to farm a tract of land to the north of the Old City. This project will be treated in greater depth in the second volume of this work.

In his summary of missionary activity in Jerusalem, Frankl (1856) mentions the sewing institution, which provided employment for eighty to one hundred women; the vocational school, where six youths studied carpentry; and the agricultural project, which employed about 100 workers at a salary of four piastres a day.[46]

In the early 1860's, Pierotti lists the Protestant institutions as follows: a boys' school; a girls' school; another girls' school and a hospital run by the Prussian Deaconesses; a Prussian hospice; an English hospital; and a carpentry school. The Protestants also owned several buildings in the city, and ran a reading room.[47] (Pierotti makes no mention of Miss Cooper's workshop and the English college, which may already have closed down by his time.)

During his second visit to Jerusalem, Robinson writes, on April 28, 1852, of the changes since his first visit in 1838:

> As we thus again looked abroad upon the Holy City, after an interval of fourteen years, signs of change and a measure of general improvement were everywhere visible.... A powerful foreign influence had been brought in, and was still exerted... all had served to increase the circulation of money and to stimulate the native mind to like efforts. The convents had erected several large buildings, and established schools; and there was a process going on in Jerusalem, of tearing down old dwellings and replacing them by the new ones which reminded me somewhat of New York. There were at this time more houses undergoing this transformation in the Holy City, than I had seen the year before in six of the principal cities of Holland. As a natural result, there was more activity in the streets; there were more people in motion, more bustle and more business.[48]

The Location of Protestant Buildings; the Protestant Quarter

Strauss discusses the location of the various Protestant institutions, pointing out that all of them were on "Mount Zion," that is, near the Citadel of David and Christ Church. These included the home of the British consul; the home of the missionary, Nicolayson; the German Deaconesses' House; the Anglican school and the English Mission hospital.[49] Most Protestant homes and institutions clustered around Christ Church, thus forming what we may call the "Protestant Quarter." When we considered the location of other population centers in Jerusalem, we saw that each group stayed close to the historical shrine most sacred to it. Thus, it is interesting that the Protestants, who had no such shrine, rallied around a nucleus of their own making. Even when they expanded outside the Old City, they did not at first go farther than the area near "Mount Zion."

260

45   Bartlett, *Revisited*, p. 48.
46   Frankl, pp. 190-193.
47   Pierotti, I, pp. 277-279.
48   Robinson, *Later Biblical Researches*, p. 164.
49   Strauss, p. 204.

The Mission and the Jews; Jewish Converts and the Growth of the Protestant Community

Much of the Anglican Protestant missionary activity in Jerusalēm was directed at the Jewish community, the Arabs becoming a focus of interest only later on. This subject has already received much attention from researchers, and we shall limit ourselves here to a few accounts of the form taken by such activities in the Old City, especially at their outset. We must remember that one of the main reasons for this concentration on the Jews was the belief that the return to Zion and the conversion of the Jews to Christianity were important steps towards salvation. This belief, extremely popular in early nineteenth-century English society, was also current in political circles; it forms the background of the repeated calls for a return to Zion and the offers of British assistance to those settling in the Holy Land made in the days of Lord Palmerston.

As we said earlier, there was no Protestant community in Jerusalem at the beginning of the nineteenth century. Missionary activities, especially those of the Anglican Church, commenced only in the 1830's. The most enterprising missionary was Nicolayson, but his success seems to have been limited. In 1840, Olin writes that only five or six Jews had been baptized, and that these had been from the periphery of Jewish society. In Olin's opinion, the Mission had not been able to convince the Jews at all, only evoking their bitter hatred instead.[50] Strauss (late 1840's) gives the Protestant Mission more credit. He relates that, on Good Friday, the Protestant church held services in various languages. First, twenty Jewish converts recited prayers in Hebrew. Then, there was a service in English and, in the afternoon, one in German. On Easter Sunday, 100 Protestants attended church. There was a German service on that afternoon, during which an Austrian Jew was publicly baptized. On holidays, Nicolayson, the head of the community, received gifts from his congregants, and from Muslims and Jews, too.[51] The missionary-convert Woodcock (1848) cites an 1847 report by the Jerusalem bishop, saying that thirty-one Jewish adults and twenty-six young people had been converted to Christianity since 1839. Woodcock says that, on the day he left the city, fourteen Jews belonging to two families arrived from Jaffa to be baptized. He also tells of the baptism of a rabbi from Salonika, one Rabbi Shuffami, at the Protestant church.[52] Another source mentions the conversion of twelve or thirteen Jewish men and women in 1848. They were very poor and unemployed. Five of them were learning shoemaking and two, tailoring. According to this source, the Mission school had eighteen pupils.[53] A source for the 1840's reports that, by 1847, after thirteen years of missionary activity, there had been a total of sixty conversions.[54]

Tobler writes that, in 1845, over 100 persons attended prayers at the Anglican Protestant church. This was a very large rise for a fifteen-year period. Tobler also ·provides a detailed account of the Jews who converted to

50   Olin, II, pp. 313-314.
51   Strauss, pp. 171-180.
52   Woodcock, p. 124; Ish-Shalom, p. 574.
53   Margoliouth, p. 294.
54   Martineau, pp. 466-468.

Christianity, supplying names and dates. Nevertheless, he criticizes the Mission's methods severely and describes the suffering of families that had been sundered as a result. He says that the number of converts was no indication of success, considering the poverty of the Jews. In his view, the Mission was inappropriate in such a concentration of fanatically religious Jews as there was in Jerusalem. Only material inducement, the sum of 6,000 piastres promised to converts, motivated a few Jews to change their faith. Most converts required support for the rest of their lives. In 1847, Gobat allotted 800 gulden to maintain these converts (about ninety souls altogether) but, in 1848, he was forced to rule that no Jew was to be baptized unless he could earn at least part of his livelihood. There was only one Jewish convert, a tailor, who was not financially dependent upon the Mission. Tobler goes on to mention the missionary bookshop near the Jaffa Gate. The failure of the Mission was all the more blatant in view of the recognition it had received from the sultan and the large sum of 60,000 gulden placed at the disposal of the Protestant Church each year.[55]

Neumann also denounces the Mission. He claims to have been witness to the unspeakable suffering inflicted upon the Jews by the English missionaries during the fifteen years he lived in Jerusalem. The Mission's methods were illegitimate, and the reports of its so-called success, he says, grossly distorted. The enormous sums spent on proselytizing activity, 60,000 gulden or 40,000 pounds sterling a year, were equal to about a quarter of its entire income in England.[56]

Petermann says that, in 1853, there were about 200 Protestants in Jerusalem: 150 belonged to the Anglican Church and fifty to the German Church. The Protestants engaged in missionary activity among the Jews, holding a Hebrew prayer service every morning from six to seven a.m. Apart from the English and German services on Sundays, they were also planning to hold prayers in Arabic. The head of the Mission, Mr. Nicolayson, was the first Anglican preacher in Jerusalem. He had been sent there in 1827 by the London Jews Society. Petermann also notes that missionaries were least successful in cities sacred to the Jews. In Jerusalem, only eighty people had been converted so far.[57]

After his second trip to Jerusalem in 1853, Bartlett relays the following:

> The Bishop is also head of the establishment of the London Society for Promoting Christianity among the Jews. This consists of a missionary staff under the Rev. J. Nicolayson, a House of Industry, for the employment of the Hebrew converts, and a medical staff under E. Macgowan, Esq. M.D. who, together with a surgeon, apothecary, steward, &c., work the noble hospital for the relief of poor Jews. The Rev. H. Crawford is clerical missionary. Many of the Hebrew converts have settled in other countries, some as clergymen, schoolmasters, and artisans, and others live in Jerusalem, and form the Hebrew congregation. For these there are daily morning prayers of the Anglican liturgy in Hebrew, and on every second Sunday afternoon Anglican prayers and sermon in the German language; besides a service in Spanish on Sunday at the house of the Rev. H. Crawford.[58]

262

55   Tobler, *Topographie*, I, p. 380.
56   Neumann, p. 284.

57   Petermann, I, pp. 214-215.
58   Bartlett, *Revisited*, pp. 47-48.

Scherer (1859) plays down the influence of Protestant missionary activity in the city. He says the phenomenon was nothing to be surprised about, since all religious sects sought new souls. Moreover, Protestant activity was not very great. He claims, for example, that the Prussian hospice had nothing to do with such activity. Despite rumor, the main objective of the Prussian-Anglican Mission in Jerusalem was the education of the city's residents, and it was making important progress in this respect. The Mission schools were undoubtedly the best in the city, and the Deaconesses' House provided its patients with fine medical treatment. The Prussian hospice offered accommodation to pilgrims and tourists alike.[59] Halsted, who sums up the activity of the Anglican Mission in the Holy Land until 1866, notes that only nineteen persons joined it during its first three years. By the end of 1844, the number had risen to fifty-four, and ten more had been baptized but not yet accepted as members. By 1851-1852, eighty-eight adults and forty-three children had joined the church, but only thirty-seven of the adults and twenty-five of the children were Jewish.[60] Frankl, on the other hand, says the Mission enjoyed considerable success. After visiting the country in 1856, he writes that the Anglican Mission had converted 131 Jews: seventy-one Ashkenazim and sixty from other countries. Four Austrian Jews had converted to Islam.[61] These figures seem excessive and inaccurate.

Summary

On the whole, the London Jews Society had little success attracting converts, particularly among the Jews. In spite of the enormous growth of the Jewish community, from 2,000 souls at the beginning of the century to 11,000 by the end of the 1860's, and despite the fact that so many Jews were poor, sick and led wretched lives, the total number of converts was not more than a hundred by the end of this period.

The failure of the Protestant mission to the Jewish community led it to direct ever more of its efforts towards other Christian sects in Jerusalem. In the course of the nineteenth century, another Protestant missionary society began to operate in the city, the Church Missionary Society; it worked mainly among the Arabs. With the dissolution of the joint Protestant bishopric in 1887, a third Anglican missionary society arose, headed by Bishop Blyth and financed by the Jerusalem Bishopric Fund.[62] All three Anglican missionary societies will be examined more thoroughly in our second volume.

Concentrated missionary effort directed at the Jews was characteristic mainly of the first half of the nineteenth century. From the middle of the century onwards, Anglican Protestant activity assumed a more general nature, and was aimed at the Jerusalem population as a whole. In contrast to the Anglicans, German Protestant organizations such as that of the Deaconesses devoted themselves from the outset to the Christian Arab population.

59   Scherer, pp. 177-181.
60   Halsted, pp. 164, 172.
61   Frankl, pp. 190-191.
62   Baedeker (1912), p. 22; Jessup, pp. 475, 568, 573.

Generally speaking, Protestant activity in Jerusalem was important because of the response it provoked in other communities. This response was particularly significant because the Protestants initiated projects in areas crying out for action: public health, welfare and education. As we have seen, Protestant projects had a very considerable impact on other Christian sects and, later, on the Muslims and the Ottoman government. No group, however, was so profoundly affected as that of the Jews. The challenge to the Jewish community, and the subsequent establishment of parallel Jewish institutions, will enter our discussion of the Jewish Quarter in the next part of this volume.

Part Four

**The Jewish Community of Jerusalem
Before Expansion Beyond the
Old City Walls (1800-1870)**

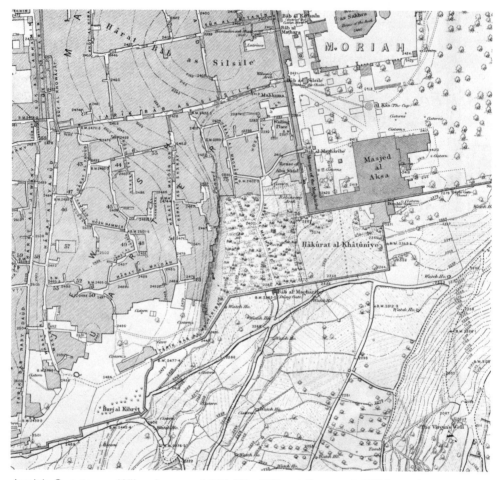

Jewish Quarter on Wilson's map, 1865 (Ch. Wilson, *Survey*, 1:2500 map)

266

Chapter One

GROWTH OF THE JEWISH POPULATION BEFORE 1870

Introduction

When dealing with the Muslim and Christian populations of nineteenth-century Jerusalem, we discussed the difficulty of determining exact figures for these communities. The same difficulty applies to the Jewish community. Demographic information about the Jews, however, differs from that about other communities in that Ottoman government sources concerning Jews become progressively less reliable, since more and more Jews acquired foreign nationalities and were eliminated from local government records. Evidence from local Jewish records, not always impartial, is much more reliable than that of the Ottoman officials. Foreign consulates are especially valuable sources of Jewish demographic information. The British consulate, in particular, regarded itself at this time as the patron of the Palestine Jewish community, and made sure that it was well-informed about community life.[1]

The major difficulty in correctly determining the size and development of nineteenth-century Jerusalem's Jewish community lies in an abundance of conflicting population estimates. Our use of these must be careful and selective. Even if we depend on relatively reliable sources, we must remember their limitations, and make comparisons before we draw conclusions. Under these circumstances, it seems that slight fluctuations in population growth will have to be ignored in favor of an examination of general trends and major changes.[2]

This chapter will not deal with the growth of Jerusalem's Jewish population throughout the nineteenth century, but rather with that preceding the establishment of new neighborhoods outside the Old City in the 1870's. Until that time, the growing population had been confined to the Old City itself, and this was one of the major reasons for expansion outside the walls. Thereafter, the number of Jews rose steadily both inside and outside the city walls; rapid growth continued until World War I.

The First Thirty Years of the Nineteenth Century

How large was the Jewish community of Jerusalem at the turn of the century? Seetzen writes that, on his visit to Jerusalem in 1806, he obtained information from the Turkish governor according to which there were about 2,000 Jews in a total population of 8,750. Jerusalem was the only place in the Levant for which

---

1   Hyamson, *British Consulate*.
2   Robinson, *Biblical Researches*, p. 83; Spencer, pp. 273-277.

Seetzen thought the population figures given him were too low: he believed there were 12,000 persons in the city, 3,000 of them Jews.[3] The figures cited originally seem more accurate.

Seetzen's first estimate fits in with what we know about this period from Jewish sources. These indicate that there had been a decline in the number of Ashkenazim in Jerusalem in the late eighteenth century, and that the Jewish community as a whole, composed mostly of Sephardim, had declined in importance. The figure of 2,000 to 2,250 Jews for the early nineteenth century will therefore serve as the basis for our study of subsequent growth and changes in the Jewish community.

The first thirty years of the nineteenth century, especially its second and third decades, saw some strengthening of the city's Jewish community. Various Jewish sources tell of the return of some Ashkenazi Jews to Jerusalem, emphasizing the arrival of the disciples of the Gaon of Vilna and some members of the "Perushim." We will deal with them later, when we discuss the different groups comprising the Jewish community. Now, let us note only that this growth was more of quality than of quantity.[4]

The Thirties — Under Egyptian Rule

The conquest of Palestine and Syria by Muḥammad 'Ali and his stepson Ibrahim Pasha in the early 1830's proved a turning point for Jewish Jerusalem. We have already seen how, during this period, Jerusalem attained an importance in the region second only to that of Damascus. Egyptian rule over the city from 1831 to 1840 was more flexible than that of the Turkish government which had preceded it, and was influenced by the European powers. There was more tolerance of the minorities, who were allowed relatively greater freedom of action. In addition, the Egyptian government, more powerful than the Turkish, enforced law and order. The Bedouins were restrained and highway robbery was ended; security prevailed. As a result, the number of Western travelers reaching Jerusalem increased. Jewish immigration to the Holy Land also grew. The Jews of Jerusalem were permitted to renovate and rebuild their synagogues, after having been forbidden to do so in the time of the Turks. They were also allowed to pray more freely at the Wailing Wall, no longer needing a special permit from the authorities to do so.[5]

The growth of the Jewish community of Jerusalem under Egyptian rule is difficult to assess. The period should be divided into the years that preceded the earthquake of 1837 and those that followed. Before the earthquake, there was a continuation and possibly an acceleration of the slow growth of the 1820's. Many of the new arrivals were active in communal work; among these were members of the well-known *Kolel Hod* (see below, p. 293). Apparently, however, there was no substantial increase in the Jewish population. It was the 1837 earthquake, which severely affected the Jewish communities of Safed and

268

3   Seetzen, II, p. 18.
4   Ben-Zvi, *Eretz-Israel*, pp. 305-306.
5   *Ibid.*, p. 346.

Tiberias, that caused many of their members to move to Jerusalem, spurring the city's growth. This migration was probably not an immediate one, taking place only when the survivors realized that their chances of rehabilitation at home were negligible.

Robinson, who visited Jerusalem in 1838, recorded his estimate of its current population. As was then customary, Robinson multiplied the Egyptian census figure of 500 Jewish males by four, so as to provide for their dependents. Considering the result too low, he added a thousand persons. He also consulted the Reverend Nicolayson, who as a missionary was familiar with the Jewish community. Using both sources, he concluded that there were 3,000 Jews then living in the city.[6]

If we consider Robinson's figures in the light of the Jewish community's composition, we find that most of the 500 adult males and their families belonged to the Sephardi community, which had not changed significantly in size since the beginning of the century. By contrast, there had been a conspicuous increase in the number of Ashkenazi Jews: in the 1830's they already numbered between 500 and 1,000.

An estimate quite similar to Robinson's appears in a Jewish source of about the same time. Montefiore's census, carried out by Dr. Eliezer Halevi in 1839, counted 2,943 Jews, of whom 2,450 were Sephardim and Oriental Jews, and 493, Ashkenazim (including 418 Perushim, 41 Hasidim, and 34 Dutch or Hungarian Jews).[7]

Tobler, too, gives details about the growth of the Ashkenazi community during the 1830's; he says there were 820 Ashkenazi Jews in the city in 1839, including 520 to 540 of Russian, 250 of Polish, and thirty of German origin.[8]

From the accounts of Robinson and Montefiore we may conclude that, at the end of the 1830's, the Jews of Jerusalem numbered between 3,000 and 3,250, most of them Sephardim. By 1840, the Ashkenazi community had grown, but it was still a minority of Jerusalem's Jewish population.

The Jewish community continued to expand in the 1840's. Various sources cite figures for the beginning of the decade far in excess of those noted above, but these large figures are probably inaccurate. We cannot, for example, accept the assertion of Rabbi David de-Beth Hillel that there were over 3,000 Jewish *families* in Jerusalem in 1824. His other figures are equally unrealistic and are, apparently, mere generalizations.[9] Another assessment which appears general and inexact is that of Rabbi Eliezer Bergmann, who noted that the Jewish community comprised 2,000 Sephardi and Ashkenazi heads of households in 1835.[10]

Some Jewish sources do correspond with our estimate. Rabbi Menaḥem Mendel of Kamieniec calculated that, in 1834, there were 3,000 Jews in Jerusalem.[11] This figure was also given by Rabbi Joseph Schwarz in a letter of 1841.[12]

Christian travelers also estimated the size of the Jewish population of

6   Robinson, *Biblical Researches*, II, pp. 85-86
7   Meisel, "Jewish Settlement," p. 429.   10   Bergmann, p. 79.
8   Tobler, *Denkblätter*, pp. 360-361.   11   Kamieniec, p. 30.
9   Yaari, *Travels*, pp. 502, 505.   12   Gat, p. 19.

Jerusalem, suggesting anything from "a few Jews" to 10,000 souls. Some travelers placed the number at 3,000, but most of their estimates are unreliable.[13]

In or about 1840, a significant change occurred in the size and status of the Jewish population of Jerusalem; the responsible agents were the catastrophic earthquake of 1837, which caused an influx of Jews from Safed and Tiberias, and the substantial increase in immigration from abroad.[14]

The first relatively reliable estimates giving fairly high figures for Jerusalem's Jewish population date from 1839. The Mission of the Church of Scotland, which visited the country in that year and took a particular interest in the Jewish community, records very high figures for this period. It notes that, of three sources, one suggested 5,000 Jews, a second 6,000, and a third 7,000.[15] These figures are not devoid of a certain bias, reflecting a vested interest in finding a Jewish population large enough to justify missionary activity in the country. Nonetheless, they do seem to indicate a sudden growth of Jerusalem's Jewish population. Only two years after telling Robinson (in 1838) that there were 3,000 Jews in Jerusalem, Nicolayson informed Dr. Olin that they numbered 5,000.[16]

Robinson remarks that while he was writing up his material in London (October 1840) he received additional demographic data, setting the Jewish population of Jerusalem at 7,000. Robinson treats this figure, which hearsay attributed to Montefiore's census, with considerable skepticism, commenting that, since this census was carried out for the purpose of distributing money, its figures were probably inflated. He doubted whether these were indeed the findings of Montefiore's census for, when he attempted to clarify the results, he was told they had not yet been made public.[17] Robinson, it turned out, was right: Montefiore's census revealed that there were only 3,000 Jews in Jerusalem. Robinson goes on to discuss the figures noted by the Mission of the Church of Scotland. The only one he cites is that of 5,000; he adds that Mr. Calman of the Mission had heard from his Jewish guide that the number of Jews in Jerusalem did not exceed 3,000.[18]

Some explanation is required of these contradictory population statistics for 1839, ranging from 3,000 to 7,000 persons. There does seem to have been rapid growth in the Jewish community, but observers were either unaware of it or tended to exaggerate its scope. Hyamson's figure of 5,500 persons, from the British consulate archives in Jerusalem for May of 1839, appears to be the most reliable for this period, taking into account the many earthquake survivors from Tiberias and Safed who moved to Jerusalem at this time. According to this source, there were 500 totally destitute persons in the city and another 500 poor who were somewhat better off.[19] The large number of refugees is also mentioned by the Mission of the Church of Scotland, and by many Jewish sources.[20] There was even a popular saying during this period to the effect that

13 Tobler, *Denkblätter*, pp. 534-535.
14 *Ibid.*, pp. 360-361.
15 Bonar—M'Cheyne, pp. 143-163.
16 Olin, II, pp. 311-312.
17 Robinson, *Biblical Researches*, II, pp. 85-86.
18 *Loc. cit.*
19 Hyamson, *British Consulate*, I, p. 5.
20 Bonar—M'Cheyne, pp. 143-163.

Rabbi praying (Bonar—M'Cheyne, p. 408)

Jerusalem had been built on the ruins of Safed and Tiberias.[21]

The British consulate estimate appears to be slightly high. It is more likely that, in about 1840, there were no more than 5,000 Jews in Jerusalem, including 1,000 to 1,500 refugees from Tiberias and Safed.[22]

The Forties

During the 1840's, the Jewish community of Jerusalem continued to expand as a result of increased immigration. Tobler writes that between 300 and 500 immigrants reached Palestine each year between 1845 and 1850. Not all of them settled in Jerusalem, but those who did made a significant contribution to the size of the Jewish community.[23] According to Mrs. Finn, the number of Jews in Jerusalem rose especially after Montefiore's visit of 1839.[24] Indeed, Montefiore's philanthropy and interest in the residents of Jerusalem seem to have promoted the growth of the city's population from the 1840's on. The impact of his visits to the city is dealt with at length by the British consul, James Finn, and by others. Some sources mention the fantastic rumors then current of the impending national rebirth of the Jews. Basili, the Russian consul, attributes the expanding immigration to the good travel facilities from the "Barbary States," Germany and Russia, as well as to the reports of religious tolerance and decent administration in the East. He also reports that newspaper accounts of imaginary negotiations between the Sultan and rich Jewish bankers had raised hopes for the re-establishment of the Kingdom of Judah and the rebuilding of the Temple.[25]

There are three relatively reliable sources for the size of the Jerusalem Jewish community in the mid-1840's. According to the Prussian consul Schultz there were 7,120 Jews out of a total population of 15,150 in 1845. Of these Jews, 6,000 were Sephardim (and Turkish subjects) and 1,100 were Ashkenazim (and

21 Ben-Zvi, *Eretz-Israel*, pp. 301, 361-362; Press, *Travel Handbook*, p. 94.
22 Gat, p. 19.
23 Tobler, *Denkblätter*, pp. 360-361.
24 Mrs. Finn, *Reminiscences*, p. 94.
25 Basili, p. 311.

Simḥat Torah dancing
(Bonar—M'Cheyne, p. 438)

foreign subjects). The latter included 520 to 540 Jews of Russian, 250 of Polish, and seventy of German origin as well as twenty Karaites.[26]

Tobler cites a similar figure for 1846: 7,500 Jews in a general population of 17,200 (including 1,500 Turkish soldiers), of whom 6,000 were Sephardim, 1,500 Ashkenazim, and fifteen Karaites.[27] Mrs. Finn's estimate for the same year is 7,000 Jews in a population of 15,000 (of whom 4,000 were Sephardim and 3,000 Ashkenazim).[28]

Additional interesting information about the size of the Jewish community is provided by Churton. Of the various population estimates for 1847 (5,000; 7,000; 9,000 persons, and even more), he believes that 8,000 is correct. For 1850, he raises this figure to 8,500, pointing out the increasing number of Jews in contrast to the declining Muslim population. Finding housing in the Jewish Quarter was therefore difficult, he says, while easy in the Muslim Quarter.[29]

Considering the various estimates, we again conclude that the Jewish community was steadily increasing in size. This, however, is not to say that the figures we have cited are completely accurate. The estimate of Schultz and Tobler, giving 6,000 members of the Sephardi community in the mid-1840's, seems too high. There may have been Sephardim among the earthquake survivors who moved to Jerusalem and among the immigrants from abroad, but an increase from 2,500 to 6,000 persons in the interval between Montefiore's census (1838-1839) and the mid-1840's seems unreasonable. These high figures seem to reflect the use by some observers of a factor of five, rather than one of four, to arrive at the number of dependents per tax-liable male in the Turkish records.

On the other hand, Mrs. Finn, using British consulate data, sets the number of Ashkenazi Jews at 3,000. Though appropriate for a somewhat later period, this seems too high an estimate for the 1840's, and may reflect the incorporation of revised figures when her husband's book was published several years later.

An average of these three population estimates will provide us with a reasonably accurate figure. Thus we can say that, in 1845, there were some 5,500 Jews in Jerusalem: about 4,000 Sephardim and 1,500 Ashkenazim. By

272

26 Williams, II, pp. 613-614.
27 Tobler, *Denkblätter*, p. 352.
28 Mrs. Finn, *Reminiscences*, p. 94.
29 Churton, pp. 135, 178-179.

the end of the decade, this figure had risen to 6,000, with the number of Sephardim possibly in excess of 4,000, and that of the Ashkenazim, nearly 2,000.

The Fifties

The population growth of the 1840's continued in the 1850's and 1860's. The splitting of the Ashkenazi community into many different *kolelim* at this time, largely the result of the population increase, will be dealt with later. Here, we will limit ourselves to a discussion of population growth. It is clear that the main reason for this growth was the steady influx of immigrants,[30] most of whom settled in Jerusalem.

Sources basing themselves on the data of the Turkish authorities provide us with several estimates of the number of Jewish residents in the 1850's. These figures, interestingly enough, show a continual decline in the number of Jews registered with the city authorities. According to Stewart, 970 Jews appear in the 1851 records.[31] Petermann reports a drop to 895 by 1853, according to information obtained from Turkish sources by the Prussian consul.[32]

As foreign consulates attained greater status in Jerusalem, and as many of the new immigrants maintained their foreign nationality, members of the veteran Jewish community of Jerusalem tended to change their nationality or to refrain from registering with the Turkish authorities. It is therefore certain that information from Turkish government sources does not give us a true picture of population growth, either in the Ashkenazi community or for the Jewish community as a whole.

Stewart himself stresses that the official figure of 970 Jews did not represent the entire Jewish population. On the basis of a census carried out by the rabbis for the Rothschild family, Stewart estimates that there were then 6,000 Jews in Jerusalem, including 4,000 Sephardim and 2,000 Ashkenazim.[33] (These figures are identical with ours for the end of the 1840's.) Petermann does not accept the official figure either. In his opinion, the number of Jews in Jerusalem in 1853 was 6,000 to 8,000.[34]

While these figures are reasonable, other sources offer excessive estimates. Van de Velde, for example, claims there were over 10,000 Jews in the city in April of 1852.[35] Zimpel also indicates this figure, saying it comprises 7,600 Sephardim and 2,400 Ashkenazim.[36] After his second visit to Jerusalem in 1853, Bartlett concluded that the Jews constituted the largest community in the city, numbering 11,000 souls, 6,000 Sephardim and 5,000 Ashkenazim.[37] (After his first visit in 1842, he had said there were 4,000 Jews, representing one third of the city's total population.)[38] These figures are undoubtedly exaggerated, particularly those for the Sephardi community, but they indicate, correctly, that several thousand immigrants had arrived in the intervening years.

30 Allen, II, p. 111.
31 Stewart, p. 295.
32 Petermann, II, pp. 232-233.
33 Stewart, p. 295.
34 Petermann, II, pp. 232-233.
35 Van de Velde, p. 211.
36 Zimpel, p. 38.
37 Bartlett, *Revisited*, p. 79.
38 Bartlett, *Walks*, pp. 187-201.

Dr. Frankl's population figures are comparatively low. He reports that there were 5,700 Jews in Jerusalem in 1856, of whom 4,000 were Sephardim and 1,700 Ashkenazim.[39] It is interesting that, while his estimate for the Sephardi community is similar to earlier ones and was probably based on information from the Ottoman authorities and, possibly, the Sephardi leadership, his figure for the Ashkenazim is too low. Perhaps this was due to the cold welcome he received from the Ashkenazi community; another possibility is that his information was out-of-date.

According to Dr. Neumann, there were 6,500 Jews in Jerusalem in 1853, including 5,000 Sephardim and 1,500 Ashkenazim.[40] In 1854, Hausdorf says, the community numbered 7,070, or 5,000 Sephardim and 2,070 Ashkenazim.[41] In both cases, the number of Sephardim is somewhat high, and seems to be a rounded approximation. The Hebrew newspaper *Ha-Maggid* reports a total of 7,000 Jews in 1857. Although, according to this newspaper, the Jewish population of Jerusalem was clearly increasing steadily, there had been a decline in the growth rate during the preceding years, due to the "high cost of living and other factors."[42]

According to Consul Finn's estimate for 1853, in the British consulate archives, there were 8,000 Jews in Jerusalem, nearly half the total population of the city.[43] Elsewhere, Finn quotes a figure of 10,000 Jews for 1856.[44] However, since this figure appears in a book published in 1878, it may refer to a later period.

Thomson also states that, by the end of the 1850's, there were 10,000 Jews in Jerusalem. He notes the difficulty in providing an accurate figure; owing to the unreliability of Turkish census figures, anything based on them was a rough estimate at best. In any case, it is clear that the population of Jerusalem was growing, albeit slowly. Thomson's contacts with Jerusalem continued for over twenty-five years. During this interval, he claims, the number of residents rose from 12,000 persons in 1833 to about 25,000 in 1858. The Jewish community in the city was the fastest growing of them all, and numbered about 10,000 souls.[45]

Thomson's figures also seem too high. The most reasonable estimate for the Jewish population of the late 1850's seems to be that of the British consulate: 8,000 persons, of whom some 4,750 were Sephardim and more than 3,000, Ashkenazim.

Various observers have sought to explain the rapid expansion of the Jewish community during the 1840's and 1850's. Bartlett, for instance, attributes it mostly to immigration from abroad and hardly at all to natural increase. Jewish population figures, he points out, were only approximations; the Jews were strongly opposed to a census for religious reasons. Bartlett also tells of the

39   Frankl, pp. 172-179.
40   Gat, p. 19.
41   *Loc. cit.*
42   Ha-Maggid, 13 Adar, 1857, vol. I, no. 14, p. 55.
43   Hyamson, *British Consulate*, I, p. 257.
44   J. Finn, *Stirring Times*, I, p. 101.
45   Thomson, p. 559.

ws of Jerusalem (Porter, *Jerusalem*, p. 69)   By the Wailing Wall (Porter, *Jerusalem*, p. 41)

great efforts of Sir Moses Montefiore to improve the living conditions of the Jews of Palestine, especially of those of Jerusalem.[46]

The advent of the steamboat, too, was instrumental in the growth of the Jewish community, along with the improved organization of the *kolelim* (which were responsible for distributing *ḥalukka* funds). Luncz relates how, in the 1840's, "steamboat companies began sending their ships to Palestine, increasing the number of immigrants year by year.... Meanwhile, financial support for residents, the *ḥalukka*, became institutionalized... these small sums and the aid that most received from their relatives and from their *kolel*... were sufficient to meet their minimal needs, enabling them to devote themselves to prayer and study."[47]

The continuing population growth is also reflected in general descriptions of the city's development. In her memoirs, Mrs. Finn writes that the housing situation in the Jewish Quarter was critical between the years 1846 and 1863, making it very difficult to find an apartment. Rent was very high, and tenants sometimes were even required to pay for three years in advance.[48]

46 Bartlett, *Revisited*, p. 83.
47 Luncz, *Almanac*, XX, 1914-1915, p. 148 (translated from Hebrew).
48 Mrs. Finn, *Reminiscences*, p. 172.

According to British consular data, there was a rise in the number of Ashkenazim at the beginning of 1858, primarily because of immigration from Russia.[49] The status of Jews protected by foreign nations improved after the Crimean War (1856). The Protestant countries, particularly Great Britain, were of great assistance to the Jews. During the war between the Turks and Muḥammad 'Ali (1839-1841), Britain had responded to the French support of the Maronites by assuming the role of "protector" of the Jews (and the Druze) of Palestine. Consul Finn recalls that in 1839, only one year after the establishment of the British consulate in Jerusalem, Lord Palmerston instructed the consul to grant protection to the Jews of the Holy City.[50] The Jews, on their part, were eager for this protection, all the more so after the 1840 blood libel in Damascus and the expulsion of Muḥammad 'Ali in the same year. Also of great assistance was Sir Moses Montefiore, who at this time intensified his activities on behalf of the Jews of Jerusalem. Consul Finn gives a detailed account of how Russian Jews were granted British nationality, and of the extensive assistance given them.[51]

Warren reports that Ashkenazi Jews coming to live in Jerusalem were either Austrian, Prussian or Russian nationals. Those with Austrian or Prussian nationality were taken care of by their respective consulates, but Russian or Polish Jews lost their consulate's protection if they failed to return to Russia within six months. Since they refused to do so, they might become Ottoman subjects. The intervention of Consul Finn, however, made it possible to grant them British nationality when their Russian nationality expired. Both Russia and Poland were interested in ridding themselves of the Jews and such action suited their aims perfectly.[52] Mrs. Finn writes that the British consul in Jerusalem was instructed to take under his protection all Russian Jews presenting a document of release from the Russian consul (an arrangement in effect until 1890). Hundreds of Jews became British subjects in this way while the Finns were in Jerusalem.[53]

Dr. Neumann points out the success of these British endeavors. Although very few Jews had immigrated from England, some twenty percent of all Jews in Jerusalem having foreign nationality were British subjects by the mid-nineteenth century (that is, some 1,000 of the city's 5,000 foreign citizens). Another 3,000 Jews were protected by the Austrian consul, who also extended aid to various Jewish institutions. The remaining Jews came under the aegis of Prussia (Germany), Russia, France, Holland and the United States.[54]

The Sixties

Pierotti, who was the Jerusalem city engineer during the time of Suraya Pasha, notes that in 1861 there were 5,200 Sephardim, 2,500 Ashkenazim and 38 Karaites resident in the city, for a total of 7,738 persons.[55] He apparently

49   Hyamson, *British Consulate*, I, p. 257.
50   *Ibid.*, p. 2; J. Finn, *Stirring Times*, I, pp. 101-130; I. Friedman, "Palmerston".
51   Finn, *loc.cit.*
52   Warren, *Underground*, pp. 374-377.
53   Mrs. Finn, *Reminiscences*, pp. 81-82.
54   Neumann, pp. 231-233, 375.
55   Pierotti, I, pp. 10-11.

obtained his information from the Turkish authorities. His numbers come close to ours for the end of the 1850's, but are biased in favor of the Sephardim. Pierotti apparently could not be wholly accurate because he was too remote from what was happening in the Jewish community.

The other comparatively reliable figures for the first half of the 1860's are, again, those of the British consulate. According to one estimate for May of 1864 (in the British consul's report to the Foreign Office), the city's Jewish community numbered 8,000 souls.[56] Another report, for March of 1865, suggests a larger figure: 8,000 to 9,000 persons.[57] (These two reports may refer to a slightly earlier period.)

Montefiore's second census, in 1866, showed that there were then only 5,650 Jews in Jerusalem.[58] This is not in keeping with the figures we have noted above, whether derived from Turkish data or consular sources. It also conflicts with the many reports of crowded conditions in the Jewish Quarter and with Jewish initiatives to move outside the city walls. The data from the 1876 census sponsored by the Board of Deputies of British Jews do not accord with such a low figure either.[59] It is true that a severe cholera epidemic in Jerusalem during the year of Montefiore's census had resulted in many deaths, and may have been one reason for the deceleration of Jewish population growth in the 1860's. However, it would not have caused such a drop in population. Thus, we cannot accept the Montefiore census data as complete.

In his book, *Sha‘arei Yerushalayim,* first published in 1867, Reicher estimates that there were 12,000 Jews then living in Jerusalem.[60] One year later, the Hebrew newspaper *Ha-Levanon* gives the figure 11,700.[61] The almanac, *Luaḥ Eretz Israel,* states that, in 1869, the Jerusalem Jewish community was composed of 6,000 Sephardim and 4,000 Ashkenazim.[62] According to the June 1868 issue of *Ha-Levanon,* the Holy Land was becoming a prime target for immigration, with Jews being the majority of new arrivals.[63]

, The 1860's also saw the arrival of several scientific research expeditions. Warren, whose expedition remained in Jerusalem from 1867 to 1869, claims that an exact figure for the Jewish population was difficult to establish. Nevertheless, he estimates that there were 10,000 Jews, including 6,000 Ashkenazim and 4,000 Sephardim. Warren also notes the fact that the number of Jews was growing year by year.[64] Elsewhere in his book, he cites Liévin de Hamme's figure of 8,000 persons for 1869. Although he usually accepted Liévin's figures as correct, in the case of the Jews, Warren says, his number should be raised to 10,000.[65]

The survey of the Palestine Exploration Fund (PEF), which relies on the figures of both the British consul Moore and of Frère Liévin, reports a Jewish population of 10,600 at the end of the 1860's or in the early 1870's.[66] Although the figures of the Palestine Exploration Fund and of Liévin are usually quite

56   Hyamson, *British Consulate*, II, p. 331.
57   *Ibid.*, p. 336.
58   Schmelz, pp. 119-120.
63   *Ha-Levanon*, 27 Sivan, 1868, vol. V, no. 24, p. 387.
64   Warren, *Underground*, pp. 356-357, 493.
65   *Ibid.*, pp. 490-496.
66   Conder—Kitchener, II, p. 162

59   Ben-Zvi, *Eretz-Israel*, p. 366.
60   Reicher, p. 51.
61   Gat, p. 20.
62   *Loc. cit.*

similar, it is always important to note the period to which they refer. The first edition of Liévin's book was printed in 1869, but its figure of 8,000 Jews relates to a slightly earlier period. Similarly, the estimate of 10,000 Jews which appears in the work published by Warren's research expedition in 1876 apparently relates to the years the expedition spent in Jerusalem, i.e., 1867-1869. The correct figure for the end of the decade seems to be that given by the PEF survey: nearly 11,000 residents. This work was published in the years 1881-1884, but the population figures it presents are valid for the early 1870's and possibly even for the late 1860's.

The Subdivision of the Jewish Community; Summary

It is difficult to establish the relative sizes of the Ashkenazi and Sephardi communities during the nineteenth century. Immigration was the chief factor in Jewish population growth, and it led to the renascence of various Oriental-Jewish communities in the city. The Maghreb (North African) community is said to have re-established itself in 1854, and the Georgian community in 1863. The Bukharan Jews' community made its first appearance in Jerusalem in 1868.[67] Still, the majority of new immigrants were apparently of Ashkenazi origin. Ashkenazim and Sephardim seem to have been present in equal numbers by the end of the 1860's. This suggestion is reinforced by reports in later decades that the Ashkenazi community was then larger than that of the Sephardim.

The following two tables summarize our estimates of the growth of the Jewish and the general population of Jerusalem prior to Jewish settlement outside the Old City walls. The first table is based on this chapter, and the second on the chapters dealing with the Muslim and Christian populations. These figures should not be taken as exact ones, but rather as indicators of the developmental trends of the period.

Table 1

The Jewish Population of Nineteenth-Century Jerusalem prior to Expansion outside the City Walls (approximate figures)

Year	Sephardim	Ashkenazim	Total
1800	2,200	minimal	2,250
1836	2,600	650	3,250
1840	3,500	1,500	5,000
1850	4,000	2,000	6,000
1860	4,750	3,250	8,000
1870	5,500	5,500	11,000

67   Palestine Zionist Organization, *Censi, Judaea*, I, p. 5.

Table 2
The Population of Jerusalem by Communities (1800-1870)
(approximate figures)

Year	Jews	Muslims	Christians	All Non-Jews	Total
1800	2,250	4,000	2,750	6,750	9,000
1836	3,250	4,500	3,250	7,750	11,000
1840	5,000	4,650	3,350	8,000	13,000
1850	6,000	5,400	3,600	9,000	15,000
1860	8,000	6,000	4,000	10,000	18,000
1870	11,000	6,500	4,500	11,000	22,000

These tables show that the Jewish population of Jerusalem increased from some 2,000 to about 11,000 persons during the first seventy years of the nineteenth century. The community itself also underwent considerable change: made up almost entirely of Sephardim at the beginning of the century, the community included equal numbers of Sephardim and Ashkenazim by 1870.

A comparison with two other religious groups shows the Jewish community to have been the smallest of the three at the start of the century but the largest by about 1870, at which time it had even begun to outnumber the other two groups combined. This rapid increase in population brought with it a rise in the number of Jewish groups and of *kolelim,* as we will see in our next chapter.

Taken in their entirety, the demographic statistics we have dealt with at such length may seem fairly insignificant. But, as with many important towns in past ages, the character of Jerusalem was determined by a relatively small population. The period we have been reviewing marked the rise of the Jewish element in the city to the point where Jews came to outnumber all other Jerusalemites, as they have continued to do ever since.

Chapter Two:
THE SUBDIVISION OF THE JEWISH COMMUNITY

Introduction

Much has been written in Hebrew about the structure and composition of the Jewish community of nineteenth-century Jerusalem, including parts of Ben Zion Gat's recently reprinted intensive study of the Jewish community of Palestine from 1840-1880, which first appeared in 1950.[1] Rather than repeat his detailed study, we will present a *general* account of developments in Jewish Jerusalem and see how they fit in with the development of the city as a whole.

The Jewish Community at the Beginning of the Nineteenth Century

Very little is known about the Jewish community of Jerusalem in the first thirty years of the century, before Muḥammad 'Ali's occupation of Palestine. We have already noted that it consisted chiefly of the descendants of Jews who came after the Expulsion from Spain (1492), especially of those who fled the persecutions of the sixteenth century. Alongside them were the so-called "Arabized" Jews (*Mista'arvim*), who had lived in the country all along, and the Oriental Jews, who had trickled in from the Eastern countries and the Maghreb. The community was further reinforced by the influx of Sephardi Jews from the Balkan states and Asia Minor that intensified in the nineteenth century, particularly in its second half, and radically altered the community's composition.[2]

At the start of the century, the Jewish and Christian inhabitants of Jerusalem were treated by the Ottoman authorities as second-class citizens. This was in keeping with the *shari'a* or Muslim law, which was enforced throughout the Ottoman empire. They had to pay special taxes such as *jizye*, or poll-tax, and, although Islam forbade their being subject to religious coercion, their freedom of worship was limited in various ways. Particularly onerous to the Jews was the prohibition to build new synagogues. In addition, repairs to existing synagogues required a special permit that was very costly. Jews were discriminated against in the law courts, and could not bear witness against a Muslim. They were forced to wear clothing of a distinctive color, were forbidden to ride horses in the city, and were denied various political rights, such as participation in most departments of government.[3]

1   See Bibliography.
2   Gat, p. 22; Ben-Zvi, "Mista'rabs," pp. 379-386.
3   Heyd, "Jerusalem," p. 199; Ma'oz, *Reforms*, p. 10.

The Protestant missionary, Pliny Fisk, who visited Jerusalem in 1825, tells of contemporary discrimination against the Jews. Although the government was tolerant in matters of religion, there was severe oppression of the Jews in the secular sphere.[4] According to Light (1814), the Jews paid very heavy taxes to the Aga of Jerusalem. Jewish pilgrims also paid the Aga of Jaffa when they landed there, and the Sheikh of Abu Ghosh on their way to Jerusalem.[5]

In the early part of the century, only Sephardi Jews were accepted by the Turkish government as representatives of the country's Jewish population. Some claim that this policy changed after 1822,[6] but the Sephardim seem to have retained this representative function till considerably later by virtue of their being Ottoman subjects.[7]

The Renascence of the Ashkenazi Community

Very few Ashkenazi Jews lived in Jerusalem in the early nineteenth century. Their desertion of the city during the eighteenth century because of harassment by creditors, and their subsequent return, have been discussed elsewhere. It is generally accepted that the first organized group of Ashkenazim settled in Jerusalem between 1810 and 1820. It was composed of ten families belonging to the Perushim sect, and was led by Rabbi Menahem Mendel of Shklov and Rabbi Abraham Shlomo-Zalman Tzoref.[8] Rabbi Joseph Schwarz indicates that the Perushim were able to return to Jerusalem only after the hatred of the Muslims had abated. By then there were already about twenty followers of R. Elijah, the "Gaon of Vilna," living in the city.[9] Reicher describes these first steps as follows:

> With God's help, an Ashkenazi community settled in the Holy City of Jerusalem... in 1816, and now some forty householders have obtained a Firman from the Sultan... that the Gentiles cannot require them to pay old debts and they may rent houses from them.... Several years later, Ashkenazi Jews began arriving from Lithuania and Russia. A few of them built houses and study houses over the ruins of Rabbi Judah Hehasid's court... and later, the saintly Rabbi Aaron Moshe, a descendant of Zvi of Brod of saintly memory, purchased a ruined building in Jerusalem where he established a large study hall, but he could not find ten male Polish Jews to pray there. Finally... men, women and children began coming to join the Lord's community in the holy mountain of Jerusalem from nations far and near.... The Ashkenazim were subjugated by the Sephardim, who took all the money sent to the Ashkenazim from abroad to set up a holy society, until the Ashkenazim... increased in number and separated from them following serious disagreement.[10]

The newspaper *Ha-Levanon* reports that the Ashkenazim living in Jerusalem were considered to be inferior Jews by the Sephardim, and were unable to

---

4   P. Fisk, p. 263; Gat, p. 80.
5   Light, p. 184.
6   Gat, p. 23; Luncz, *Jerusalem*, IX, pp. 1-16.
7   Mrs. Finn, *Reminiscences*, p. 54.
8   Yaari, *Memoirs*, pp. 118-128; Gat, pp. 26-27; Eliav, *Love of Zion*, p. 13.
9   Schwarz, *Produce*, 1900 ed., p. 471.
10   Reicher, pp. 43-44 (translated from Hebrew).

Turk pulling a Jew by the beard (Turner, part of frontispiece)

obtain permission to work as ritual slaughterers. They had to purchase their meat from the Sephardim and pay a special tax on it, although they themselves did not benefit from the money: all of it was used by the Sephardim, who did not accept the Ashkenazim as *bona fide* Jews.[11]

Another Hebrew newspaper, *Ḥavatzelet,* writes that the two communities merged when the Ashkenazim first moved to the city. Ashkenazi Jewis prayed in Sephardi synagogues, buried their dead in Sephardi cemeteries and followed Sephardi customs. They even changed their style of dress and were no longer recognizably European. Only later, with the arrival of a large number of Ashkenazim, did they establish a separate community.[12]

Luncz writes of a terrible plague in the Holy Land which began in 1812 and lasted for over two years. Especially hard hit was the Galilee, where thousands died. Many fled to Jerusalem because there were very few cases of the disease there. Among these refugees were Rabbi Abraham Shlomo-Zalman Tzoref and Rabbi Menaḥem Mendel of Shklov, who decided to establish an Ashkenazi community in Jerusalem. There were dozens of refugees from Safed but, since some of them were afflicted with plague, they were not allowed to enter the city.

> Through the efforts of a Sephardi community official, they were brought to the large cave in the north of the city called "Magharet al-Maḥjar" (commonly known as the Cave of Zedekiah), where they remained for eight days. The official then rented two small Arab houses near the city wall for them; he subsequently paid the required tax for them when they were allowed into the city itself in September 1814. Some of them undoubtedly stayed in Jerusalem after the plague had subsided, but their exact number is unknown. Neither do we know whether any new Ashkenazi families settled in Jerusalem during the next two years.

282

11   *Ha-Levanon*, 22 Adar B, 1867, vol. IV, no. 7, p. 104.
12   *Ḥavatzelet*, 8 Sivan, 1872, vol. II, no. 33, pp. 257-258.

The Ashkenazi community continued to grow because of immigration from overseas, and it was eventually recognized by the government as a separate entity (except for taxation purposes). Slaughter-houses, cemeteries and other such facilities remained under Sephardi control many years after the establishment of the Ashkenazi community.[13]

The Sephardi Community and the "Ḥalukka"

What was the composition of the Sephardi community and how did it survive financially? According to Luncz, it included four categories: a) scholars and students, who received contributions from abroad; b) craftsmen and laborers, most of whom were natives of Palestine; c) merchants, who made a living from trade; d) the rich, who came to live out the remainder of their lives in the Holy Land and be buried there. The last, some of whom were widows of means now married to poor scholars, derived their income from assets left abroad in the hands of relatives.

The Sephardi community obtained its funds from both local and foreign sources. Local income came from the inheritance laws instituted by the rabbis of the Holy City in the sixteenth century. According to these laws, known as *Takkanot Yerushalayim,* any Jerusalem resident, whether native or foreign born, dying in Jerusalem without a legal heir in the city at the time of his death, had to leave his money and effects to the Jerusalem *kolel* officials. Since most immigrants to Jerusalem were elderly persons, this brought considerable sums into the community coffers. The rabbis, however, claimed it was barely enough to pay taxes, purchase burial grounds, and so on, forcing them, among other things, to levy a tax (the *gabella*) on the manufacture and sale of wine. When these sums also proved insufficient, they had to be supplemented by outside sources like the regular *halukka* collections in Turkey, the Maghreb (Morocco and Algeria) and Western Europe.[14]

Press also writes that, before the establishment of the Ashkenazi community, the Jews of Jerusalem received financial support from North Africa, Turkey and Western Europe. The central charity office was in Amsterdam. Once established, the Ashkenazi community received aid from Shklov and then, after 1820, from Russia, Lithuania and Poland, with the central collection office being located in Vilna.[15]

Money from overseas was sent to the Sephardi leadership, which divided it into three parts. One part went for community needs and municipal expenses, another to scholars recognized as such by a committee elected by the city's rabbinic scholars. This was in keeping with the belief that the purpose of the *halukka* was to support gifted Torah scholars, whose studies benefited the Jewish people as a whole. The remainder was doled out to the poor as haphazard gifts. Unable to rely on such erratic income, needy Sephardim tried to earn their livings from trade and craftsmanship. Until the establishment of a

283

13 Luncz—Kressel, pp. 166-169 (*Jerusalem*, XIII, 1919).
14 *Ibid.*, pp. 163-164.
15 Press, *Travel Handbook*, pp. 129-130.

separate Ashkenazi community, the money in the Sephardi community treasury seems to have served all the Jews in the city.[16]

The *halukka* was a phenomenon unique to the Jewish community of Palestine. This was due in large measure to the dismal economic plight of the country, and to the fact that most immigrants came with the intention of devoting their lives to study and prayer. Living in Palestine meant continual sacrifice and hardship, yet Jews continued to come, giving up mundane pleasures in order to express their devotion to the land and saturate its dry soil with their tears. Thus, the Jews of Jerusalem regarded the *halukka* not as charity, but as the compensation due every Jew who lived and studied there. This view gave rise to innumerable difficulties because even the wealthy thought they had a right to a portion of the *halukka*.[17]

At first, the emissaries sent to bring back contributions from the Diaspora represented individual communities and bore letters of introduction from their rabbis. Fund-raising was reorganized by the Amsterdam merchant, Rabbi Zvi-Hirsch Lehren, early in the nineteenth century. Between 1810 and 1822, a central collection center in Amsterdam maintained ties only with the Sephardi community, and *halukka* funds were distributed only to Sephardim. The system was reorganized again in 1822 and many other *halukka* distributors eventually began to function.[18]

The existence of a central *halukka* office in Amsterdam caused a decline in the importance of individual emissaries. In 1830, the new trustees of the Jewish Yishuv—the Amsterdam staff—launched a fierce battle against the independent emissaries, in an effort to reduce the undisciplined activity of various institutions and enforce order in the *halukka*. Led by the Lehren brothers, they began to organize the collection of charity from all of Western Europe and, later, from Central Europe as well. Those heading the operation bestowed the title of *Nasi* or "President of Palestine" on themselves and believed that, because of their extensive activities on behalf of the Jewish community, they were entitled to intervene in all its affairs, including the appointment of rabbis and lay officials. This intervention was the cause of endless quarrels and conflicts among the various Jewish groups in Jerusalem.[19]

Changes during Egyptian Rule (1831-1840)

An important change occurred following the Egyptian occupation of Palestine. In a letter written to his father-in-law on March 24, 1835, Rabbi Eliezer Bergmann writes that the Jews were now allowed to purchase homes in the Old City:

> In particular, it should be noted that our people (may God guard and preserve them) may now buy houses outright for themselves in the city... and indeed, several Ashkenazim from Poland... have purchased homes outright in one of the corners of the city, not far from one of the city gates where prices are very low,

16   Gat, pp. 101-103.
17   *Ibid.*, p. 94; Luncz, *Jerusalem*, IX, 1911, pp. 187-220; Rothschild.
18   Gat, pp. 94-95; Eliav, *Love of Zion*, pp. 14-18.
19   Gat, pp. 98-99.

homes within the Holy City (may it be speedily rebuilt and restored in our day, Amen) being very much more costly.[20]

From a later letter, it appears that Bergmann was referring to the Bab Ḥuta district, northeast of the Muslim Quarter, and near Herod's Gate.

A noteworthy event at the outset of Egyptian rule was the granting in 1834 of a charter (*firman*) for the renovation of the Sephardi synagogues, which were almost in ruins. A stone dome, and room for 1,000(!) worshippers were provided, at a cost of over *one million* piastres.[21]

1834 was also the year of the peasants' revolt against Muḥammad 'Ali. The Jews of Jerusalem, unlike those of Safed and Hebron, were not affected much by this. Another important event under Egyptian rule was the construction of the first wing of the Ḥurva synagogue, Menaḥem Zion, in 1836. (This will be discussed in greater detail later, when we deal with the synagogues of the city.)

There seems little doubt that the Jewish community was showing signs of recovery and development under the Egyptians before the earthquake of 1837. Further evidence of this is provided by the relative increase in the number of Jews, the strengthening of the Perushim sect, and the beginning of the *kolel* of German and Dutch Jews.

After the disastrous earthquake of 1837, there were important changes in the Jewish community of Jerusalem. The number of Perushim increased greatly. Instead of the few families present before 1820, the Perushim numbered 418 souls in Montefiore's census of 1838, the year after the earthquake.[22] Some sources stress that there was also a substantial increase in immigration from Germany, Holland and Hungary after the death of the Gaon of Vilna. These immigrants joined the Perushim in the establishment of public institutions which formed the foundations of Jerusalem's "Old Yishuv," and which were imbued with the Gaon's teachings.[23]

After the earthquake, large numbers of Ḥasidim began arriving in Jerusalem, and formed the city's Ḥasidic community.[24]

The Improved Status of the Jews during the 1840's

The Jewish community of Jerusalem was strongly affected by the resumption of Turkish control over Palestine. These years also saw the establishment of the first foreign consulates in Jerusalem. As the influence of the foreign powers grew, their consuls in Jerusalem gave substance to the "Capitulations" system, which had been in force until then only on paper. Many newly-arrived Jews, as well as many local ones, were recognized as foreign nationals enjoying consular protection. The Muslims now had to beware of causing injury to Jews of foreign nationality; such Jews were entitled to be tried in the presence of their consul or his representative. The homes of foreign nationals could not be entered by the authorities without consular permission and, if the Turkish governor attempted to bring one of these people to trial without the consul's

20 Bergmann, p. 93 (translated from Hebrew).
21 Spyridon, p. 125.
22 Ben-Zvi, *Eretz-Israel*, p. 362.
23 Malachi, pp. 9-21.
24 Press, *Travel Handbook*, pp. 129-130.

285

assent, the latter, who jealously upheld his country's prestige, was quick to intercede.[25]

As a result, the Jews of Jerusalem belonged to one of two categories: they were either *raya* (Ottoman subjects), or "Franks" (Europeans enjoying foreign protection). In the 1840's the first category was still the largest, but there was an increase in the second from the middle of the century.[26] This is emphasized by Neumann, who adds that Ottoman subjects enjoyed total freedom and paid only a poll-tax of fifteen, thirty, or sixty piastres per year, according to their means; the community paid for the poor. Jews protected by foreign countries were exempt from this poll-tax, and paid very little in customs duties. Charitable organizations were not charged customs duty on their imports, and had the same rights as "Frankish" institutions.[27]

At the beginning of the 1840's, representatives of the non-Muslim communities began to be recognized by the Turkish authorities. Istanbul ordered the Jews of Jerusalem to choose a chief rabbi, or *Hakham Bashi*. This issue immediately became controversial: some Jews wholly opposed such an appointment, while others battled against the chief contender, Rabbi Hayim Gagin, the chief rabbi of the Sephardim. Nevertheless, Gagin was elected, and recognized by the Sultan. This new office enhanced the status of the Sephardi community, because the *Hakham Bashi* or the *Rishon le-Zion* ("Foremost of Zion") was always selected from among its members. Although some of the later chief rabbis were recognized only by the local authorities and not granted the imperial *firman,* the status of the *Hakham Bashi* was undoubtedly beneficial for the Jews.[28] One writer notes in 1843 that the *Hakham Bashi* was responsible for the collection of taxes in his community and had several officials at his command, and that his authority extended over nearly all the Sephardi Jews in Palestine.[29]

It should also be pointed out that non-Muslim communities were still organized in "milets," with autonomy in the educational and religious spheres, as well as jurisdiction concerning matrimonial law. Ottoman Jews and Christians were represented in the *Majlis* or administrative council of Jerusalem, where their delegates were treated fairly and were active members. However, Jews and Christians had fewer representatives, proportionately, than the Muslims, and they were seen as being inferior to Muslim council members.

The Sephardi Community

There are many descriptions of the Sephardi community of Jerusalem in western travel literature of the mid-nineteenth century. Mrs. Finn, for example, makes these comments:

> To the Turkish authorities the Sephardim were then the only people recognised as Jews. They were permitted to settle on the eastern slopes of Mount Zion and had

25 Hyamson, II, p. 2; Temperly, pp. 443-445.
26 Gat, p. 80; Eliav, *Love of Zion*, p. 14; and see sources cited in both.
27 Neumann, p. 375.
28 Gat, p. 72; Luncz, *Jerusalem*, IV, p. 210; Grayevsky, *Hidden Treasures*, I & II.
29 J. Wilson, I, pp. 453-459.

the privilege, in return for payment of annual fees, of worshipping at the western wall of Solomon's Temple, the "Wailing Wall." Their Chief Rabbi was recognised by the Turkish Government and also given certain privileges, including jurisdiction over their people and the right to employ a Kawass. Like all other non-Moslems, the Jews were exempt from military service, but had to pay a capitation tax. A good many of the Sephardi Jews were rough carpenters and glaziers. They spoke the old Spanish of the fifteenth century, with some Hebrew intermixture. They never went beyond the walls of Jerusalem except for the monthly prayers at Rachel's Sepulchre near Bethlehem or to Hebron. The women never veiled their faces, but were seldom out of doors. They had an old synagogue and, as a community, were excessively poor.[30]

Another Western writer, W.H. Bartlett, had this to say:

> The Sephardi, or Spanish, community, numbers six to seven thousand, and includes... the descendants of those Jews expelled from Spain by Ferdinand and Isabella in the fifteenth century, many of whom found a refuge in Jerusalem among the Moslems. The Morocco and other Oriental Jews also belong to this division. Not only have the majority of these Jews no trades, but they have no allowance from the fund of the community, which is burthened with an increasing debt of two million piastres.... The money collected abroad is not enough to pay the interest upon this debt.... Every Friday the synagogue servants go to the houses of those few who are a little better off, and beg loaves of bread, which they then distribute among the most needy. The disease and suffering occasioned by bad food, close crowded dwellings, and scarcity of water, are beyond description, and would surely, if known, awaken the compassion and active benevolence of happy England. Any one of the medical residents could testify that death from starvation is not uncommon. A well-directed system of employment is what would more than anything raise the poor Israelites of Zion from their mental and bodily degradation. The chief rabbi and head of both divisions must be a Sephardi; and the Spanish Jews generally despise and dislike the Ashkenazim. Each class has its own synagogues, rabbis, and councils, and all are tyrannised over and kept in bondage by those rabbis who hesitate at no means of keeping up their authority.... The Jews speak Hebrew among themselves, and the Ashkenazim have a dialect of German, and the Sephardim a dialect of Spanish in various shades of admixture with Greek and Turkish; but the high families speak a good dialect, and preserve in it many antique words no longer used in Spain. The Oriental Jews also speak Arabic and several other languages.[31]

He also notes that "the financial affairs of the community are administered by its own officers; but its debt is enormous, with interest on the obligations paid to Moslems and the convents at an excessively high rate." Other western sources noted that the Sephardi community was better organized than that of the Ashkenazim, and that most of the Sephardim were natives of the country and Ottoman subjects. On the other hand, the educational level of the Sephardim was lower and their women, unlike the Ashkenazi women, were almost all illiterate, as was customary in the Orient.[32]

A Jewish writer, Dr. Frankl, describes the financial state of the Sephardi community in 1856. He says it had several sources of income: contributions from the Jewish community of Amsterdam; contributions from other countries (especially those of North Africa); money from the sale of burial plots; fees for

30 Mrs. Finn, *Reminiscences*, p. 54.
31 Bartlett, *Revisited*, p. 43-44; on the languages spoken by the Jews see also Press, *Hundred Years*, p. 129.
32 Zimmerman, pp. 6-8.

Jewish family on "Mt. Zion" (=the Jewish Quarter) (Bartlett, *Walks*, frontispiece)

circumcisions and weddings; taxes on meat and wine. The community enjoyed a monopoly on ritual meat slaughtering. Its expenses included taxes and duties paid to the Turkish authorities; payments made to Arab villages and Muslim leaders to insure access to the Wailing Wall and Rachel's Tomb, and to prevent desecration of graves on the Mount of Olives and in the Kidron Valley; internal community expenses; the salary of the *Ḥakham Bashi*; the wages of the community scribe and functionaries; allowances for the study of the Torah; the maintenance of the poor, and of widows and orphans. Frankl cites figures for the expenditures and revenues during the year of his visit, commenting that the Sephardi community had cut its expenses to 20,000 piastres a year by closing down its only *Talmud Torah* and selling the building to the Rothschild family for use as a hospital.[33]

The Ḥakham Bashi and His Court

As we have noted, only the Sephardim were considered Jews by the Ottoman authorities, and the *Rishon le-Zion* had to be a member of this community. He was elected by the *ḥakhamim* (Sephardi rabbis), and confirmed in office by the Turkish administration. His official status was similar to that of other religious leaders recognized in Turkey, and his representative was a member of the Pasha's council.[34] Neumann writes that the elected *Ḥakham Bashi* was

33   Frankl, pp. 173-175.
34   Bartlett, *Revisited*, pp. 79-83; Mrs. Finn, *Reminiscences*, p. 54.

Jewish family on "Mt. Zion" (Porter, *Jerusalem*, p. 35)

presented with a document signed by the Sultan himself, as well as the *medjidi* medal and an embroidered tarbush. He presided over a council of eighty rabbis, three of whom sat as the *beth din,* or religious court of law, in monthly rotation. This court delivered its verdict as soon as each case was heard, and received no fee. It was held in esteem by members of other religions who, in cases of disputes with Jews, often turned to it for help. The government authorities recognized its verdicts and saw to their execution. Important issues were dealt with by the *Beth Din Gadol* or superior rabbinical court, composed of the seven most respected rabbis. The committee in charge of community affairs consisted of three officials, three substitutes, and three supervisors. The community owned several synagogues, houses, and vacant lots, but there were no communal taxes and its income was minimal and irregular. Immigrants were required to pay an admission tax commensurate with their means. The community's expenses far exceeded its income; the deficit sometimes forced the sale of community real estate, but this did not keep the community from sinking deeper and deeper into debt.[35]

After his election, the *Rishon le-Zion* was installed with great ceremony and honored by the Turkish authorities and various European governments, who regarded him as the representative of Palestinian Jewry. A new pasha would make a special courtesy visit to the *Rishon le-Zion* upon his arrival in the city. The government posted special guards outside his door. This, however, proved

35 Neumann, pp. 366-368; Finn, *Stirring Times*, I, p. 103; Mrs. Finn, *Reminiscences*, p. 182; Gorion, pp. 49-50.

an expensive luxury and was dispensed with by the community in favor of two *kawasses* who escorted him through the streets.[36]

An interesting description of the election of the *Ḥakham Bashi* appears in the newspaper *Ha-Levanon:*

> The person chosen to be leader must belong to a rabbinic family and be sixty or seventy years old, the older the better.... On the day of his inauguration, all the scholars, rabbis and other dignitaries assemble at his home. The eldest among them dresses the chosen rabbi in a new mantle *(joba)* and turban, while reciting the *She-heḥeyanu* benediction ("Blessed art Thou... who has kept us alive and preserved us..."). All the guests say *"be-siman tov"* (may it be under a propitious sign) and approach the rabbi to kiss his hand and the hem of his garment. The rabbi then delivers a sermon. Apart from the power vested in him by the rabbis and Turkish authorities of the city, he is awarded the *nis'an* or medal of honor of the government and is sent the official seal, inscribed in Hebrew and Turkish. He is empowered by law to reign over the Jews in the same way that the *qadi* reigns over the Ishmaelites. Any request he submits in keeping with his office to the pasha must be acted upon, by decree of the sultan.

The newspaper goes on to describe the *Ḥakham Bashi's* special court called *Beth Din Haz'man* ("court of the times"), which dealt mainly with matters of ritual prohibition and permission, or relations between man and man, and was made up of an unspecified number of rabbis and scholars. Its judges were rotated every three months. Since this court was subordinate to the chief rabbi, any decision made by him was binding on it. Another court meeting once or twice a week was presided over by the chief rabbi together with two scholars of his own choice. A further task of the *Ḥakham Bashi* was to supervise the sending of agents to collect contributions abroad, and to negotiate with them in advance how much of the money they collected would go to the *kolel* treasury. In addition, he appointed these agents, determined their destinations, and kept an eye on the community's financial affairs.[37]

As time went on, the *Rishon le-Zion* declined in importance in the eyes of non-Sephardi Jews, most of whom were foreign subjects enjoying privileges under the Capitulations and not subject to his jurisdiction. After an extended struggle they achieved a considerable degree of autonomy, and their ties to the *Rishon le-Zion* weakened even more. The chief responsibility of the *Rishon le-Zion* as head of the Jewish community was to present the poll-tax to the Ottoman authorities. Since there were many poverty-stricken Jews in the city, he had to supplement what was collected in taxes by sums from the general funds of the community. Although at first he tried to shift part of the burden onto the shoulders of the Ashkenazim, this was no longer possible once they were exempted from this tax by virtue of their acquiring foreign nationality. In the end, however, the Ashkenazim paid indirectly by means of the meat tax, which the chief rabbi collected whenever government taxes were collected. In theory, the influence of the *Rishon le-Zion* extended over all Jewish groups in the country; in practice, his power was limited to the Sephardi community, especially to representing it before the Ottoman authorities. His hegemony in this respect continued almost until the British conquest of 1917.[38]

290

36 Frankl, pp. 158-160; Gat, pp. 73-75.
37 *Ha-Levanon*, 21 Shevat, 1865, vol. II, no. 4, pp. 52-53.
38 Gat, pp. 73-80; Neumann, p. 375.

The Differences Between the Sephardi and Ashkenazi Communities

The Jewish sources make much of the fact that the Sephardi community tried to prevent the Ashkenazim from becoming independent. For example, the Ashkenazim were not allowed to do their own ritual slaughtering. As we have seen, an important economic consideration was involved: the price of properly slaughtered meat (which was also bought by Muslims) included a tax levied for the Sephardi community committee. Neither were the Ashkenazim allowed to have a separate burial society, because this service too produced a substantial income. The property of the many persons dying without heirs, including Ashkenazim, went to the Sephardi community committee.[39] This caused a great deal of tension between the two communities, and their relationship deteriorated to the point where *Ha-Levanon* complains of the Sephardi rabbis' total refusal to recognize or aid the Ashkenazi rabbis, despite their being fellow Jews.[40]

The Sephardim and Ashkenazim of Jerusalem could be told apart by their attire although, at the beginning of the century, some Ashkenazim dressed like Sephardim; at a later date, the Dutch and German members of *Kolel* Hod also wore Sephardic garb. Cahanyu writes extensively about the differences in dress between the two communities:

> The Ashkenazim speak the same language they spoke abroad and follow the same manners and style of dress as did the preceding generation in their native lands. Only a few of them have begun to dress like Sephardim, with some modifications. The Sephardim wear flowing robes, with red hats (*fez*) and shawls on their heads. The *hakhamim* also tie a costly scarf around their necks in various ways. The city of Zion is unlike other European towns and cities, where everyone pays attention to what others do, say and wear. The inhabitants of Zion are not concerned with such things. On a single street you can see a multitude of people from various countries, each dressed differently. Some are wrapped in white robes and covered with scarves, others wear black coats. Some don clothing of a red, others of a green hue — each according to his national custom or personal whim...."[41]

In the second half of the nineteenth century, the Sephardi community began to split into various factions, but to a lesser extent than the Ashkenazi community. Frankl tells us that, as early as 1856, Tunisian, Algerian and Moroccan Jews began to rebel against their subjection to the Sephardic community, and sought to establish a separate one of their own.[42] In the same year, Montefiore mentions the existence of a *kolel* composed mainly of Moroccans, *Kolel Ha-ma'araviim*. The distinguished rabbi of this community, Rabbi David ben Shim'on, immigrated to Jerusalem in 1854, and many Jews of the Maghreb followed in his wake.[43]

The second group to part from the Sephardi community was that of the Georgian Jews ("Gurjim"). Montefiore reports the presence of *Kolel "Gurjistan"* in 1856. While Graetz (1872) does not mention this *kolel*, it

---

39   Y. Yellin, *Memoirs*, pp. 99-112, Reicher, p. 44.
40   *Ha-Levanon*, 27 Nisan, 1866, vol. III, no. 8, p. 115.
41   Cahanyu, p. 50; on the Jews' clothing see also Luncz—Kressel, p. 218; Press, *Hundred Years*, p. 21.
42   Frankl, p. 173.
43   Gat, p. 24.

reappears in a list of *kolelim* compiled in 1875, following the considerable immigration from Georgia after 1863.[44]

The Growth of the Ashkenazi Community

The ˊPerushim. We will now return to the development of the Ashkenazi community in the period before Jews began settling outside the Old City walls. The two major Ashkenazi groups in Jerusalem in the early 1840's were the Perushim and the Ḥasidim. The older and larger of the two was that of the Perushim, who were followers of the famed Rabbi Elijah, the "Gaon of Vilna." Since they received *ḥalukka* money from the Jews of Vilna, they were often called *Kolel Vilna*.[45] Frankl (1856) writes that they were led by Rabbi Bardaki of Minsk, and were all Russian-born. The Russian authorities demanded their return to Russia, and removed their protection from them when they refused. Some of these Perushim became British subjects, and most of the others, Austrian ones. They receive, he notes, 300,000 piastres in donations from Vilna and 80,000 from elsewhere. The money collected in Austro-Hungary came only from Vienna and Eisenstadt.[46] According to Reicher, the *Kolel Perushim* included Jews from Russia, Lithuania, Vilna, Grodno, Pinsk and Minsk, all of whom were followers of Rabbi Elijah, the Gaon of Vilna. Originally, he says, they lived in Safed; most fled to Jerusalem after the earthquake of 1837 and subsequently constituted the majority of Jerusalem's Ashkenazi population Some of these Perushim were important rabbis and scholars. The community ran its own courts, *Talmud Torah, yeshivot*, synagogues and study halls. Most *kolel* members had brought some capital with them from their native lands; the few who engaged in trade were generally successful.[47]

Opinions are divided over the origin of the name Perushim. There is, of course, no connection between these Perushim and the Perushim, or Pharisees, of the second Temple period. The name Perushim, or "those who break away," seems to have been used to emphasize their separation from the Ḥasidim.[48] (In Eastern Europe, the Perushim were known as Mitnagdim or "opposers.")

When the Perushim first began to settle in the city, Rabbi Isaiah Bardaki served as community leader. Later, Rabbi Joseph Sundel Salant, who immigrated to Jerusalem in 1839, and his son-in-law, Rabbi Samuel Salant, who followed in 1841, shared the responsibility with him. This partnership was a stormy one and, before long, the community split into two factions over the question of building a synagogue: the Ḥurva Party, headed by Rabbi Samuel Salant, and the Ḥatzer Party, headed by Rabbi Isaiah Bardaki.[49]

The Ḥasidim. The Ḥasidim formed the second largest Ashkenazi community in Jerusalem. Since the Perushim were initially the sole representatives of Ashkenazi Jewry in Jerusalem, the first Ḥasidim to move to the city joined this community. However, they continued to receive their portion of the *ḥalukka*

44   *Ibid.*, p. 116; Meisel, *Testimonial Fund*, p. 21; Ben-Zvi, *Population*, pp. 37-97.
45   Gat, p. 117; Luncz, *Jerusalem*, V, pp. 217-218; 221-222.
46   Frankl, pp. 175-176.   48   Gat, pp. 27-28.
47   Reicher, pp. 51-52.   49   Y. Yellin, *Memoirs*, p. 10.

Samuel Kaufman, 73-year-old Jewish resident of Jerusalem (Hedin, p. 71)

from *Kolel Ha-Ḥasidim* of Safed and Tiberias, and remained a distinct group for this reason.[50]

A separate Ḥasidic community began to take shape in Jerusalem after the earthquake of 1837, and especially after 1840. The Perushim, however, retained the upper hand for a long time to come. Dissatisfied with this state of affairs, the Ḥasidim began to complain of being deprived of *ḥalukka* monies and of being dominated by Perushim officials. They remained subject to the Perushim-controlled Ashkenazi superior rabbinical court until 1873. Only in 1877 were the Ḥasidim granted permission to do their own ritual slaughtering. The inferior status of the Ḥasidim may have been one of the reasons why this community produced men who sought to change the character of Jerusalem. These people denounced the *ḥalukka* system and demanded radical reorganization of the contemporary way of life. They were also much more receptive to new educational ideas than the Perushim.[51]

Kolel Hod. The first *kolel* to break away from the General *Kolel* of the Perushim as early as the 1830's was *Kolel* Hod (*Ho*lland-*D*eutschland). It consisted of eight families from Germany and Holland who were apparently dissatisfied with their share of *ḥalukka* funds. Since the Jews in Germany and Holland contributed large sums, they thought that they should receive more

293

---

50   Gat, pp. 122-123.
51   *Ibid.*, p. 28-29; Ben-Zvi, *Eretz-Israel*, p. 388; Frankl, p. 177.

than other Jews. They hoped to accomplish this by founding a separate *kolel*. Rabbi Moses Sachs, who moved to Jerusalem in 1830, was the first member of this group. When Rabbi Eliezer Bergmann, a German Jew, arrived in 1835, he found four other "German" Jews already in the city: three Jews from Amsterdam and Rabbi Joseph Schwarz. By 1848, the number of German Jews in Jerusalem had reached fifty-seven.[52]

Even non-Jewish writers such as Tobler noted the lack of German-Jewish families in Jerusalem prior to 1830. By 1842, however, there were twelve such families.[53] G.H. Schubert, who visited Jerusalem in 1837, writes that a letter of introduction to Rabbi Bergmann was given to him in Bavaria. He also mentions the German-Jewish families of Schwarz and Hirsch.[54] Petermann, writing of 1853, tells us they had a small synagogue, and shared the money arriving from Germany with the other Jews. The community then consisted of twelve families, most of them poor, and numbered sixty persons.[55] Frankl (1856) confirms this figure. He claims the German Jews constituted a separate community, which received annual contributions of 60,000 piastres from Amsterdam and 2,000 piastres from other countries.[56]

The Splintering of the Community

The sub-division of the Ashkenazim into numerous *kolelim* began in the early 1850's, and continued for several decades. By the 1860's, there were nineteen *kolelim* in Jerusalem.[57] Among the first to secede from the General *Kolel* of the Perushim, apparently for economic and social reasons, was the Warsaw *kolel*. With increased immigration to Palestine, a number of distinguished rabbis arrived from Poland. When they were not given preferential treatment, they complained to their colleagues in the Diaspora about financial matters in Jerusalem, and decided to create a *kolel* of their own. This *kolel* was established on a geographical basis and included all Jews stemming from the Warsaw district; both Perushim and Ḥasidim joined it. According to Frankl (1856), the Warsaw *kolel* had 150 members, some of whom had the status of British, Prussian or Austian nationals. It received 90,000 piastres in contributions from Galicia, and 5,000 from other countries.[58]

A short while later, Jews from Russian Poland founded the Grodno *kolel*, seemingly in an attempt to undermine the General *Kolel* of the Perushim. In 1858, the Hungarians established the *Kolel Shomrei Haḥomot* ("guardians of the walls"), most of whose members were followers of the Ḥatam Sofer of Pressburg, and violent opponents of change in the Jewish educational system. Some of them, however, settled in agricultural colonies. This period also saw the establishment of *Kolel Minsk* (1856-1857), *Kolel Lomza* (1856-1858), *Kolel Slonim* (probably in 1856), and *Kolel Reissin* (probably in early 1860's).[59]

---

52 Luncz, *Jerusalem*, IX, pp. 17, 43; Eliav, *Love of Zion*.
53 Tobler, *Denkblätter*, pp. 360-361.
54 Schubert, II, p. 555.
55 Petermann, I, p. 230.
56 Frankl, p. 178.
57 Luncz, *Jahrbuch*, pp. 61-67; Gat, p. 112; Hannani, *Enlightenment*, pp. 7-8.
58 Frankl, p. 178.
59 Gat, pp. 119-123.

The Ḥasidim, too, after having all belonged to a single *kolel* until 1845, and having shared in the *ḥalukka* funds of the large Ḥasidic community of Safed, began to split into many *kolelim*. The first separate *kolel* was *Kolel Volhyn,* led *inter alia* by the well-known Bak family. The size and active leadership of this *kolel* helped establish its predominance in the Ḥasidic community.[60]

Kolel Ḥabad was the second Ḥasidic *kolel* in Jerusalem. At the behest of their revered leader, the Rabbi of Lubavitch, a group of Ḥabad Ḥasidim had settled in Hebron in 1821, founding the first Ashkenazi settlement there. In 1856, a few of these Ḥasidim moved to Jerusalem, and founded *Kolel Ḥabad,* which soon became one of the most prestigious in the city. Frankl (1856) writes that only forty or fifty members of this *kolel* lived in Jerusalem; they received annually 40,000 piastres from Russia, and 5,000 piastres from other countries. Reicher (1867) adds that they had their own study hall and that a few of them were shopkeepers.[61]

The third Ḥasidic *kolel* broke away from *Kolel Volhyn* in 1853 because of a financial dispute. It included Jews from Austria, Galicia and Cracow. Frankl (1856) reports that it had 150 members, some of whom lived in Safed and Tiberias. They received contributions of 80,000 piastres from Galicia and some 6,000 from other countries. *Kolel Karlin* separated from this *kolel* in 1870, and *Kolel Zhitomir* left *Kolel Volhyn* in 1872. Thus, the number of Ḥasidic *kolelim* in Jerusalem grew steadily.[62]

At the end of the 1860's, Dr. Neumann stresses, the Ashkenazim of Jerusalem formed not a single community but many different groups. Their primary division was between Perushim and Ḥasidim, but these were again divided, chiefly by places of origin. There were 3,000 Perushim from Russia, 700 from Warsaw, 500 from Hungary, and 100 from Germany and Holland. The Ḥasidim included 1,000 Jews from Volhyn and 500 from Galicia, as well as 200 members of Ḥabad.[63]

The General Kolelim Committee

The sub-division into *kolelim* continued into the 1870's and beyond. In an effort to minimize differences and draw all the various *kolelim* together, the "General Committee for All Ashkenazi *Kolelim*" was founded in 1866. Its aim was to supervise community needs, and represent the Ashkenazi Jews of Jerusalem in their dealings with outsiders. This, however, did not unify the *kolelim*: internal affairs, such as alms distribution, continued to be dealt with separately.[64]

As for official matters, we have already indicated that, initially, only the Sephardi community and the *Ḥakham Bashi* were recognized as community representatives by the government. As the Ashkenazi groupings in the city gained in strength, they began to appoint leaders, alongside their rabbis, to manage their secular affairs. One such leader was Rabbi Isaiah Bardaki, who

60   *Ibid.*, pp. 123-125.
61   Luncz, *Jerusalem*, IX, 1911, pp. 187-213; Frankl, p. 177; Reicher, pp. 51-52; Gat, p. 123.
62   Frankl, p. 177; Gat, p. 124.
63   Neumann, pp. 369-371.
64   Press, *Travel Handbook*, pp. 129-130; Gat, pp. 114-115.

ruled the Perushim with an iron hand from 1840-1860. Some considered him to be the *Ḥakham Bashi* of the Ashkenazim. Since Bardaki also served as vice-consul of Austria, he had a *kawass* to walk before him with a silver-tipped cane, and a dragoman to aid him in his dealings with the authorities.[65]

Following the death of Rabbi Isaiah Bardaki in 1863, a new generation of Ashkenazi leaders appeared on the scene. These were active in founding the union noted above of all the Ashkenazi *kolelim,* including those of the Perushim and those of the Ḥasidim alike. Joseph Rivlin served as secretary of this union, and was its moving spirit. Rabbi Samuel Salant became a prominent leader, and it was the existence of the General Committee that enabled him to be elected both local rabbi and chief rabbi of the Jerusalem Ashkenazi community (for both Perushim and Ḥasidim). Although he did not receive this title from the government, the Ashkenazi chief rabbi began to be regarded on a par with the *Rishon le-Zion,* and the Ashkenazim began to be recognized by both Jews and others as being an independent community.

Summary

The developments of the late 1860's marked the growth and strengthening of Jerusalem's Jewish community. It was not long before this growth found its expression in settlement outside the walls of the Old City. This period also saw considerable respect paid to the city's Jewish leadership. Because of the unique status of religious communities in the Ottoman Empire, Sephardi and Ashkenazi leaders were granted the authority to establish an independent judicial system and the power to have both their own verdicts and those of the Turkish authorities implemented. They made use of this authority not only to deal with matters concerning daily life but also, and even more so, to punish religious offenses. Thus, for example, the ritual bath in Rabbi Isaiah Bardaki's courtyard was used as a jail as well, and there were stocks in the courtyard of the Ḥurva synagogue, where sinners might be confined and displayed to the entire community.[66] The Jewish community was so independent that it even issued its own money, backed by the *halukka* and accepted as legal tender in Jerusalem markets. Frankl describes these coins as square bits of metal inscribed with the words *bikkur ḥolim* (visiting the sick). They seem to have been designed originally for charitable purposes, but the Jews came to regard them as current coin. Sometimes they were even accepted by foreign merchants. Consul Finn reports that the Jews used various types of coin, and that this was disapproved of by the Turks. He also indicates that the Jews demonstrated the trappings of independence in other ways.[67]

A most powerful weapon in the hands of the Jewish leadership was, of course, the control of the *halukka* funds. By threatening to withhold these funds, or by excommunicating anyone who challenged their authority, the leaders were able to enforce their will and command public obedience.[68]

296

The sizable population growth and development of numerous community groupings during the nineteenth century brought with it a proliferation of synagogues in the city. We will deal with the synagogues in the next chapter.

65 Y. Yellin, *Memoirs*, p. 9; Gat, p. 76.
66 Gat, pp. 75-80.
67 J. Finn, *Stirring Times*, I, pp. 101-103.
68 Gat, pp. 77-88.

Chapter Three:
SYNAGOGUES, TALMUDEI TORAH AND YESHIVOT; THE WAILING WALL AS A PRAYER SITE

Introduction

There is no doubt that the number, size and splendor of synagogues in the Old City during the nineteenth century reflected the size and development of the Jewish community at that time. As we saw above, there were very few Jews in Jerusalem during the early part of the century; their synagogues reflected the trying conditions in which they lived. This did not escape the attention of nineteenth-century travelers who visited the city. In 1807 Ali Bey (El-Abbassi) describes the synagogues of Jerusalem as pitiful.[1] According to Richter, they were wretched and small in 1818.[2] Seetzen writes that during his visit there were only five synagogues in the whole city, one of which belonged to the Karaites.[3]

The Sephardi Synagogues

The Old City's main synagogues in the beginning of the nineteenth century were the four famous, interconnected Sephardi synagogues known collectively as the Rabban Yoḥanan ben Zakkai synagogues. Buckingham (1816) describes his visit together with a friend to these synagogues on the Sabbath. Despite several inaccuracies as to the number of rooms and worshippers (particularly the women), he gives a fair account of what it was like to pray there.[4] Joliffe (1817) was probably referring to these synagogues when he described his impressions of a Jewish prayer service.[5] These Sephardi synagogues are mentioned by Forbin in 1818,[6] and by John Carne (in 1821), who tells of a group of synagogues reached by descending a flight of stairs.[7] Madden was taken in 1827 to see a Jerusalem synagogue, apparently that of the Sephardim, by Mr. Amzalag, the wealthiest Jew in the city.[8]

In 1831, Geramb writes, there was a large synagogue in Jerusalem that was famous abroad. Partially built of wood, it looked very old and neglected, and housed many bookshelves bearing ancient religious texts.[9] Geramb speaks of

1   El-Abbassi, II, p. 239.
2   Richter, II, p. 263.
3   Seetzen, II, p. 19.
4   Buckingham, pp. 254-258.
5   Joliffe, pp. 145-146.
6   Forbin, pp. 34-36.
7   Carne, p. 351.
8   Madden, pp. 242-248.
9   Geramb, II, pp. 86-89.

Ancient Jewish synagogue in the Kidron Valley (Pierotti, II, pl. LVII)

the four synagogues as if there were only one, including a school and a *beth midrash* (study hall) which was less well known than that in Tiberias.[10]

Jewish sources also dwell upon the poor condition of the Sephardi synagogues in the early nineteenth century. Over the years, the buildings had fallen into disrepair and their ceilings had become so damaged that it was almost impossible to pray there when it rained or during a heat wave. Rabbi Raphael Makhluf Abraham Ḥayyat, who was sent as an emissary to Morocco, writes as follows:

> The five synagogues (Rabban Yoḥanan ben Zakkai)... are so old that it is a miracle they are still standing.... Because of their poverty, the Jews have been forced to build from tin and boards which cannot withstand the wind and provide no shelter from the heat.... The rain pours in and drives the worshippers from one corner to the other. They cover their faces with their cloaks and hasten to complete their prayers before the synagogue is flooded. Then they leave, weeping that things have come to this.[11]

Restoration was first begun in 1834; it included the replacement of the wooden dome by a stone one to keep the rain out.[12] Bartlett writes that the four Sephardi synagogues had been renovated a few years earlier by the Minkhas (actually: Meyuḥas) family.[13] Frankl and Neumann add that the Rabban

298

10   *Ibid.*, pp. 90-92.
11   Yaari, *Emissaries*, pp. 724-725 (translated from Hebrew).
12   Spyridon, p. 125.
13   Bartlett, *Revisited*, pp. 78-83.

Yoḥanan ben Zakkai synagogue, which was about to collapse, had been repaired by permission of Ibrahim Pasha.[14]

Later descriptions of the unique structure of the Sephardi synagogues include that of Consul Finn (in the 1850's), which tells us that the four synagogues of the Sephardim, the large, the middle, the *Talmud Torah* and the "Istambuli" synagogues, were all grouped together in a single complex.[15] Mrs. Finn adds that the door of one synagogue opened into the next. The furnishings were of plain wood and the synagogues were used as schools for children of all ages.[16] Reicher provides us with a similar account for 1867.[17] In the 1870's Neumann describes the synagogues as follows:

> The Sephardi synagogues are wrapped in an aura of antiquity and all who enter their underground rooms feel a sense of mystery and holiness. The present synagogue, Kahal Zion, was founded by the Sephardim in what was believed to have been the study hall of Rabbi Yoḥanan ben Zakkai, before the destruction of the Temple. When the community expanded, another synagogue, Kahal Talmud Torah, was built alongside it. Some time later, a third was added: Kahal Medio [=middle in Ladino]. Finally, in the eighteenth century, Kahal Les Stambulis (for the Jews of Istanbul) was added.... Ibrahim Pasha of Egypt allowed them to renovate the buildings; this work was completed in 1845. It was then that an inscribed stone was discovered that proved the building to be 460 years old...[18]

Aside from these Sephardi synagogues, the Beth El synagogue and the Rabbi Ḥayyim ben Attar *yeshiva* (later called Or Ha-Ḥayyim) apparently served for prayer and study early in the century. They were rented by the Ashkenazi community later on for these purposes.

The Ashkenazi Synagogues

At first, the Perushim were unable to build a synagogue of their own, and held services in the *sukka* of the Sephardi synagogues, as well as in the Beth El synagogue and the Rabbi Ḥayyim ben Attar *yeshiva*. According to Luncz, this last was opened without permission from the authorities, and so prayers were conducted there at first only on week-days. Sometimes the congregants even removed the Torah scrolls in the middle of the night, for fear of discovery.[19]

The first Ashkenazi synagogue and study hall to be built in Jerusalem was "Menaḥem Zion," the first wing of the Ḥurva synagogue. Luncz tells of the founding of the Menaḥem Zion synagogue:

> The Ashkenazi community was growing steadily and had only one synagogue—Or Ha-Ḥayyim—which they rented with financial assistance from Akiva Lehren of Amsterdam. One of the community leaders, Rabbi Abraham Shlomo-Zalman Tzoref, decided to request permission to establish a synagogue in the courtyard called Ḥurvat Rabbi Judah He-Ḥasid, or Deir Shiknaz [Ashkenaz] by the non-Jews, which had been purchased by the Ashkenazi leadership a century earlier. However, another leader, Rabbi Isaiah Bardaki... was convinced that, even if the authorities agreed to return this property to the Jews, the Arabs who had confiscated it because of debts owed by the Jewish leaders of the

299

14 Frankl, p. 169; Neumann, p. 393.
15 J. Finn, *Stirring Times*, I, pp. 101-104.
16 Mrs. Finn, *Home*, pp. 200-201.

17 Reicher, pp. 61-62.
18 Neumann, p. 393.
19 Luncz, *Jerusalem*, XIII, pp. 222-225.

previous century would be a continual source of harassment. He therefore advocated purchasing another site for the community synagogue. Supporters ... were found for both viewpoints, and a fierce controversy followed.[20]

Other Jewish sources report that, a few years prior to the Egyptian occupation, the Ḥurva became the property of the Ashkenazi community. The *qadi* of Jerusalem declared that the Ashkenazim were its rightful owners; later, they received a *firman* from Muḥammad ʿAli allowing them to build there.[21] Rabbi Joseph Schwarz relates how this permit was obtained:

> ... Meanwhile the number of persons immigrating to Jerusalem increased. In 1836, they decided to request permission from the king of Egypt, Muḥammad ʿAli Pasha, to build on their ancestral property. Rabbi Abraham Shlomo-Zalman [Tzoref] went to Egypt and persuaded the consuls-general of Austria and Russia to speak to the king on behalf of the Ashkenazi Jews.... I also assisted him to the best of my ability by composing clear, well-written petitions for him. These were found acceptable by the king, who promptly wrote out an explicit order authorizing the Ashkenazim to build in Deir Ashkenaz and forbidding anyone to extort payment from them for the debts of their ancestors.[22]

Once the *firman* was in their hands, the Ashkenazim set out vigorously to establish the Menaḥem Zion synagogue. Rabbi Joseph Schwarz, who took part himself in the building activities, writes:

> On Thursday, the nineteenth of Elul (1836), we cleared the site of rubbish and began to build. By the eighteenth of Shevat (1837), the synagogue was complete and we were able to pray there. It was consecrated on that day with great joy... and named Menaḥem Zion....[23]

Another source adds:

> ... even dignitaries and important personalities rolled up their sleeves and participated in the labor, digging with their own hands and carrying away the rubbish and soil on their own shoulders. The elderly, too, helped to cart away the soil, all the while singing songs of praise to God....[24]

From the outset, Menaḥem Zion served as a focal point for the Perushim sect. It provided a sanctuary for prayer and study, and a meeting place for scholars. The religious court convened there as well. It also included a women's gallery and a ritual bath.[25] Although the synagogue was dedicated in 1837, it was not yet as complete as the builders had hoped. According to Schwarz, "to this day the great synagogue remains incomplete, because the king of Egypt... was overthrown in the meantime."[26]

The establishment of Menaḥem Zion had been violently opposed by the group led by Rabbi Isaiah Bardaki. Luncz points out that Bardaki wanted the Ḥurva to be used for housing members of the community, and the synagogue to be built elsewhere. His father-in-law, Rabbi Israel of Shklov and another prominent rabbi agreed with him. In the end, their opposition was overridden

20 *Loc. cit.* (translated from Hebrew).
21 *Ibid.*, V, pp. 229-235.
22 Schwartz, *Produce*, 1900 ed., p. 472 (translated from Hebrew; the version in the English edition, p. 282, is slightly different).
23 *Loc. cit.*; Gat, p. 16.
24 Tokachinsky, "Court," p. 126.
25 A.L. Frumkin, *Sages*, III, p. 156.
26 See above, note 22.

and the Menaḥem Zion synagogue erected. Immediately afterwards, work was begun on the additional buildings planned for the courtyard. A small sum of money obtained from individuals enabled some shops to be built along the street front.[27]

"Sukkat Shalom" and Other Synagogues

Rabbi Isaiah Bardaki's opposition to the Ḥurva plan led to the establishment of yet another synagogue in Jerusalem. With the financial assistance of the Lehren brothers of Amsterdam, who purchased a *hatzer* (courtyard), Bardaki founded the Sukkat Shalom synagogue; he thereby split the Perushim into the Ḥurva party and the *Ḥatzer* party. There were numerous conflicts between them, and these formed the basis of much impassioned polemic.[28]

Christian travelers visiting Jerusalem noted the increase in the number of synagogues. Stephens (1837) mentions a new synagogue, probably Menaḥem Zion.[29] In March of 1838 Wilde writes that he was asked to visit a new synagogue built on a plot of land that had been declared the rightful property of the Jews after lengthy deliberations.[30] The archives of the British consulate mark the building of Jerusalem's first Ashkenazi synagogue.[31] The recent construction of a synagogue in the Jewish Quarter was noted by Robinson on April 27, 1838.[32]

The Jewish community grew rapidly after the 1840's, and the number of synagogues increased accordingly. Often rooms and buildings were rented for use as places of prayer. Here, we will concentrate on the most important synagogues, those specifically designed as such and those which came to play a significant role in Jewish community life.

The Perushim had two central synagogues: the Menaḥem Zion synagogue of Rabbi Samuel Salant and the Ḥurva party, and the Sukkat Shalom synagogue of Rabbi Isaiah Bardaki and the *Ḥatzer* party. In the early 1840's, the Ḥasidim began to establish synagogues of their own. John Wilson, who visited Jerusalem in 1843, reports that there were two Perushim synagogues, one private, and another being reconstructed with donations collected all over the world. The Ḥasidim, he notes, had two small synagogues, one of them in the home of Rabbi Israel, who ran a printing press.[33] Strauss also says there were two small Ḥasidic synagogues.[34] According to one Jewish source, the Ḥasidim of Volhyn bought a large tract of land in 1845, upon which they built homes and a synagogue named "Beth Ya'akov," in honor of Rabbi Abraham Ya'akov of Sadigora.[35]

Petermann (1853) writes that the Russian Jews had three synagogues, located near one another, and that the Jews of Warsaw had a separate synagogue (probably the *Kolel* Warsaw synagogue, founded in 1850).[36] Stewart tells us in 1854 that the synagogue belonging to the Sephardim was large and

27 Luricz—Kressel, pp. 178-179.
28 Gat, p. 195.
29 Stephens, p. 116.
30 Wilde, p. 524.
31 Hyamson, I, p. 257.

32 Robinson, *Biblical Researches*, I, pp. 359-360.
33 J. Wilson, I, pp. 453-459.
34 Strauss, pp. 232-236.
35 Gat, pp. 193, 200; Goldmann, *Ha-Assif*, III, p. 75.
36 Petermann, I, pp. 228-231.

Ḥurva Synagogue in the early 1870's (Sepp, I, p. 909)

shabby, and that whenever he visited the nearby Ashkenazi synagogue (which was much smaller), it was always filled to capacity.[37]

In the 1850's, *Kolel* Hod also had a synagogue of its own, Ahavat Zion, in one of the houses in the Ha-Ḥosh courtyard, owned by Rabbi Zadok Halevi.[38] An upper story was taken over by the Beth Hillel synagogue of *Kolel* Grodno in later years.[39]

As various community groupings and *kolelim* established themselves in Jerusalem during the 1850's and 1860's, more synagogues came into being. In 1850, Luncz considered the large number of its religious institutions the most outstanding feature of the Jewish Quarter. He estimates that there were thirty such institutions.[40]

In 1854, the Perushim built another synagogue in the Ḥurva courtyard: Sha'arei Zion, also known as "Beth Midrash Ḥadash" or the "new synagogue," while Menaḥem Zion began to be called "Beth Midrash Yashan" or the "old synagogue." Even this was not enough to meet the growing needs of the community.[41]

The synagogue of the Ḥabad Ḥasidim, still to be seen at the southern end of Ḥabad street, west of the Ḥurva, was established in 1858. Approximately two years later, another synagogue was founded by the rabbi of Kalish, Rabbi Meir

302

37   Stewart, pp. 295-297.
38   Goldmann, *Ha-Assif*, III, p. 75.
39   *Loc. cit.*
40   Luncz, *Almanac*, XV, p. 30.
41   Gat, p. 196; A.L. Frumkin, *Sages*, III, p. 156.

Mosque of Omar and the Jewish Quarter (Vincent—Lee—Bain, p. 129)

Auerbach, who came to Jerusalem in 1859. It was located in the southern part of the Jewish Quarter, at the end of the Street of the Jews.[42] In 1868, *Kolel Polin* (Poland) built a synagogue in the north of the Jewish Quarter, east of the street of the Jews, with contributions from Poland, especially from Rabbi David Reiss Janover.[43]

The Ḥurva Synagogue

The considerable growth of Jerusalem's Jewish population spurred community leaders to establish large synagogues in the city. In 1854, the Perushim leaders applied for a permit to build such an institution in the Ḥurva courtyard.[44] A royal *firman* was obtained only after two years, when Sir Moses Montefiore visited Constantinople on his way to Jerusalem.[45] The *Ḥavatzelet* newspaper reports that when Lord Napier, the British ambassador at the Sultan's court in Constantinople, visited Jerusalem in 1854, he agreed to speak to the Turkish government about the construction of a large synagogue in the Ḥurva courtyard. His recommendation helped the Jews to secure a *firman*.[46]

The arrival of this *firman* was a joyous occasion for the Jewish community.

303

42   Freiman, pp. 82-87; Cahanyu, p. 58.
43   Shapira, p. 53; Press, "If I forget thee" (list at end), in *Studies*, p. 104.
44   Tokachinsky, "Court," pp. 121-167; Gat, p. 196.
45   Gat, p. 196-197; Salomon, p. 117.
46   *Ḥavatzelet*, 15 Sivan, 1872, vol. II, no. 34, pp. 265-266.

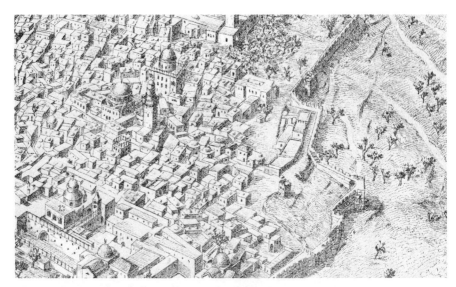

Jewish Quarter in 1870's—aerial view (Illes)

The scenes of twenty years earlier were repeated as young and old as well as leaders and dignitaries volunteered to clear the building site. Excavation for the foundations was begun in 1856, and preparations made for construction. Some of the stone was purchased from Mrs. Finn's Kerem Abraham quarry, at a cost of £70. Thus the construction of the Ḥurva indirectly assisted the project that Mrs. Finn had initiated to provide employment for poor Jews.[47] To the delight of the Ḥurva *gabbaim*, the architect appointed by the Sultan to plan and supervise the renovation of buildings on the Temple Mount agreed to design and oversee the construction of the Ḥurva synagogue. Lack of funds, however, slowed down the building process. Jewish sources record the many efforts to recruit money, and the difficulties encountered. Among those offering financial assistance was the king of Prussia, whose name was later inscribed on the cornerstone and over the doorway, along with the names of other benefactors. The Rothschild family also donated money towards this project. Construction was completed only at the end of 1864. The synagogue was dedicated on the 24th of Elul, and named "Beth Ya'akov" in honor of Baron Jacob (James) de Rothschild.[48]

An 1864 issue of the newspaper *Ha-Maggid* provides a detailed description of this synagogue, as well as a discussion of the construction materials, architectural design and esthetic merit of the building.[49] The newspaper *Ha-Levanon* gives the following account:

> The magnificent Great Synagogue has just been completed, splendidly built with a large study hall and a beautiful guest house surrounded by a garden. This synagogue is a large, attractive structure... made of hewn stone and brick and,

47   Solomon, pp. 119-124; Mrs. Finn, *Reminiscences*, p. 134.
48   Gat, pp. 197-198; Press, *Hundred Years*, pp. 31-32.
49   *Ha-Maggid*, 26 Tishrei, 1864, vol. VIII, no. 41, p. 524.

like the buildings of Europe, has an imposing clock-tower visible from afar. The building itself has already cost £15,000, with the interior yet to be paid for...[50]

Two years later, the newspaper reports that an ornate, solid candelabrum as tall as a man, made of thirty-six pounds of silver, had been installed in the synagogue on the seventh day of Hanukka.[51]

During his sixth visit to Jerusalem, in 1866, Montefiore "went to see the large new synagogue in Hurvat Rabbi Yehuda Hasid, where he was received with great honor.... He went up to the pulpit, opened the Holy Ark, and placed a silver breastplate on one of the Torah scrolls. Then he thanked God, blessed the congregation, and returned home...."[52] The next time Montefiore visited the synagogue, in 1875, he was welcomed by some 3,000 Jews.[53] This splendid synagogue was the pride and glory of the Jews of Jerusalem for many years, and many important events in the life of the Jewish community were celebrated within its walls.

The Tif'eret Israel Synagogue—Nisan Bak

After seeing how successful the Perushim had been in building their Great Synagogue, the Hasidim determined to emulate them. Rabbi Nisan Bak, a dedicated community worker, devoted himself to this project and saw it through to its completion. When Frankl visited Jerusalem in 1856, the Hasidic community had already purchased a plot of land but had not yet begun to build. At the request of community spokesmen, Frankl included a fervent plea for contributions in his book *Nach Jerusalem*. The new synagogue was finally finished in 1872, and named "Tif'eret Israel" in honor of the saintly Rabbi Israel of Rozin.[54] According to Luncz (1891), construction had begun in 1862 but the building lacked a dome for several years because of a shortage of funds. In 1871, sufficient money was brought from abroad to complete the building and decorate its interior. The first floor was rented out as living quarters, while the second housed the synagogue. There was an elaborate dedication ceremony that summer, with both Ashkenazim and Sephardim participating; the Sephardic chief rabbi and other prominent rabbis carried the Torah scrolls. *Havatzelet* carried a three-page description of the building of the synagogue and of the joyful dedication ceremony.[55]

Neumann writes that a generous contributor from Baghdad, one of the Sassoon family heirs, had donated 100,000 piastres towards the construction of the Hurva synagogue, and that the total building costs had exceeded a million piastres. He adds that the sum of 800,000 piastres required to establish the Tif'eret Israel synagogue had been collected through the fund-raising activities of Rabbi Jacob Freedman of Sadigora.[56]

The completion of Tif'eret Israel in the early 1870's may be taken as a sign

---

50 *Ha-Levanon*, 21 Shevat, 1864/5, vol. II, no. 4, p. 54 (translated from Hebrew).
51 *Ibid.*, 27 Tevet, 1866/7, vol. IV, no. 7, p. 15.
52 Gat, p. 198 (citing *Ha-Maggid*).
53 *Ha-Levanon*, 1 Elul, 1875, vol. XII, no. 4, p. 31.
54 Gat, pp. 198-199.
55 Luncz, *Guide*, pp. 154-155; *Havatzelet*, 19 Av, 1872, vol. 2, no. 43, pp. 333-335.
56 Neumann, pp. 395-397.

that the Jewish community within the Old City was flourishing. At the same time, however, important developments were taking place outside the city walls. By 1875, three years after the founding of Tif'eret Israel, the Me'a She'arim neighborhood was already in existence. Other neighborhoods followed, and before long the center of the Jewish community had begun to shift outwards from the Old City. It is true that the community inside the walls continued to thrive until the 1890's and even beyond, but the stirrings of change were felt as early as the mid-1870's.

The Yeshivot of the Sephardim

It should be borne in mind that the Sephardi *Yeshiva* of the nineteenth century bore little resemblence to the *yeshiva* of today, where boys and young men study the Torah and Talmud. It was attended by renowned scholars, and was designed to provide them and their families with financial support.[57] The amount of support varied from *yeshiva* to *yeshiva;* some scholars belonged to several, in order to increase their income. During the seventeenth and eighteenth centuries, most *yeshiva* funds were drawn from communities in the Ottoman Empire, especially from Constantinople. In the eighteenth century, the Jews of Italy were very active contributors as well. The beginning of the nineteenth century saw the countries of North Africa become prominent, and most of the *yeshiva* fund-raisers were sent there. From the 1820's, donations began to pour in from the Jews of Western and Central Europe through a new central office in Amsterdam. According to Rabbi Joseph Schwarz, the *yeshivot* of the Sephardim had been founded by the Jews of Babylonia (Iraq), Asia Minor, Italy, the Barbary states (North Africa), Holland, Germany, England, Poland, and other countries, who contributed large sums.[58]

The *yeshivot* of the Sephardim were small in size and had few members. The largest were the veteran *yeshivot,* Beth El and Ferrara, each with twenty-five students. Others had ten or fewer.[59] The sizable increase in the Sephardi population of Jerusalem brought with it a rise in the number of *yeshivot.* Fund-raisers searched for rich Jews from overseas who were willing to establish a *yeshiva* in Palestine, intending to join it themselves at a later date. Many of these *yeshivot* eventually closed down for financial reasons; new ones replaced them.[60]

Frankl regarded the *yeshivot* of the Sephardim as being "charitable institutions" in 1856. He says there were thirty-six of them, most of which were financed by contributions from abroad. Reicher claims there were only nineteen in the 1860's.[61] Non-Jewish sources also report the existence of numerous *yeshivot* in Jerusalem, probably referring to those of the Sephardim. J. Wilson reports in 1843 that there were twenty-nine *yeshivot* in the city. Strauss gives the figure thirty-six, and tells of rabbis who, aside from being well-versed in the Talmud, were knowledgeable in worldly affairs. One of these was Rabbi Joseph Schwarz of Bavaria, who had recently published a book on

57   Luncz—Kressel, pp. 163-165; Gaon, *Oriental Jews*, I, pp. 123-125.
58   Schwarz—Landau, p. 75.   60   Luncz—Kressel, p. 165.
59   Gaon, *Oriental Jews*, I, pp. 132-135.   61   Frankl, p. 173; Reicher, p. 61.

Jerusalem. Tobler lists the names of twenty-eight study halls and private synagogues in 1853.[62]

Knesset Yeḥezkel (Ezekiel) and Ḥessed El, both founded in the nineteenth century, were typical Sephardi *Yeshivot*. Knesset Yeḥezkel was established by Rabbi Solomon Yehuda, who immigrated from Baghdad in 1857, in memory of his father, Ezekiel of Calcutta. Rabbi Solomon also set aside a room in his courtyard for a *yeshiva* shortly after his arrival, and supported ten scholars who studied there regularly.[63] (Another source claims that the Knesset Yeḥezkel *yeshiva* was in existence by 1844.[64]) It was headed by the Sephardi rabbi, Moses Naḥmias, and the Ashkenazi rabbi, Isaac Oplatka of Prague. The latter was a follower of the *Ḥatam Sofer,* and was the head of the Doresh Zion institution. Students at Knesset Yeḥezkel studied only the Talmud and rabbinical literature, and were provided for handsomely by Rabbi Solomon, a very wealthy man.[65]

Joshua Yellin, Rabbi Solomon's son-in-law, writes that the Ḥessed El *yeshiva* was also founded (in 1860) and maintained by Rabbi Solomon. It was housed next door to the home of Rabbi Zadok Halevi and became a source of contention between Rabbi Solomon and Halevi. (M.D. Gaon claims the *yeshiva* was actually established earlier by the Kabbalist, Rabbi Abdullah Moshe Ḥayyim, but that Rabbi Solomon was considered its founder because he financed it.) The scholars of Ḥessed El studied day and night, particularly Kabbala; they went home only for the Sabbath, and returned as soon as it was over. Rabbi Solomon Yehuda's brother and sister, Sasson and Ruḥama, also contributed to the *yeshiva.* Thus, unlike the other *yeshivot* where only a few hours a day were devoted to study, the students of Ḥessed El could devote themselves wholly to the study of the Torah. After the death of Rabbi Solomon, Knesset Yeḥezkel and Ḥessed El joined and became one *yeshiva.*[66]

In addition to study halls and *yeshivot*, the Sephardim also ran elementary institutions for their children. Classes were usually held in synagogues or in adjoining buildings. Repeated mention is made of such schools in the four-synagogue complex (Rabban Yoḥanan ben Zakkai).

The Ashkenazi Yeshivot

With the revival of the Ashkenazi community in Jerusalem, its members also began to establish *yeshivot*. One source reports that such a *yeshiva* was set up near the Wailing Wall in the early part of the century by Rabbi Menaḥem-Mendel of Shklov, one of the leaders of the Perushim community.[67] According to another source, a small Ashkenazi *yeshiva* called "Midrash Eliahu" (Elijah) named after the "Gaon of Vilna," was founded in the 1820's.[68]

From the 1830's on, the growth of the Ashkenazi community dictated the establishment of a growing network of elementary institutions, study halls and *yeshivot*. The most important of these institutions was the Etz Ḥayyim *yeshiva.*

62   J. Wilson, I, pp. 453-462; Strauss, pp. 232-236; Tobler, *Topographie*, pp. 614-632.
63   Y. Yellin, *Memoirs*, p. 24.
64   Ben-Jacob, pp. 89-99.
65   Gaon, *Oriental Jews*, I, p. 144.

66   *Loc. cit.*; Y. Yellin, *Memoirs*, p. 26.
67   Malachi, pp. 16-17.
68   Horowitz, p. 121.

A *Talmud Torah* of this name seems to have been opened in the Menaḥem Zior synagogue in 1841-1842, but the prestigious Etz Ḥayyim *yeshiva* of the 1860's grew from a small *yeshiva* founded in the Ḥurva considerably later.[69] We will deal with the further development of religious institutions in Jerusalem later.

The Wailing Wall as a Prayer Site

Access to the Wailing Wall for prayer, and the number of Jews who prayed before it, changed constantly during the nineteenth century. Later, in Mandatory times, the Muslims contested the right of the Jews to worship and place furniture and ritual objects there. An international investigating committee, the "Wailing Wall Commission," was established; it gathered extensive testimony about the importance of the Wailing Wall to the Jews at different periods in history, particularly during the nineteenth century and early twentieth century. Its findings indicated that a special permit from the authorities had been necessary for Jews to pray at the Wailing Wall at the start of the nineteenth century. Even if the Jews made no official request for such a permit, however, it appears that prayers were held there anyway, without any special ceremony. When Seetzen (1806) visited Jerusalem, he found that the Jews were forbidden to approach the Temple Mount freely.[70] However, the records of the Sephardi community show that the area of the Wailing Wall was cleaned on various occasions on the initiative of the Jewish community. In 1768, for example, the Sephardim spent fifteen aries to have the Wailing Wall area cleared of mud. A similar payment is recorded in 1812, and another in 1815. Payment was also made for the removal of some camels abandoned near the Wall.[71]

The missionary Thomson relates the following:

> No sight [that] meets the eye in Jerusalem is more sadly suggestive than this wailing of the Jews over the ruins of their Temple. It is a very old custom, and in past ages they have paid immense sums to their oppressors for the miserable satisfaction of kissing the stones and pouring out lamentations at the foot of their ancient sanctuary.[72]

Opportunities for Jewish access to the Wailing Wall improved markedly when Ibrahim Pasha assumed power. Robinson, who visited Jerusalem towards the end of Ibrahim Pasha's rule, offers a vivid description:

> In the afternoon of the same day, I went... to the place where the Jews are permitted to purchase the right of approaching the site of their temple, and of praying and wailing over its ruins and the downfall of their nation.... Two old men, Jews, sat there upon the ground, reading together in a book of Hebrew prayers. On Fridays they assemble here in greater numbers. It is the nearest point in which they can venture to approach their ancient temple; and fortunately for them, it is sheltered from observation by the narrowness of the lane and the dead walls around. Here, bowed in the dust, they may at least weep undisturbed over the fallen glory of their race; and bedew with their tears the soil, which so many thousands of their forefathers once moistened with their blood.[73]

69   Malachi, pp. 105-119.
70   Seetzen, II, p. 19.
71   Triwaks, *Trial*, pp. 54-55.

72   Thomson, pp. 512-513.
73   Robinson, *Biblical Researches,* I, pp. 349-350.

In 1840, Rabbi Menaḥem Mendel of Kamieniec writes:

> I went to pray at the western wall of the Temple Mount, as is the custom here every Sabbath eve. A few poor people sit there and collect alms. Then they recite a few chapters of Psalms, follow this by the *Minḥa* service, and proceed to usher in the Sabbath (and I must say, prayers here are truly from the heart). The cantor stands next to the stone where the divine presence is said to have appeared before a certain *tzaddik* (saint). All those approaching the Wall remove their shoes.[74]

It seems, however, that the Jews were still afraid to enter the houses near the Wailing Wall during the period of Egyptian rule. Eliezer Halevi, who visited Jerusalem in 1838, writes that a Jewish resident told him about a tall building near the Wailing Wall which afforded a view of the Temple Mount. This Jew dared not accompany him there because of Halevi's Polish-style clothing and ignorance of Arabic. Halevi tried to go there by himself, but changed his mind after being warned by a Muslim.[75]

When the Turks recaptured Jerusalem in 1840, the Jewish community did not suffer. On the contrary: it continued to expand, and the Wailing Wall increased in importance as a Jewish prayer site. In 1840, the Jews asked for permission to pave the area adjacent to the Wall. The request was rejected on the grounds that the area concerned bordered on the *haram* (Temple Area) and belonged to the *Waqf* of Abu Madyan, but the Jews were allowed to visit the site as before.[76]

In 1841, the authorities presented Chief Rabbi Gagin with a *firman* concerning the holy places, that declared "there would be no interference in their synagogues or shrines, in their mode of worship, or in their religious customs."[77] Indeed, it seems that Jews began to frequent the Wailing Wall after 1840 in ever greater numbers.

When Bartlett visited Jerusalem in 1842, he was greatly impressed by the prayers at the Wailing Wall. He describes his experience as follows:

> Not a hundred yards further to the north is a spot immediately under the wall and quite concealed from observation, where they have purchased permission from the Turks to approach the boundary of the temple, to wail over the desolation of Judah, and implore the mercy and forgiveness of their God. We repaired to this place on Friday, when a considerable number usually assemble. In the shadow of the wall, on the right, were seated many venerable men, reading the book of the law, wearing out their declining days in the city of their fathers, and soon be gathered to them in the mournful Valley of Jehoshaphat.[78]

In the same year, Ewald reports that the Jews had paved an area ninety-two feet long and fifteen feet wide in front of the Wall (this is the first mention of this event in the sources).[79]

According to Durbin (1845),

> [The Jews] have purchased of the Turks the privilege of approaching the ancient Temple wall at this spot, which is called their Place of Wailing, to weep over the

74   Yaari, *Travels*, p. 542 (translated from Hebrew).
75   Eisenstein, p. 297.
76   Ben-Zvi, *Eretz-Israel*, p. 350.
77   Luncz, *Jerusalem*, IV, 1892, pp. 202-209.
78   Bartlett, *Walks*, pp. 140-141.
79   Cited in Triwaks, *Trial*, p. 105.

fallen glory of their race, under the very ruins of their once magnificent sanctuary.... On Friday they assemble here in considerable numbers, and cry, "Our inheritance is turned to strangers, our house to aliens." The Book of the Law is read by aged men, and women walk up and down the small area, occasionally approaching the wall to kiss it, pouring forth lamentations and prayers.[80]

We also have Rabbi Joseph Schwarz's comments on the same period:

This wall is visited by all our brothers on every feast and festival; and the large space at its foot is often so densely filled, that not all can perform their devotions here at the same time. It is also visited, though by lesser numbers, on every Friday afternoon, and by some nearly every day. No one is molested in these visits by the Muslims, as we have a very old *firman* from the Sultan of Constantinople that the approach shall not be denied to us, though the Porte obtains for this privilege an especial tax, which is, however, quite insignificant.[81]

Picturesque descriptions of the Wailing Wall were also recorded in the 1850's. De Saulcy, for example, wrote:

I was aware long since, that there exists in the interior of Jerusalem... a portion of wall which the Jews have in all times considered as a fragment of the original building. I also knew that the foot of this wall, which the Jews were permitted to approach, was considered by them a sort of sanctuary, where they came to pray every Friday evening; and where they were often seen lamenting, crying and thrusting their heads into the cavities of the holy wall,—so that their tears might water it, while they pondered over the fall of Jerusalem, and the destruction of the temple.[82]

According to Consul Finn, describing the situation in 1853,

... The Jews are humiliated by the payment through the Chief Rabbi, of pensions to Moslem local exactors, for instance the sum of 300 l. a year to the Effendi whose house adjoins the "wailing place," or fragment of the western wall of the Temple enclosure, for permission to pray there... All these are mere extractions made upon their excessive timidity, which it is disgraceful to the Turkish Government to allow to be practised. The figures are copied from their humble appeals occasionally made to the Synagogues in Europe.[83]

Stewart writes that, as of 1854, the area "has been lately paved by a Jew for the benefit of his brethren.... The Jews have purchased from the Government the privilege of resorting to this place; and, on every Friday, many of both sexes are seen to be sitting in the court.... At the northern end of the Jews' Wailing Place is the Mekhémeh or Cadi's Court...[with] a large portal or bow-window [looking] out upon the Harám."[84]

Frankl points out in 1856 that the Jews had a perpetual *firman* from the government enabling them to visit Wailing Wall freely upon payment of a small fee.[85] The text of this *firman,* which is mentioned in several sources, has not yet been discovered. Many other descriptions of the Wailing Wall in addition to those we have cited exist; quite a few of them stress the large number of Jews who flocked to the Wall on Fridays.[86]

80 Adler, *Memorandum*, p. 47.
81 Schwarz (English edition), p. 260.
82 De Saulcy, II, p. 78.
83 J. Finn, *Stirring Times*, I, pp. 118-119.
84 Stewart, pp. 272-274.
85 Frankl, p. 164.
86 Adler, *Memorandum*, pp. 50-52.

Wailing Wall (Bernatz, pl. 22)

It seems that week-day prayers were not customarily recited at the Wailing Wall three times a day during the 1850's and 1860's. Rabbi Moses Meshil Gelbstein does relate that a celebrated rabbi had official permission to hire a quorum of ten men to pray at the Wall every morning, afternoon and evening, but this practice was discontinued after the rabbi's death in 1865.

During the 1860's, important meetings reportedly took place at the Wailing Wall, and various improvements were made at the site. In the early 1860's, the Prince of Wales met there with the chief rabbi and other dignitaries of the Jewish community. After his visit to the Wall in 1866, Montefiore told the Board of Deputies of British Jews that the governor of Jerusalem (Izzat Pasha) had granted a *firman* for the erection of an awning over the area to protect worshippers from sun and rain.[87]

Warren writes, referring to the late 1860's:

> Some time after the fourth century, the Jews were turned out of the Temple Enclosure, and only allowed to approach its walls, and there lament; but where they did this at first, we have no evidence; probably not at the present Wailing Place, for there we find signs of vaulted chambers having once been built against the wall, and it was probably not until these chambers fell, or had been pulled down, that the mourners were here able to congregate.
>
> A few years ago, this Wailing Place was of greater length than at present, but a portion of its northern end has been taken into the grounds of the Council House.

311

87 *Ibid.*, p. 28.

At present, the portion that remains free and open to the Jews is the west wall of the Temple Court, reaching for about one hundred feet to north from the Prophets' Gateway... a stone-paved court, in which the Jews assemble on the afternoon of Friday, to read the Book of Lamentations, and rock themselves..., for they still follow in this the practice of their forefathers.

Above this pavement, rises fifteen feet more of this old wall..., in which four courses of drafted stones are visible; many of them are very much worn, and the people in prayer thrust their hands into the interstices, and also push as far into the crevices as they can, prayers they have written to God, thinking that they will be carried from thence up to heaven. If afterwards they come and find these paper scraps gone, they think their prayers will be answered.

... It is a most remarkable sight; these people all thronging the pavement, and wailing so intensely, that often the tears roll down their faces.[88]

In the early 1870's, the *Baedeker Guide* prints the following:

This spot should be visited repeatedly, especially on a Friday after 4 P.M., or on Jewish festivals, when a touching scene is presented by the figures leaning against the weather-beaten wall, kissing the stones and weeping. The men often sit here for hours reading their well-thumbed Hebrew prayer-books.[89]

Rabbi Isaac Yeḥezkel Yehuda, one of the Sephardi community elders, who testified before the wailing Wall Commission in 1929, had this to say:

... After my grandmother's father, the great and pious Kabbalist Rabbi Abdullah... immigrated to Palestine in 1841, my grandmother's mother... was accustomed to go to the Wailing Wall every Friday afternoon, winter and summer, and remain there until candle-lighting time, reading the entire Book of Psalms and the Song of Songs. In those days, the city was forsaken and desolate. There were no Jews at the Wall before noon, but as the day progressed they would begin to arrive for the Sabbath-Inauguration service. Thus she would sit there by herself for long hours. She was never reproached, on the contrary, the local residents respected her.

When I was six years old my father began to take me there to pray with his rabbi... Eleazar Halevi... on the eve of the Sabbath. We would finish our prayers when the sun was still shining. There were tables with large lanterns upon them which the Ashkenazim lit in honor of the Sabbath. Sometimes, when my father's business detained him, we would pray with the Ḥasidim and their rabbi, Eleazar Mendel Biedermann. Prayers would end after dusk, and a non-Jew would carry the lanterns before us to light our way.

As a youth, I used to go to the Wailing Wall between morning and afternoon prayers on Yom Kippur, to recite "Solomon's Prayer." The Ḥasidic rabbi, Moses Meshil Gelbstein, would be there with his followers chanting the Additional service. Sometimes they would be reading the Torah portion.... An awning was stretched across the courtyard and there were tables, a Holy Ark, a Torah scroll, chairs and benches there. The weak old people would sit on feather pillows. Prayers were conducted quietly and peacefully. The local residents would pass by without disturbing the worshippers.

Poor Sephardi scholars would sit there all day long and read to people in... Ladino. The old men and women sat around in a circle to listen.... I also remember that, when Russia was fighting the Turks in 1878, the government asked the Jews to pray for the Turks' success at the Wailing Wall. The pupils of the Sephardi and Ashkenazi *Talmudei Torah* were escorted there by an honor guard of soldiers.

312

88   Warren, *Underground*, pp. 366-368.
89   Baedeker, 1876 (1973 reprint), p. 68.

313

Wailing Wall (Wilson, *Picturesque Palestine*, I, p. 43)

Sheikh Raḥamim, the sainted kabbalist Rabbi Raḥamim Antebbi, was one of the "Mourners of Zion." He wore no shoes, but only open sandals... without stockings.... He was in the habit of visiting the Wailing Wall every midnight, winter and summer, to recite midnight lamentations and weep. Neither rain nor wind prevented him from appearing there nightly until the day he died. The Muslims respected him and never did him any harm.[90]

Summary

These descriptions lead us to the obvious conclusion that the larger the Jewish community became, the greater the number of worshippers at the Wailing Wall and the more importance the Wall assumed as the spiritual focus of the community. At the beginning of the century, worshippers were few and prayers there lacked any special distinction. But, as time went on, and particularly after 1840, prayers began to assume a fixed character, first on Fridays and holidays, and then on week-days and throughout each day. The area before the Wall was paved, and attempts were made to make the site more like a synagogue. In the course of the nineteenth century, the Wailing Wall became a center of national importance for the Jews of the country and the world, and was used as a gathering place for important royal assemblies and festive prayer services.

314

90 Triwaks, *Trial*, pp. 28-30 (translated from Hebrew; for a different translation of the entire testimony see Adler, *Memorandum*, pp. 37-40).

Chapter Four:
THE JEWISH QUARTER

Introduction

In the last three chapters, we examined the changing character of Jerusalem's Jewish community as it grew from 2,000 to 11,000 souls between 1800 and 1870. The physical boundaries of the Jewish Quarter were changing too. The Quarter was not a clearly-defined and well-delineated area, but one whose boundaries were constantly shifting. Nonetheless, it had a distinct nucleus, and we can establish a reasonable basis for the Quarter's expansion before the 1870's.

The Nucleus of the Jewish Quarter

At the beginning of the nineteenth century, when only Sephardi Jews lived in Jerusalem, the Sephardi synagogue region seems to have been the nucleus of the Jewish Quarter. When the Ashkenazim began to return to Jerusalem, they lived alongside their Sephardi brethren, and the original nucleus expanded. At first the Ashkenazim prayed in the *yeshiva* of Rabbi Ḥayyim ben Attar (or "Or Ha-Ḥayyim"); later, they built Menaḥem Zion—the first wing of the Ḥurva synagogue—and the Sukkat Shalom synagogue. All three of these buildings were located near the Sephardi synagogues, and helped to form a Jewish enclave. Other synagogues built at about this time were also concentrated in the Jewish Quarter. The Jews began to expand from the Jewish Quarter to parts of the Muslim Quarter in the latter half of the nineteenth century, but this expansion was not permanent. The establishment of new Jewish neighborhoods outside the city walls, and the beginnings of rioting in the Muslim Quarter, encouraged the Jews to withdraw to their established center in the Jewish Quarter.

The sole exception to this tendency was an attempt made by Ashkenazi Jews to settle in the Bab Ḥuta region in the northeastern part of the city at the beginning of the century. Luncz relates that the first Ashkenazim to return to Jerusalem made their homes in that district. Confirmation of this is provided by Rabbi Eliezer Bergmann, and by Joshua Yellin. The latter indicates that his

"David's Tomb" on Mt. Zion (Barclay, p. 209)

parents' family settled among the Ashkenazim in Bab Huta after a futile attempt to establish itself in Safed.[1] However, Jewish settlement in Bab Huta appears to have been less than successful, with most Ashkenazim moving eventually to the Jewish Quarter. Joshua Yellin describes the move made by his own family, with other families apparently following suit. This episode emphasizes the growing importance of the established center, the Jewish Quarter, in the southwestern part of the city.

The Location of the Jewish Quarter

Why has the Jewish Quarter been located in roughly the same area from the thirteenth century until today? It seems that there are two main reasons for this: no Muslim or Christian holy places were located there, and the area therefore held no attraction for either community; it was near the Wailing Wall, and offered a view of the Mount of Olives. Some say the Jewish community grew up in this spot because it was here that the Ramban (Nahmanides), the famous Jewish rabbi and scholar, decided in 1267 to establish the synagogue which bears his name today. However, it is quite likely that the Ramban's choice of this ruined area was influenced by the factors we have just considered. The fact that the Jewish Quarter was built on a slope allowed the Jewish immigrants of the early nineteenth century to see the city's most important sites from their homes: the Wailing Wall, which symbolized the nation's glorious past, and the Mount of Olives, which symbolized its future and the resurrection of the dead.

316

1   Luncz and Bergmann are cited above, pp. 282, 284f., see also Grayevsky, *First Lovers*, XI, p. 32; Y. Yellin, *Memoirs*, pp. 6-8.

At the beginning of the nineteenth century, the core of the Jewish Quarter was the region running from the Street of the Jews eastwards to the Wailing Wall. Tobler writes that there were two Jewish streets in 1846, located near the Wailing Wall.[2] Other travelers of the first half of the century state that the Jews lived on Meidan street (known today as Misgav Ladach street) and the Street of the Jews.[3]

Thus the Jewish population—especially that of the Sephardim—lived close to the Sephardi synagogues, east or north of them, approaching the Wailing Wall. When the Ashkenazim began to settle in the city, they resided on the Street of the Jews, near the Hurva, or to the west, towards the Sukkat Shalom synagogue.

The Expansion of the Jewish Quarter

From the start, the Ashkenazi neighborhood expanded westwards along the slope of Mount Zion, in the direction of the Armenian Quarter.[4] By 1826, the leaders of the Perushim were negotiating for the purchase of a large tract of land extending from the Jewish Quarter to the Kishleh (the prison near the Citadel of David).[5]

Grayevsky relates that a large courtyard, later known as Hatzer Ha-Kotel, bordering on the Armenian Quarter, was purchased in the 1830's. Located on the Street of the Armenians, it marked the beginning of the expansion of the Jewish Quarter. In the 1830's, the leaders of the Jewish community rented this courtyard from the Armenian monastery, and let its rooms to Jewish tenants on a non-profit basis until 1901, when it was returned to the Armenians. It consisted of forty apartments, some large and some small; each tenant enjoyed the use of part of the property, and paid an annual rent to the monastery. Not far away was another Jewish courtyard, Hatzer Ha-Shkola; Hatzer Or Ha-Hayyim was adjacent to it, and others were nearby. Seven steps led from the slope down to the Street of the Jews.[6]

An important courtyard west of Habad street was Hatzer Ha-Hosh. Hamburger writes that a rich Jew named Rabbi Zadok Halevi came to Jerusalem from Shklov in Russia with his wife and only daughter in the 1830's, and bought the "Hosh" from the Arabs. This area derived its name from the Arabic word for a cattle pen or shed, used figuratively to denote a narrow, dark alley. Rabbi Zadok's "Hosh" eventually became one of the most densely populated sections of the Jewish Quarter. It was entered through a narrow passage whose gate was locked at night. Only in later years, when the fear of thieves had lessened, was this gate left open.[7]

In the 1850's the Jews began to settle on Habad street, thereby strengthening the nucleus' expansion to the west (towards the Armenian Quarter) and to the north (towards the Muslim Quarter). The construction of the Batei Mahseh houses to the south followed, and an attempt was made to populate the area up to the southern wall of the city.

All this indicates that the Jewish Quarter was growing as the years passed.

317

2 Tobler, *Topographie*, I, pp. 197-198.
3 Chateaubriand, p. 345.
4 Luncz—Kressel, p. 172.
5 Horowitz, pp. 119-120, 128.
6 Grayevsky, *First Lovers*, XIII, 1928, p. 36.
7 Hamburger, II, p. 18.

Mt. Zion from the north (Schwarz, English ed.)

Tobler writes that, in the middle of the nineteenth century, the Jewish Quarter was bounded by the Armenian Quarter on its west, the Muslim Quarter on its north, the valley of the Mughrabi Quarter on its east, and a sparsely settled area reaching the city walls on its south. Even so, the Jewish Quarter comprised no more than a twelfth of the total area of the city at that time.[8] That the Jewish Quarter was so very small is also mentioned by other writers. Barclay, for example, records that although it was only a third of the size of the Christian Quarter, and one-fifth the size of the Muslim Quarter in 1857, it was the most densely populated quarter of all, because nearly half of the city's inhabitants lived there.[9]

As the Jewish Quarter grew, its various community groups began to segregate themselves to some extent. While the Sephardim continued to live to the east and north of the Sephardi synagogues, the Ashkenazim congregated on the Street of the Jews, expanding to the north and west. *Kolelim* and groups of Jews from the same part of the Diaspora tended to concentrate in specific areas. Western travelers describe this cluster-phenomenon among the Sephardim, Ashkenazim, Karaites, and Jews from various foreign countries.[10] The Jews did not penetrate into the Christian Quarter, apparently because their relations with the Christians were far worse than those with the Muslims. According to one source,

> the professing Christians here — Greeks, Armenians and Roman Catholics — are even more bitter enemies to Jews than Mahometans; so that in time of danger, a Jew would betake himself to the house of a Turk for refuge, in preference to that of a Christian.[11]

8   Tobler, *Denkblätter*, pp. 125-126.   10   Ritter, IV, p. 189; Petermann, I, p. 199.
9   Barclay, pp. 432-444.   11   Bonar—M'Cheyne, pp. 147-149.

Mt. Zion from the south (Schwarz, English ed.)

This phenomenon may also have been connected with the fact that Jews were strictly forbidden to approach the Church of the Holy Sepulchre. Various sources attest that no Jew dared to walk nearby, and describe violent attacks upon Jews who happened there by chance.[12]

Harsh Living Conditions

The Jewish Quarter was full of neglected buildings, narrow streets and dark corners; it was dirty and strewn with rubbish. Living conditions in the Quarter were very bad. The Jews lived in damp houses, or in cellars that were, perhaps, the foundations of ancient buildings. Scherer (1859) describes the Jewish "ghetto" in Jerusalem as one of the most miserable in the East.[13]

Jewish writers also comment on the distressing state of the Jewish Quarter, particularly in the beginning of the nineteenth century, indicating that the poor condition of the Sephardi synagogues was tangible evidence of it. According to one source, "it was as though Jewish property was free for the taking. Highway robbers proliferated outside the city walls and, within the city, doors had to be locked at dusk for fear of them."[14]

The harsh conditions in the Jewish Quarter resulted from its large number of dilapidated buildings and ruins; its inhabitants' low economic level; its perennial water shortage; and the hostile attitude of the local authorities, who preferred to make life more burdensome for its residents.

319

12 Petermann, p. 116; Martineau, p. 145.
13 Scherer, pp. 189-190.
14 A.L. Frumkin, *Sages*, III, p. 153.

The Slaughterhouse and Other Non-Jewish Sites

A particularly offensive feature of the Jewish Quarter was the slaughterhouse located near the Sephardi synagogues.[15] Seetzen (1806) writes that the Jewish Quarter smelled bad because of this slaughterhouse; the Jews believed it had purposely been established there by the Muslims in order to harass them.[16] In his British Admiralty Map notes (1849), Williams claims that the slaughterhouse had existed as early as the time of the Crusades, and that it had been left in its present location to annoy the Jewish population. A request to have it moved had been submitted to the Turkish governor, but no satisfactory answer was received.[17]

Schulz relates that in 1851 there was a narrow path leading to the slaughterhouse, which consisted of a square, open yard surrounded by walls and cold-storage lockers. In the middle there were columns beside which the animals were slaughtered. Their internal organs were flung on the ground, blood flowed everywhere and refuse was never removed.[18]

According to Consul Finn, the slaughterhouse had already been moved outside the city by 1856 because of the intervention of Sir Moses Montefiore.[19] Another source says that complaints by the foreign consuls in Jerusalem brought about the relocation of the slaughterhouse outside the city walls, near some burial caves.[20] The PEF QSt also reports in 1880 that the slaughterhouse and tannery had been moved outside the city walls.[21]

The Jewish Quarter had several other non-Jewish landmarks as well. One of these was the minaret still in the heart of the Jewish Quarter today, south of the Ramban synagogue. Williams notes that this minaret was built after 1398 and suggests that its location illustrated the competition that existed then between Jews and Muslims. When a nearby structure owned by the Ramban synagogue collapsed, the Muslims tried to take over the area. However, the case was brought to court, and the Jews won.[22]

Another conspicuously alien structure was the Greek Convent of St. George, located at the edge of the Armenian Quarter. In Christian sources, it is referred to as the "Jewish Convent" because of its proximity to the Jewish Quarter.[23] The Jewish Quarter also contained ruins dating from the Crusader period. The PEF Survey of Jerusalem reports that Conder and Chaplin investigated the site of an old church south of Meidan street, where a Moroccan Jew lived, in 1881. Further east, there were ruined arches, suggesting that there had been large buildings on the site during the Middle Ages — probably the old hospice of St. Mary of the Germans.[24]

15   Tobler, *Planographie*.
16   Seetzen, II, p. 17.
17   Williams, I, Supplement.
18   Schulz, p. 124.
19   J. Finn, *Stirring Times*, II, p. 333.
20   Bovet, pp. 254-255.
21   *PEF QSt*, 1880, p. 188; Luncz, *Almanac*, 1907, pp. 31-32.
22   Williams, I, p. 443 and Supplement.
23   *Ibid.*, Supplement.
24   Warren—Conder, *Jerusalem*, pp. 272-273.

Jewish moneychanger
(Lortet, p. 247)

Jewish Occupations in the Old City

The Jewish Quarter, desolate and decaying in the early part of the nineteenth century, slowly filled with Jews who built new houses and renovated old ones. However, it continued to look somewhat neglected and poverty-stricken. One of the main reasons for this was the perennial lack of financial resources, since most of the Jewish community lived on charity from abroad.

Some Jews, however, did engage in craftsmanship and commerce, and their number increased as time went on. At the beginning of the century, Seetzen recorded the presence of three physicians; five coppersmiths and blacksmiths; two or three tinkers; two cloth-dyers; two thread-and-rope makers; ten tailors; six pedlars of sewing articles; ten to twenty-five pedlars of other types; ten ritual slaughteres; ten butchers; ten spice merchants; six coffee-grinders; five teachers and one bookbinder.[25] Thus, most working Jews seem to have been in the metal and textile industries, or were shopkeepers or pedlars.

321

25   Seetzen, II, pp. 17-23; see also Ritter, IV, p. 211; Norov, I, pp. 209-214.

Jewish cotton-maker (Wilson, *Picturesque Palestine*, p. 44)

Much of our information about the Jews of Jerusalem at the beginning of the century (1800-1815) is derived from Luncz. He emphasizes the low standard of living in the sparsely-settled Jewish Quarter:

> Many houses stood empty and rent was low. Food and other basic human necessities were very inexpensive. The inhabitants made do with little, and lived in an extremely simple way. Their eating habits, family lives and dress followed those of their countries of origin, and they did without luxuries. On the other hand, they also earned very little.[26]

Luncz points out that there were Jewish craftsmen and laborers in the Old City between 1810 and 1840, drawn mostly from the ranks of the Sephardim. Their main occupations were

> tailoring, shoemaking, carpentry, tinkering, gold- and silversmithing, black-smithing, and pillow- and quilt-making. They worked in shops on the Street of the Jews as well as in special markets devoted to each trade, and had many customers because the Arabs scorned craftsmanship, with even those who could

322

---

26   Luncz—Kressel, p. 160 (translated from Hebrew).

not make a living from farming preferring to deal in wheat, vegetables, spices or animals with the fellahin, rather than engaging in the crafts. There were also Jews who performed all types of difficult physical labor. Most of them were natives of Palestine... uneducated, simple folk commonly known as "Moriscos"; they could recite the prayers and read the Torah by rote, but had no conception of their meaning.[27]

This "Morisco" group is also described by *Ha-Levanon* in 1869. The newspaper points out that most of the residents of the Holy Land were not native-born, but were refugees from enemy lands, and classifies the Jews of Jerusalem in three groups: elderly persons from the East, Morocco and, to a lesser extent, Persia, with little money and less time left to live; rabbis, scholars and aspiring scholars; and, at the bottom of the ladder, the largely native-born "Moriscos," as the Sephardim called them. The Moriscos, who earned their living as laborers, could speak the local language; they made the rounds of the local villages to bring the city dwellers whatever they needed. Some worked as porters. Others performed all the difficult, repugnant tasks that no Arab or Christian would do.[28]

Luncz writes that the Jews of this period also played an important role in commerce. They dealt particularly in

> textiles, which they almost monopolized, importing their goods from Beirut or Damascus, and in money-changing, exchanging gold coins for silver and copper or vice versa, and buying and selling small gold coins for women's jewelry. Sometimes they also exchanged bills for the merchants of Beirut (money-changing was controlled by the Jews). A few of them ran food shops in the Jewish Quarter.[29]

Another trade engaged in by the Jews of Jerusalem was stone-cutting. Luncz writes about one Mórdechai of Jerusalem, who had once been famous for his workmanship in Vilna and might have fared equally well in Germany, but who renounced prestige in order to eke out a meager living in Jerusalem. There were several other skilled stone-masons, learned in German culture, whose great faith had inspired them to come to the Holy Land.[30]

According to Montefiore's census of 1839, most of the Jews engaged in productive work were Sephardim. Out of a total of 1,751 breadwinners, 229 Sephardim and only twenty-eight Ashkenazim earned their living from craftsmanship and physical labor.[31] Western travelers point out that the low level of employment among Jews was not due to their unwillingness to work but to their belief in the importance of studying the Torah, especially in the Holy Land. The Jews devoted all their time to study, relying on foreign philanthropy for their upkeep. Bartlett says:

> It is true that but little handicraft trade is to be found in Jerusalem, but it is also true that the system of the Rabbis discourages such employment—its efforts being directed to the sustenance of a population reading "the law day and night" (Ps. I. 2). This system, by its erroneous mode of practice, indirectly creates a nation of paupers depending upon them for bread.[32]

323

27   *Ibid.*, pp. 165-166 (translated from Hebrew).
28   *Ha-Levanon*, 15 Tamuz, 1869, vol. 6, no. 25, p. 195.
29   Luncz—Kressel, pp. 165-166 (translated from Hebrew).   30   *Ibid.*, p. 174.
31   Ben-Zvi, *Eretz-Israel*, p. 366.   32   Bartlett, *Revisited*, p. 81.

In the course of the nineteenth century, there was a rise in the number of Jews in Jerusalem engaged in manual labor. It is doubtful whether this growth was proportionate to the increase in population, but it was conspicuous. Consul and Mrs. Finn both note the fact that most of the tinkers, glaziers, shoemakers and tailors in Jerusalem were Jewish. In effect, the Europeans in the city found themselves keeping the Sabbath almost in the manner of the Jews, because all the shops were closed. The Finns also mention that there were many watchmakers, silversmiths, carpenters and tailors among the Ashkenazim.[33]

Frankl records that, in the mid-1850's, there were enough Jewish artisans in the city to renovate the house he rented. He also provides a list of Jewish craftsmen: one fence-builder; two stone-masons; one sculptor; twelve money-changers; one locksmith; two blacksmiths... six tinkers; five watchmakers; one polisher; two engravers; five silver- and goldsmiths; five bookbinders; six gem-setters; twenty-four tailors; fifteen shoemakers; two house-painters; five barbers; ten bakers; three pastry-cooks; some forty brandy distillers (all natives of Poland and Russia) and wine merchants, who bought grapes in Hebron. There were also forty teachers; five scribes; two musicians; twelve merchants; twenty traders; three bankers and about twelve pedlars. A total of 239 persons, or about four percent of the population, worked for a living. The remaining 5,461, including women and children, did not. Frankl adds that the Ashkenazi craftsmen were predominant, because they had learned their skills in Europe and outnumbered the Sephardi craftsmen.[34]

The number of Jews engaged in manual labor, however, was proportionately very small; even at the beginning of the second half of the century, most of the Jewish population lived on *ḥalukka* funds. For the most part, Jews avoided taxing physical labor. Warren comments that very few Jews participated in the extensive archaeological excavations in Jerusalem at the end of the 1860's because Jews were not accustomed to such difficult work.[35]

Neumann divides the Jews living in Jerusalem in the 1860's and 1870's into three categories. His first included pensioners—elderly persons receiving annuities, merchants, money-changers, landlords and businessmen; that is, those who were independent and relatively well-to-do. They numbered 2,000 out of a total Jewish population of 13,000. His second category included the majority of the Jews of Jerusalem: owners of small businesses, pedlars, artisans, piece-workers and housewives. There were 8,000 such persons, 3,000 of whom required financial aid on occasion. His third category included those engaged in spiritual activities, such as scholars and *yeshiva* students, who numbered 3,000. Neumann says that about half the Jewish population required financial assistance, and that their numbers grew in times of trouble. He also stresses that the Jews were wholly free to engage in commerce and craftsmanship. No permit was necessary, and there was no jealousy on the part of the Muslims. The Jews worked in about forty different professions, most of

324

33   J. Finn, *Stirring Times*, p. 63; Mrs. Finn, *Reminiscences*, p. 55.
34   Frankl, pp. 160-162; 218-221.
35   Wilson—Warren, *Recovery*, pp. 67-68.

which they had learned abroad. The Ashkenazim, who made up the majority of the craftsmen, were considered to be fine workers; most of them plied their trades in open shops in the market place.[36]

In 1877, Luncz carried out a detailed survey of the occupations of the Jewish population according to community groupings, dividing his subjects into three categories: merchants, artisans, and laborers. (Sometimes, he included different branches of the services in the artisans' category.) His survey shows that there were 493 Jewish workers, including many shoemakers, tailors, and metalworkers in 1877.[37] Another source notes that there were many Jewish workers in the souvenir industry, particularly in the manufacture of olive-wood artifacts.[38]

At the end of the nineteenth century, despite the swift growth of the new neighborhoods beyond the city walls, Jewish merchants continued to play an important role in commerce and brokerage in the markets of the Old City. David Yellin writes that at this time the Ashkenazim owned many small shops on the Street of the Jews. There were also well-known Sephardi merchants in the Old City who imported goods from Syria and other parts of the Ottoman Empire, or from Europe. Their shops were located on the main streets of the Old City, particularly in its "Bazaar" (David Street) and on the Street of the Christians.[39]

Pockets of Wealth amidst Widespread Poverty

Despite the difficult economic circumstances at the beginning of the century, there were always a few wealthy Jews to be found in Jerusalem. Richter, who visited the city in 1818, tells of prosperous Jewish property-owners whose homes were outwardly shabby but comfortable and well-appointed inside.[40] Geramb reports that wealthy Jews lent money to members of the Christian clergy during the 1830's when delays in transferring funds from Europe occurred. He says the Jews of that time were highly cultured and fluent in several languages.[41] Zimmerman estimates that ten percent of the Jews lived more or less comfortably in the 1850's, but that all the rest were extremely poor.[42] Although these travelers may have overestimated the extent of prosperity because they had been impressed by the cleanliness and pleasant external appearance of some Jewish homes and of some Jews, it does appear as if Jerusalem had a few relatively wealthy Jewish residents.

The sources abound in descriptions of a particularly rich family—the Amzalags. Mr. Amzalag is often referred to as "the richest Jew in the city"; a native of Portugal, he had come to Jerusalem from Gibraltar.[43] Slightly later, Frankl cites Zadok Halevi of Galicia as the richest of the Austrian Jews in Jerusalem, and notes that he owned three homes in the city. Other rich Jews

36   Neumann, p. 222.
37   Luncz, *Jerusalem*, VI, 1882, English Section, pp. 53-58.
38   Avitzur, *Daily Life*, pp. 272-274 (citing *Havatzelet*, 1878, nos. 34-37).
39   D. Yellin, *Writings*, II, pp. 249-250.   41   Geramb, II, pp. 90-92.
40   Richter, II, p. 261.   42   Zimmerman, p. 5.
43   Stephens, pp. 116, 184-186; Madden, pp. 242-248; Gaon, *Oriental Jews*, II, pp. 106-107.

Jewish shoemaker's shop in Jerusalem (Wilson, *Picturesque Palestine*, p. 27)

continue to be mentioned but, on the whole, the Jewish community lived in very straitened circumstances.[44]

Ha-Levanon describes the plight of the Jews in 1869. Unable to engage in agricultural work, most of the Jews relied entirely upon contributions and were on the verge of starvation. Rabbi Cahanyu offers the following description of privation in the Jewish community:

> There is no devil worse than poverty and need. My dear brother, if you only knew a small portion of what the Jews of Jerusalem suffer every day of their lives! They all live in tiny, cramped, dilapidated quarters—those who live alone, elderly married couples, the aged, who have no one to care for them. Only one Ashkenazi in a thousand had a servant in this city. What, for instance, would these poor souls do if someone in their family were to become ill, God forbid? Who would send for the doctor?

Financially, Cahanyu writes, the Jews were in a very bad state. Funds were usually received at the beginning of the year, but ran out before Passover, when the next year's rent had to be paid. As a result, the *kolelim* would advance rent money, and have almost nothing left to distribute for other purposes throughout the year. Cahanyu adds that

> ... It costs a man and his wife at least 500 piastres a year to rent an average-sized, one-room apartment in the Holy City. Coal for cooking purposes costs about 200 piastres a year. When water must be purchased over a period of several months, another 100 piastres are needed. This expenditure depends on the courtyard because some have good cisterns and relatively few residents. If rain has been plentiful, there may be enough water for the whole year's needs. Other cisterns may contain only enough for half a year, as a result of which one has no money left to buy even oil for lighting. How, I ask you, will such an unfortunate person obtain bread to eat, clothing for the winter, and other basic human necessities?[45]

326

44 Frankl, p. 163.   45 Cahanyu, pp. 61, 70-72 (translated from Hebrew).

Housing and the "Ḥazaka" System

The first problem facing a Jew who wished to build a house in Jerusalem was the acquisition of land. There were two types of land in the city: *Mulk,* or strictly private property, which was as a rule sub-divided among so many heirs that it was difficult to reach an agreement, and *Waqf,* or property owned by the Muslim religious authorities, which could not be sold but only rented for long periods. At the beginning of the century, Ottoman laws also forbade the sale of land to foreign subjects.[46] Sometimes an exception was made, as in the case of Sir Moses Montefiore, who received a special *firman* to purchase the "Kerem Moshe vi-Yhudit" (Moses and Judith) plot, later the site of the Mishkenot Sha'ananim quarter, and to register it in his name.[47] Ottoman law reforms, particularly the *Ḥatt-i Humayun* of 1856, eased the situation somewhat. It seems, however, that the land-sale prohibition was abolished in full only at the end of the 1860's. As a result, few Jews owned property, and most of the Jewish Quarter belonged to Muslim landlords who insisted on receiving rent a year in advance. When increased immigration to Jerusalem intensified the demand for housing, the Muslim landlords tried to exploit the situation by raising the rent. As a countermeasure, the Jews put the *"Ḥazaka"* system into practice. This was an ancient regulation of the Sephardi rabbis to forestall the loss of Jewish funds to non-Jewish landlords as a result of increases in rent produced by competition among Jews for rental housing. The rabbis had declared that the first Jew to rent a house from a non-Jew established a claim to it, and that other Jews could rent it only from him. Anyone who disobeyed this regulation was excommunicated, and no Jew was allowed to rent the house from him. If the original tenant appeared before a rabbinical court and produced a document proving his status, the court would give him a Bill of *Ḥazaka,* establishing his legal right to sell or mortgage this protected tenancy as if it were his own property. This, of course, proved to be very good business.[48]

Luncz confirms that the Jewish Quarter included very few houses and courtyards owned outright by Jews, and that most Jews lived in homes rented from Muslims in accordance with the *Ḥazaka* system. He adds that only the original tenant, whose *Ḥazaka* rights derived from a tenancy of three successive years, could sub-let it to other Jews at a fixed margin of profit. Some Jews enjoyed possession of several such protected-tenancy rights in Jerusalem, either inherited or acquired, which helped them to pay their own rent or supplement their family income. Luncz states that the Jewish community as an entity owned almost no public buildings or institutions at the beginning of the nineteenth century, other than the four interconnected synagogues and their adjoining courtyards, the *Talmud Torah* buildings, and a few other courtyards bequeathed or donated to the community. There was a large courtyard on the main Jewish street known as Deir Shiknaz, which had belonged to the Ashkenazim ever since the eighteenth century; the surrounding buildings had

---

46   Mrs. Finn, *Reminiscences*, p. 142; Y. Yellin, *Memoirs*, p. 31.
47   J. Finn, *Stirring Times*, II, p. 335.
48   Y. Yellin, *Memoirs*, p. 20.

been burned down by the Arabs in 1721, when the Jews were unable to repay a massive debt, and it had lain in ruins ever since.[49]

Frankl writes that he rented a house for three years in the 1850's, paying a total of 6,150 piastres. He later obtained a Bill of *Hazaka* and comments that such a document was considered to be very valuable. It was passed down from generation to generation in Jerusalem, and could be sold for thousands of piastres.[50]

The housing situation is also examined by other late nineteenth-century writers. Gad Frumkin relates that "a person with *Hazaka* would rent rooms out to sub-tenants. A Jew dared not ignore the *hazkir* [as a person with *Hazaka* was called] and rent a room directly from its Arab owner, because the matter would be brought before the religious court."[51] According to J.I. Yellin:

> The Jewish community of Jerusalem was totally dependent upon these courtyards and protected-tenancy rights. Apart from the *Hurva* courtyard, where many important members of the community lived, and a few other courtyards publicly or privately owned by Jews, all the other courtyards belonged to Arabs, and leasing rights in them were held by Jews.... This was a sure defence against profiteering on the part of the Arab owners. In this way the *Hazaka* system became both a fundamental institution and a valuable asset to the Jews of Jerusalem.

Yellin also tells about the Arab landlord of a large number of courtyards who had tried to raise the rent. The community joined forces against him and, in response to his threats, established the Nahalat Shiv'a neighborhood outside the city walls. Thus, instead of raising the rent, the Arab in fact lowered it.[52]

Some writers considered the *Hazaka* system detrimental to the development of Jerusalem's Jewish community, since it discouraged Jews from purchasing homes and shops of their own, although these were relatively inexpensive. The *Hazaka* also became an important source of income for the *hazkir,* who made a living from renting his flat to other Jews. Some Jews who moved to the new neighborhoods outside the city walls leased their homes in the Old City to others.[53]

The restrictions on land purchase by Jews were greatly relaxed under Egyptian rule. This remained the case when the Ottoman government returned, especially after the post-Crimean War law reforms (1856). Encouraged by the growth of their community, the Jews began to weigh the possibility of new construction inside the Old City. Thus the Batei Mahseh housing complex came into being.

The Batei Mahseh Neighborhood

The immediate incentive for initiating the Batei Mahseh plan was the opportunity to purchase a large tract of land at the southwestern end of the Jewish Quarter, afforded by the death of its Sephardi owner, Joseph Peretz. In 1857, Rabbi Meir Sheinbaum, a Hungarian immigrant and official of *Kolel*

49 Luncz—Kressel, p. 161. 52 J.I. Yellin, *Forefathers*, pp. 44-46 (translated from Hebrew).
50 Frankl, pp. 218-221. 53 Y. Yellin, *Memoirs*, p. 20.
51 G. Frumkin, *Judge*, p. 10.

Hod, which included Jews from the Austro-Hungarian Empire as well as from Holland and Germany, purchased the plot for the *kolel*. He paid 83,872 Turkish piastres for it, a very considerable sum in those days. The members of *Kolel* Hod financed the purchase by pledging their *ḥalukka* money to this end. At first, this purchase had been opposed by the officials in Amsterdam to whom *Kolel* Hod was subordinate, but they too were finally convinced to help. In 1858, *Kolel* Hod appealed to the Jews of the Diaspora to contribute money for the construction of housing for poor persons and guests on Mount Zion.[53*] Rabbi Azriel Hausdorf, dragoman of the Austrian consul, Pizzamano, and a leader of *Kolel* Hod, went to Europe to raise money. He was even granted permission by the Austrian Ministry of the Interior to appeal for funds all over the Austrian Empire.[54]

Another supporter of the project was Rabbi Azriel Hildesheimer of Berlin, who requested the Austrian consul in Jerusalem to handle the project's legal aspects on the assumption that it would operate under Austrian auspices. Consul Pizzamano obtained the necessary *firman*, and negotiated for the Jewish community on building matters. On August 24, 1858, the original documents pertaining to the transfer of land ownership were filed at the Austrian Consulate in Jerusalem. Pizzamano sent the bill of transfer to Mr. Lehren, and a copy to the officials in Holland. He was then asked to oversee the drafting of regulations to govern the allocation of apartments. The next Austrian consul, Von Wolfsburg, was asked to continue the activities of his predecessor, and agreed to supervise the project's construction.[55]

The "Batei Maḥseh Society for Housing the Poor and Guests on Mount Zion in the Holy City of Jerusalem, May it be Speedily Rebuilt in Our Day, Amen" was founded in 1859. As soon as the building permit was received in 1860, the Jewish community began amassing stones and lime — the main building materials of the time. Actual construction began a year later. The first eight apartments, completed in 1862, were by far the most attractive dwellings and had the best sanitary facilities to be found in the Old City. Within a year, four more houses were ready. The neighborhood charter was drawn up in 1863 and made public in 1865.[56] The regulations show that one room was set aside for guests (following the Christian custom of using monasteries as tourist hostels). One source reports that

> ...all the apartments are airy, sunny, and comfortably appointed. Each consists of two rooms and a kitchen. Their location near the southern wall of the city offers an attractive view of the Mount of Olives and the surrounding area. There is room for another 400 apartments. All the houses on this large, open plot are so well situated that those living here suffer much less illness than do all the other Jews in Jerusalem.[57]

Some buildings in the Batei Maḥseh neighborhood were donated by benefactors wishing to create memorials of themselves or of their dear ones.

53* The term "Mount Zion" also referred then to part of the area within the walls.
54 Eliav, *Love of Zion*, pp. 266-286; Bartura, "Batei Maḥseh," pp. 122-128.
55 *Loc. cit.*
56 Eliav, *ibid.*, p. 271.
57 Bartura, *Eye of the Beholder*, p. 77 (translated from Hebrew); for further information, see *PEF QSt*, 1898, p. 81.

Neve Shalom, the first such building, was established by the wealthy Hirsch brothers of Halberstadt in memory of their brother, Rabbi Shalom, who had died young and childless. It contained six apartments, and was governed by special regulations. Two other buildings (the largest ones in the neighborhood, and still standing today) were financed by Baron Karl Wilhelm Wolf Rothschild of Frankfurt to house renowned scholars. Ohel Shlomo was established in memory of Rabbi Salomon Ullmann, the chief Rabbi of France, and another two-family house in memory of Rabbi Jacob Ettlinger, the chief rabbi of Altona. The large, attractive, neighborhood synagogue, "Beit Meir ve-Ohel Yitzḥak," commemorated Rabbi Meir ben Isaac Frankl Eismann of Frankfurt. A ritual bath was constructed nearby; its water came from an ancient cistern.[58]

When the first group of apartments was completed, the Austrian consul held a lottery to allocate them. According to the neighborhood charter, new tenants were to be chosen in this way every three years. Certain houses had different regulations. For example, those built by the Rothschilds offered tenants a permanent residence. The Austrian consul was appointed to supervise the proper maintenance and cleanliness of Batei Maḥseh. When Emperor Franz-Josef of Austria visited Jerusalem in 1869, he was so impressed by this project that he donated money for the erection of an entrance gate to the neighborhood which would bear his name.[59] Several Jewish sources, which call the neighborhood "Batei Maḥseh for Housing the Needy and Widows on Mount Zion," describe the construction of a study hall, a synagogue and *yeshivot*; they also note the discovery of eight large cisterns containing potable water in the area.[60]

The large and spacious Beth Rothschild was completed in 1871, by which time there were twenty-two houses in the neighborhood. By 1885, this number had risen to seventy, with even more houses under construction. Once the major building activity was completed, supervision of the project passed from the Austrian consul to the various *kolelim*. It is worthy of mention that, although the founders of Batei Maḥseh intended the neighborhood to serve only *Kolel* Hod, it actually housed the needy members of all the *kolelim*.

In 1891, Luncz writes that there were seventy-six houses in the Batei Maḥseh neighborhood:

> Five houses are set aside for guest accommodations and the rest allocated by lottery, two-thirds to the Jews of Germany, Holland, Austria and Hungary, who built the place, and one-third to members of other community groups. Residence is free for three years, or for seven years in those houses built by individual contributors. This institution is noteworthy for its cleanliness and orderly administrative procedures, which are handled by a local committee under the jurisdiction of the learned... Rabbi Azriel Hildesheimer.[61]

In the 1880's, the newspaper *Ha-Tzevi* cites Batei Maḥseh as an example of how apartments were leased in Jerusalem. There were two ways to acquire

58   Bartura, "Batei Maḥseh," pp. 126-127; Eliav, *Love of Zion*, p. 175.
59   Eliav, *ibid.*, pp. 171-173.
60   See, e.g., Reicher, pp. 61-62.
61   Luncz, *Guide*, pp. 108-109 (translated from Hebrew).

housing: one was Montefiore's three-year rotating lottery system, which was used in Batei Maḥseh, and the other was the "Mazkeret Montefiore" grant system, which offered building loans to be repaid after fifteen years had passed. The *Ha-Tzevi* columnist advocates the latter because it was not a short-term gift but a loan, repayable by means of monthly rent.[62]

Construction in the Batei Maḥseh quarter continued into the early twentieth century. As late as 1910, the newspaper *Ha-Or* reports the completion of an attractive building to serve as a rabbi's study house and residence.[63]

Batei Maḥseh, or "der Deutscher Platz" (the German compound), as it was called then, consisted of a large, square courtyard surrounded by houses, able to accommodate several dozen families. Each family received one room, an entrance hall, and a kitchen.[64] A protective wall encircled the neighborhood, and heavy iron or wooden gates locked at night made the inhabitants feel safe.[65] The establishment of Batei Maḥseh led to the paving of a road (still in use) in the southern part of the neighborhood, alongside the city wall, between the Armenian Quarter and the Wailing Wall.[66]

Whereas various sources lavish praise on the Batei Maḥseh project, David Yellin ridicules the fact that the Jews of Hungary, Holland and Germany left only one-third of the available dwellings for all the rest of the Jewish population:

> For thirty-five years, the learned Rabbi Azriel Hildesheimer and his colleagues appealed to the Jews of Germany and Hungary to contribute towards the construction of housing for the needy scholars of Jerusalem. When they had amassed enough money, they bought a large plot of land known as *Tel Hagofrit* (the mound of sulfur)... on the eastern slope of Mount Zion, and built over fifty houses called Batei Maḥseh on it. When the time came to divide the dwellings among the needy scholars of Jerusalem, the Jews of Hungary took the lead, for who are the Jewish people if not the scholars of *Shomrei Haḥomot?* Next in line were the Jews of Holland and Germany. The leaders of the project from abroad decided to divide the residency rights in these buildings three ways: a third was reserved for the Jews of Hungary, a third for those from Holland and Germany, and a third for the Jewish people as a whole and the truly needy, who did not have the holy privilege of being born in Hungary or Germany—including Ashkenazim, Sephardim, North Africans, Yemenites and all other kinds of Jews. Thus the whole Jewish people sat on one side of the balance, and the Jews of Hungary, Holland, and Germany, with their double portion, on the other.[67]

Other charitable institutions were established especially for Oriental Jews. The newspaper *Yehuda vi-Yrushalayim* reports the construction of *Talmud Torah* institutions for the Sephardi *kolelim,* and an almshouse for 140 poor widows called *Gevul Ha-Almana,* both on Mount Zion.[68] *Ha-Levanon* adds that the *Talmud Torah* institutions were intended for orphans, and for children from poor families.[69] Gaon reports that, in 1876, *Gevul Ha-Almana,* the North

62 *Ha-Tzevi*, vol. II, no. 25, p. 2.
63 *Ha-Or,* 21 Ḥeshvan, 1910, vol. II, no. 30-205, p. 2.
64 G. Frumkin, *Judge*, p. 48.
65 Bartura, "Batei Maḥseh," p. 126.
66 Horowitz, p. 130.
67 D. Yellin, *Writings*, I, pp. 64-65 (translated from Hebrew).
68 *Yehuda vi-Yrushalayim,* p. 76.
69 *Ha-Levanon,* 7 Tamuz, 1873, vol. IX, no. 44, p. 384.

African almshouses in Jerusalem, housed three widows in each of its 106 apartments. There were also eight dwellings for scholars, an administrative office, a soup kitchen, and two organizations to aid the sick.[70] These houses must have been quite poorly constructed, because the *Sha'arei Zion* newspaper reports two years later that a storm had wrecked two *Gevul Ha-Almana* dwellings and had left others on the verge of collapse.[71]

Summary

The building activities of the second half of the nineteenth century, particularly the Batei Maḥseh project, which coincided with the establishment of Mishkenot Sha'ananim, indicate the growing importance of the Old City as a center of Jewish life. The apartments of Batei Maḥseh, distributed by lottery for short leases, were much in demand. The rent-free apartments of Mishkenot Sha'ananim attracted very few tenants at first. This was because the attractive Batei Maḥseh neighborhood was in the heart of the Jewish Quarter, close to the Wailing Wall, while Mishkenot Sha'ananim, the first neighborhood outside the city walls, was exposed to danger and insecurity. Despite the initial success of Batei Maḥseh, however, it was Mishkenot Sha'ananim which showed the pattern of the future. The construction of homes and neighborhoods inside the Old City could be no more than a partial and temporary solution for a growing Jewish community: the real solution was to create a new city outside the walls. However, the contribution of Batei Maḥseh to the community's development should not be underestimated. It was the first serious attempt to deal with the increasingly severe housing shortage in the Old City. Overcrowding, unspeakably bad living conditions, and inflated rental fees had encouraged *Kolel* Hod to help the Jews by providing new housing. Never before in the nineteenth century had a project of such scope been envisioned. The *kolel's* purchase of a large tract of land and its construction of dozens of apartments was an act of true community pioneering.

70   Gaon, *Oriental Jews*, p. 133.
71   *Sha'arei Zion*, 27 Shevat, 1878, vol. II, no. 42, p. 178.

Chapter Five:
CHRISTIAN MISSIONARY ACTIVITY:
INSTITUTIONS FOR HEALTH, EDUCATION AND
WELFARE; THE KARAITES

Introduction

The poverty and neglect characteristic of Jerusalem's Jewish community during the early part of the nineteenth century provided fertile ground for Protestant missionary activities. The Jewish community's response was twofold: laying down prohibitions and excommunicating anyone who dared to accept aid from the missionaries, and establishing Jewish social-welfare institutions.

Nineteenth-century Christian travelers, many of them missionaries themselves or connected in some way with the Mission, provide detailed accounts of missionary activities and of the Jewish community's opposition to them. Let us consider their comments, and also several Jewish sources dealing with this activity.

The Jewish Response to Missionary Activity

F.A. Strauss, writing in the 1840's, stresses that the nature of the internal leadership of the Jews should be considered carefully by Christian missionaries, since the chief rabbi of the Sephardim, who was also their political leader, could easily punish any Jew involved with missionaries. He adds that, in the Turkish Empire, only non-Muslims were free to change their religion. Hence, missionary activity in Jerusalem centered on non-Muslims, and on Jews in particular. The Ashkenazim were most easily approached because they were protected by foreign consuls prepared to help in this matter. As missionary activities increased, however, the Jews stepped up their resistance, banning contact with missionaries, burning their books, and forbidding Jews to use the English Mission hospital located near the Jewish Quarter. In addition, wealthy Jews began to offer aid, financial and other, to keep the Jews of Jerusalem away from Mission institutions. Sir Moses Montefiore, for example, was active in this respect, as was the Rothschild family, which sent its representative, Albert Cohn, to establish institutions competing with those of the British. A pilot attempt was made to interest Jews

333

Ashkenazi Jews praying in Kerem Abraham at end of 19th century (Boddy, p. 257)

in agricultural work, something for which they had shown little inclination previously.[1]

Bartlett declares:

> One thing that tends to withhold any Jews who might feel disposed to embrace Christianity from making an open confession, is the almost despotic power exercised over them by the rabbis. As the law stands at present... he must be prepared to separate from his wife and children.... Another obstacle is the loss of employment or alms among his brethren, and his being thrown entirely upon the missionaries for the means of support.[2]

Zimmerman notes (in 1852) that all the Christian sects had begun lately to pay more attention to the Jews, establishing schools and hospitals for their benefit, under British, Prussian or French auspices. The Jews' attitude towards them was one of distrust. They avoided Christian welfare institutions, preferring to risk disease and death rather than expose themselves to religious coercion in such places as hospitals. Because of this, Sir Moses Montefiore established a pharmacy in Jerusalem and sent Dr. Simon Fraenkel to work there, covering all of his expenses.[3]

Van de Velde also discusses Jewish resistance to the Mission:

> A great hindrance, however, arises from the difficulty of finding access to the Jews. The bitter hatred entertained by the Rabbis towards a living Christianity, and, in particular, towards the missionaries, makes it almost impossible for the latter to speak to the Jews about the concerns of their souls.... On this account, the London society has very wisely attached to its agency at Jerusalem a medical

334

1   Strauss, pp. 232-236.   2   Bartlett, *Revisited*, pp. 78-83.   3   Zimmerman, pp. 8-13.

institution in the form of an hospital, in which gratuitous attendance is given to sick Jews. The haughty heart, when broken by the disease of the body, is willing to listen to the voice of Divine compassion, especially when the lips of those from whom that voice proceeds are in correspondence with the benevolent hand of human sympathy and tenderness. This is the way pointed out to us by our Lord Jesus Christ Himself....[4]

Tobler attacks the activities of the Mission, claiming that its hospital admitted only Jewish patients and sometimes even kept healthy persons there to benefit its statistics. The rabbis excommunicated anyone making use of the hospital's services; in 1846, they even stationed private guards near the hospital building. The Mission purchased land near the Jewish cemetery to bury Jews who had died in its hospital and were consequently denied Jewish burial. In 1853, Tobler tells us a body was carried back and forth between the two cemeteries until the authorities ordered it buried in neutral territory.[5]

Christian missionary activities are also described by many Jewish writers of the period. Neumann repeats Tobler's accusations, noting that the Mission was still active in his time and had even greater resources at its disposal. He believes it was not the apathy of the Jewish community but its inability to withstand material temptation that led to its dependence on Mission services. He advocates increasing the resources available to Jewish charity institutions in order to solve the problem. Neumann also charges Consul Finn with complicity in the proposed conversion of the Jews, and of acting on his own when the mission failed. Finn appointed a notorious Jew to serve as vice-consul in his absence, purchased land for Jews to farm, and established charitable institutions, all with the purpose of converting Jews to Christianity.[6]

According to Luncz, the Mission was active primarily in providing a medical specialist who made house calls and distributed medicine free of charge. As time passed, the Mission's philanthropic activities expanded until they became a stumbling block for the Jewish community of Jerusalem.[7]

In 1871, *Ha-Levanon* reports that missionaries posted provocative placards on the walls of homes in Jerusalem. The Jews complained to the pasha, who ordered them removed.[8] Eight years later, the newspaper notes, the schools established by the Mission provided free meals for the children, in order to attract them to Christianity. Any Jew sending his children there was excommunicated. In the same year, the newspaper appealed to the Jews of Jerusalem to beware of missionary activities as there had already been cases of needy Jews giving their children up to the Mission.[9] Among the means employed by the Jewish community to prevent Jews from using the Mission hospital were excommunication, exclusion from prayer groups (*minyanim*), and denial of burial in a Jewish cemetery.[10]

The Mission continued its activities late into the nineteenth century, posing a profound threat to the Jewish community. The *Benei Israel* society was formed in 1898 in order to unite the Jewish community in its fight against the Mission,

4   Van de Velde, p. 219.
5   Neumann, pp. 231-233, 284.
6   *Loc. cit.*
7   Luncz—Kressel, p. 70.
8   *Ha-Levanon*, 8 Tevet, 1871, vol. VIII, no. 15, p. 118.
9   *Ibid.*, 2 Iyyar, 1879, vol. XV, no. 37, p. 295; *ibid.*, 19 Av, 1879, vol. XVI, no. 2, p. 9.
10 Yaari, "The Suffering," p. 270.

most of whose activities were directed towards needy Oriental Jews. The Mission offered them an extensive range of free medical services (including an excellent, large hospital) and an opportunity to send their children to schools providing free meals and clothing. The *Benei Israel* society banned contact with the Mission and its institutions, and hired its own doctor, who opened a clinic for needy Jews from all community groups. This doctor also made free house calls, and dispensed medicines at very low cost. With the approval of the rabbis and Jewish community leaders, the society declared that any Jew or Jewess who died in the Mission hospital would be denied Jewish burial. It was not long before this threat was carried out: a Sephardi woman who died there was buried outside the cemetery on the Mount of Olives. Thereafter, the Mission hospital refused to admit Jews in critical condition and, if a patient's health took a turn for the worse, he was moved, if possible, to a Jewish hospital. The *Benei Israel* society functioned for several years; for various reasons, its activities decreased and eventually ceased altogether.[11]

Jewish Health Institutions; Simon Fraenkel's Clinic

The battle against the Mission led to the establishment of Jewish institutions for health, welfare, and education, so that Jews would not have to resort to the services of the Mission. The first such project was the clinic of Dr. Simon Fraenkel, who resided in Jerusalem from 1842 to 1858.[12] Moses Montefiore had sent Fraenkel to the Holy Land, paid his travel expenses, equipped him with a pharmacy and surgical instruments, determined an appropriate salary, and promised him the protection of the British consul and Turkish pasha.[13] Barclay reports in 1857 that the Jewish clinic run by Dr. Simon Fraenkel was located in the northwestern sector of the Jewish Quarter.[14] Of the two Jewish hospitals in the Jewish Quarter shown by the Tobler-Van de Velde map of 1857, the one in the west was probably Fraenkel's clinic, and that in the southeast, the Rothschild hospital. (The German-Jewish leader, Ludwig Phillipson, had proposed the establishment of a Jewish hospital in 1842, when Fraenkel's clinic was opened, but his hospital never came into being.)[15]

The Rothschild Hospital

The Rothschild family founded Jerusalem's first Jewish hospital in 1854, after the outbreak of the Crimean War in 1853 had left the Jewish community of Jerusalem in dire straits.[16] The Rothschild family sent Dr. Albert Cohn to Jerusalem to establish welfare and medical institutions, the most important of which was the Mayer Rothschild hospital, whose chief physician from 1854 to 1862 was Dr. Neumann. According to Dr. Neumann, the hospital staff included a chief physician; a surgeon; two pharmacists (with one or two assistants); and an administrator. About 600 patients were treated annually and some 30,000 prescriptions filled.[17] The hospital was housed in the rented

11   Schirion, pp. 39-40.
12   Eliav, *Love of Zion*, pp. 287-288.
13   Gat, pp. 126-127; 131-132.
14   Barclay, p. 444.
15   Eliav, *Love of Zion*, pp. 287-288.
16   Gat, pp. 127-129.
17   Neumann, pp. 399-413.

building in which Dr. Albert Cohn had resided during his sojourn in Jerusalem. Later, a building was purchased for the hospital in the southeastern corner of the Jewish Quarter. The hospital also served the non-Jewish population.[18]

Grayevsky offers the following account of the hospital's establishment:

> The Sephardi community owned an ancient courtyard in Jerusalem, called the *Talmud Torah* courtyard... near the Batei Maḥseh neighborhood. In 1854, Dr. Albert Cohn arrived from Paris to found a hospital in Jerusalem on behalf of the Rothschilds. Since a foreigner was not allowed to buy land in his own name... Cohn established the Rothschild hospital in a courtyard he purchased from the Sephardi community for 20,000 francs on condition that, if the hospital were ever closed, the courtyard would be sold back to the community at its original price.[19]

Hausdorf also writes extensively about Albert Cohn's visit to Jerusalem, and mentions his numerous plans for welfare institutions in the city.[20] The newspaper *Sha'arei Zion* reports that Rothschild had bought a courtyard opposite the al-Aqṣa mosque, on the southern slope of Mount Zion, to house a hospital. The courtyard had buildings on all four sides. They included a treasury; a pharmacy; a synagogue; a kitchen; servants' quarters; and three rooms for patients, one for men and two for women, with a total of eighteen beds.[21]

After his third visit to Jerusalem, in 1857, Tobler reports the existence of a new hospital founded by the Rothschild family. He says that its order and cleanliness made an excellent impression. In 1856, he records, 573 patients had been treated there, and 21,342 medicines prescribed. Tobler also enumerates the countries of origin of the patients, their occupations, their illnesses, and so on.[22] Frankl also provides details about the patients in 1857, pointing out that the hospital itself admitted only Jews, but its clinic treated Christians and Muslims as well, and provided free medication. Frankl adds that the Rothschild family had donated another 300,000 francs recently to expand the building, but that there was not enough money to equip it.[23]

The Bikkur Ḥolim Hospital

The Rothschild hospital was too small to meet the needs of the Jewish community. Taking into account the activities of the Mission, the leaders of the Perushim community decided another hospital was required. Thus, in 1857, the Bikkur Ḥolim hospital came into being. The Bikkur Ḥolim Society which founded it rented two courtyards for the purpose, one on Meidan Street and the other on Hebron Street. In 1864, the hospital moved to new quarters west of Ḥabad Street. An appeal for donations was published that year in the newspaper, *Ha-Maggid*. Montefiore laid the cornerstone of the new building, which included a pharmacy and clinic.[24] Its location near the English Mission hospital may have been chosen to deter Jews from using Mission facilities.

18   Gat, pp. 133-137.
19   Grayevsky, *Sefer Hayishuv*, p. 27 (translated from Hebrew).
20   Gat, p. 135.   22   Tobler, *Dritte Wanderung*.
21   *Sha'arei Zion*, 19 Tevet, 1879, vol. IV, p. 54.   23   Frankl, pp. 226-227.
24   *Ha-Maggid*, 29 Av, 1864, vol. VIII, no. 34, p. 268; Yaari, *Memoirs*, I, p. 217.

Jewish hospital (Bartlett, *Jerusalem Revisited*, frontispiece)

At first, the Bikkur Ḥolim hospital could accommodate no more than twelve persons at a time, and its expenses reached 400 francs a month.[25] Luncz reports that it had three rooms and twelve beds in 1869,[26] and that, by 1891, it comprised five "houses" and thirty-six beds. Patients were examined by the house physician on three days each week, free of charge; medicines were provided for a small fee.[27] Freiman (1914) says the hospital consisted of thirteen "houses."[28] Schirion describes how it started out in a small building purchased by members of the Perushim *kolelim* and expanded until there were more than fifty beds. Throughout its existence, Bikkur Ḥolim was supported by donations, especially those sent from Russia, America, Germany, Austria and Hungary. Jerusalem residents also contributed and, in the beginning, the *kolelim* of the Perushim donated fixed annual sums. Thus, needy patients belonging to these *kolelim* paid only ten Turkish grush a day while members of

338

25 *Ha-Levanon*, 18 Tamuz, 1868, vol. V, no. 27, p. 428.
26 Luncz—Kressel, p. 210.
27 Luncz, *Guide*, pp. 113-114.
28 Freiman, p. 19.

the Hasidic *kolelim* paid twenty. Poor members of *Kolel* Habad paid fifteen grush a day because the president of the *kolel*, Rabbi Moses Wittenberg, made substantial monthly contributions to the hospital. Bikkur Holim also derived some income from its monopoly of the sale of shrouds to the *kolelim* of the Perushim. Patients without means received medication free or for a very small charge. Until the First World War, the hospital operated under the auspices of the German consul. When Jerusalem expanded outside the Old City, Bikkur Holim hospital moved to its present location on the Street of the Prophets, and its former building became a hospital for the chronically ill.[29]

These three medical establishments were the first Jewish public-health institutions in Jerusalem. As time went on, the number of medical orderlies and of physicians in the city grew, and medical care improved. Still, sanitary conditions in the city left much to be desired, and contagious diseases continued to plague Jerusalem. A severe cholera epidemic broke out in 1866, taking a heavy toll in lives; it moved the Hebrew press to appeal to Jewish doctors to come to the aid of Jerusalem's Jews, lest they turn to the Mission Hospital.[30]

Charity and Welfare

The leaders in the areas of charity and welfare were again Montefiore and the Rothschilds. The various projects undertaken by Dr. Albert Cohn for the Rothschild family included a pawnshop; a bread-distribution fund; and a poor women's maternity fund. According to Neumann, the pawnshop had 100,000 piastres in assets, while the fund for new mothers assisted 120 women each year; 600 loaves of bread were distributed to the poor for the Sabbath and holidays.[31]

Montefiore established another maternity fund, as well as a loan fund. In 1854, the Society for the Support of Sewers and Launderers in England sent a shipment of textile materials to Palestine at Montefiore's request, to enable widows and orphans to sew clothing for a living. (Montefiore had earlier attempted to establish a weaving mill in Jerusalem, but it had failed; see below.) Montefiore also tried to offer assistance in other areas.[32]

Charitable institutions, such as an Ashkenazi burial society (1861); loan funds for the poor; *Bikkur Holim* societies to aid the sick; soup kitchens for the elderly and destitute; and guest hostels began to be established by various Jewish groups and *kolelim*. Luncz gives a long list of welfare societies in Jerusalem run by the Perushim, Hasidim, Sephardim, and Mugrabim (North Africans).

One institution worthy of mention is the Sanders Old Age Home. Luncz describes it as follows in 1891:

29 Schirion, pp. 149-151.
30 *Ha-Levanon*, 25 Elul, 1873, vol. X, no. 5, p. 33; *ibid.*, 2 Heshvan, 1873, vol. X, no. 10, pp. 78-79.
31 Gat, p. 140; Neumann, pp. 339-413.
32 Yellin, in Yaari, *Memoirs*, pp. 164-165; *Havatzelet*, 1 Kislev, 1870/1, vol. I, no. 5, p. 17; Malachi, pp. 150-167.

This home was established in 1879 by Samuel Baruch Sanders of Australia. At first it was very small, and no one, including the founder himself, believed this institution would become one of the largest in the Old City. Slowly, however, Sanders managed to build it up and increase its profits to such an extent that, by 1889, he was able to purchase a large building for 24,000 francs. Later on, a plot of land was acquired outside the city [walls] on the Jaffa highway. The old building was eventually sold and the money used for the upkeep of the institution, which provided a home for sixty-three elderly people.[33]

Culture and Education

As more educated, cultured Jews immigrated to Jerusalem, and Europe and the country became more closely linked by means of the Hebrew press, a yearning for education began to be felt. It led to the establishment of various organizations, some dedicated to spreading modern education and others trying to limit it; this was in addition to the social functions assumed, apparently, by all Jerusalem organizations. Most of these organizations were established after 1870, and therefore will be discussed later, in the second volume of this work.

Until the early 1840's, Jerusalem's educational institutions were much like the *hadarim* and *yeshivot* of the Diaspora, devoting themselves mainly to religious studies.[34] It is interesting to see how a foreign Christian viewed the Jewish educational system in Jerusalem. Tobler writes, for example, that the Jews' elementary schools (*hadarim*) were extremely disorganized, and were run privately. The Sephardim had such a school alongside their synagogue. This did not mean, he said, that Jews were uneducated or illiterate. On the contrary, they attained a high level of education through their own special methods of study. Despite the lack of organized elementary schools, there were many higher schools (*yeshivot*) where the students, both young people and adults, specialized in the scriptures and learned to think logically and deductively.[35]

Vocational Schools and Girls' Schools

Beginning in the mid-nineteenth century, new types of schools began to be established in Jerusalem. The first to open were those which specialized in vocational training. Schools designed to broaden their students' general knowledge appeared only later on, and were a source of controversy in the Jewish community. Schools for girls were of the vocational type. Since girls did not attend *heder* or *yeshiva,* a need was felt to give them some kind of education, with training in sewing, embroidery, and the like seeming to be most appropriate.

It was Montefiore and the Rothschilds who took the first steps for the establishment of Jewish vocational schools in Jerusalem. Representing the Rothschilds, Dr. Cohn founded a boys' vocational school and a school for girls.[36] The vocational school was attended by thirty boys and also provided

33 Luncz, *Guide*, pp. 153-154 (translated from Hebrew).
34 Grunwald, p. 170.
35 Tobler, *Denkblätter*, p. 462; Neumann, pp. 397-399.
36 Gat, p. 149; Neumann, p. 399.

religious instruction, but it proved a failure and was closed down.[37] According to Cohen-Reiss, it was supported by private craftsmen and its Ashkenazi and Sephardi pupils studied in separate classes, each of which was conducted in the spoken language of its community.[38] Consul Finn writes that Albert Cohn established several important institutions in Jerusalem in 1854, among them vocational schools for children and for women.[39] Montefiore also tried to establish a type of vocational school: a linen-weaving mill to train forty apprentices, but this too met with little success.[40]

Some writers see a continuation of the efforts of Albert Cohn to establish a vocational school in the abortive attempt of the Jewish official and dragoman, Joseph Krieger, to do so. In 1867, Krieger went before the Central Committee of the Alliance Israélite Universelle in Paris to propose the establishment of a school in Jerusalem. This school opened on a part-time basis in 1868 under Krieger's administration, but was forced to close in 1870 because of the opposition of religious fanatics and because of other difficulties. It was only ten years later that the first real vocational school, known briefly as the "Alliance" school, came into being.[41]

During his fourth visit to the country, in 1855, Montefiore set up a girls' school in Jerusalem. Frankl writes that there were two such girls' schools when he visited in 1856. One was affiliated with the boys' school erected by the Rothschild family, and taught handicrafts, reading, and prayer; it had three girls in one class, and five in another. The building itself was on the verge of collapse. The twenty-four member school committee met only three times in the course of its existence and dealt mainly with trivial matters such as whose signature would appear first on official correspondence. The second such institution was Montefiore's sewing school, which was housed in a dilapidated building and had twenty-one girls working together in one classroom. Frankl also comments that parents were in no rush to send their daughters to these schools, and would do so only in return for payment.[42] Mrs. Rogers, who also visited the city in 1856, writes:

> There were thirty-one girls ranging in age from seven to fourteen in one classroom but the full number usually assembled there was thirty-five. All were engaged in needlework. The second class of thirty girls were likewise engaged. These two rooms were set apart expressly for Sephardi youngsters. The school for Ashkenazim had fifteen pupils. In one class all the children seemed to be under seven years of age and in the other, between thirteen and fifteen.[43]

Montefiore and his wife returned to England to present an enthusiastic report about the sewing school, but it too closed down in 1857, unable to cope with the many difficulties it encountered. When Mrs. Rogers revisited the city in 1859, she was told that both these institutions were no longer in existence.[44]

37 Frankl, pp. 221-222.
38 Cohen-Reiss, p. 77.
39 J. Finn, *Stirring Times*, II, p. 321.
40 Neumann, pp. 414-417; Meisel, *Testimonial Fund*, pp. 9-18; Malachi, pp. 150-168.
41 Gat, pp. 239-241; Leven, p. 110; Grunwald, pp. 173-174.
42 Frankl, pp. 222-223; Cohen-Reiss, pp. 77-78.
43 Rogers, pp. 313-317.
44 *Loc. cit.*; Gat, p. 242.

Jewish old age home in early 20th century (Goodrich-Freer, p. 60)

The establishment of boys' vocational schools and of schools for girls was violently opposed by fanatical religious leaders, but their antagonism towards modern, general, educational institutions was greater still.[45]

The Laemel School

Through the efforts of Ludwig Frankl, another educational institution was founded in Jerusalem: Aliza Hertz established the Laemel school in memory of her father, Simon von Laemel. Despite opposition by religious fanatics, the school's opening was marked by a festive celebration in the Austrian style. In attendance were the pasha, the consuls of various countries, and the chief rabbi and his court. Frankl, who made the opening remarks, did not forget to mention that the Emperor of Austria also bore the title of "King of Jerusalem," and that his flag was now flying once again in the Holy City.[46] The Laemel school was located on the street leading from the Street of the Chain to the Meidan, in the northeastern corner of the Jewish Quarter.[47] Formally under the auspices of the Austrian government, this school was supervised by the Sephardi community, and accountable to the chief rabbi. Opinions differ over the subsequent development of this institution. Some praise the school's advanced methods of study, its order and cleanliness, while others say it was no

342

45   Gat, pp. 224-236; Ḥannani, *Enlightenment*, pp. 28-36.
46   Gat, pp. 229-237; Frankl, pp. 255-257.
47   Grayevsky, *Hidden Treasures*, XV, p. 20.

different from a *heder*, its only innovation being that the boys also studied Arabic and a little arithmetic. These contradictory opinions apparently reflect both the outlooks of their authors and periodic fluctuations in the school's fortunes. From time to time attempts were made to improve the educational level of the school, but without any lasting success. After uniting with the Orphanage school in 1879, the Laemel school was completely reformed, and thereafter progressed at a steady rate.[48]

The establishment of the Laemel school was undoubtedly a turning point in the development of Jerusalem; the cultural conflict it sparked brought about important changes in the city. The school fought fiercely against its numerous opponents, and, although it was not notable for a high educational level or for special achievements, its very existence stimulated further development.

The Rothschild School

Another educational institution established prior to 1870 was the Evelina de Rothschild School for Girls. As we have seen, the girls' school established by Montefiore closed in 1857. The Rothschild school, however, continued to exist and therefore may be regarded as the oldest of Jerusalem's modern schools. The early period of this school's existence was a difficult one, but the situation improved later on, and the number of pupils and teachers rose considerably. When Evelina de Rothschild, daughter of the school's founder, died in 1864, her three brothers assumed financial responsibility for it, and named the school after her.[49] (For this reason, some sources state that the Rothschild school was founded in 1864, not in 1855.)[50]

According to the newspaper *Sha'arei Zion,* the school was housed in a rented building on Kanatir Aḥdar street, and occupied five rooms: three classrooms, a room for the headmistress, and a room for the cleaning woman. Girls attended the school until the age of sixteen; thereafter, each graduate was given a sum of money to help her when she married.[51] The Rothschild school was one of the first educational institutions to move outside the Old City.

The Doresh Zion-Blumenthal School

The Doresh Zion school was founded in 1866 with far less publicity than the other schools, though it was no less important. It was established by the *Dorshei Shelom Yerushalayim* society at the initiative of the elderly philanthropist Rabbi Joseph Blumenthal of Paris, who had been inspired by the activities of Montefiore and Albert Cohn, and who had made three trips to Jerusalem in this connection.[52]

According to *Ha-Levanon* in 1867, the Doresh Zion school was established

---

48 Gat, pp. 229-257; Cohen-Reiss, pp. 76-78; Grunwald, pp. 171-173; on the Laemel School in general see Press, *History.*
49 Gat, p. 243.
50 *Sha'arei Zion,* 6 Shevat, 1879, vol. IV, p. 10; Luncz, *Guide,* p. 142.
51 *Sha'arei Zion, loc. cit.*; for a detailed account of the Rothschilds' activities in Jerusalem see Luncz, *Almanac,* XI, pp. 169-203.
52 Gat, pp. 237-239.

for the benefit of the orphanage located alongside it. Its benefactor had also hired *kashrut* supervisors. Part of the remaining funds was given to an alms fund, and the rest distributed among the poor Jews of Jerusalem and Hebron.[53] A year later, the newspaper reports that Doresh Zion had forty pupils, all of them Sephardim, and three teachers.[54] Three years after its establishment, the school purchased a large courtyard in the Old City, and renovated a house with fifteen rooms. *Ha-Levanon* reports that this was used as a home for orphans and children from needy families, and was established by Rabbi Joseph Blumenthal.[55] The dedication ceremony in 1869 was attended by many dignitaries, among them the city's foreign consuls. However, the "magnificent" building was undermined by heavy rains in 1875, only six years after its purchase, and had to be reinforced.[56]

The Sephardi *Talmud Torah* adjoining the Doresh Zion school expanded as time passed. Neumann writes that it had five classrooms, and ninety students from Sephardi, North African, Georgian and Yemenite families. Studies included religious instruction, writing, Hebrew, Arabic, and arithmetic. In 1877, *Yehuda vi-Yrushalayim* reports that Doresh Zion belonged to both Ashkenazim and Sephardim. The land had been purchased by contributors from France, and there was a Sephardi *Talmud Torah* alongside it, with windows facing Batei Maḥseh. According to Luncz (1891), this *Talmud Torah* had fifteen classrooms and 300 pupils. (Nearby were the *Gevul Ha-Almana* houses noted above, which provided free accommodation for needy persons and widows of Sephardi origin.) In 1897, David Yellin states, the *Talmud Torah* had fourteen teachers and over 300 students.[57]

Understandably, both the Laemel and Doresh Zion schools were located near the Sephardi neighborhood in the eastern sector of the Jewish Quarter. The Sephardim were more receptive to "modern" schools, and most of the schools' pupils were from Sephardi families.

The needs of the nearby orphanage seem to have been a major consideration when Doresh Zion purchased a new building. It was accepted practice at this time to establish separate *Talmudei Torah* for the city's many orphans.[58] In 1869, *Ha-Levanon* writes that the orphanage established near Ḥurvat Rabbi Judah He-Ḥasid was a *Talmud Torah* for poor children and orphans run by Rabbi Saul Benjamin Ha-Cohen. These children were taught the rudiments of reading to enable them to pray; they then studied advanced reading and Talmud.[59]

Ha-Levanon lists the modern schools in 1869 as follows: Dr. Frankl's boys' school (Laemel); the Blumenthal school (Doresh Zion) directed by a Mr. Oplatka; and the Rothschild girls' school (Evelina de Rothschild). It adds that

53 *Ha-Levanon*, 5 Iyyar, 1867, vol. IV, no. 9, p. 139.
54 *Ibid.*, 12 Shevat, 1868, vol. V, no. 6, p. 94.
55 *Ibid.*, 20 Shevat, 1869, vol. VI, no. 23, p. 182.
56 Gat, pp. 237-239.
57 Neumann, pp. 397-399; *Yehuda vi-Yrushalayim*, pp. 97-98; Luncz, *Guide*, p. 110; D. Yellin, *Writings*, I, p. 104 (1897).
58 *Ha-Levanon*, 8 Adar B, 1867, vol. IV, no. 6, p. 88.
59 *Ibid.*, 5 Tevet, 1868/9, vol. VI, no. 1, p. 7.

another school was planned by Krieger and the Alliance Israélite Universelle society. All of these schools provided their pupils with clothing, and offered financial assistance to parents as inducement to send their children there.[60]

As time went on, the *Talmud Torah* institutions of the Perushim and other Jewish groups also became "modernized." In 1876, *Ha-Levanon* summarizes the schools' student populations as follows: the Doresh Zion school, 45 pupils; the Laemel school, 33; the Evelina de Rothschild school for girls, 119; *Talmudei Torah* of the Perushim, 128; *Talmudei Torah* of the North Africans, 65; *Talmudei Torah* of the Sephardim, 326.[61]

Summary

The development of educational institutions in the Old City paralleled a general process of re-awakening in all aspects of life. Although this process manifested itself mainly after 1870, first signs became evident much earlier. Throughout the thirty years of Ottoman rule over Palestine (1840-1870), the Jewish community of Jerusalem took enormous strides forward in its development and also "incubated" new ideas and processes which would come to fruition later on.

Between 1840 and 1870, the community grew from between 3,000 and 4,000 persons to 11,000. It grew from a tiny, almost exclusively Sephardi group to a vibrant community abounding in *kolelim*. It progressed from a small, shabby neighborhood with few public institutions to an expanding quarter bursting with life and hardly able to contain its ever-increasing population. Its religious establishments, synagogues, study halls, *yeshivot* and *hadarim* flourished as never before. New types of schools began to appear: vocational schools; schools for girls; and schools offering general education. And, above all, there arose a drive to expand beyond the confines of the Old City, although it was not universal. Among those who remained were the Karaites.

The Karaites

One of the historical remains to be found in nineteenth-century Jerusalem was its Karaite community, which had dwindled over the years to no more than a few families.[62] The Karaites took no part in Jewish community life, but lived a totally separate existence. They refused to accept the Rabbinical interpretation of scripture. This tiny sect is mentioned frequently in nineteenth-century sources. Strauss (1845) writes that there were only two Karaite families in Jerusalem at the time of his visit.[63] Petermann (1853) reports three such families present, and says they prayed in a very small, underground synagogue reached by descending fifteen steps. Once there had been more Karaites in the city, but many had left following harassment by the Sephardim. Nevertheless, it was in the Sephardi synagogue that Petermann met three Karaites. The Karaite community believed that if it ever reached a total of ten families, it

345

60   *Ibid.*, 18 Iyyar, 1869, vol. VI, no. 17, p. 128.
61   *Ibid.*, 12 Adar, 1876, vol. XII, no. 28, pp. 233-234.
62   Gat, p. 26; Neumann, pp. 365-371.
63   Strauss, pp. 232-236.

would disappear from Jerusalem. Therefore, it tried not to exceed nine. It seemed to Petermann that most of the Karaites were relatively wealthy. He also notes that they did not wear beards.[64] Frankl (1856) relates that the Jerusalem Karaite community received financial support from members of the sect in the Crimea, and that the majority of Karaites worked for a living nonetheless. Two decades before Frankl's trip to Palestine, twenty Karaite families had immigrated to Jerusalem from the Crimea, but many of them had died of plague. He describes his visit to a Karaite home as follows:

> We came to a spotlessly clean house whose courtyard walls were inlaid with marble slabs engraved in gold and in ancient script with the names of Karaites who had come to the Holy Land from afar. We walked up a flight of stairs flanked by small marble columns to the carpeted quarters of the community official, whom we found reading a book in the company of his wife and sons. He bade us a cordial welcome.... "We now number only four families with a total of thirty-two persons. It grieves us that we are scorned by your fellow Ashkenazim.... The Sephardim visit us occasionally and we them, but we choose wives only from our own community and cannot bury our dead in their cemetery...." Even though they live apart because of their religious beliefs, the Arabs regard the *Hakham Bashi* as the Karaites' rabbi and spokesman.[65]

Bonar (1865) writes that the name of the Karaite chief rabbi was Daoud. The community consisted of eight or nine families, all of whom lived together in one large house.[66] Neumann states that there were between eight and ten families at this time, and that, although the Karaites lived according to their own customs, they depended upon the "Rabbanite" Jews to supply circumcisers and ritually slaughtered meat. Neumann adds:

> The Karaites have a small underground synagogue illuminated by a single square skylight. The tiny room is kept clean and the floor covered with beautiful rugs. On the eastern wall... above the Holy Ark is a silver plaque inscribed with the *Shema* prayer in large gold letters. Near the ordinary Torah scrolls in the ark is a Pentateuch in book form, written on parchment and decorated with gold illuminations and arabesques. A date showing the manuscript to be 550 years old appears on its last page. The Karaites say this synagogue is the same one established in the eighth century by Anan, the founder of their sect, after his immigration from Babylonia. He is said to have obtained a *firman* from the Muslim authorities to build a synagogue, but only on condition that it be undergroud so as not to defile the land.[67]

At the end of the nineteenth century, the Karaites were still few in number: only twenty-five souls. Their only synagogue was the one located underground, and their courtyards were community property. One writer states that the sect was said to have originated in Egypt.[68] In 1891, Luncz writes:

> The Karaite community here is very small. It numbers only twenty-five, and has been in the Holy City ever since the days of Anan. The courtyards in which they all live are community-owned. The community leader is the Hakham... Moses Halevi, who receives all who visit him with open arms. They have a small synagogue beneath the courtyard, reached by going down many stairs. It contains nothing ancient apart from a Bible with the traditional text and commentary

64 Petermann, I, pp. 231-232.
65 Frankl, pp. 186-187.
66 Bonar, p. 198.

67 Neumann, pp. 371-375.
68 Luncz, *Guide*, p. 155.

Jewish schoolchildren in early 20th century (Adler, *Von Ghetto zu Ghetto*, p. 39)

written on parchment in square script. The traditional text and commentary fill both sides of the page, and are beautifully illustrated....[69]

In early Mandatory times, Press relates that there were fifteen Karaites left in Jerusalem, and that they lived together in a single courtyard located on the Street of the Jews, speaking Ladino and wearing local Sephardi garb. There was no social contact between them and the Jews.[70] Zuta and Sukenik (1920) tell of the Karaite house of prayer located opposite the Nisan Bak synagogue:

> The courtyard was half-ruined. A few Karaite families lived there, mostly women.... Thirty years ago they numbered twenty-five, but now there are only thirteen.... The synagogue of the Karaites is in a dark cellar, with only one small window for light....[71]

Many sources note that the Karaite cemetery, still in existence today, was in the Valley of Hinnom. Inscriptions on the tombstones reveal that it was used by the Karaites throughout the nineteenth century. Clarke (1812), however, claims that the Karaites buried their dead in the Tombs of the Kings.[72]

This brief glimpse of the Karaite community of Jerusalem reveals several phenomena. The sect had a deep attachment to the Holy City, in which their synagogue and remnants of their ancient community were to be found. The location of the Karaite synagogue near the cluster of important Jewish synagogues in the Jewish Quarter indicates that, in spite of everything, the Karaites maintained strong ties with the Jewish community. Furthermore, the Karaites evidence a basic fact of life: that much of what nineteenth-century Jerusalem had to offer, both physically and spiritually, derived from earlier periods. Some of these physical and spiritual remnants flourished; others withered and died or, at most, continued to exist as historical relics. An example of the last is the Karaite community of Jerusalem.

347

69   *Loc. cit.* (translated from Hebrew).
70   Press, *Travels*, p. 52.

71   Zuta—Sukenik, pp. 106-107.
72   Clarke, II, p. 551.

348

Jewish Quarter (Taylor, *Syria*, p. 276)

Part Five

The Jewish Community of Jerusalem at the End of the Ottoman Period (1870-1914)

Built-up area of Jerusalem at end of Ottoman period

Chapter One:

THE CONTINUED GROWTH OF THE JEWISH POPULATION, AND THE PROLIFERATION OF *KOLELIM*

Introduction

The rapid growth of Jerusalem's Jewish community was perhaps the city's most important characteristic at the end of the Ottoman period. Up to now, we have dealt with the Old City in isolation, without considering developments outside the walls. It is impossible, however, to discuss population growth in this manner. Our survey of Jewish expansion in the final forty years of Ottoman rule will thus encompass the entire Jewish community, both inside and outside the Old City walls.

The Seventies

In the 1870's, the PEF carried out the first scientific survey of Palestine west of the Jordan River. It included an estimate of the population of Jerusalem. Based on the estimates of the British consul, Moore, and of the Franciscan friar, Liévin, the Jewish community was reported to number 10,600 souls. As we noted in the last chapter, this figure relates to the end of the 1860's or, at most, to the early 1870's. Indeed, the PEF researchers elsewhere note their personal impression that the number of Jews had risen significantly during the 1870's, especially after 1875. They claim that this increase amounted to between 1,000 and 1,500 persons per year, with the Jewish population reaching between 15,000 and 20,000 during the latter half of the decade.[1]

In December of 1875, *Ha-Levanon* reports slightly lower figures: from 11,000 to 20,000 Jews, with an average of 13,000, including 6,000 Sephardim and 7,000 Ashkenazim.[2] Another relatively reliable source is the census taken by the Board of Deputies of British Jews that showed a Jewish population of 13,920 for 1876.[3]

Montagu and Esher, whose sources were probably those of the Board of Deputies, say that there were approximately 13,000 Jews in 1875 (7,000

---

1   Conder—Kitchener, III, p. 162.
2   *Ha-Levanon*, 24 Kislev, 1875, vol. XII, no. 19, p. 146.
3   Ben-Zvi, *Eretz-Israel*, p. 365.

Ashkenazim and 6,000 Sephardim), in 5,000 families.[4] They write that an examination of *kolel* records revealed a doubling of Jerusalem's population within nine years.[5] Neumann, probably referring to 1876, also maintains that there was a Jewish population of 13,000.[6] Some Jewish sources give lower figures. In a letter to Montefiore, written in 1875, Rabbi Meir Auerbach and Rabbi Samuel Salant of Jerusalem note a population of 11,000,[7] but this figure was probably somewhat out-dated.

Population estimates in non-Jewish sources are not much different. Orelli writes that there were 13,500 Jewish residents in March of 1876. He discusses what he considers the amazing growth of the Jewish community, and states that his figures correspond with those of the German consul. He also emphasizes that the Jews outnumbered Muslims and Christians put together.[8] According to Neil, the Jewish population of Jerusalem numbered 15,000 in the mid-1870's, having doubled during a decade.[9] Seven years passed between the first and second editions of Liévin's travel guide; his figures rose from 8,000 to 12,000 between editions.[10] Although Liévin's estimates are usually reliable, those given in the first and second editions probably pre-date their publication by several years.

In 1880, Luncz writes that there were 13,920 Jews in Jerusalem (7,260 Sephardim and 6,660 Ashkenazim).[11] This figure corresponds with the Board of Deputies' data for 1876 and may have been taken from this source. Elsewhere, Luncz presents the figure 8,000 for 1876, the figure given by Liévin.[12] Once again, his information is clearly not up-to-date but was, most likely, derived from sources relating to a much earlier period.

The data in the first English edition of the Baedeker Guide, published in 1876, also appear to be inaccurate. Here, we are told that there were 4,000 Jews (with Liévin's figure of 8,000 being given in parentheses).[13] This seems very unlikely, and must be due to the faulty calculations of nineteenth-century researchers, who often multiplied the Turkish census figures for males by four and failed to add to the result residents who were foreign nationals. This procedure usually gave a correct average figure for the Muslim and Christian populations, but could not do so for the Jews, very few of whom were then registered as Ottoman subjects.

A summary of the demographic data for the Jewish community of the 1870's indicates that this decade was an important turning point in Jewish population growth. There were 11,000 Jews at the beginning of this period, 14,000 by its middle, and 17,000 to 18,000 by its end. The division into community groups can no longer be determined. Natural increase and immigration seem to have had an important role in raising the number of Sephardim in the city, but the Ashkenazim retained their numerical superiority nonetheless. According to reliable sources at the end of the century, the Ashkenazim even increased their relative superiority in numbers.

4   Kellner, pp. 187-205.
5   *Loc. cit.*
6   Neumann, p. 365.
7   Ish-Shalom, p. 153, n. 28.
8   Orelli, pp. 108-109.

9   Neil, pp. 8-10.
10 Liévin (1876), I, p. 137.
11 Luncz, *Almanac*, 1899, pp. 39, 48.
12 Luncz, *Ways of Zion*, p. 31.
13 Baedeker (1876), p. 161.

As the 1870's drew to a close, there were 15,000 Jews living inside the Old City, but there were already nine Jewish neighborhoods outside it and their population was approaching 2,000.[14]

The Eighties and Nineties

The number of Jews continued to rise throughout the 1880's. After his visit to Jerusalem in July of 1885, Oliphant writes that the city's population had nearly doubled in the last twenty years owing to the growth of the Jewish and Christian communities.[15] In 1889, the newspaper *Ha-Tzefirah* reports a Jewish population of 20,000, including 11,000 Ashkenazim and 9,000 Sephardim.[16] According to British consular information dating from February of 1890, the population of Jerusalem had grown from 20,000 to 40,000 in the twenty-five years between 1865 and 1890, with the Jews responsible for nearly half of this growth.[17]

The estimates of both *Ha-Tzefirah* and the British Consulate are too low for 1890, the actual number of Jews at this time being closer to 25,000.[18] Luncz gives this last figure in his 1891 travel guide, together with the following details: total Jerusalem residents, 41,335; Jews, 25,322, with the "Sephardi" community numbering 11,748 (7,300 Sephardim; 2,280 North Africans; 660 Georgians; 500 Bukharans and 1,068 Yemenites), and the Ashkenazi community numbering 13,574 (11,043 Russian and Polish Jews; 1,850 Austro-Hungarian Jews; 170 Dutch and German Jews; and 511 Rumanian Jews).[19]

The 1880's were marked by extensive construction activity outside the Old City. Fourteen new neighborhoods were added, while the nine existing at the start of the decade continued to grow. Of the 25,000 Jews in Jerusalem during this period, some 6,500 already lived outside the walls. But the overwhelming majority—18,500 Jews—remained within the Old City, in a period of record growth for its Jewish community.[20]

This growth continued into the 1890's. Luncz says that, by 1895, the number of Jews had risen to 28,112.[21] The population figures offered by many sources, especially at the end of the 1890's, are very high. The fifth edition of the Baedeker Guide in German, published in 1900, and the parallel English and French versions report an overall population of 60,000, with 40,000 of them Jews (i.e., two-thirds of the population).[22] The later editions of Liévin's guide also testify to a large increase in Jewish population. The third edition, of 1887, counted 28,000 Jews in an overall population of 42,630.[23] Ten years later, Liévin's guide said there were 55,000 Jews out of a total Jerusalem population

14   Ben-Arieh, "Initial Jewish Quarters."
15   Oliphant, pp. 296-318.
16   *Ha-Tzefira*, 12 Adar B, 1889, vol. XXXVII, no. 6, p. 219.
17   Hyamson, II, p. 450.
18   *ZDPV*, XIV, 1891, pp. 148-150.
19   Luncz, *Guide*, p. 103.
20   Ben-Arieh, "Legislative and Cultural Factors."
21   Ben-Zvi, *Eretz-Israel*, p. 414.
22   Baedeker (English ed., 1906), pp. 22-24.
23   Liévin (1887), I, p. 161.

of 73,000.[24] These figures are grossly exaggerated, but they reinforce other reports of rapid population growth at the end of the nineteenth century.

Mrs. Carpenter notes, in 1894, that the "Jewish people in and about Jerusalem number about 40,000, nearly one-half of the entire population."[25] Her figure for the total population seems slightly high. At the end of the nineteenth century, the British consul, Dixon, cites a similar figure for the Jewish population.[26]

Also indicative of the vast development of Jerusalem is Luncz's claim that forty-six Jewish neighborhoods, consisting of 3,430 homes, had been built outside the Old City between 1869 and 1897.[27] In 1893, the quarterly of the DPV notes the large number of new neighborhoods, and describes the various societies responsible for their establishment.[28] An 1894 issue of the PEF QSt gives an account of the establishment of the Bukharan neighborhood, and notes that the Jewish population of Jerusalem was constantly expanding despite government restrictions.

Many of the immigrants had come from Muslim countries, bringing numerous possessions with them.[29] One source for 1903 says that there were already 14,000 Sephardim in the city, more than one-third of their total number in the three holy cities, Jerusalem, Safed and Hebron.[30] At the end of the century, the Turkish authorities began to place strict limitations on Jewish immigration to the country. In many cases, would-be immigrants were admitted to the country for only one month, and were threatened with forcible expulsion if they did not leave of their own accord. Those requesting Turkish citizenship were taxed heavily.[31]

The Early Twentieth Century

Population figures given for the Jewish community of Jerusalem in the early twentieth century are very high, reinforcing the generous estimates of the 1890's. According to Luncz, there were 50,000 Jews included in the city's total population of 75,000 in 1905. This figure is believed by some to relate to the period 1905-1908.[32] The 1912 edition of the Baedeker Guide reports a Jewish population of 45,000 in a general population of 70,000.[33] Both Ruppin and Gurevich offer the same estimate in 1914.[34] Watson claims that the Jews numbered 50,000 by 1913, in a total population of 68,000.[35] Press reports a pre-World War I population of 80,000, including 50,000 Jews. Most of the Jews who were nationals of countries hostile to Turkey left Palestine at the outset of the fighting. Many other Jews died of hunger and disease in the course of the war.[36]

24 *Ibid.* (1897), I, pp. 186-187.
25 Carpenter, pp. 199-202.
26 Hyamson, II, p. 558.
27 Luncz, *Almanac*, III, 1898, pp. 59-71.
28 *ZDPV*, XVI, 1893, pp. 196-197.
29 *PEF QSt*, 27, 1894, p. 262.
30 *Keep ye Righteousness...*, p. 12.
31 *PEF QSt*, 1888, p. 21.
32 Ben-Zvi, *Eretz-Israel*, p. 414; Palestine Office, *Censi*, I, *Judaea*, p. 5.
33 Baedeker (1912), p. 24.
34 Ruppin, *Soziologie*, p. 146 (see also Ruppin, *Der Ausbau*); Gurevich, p. 14.
35 Cited by Zuta—Sukenik, p. 67.
36 Press, *Travel Handbook*, p. 126.

According to the newspaper *Ha-Or,* there were already 110,000 Jews in the country by 1910, with 60,000 of them living in Jerusalem. Only 15,000 of them were Ottoman subjects. About 20,000 of them were elderly persons, who no longer worked and had little influence on society. Some 25,000 Jews lived on charity; only 15,000 earned a proper living. These figures seem exaggerated; those for Jerusalem are undoubtedly inflated.[37]

In his book, *Sefer Hazikaron Hayerushalmi,* Freiman says the number of Jews present in Jerusalem in 1913 was 58,390: 32,918 Ashkenazim; 19,218 Sephardim; 2,874 Yemenites; 1,987 North Africans; 917 Bukharans and 476 Georgians.[38] Freiman's assessment is too high. The pace of Jerusalem's development had slowed considerably by 1908; in that year, accelerated building activities were abruptly halted, despite the great hopes raised by Sultan Abdul Ḥamid's ratification of the Turkish constitution. The unstable political situation, the political crises in Europe, the Balkan wars, all influenced local development. Only two small neighborhoods were founded between 1908 and the outbreak of World War I.[39]

Even Luncz's estimate of 50,000 Jewish residents in 1905-1908 may be inflated. It is indisputable that World War I brought about a drop in the Jewish population of Jerusalem. The banishment of foreign subjects, the unavailability of *ḥalukka* funds, and the high mortality rate all took their toll. It is the extent of Jewish emigration from Jerusalem that concerns us.

In 1917, Colonel Zaki Bey, head of the Jerusalem Wheat Syndicate, reported to Jamal Pasha that Jerusalem had 31,147 Jews in an overall population of 53,410. These figures were based on birth certificates and police records;[40] their accuracy is proven by the first comprehensive census in Jerusalem, made by the British in 1922. This census showed a general population of 62,000, including 34,300 Jews.[41]

The census made by the Palestine Office of the World Zionist Organization between March and June of 1916 revealed a Jewish population of only 26,605, but it may have been incomplete.[42] Zuta and Sukenik claim that neither the figures of the Turkish Police nor the detailed calculations of the Palestine Office are accurate, because the fact that they were carried out during the war made the public suspicious.[43] Nonetheless, both surveys provide useful general estimates, and correspond favorably with the results of the British census of 1922.

If, for the sake of argument, we accept the exaggerated pre-war figures cited above, we would have to admit a drop of 20,000 to 30,000 persons during the first two or three years of the war. A decrease of 10,000 to 15,000 seems much more reasonable. Thus, there were probably no more than 45,000 Jews in Jerusalem before the war, and about 35,000 earlier, at the end of the nineteenth century.

---

37 *Ha-Or,* 13 Av, 1910, vol. I, no. 136, p. 1.
38 Freiman, pp. 8-14.
39 Palestine Office, *Censi,* I, *Judaea,* p. 5.
40 *Loc. cit.*
41 Barron.
42 Palestine Office, *Censi,* I, *Judaea,* p. 6.
43 Zuta—Sukenik, p. 66.

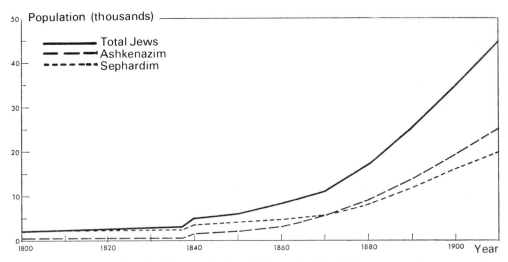

Increase in Jewish population of Jerusalem in 19th century, by community

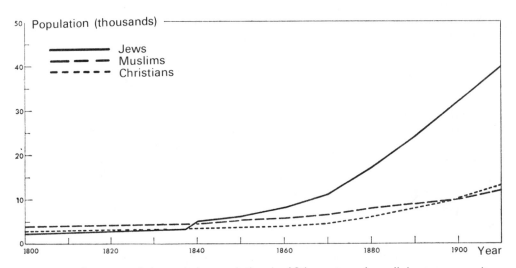

Increase of Jerusalem population in 19th century, by religious community

Jewish Community Groups; A Summary of Population Figures

356

It is difficult to establish the relative size of the various Jewish community groups between the end of the nineteenth century and World War I. On the basis of Luncz's figures of 13,754 Ashkenazim and 11,748 Sephardim for 1891, and of Freiman's inflated estimate of 33,000 Ashkenazim and 25,500 Sephardim for 1913, we may conclude that in 1900 the total Jewish population of 35,000 was composed of 18,500 Ashkenazim and 15,500 Sephardim. The

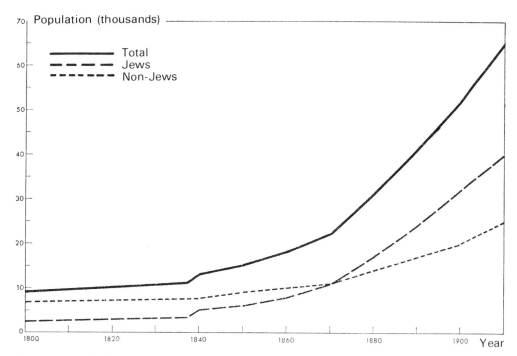

Population (thousands)

Total
Jews
Non-Jews

Year

Increase in Jewish and non-Jewish population of Jerusalem in 19th century

Jewish population of 45,000 on the eve of the war included 25,000 Ashkenazim and 20,000 Sephardim. Despite the fact that more Ashkenazim were expelled from the country because of their foreign nationality, the war seems to have affected both communities. By 1916, they were almost the same in size: 13,125 Ashkenazim and 13,446 Sephardim.[44]

Jewish Population in Jerusalem by Community
from 1870 to the British Mandate[45]
(Approximate Figures)

Year	Sephardim	Ashkenazim	Total
1870	5,500	5,500	11,000
1880	8,000	9,000	17,000
1890	11,750	13,250	25,000
1900	16,000	19,000	35,000
1910	20,000	25,000	45,000
1916	13,446	13,125	26,571
1917			31,147
1922 (census)			34,300

44 Palestine Office, *Censi*, I, *Judaea*, p. 7; according to these data the "Sephardim" category includes all other Oriental communities.

45 The data in this table for the Ottoman period are the results of our discussion of the sizes of the three communities in this book. The 1922 data are from the official British census of that year; see Barron.

Our findings with regard to the size of the Jewish community during the final forty years of Ottoman rule may be summarized as follows:

Population of Jerusalem by Religious Community
from 1870 to the British Mandate[45]
(Approximate Figures)

Year	Jews	Muslims	Christians	Total Non-Jews	Total
1870	11,000	6,500	4,500	11,000	22,000
1880	17,000	8,000	6,000	14,000	31,000
1890	25,000	9,000	8,000	17,000	42,000
1900	35,000	10,000	10,000	20,000	55,000
1910	45,000	12,000	13,000	25,000	70,000
1916	26,571				
1917	31,147				
1922	34,300	13,500	14,700	28,200	62,500

A review reveals that the Jewish population of Jerusalem quadrupled during the last forty years of Turkish administration, becoming twenty-two times larger than it had been at the beginning of the nineteenth century. While this growth was a major factor in the establishment of new neighborhoods outside the city walls, it also strengthened the Jewish community inside them and led to changes in the relative numbers of Sephardim and Ashkenazim.

By the early 1890's, as stated above, the Old City's Jewish population (inside the walls) reached 18,500 persons, or between eight and nine times what it had been at the start of the century. With the continued development of new neighborhoods outside the city between 1890 and 1910, growth within the city walls ceased, and the number of Jews there even declined to some extent. At the end of the Ottoman period, population was distributed roughly as follows:

Jewish Population Inside and Outside the Old City
towards the End of Ottoman Rule[46]

Year	Inside Old City	Outside Old City	Total
1870	11,000	negligible	11,000
1880	15,000	2,000	17,000
1890	18,500	6,500	25,000
1900	19,000	16,000	35,000
1910	16,000	29,000	45,000

358

46   Ben-Arieh, "Legislative and Cultural Factors".

The Proliferation of Kolelim at the End of the Century

The growth of Jerusalem's Jewish population led to changes in the community's composition. As we have noted, the Jewish community was composed of two main groups, the Ashkenazim and the Sephardim, which were, in turn, divided internally. Our discussion of the Ashkenazi community reached the establishment of the General Committee *(Va'ad Kol Ha-Kolelim)* in 1866, and dealt with the community in the 1860's. Let us now consider additional developments during the final forty years of the Ottoman period.

In 1878, Frumkin writes, there were eighteen Ashkenazi *kolelim* in the city: eleven of Perushim, and seven of Ḥasidim. Each one had several trustees and vice-trustees, a scribe, an agent, a treasurer, a *gabbai,* a burial society, and a synagogue, as well as beadles to serve the *kolel,* synagogue and cemetery.[47] In 1901, Luncz says, there were twenty-five Ashkenazi *kolelim,* and lists them by name. Freiman does the same.[48]

Press relates that the Ashkenazi community continued to split into *kolelim* during the early days of the British Mandate. Before the war, they numbered twenty-seven. He distinguishes between large *kolelim* having 1,000 to 2,500 members, and small ones having only forty to one hundred. Press says that the financial aid received by these *kolelim* and other public institutions of the Jewish community exceeded five or six million francs a year. During the war, the *ḥalukka* funds were blocked, one after another; this affected the *kolelim* of Russia, Austria, Hungary and Rumania in particular. The *ḥalukka* method of support had to be abandoned almost completely; a relief committee raised money in America instead.[49]

One *kolel* notable for its activities in the Old City was *Kolel Ungarn* (Hungary). Its members were followers of the Ḥatam Sofer of Hungary, and had come to settle in the Holy Land at their leader's bidding. Once in Jerusalem, they never left it; they titled themselves "Shomrei Ha-Ḥomot," guardians of the walls, and have retained this name ever since. Grayevsky points out that several prominent scholars, as well as the early directors of the Doresh Zion school, belonged to this *kolel.* One of them, Moses Aaron Baumgarten, was the first Jew who dared to live on Hebron Street, near the Temple Mount. In 1876, the Jews of Hungary established a society called *Avodat Ha-Adama u-Geulat Ha-Aretz* ("redemption of the land through agricultural labor"). Rabbi David Guttmann, Rabbi Joshua Stampfer and Rabbi Akiva Joseph Schlesinger, three members of this community, helped found Petaḥ Tikva, known as the "mother of the colonies." Later, they established a neighborhood outside the Old City, near Mea She'arim.[50]

Kolel Ḥabad was also one of the more important *kolelim* in Jerusalem. Schirion writes that, after the establishment of a Ḥabad community in Jerusalem in 1852, the Lubavitch Rabbi and others began to send the "Rabbi Meir Ba'al Ha-Nes" funds to *kolel* trustees in Jerusalem, who apportioned them to Ḥabad communities all over the country.[51] Schirion also describes the

359

47   I.D. Frumkin, *Selected Writings*, p. 39.
48   Luncz, *Almanac*, 1902, pp. 168-171; Freiman, pp. 59-70; Luncz, *Jerusalem*, IX, 1911, pp. 43-62; 187-213.   49   Press, *Travel Handbook*, pp. 129-130.
50   Grayevsky, *Sefer Hayishuv*, pp. 42-43.   51   Schirion, pp. 67-68.

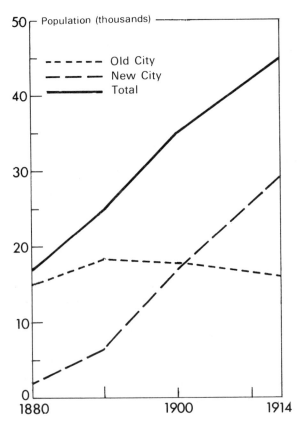

50 ⌐ Population (thousands)

- - - - - Old City
- - - New City
Total

40

30

20

10

0

1880　　　　　1900　　　1914

Jewish population of Jerusalem in 19th century, in Old City and outside

difficulty of sending these funds to Palestine during the Russo-Turkish War of 1878, and the activities of Rabbi Moses Wittenberg, who was appointed *kolel* treasurer when he came to Palestine in 1882.

Wittenberg demanded that the "Rabbi Meir Ba'al Ha-Nes" funds be sent directly to Jerusalem, without the intervention of emissaries. Most of the money was divided equally among members of the *kolel* regardless of their financial need. Even those members who were well-to-do were reluctant to give up their claim to this, so-called "ordinary *halukka*." The rest of the money was divided among acknowledged scholars and rabbinic families, as a supplement to the *halukka* funds they received. This supplement was known as *demei kedima* ("priority money"). Distribution of *halukka* funds was carried out at fixed times, twice a year. Various sums of money were also received from different cities abroad, together with instructions for them to be distributed immediately among the *kolel* members, rather than to be added to the ordinary *halukka* funds. The same was done with the money obtained from the General Committee in Jerusalem. This "small *halukka*" was divided among all the *kolel* members; although each received only a few grush, the members would wait on line for hours to receive this money. Sometimes the *kolel* administration would receive donations for individuals specifically named by the contributor. This was called *me'ot yaḥid* (individual alms).[52]

Another *kolel* established at the end of the nineteenth century was *Kolel America*, also known as Tif'eret Yerushalayim. Schirion writes that, until World War I, the money sent to the General Committee in Jerusalem was distributed to the various *kolelim*, after certain sums for the religious and general needs of the community were deducted. In 1896, the few Jewish Americans in Jerusalem founded their own *kolel*, Tif'eret Yerushalayim. After the war, a considerable number of orthodox Jews from America began to immigrate to Jerusalem, among them rabbis, scholars, Jews of all ages, and poor people.[53]

At the end of the century, the various *kolelim* took an active part in the construction of houses and neighborhoods outside the Old City; these will be discussed in the second volume of this work.

The Subdivision of the Sephardi Jewish Community

In the course of the nineteenth century, various groups broke away from the Sephardi community. Zuta and Sukenik say that the North Africans took this step in 1854, the Georgians in 1863, the Bukharans in 1868 and the Yemenites in 1883. The Jews of Kurdistan, Iraq, Aleppo, Damascus, Urfa (in southern Turkey) and Daghestan also organized themselves in independent communities. Zuta and Sukenik provide us with a detailed table of population figures for each group:[54]

The Jewish Population of Jerusalem by Community Groups

Year	Ashke-nazim	Sephar-dim	North Africans	Georg-ians	Bukha-rans	Yemenites	Persians
1876	6,600	7,260					
1891	13,574	7,300	2,280	600	500	1,068	
1901	15,180	7,900	2,420	670	530	1,288	230
1909*	27,170	6,000	1,500	1,000	500	3,000	1,200
1913	32,918	19,218***	1,987	476	917	2,874	
1917**	13,125	7,636	1,029	572	762	1,956	1,509

*   Barzilai census.
**   Palestine Office.
***   For 1913, the "Sephardim" category included all the Persian Jews.

The table below is based on the figures of the Palestine Office for 1916 as they are given by Zuta and Sukenik. There were 8,862 Jewish families in 1917; 3,734 of them were surveyed by the Palestine Office. Their activities and sources of income were classified by community as follows.

361

52   *Ibid.*, pp. 66-80.   53   *Ibid.*, pp. 79-80.   54   Zuta—Sukenik, pp. 68-69.

Sources of Family Income by Community

Community	Commerce	Industrial workers	Craftsmen	Clerks	Teachers	Religious Ministrants	Professional Men	Miscellaneous workers	Scholars	Rent	Charity	Total
Ashkenazim	225	24	321	113	130	123	46	273	525	25	6	1811
Sephardim	127	3	230	23	19	55	3	117	20	4	1	602
Yemenites	27	—	183	11	6	20	—	121	8	—	8	384
North Africans	16	—	51	1	1	16	—	23	9	2	5	124
Georgians	49	—	7	2	—	6	—	10	1	—	1	76
Persians	58	1	63	—	3	3	—	92	3	1	6	230
Bukharans	21	—	10	1	1	3	—	7	9	3	—	55
Aleppo Jews	48	—	58	—	5	20	—	19	6	—	1	157
Others	55	—	66	—	8	10	—	141	5	3	7	295
Total	626	28	989	151	173	256	49	803	586	38	35	3734

Freiman (1913) describes property owned by the Sephardi community and by the Ashkenazim, but these details do not concern us at present.[55] Schirion mentions the election in 1898 of a committee to deal with the non-religious affairs of the Sephardi community. One of its tasks was to carry out an accurate census of community members, recording places of birth, national groupings, occupations, and so on. A similar committee was set up the following year by the Ashkenazim; it was active for only a year or two.[56]

The North Africans, led by Rabbi David ben Shim'on, were the first group to break away from the Sephardim. Several wealthy and distinguished North African families built synagogues in the Old City and were active in the community; according to Luncz, however, their activity did little to improve the financial situation of the community. The North Africans remained one of the poorest Jewish groups in Jerusalem, and many left the city in 1880 because of hunger and deprivation.[57] Freiman reports that this community numbered 1,987 souls on the eve of World War I. It had one religious court, a *Talmud Torah*, two *yeshivot* and five synagogues, but made use of the almshouses of the Ashkenazim and Sephardim.[58]

The Georgian Jews were the next to form a separate community. *Ha-Levanon* (1875) notes the presence in Jerusalem of Jews from Georgia and the Caucasus.[59] According to Gat, when Montefiore visited Palestine in 1875 for the seventh time, he was approached by this community for help. Their written appeal described how they had received official permission to leave Russia. Two hundred of them were now living in Jerusalem and more were arriving every day. Although they had brought with them sufficient money to live on,

55 Freiman, pp. 9-10.
56 Schirion, pp. 162-163.
59 *Ha-Levanon*, 18 Ḥeshvan, 1875, vol. XII, no. 14, pp. 105-106.
57 Luncz, *Jerusalem*, I, p. 143; VII, pp. 113-135.
58 Freiman, pp. 11-12.

they did not have enough to build a synagogue or to support the poor. Therefore, Montefiore was asked to come to their aid.[60] Grayevsky says that the Georgians made a great impression in Jerusalem because of their striking appearance. Most of them were men of valor; some had been decorated for bravery by the Czar. Their leader was Rabbi Ephraim Halevi Kukiah. The Georgians were in no need of financial assistance, he adds. They had brought money with them, and now engaged in commerce. Some even owned property.[61] According to Freiman, there were 476 Georgian Jews in Jerusalem on the eve of World War I. They had their own religious court, *kolel, 'Ezrat Dalim* society to aid the needy, *Talmud Torah* (called *She'erit Yisrael,* with Hebrew as the language of instruction), and six synagogues. They too utilized the almshouses of the Ashkenazim and Sephardim. The Georgian community had lived in Jerusalem ever since 1865.[62]

Another "oriental" community established in the 1880's was that of the Yemenites. According to Freiman, the Yemenites numbered 2,874 before World War I. Their community had its own religious court, *kolel,* slaughter house and cemetery. There were twenty Yemenite synagogues, as well as two schools and two *yeshivot,* one for youngsters and the other for adults. This community also depended upon the almshouses of the Ashkenazim and Sephardim.[63]

The Bukharans strove to achieve special status within the Sephardi community. *Ha-Tzefirah* says they were considered something of a privileged class. No longer willing to be led by the *Ḥakham Bashi,* the Bukharans appealed to the Russian consul, who helped them obtain a certain degree of independence. They could not, however, appoint a chief rabbi of their own. The consul was authorized to grant them legal documents without the intervention of a rabbi.[64] Prior to World War I, Freiman reports, there were 917 Bukharan Jews in Jerusalem. They lived in their own neighborhood, Reḥovot Ha-Bukharim, and wealthy members of their community supported Sephardi institutions. The Bukharans broke away from the Sephardi community in 1912, and established their own religious court. Bukharans had been living in Jerusalem since 1870.[65]

At the end of the nineteenth century (1892), a group of Persian Jews came to seek refuge in Palestine. The Sublime Porte in Constantinople ordered the pasha to expel them from the country and return them to Persia. Cohen-Reiss witnessed the terrible scene of weeping men, women and children being led to the police station near the Jaffa Gate. He and two of his colleagues were able to secure the release of these Jews by guaranteeing their orderly departure from the country. The immigrants were then housed temporarily at the "Alliance" school, and the *kolelim* of both Sephardim and Ashkenazim came to their aid. Meanwhile, the chief of police and his assistants received due "compensation," and the Persian Jews were not deported after all. For the sake of appearances, most of them left Jerusalem and settled in other parts of the country.[66]

363

60   Gat, *Jewish Community*, p. 25; see also sources cited there.
61   *Ibid.*, p. 26 n. 35.
62   Freiman, pp. 13-14.   64   *Ha-Tzefira*, 23 Elul, 1913, vol. XXXIX, no. 209, p. 3.
63   *Ibid.*, pp. 10-11.   65   Freiman, pp. 12-13.
                                   66   Cohen-Reiss, pp. 116-117.

Chapter Two:
JEWISH RELIGIOUS INSTITUTIONS AND THE GROWING IMPORTANCE OF THE WAILING WALL

Ashkenazi Talmudei Torah and Yeshivot; the Etz Ḥayyim Yeshiva

In the last part of this book, we discussed the synagogues and *yeshivot* established in the Old City by the early 1870's. More made their appearance during the last forty years of Ottoman rule. Let us take a closer look at some of them.

One of the most important *yeshivot* in the Old City was the Etz Ḥayyim yeshiva. It began in 1850 as an extension of an existing *Talmud Torah;* the latter was reorganized in 1855. The devoted efforts of its new director, Rabbi Saul Benjamin Ha-Cohen, who renovated parts of the Ḥurva and added new buildings, led to the growth of this institution and the opening of a *yeshiva* in 1862. A courtyard was purchased for it, with some of the houses being named for Jews in the Diaspora who had paid for them and contributed the rent for *yeshiva* expenses.[1]

In 1877, the newspaper *Yehuda vi-Yrushalayim* gives the following account of the Etz Ḥayyim yeshiva:

> In Naḥalat Ha-Ashkenazim (as the Ḥurva was called) stood the *Talmud Torah,* a splendid building consisting of fourteen spacious, ... well-ventilated rooms with large windows. There were 170 students in fourteen grades, ranging from very young children learning the alphabet to older ones studying the Bible, Gemara and commentaries. In the highest grade, outstanding pupils were taught Gemara and commentaries by a famous rabbi. There was also a class for ordinary boys who had reached the twelfth level but showed no capability for studying Gemara. These boys studied the Bible, religious laws and customs... and then went out to acquire a trade.... Those completing their studies through the highest grade were sent to the Etz Ḥayyim yeshiva to study under the great rabbis....

The reporter goes on to argue the need for a vocational school for those youngsters not gifted enough to continue their studies in a *yeshiva.* Such boys were now apprenticed to various craftsmen, but there were many negative aspects to this arrangement.[2] As time went on, the *yeshiva* found itself in

---

1   Malachi, pp. 105-106.
2   *Yehuda vi-Yrushalayim*, pp. 93-96 (translated from Hebrew).

financial straits. In 1871, *Ha-Levanon* reports fund-raising efforts in America on behalf of the Etz Ḥayyim *yeshiva*.[3] In 1881, it writes that the *Talmudei Torah* of the Perushim and the Etz Ḥayyim *yeshiva* were on the verge of closing for financial reasons.[4]

The Etz Ḥayyim *yeshiva* was supported mainly by the "Rabbi Meir Ba'al Ha-Nes Fund." Other sources of income were regular funds from overseas, religious property endowments in Jerusalem, and donations collected by emissaries. In 1891, Luncz says the *yeshiva* consisted of seventeen rooms, and that it included writing and arithmetic in its course of studies. The *Talmud Torah* had 250 pupils, and the *yeshiva* about forty.[5] In 1899, David Yellin writes, a large new *yeshiva* building was dedicated in Ḥurvat Rabbi Judah He-Ḥasid.[6] The Etz Ḥayyim *yeshiva* also opened branches in the new neighborhoods outside the Old City. In 1889, the general *Talmud Torah* in the Ḥurva reportedly took the *Talmudei Torah* of Naḥalat Shiva, Mishkenot Yisrael and Beth Yaakov under its wing.[7]

In around 1910, the newspaper *Ha-Or* reports that the Etz Ḥayyim *yeshiva* was preparing to move into its new quarters near the Maḥane Yehuda neighborhood. At this point, it was no longer interested in financing the small neighborhood branches of the *yeshiva,* and parents were suddenly faced with the problem of where to send their sons, other *yeshivot* such as those in Me'a She'arim being too far away.[8]

The Etz Ḥayyim *yeshiva* was the first Ashkenazi *yeshiva* in Jerusalem to offer something new in both size and aims. In its prime, it was a large, well-organized educational institution with hundreds of students, incorporating a *Talmud Torah* for children, a junior *yeshiva* for boys and a senior *yeshiva* for advanced students and married men. Its chief goal was to provide a religious education for all, with particular emphasis being placed on the younger generation. In his memoirs, Ephraim Cohen-Reiss describes the *yeshiva* as it was in 1876:

> This *yeshiva* differed from the *yeshivot* in Russia. Its students did not aspire to be teachers, rabbis or judges, because priority was usually given to qualified rabbis and judges arriving from the Diaspora. Nearly all the students were married, the *yeshiva* constituting for them a source of income in addition to the *ḥalukka*.[9]

The Etz Ḥayyim *yeshiva* was yet another step in the development of the center of the Perushim that had sprung up around the Ḥurva. This trend was begun with the establishment of the Menaḥem Zion and Sha'arei Zion synagogues, and continued through the establishment of Etz Ḥayyim and of the central synagogue in the Ḥurva itself. The religious court of the Perushim and the home of Rabbi Samuel Salant were also there. Etz Ḥayyim was probably the most important educational institution in Jerusalem in the nineteenth century.

3   *Ha-Levanon*, 8 Ḥeshvan, 1871, vol. VIII, no. 6, p. 45.
4   *Ibid.*, 18 Sivan, 1881, vol. XVII, no. 45, p. 358.
5   Luncz, *Guide*, pp. 112-113.
6   D. Yellin, *Writings*, I, p. 344.
7   Michlin, p. 19.
8   *Ha-Or*, 13 Tishrei, 1910, vol. II, no. 181, p. 2.
9   Cohen-Reiss, p. 51 (translated from Hebrew).

It played a significant role in the cultural development of the city and, until the 1890's, it was here that most Ashkenazi youth and the overwhelming majority of Jerusalem's Jewish leaders, Orthodox and non-observant alike, were educated.[10]

Other Ashkenazi Talmudei Torah and Yeshivot

In 1884, the newspaper *Ha-Tzevi* lists five Ashkenazi *Talmudei Torah* in the Old City: the general *Talmud Torah* in the Hurva, with its 175 pupils; the *Talmud Torah* of *Kolel Ungarn* with 16; the *Talmud Torah* in Me'a She'arim with 60; the *Talmud Torah* in Mishkenot Yisrael with 23; the *Talmud Torah* of the Ashkenazi orphanage, with its 35. There were about sixty-five teachers.[11] The newspaper also reports a demand for the establishment of a central *yeshiva* in Jerusalem to train rabbis and teachers.[12] Dissatisfied with the general *Talmud Torah, Kolel Ungarn* founded a *Talmud Torah* of its own (in 1885),[13] as did *Kolel Volhyn*.[14] Other Jews from Russia began to organize themselves too, renting quarters for a synagogue and requesting funds to open a school for their children.[15]

The extensive growth of the Jewish community led to the establishment of another large *yeshiva* in 1886: the Hayyei Olam *yeshiva*.[16] This *yeshiva* was originally located east of Meidan (Misgav La-dakh) Street, on the edge of the slope leading down to the Wailing Wall, but was later moved to the Muslim Quarter. Hayyei Olam was to the Hasidic *kolelim* what Etz Hayyim was to the Perushim. It consisted of several departments: a *Talmud Torah* for young children; a *yeshiva* to train outstanding *Talmud Torah* graduates as rabbis, teachers, ritual slaughterers and judges; a senior *yeshiva* for rabbis and scholars; a soup-kitchen for orphans (which also provided them with clothing); and a library.[17] The Hayyei Olam *yeshiva* developed especially rapidly in its new location in the Muslim Quarter and by 1913 had 110 pupils.[18] (The reasons for the move will be examined later, when we discuss Jewish expansion outside the Jewish Quarter.)

The third large Ashkenazi *yeshiva* in the Old City was that known as Torat Hayyim. As this *yeshiva* was located in the Muslim Quarter from the outset, we will discuss it in the next chapter.

In 1895, another *yeshiva*, Ohel Moshe, was established in the heart of the Jewish Quarter, north of the Street of the Karaites and west of Tif'eret Yisrael street. Named after the famous Rabbi of Brisk, Rabbi Moses Joshua Leib Diskin, its founders were Rabbi Isaiah Orenstein and his son, Rabbi Jacob, who eventually became head of the *yeshiva*. Ohel Moshe represented the

10   G. Kressel in I.D. Frumkin, *Selected Writings* (Introduction), p. 30.
11   *Ha-Tzevi*, 24 Kislev, 1884, vol. 1, no. 8, p. 2.
12   *Ibid.*, 12 Tamuz, 1885, vol. I, no. 34, p. 2.
13   *Ibid.*, 9 Tishrei, 1885, vol. II, no. 1, p. 1.
14   *Ibid.*, 14 Heshvan, 1885, vol. II, no. 4, p. 1.
15   *Ibid.*, 20 Tamuz, 1885, vol. I, no. 35, p. 1.
16   Freiman, p. 36, 49.
17   *Our Spiritual Possessions.*
18   Freiman, p. 49.

religious zealots who regarded Rabbi Diskin as their spiritual leader.[19] Its establishment was fiercely opposed by the older *yeshivot,* who feared competition in fund-raising. As a result, Ohel Moshe received no money from the Rabbi Meir Ba'al Ha-Nes Fund. It found itself in severe financial difficulties, barely able to exist on sporadic contributions from overseas. Ohel Moshe was a small *yeshiva* compared to Etz Ḥayyim, Ḥayyei Olam and Torat Ḥaim. At first, it had only ten students; by 1898, this number had increased to fifty.[20] According to another source, there were fifty-six students in 1913.[21]

The Sha'ar Ha-Shamayim *yeshiva,* also an Ashkenazi one, was established by Rabbi Ḥayyim Judah-Leib Auerbach and Simon Zvi Hurwitz in 1906. It was situated in a house with seven rooms, located east of the four Sephardi synagogues, in an alley that linked Beth-El street to the Batei Maḥseh neighborhood. Sha'ar Ha-Shamayim was the first Ashkenazi *yeshiva* to teach *Kabbalah.*[22] Before its establishment, *Kabbalah* was taught only in Sephardi *yeshivot,* notably Beth-El and Ḥesed El.[23] In Sha'ar Ha-Shamayim, *Kabbalah* was taught in an orderly, systematic fashion, by instructors. In other Kabbalistic *yeshivot,* these studies were generally pursued on an individual basis. In addition, these *yeshivot* only admitted acknowledged scholars who were married and had families. Sha'ar Ha-Shamayim accepted boys from the age of sixteen. It seems to have been one of the first schools in the world where a *yeshiva* student was guided in his study of *Kabbalah.* This was to prevent his being led astray, and was perhaps a reaction to the methods of *Kabbalah* study in the *yeshivot* of the Sephardim. Sha'ar Ha-Shamayim held that before one proceeded to the study of the esoteric, one had to learn the exoteric. Thus, it had two main departments: one for exoteric studies, and one for *Kabbalah* or esoteric studies.[24] In 1913, Freiman says, the *yeshiva* and its various branches had a total of 113 students, some of them Sephardim.[25] A 1910 issue of *Ha-Or* reports that, while the Beth-El synagogue stood empty, the younger generation of Ashkenazim had established the Sha'ar Ha-Shamayim *yeshiva* which, in the course of four years, had attracted students from the Sephardi, Georgian and Bukharan communities as well, and had opened a branch outside the city called Kehal Ḥasidim.[26]

The newspaper *Ha-Yehudi* of 1899 carries a notice about the establishment of the first *beth musar* (ethical study house) in Jerusalem. A large thirty-room house was rented for this purpose; as the students were provided for, they could study Torah without fear of going hungry.[27] In addition, *Ha-Moriah* reports the opening in 1912 of a new *yeshiva* in the house where the "Ari" (Rabbi Isaac Luria) had been born.[28]

---

19 Gellis, *Jerusalem Personalities,* pp. 281-284.
20 *Loc. cit.*
21 Freiman, pp. 50-51.
22 *Yeshivat Sha'ar Ha-Shamayim.*
23 On these *yeshivot* see above, p. 307.
24 *Yeshivat Sha'ar Ha-Shamayim.*
25 Freiman, p. 51.
26 *Ha-Or,* 6 Kislev, 1910, vol. II, no. 217, p. 2.
27 *Ha-Yehudi,* 12 Tevet, 1900, vol. III, no. 10, pp. 2-3.
28 *Ha-Moriah,* 28 Nisan, 1912, vol. III, no. 1, p. 2.

Sephardi Yeshivot

One important Sephardi *yeshiva,* Tif'eret Yisrael, was the first modern educational institution of the Sephardi community; it was established before the Porat Yosef *yeshiva.* Although supported by communal funds, Tif'eret Yisrael received most of its money from the donations of Diaspora Jews, especially from the Jews of Calcutta, India. Montefiore and Rothschild also contributed large sums towards its establishment. At first, Tif'eret Yisrael was simply a continuation of the traditional *Talmud Torah* affiliated with the Sephardi synagogues.[29] It was modernized in 1874, and a *yeshiva* to train Sephardi rabbis and scholars was added in 1890. Tif'eret Yisrael was located in the southern part of the Jewish Quarter, west of Batei Maḥseh, and had three wings: one for Torah study, one for residential purposes and one for vocational training. The two-story *yeshiva* building had fourteen rooms and 300 students in 1887; there were 400 Sephardi, Georgian and North African students in 1894. Later, when the school was taken over by Rabbi Kowinka, their numbers increased to between 500 and 600. Rabbi Uziel, later the chief rabbi of the Holy Land, directed the institution after him. Hebrew studies were added to the curriculum, and the *yeshiva* was adopted by the Alliance Israélite Universelle Society. In the course of its existence, Tif'eret Yisrael faced many crises. First, there was a drop in donations from the Jews of the Ottoman Empire, because of the unstable political situation. Then, Jerusalem suffered severe epidemics which reduced its student population, and educational reforms instituted at the *yeshiva* resulted in the dismissal of many teachers. Worst of all was World War I: the *yeshiva* closed because of a lack of funds, and only the *Talmud Torah* remained in operation.[30]

The Porat Yosef *yeshiva,* the most important Sephardi *yeshiva* in the Old City, may be regarded as the successor of Tif'eret Yisrael. It was located in the southeastern corner of the Jewish Quarter, to the east of Misgav La-dakh Street and opposite the Wailing Wall, and was named after Joseph ben Shalom of Calcutta who, in 1909, had purchased the land on which it was built. Although its cornerstone was laid in 1914, World War I delayed the construction of Porat Yosef: the *yeshiva* was dedicated only in 1923.[31]

The Sephardi community had many junior *yeshivot.* For example, there were four *yeshivot* exclusively for Jews from Bosnia: Shevet Aḥim, founded in 1871; Ḥaverim Makshivim, in 1880; Shelom Yerushalayim, in 1892; Shivḥei Yerushalayim, in 1897. During the 1870's and 1880's, many Bosnian Jews, most of them elderly, wealthy and supported by their families abroad, came to spend their last years in the Holy Land. This wave of immigration produced the Shevet Aḥim *yeshiva,* founded by Abraham Ḥai Musufiyya ("Aḥim") and Moses Pincho. Rabbi Abraham Uziel, also director of the Kabbalist Beth-El *yeshiva,* headed Shevet Aḥim, whose students met in his home for eight years. After Uziel's death, the wealthy Shabbetai Pincho established another *yeshiva,* and Shevet Aḥim closed. The various Bosnian *yeshivot* ceased to function when

29 Freiman, p. 34; Gaon, *The Sages,* pp. 54-64.
30 Press, "If I forget thee...," in *Studies* (list at end), p. 104; Shapira, pp. 48-49; Yehoshua, III, pp. 97-112.
31 *Ha-Moriah,* 11 Tevet, 1914, vol. V, no. 414.

World War I led to a decreased flow of funds and weaker links to the Balkans.[32]

Two lists drawn up by Freiman enumerate the important *yeshivot* and *Talmudei Torah,* and their dates of establishment: the Etz Ḥayyim *yeshiva,* 1850; the Pri Etz Ḥayyim *yeshiva,* 1884; the general Ḥayyei Olam *yeshiva,* 1886; the general Torat Ḥayyim *yeshiva,* 1887; the general Ohel Moshe *yeshiva,* 1895; the Beth-El and general Ziknei Talmidei Ḥakhamim *yeshiva,* 1907; the Sha‘ar Ha-Shamayim *yeshiva,* 1907; the Ohel Torah *yeshiva,* 1912; the Har Zion— Batei Maḥseh *yeshiva,* 1912.[33]

Freiman's second list includes the important *Talmudei Torah: Talmud Torah* Tif'eret Yisrael, the general *Talmud Torah* of the Sephardim founded many years earlier; *Talmud Torah* Etz Ḥayyim in Ḥurvat Rabbi Judah He-Ḥasid, established in 1841 (with a new building in Maḥane Yehuda and branches in Mazkeret Moshe, Beth Yisrael, Yemin Moshe, Naḥalat Shiva, Kerem Aḥava, Sha‘arei Ḥesed and Giv‘at Shaul); *Talmud Torah* Pri Etz Ḥayyim in Me‘a She‘arim; the Ḥasidic *Talmud Torah* Ḥayyei Olam founded in 1886; the Doresh Zion (Blumenthal) school, 1866; the *Talmud Torah* of the North African community, 1865; the *Talmud Torah* of the Persians, 1900. The *Talmud Torah* of the Bukharans, *Talmud Torah* Torah Or of the Yemenites, and *Talmud Torah* She'erit Yisrael of the Georgian Jews were also established in the Old City at the end of the nineteenth century.[34]

Synagogues

There was a vast increase in the number of synagogues in the Old City during the nineteenth century. The largest and most important of them were dealt with above, in Part Four. There were also dozens of smaller ones. Gaon (1897) reports over thirty Sephardi synagogues and study halls, including the Beth-El synagogue (also called the Ḥasidim synagogue); the Ḥesed El synagogue on Ḥabad street; the Great Synagogue of the North African community; the New Synagogue of the North African community; the David Ḥai synagogue; the synagogue in the home of Shlomo Amzalag; the Georgian synagogue and the Saloniki synagogue.[35] On the eve of World War I, Freiman lists some eighty synagogues and forty-five private places of worship, most of them located in the Old City.[36]

An important synagogue in the Old City, mentioned briefly in the last chapter, was the Ḥabad synagogue on the southern end of Ḥabad Street. This synagogue was also known by three other names: Beit Menaḥem, after Rabbi Menaḥem-Mendel Schneersohn, president and head of the Ḥabad (Lubavitch) movement; Tzemaḥ Tzedek, after a book written by the Lubavitch leader in about 1860; Kneset Eliahu, the official name of the synagogue, after Elijah Sassoon of Bombay, India, who contributed most of the funds for the

32 Gaon, *Oriental Jews*, pp. 145-146.
33 Freiman, pp. 48-52.
34 *Ibid.*, pp. 34-37.
35 Gaon, *Oriental Jews*, pp. 129-132.
36 Freiman, pp. 79-87; Press, *Hundred Years*, p. 33.

synagogue's upper level. According to Freiman, this synagogue was founded in 1858, at which time its ground floor was built. The second floor was added in 1879. The ground-floor synagogue seems to have retained the names Tzemaḥ Tzedek and Beth Menaḥem, while the large new one was known as Kneset Eliahu. However, the building as a whole was called the Ḥabad synagogue.[37]

Another prominent synagogue was that founded by Rabbi Meir Auerbach of Kalish, one of Poland's most famous rabbis, who immigrated to Jerusalem in 1859. *Kolel* Warsaw had just established its independence from the general *Kolel Perushim,* and the arrival of such a learned and wealthy man did much to enhance its prestige. Two months later, Rabbi Auerbach purchased a large courtyard for the Warsaw *kolel* at the southern end of the Street of the Jews. It was known as the Warsaw courtyard or "House of the Rabbi of Kalish," and a synagogue was founded in it in 1860.[38]

The *Kolel Polin* (Poland) synagogue was located at the opposite, northern end of the Jewish Quarter, east of the Street of the Jews. It was established in 1868 in the courtyard of Rabbi David Reiss Yanover, who was one of the major contributors. This courtyard had fourteen rooms set aside to house rabbis and scholars immigrating from Poland.[39]

Not far from the *Kolel Polin* courtyard was a synagogue belonging to the Jews of North Africa. It was founded by Rabbi David ben Shim'on, who immigrated from Morocco in 1854. Light filtered in through its dome, which was surrounded by windows; at one time, a corner of the synagogue was used as a religious court.[40]

The Shoneh Halakhot synagogue was located in an alley at the southern end of the Street of the Jews. It was built by a philanthropist named Neuten, and received its name because a group of people convened there to study the *Shulkhan Arukh* code of law. Another synagogue in this alley was that of the Karlin Ḥasidim, opened in memory of the Rabbi of Stolin. It was the main building in the courtyard of *Kolel* Karlin, which comprised eight apartments.[41]

We will conclude our list with the Aḥvat Zion synagogue of *Kolel* Hod and the Beth Hillel synagogue of *Kolel* Grodno, both located in the Ḥosh courtyard.[42]

Aside from their religious function, the synagogues served as a meeting place for memorial ceremonies and public events. In 1884, the newspaper *Ha-Tzevi* reports there were memorial gatherings held in honor of Montefiore at the Misgav La-dakh hospital; the Great Synagogue in Ḥurvat Rabbi Judah He-Ḥasid; the Or Ha-Ḥayyim synagogue; the Sephardi community's Istanbuli synagogue; the Shenot Eliahu *yeshiva* headed by Rabbi Jacob Mordecai Hirschensohn; the home of a member of the Mazkeret Moshe Committee; the Etz Ḥayyim *yeshiva*; the Doresh Zion school; the Diskin orphanage and Sanders Old-Age Home.[43]

37   Freiman, p. 83; Grayevsky, *Avnei Zikkaron*, I, pp. 7-8.
38   Yellin, Memoirs, pp. 11-12; Cahanyu, p. 55.
39   Shapira, p. 53; Press, "If I forget thee...," in *Studies* (list at end), p. 104.
40   Shapira, p. 53; Grayevsky, *Avnei Zikkaron*, I, pp. 10-11.
41   Shapira, pp. 53-54; Press, "If I forget thee...," in *Studies* (list at end), p. 103.
42   Freiman, pp. 82, 86; Press, *loc. cit.*
43   *Ha-Tzevi*, 12 Ḥeshvan, 1884, vol. I, no. 2, p. 2; *ibid.*, 19 Ḥeshvan, 1884, vol. I, no. 3, p. 3.

Wailing Wall (Geikie, p. 480)

The Wailing Wall

The Wailing Wall was, without a doubt, the most important Jewish prayer site in the Old City. This importance attained even greater proportions at the end of the nineteenth century in view of the extensive growth of the Jerusalem Jewish community. Several descriptions illuminate this.

In the early 1880's, Luncz relates, the Jews of Jerusalem lit oil lamps at the Wailing Wall every Friday evening. This custom continued for thirty-two years, until the government put a stop to it in the summer of 1913. Luncz also points out that the leaders of the Jewish community never received a *firman* or special permit to pray at the Wall:

> This is not surprising, because there was no need for it. The Muslims never showed intolerance towards those who worshipped the One God in whom they too believed. Thus they did not hinder us from praying here to our heart's content.... In our favor, we have the following: the indisputable historical document which proves the Wailing Wall is a remnant of the wall once surrounding our Temple; ancient possessory rights dating back 400 years or more (of considerable legal value in Palestine), showing that our forefathers had prayed here undisturbed for centuries....[44]

Luncz tells us that, during Montefiore's sixth trip to the Holy Land in 1866, the latter sought permission to erect a shelter at the Wailing Wall to protect worshippers from the elements. At first the pasha promised to grant his request, but then he withdrew his agreement, either because the higher authorities had not been consulted in advance or because "our enemies were working against us." An application to build benches along the Wall was also

371

---

44 Luncz, *Jerusalem*, X, pp. 1-58; Luncz—Kressel, pp. 152-153 (translated from Hebrew).

rejected. On the other hand, the Jews were allowed to place several large stones near the Wall for people to sit on, but these disappeared one by one.[45]

Luncz describes his own impressions of the Wailing Wall in this way:

> A few inhabitants of the Holy City may be found at the Wailing Wall every day of the year. Some read the Scriptures, others come to mourn.... But the fixed times Jews pray here are the eve of Sabbath, the eve of Passover... the first and last days of the three festivals..., the ninth of Av, the eve of the New Year, and the eve of the Day of Atonement. On these days the site is crowded with men, women and children from one end to the other, and those who arrive late sometimes must stand in nearby alleyways.[46]

This is how Luncz portrays Jerusalem on Fridays at a later date:

> Every Sabbath eve, masses of Jewish men, women and children from all of the various community groups hasten to the Wailing Wall from noontime onwards.... One hears the noise of hurried preparations emanating from every home in the city as people ready themselves to go to the Wall. Dressed in their best clothing and clutching holy texts, they rush through the streets from all directions. Old men and women leaning on their canes, little children holding their parents' hands, all with a common destination. Neither burning sun, wind and cold, storm, snow or teeming rain will stop them.... This scene so amazes anyone who sees it that foreigners visiting the country try to be present at these times; they write endless descriptions of the event in their diaries so as to etch it in their minds forever.[47]

The Wailing Wall continued to make a strong impression on foreign visitors through the end of the century. Philippe Berger, a French archaeologist and scholar, describes his visit to the Wall on April 7, 1894:

> In the broad sunshine we followed little unpaved lanes hemmed in by wretched hovels. As we went on we met men and women dressed in a sort of big white shroud; who were taking the same road as we were. The crowd became more and more dense; walking side by side jostling one another. At last at the corner of a little alley jammed with people we came to the wall of the Jews. Beda's beautiful engraving of the Jews weeping at the wall of "Sion" gives an impression of size which the reality lacks. You expect to see huge wall reminiscent of Herod and Solomon, with the sky and countryside as a horizon. Instead you are in a narrow passage so crowded with people that you must use your elbows to get through. There is a procession to-day, it is the first of Nisan, and it is hardly possible to pass. Some children led by a cantor sing with extraordinary energy. The Jewish women are in white, the men dressed in robes of purple or blue velvet, fur hats on their heads, long beards, their curls of hair combed in front of their ears hang on their temples, in their hands are old worn Bibles bound in black.[48]

Margaret Thomas writes:

> ... spending the afternoon in one of the most remarkable scenes in the world, the Wailing-Place of the Jews at the wall of their ancient temple. It should be seen on Friday to be seen at its best.... Leaning tenderly against these stones, as if they were human and could sympathize with their misery, and throwing themselves with outstretched arms against them, may be seen sometimes as many as two

45   Luncz—Kressel, p. 145.
46   Luncz, *Guide*, p. 106 (translated from Hebrew).
47   Luncz, *Jerusalem*, I, 1882, pp. 31-32 (translated from Hebrew).
48   Adler, *Memorandum*, p. 61.

Wailing Wall (Pro-Jerusalem Society)

hundred Jews, reading, praying aloud, and weeping, men in one group and women in another.[49]

Luncz relates that there were, alongside the Wall, a small table, a prayer stand, a lantern and oil lamps, benches and chairs, a small tent and a curtain. These had been placed there by the Jews in an effort to make the site more like a synagogue; when the Muslims noticed what was happening, they notified the

373

49   *Ibid.*, pp. 61-62.

Ottoman authorities, and some of the Jews' activities were brought to a halt.[50]

In the 1890's, the area near the Wailing Wall was paved by the municipality, along with other areas throughout the Old City. The narrow lanes leading to the Wall were also paved in order to keep the area clean.[51] The paving of the Wailing Wall area was mentioned before the Wailing Wall Commission during the British Mandate. It was stated that three elders of the Jewish community had complained to municipal officials about the offensive sewage-canalization work being carried out near the Wailing Wall, which defiled their holy place. They had also requested permission to pave this area in a more attractive manner than was usual in the Old City. The Jews were allowed to undertake this project at their own expense within the framework of the general paving activities under way in the city, using large paving stones ordered from Bethlehem.[52]

Such testimony was of great importance, because it proved that the Muslims recognized the Wailing Wall as a Jewish holy place. Other information presented to the Wailing Wall Commission showed that it was the Jews who were responsible for its maintenance. The financial report of the General Committee of Jerusalem for 1894-1895 lists an expenditure of 10 napoleons for carrying out repairs at the Wailing Wall.[53] The minute books of the joint *kolelim* committee record two sums devoted to the same purpose in 1895, of 218 and 545 Turkish grush respectively, and another, of 327 Turkish grush, in 1896. From 1909 on, there are records of expenditure for water and for guarding the benches near the Wall.[54]

The Jewish community had already begun to contemplate the development of the Wailing Wall area, and the purchase of the nearby residential areas, in the 1880's.[55] Cahanyu writes about attempts made to acquire the entire Muslim Mughrabi neighborhood in order to eliminate disturbances during Jewish worship. He says that the Baron de Rothschild took an active interest in the matter in 1897, but that nothing ever came of it. Serious efforts were made again in 1908, with the support of important Jerusalem rabbis, but to no avail.[56] Zuta and Sukenik offer details of efforts to obtain the land as well as of attempts to improve conditions at the Wailing Wall.[57]

Luncz writes:

> ... The best proposition for improving the site was put forward by Baron Edmond de Rothschild. When he saw the run-down dwellings surrounding the Holy Wall and the twisting, unrepaired, garbage-strewn roads leading to it, he decided to purchase all the homes in the Muslim Mughrabi neighborhood, raze them to the ground and build an iron fence around the leveled area, making it the property of the Jewish community. Since the laws of the country forbid the sale of *Waqf* land, the Rothschilds' emissary suggested a property exchange: the Baron

---

50   Luncz, *Jerusalem*, X, pp. 1-58; Luncz—Kressel, pp. 129-139, 155-159.
51   Schirion, p. 161.
52   Adler, *Memorandum*, p. 79.
53   *Ibid.*, p. 80.
54   Triwaks, *Trial*, pp. 54-55.
55   *PEF QSt*, 1887, p. 215.
56   Cahanyu, pp. 76-77.
57   Zuta—Sukenik, p. 85; Yaari—Polskin, pp. 206-219.

would buy suitable real-estate elsewhere, and build the same number of homes there as in the present neighborhood. (The land and homes were reportedly assessed at 740,000 francs. According to the laws of the *Waqf,* land could be exchanged only if the property were valued higher than its true worth, to exclude the possibility of fraud. Thus each of the thirty-seven courtyards in the neighborhood was valued at 20,000 francs.) Realizing the benefit of this project from the standpoint of health in general and that of the residents of this quarter in particular, the pasha gave his approval, and said he would seek the authorization of the Sheikh al-Islam and the royal authorities. Suddenly, however, he reversed his decision. (I heard from the most learned Rabbi Jacob Saul Eliashar, the *Hakham Bashi* of the time, that the project was canceled because Sayyid Bashir, the son of 'Abd al-Salam al-Huseini and guardian of *Waqf* property, discovered that the exchange had been decided upon without his knowledge.) He then sought and produced a document of Sayyid Abu Madin al-Jus, in whose honor the neighborhood had been built and dedicated, which cursed and threatened to excommunicate anyone who tried to take the neighborhood from the Muslims and give it to infidels, even in exchange for a better one in keeping with the law. A telegram was sent to the Sheikh al-Islam, who replied that such a holy man's threat of excommunication should not be taken lightly. Intimidated, the pasha announced that the homes might be demolished, but that the property would belong to all Jerusalemites and could not be fenced in by the Jews. The famous philanthropist, of course, would not agree to this...[58]

On the eve of World War I, the Anglo-Palestine Bank also tried to purchase this neighborhood, but met various difficulties, financial and otherwise, along the way. Meanwhile, World War I broke out and the purchase negotiations were halted.[59] (It may be noted that a broad, open area adjacent to the Wailing Wall, for the accommodation of a multitude of visitors and worshippers, was created only after the Six Day War of 1967.)

375

58   Luncz, *Jerusalem*, X, p. 1-58; Luncz—Kressel, pp. 153-154 (translated from Hebrew); Druyanov, II, 1888, pp. 227-231.
59   Levontin, II, pp. 237-240; G. Frumkin, pp. 176-179.

Chapter Three:

THE EXPANSION OF THE JEWISH QUARTER AND THE BEGINNING OF ITS DECLINE

The Overcrowding of the Jewish Quarter

The vast increase in Jewish population led to a severe shortage of housing in the Old City; intense overcrowding in the Jewish Quarter worsened as time went on. By the early years of the British Mandate, according to Zuta and Sukenik, conditions in the Jewish Quarter were much worse than in the rest of the city. Its courtyards were not particularly clean and, aside from Batei Maḥseh and a few synagogues, its architecture was unimpressive. The Street of the Jews was narrow, dirty, and dark except at high noon. It was lined with small food shops, whose upper stories were used as dwellings. The parallel streets, Ḥabad and Meidan (Misgav La-dakh), were slightly wider, but of the same character as the Street of the Jews.[1]

Many other sources at the end of the Ottoman period offer similar descriptions of the Jewish Quarter.[2] Nevertheless, many Jews still seemed to prefer living there to moving outside the Old City. In 1891, Luncz reports, homes in the Old City were more expensive than those outside the walls. Inside the city, the rent for an average one-room apartment with a small kitchen was 650 grush a year; outside, it would cost 550 grush.[3]

The Jewish Quarter was made even more congested by the large number of shops and businesses in it. Gad Frumkin writes that the Street of the Sephardim (Meidan Street) contained several small shops for baked goods, candy and Sephardi-style sweets, as well as a bookstore where books could be exchanged for a fixed weekly subscription. Behind the large Yoḥanan ben Zakkai synagogue was the "Ḥakura," an overcrowded almshouse where needy Sephardim, mainly widows, lived several to each tiny room.[4] Living conditions in other courtyards, *Ḥatzer Ha-Ḥosh* for example, were equally trying.

The Beginnings of Expansion Outside the Jewish Quarter

376   The lack of sufficient housing for the growing population of the Jewish Quarter led to expansion into other areas of the Old City. Luncz writes that the

1   Zuta—Sukenik, p. 103.   3   Luncz, *Guide*, p. 10.
2   See, e.g., Hurlbut, pp. 45-86.   4   G. Frumkin, pp. 45-46.

few streets in the Jewish Quarter could not possibly contain all the immigrants from Russia and Poland arriving in the 1850's. Some members of the Ashkenazi community had the courage to move out of the Jewish Quarter, settling to its north, on the streets to the left of the vegetable market. This region became known as the Hebron market, because its first settlers were natives of that city. Jews continued to settle in the north until they reached the Damascus Gate.[5]

Luncz describes the developments of the late 1860's as follows:

> The Jewish Quarter began to expand into Hebron street, reaching the other side of the Saraya where the wealthy Rabbi Fischel [Ha-Cohen] Lapin owned a large courtyard with many houses and a study hall. This served as the border of Jewish settlement. Only two or three Jews of foreign nationality were courageous enough to move to the Bab Huta area because of its fine air; no Jew dared to walk alone past Batrak Street in the Christian Quarter, lest he enter "Treifa" [non-kosher] street (as the Jews called the street where the Church of the Holy Sepulchre was located) and be cruelly beaten as a result by the Christians.... The Jewish Quarter began at the edge of the Armenian convent (Deir al-Arman), where the area still known as the *kolel* courtyard, rented from the convent in the 1830's, was situated. Two large buildings were set aside for baking matza. The others were leased on a non-profit basis to persons who have protected tenancy rights to this day.... Although this region was called the Jewish Quarter, few houses in it actually belonged to Jews. With the exception of the synagogues, *Talmudei Torah* and hospitals, all the buildings in it were rented to Jews according to a protected-tenancy system.... When the Jewish community began to expand greatly at this time, the Jewish Quarter became very crowded and housing costs soared. Five years later, the Jews broke through the imaginary "ghetto" line and rented courtyards in the region of Bab Khan al-Zeit (near the Christian Quarter and the street known to the Christians as Via Dolorosa), following the protected-tenancy system. Settlement here was not extensive; the Jews soon realized the need for establishing new neighborhoods outside the Old City to accommodate an ever-increasing number of immigrants.[6]

Grayevsky mentions Rabbi Fischel Ha-Cohen Lapin's two courtyards in the Muslim Quarter: one located opposite the Torat Hayyim *yeshiva,* later used as a *Talmud Torah* and synagogue by the Georgian community, and another, called the Rabbi Fischel Ha-Naggid courtyard, near one of the gates to the Temple Mount. On the second floor of this courtyard, there was a synagogue where the students of the Degel Ha-Torah and Torat Hayyim *yeshivot* met later on. From his letters, Lapin seems to have moved to Jerusalem in the early 1860's.[7]

Neumann (for the same period) repeats that the Jewish Quarter was too small to house all the Jews and that many of them had begun moving to other parts of the city (excluding the Christian Quarter).[8] Elsewhere he stresses that the Jews were strictly forbidden to walk in the alleyways near the Church of the Holy Sepulchre; he himself was never there, but had to rely on the descriptions in Tobler's book, *Golgotha.* Many other writers mention this restriction, claiming that any Jew found walking in this area was severely beaten.[9]

377

5   Luncz, *Almanac*, III, 1898, pp. 59-71.
6   Luncz—Kressel, pp. 200-201 (translated from Hebrew).
7   Grayevsky, *Hidden Treasures*, II, pp. 1-10.
8   Neumann, p. 219.
9   *Ibid.*, p. 294.

The Bab Ḥuta Neighborhood

The first area in which the Jews settled beyond the confines of the Jewish Quarter was Bab Ḥuta. An attempt to settle there had been made by the Ashkenazi Jews returning to Jerusalem at the beginning of the century, but their efforts had been unsuccessful.[10] Now that the Jewish Quarter was so overcrowded, it was decided to try again. According to one source, the heads of the various *kolelim* wished to establish the Bab Ḥuta neighborhood simultaneously with the construction of Batei Maḥseh. For this purpose, they purchased a large tract of land and several ancient courtyards which they planned to demolish, building a new neighborhood in their stead. A series of obstacles prevented this plan from being carried out; however, the courtyards remained Jewish property from the time that the Etz Ḥayyim *yeshiva* established a synagogue and office there.[11]

Goldmann describes this endeavor in an 1888 issue of *Ha-Asif.* He says that almshouses for poor members of the Warsaw *kolel* had just been completed when the rabbis decided to purchase a few courtyards in the desolate Bab Ḥuta region in the north of the city. In 1886, the rabbis bought one large courtyard and three small ones for the sum of 1,395 French "lira." They planned to rent apartments to *kolel* members for a three-to-five year tenancy, on a rotation basis.[12] Their scheme met with limited success, as we see from Luncz's description of Bab Ḥuta in 1891:

> This quarter of the city, which included the entire hill of Old Bezetha, consisted largely of ruins and vacant lots. It was inhabited by a few poor Muslims and members of twenty Jewish families, most of whom lived in the courtyard belonging to the Warsaw *kolel.*[13]

Jewish Penetration into the Nearby Part of the Muslim Quarter

Bab Ḥuta was far from the Jewish Quarter. The other focus of Jewish expansion in the Old City was not: it was the section of the Muslim Quarter which bordered on the Jewish Quarter and which constituted its natural extension. As we have seen, Rabbi Fischel Lapin's courtyard was located in this area; so too was the first Jewish guest-house, run by Menaḥem Mendel of Kamieniec, where Eliezer Ben Yehuda lived when he first came to Jerusalem.

Another Jewish stronghold in the Muslim Quarter, established at the outset of Jewish expansion in the Old City, was *Kolel Ungarn.* We have already mentioned Rabbi Moses Aaron Baumgarten, an active member of this *kolel,* who came to Jerusalem in 1834 and dared to settle alone on Hebron Street, near the Temple Mount. In his courtyard, known as the "Rabbi Moses of Pressburg" courtyard, Baumgarten extablished the Ohel Moshe synagogue in memory of his teacher, Rabbi Moses Sofer. This synagogue attracted many new residents, including great scholars and public figures.[14]

10 Bartal, *Montefiore,* pp. 287-288.
11 Horowitz, *Mosad Hayesod,* p. 130.
12 Goldmann, *Ha-Assif,* IV, 1888, p. 43.
13 Luncz, *Guide,* p. 147 (translated from Hebrew).
14 Grayevsky, *Sefer Hayishuv,* pp. 42-43.

Other institutions belonging to *Kolel Ungarn* grew neaby. Several sources mention the Neḥamat Zion synagogue, which was originally established in 1862 as the first synagogue of the Hungarian *kolel* and had a bath-house beside it. Another synagogue, Ohel Yitzḥak, was founded near Neḥamat Zion in honor of Rabbi Ratzesdorfer of Hungary, who donated the funds to establish it when he visited the country in 1891. The Hungarian *kolel* abandoned this neighborhood during the riots of 1929, after the Arabs attacked a synagogue there. They killed the Jewish worshippers, tore off the synagogue roof, stole its doors, windows and cabinets, and left only the bare walls.[15]

Another *kolel* that settled in the Muslim Quarter was *Kolel* Reissin. Grayevsky cites a cornerstone inscription indicating that the courtyards of *kolel* Reissin and the Kehillat Yeshurun synagogue were donated by Sa‘adia ben Yeḥezkel Shorr in 1871. Another inscription reports an additional donation towards the purchase of these courtyards.[16] According to *Ha-Levanon,* Rabbi Sa‘adia Shorr of Moghilev purchased a large courtyard in the Muslim Quarter for 12,000 silver rubles, dedicating it to *Kolel* Reissin. He also established a study hall there for ten noted scholars. The newspaper also describes the beauty of the houses in this courtyard and the fine materials used to build them.[17]

Two other prominent structures in the Muslim Quarter were the houses of Rabbi Moses Wittenberg who, according to Schirion, was a very wealthy man, with half a million Russian rubles to his name. The two large houses he purchased near the Damascus Gate in 1884 contained some twenty apartments, each of two or three rooms.[18] These houses belonged originally to a Christian Arab who, in the middle of negotiating with Rabbi Wittenberg, sold them to the Latin Monastery. His heart set on owning these buildings, which were the most beautiful in the Old City, Rabbi Wittenberg resolved to buy them back from the monastery regardless of cost—a daring proposition in view of the monastery's vast financial resources and of the fact that the buildings were located on the Via Dolorosa, historically linked to Christianity. He sought out persons close to the dragoman and confidant of the Latin Patriarch, who was a Christian Arab with a weakness for gold, and succeeded in this way to initiate negotiations with the Patriarch. A year later, the buildings were his for the cost of the property plus 500 gold napoleons for the monastery and the same amount for the dragoman. As the Patriarch spoke only French, Eliezer Ben Yehuda, who knew French, served as the go-between during the negotiating process. Rabbi Wittenberg selected the best rooms in one of these buildings for himself, and rented the others to various individuals. He also established a synagogue for the benefit of his tenants and of Jews from the surrounding area.[19] Rabbi Moses Wittenberg is also mentioned by Gad Frumkin, who writes that the rabbi was a member of the Ḥabad Ḥasidim from

---

15 Freiman, pp. 84-86; Luncz, *Guide*, p. 151; Press, "If I forget thee," in *Studies* (list at end), p. 105.
16 Grayevsky, *Avnei Zikkaron*, I, p. 109.
17 *Ha-Levanon*, 15 Ḥeshvan, 1871, vol. VIII, p. 62.
18 Schirion, p. 50.
19 *Ibid.*, pp. 53-54.

Important Jewish institutions and residences in Muslim Quarter of Old City

1. Hospice of North African *Kolelim*
2. Ḥayyei Olam *Yeshiva*
3. Torat Ḥayyim *yeshiva*
4. *Kolel* Shomrei ha-Homot
5. Diskin orphanage
6. *Kolel* Reissin synagogue
7. Georgian synagogue and *Talmud Torah*
8. Wittenberg House — Tefillah le-Moshe synagogue
9. *Kolel* Galicia
10. Beth Rand
11. "Havatzelet" House — Frumkin family

Vitebsk and the owner of a courtyard near the Via Dolorosa, which he had purchased from the Arabs.[20]

In 1912, the newspaper *Ha-Moriah* tells of another important residence in the Muslim Quarter: Beth Rand.

> Mr. Rand has demolished part of his courtyard to build a new house in place of the dilapidated one. Construction was stopped because he was ordered to build the wall further in to permit the widening of the street. It is hoped that building activities will be allowed to resume, since the building is not a new one but only to be renovated.[21]

The Bak family also lived in the Muslim Quarter. Their home, which housed a printing press, was known as the *Havatzelet* courtyard, because the newspaper *Havatzelet* was published there. In his memoirs, Gad Frumkin describes the Bak home in detail. It consisted of three terraced apartments, with the roof of the one serving as the courtyard of the next. Both Jewish and Christian tenants lived on the ground floor, together with an Arab attendant. As the printing shop expanded, storage rooms were set aside for paper and books, and a bookbindery was opened. A flight of stairs led from the courtyard of the ground floor down to a yard where chickens, a goat and a donkey were kept. The courtyard on the next floor served the printing shop. The one above it had neither been paved nor made into a garden. Along its left wall, there was a large pile of stones with an opening through which one could reach the large home of the Huseinis. Near the entrance there was a wine and grain cellar, and a storage room for firewood, oil, and so on. Facing the stairs were the windows of a synagogue, located in a room on the second floor. The courtyard of the top floor, where Gad Frumkin lived, offered a view of the Temple Mount and the Mount of Olives. A pipe with a wooden receiver led down to the printing shop and served as a speaking tube.[22]

Gad Frumkin also gives a general description of Jewish life in his neighborhood. He points out that the Saraya building was surrounded by Jewish homes on all sides, most of them occupied by Jews from North Africa. He includes in his book a map of the al-Wad (Valley) Quarter, the Saraya, and Hebron street, indicating where Jewish homes and *yeshivot* were to be found.[23]

Isaiah Press provides many descriptions of the Jewish courtyards in the Muslim Quarter. He himself was born in 1874 in the courtyard of Rabbi Nahum of Shklov, opposite "the stores" (the Cotton Market), on the Street of the Steps leading to the Tyropoeon valley. As the Jewish population grew in the 1860's and 1870's, Jews began to settle in this valley, from the Damascus Gate to the street leading to the Street of the Chain, as well as in the Bab Huta neighborhood. Frumkin lists the large courtyards of Mendel Rand (near the Cotton Market); of Fischel Ha-Naggid (near the Third Gate of the Temple area) and of Rabbi Haim Avraham Gagin (where the newspaper *Sha'arei Zion,* edited by his father, was published). He also mentions the *Havatzelet* courtyard; a large building belonging to the Torat Hayyim *yeshiva* in the

---

20 G. Frumkin, p. 40.
21 *Ha-Moriah*, 1 Adar, 1912, vol. III, no. 46, p. 1 (translated from Hebrew).
22 Frumkin, *Selected Writings*, pp. 215-221.
23 G. Frumkin, pp. 7-21.

middle of the Valley Street; and the large courtyard near the Damascus Gate that Rabbi Moses Wittenberg donated to charity.[24]

Other homes, courtyards and public institutions in the Muslim Quarter included the almshouse of the North African *kolelim;* the *Kolel* Galicia synagogue on Hebron street; the Diskin orphanage on Saraya street; the Georgian synagogue and *Talmud Torah* on the corner of the Via Dolorosa and the Street of the Valley; and others.[25]

Luncz writes about some of these structures in his 1891 travel guide. Near the Cotton Market, he says, there was a new synagogue for Moroccan Jews, which included a *Talmud Torah* and an almshouse for widows and needy members of the community. Opposite this was the *Talmud Torah* of the Volhyn community, established in 1858 with the assistance of Pinḥas Numinsky, who purchased the courtyard and donated monthly sums towards its upkeep. In this region there was also an orphanage, founded by the Rabbi of Brisk, which housed over sixty youngsters.[26]

One source maintains that, over the generations, the Muslim Quarter served as a refuge for thousands of immigrants, and that more than ten synagogues and study halls were established there. These included the Torat Ḥayyim *yeshiva;* the Ḥayyei Olam *yeshiva;* two Moroccan synagogues; the New Synagogue; the Kehillat Yeshurun synagogue; two Hungarian synagogues (with their own ritual bath); the Zion Hametzuyyenet synagogue of the Austrian Jews; the Ohel Yitzḥak synagogue; Nefesh Ḥayya synagogue (also known as the "Aguna" synagogue); and others.[27]

Important Yeshivot in the Muslim Quarter

The establishment of the Torat Ḥayyim *yeshiva* on the Street of the Valley (al-Wad) in the 1890's was a major event in the penetration of Jews into the heart of the Muslim Quarter. This *yeshiva* was founded by Rabbi Isaac Winograd of Pinsk, who named it after his father, Rabbi Ḥayyim Winograd. Before immigrating, he sought approval for the *yeshiva* from the famous rabbis of Lithuania and Russia, hoping to forestall the anticipated opposition of veteran Jerusalem *yeshivot,* Etz Ḥayyim in particular, which regarded any new *yeshiva* as a financial rival. Nevertheless, a fierce controversy ensued, accompanied by a battle of insults between Torat Ḥayyim and the General Committee of the Perushim *kolelim,* then responsible for the distribution of *halukka* funds.[28]

The neighboring Christian institutions also tried to drive the *yeshiva* away. Located on the Street of the Valley, close to the Fourth and Fifth Stations of the Cross on the Via Dolorosa, the large, impressive *yeshiva* building was a thorn in their side. They tried to remove it by means of persuasion, tempting financial offers and even violence.

The Torat Ḥayyim *yeshiva* was more forward-looking and innovative in its approach than the older *yeshivot,* Etz Ḥayyim and Ḥayyei Olam. Its main goal

24   Press, *Hundred Years*, pp. 15-18.
25   Bier, map and text.
26   Luncz, *Guide*, p. 150.
27   Shapira, pp. 46-47; Grayevsky, *Hidden Treasures*, 1933, pp. 15-16.
28   Eliyahu Goldberg, *Justice and Righteousness*, Jerusalem, 1898 (Hebrew).

was to train rabbis of distinction, and it constituted in many ways a combination of the higher *yeshiva* and rabbinical seminary.[29] Luncz writes that the Torat Ḥayyim *yeshiva* was an important spiritual project, founded in 1887, designed to glorify Torah study by increasing the financial support extended to *yeshiva* students. Exploiting his talent for fund-raising, its founder gradually improved the institution, built a large, handsome building, and increased the number of students to 200. Those who were successful in their studies were ordained as rabbis.[30]

Porush states that another aim of this *yeshiva* was the absorption of rabbis who had escaped from Russia during the pogroms of the 1890's. Several outstanding scholars from the *yeshivot* of Poland and Lithuania came then to continue their studies in the Holy Land. The pressing financial situation of the Etz Ḥayyim *yeshiva* prevented it from accepting new students. Rabbi Isaac Winograd therefore initiated the establishment of Torat Ḥayyim, to serve talented immigrant scholars as well as Jerusalem residents. This *yeshiva* increased its students' incomes to such an extent that other *yeshivot* were forced to follow suit.[31]

Rabbi Isaac Winograd was both founder and head of the *yeshiva,* and dealt for the most part with money matters. His brother, Joseph Winograd, served as its spiritual leader. After the death of Isaac Winograd in 1913, Joseph also assumed financial responsibility. At this time the *yeshiva* had 102 students; according to Freiman, there had formerly been twice as many. Rabbi Joseph Winograd died in 1918.[32] The *yeshiva* ceased to function in the Old City at the beginning of the British Mandate. According to Weiss it was destroyed in the riots of 1921.[33] Others say its destruction took place during those of 1929. In his 1932 survey of Jewish property in the Old City, Press writes that the Torat Ḥayyim building had been abandoned, along with twenty-two *hadarim* and two Jewish shops in the same region.[34]

The Ḥayyei Olam *yeshiva* also acquired property in the Muslim Quarter; it proposed to erect a handsome *yeshiva* building on Hebron Street. Its first courtyard was purchased by the philanthropist, Numinsky. Then, the neighboring courtyard was acquired; this made it possible to construct large buildings and concentrate students in one place. Another, nearby courtyard was purchased in 1908, and the central *yeshiva* building constructed there. This *yeshiva,* like the rest of the Jewish community of Jerusalem, was severely affected by World War I. It managed to remain in existence only by virtue of contributions from the United States. It continued to develop in the Old City during Mandatory times, adding a second floor in 1927 and doubling its student capacity. However, the building was damaged by an earthquake in the same year, and damaged again during the riots of 1929. Along with other Jewish institutions, the Ḥayyei Olam *yeshiva* was forced to abandon its

29 Gellis, *Jerusalem Personalities*, pp. 219-220.
30 Luncz—Kressel, p. 253; Weiss, p. 84.
31 Porush, p. 152
32 Freiman, p. 49; *Yeshivat Torat Ḥayyim...*
33 Weiss, p. 189.
34 Press, "If I forget thee," in *Studies* (list at end), p. 105.

quarters and move to the New City.[35] Press's survey of 1932 found the *yeshiva* building and nearby structures dilapidated and deserted.[36]

Jewish Expansion into the Markets of the Old City

Another interesting phenomenon was the penetration of Jews into the commercial zones of the Old City and their acquisition of shops there. By 1872, *Ha-Levanon* reports, most of the stores on the street leading from the Upper Market to the Lower Market belonged to Jews who were respected merchants.[37] In 1891, Luncz writes that most of the storekeepers in the goldsmiths' market were Jewish.[38] The fact that so many stores in the Old City markets were closed on the Sabbath made a profound impression on David Yellin at the end of the century:

> I entered the city through the Jaffa Gate. From here to Batrak Street (the Greek Patriarchate), it is true that many shops were open; of the seventy-five shops located along the western side of the street, most of them selling fruit, vegetables and other foodstuffs, only about twenty belonged to Jews. The square opposite the citadel of David, however, was empty of the crowd of farmers who came there daily to display their wares....
> As I continued walking, I passed the city's first bank, owned by a fellow Jew, Mr. Valero [founded by his father in 1848, it was the first public financial institution in the country, was used by both Jews and Christians, and had dealings with most of the cities of Palestine and Syria]. In contrast to the other two, Christian-owned banks (the Frutiger bank and the German bank), it had not succumbed to the times. Then I reached the end of Batrak Street.
> Here the Sabbath Queen reigned supreme. To my left was Batrak Street leading to the Church of the Holy Sepulchre, and, before me, Bazaar Street (the Grain Market).... These, the two most important commercial streets in the city, were slumbering. There were many passersby on Batrak Street, because all the gentiles had to go that way to reach the burial place of their messiah, but it was a day of rest from business, and most of the stores were closed. Over forty of the sixty stores here were rented by Sephardi Jews who sold thread, ribbons, needles, knives and other such merchandise, which they imported from Constantinople.... No Ashkenazi Jews engaged in this branch of trade. I left Batrak Street and descended to Bazaar Street, which was deserted. Only eight of the seventy large stores here belonged to non-Jews. Most of the storekeepers on this street were Sephardi, Georgian or North African Jews who sold cloth, wool and all types of woven fabric. Even more of them were money-changers; they sat in small stores or beside the large ones belonging to merchants who imported their goods from Beirut, Syria's city of commerce.... A non-Jew opening his store here on the Sabbath would not have had much business: what Muslim or Christian woman would decide to shop when she knew most of the stores were closed? So she too would sit home on the Sabbath.... There were very few Jewish businesses on the street leading to the Damascus Gate. Only fifty stores out of a total of 300 were run by Sephardi and Moroccan Jews, who sold sewing articles to the villagers or worked as flax-beaters, gold- and silversmiths, or as shoemakers-cum-saddlers.... There were also a few Jewish stores in the Vegetable Market, ten out of a total of sixty. From here to the Temple Mount, the Jews accounted for twenty-five out of sixty stores, most of them being of saddlers.
> The situation was different on the Street of the Jews, where some 250 tiny, crowded stores were owned largely by Ashkenazim. Here they were among their own people and could freely use the language they had spoken in the Diaspora.

384

35 *Our Spiritual Possessions.*
36 Press (see above, n. 34).
37 *Ha-Levanon*, 15 Elul, 1873, vol. IX, no. 4, p. 30.
38 Luncz, *Guide*, p. 156.

Even the Sephardi Jews and gentiles who had businesses on this street spoke Yiddish....[39]

Using this description, a list of Jewish stores in the Old City may be prepared:

Jewish stores in Old City Markets at the End of the Nineteenth Century

Section of the Market	Total Stores	Jewish Stores
From Jaffa Gate to Batrak Street	75	20
Batrak Street	60	40
Bazaar Street (from Batrak Street to the main crossroad)	70	62
From the main crossroad on David Street to the Damascus Gate	300	50
From the main crossroad on David Street to the Vegetable Market on the Street of the Chain	60	10
From the Vegetable Market on the Street of the Chain to the Gate of the Chain	60	25 (saddlers)
The Street of the Jews and its satellite streets	250	250
Total	875	457 (52.2%)

Press also writes that Jews played a vital role in Old City commerce at the end of the nineteenth century. Most of their workshops and places of business were outside the Jewish Quarter, extending in the direction of the city's main markets. While these were designed for a wider clientele, the stores in the Jewish Quarter catered only for local needs.

Press offers the following account of the Old City markets:

David Street was the main shopping thoroughfare of the Old City of Jerusalem.... In the passage beneath the Grand New Hotel, one could buy the oriental wares and souvenirs so much sought after by tourists. Along the rest of the stepped street was the Arab fruit, vegetable and fish market, followed by the textile market, wholly owned by Jews. After this was a large, high-ceilinged hall

385

39   Yellin, *Writings*, I, pp. 15-16 (translated from Hebrew).

that was used as a caravanserai during the Crusader period, as grain market during the nineteenth century, and as Jerusalem's central fruit and vegetable market in the twentieth century. The vaulted continuation of David Street held an Arab textile market with closet-like shops whose owners sat cross-legged on the curb and offered their wares to customers standing in the road. The next section of the street was also vaulted, and was known to the Jews as "the dark stores." These stores served as a market for vegetables and other food products. The market was owned wholly by Arabs, but most of its customers were Jewish since it was adjacent to the Jewish Quarter on its east and south.... Batrak Street, the street of the Christians, turned off to the north from the upper end of David Street. Here, all the stores belonged to Jewish merchants selling sewing articles and other small items.... Batrak Street led to the new market, built on the site of the the Muristan ruins at the beginning of the twentieth century. Jewish textile and sewing-article stores were located here. The bottom of David Street branched off to the north, leading into three narrow, vaulted roads running parallel to one another and joined by high, open gates. The first of these was the Meat Market (Suq al-Laḥmin); the second, the Spice Market (Suq al-Attarin); the third was the Squires' Market (Suq al-Khawajat), where Jewish gold- and silversmiths practised their trade. Most of them were from North Africa, where this was a typically Jewish occupation. The Street of the Jews lay opposite this street, continuing southward towards the Zion Gate. A large Arab market place was situated in the north of the city, between the Damascus Gate and the Muristan. Here, there were grocery stores, soap factories and oil presses for the production of sesame and olive oil.[40]

The first Jewish banks were also located in the market places. According to Press, a Sephardi ritual slaughterer by the name of Jacob Aaron Valero established Jerusalem's first bank in 1848. Press visited this bank forty years later, when the founder's son, Aaron, had taken over. It was housed in two small rooms on David Street overlooking the Pool of Hezekiah. Opposite the grain market on David Street was another Jewish bank, which was owned by the well-known ritual circumciser, Rabbi Nathan Netta Hirsch Hamburger. Operating out of a small store, this bank provided such special services as relaying letters of credit and registered mail between Jerusalem and merchant ships anchored in the port of Jaffa.[41]

The vast development of the Old City market places at the end of the Ottoman period spurred the Pro-Jerusalem Society to undertake the cleaning and reorganization of the Cotton Market at the beginning of the British Mandate, instituting order in the Jewish and Muslim spinning shops located there.[42]

A Summary of Jewish Settlement Outside the Jewish Quarter

Jewish expansion within the Old City took two major directions. A large number of Jews preferred to settle on the streets to the north of the Street of the Chain (Market Street), remaining near the Jewish Quarter; in effect, they expanded the Quarter to the north. Many others chose to settle in more remote parts of the Muslim Quarter, such as the top of the Street of the Valley leading to the Damascus Gate; the area north of the Saraya; the Bab Ḥuta

40 Press, *Hundred Years*, pp. 34, 39-41 (translated from Hebrew).
41 *Loc. cit.*
42 Zuta—Sukenik, p. 115.

neighborhood; and similar sites. On the other hand, there was no Jewish penetration whatsoever into the Christian Quarter. There seem to have been three reasons for this. The Muslim Quarter was the largest and least populated neighborhood in the Old City, whereas the Christian Quarter was small and overflowing with people and institutions such as monasteries, churches and hospices. The dwellings in the Muslim Quarter were owned as a rule by private persons prepared to sell or lease their homes. The monasteries, which owned many of the homes in the Christian Quarter, were reluctant to do so. Finally, Jewish-Muslim relations seem to have been much better than Jewish-Christian relations in the nineteenth century. The Christian Quarter was dominated by monks and monasteries, and Jews were forbidden even to walk in the vicinity of the Church of the Holy Sepulchre.[43] The Jews also viewed Christianity as a hostile religion. The Muslims, on the other hand, seemed to the Jews to be no more than the local residents among whom they lived.[44]

The extent of Jewish settlement in the Muslim Quarter is brought home by the results of the census carried out by the World Zionist Organization's Palestine Office during World War I. More Jews were found living on Hebron Street (557 households or 1,355 persons) than on the Street of the Jews (436 persons) and Ḥabad Street (781 persons).[45] Even if these figures are not totally accurate, they show how large the concentration of Jews in this area was during the war.

The penetration of Jewish merchants into the Old City market places, particularly the lower portion of the central thoroughfare between the Temple Mount and David Street, was, in effect, expanding and reinforcing the so-called "Jewish Quarter." It would seem, therefore, that we cannot speak of the Jewish Quarter as a neighborhood with definite, clear-cut borders, because these borders were constantly in a state of change. During the first forty years of the nineteenth century, Jewish settlement centered around the Sephardi synagogues. This nucleus expanded with the return of the Ashkenazi community to Jerusalem, and it remained the focus of Jewish activity until the shift towards the Muslim Quarter began in the early 1870's. Residential preferences were also influenced by the subdivision of Jews into community groups, with each *kolel* setting up its own central courtyard and synagogue. The Sephardim preferred to live near the Sephardi synagogues and Meidan Street, the Perushim near the Ḥurva and Sukkat Shalom synagogues, and the Ḥasidim, near the Tif'eret Yisrael and Ḥabad synagogues. Jewish settlement in the Muslim Quarter followed a similar course. It seems, however, that the various Jewish groups had much more to bind them together than to separate them. Life among the Muslims and Christians was fraught with difficulty, and so the Jews had to maintain some degree of unity despite their differences. Thus the different groups always made an effort to live close to each other. In this way, a pattern of concentric development evolved, wherein each territorial addition, including the areas outside the Jewish Quarter, constituted a continuous enlargement of the original Jewish nucleus.

43 Luncz—Kressel, pp. 200-201.
44 Ma'oz, "Jerusalem," pp. 160-163.
45 Palestine Office, *Censi*, I, *Judaea*, p. 5.

The Onset of the Jewish "Exodus" from the Old City

Most of the Jewish expansion within the Old City took place at the same time as the Jewish exodus from it. However, unlike the process of development outside the walls, this expansion did not continue during the British Mandate. The difficult living conditions in the Old City, compounded by precarious security and the bloody riots that broke out in 1921 and 1929, led the Jewish community to prefer the new neighborhoods outside the walls. At this time, the Jews in the Old City began to withdraw from peripheral areas, concentrating once again in the Jewish Quarter. This ancient core continued to be the major Jewish stronghold in the Old City during the British Mandate; it was the last part of the Old City to fall into the hands of the Arab Legion in 1948, during the War of Independence.

In the final years of Ottoman rule (1870-1914), the Old City was still an important center of Jewish activity despite the expansion outside the walls. The 1880's were peak years for Jewish residence there: in 1890, some 19,000 Jews out of 25,000 lived inside the city walls, only 6,000 outside them. In the 1890's, the tide turned, and it was the new neighborhoods that grew and developed. By the end of the decade, the number of Jews inside the walls was equal to that outside the walls; those outside took the lead shortly before World War I. However, we must remember that, until the end of Ottoman rule, a large concentration of Jews remained in the Old City. This part of Jerusalem still retained its special holy status, and the Old City continued to be the preferred location for religious institutions such as large *yeshivot.* Modern secular institutions, on the other hand, had been housed in the New City for some time.

Evidence of the start of the Jewish exodus from the Old City at the end of the Ottoman period may be found in contemporary literature. Gad Frumkin writes as follows:

> In 1905, my father decided that the time had come to leave the home in which I had been born and raised, and to move outside the city. This had been Mother's desire for years, but Father, who was bound heart and soul to the Old City, would not hear of it.... Some of our close friends and relatives had left the Old City long before, and making visits to their new neighborhoods was arduous and time-consuming. It had also become increasingly difficult for women to go out alone, because the number of Jews was steadily declining.[46]

Most of those remaining in the Old City were members of poor families who could not afford to move. The Jewish exodus was considered to be a positive and vital development in those days, and was favored by Jewish leaders on the spot and abroad. Thus, masses of people made the move, seeking better living conditions and a more modern life-style. Government and municipal bodies, medical and financial institutions, hospitals, businesses and banks all left for new premises outside the city walls.

388

Reflecting on the future of Old City Jewry before the war (1913), David Yellin asked himself what importance the Old City still had, aside from its historical significance. He noted that it had religious importance, with the

---

46   G. Frumkin, p. 125 (translated from Hebrew).

Wailing Wall and important synagogues being located there; it had commercial importance as well, since the area was densely populated and Old Jerusalem had its own power of attraction. Yellin believed that action should be taken to preserve the concentration of Jews in the Old City and to keep them from leaving. He lamented the lack of action in this connection: "What did our ancestors and leaders do to secure themselves a foothold in Zion and Jerusalem? And what have we done ourselves?"[47]

Ussishkin, too, was among those who called for the continued purchase of land and buildings in the Old City. He even proposed that ownership of Jewish courtyards there be made over to the Jewish National Fund.[48] But all this was of no avail. Even the *kolel* trustees, previously noteworthy for their determined efforts to purchase courtyards from non-Jews, began to direct more and more of their attention towards settling in the new neighborhoods.[49]

Thus, the development of the Jewish Yishuv in the Old City came full circle: from a tiny group of Jews in the early nineteenth century to a flourishing community as time passed, and then back again to a group of dwindling proportions as the New City of Jerusalem grew.

389

47   Yellin, "Ancient Jerusalem," pp. 65-70 (translated from Hebrew).
48   Ussishkin, *Anniversary Volume,* pp. 138-141, 221-224.
49   This will be discussed more fully in the second volume of this work.

Epilogue
THE OLD CITY IN CONTEXT

A Historic Middle-Eastern City

It is hard to summarize an unfinished essay; it is no easier to draw conclusions about half a city. Nonetheless, we will try to do so, because the nineteenth-century Old City of Jerusalem was essentially different from the new one being built outside the walls. Indeed, the latter was a new creation, springing up in unoccupied terrain alongside an ancient city. The Old City, by contrast, exemplifies the influence of a period on a metropolis existing in the present but steeped in the past.

The urban geography of the Old City can only be understood in its historical context. Nineteenth-century Jerusalem was the product of hundreds, even thousands, of years of development. Its built-up area, population composition, economy, way of life, unique universal status and special characteristics were all determined long before the nineteenth century.

Some have tried to attribute to Jerusalem the geographical characteristics of a typical Middle-Eastern city—that is, of a Muslim city. Such traits are there, but anyone who delves deeply enough will find that they form only a thin veneer for the many strata of complexity that make Jerusalem the city it is.

Students of Middle-Eastern, Muslim cities have tried to establish the common characteristics of cities of this kind. They include: a large central mosque, the "Friday mosque," located in the city center; a religious school, or "madrasa," adjacent to the mosque and occasionally a center of higher learning; a central government building, a palace or citadel, usually near the large mosque, but sometimes found in an outlying area on a high, easily-defended site, which may also serve as the governor's official residence; a Turkish bath (*hammam*) and an inn (*khan*), usually located in the city center, sometimes near the city gates; a permanent central market (bazaar) with functional and hierarchic divisions according to the type of merchandise. Also characteristic are stores of the same kind, grouped together as follows: in the center, near the mosque, one might find stores selling candles, incense and other ritual items used in the mosque; vendors of religious books and bookbinders serving the *madrasa*; the *kaisariyya*, vaulted structures on either side of the road, closed by gates, and used for expensive merchandise, such as textiles; and coppersmiths, carpenters and locksmiths. Near the city gates, or beyond them, grocers, saddlers and wool-weavers from the neighboring villages might be found; on the outskirts of the city, such trades as require a great deal of space or constitute a public nuisance such as pottery-making, wool dyeing and leather-tanning might be located. This typical city would be protected by a wall and gates, as a rule, and its distinct neighborhoods house various religious and ethnic groups separately. Each neighborhood is a unit, with its own mosque, Turkish bath and market place; sometimes, it even has its own wall and gates. The Jewish quarter is usually located near the governor's palace, for reasons of security. The streets of the city are narrow and winding. Houses are turned towards an inner courtyard, and away from the street. The cemetery is outside the city walls, and usually contains the tomb of a holy man.

Some researchers believe these typical cities follow a concentric, relatively fixed hierarchical plan, with the large mosque, the government buildings and the markets in the center, surrounded by the residential districts and, finally, the semi-rural areas and cemeteries. Scholars also differentiate between two types of Muslim cities: new cities established and planned by Muslim rulers after the birth of Islam, and ancient cities taken over by Islam. In either case, the city-street plan becomes rambling and disorderly with time, due to an absence of municipal organization. This is particularly noticeable in the commercial zones, where stores may be built in any open space, and less so in the residential districts, where inhabitants often build their homes over the foundations of older structures.

Only some of the attributes of such a typical Muslim city apply to Jerusalem. The "Friday mosque," al-Aqṣa, is not located in the city center but, rather, on a historic, holy site: the Temple Mount. Another Muslim structure, no less sacred, is found near by: the Dome of the Rock. Both are much holier than the Friday mosques of other Muslim cities. Jerusalem is surrounded by a wall and gates, but these were built before the Muslim period. The city wall closely follows the outlines of the Roman city (Aelia Capitolina) built by Hadrian, and its main gates, facing in all four directions, are located either above the ancient gates or very close to them. Jerusalem's two government fortresses—the main one located in the Citadel of David, and the other one in "Pilate's Palace" at the northwestern corner of the Temple Mount—are both on sites that have been used for these purposes ever since the days of the Second Temple. The location of the main thoroughfares also antedates the Muslim period. Al-Wad Street, which runs along the foot of the Temple Mount from the Damascus Gate to the Dung Gate, seems to date from the Second Temple period, while the two principal, intersecting streets—one leading from the Damascus Gate to the Zion Gate, and one from the Jaffa Gate to the Temple Mount—are the Cardo and Decumanus of Roman Jerusalem. The location of other important historical sites, too, such as the Church of the Holy Sepulchre, for example, was set long before Muslim rule. There is indeed a typical Muslim market in Jerusalem, and its shops are sometimes grouped by the type of merchandise; however, the anticipated, concentric arrangement and hierarchic divisions are here substantially modified. There are public bathhouses, but their organization and location differ from that in other Muslim cities, and may date

391

back to earlier times. Jerusalem had small *khans,* but these did not play an important role, because the city was never a major caravan station or a commercial center. Finally, although the city is divided into quarters and neighborhoods, some of them walled, their structure and plan are infinitely more complex than that associated with the "typical" Muslim city.

Three factors seem to have kept Jerusalem from assuming the features of a typical Muslim city. First, if we insist on fitting Jerusalem into a category, it would come closest to the second type of Muslim city, that of ancient cities taken over and molded by Islam to suit its needs. However, it is extremely doubtful whether these should be considered Muslim cities at all. Indeed, many researchers have shown that many of the geographical characteristics cited as typical of the Muslim city are equally typical of other old cities, having no connection with Islam. (Medieval cities are a case in point.) Furthermore, walls and gates, government fortifications, bathhouses, winding streets, and even markets and quarters have been found in many other ancient cities. According to some scholars, there may be nothing unique about the Muslim city at all. Even if we reject this contention, it is clear that, in the case of Jerusalem, many features that could be attributed to the so-called Muslim city were actually in existence before the Muslim occupation, and they are characteristic of the ancient city in general.

The second factor which kept Jerusalem from becoming a typical Muslim city was its being a city sacred to three great religions. This led to the development of special geographical features that we may call religio-geographic, which largely obscured the city's Muslim nature. Alongside the Friday mosque and Muslim buildings stood both the Church of the Holy Sepulchre and other Christian structures, and the Wailing Wall and additional Jewish structures. The ctiy's population comprised members of three different faiths, and its economy was based on the religious activities conducted in it. The plan of Jerusalem's buildings and quarters, and its way of life, derived primarily from its being a city of religion: Muslim influence was secondary.

The third element that helped keep Muslim influence to a minimum was the fact that, aside from the early years of the Umayyad dynasty and a few short-lived efforts of a later date, the Muslim administration made no special contribution towards the city's development. There is no comparison between the enormous amount of building in the city during the Second Temple, Byzantine and Crusader periods, and the situation during the time of Muslim control. Relatively speaking, Jerusalem lay dormant for over 500 years, from the end of the Crusader period until the nineteenth century (except for part of the Mamluk period and the sixteenth century). The Holy Land and Jerusalem were peripheral and unimportant in the Muslim empire in the Middle East. Its religious standing aside, Jerusalem played no role in this empire, and it could not compete with such Muslim cities as Cairo, Baghdad and Damascus. It was always sparsely populated, and may not even have merited description as a city at all in those days. This lack of development helped preserve Jerusalem's historical and religious character, and made it relatively impervious to Muslim influence.

Nonetheless, the Old City does have certain Muslim or, to be more precise, Oriental, features. We have emphasized them in our reconstruction of the

392

nineteenth century and, to a certain extent, they continue to characterize the city today. These features were external. They did not find expression in the city's plan, its internal structure, or the general organization of its institutions but rather in the "oriental" culture common to all its inhabitants—Muslim, Christian and Jewish alike. This culture encompassed food, dress, dwellings, behavior patterns at home and in the streets, and bargaining in the market places, as well as the use of animals for the transporting of goods, and special means of collecting water. It was marked by a lack of esthetic appreciation, by an outward respect for traditional values, by an inward orientation of private life and an outward orientation of commercial life. These features and others are those that lend a unique appearance to Muslim cities, and they gave the Old City of Jerusalem a distinctly oriental flavor in the nineteenth century.

A Religious City

We have called Jerusalem an ancient city, as well as an oriental, Muslim city. It was also a spiritual city, the only one in the world sacred simultaneously to Judaism, Christianity and Islam. Religion constitutes a key factor in understanding the city's development. Economically, as we have seen, Jerusalem never assumed any measure of importance. It has no natural resources or sources of energy, and the rural district surrounding it is relatively poor, hardly an agricultural hinterland. International trade routes, which prompt economic and population growth, have never been established close to the city.

We cannot accept the theory that Jerusalem's importance in historic times derived from its location at the crossroads between the longitudinal mountain road and the latitudinal road joining the coast and Transjordan. Many other sites, such as Giv'at Binyamin, Beth El and Giv'on, would have been more suitable from this point of view. The fact is that Jebusite Jerusalem was not located on the mountain highway at all, but alongside it. The road ran along the watershed line of the mountain region: the city of Jebus was a little to its east, in a low area near the Kidron valley. Jebus had the advantage of a source of fresh water, the Gihon spring, flowing within its boundaries, and it was situated on a topographical spur almost entirely ringed by valleys. This enabled the establishment of an effective system of fortification, considered extremely strong for those days. However, a whole host of cities in the country enjoyed similar endowment, and these features cannot explain Jerusalem's exalted status in later periods. Moreover, the region was not especially conducive to urban expansion. Ancient Jerusalem did not face west but rather east, towards the desert.

At times, the city served as a political capital for its region, but this was not its major source of importance either. It was Jerusalem's religious position that led to its world-wide significance.

King David seems to have been the first to grant Jerusalem special status. His considerations were essentially political: he sought to establish the capital of his united kingdom in a neutral city, unaffiliated with a particular Israelite tribe, especially not with the strongest of the tribes, Judah and Benjamin. King David then bestowed a sacred status upon Jerusalem, by bringing the Holy

393

Ark to it, and by proposing to build a Temple there, a project carried out by his son, King Solomon.

Jerusalem has maintained its aura of sanctity ever since. The schism following the death of Solomon, the destruction of the First Temple, the Babylonian exile, the destruction of the Second Temple—none of these events lessened Jerusalem's holiness in the eyes of the Jewish people. On the contrary, the more the Jews suffered, the greater was their yearning for the Holy City. We may even say that this longing for Zion and the prophetic visions of the rebuilding of Jerusalem, the City of David and the Temple were among the factors that kept the Jewish people together in the Diaspora.

It is noteworthy that, even after the destruction of the Temple, there was almost always a Jewish community in Jerusalem. There were times of persecution such as the Crusader period (and even then, perhaps only at the beginning), when Jews were forbidden to live in the city. But they always returned to Jerusalem as soon as they could, however few in number they might be. Jerusalem's importance to the Jewish people has never been measured by the *size* of its Jewish community; its importance has always been related to the Jews' intense longing to return to the Holy City and rebuild it.

After the destruction of the Second Temple, Jerusalem began to be sacred for non-Jews as well. When Christianity was proclaimed the official religion of Rome in the days of Constantine, Jerusalem became a Christian city. In Byzantine times, it served as an important Christian center, attracting pilgrims from all over the empire. As the Christian church split into factions, monks and clergy of various sects settled in Jerusalem; Christians from all over the world began to stream to the city as pilgrims or permanent residents. Little by little, the number of Christian holy places increased; their special mark on Jerusalem may be seen to this very day.

A new religious power, Islam, seized Jerusalem (and the whole of the Holy Land) in 637, and it soon became a religious center for Islam, too. Under Umayyad rule, Islam flourished, establishing splendid mosques such as the Dome of the Rock and al-Aqsa. Jerusalem's special standing as Islam's third holiest city (after Mecca and Medina) did not diminish even in later periods.

The various Christian communities continued to maintain themselves throughout the Muslim period. In Crusader times, the Christians gained control of Jerusalem, and instituted a Christian way of life that lasted for ninety years. Jerusalem was reorganized by sects, and ecclesiastical building moved swiftly ahead. Christian links with Jerusalem were not severed by the return of the Muslims. Its various sects continued to live there, and pilgrims never ceased to arrive, in spite of the Muslim domination of the city.

The nineteenth century found Jerusalem under Ottoman-Muslim rule, but both the Jews and the Christians maintained large, active communities there. The continuing activities of the three major religious groups left an indelible mark on the city's geographical character—so much so, that Jerusalem of the nineteenth century is most aptly described as a city of religion. Jerusalem's geographical aspects most affected by contemporary religious activity (and, presumably, this is true of earlier periods as well) are five in number:

A) *Population.* Throughout the centuries, Jerusalem has been the home of three major religious communities that have branched out into sects and subgroups because of differences of opinion on matters of belief and ritual, or because their members hailed from different countries. Strong religious sentiments drew to the city a diverse religious population, whose singular devotion enabled it to withstand the harsh living, financial and sanitary conditions. A large part of this population was made up of men of religion: Jewish rabbis and scholars, Christian priests and monks, Muslim dervishes and other religious ministrants. Jerusalem's status as a city of religion attracted religious institutions of learning such as *yeshivot, madrasas* and monasteries. In addition, its population was continually reinforced by the masses of pilgrims of all three religions who arrived each year, especially for religious festivals. Sometimes, these pilgrims even outnumbered the city's permanent inhabitants.

B) *The Plan of the Built-Up Area.* Religion affected this in the following ways:

1) There were three major religious centers in the city: the Temple Mount for the Muslims, the Church of the Holy Sepulchre for the Christians, and the Wailing Wall for the Jews. The city was divided accordingly into three main residential areas adjacent to them.

2) Religious subcenters were established, leading to the growth of additional neighborhoods, such as the Armenian Quarter, and the subdivision of the three main residential districts.

3) The built-up area was characterized by an enormous number of religious buildings, most of them large and impressive, located in extensive grounds and surrounded by walls and gates made of the finest building materials in the city.

4) A unique skyline incorporating many minarets and the domed roofs of synagogues and churches came into being.

5) Cemeteries belonging to the different religious groups and subgroups were located outside the Old City walls, in areas linked to religious traditions.

C) *The Economy.* The city's economy depended almost entirely on the pilgrims and on the support its religious institutions and groups received from co-religionists and institutions outside the Holy Land. Jerusalem's religious status also influenced commercial life; there was little industry; both trade in the market places and construction projects were designed to meet the needs of pilgrims or of religious institutions and sects.

D) *A Unique, Religious Way of Life.* The city's unique religious character was discerned easily by the senses—especially vision and hearing. Every day, and particularly on holidays, the church bells and the chanting of the Christian liturgy echo from churches and monasteries. The *muezzin* calls from his minaret, the droning of prayers and the murmurs of study issue from synagogues and *yeshivot.* Every day of the week, and especially on Sundays and Christian holidays, one sees outdoor processions by different Christian sects and monastic orders, in their diverse costumes. On Fridays and Islamic holidays, one sees the Muslims, among them villagers in traditional dress, hurrying towards the Temple Mount. On Fridays, Saturdays and Jewish holidays, religious Jews in traditional garb make their way to the Wailing Wall. Jerusalem even has a religious *odor*: the odor of incense emanating from churches and monasteries, the odor of sweaty mats and carpets from the mosques, the odor of musty old books from the synagogues and *yeshivot.* Certain foods forbidden to one religious group or another are conspicuously absent from the market places, while other, traditional, items are found in abundance. The religious atmosphere in the Old City is so alive that it is almost touchable.

E) *Spiritual Status.* Jerusalem has always been accredited with divine qualities, and has had different religious traditions and legends associated with it. Here is the navel of the earth; here the creation of the universe began; here Abraham bound Isaac on the altar; here Christ suffered, was crucified and rose to Heaven; here the prophet of Islam ascended skywards. Sacred sites such as hills, mountains, caves, walls, stones, trees and springs are everywhere to be found: at the Temple Mount, the Church of the Holy Sepulchre, Mount Zion, Gethsemane, the Kidron valley and more. These sacred associations have been accepted by millions of believers the world over. For them, Jerusalem is more mystical and spiritual than real, more celestial than earthly. Jerusalem's religious inhabitants, the masses of pilgrims streaming to it, and the even greater number of those who have prayed and longed to see the Holy City — all of these conceive of Jerusalem as a spiritual, a religious, city.

It seems that the prime motive for the development of Jerusalem in the nineteenth century was also religious. The Ottoman reforms and liberalization of policies, along with improvements in transportation, especially by sea, made it much easier to reach the country. These, however, were only the *external* conditions that made increased immigration and tourism possible. The real impetus was religious: a fierce longing for the Holy City. These sentiments were very strong among Jews and Christians alike in the nineteenth century. For many generations, Jerusalem had been out of their reach. Now that the opportunity arose, they began to exploit it, realizing their dream of visiting the Holy Land. Christians organized mass pilgrimages, especially at festivals, and initiated large-scale missionary and philanthropic activities, run by both foreign missionaries and local monastic orders. Christian building activity centered, on the one hand, around the establishment of hospitals, schools and philanthropic institutions and, on the other, around the establishment of churches, monasteries and hospices for pilgrims. Jews came to Jerusalem with the intention of living and studying in it, and some with the intention of being buried in its sacred soil. For this reason, Jewish building activity focused on the establishment of residential neighborhoods and of religious institutions (*yeshivot* and synagogues) for the growing Jewish community inside and outside the Old City. Thus, we see that religion was always a major factor in the development of Jerualem — the nineteenth century included.

A Backward, Pre-Modern City

Thus far, the characteristics we have cited are true of Jerusalem both in the nineteenth century and in other historical periods. Backwardness and pre-modernity, on the other hand, are typical only of certain periods, the nineteenth century being one of them.

Our reconstruction of nineteenth-century Jerusalem has shown that, by modern urban standards, the Old City was highly underdeveloped during most of the century. Industrial enterprises and craftsmanship worthy of the name were absent, there was no modern commerce, and advanced technology had not yet appeared. The local population continued to live in the dilapidated homes and crumbling streets of days gone by. At the beginning of the century, there were no sanitary facilities, modern schools or philanthropic institutions to speak of. Eventually there was some improvement, but even at the end of the century, Jerusalem was an extremely backward city from an urban-geographical point of view.

Why, we must ask ourselves, did a city of such historical and cultural importance persist in its backwardness until so late a date? As strange as it may seem at first, the answer lies in the basic characteristics that we have already attributed to Jerusalem—especially to its being a Middle-Eastern, Muslim city. We will begin, however, with two other factors, history and religion.

A historic and a religious character immediately imply preservation and conservation. A city of great age contains buildings, sites and infrastructures dating from earlier periods. Moreover, the existence of such historical features usually shapes the further development of an area because an effort is made to use what has gone before. From this point of view, we may speak of a sort of geographical law of historical inertia: a geographical site will be adapted, grow and develop over the years in keeping with the historical foundations upon which it lies. Only rarely, in the case of physical or cultural "revolution," will drastic changes take place in the developing area. The Old City of Jerusalem is an example of how powerful historical legacy and inertia can be. Jerusalem of the nineteenth century was heir to centuries of history. Many developments of nineteenth-century Jerusalem, such as the enormous growth in the number of its inhabitants, homes and functional buildings, and the great increase in economic and social activity, occurred while adjustments to the previous layout and structure of the city were made. Thus, Jerusalem was able to preserve its historical character, and modernization affected it but little.

Religion has an even greater impact on geography than history. A sacred site which becomes a place of worship and religious ritual maintains its historical continuity more than any other. Jerusalem is full of examples of this. Consider, for instance, the Temple Mount. Ever since it was sanctified in the days of King David, this area has been the holiest site in the Old City. It has remained so for 3,000 years, also becoming sacred to Islam as time went on. The Christians, too, considered the Temple Mount holy at certain times, such as the Crusader period and, to some extent, the Byzantine period. Other prominent examples of holy places linked to specific geographic locations may be seen in various ecclesiastical structures in the city. The most important Christian shrine, the Church of the Holy Sepulchre, has been rebuilt on the same spot since the fourth century. Christian holy places have existed for centuries on the Mount of Olives, in the Gethsemane region, on Mount Zion, at the Pool of Siloam, and so on. This phenomenon is understandable since these geographical locations were associated with religious traditions and beliefs. As long as there were people who upheld these beliefs, an effort was made to build and rebuild on the same sites. Most interesting of all, however, is the fact that a new religion sometimes sanctified the same geographical location that had been sacred to other religions before it. (This may be seen at many archaeological sites in Israel: the temples of one culture were often reused by the members of another culture at a later date.) The most obvious example is Jerusalem itself, since the whole city became sacred to three religions, one after the other.

397

As we have noted, Jerusalem's status as a hallowed city for three faiths led to the preservation and continuous rebuilding of holy places, and hence to conservatism in the location of the city's important buildings. The social and religious cohesion of various groups resulted in the establishment of residential neighborhoods around religious centers. Thus, the location of religious centers on fixed geographical sites also resulted in fixed residential patterns nearby.

Nineteenth-century Jerusalem was very much a product of its long history and its religious heritage. This alone, however, is not enough to explain why it was so underdeveloped. Two other factors were at work. We have already noted that, from the end of the Crusader period until the nineteenth century, the city progressed very little, because the ruling powers attached no importance to it (aside from its religious importance) and were unwilling to invest any effort to develop it. This standstill continued all through the nineteenth century, preserving Jerusalem's past on the one hand, but preventing progress on the other.

Secondly, the geographical features of a Muslim city that took root in Jerusalem during the Muslim occupation also took their toll. The lack of municipal organization, typical of Muslim cities, was a major factor in the city's lack of progress. Jerusalem deteriorated physically and no improvements were made in its vital services. The fact that Muslim culture tended to disregard external appearances in favor of an extreme devotion to traditional religious values was also of importance. These two factors were present throughout the Ottoman empire; in this respect, the situation in Jerusalem was not much different from that in many other cities.

All of these factors—the preservation of a historical city with its ancient street system and buildings; the conservatism of an extremely religious city with old-fashioned traditions and ways of life; the lack of interest of an indifferent and unprogressive government; the lack of municipal organization—and the strong opposition of the government and of the largest population group in the city to the intervention of outsiders in the city's development—all these made Jerusalem an urban backwater for hundreds of years. The numerous written accounts we have discussed bear witness to the great disappointment of Western travelers when they reached Jerusalem. They had expected to find a historic, religious city, the city of the Scriptures, the city of prophets and messiahs. Some thought that they would find it an exotic, oriental city. Great was their chagrin at the backwardness, the misery, the dirt and the neglect that they saw. Only the more perceptive of them could see that all this was external, and that behind this exterior lay a historic city cloaked in the majesty of the past. But these were the minority.

The Contribution of the Nineteenth Century

We have dealt mainly with the ways in which nineteenth century Jerusalem was influenced by the *past,* devoting scant attention to the changes occurring in the nineteenth century itself. Contemporary Jerusalem was subject to two opposing forces: extreme continuity with the past, and decisive changes during the century. The continuity with the past, expecially as reflected in the general plan of the city, its important buildings, its population, its market places, its sources of livelihood and its cultural-religious character, has been treated above in depth. Let us now turn to the forces of change.

The first of these forces may be called *augmentation.* The nineteenth century was marked by an increase in population, building, commerce and activity of all kinds. If there were 10,000 persons living in the Old City at the beginning of the century, there were at least 30,000, possibly even 40,000, by the end of the century in this part of the city alone. At first, there were many underdeveloped areas within the city walls, especially along its edges, and occasionally in its center, as in the case of the Muristan district. These areas eventually were filled with large, impressive buildings, many serving religious and philanthropic institutions. The Muristan and its vicinity (the Christian Quarter) was filled with buildings, including the Lutheran Church of the Redeemer and the Russian Church of Alexander among other new buildings. A new Latin Patriarchate and religious seminary, a Greek hospital and other Greek institutions were established at the edge of the Christian Quarter. The Protestants' Christ Church and additional structures were built opposite the Citadel of David. The Armenian Quarter was augmented by new houses, a religious seminary, a school and so on. The Batei Maḥseh neighborhood, large synagogues and other buildings rose in the Jewish Quarter. The Austrian hospice, the Church of the Flagellation, the church of the Sisters of Zion and other Christian institutions were established in the Muslim Quarter. New rows of shops and commercial centers were built near the Jaffa Gate and the New Gate as well as in the Muristan and on the edge of the Armenian Quarter. The various quarters were filled with new houses and the market places with stores and workshops. Jerusalem retained its former general plan, but filled it to capacity, almost to bursting point.

The Old City was too small to contain all this growth. Therefore, the *New City* rose outside the ancient walls. The large increase in population, the overcrowding, the limited space available for building, the lack of housing, the high rents and the difficult sanitary conditions within the walls—all led to a mass exodus from the Old City to the New. During the Ottoman period, it was not people and institutions from outside Jerusalem and the Holy Land that established the New City, but the residents and public bodies of the Old City itself. Immigrants and new institutions heading for Jerusalem in the nineteenth century settled in the Old City for the most part. Only later did they begin to move towards the New City. It was Old Jerusalem that built New Jerusalem.

The third important change in nineteenth-century Jerusalem was an alteration in the city's *political and cultural status.* At the beginning of the century, Jerusalem had no special political or administrative position. It was merely an urban center for the surrounding rural district. During the Egyptian occupation, and when the Ottoman government resumed power later on, Jerusalem assumed administrative significance as the capital of a district whose borders had changed. Even more important was the change in status of the city's non-Muslim institutions. At the beginning of the nineteenth century, there was not a single Western consulate in Jerusalem. As the years went by, many European consulates opened their doors, perhaps more than in any other city in the East. The consuls had a quasi-royal status, with whole "armies" of subjects. There was a vast increase in the number of non-Ottoman subjects, who now nearly equalled the number of Ottoman ones. The non-Ottomans became a sort of state within a state. The Christian churches and the Jewish community took advantage of the reforms in Ottoman law which granted them more freedom, and expanded their activities in the city. The Protestants, who had exercised no power in Jerusalem at the beginning of the century, became an active and influential force. The European powers began to show great interest in Jerusalem and, under the guise of aid to the Christian and Jewish communities under their protection, set out to strengthen their foothold in the Old City and outside it. As a result, Jerusalem's standing also rose in the eyes of the Muslim community and the authorities. In this way, Jerusalem, which at the start of the century played no role in the Holy Land, the Ottoman Empire, or the Western world, became a city of utmost importance for all three. Jerusalem was no longer a provincial town of little consequence in the Ottoman Empire, but a growing cultural and spiritual center attracting ever larger numbers of people from all over the world.

The three major changes in the Old City during the nineteenth century had an overwhelming impact on the Jewish community of Jerusalem and on the Jewish people as a whole. The "augmentation" factor was especially powerful in the Jewish sector. When the nineteenth century began, this community was tiny, and almost exclusively Sephardi. It had a minimal number of synagogues, *yeshivot* and other public institutions; the Jewish Quarter was extremely small in size. By the end of the century, the Jewish community had expanded greatly; in the Old City alone, it constituted more than half the total population. The number of community groups and *kolelim* continually increased, and Jews from Ashkenazi, Sephardi, North African and Asian communities began streaming to Jerusalem. Important Jewish institutions were established. The residential district of the Jews expanded, encompassing both the whole of the district known later as the Jewish Quarter, and a sizable section of the Muslim Quarter. There was extreme overcrowding in the Jewish neighborhoods. Jerusalem throbbed with Jewish activity as Jews took an increasingly important part in commerce and craftsmanship. The second half of the nineteenth century seems to have been a peak period for Jewish settlement in the Old City.

The population density and difficult living conditions led to a Jewish exodus from the Old City, and the construction of a new Jewish city outside the walls through the joint efforts of various community groups, *kolelim* and private building companies. At first, it was difficult for the Jews to think of leaving the Old City. Many of them had journeyed long distances and endured innumerable hardships to reach it. Others had been born there and had lived within its walls all their lives. For these people, only the Old City was the true Jerusalem. To leave it—even to build a new city which would still be called Jerusalem, even for new and roomier homes—was something they could not accept. It was only when the situation became hopeless, when the grave conditions in the Old City persisted, and when a new, healthier city began growing up outside the walls that the more extreme opponents gave in, and the building proceeded in full strength. During the last four decades of Ottoman rule, some seventy new Jewish neighborhoods rose beyond the city walls. Most of them were built and populated by Jews leaving the Old City. *It was old Jewish Jerusalem which built new Jewish Jerusalem,* as we have seen.

The Jewish community also played a key role in the third change occurring in the nineteenth century. A large part of this community had foreign nationality, and was protected by foreign consuls. Various European powers assisted the Jews in the establishment of hospitals, schools and welfare institutions, and provided support for community members. The reforms and liberalization of Ottoman law paved the way for a considerable increase in Jewish immigration. The Jews' deep longing for the Holy Land burst forth in a massive wave of Jews heading for the Old City. The philanthropic activities of Montefiore and Rothschild began to make their impact on the Jewish communities of the East, sowing messianic hopes. Jewish ties to Jerusalem may have been weak at the beginning of the nineteenth century but, as the years went by, these ties multiplied and strengthened until they became an unseverable and unending bond.

We have stressed the *positive* aspects of the Jews' exodus from the Old City in order to build the new one. It should be pointed out that this process was not without its *negative* aspects. The development of a new city resulted in the decline of ancient Jerusalem and drained it of its Jewish inhabitants. Strange as it may seem, the veteran Jewish community of the Old City, in building New Jerusalem, brought about its own demise. Only now, more than one hundred years after so many of its fathers and grandfathers left the Old City for the New, has the Jewish community of Jerusalem realized how much they erred in abandoning the Old City to its fate. But it took the Jordanians to make the Old City "*judenrein*" in 1948, as they drove its last Jews into exile before razing the Jewish Quarter. Now that the Old City is once again open to the Jews—as to all others—the citizens of Israel are striving to restore its former glory and to rebuild its private homes and public institutions of the rosy Jerusalem stone with which this beloved city has been built and rebuilt throughout the ages.

ABBREVIATIONS OF SERIAL AND OTHER PUBLICATIONS USED IN THE TEXT, NOTES AND BIBLIOGRAPHY

Cathedra:	*Cathedra for the History of Eretz-Israel and Its Yishuv.* Jerusalem, Yad Izhak Ben-Zvi.
Chapters:	*Chapters in the History of the Jewish Community in Jerusalem.* Jerusalem, Yad Izhak Ben-Zvi.
Eretz-Israel:	*Eretz-Israel: Archaeological, Historical and Geographical Studies.* Jerusalem, Israel Exploration Society.
Hamizraḥ Heḥadash:	*The New East, Quarterly of the Israel Oriental Society.* Jerusalem.
Jerusalem Quarterly History: Jerusalem Quarterly Devoted to the Study of Jerusalem and its History. Edited by J. Press, M. Ish-Shalom, M. Benayahu, and A. Shoḥat. 3 vols. Jerusalem, 1949.	
Keshet:	*Keshet, Reminiscences of Eretz-Israel 1830-1930.* Tel Aviv, 1970.
MNDPV:	*Mitteilungen und Nachrichten des deutschen Palästina-Vereins.*
NNADO:	*Neueste Nachrichten dem Orient.*
PEF QSt:	*Palestine Exploration Fund Quarterly Statements.* London, 1869 ff.
Sefunot:	*Annual for Research on the Jewish Communities in the East.* Jerusalem, Yad Izhak Ben-Zvi.
Sinai:	*Sinai, A Monthly for Torah and Judaic Studies.* Jerusalem, Mosad ha-Rav Kook.
Shalem:	*Shalem: Studies in the History of the Jews in Eretz-Israel.* Jerusalem, Yad Izhak Ben-Zvi.
Tarbiz:	*Tarbiz, A Quarterly for Jewish Studies.* Institute of Jewish Studies of the Hebrew University, Jerusalem.
Vatiqin:	*Vatiqin, Studies in the History of the Yishuv.* Bar-Ilan University, Ramat Gan.
Yad Yoseph Rivlin:	*Joseph J. Rivlin Memorial Volume.* Edited by H.Z. Hirschberg, Ramat Gan, 1964.
Yediot:	*Yediot, Bulletin of the Israel Exploration Society*, Jerusalem.
Yediot, Selected Articles: Bulletin of the Israel Exploration Society, Reader. 2 vols. Jerusalem, 1965.	
ZDPV:	*Zeitschrift des deutschen Palästina-Vereins.*
Zion:	*Zion, A Quarterly for Research in Jewish History.* Jerusalem, The Historical Society of Israel.
Zionism:	*Zionism: Studies in the History of the Zionist Movement and the Jewish Community in Palestine.* Tel Aviv, Tel Aviv University, 1970.

SOURCES AND BIBLIOGRAPHY

Abir, M.   "Local Leadership and Early Reforms in Palestine 1800-
                                  1834," in *Studies on Palestine during the Ottoman Period*.
                                  Edited by M. Ma'oz. Jerusalem, 1975, pp. 284-310.

Adler, C.   *Memorandum on the Western Wall, Prepared for the Special
                                  Commission of the League of Nations*. Philadelphia, 1930.

Adler, E.N.   *Von Ghetto zu Ghetto*, Stuttgart, 1909.

Alderson, C.R.   *Notes on Acre—Papers on Subjects Connected with the Duties
                                  of the Corps of the Royal Engineers, No. VII*. London, 1844.

Allen, W.   *The Dead Sea, New Route to India....* London, 1855.

Alsberg, P.A.   "The Israel State Archives as a Source for the History of
                                  Palestine during the Ottoman Period," in *Studies on Palestine
                                  during the Ottoman Period*. Edited by M. Ma'oz. Jerusalem,
                                  1975, pp. 533-544.

Amiran, D.H.K.   "The Development of Jerusalem 1860-1970," in *Urban
                                  Geography of Jerusalem: A Companion Volume to the Atlas of
                                  Jerusalem*. Edited by D.H.K. Amiran *et al.* Jerusalem, 1973,
                                  pp. 20-52.

Amiran, D.H.K., Schachar, A. and Kimchi, I, (eds.). *Atlas of Jerusalem*. Jerusalem, 1973.

Ashwort, J.   *Walks in Canaan*. London, 1869.

Assaf, M.   *History of the Arabs in Palestine*, vol. II: *The Arabs under the
                                  Crusaders, the Mameluks and the Turks*. Tel Aviv, 1941
                                  (Hebrew).

——   *History of the Arabs in Palestine*, vol. III: *The Arab Awakening
                                  and Flight*. Tel Aviv, 1967 (Hebrew).

Atlas of Israel. Maps and Text, VIII/1; IX/13. Jerusalem, 1970.

Avitzur, S.   *The Port of Jaffa 1865-1965*. Tel Aviv, 1972 (Hebrew).

——   *Daily Life in Eretz-Israel in the Nineteenth Century*. Tel Aviv,
                                  1972 (Hebrew).

——   "The Jewish Quarter of the Old City of Jerusalem," *Chapters*,
                                  I (1973), pp. 9-43 (Hebrew).

Bachrach, J.   *Reise nach dem heiligen Lande, unternome im Jahre 5642*.
                                  Warsaw, 1882 (Hebrew edition).

Baedeker, K.   *Palestine and Syria, Handbook for Travellers*. lst edition.
                                  Jerusalem: Carta, 1973. (First published in 1876: Leipzig—
                                  London.)

Baldensperger, P.J.   *The Immovable East*, London, 1913.

Barclay, J.T.   *The City of the Great King: or Jerusalem as it was, as it is, as it
                                  is to be*. Philadelphia, 1858.

——   *Jerusalem and Environs: From Actual and Minute Survey*.
                                  Philadelphia, 1856.

403

Baritz, L.   *City on a Hill.* New York, 1964.

Barnai, Y.   "The 'Mughrabi' Community in Jerusalem in the Nineteenth Century," *Chapters,* I (1973), pp. 129-140 (Hebrew).

――   "R. Eliezer Bergmann's Assistance to the Mughrabis in Jerusalem," *Vatiqin* (1975), pp. 117-126 (Hebrew).

Barron, J.B.   *Palestine Report and General Abstracts of the Census of 1922.* Jerusalem, 1923.

Bartal, I.   "The 'Old' and the 'New' Yishuv — Image and Reality," *Cathedra,* II (1976), pp. 3-19 (Hebrew).

――   "Settlement Proposals during Montefiore's Second Visit to Eretz-Israel, 1839," *Shalem,* II (1976), pp. 231-296 (Hebrew).

Bartlett, W.H.   *Walks about the City....* London, 1844.

――   *Jerusalem Revisited....* London, 1855.

Bartura, A.   *Jerusalem in the Eye of the Beholder: the History of "Batei Maḥseh" and "Hakhnasat Orḥim" on Mt. Zion.* Jerusalem, 1970 (Hebrew).

――   "On the History of 'Batei Maḥseh'," *Chapters,* I (1973), pp. 122-129 (Hebrew).

Basili, R.   *Syrien und Palästina unter der türkischen Regierung.* Odessa, 1918.

Bedford, F.   *The Holy Land, Egypt, Constantinople, Athens.* London, 1864.

Bell, C.D.   *Gleanings from a Tour....* London, 1887.

Belloc, J.T.   *Jerusalem.* Paris, 1887.

Ben-Arieh, Y.   "Pioneer Scientific Exploration in the Holy Land at the Beginning of the Nineteenth Century," in *Terrae Incognitae: The Annals of the Society for the History of Discoveries,* IV (1972), pp. 95-110.

――   "The Growth of the Jewish Community of Jerusalem in the Nineteenth Century," *Chapters,* I (1973), pp. 80-122 (Hebrew).

――   "The First Surveyed Maps of Jerusalem," *Eretz-Israel,* XI (1973), pp. 64-74 (Hebrew).

――   "Frederick Catherwood Map of Jerusalem—1833," *Quarterly Journal of the Library of Congress* (1974), pp. 150-160.

――   "The Initial Jewish Quarters outside the Old City of Jerusalem before 1882," *Shalem,* I (1974), pp. 331-376 (Hebrew).

――   "The Growth of Jerusalem in the Nineteenth Century," *Annals of the Association of American Geographers,* LXV (1975), pp. 252-269.

――   "Christians' Activity and Dispersion in Nineteenth-Century Jerusalem," *Journal of Historical Geography,* II (1976), pp. 49-69.

――   "Legislative and Cultural Factors in the Development of Jerusalem 1800-1914," in *Geography in Israel.* Jerusalem, 1976, pp. 54-105.

――   *The Rediscovery of the Holy Land in the Nineteenth Century.* Jerusalem, 1979.

Ben-Gurion, D. and Ben-Zvi, I., *Eretz-Israel in the Past and in the Present.* New York, 1918 (Yiddish); Jerusalem, 1979 (Hebrew).

Ben-Jacob, A. "On the History of the Yeshivot 'Kneset Yeḥezkel' and 'Ḥesed-El' in Jerusalem," *Jerusalem Quarterly History*, II (1949), pp. 89-99 (Hebrew).

Ben-Or-Kalmar, Y. *Jerusalem: Old City Sights*. Jerusalem, 1924 (Hebrew).

Ben-Zvi, I. *The Population of Eretz-Israel*. Vol. V of *The Writings of Izhak Ben-Zvi*. Tel Aviv, 1937 (Hebrew).

—— "Mista‘rabs in Eretz-Israel," *Sinai*, XXX-XXXI (1939-1940), pp. 379-386 (Hebrew).

—— *Travels in Israel and the Neighboring Countries from Travel Impressions and Diaries*. Jerusalem, 1960 (Hebrew).

—— *Eretz-Israel under Ottoman Rule: Four Centuries of History*. Jerusalem, 1962 (Hebrew).

—— *Travel Impressions*. Jerusalem, 1972 (Hebrew).

Bergmann, E. and S. *Yis'u Harim Shalom: Aliya and Travel Letters, Jerusalem 1834-1836*. Edited by A. Bartura. Jerusalem, 1969 (Hebrew).

Bernatz, J.M. *Palästina: New Album of the Holy Land; Fifty Views*. Stuttgart, 1868.

Bezanson, W.E. (ed.). *Clarel; A Poem and Pilgrimage in the Holy Land*, by Herman Melville. New York, 1960.

Bier, A. *Jewish Religious and Welfare Institutions in the Muslim Quarter of the Old City of Jerusalem*. Jerusalem, 1974 (Hebrew).

Bliss, P.J. *Excavations of Jerusalem 1894-1897*. London, 1898.

—— *The Development of Palestine Exploration*. London, 1906.

Blyth, E. *When We Lived in Jerusalem*. London, 1927.

Boddy, A.A. *Days in Galilee*..... London, 1900.

Bonar, A.E. and M'Cheyne, R.M., *Narrative of a Mission of Inquiry to the Jews from the Church of Scotland in 1839*. Edinburgh, 1846.

Bonar, H. *Days and Nights in the East*. London, 1866.

Book of Takkanot, Haskamot and Minhagim in the Holy City. Jerusalem, 1883 (Hebrew).

Bovet, F. *Egypt, Palestine and Phoenicia*. London, 1858.

Brawer, A.J. "First Use by Jews of the Privilege of Capitulations in Palestine," *Zion*, V (1940), pp. 161-169 (Hebrew).

Bremmer, F. *Travels in the Holy Land*. London, 1861.

Breycha-Vautheir, L. *Österreich in der Levante*. Vienna, 1972.

Brinker, D.N. *Jerusalem Almanac*, vol. X. Jerusalem, 1950, pp. 274-277 (Hebrew).

Brown, J.R. *Yusef, or the Journey of Franji....* New York, 1858.

Buchanan, R. *Notes of A Clerical Furlough Spent Chiefly in the Holy Land*. London, 1859.

Buckingham, J.S. *Travels in Palestine....* London, 1821.

—— *Travels among the Arab Tribes..., including a Journey from Nazareth to the Mountains beyond the Dead Sea....* London, 1825.

Busch, B. *Eine Wallfahrt nach Jerusalem: Bilder ohne Heiligenschein.* Leipzig, 1881.

Cahanyu, M.N. *Pray for the Peace of Jerusalem (Sha'alu Shelom Yerushalayim)*. Jerusalem, 1969 (Hebrew).

405

Carmel, A.   *Die Siedlung der württembergischen Templer in Palästina 1868-1918*. Stuttgart, 1973.

——   *German Settlement in Eretz-Israel at the End of the Ottoman Period—Political and International Problems*. Jerusalem, 1973 (Hebrew).

——   *The History of Haifa under Turkish Rule*. 2nd edition. Jerusalem, 1977 (Hebrew).

Carne, J.   *Letters from the East*. London, 1826.

——   *Recollections of Travels in the East, Forming a Continuation of the Letters from the East*. London, 1830.

——   *Syria, the Holy Land, Asia Minor, etc.*. London, 1836.

Carpenter, N.T.   *In Cairo and Jerusalem, An Eastern Note Book*. New York, 1894.

Catherwood, F.   *Plan of Jerusalem*. New York, 1835.

Charles, E.   *Wanderings over Bible Lands and Seas*. London, 1865.

Chateaubriand, F.A.   *Travels in Greece, Palestine....* London, 1811.

Churton, H.B.W.   *Thoughts on the Land of the Morning. A Record of Two Visits to Palestine*. London, 1851.

Clarke, E.D.   *Travels in Various Countries of Europe, Asia and Africa* (Holy Land: Chaps. III-IX). Cambridge, 1810-1823.

Cohen-Reiss, E.   *Memories of a Son of Jerusalem*. 2nd edition. Jerusalem, 1967 (Hebrew).

Colbi, S.B.   *Christianity in the Holy Land, Past and Present*. Tel Aviv, 1969.

Conder, C.R.   *Tent Work in Palestine*. London, 1878.

Conder, C.R. and Kitchener, H.H., *Map of the Palestine Exploration Fund during the Years 1872-1877*. London, 1880.

——   *The Survey of Western Palestine. Memoirs of the Geography, Topography, Hydrography and Archaeology*. London, 1881-1883.

Cowper (Countess).   *A Month in Palestine*. London, 1889.

Cramer, V.   *Ein Jahrhundert deutscher, katholischer Palästina-mission, 1855-1955*. Cologne, 1956.

Cuinet, V.   *Syrie, Liban et Palestine; Géographie Administrative....* Paris, 1896.

Curtis, G.W.   *The Wanderer in Syria*. London, 1852.

Curzon, A.   *Visits to Monasteries of the Levant*. London, 1849.

Damas, A.   *Voyages en Orient*. Paris, 1866.

Damer (Dawson), G.L. *Diary of a Tour in Greece, Turkey, Egypt and the Holy-Land*. London, 1841.

Das Deutsche Kaiserpaar im Heiligen Lande. Berlin, 1899.

De Haas, J.   *History of Palestine: the Last Two Thousand Years*. New York, 1934.

De Saulcy, F.   *Narrative of a Journey around the Dead Sea*. London, 1854.

——   *Jerusalem*. Paris, 1882.

Deverell, F.H.   *My Tour in Palestine and Syria*. London, 1899.

De Vogüe, M.   *Le Temple de Jerusalem...* Paris, 1864-1865.

Dixon, W.H.	*The Holy Land....* London, 1865.
Dmitrievskii, A.A.	*Imperatorskoe pravoslavnoe Palestinskoe Obshchestvo i ego deiatel'nost' za istekshuiu chetvert' veka (1882-1907), Istoricheskaia zapiska.* St. Petersburg, 1907.
"Doresh Zion."	*The Seventy-Fifth Anniversary of the Doresh Zion School in Jerusalem.* Jerusalem, 1941 (Hebrew).
Drori, Y.	"On the History of the Nebi Musa Celebrations," *Sal'it*, I/5 (1972), pp. 203-208 (Hebrew).
Druyanov, A.	*Writings on the History of Hibbat Zion.* [3 vols. Tel Aviv, 1919-1932.] II (1928), pp. 227-231 (Hebrew).
Dupuis, L.H.	*The Holy-Land Places.* London, 1856.
Ebers, G.E. and Guthe, H.,	*Palästina in Bild und Worte* (Nach dem Englischen herausgegeben). Stuttgart and Leipzig, 1882.
Efrati, N.	*The Role of the Eliachar Family in Jerusalem.* Jerusalem, 1975 (Hebrew).
Egerton, F.	*Journal of a Tour in the Holy Land in 1840.* London, 1841.
Eisenstein, J.D.	*Otzar Massa'ot: A Collection of Itineraries by Jewish Travelers to Palestine, Syria, Egypt and Other Countries.* New York, 1926 (Hebrew).
El Abbassi (Ali Bey).	*L'Atlas des voyages d'Ali Bey...* Paris, 1814.
——	*The Travels of Ali Bey el Abbassi... between the Years 1803 and 1807.* London, 1816.
Eliachar, E.	"The Rabban Yoḥanan Ben-Zakkai Synagogues," *Chapters*, I (1973), pp. 61-79 (Hebrew).
Eliav, M.	*Love of Zion and Men of Hod: German Jewry and the Settlement of Eretz-Israel in the 19th Century.* Tel Aviv, 1970 (Hebrew).
——	"The German Consulate in Jerusalem and the Jews in Jerusalem in the 19th Century," *Zionism*, I (1970), pp. 57-83 (Hebrew).
——	*The Jews of Palestine in the Light of German Policy 1842-1914: Selected Documents from the Archives of the German Consulate in Jerusalem.* Tel Aviv, 1973 (Hebrew).
Elmaleh, A.	"History of the North African Community," in A.M. Luncz, *Almanac*, XIV (1909), pp. 58-88 (Hebrew).
——	*The First Men of Zion: Their Life and Work.* Jerusalem, 1970 (Hebrew).
Etz-Hadar, A.	*Ilanot: On the History of the Yishuv in Eretz-Israel (1830-1920).* Tel Aviv, 1967 (Hebrew).
Ewald, F.C.	*Journal of Missionary Labours in the City of Jerusalem during the years 1842-1844.* London, 1845.
Finn, J.	*Byways in Palestine.* London, 1868.
——	*Stirring Times....* London, 1878.
Finn, Mrs. M.C.	*Home in the Holy-Land....* London, 1866.
——	*A Third Year in Jerusalem....* London, 1869.
——	*Reminiscences of Childhood.* London, 1929.

Fishbane, S.   "The Founding of Kolel America Tifereth Yerushalayim," *American Jewish Historical Quarterly*, LXIV (1974), pp. 120-136.

Fisk, G.A.   *A Memorial of Egypt... Jerusalem and Other Principal Localities Visited in 1842*. London, 1847.

Fisk, P.   *A Memoir of... Pliny Fisk, Late Missionary to Palestine*. Edinburgh, 1828.

Forbin, L.N.P.U.   *Voyage dans le Levant en 1817-1818*. Paris, 1819.

Fortescue, A.   *The Orthodox Eastern Church*. New York, 1920.

Fox, F.   "Quaker, Shaker, Rabbi: Warder Cresson, The Story of a Philadelphia Mystic," *The Pennsylvania Magazine of History and Biography*, XCV, no. 2 (April 1971), pp. 147-194.

Frankl, L.A.   *Nach Jerusalem! Reise in Griechenland, Kleinasien, Syrien, Palästina*. Leipzig, 1858.

――――   *Nach Jerusalem:* Photocopy of selected chapters from the Hebrew edition of Vienna, 1859. Jerusalem, 1973.

Franklin, G.E.   *Palestine Depicted and Described*. New York, 1911.

Freiman, D.N.   *Jerusalem Commemorative Volume*, vol. I. Jerusalem, 1913 (Hebrew).

Friedman, I.   "Lord Palmerston and the Protection of Jews in Palestine 1839-1851," *Jewish Social Studies*, XXX, no. 1 (1968), pp. 23-41.

Friedman, M.   "On the Structure of Community Leadership and the Rabbinate in the 'Old Ashkenazi Yishuv' towards the end of Ottoman Rule," *Chapters*, I (1973), pp. 273-288 (Hebrew).

Frith, F.   *Egypt, Sinai and Jerusalem*. London, 1862.

Frumkin, A.L.   *The History of the Sages of Jerusalem*, vol. III. Jerusalem, 1929 (Hebrew).

Frumkin, G.   *The Life of a Judge in Jerusalem*. Tel Aviv, 1956 (Hebrew).

Frumkin, I.D.   *Selected Writings*. Edited by G. Kressel. Jerusalem, 1954 (Hebrew).

Fulton, J.   *Palestine, the Holy Land*. Philadelphia, 1900.

Fürst, A.   *The New Jerusalem*. Jerusalem, 1946 (Hebrew).

Gadsby, J.   *Wanderings, Travels in the East (1846-1853)*. London, 1855.

Gaon, M.D.   *Oriental Jews in Eretz-Israel, Past and Present*, vol. I. Jerusalem, 1928 (Hebrew).

――――   *The Sages of Jerusalem: Selected Essays*. Edited by R. Kashani. Jerusalem, 1976.

Gat, B.   "The First Medical Institutions in Eretz-Israel," in *Jerusalem, Studies of Eretz-Israel*. Edited by M. Ish-Shalom, M. Benayahu and A. Shoḥat. Jerusalem, 1953, pp. 259-272 (Hebrew).

――――   *The Jewish Community in Eretz-Israel (1840-1881)*. Jerusalem, 1963 (Hebrew).

Geikie, C.   *The Holy Land and the Bible*. London, 1891.

Gelber, N.N.	"The Palestine Question, 1840-1842," *Zion*, IV (1930), pp. 44-46, and appendices, pp. 1-41 (Hebrew).
——	"Additional Material on the History of the Foundation of the 'Laemel' School at Jerusalem," *Jerusalem Quarterly History*, I (1948), pp. 95-108; 199-213 (Hebrew).
——	"Dr. Albert Cohn and His Visit to Jerusalem," *Jerusalem Quarterly History*, II (1949), pp. 175-195 (Hebrew).
Gellis, J.	*Jerusalem Personalities*. Jerusalem, 1962 (Hebrew).
Geramb, M.J.	*Pélérinage à Jérusalem et au Mont Sinai en 1831, 1832 et 1833.* Tournay, 1836.
Gerber, H.	"The Ottoman Administration of the Sanjak of Jerusalem 1890-1908," *Hamizrah He-hadash*, XXIV (1974), pp. 1-33 (Hebrew).
Gibb, H. R. and Bowen, H., *Islamic Society and the West*. Oxford, 1950.	
Gidney, W.T.	*The History of the London Society for Promoting Christianity amongst the Jews.* London, 1905.
Goldmann, I.	"The General Outook for Our Brethren in the Holy Land," *Ha-Assif*, I, 2nd series (1885), pp. 121-154; *Ha-Assif*, III (1886), pp. 69-98; "Charitable Organizations in Jerusalem," *Ha-Assif*, IV (1888), pp. 17-40; "Outlook on Urban and Agricultural Settlement in Eretz-Israel in the Last Four Years (1885-1888)," *Ha-Assif*, V (1889), pp. 75-95 (Hebrew).
Goodman, P.	*Moses Montefiore*. Philadelphia, 1943.
Goodrich-Freer, Adela M., *Inner Jerusalem*. London, 1904.	
Gorion, M.	*Introduction to the History of Local Government in Israel.* Jerusalem, 1957 (Hebrew).
Grabill, L.	*Protestant Diplomacy and the Near East: Missionary Influence on American Policy 1810-1927.* Minneapolis, 1971.
Graham, J.	*Jerusalem, its Missions, Schools, Convents....* London, 1858.
Graham, S.	*With the Russian Pilgrims to Jerusalem.* London, 1916.
Granovski, A.	*Land Tenure in Eretz-Israel.* Tel Aviv, 1949 (Hebrew).
Grayevsky, P.	*Avnei Zikkaron, Memorial Stones of Jerusalem*, vols. I-VI. Jerusalem, 1928-1929 (Hebrew).
——	*A Tribute to the First Lovers of Zion*, vols. I-X (Hebrew).
——	*From the Hidden Treasures of Jerusalem*, vols. I-XXIV, Jerusalem, 1927-1935 (Hebrew).
——	*Jewish Resistance to the Mission, from 1834 until Today.* Jerusalem, 1935 (Hebrew).
——	*The Visit of the Princes of England in Jerusalem.* Jerusalem, 1935 (Hebrew).
——	*Sefer Ha-yishuv: Jewish Settlement Oustide the Old City.* Jerusalem, 1939 (Hebrew).
Grunwald, K.	"Jewish Schools under Foreign Flags in Ottoman Palestine," in *Studies on Palestine during the Ottoman Period*. Edited by M. Ma'oz. Jerusalem, 1975, pp. 164-174.
Guérin, V.	*Description de la Palestine, Judée....* Paris, 1868.
——	*Terre Sainte.* Paris, 1883.
Gurevich, P.	*The Jewish Population of Jerusalem.* Jerusalem, 1940.

409

Guthe, D.   "Die Griechisch-Orthodoxe Kirche im heiligen Land," *ZDPV,* XII (1899), pp. 81-91.

Halevy, Shoshanna.   *The First Hebrew Books Printed in Jerusalem in the Second Half of the Nineteenth Century (1841-1890).* Jerusalem, 1975 (Hebrew).

Halsted, T.D.   *Our Missions: Being a History of the Principal Missionary Transactions of the London Society for Promoting Christianity amongst the Jews from its Foundation in 1809 to the Present Year.* London, 1866.

Hamburger, H.   *Three Worlds,* vols. I-III. Jerusalem, 1939-1946 (Hebrew).

Hanauer, J.E.   *Walks in and around Jerusalem.* London, 1885; 2nd edition, London, 1926.

Hannani, I.   "Artisans in Jerusalem," *Jerusalem Quarterly History,* III (1951), pp. 160-184 (Hebrew).

——   *The Enlightenment in Eretz-Israel.* 2nd revised edition. Jerusalem, 1974 (Hebrew).

Harper, A.H.   *Walks in Palestine.* London, 1888.

Harry, M.   *Das kleine Mädchen von Jerusalem.* Berlin, 1928.

Harsford, H.C. (ed.)   *Herman Melville, Journal of a Visit to Europe and the Levant.* Princeton, 1955.

Hartmann, R.   "Nebi Musa," *MNDPV,* XXXIII (1910), pp. 65-75.

Hayut, A.   *Sixty-Three Years in Jerusalem.* Jerusalem, 1953 (Hebrew).

Hechler, W.H.   *The Jerusalem Bishopric* (Documents with Translations). London, 1883.

Hedin, S.   *Jerusalem.* Leipzig, 1918.

Henniker, F.   *Notes during a Visit....* London, 1823.

Herbert, Lady M.E.   *Cradle Lands: Egypt, Syria, Palestine....* New York, 1869.

Hertzberg, H.W.   *75 Jahre deutsche-evangelische Gemeinde.* Jerusalem—Leipzig, 1927.

Herzl, T.   *The Complete Diaries of Theodor Herzl.* Edited by R. Patai. London—New York, 1960.

Heyd, U.   *Ottoman Documents on Palestine, 1552-1615.* Oxford, 1960.

——   "Jerusalem under the Mameluks and the Turks," in *Jerusalem through the Ages.* Jerusalem, 1978, pp. 193-202 (Hebrew).

Hilprecht, H.V.   *Explorations in Bible Lands during the Nineteenth Century.* Edinburgh, 1903, pp. 579-622.

Hirschberg, A.S.   *The Path of the New Yishuv in Eretz Israel.* Photocopy of the Vilna edition of 1901. Jerusalem, 1979 (Hebrew).

——   *In Oriental Lands.* Photocopy of the Vilna edition of 1910. Jerusalem, 1980 (Hebrew).

Hirschberg, H.Z.   "The Turning-Point in the History of Jerusalem in the Nineteenth Century," in *Yad Yoseph Rivlin,* pp. 78-107 (Hebrew).

Hodder, E.   *On Holy Ground.* Edinburgh, 1873.

Hofman, Y.   *The Activities of Muḥammad ʿAli in Syria.* Doctoral dissertation, Hebrew University; Jerusalem, 1963 (Hebrew).

——	"The Administration of Syria and Palestine under Egyptian Rule (1831-1840)," in *Studies on Palestine during the Ottoman Period.* Edited by M. Ma'oz. Jerusalem, 1975, pp. 311-333.
Hopkins, I.W.J.	"The Four Quarters of Jerusalem," *Palestine Exploration Quarterly*, CIII (1971), pp. 68-85.
Hopwood, D.	*The Russian Presence in Syria and Palestine, 1843-1914: Church and Politics in the Near East.* Oxford, 1969.
Horne, T.H.	*Landscape Illustrations of the Bible....* London, 1836.
Horowitz, A. (ed.)	*Mosad Ha-yesod: Selections from the History of Va'ad Ha-kelali Kneset Yisrael.* 2nd enlarged edition. Jerusalem, 1958 (Hebrew).
Hurlbut, J.L.	*Travelling in the Holy Land.* New York, 1900.
Hyamson, A.M.	*The British Consulate in Jerusalem in Relation to the Jews of Palestine 1838-1914.* London, 1939-1941.

I.D. 1215 (Naval Intelligence Division, Great Britain). *A Handbook of Syria (including Palestine).* London, 1920.

Ilan, S.	"The Germans in Nineteenth-Century Jerusalem and Their Influence on the City's Development." Research paper, Department of Geography, Hebrew University; Jerusalem, 1972 (Hebrew).
Illes, S.	*Jerusalem aus der Vogelschau. Verlag und Eigenstham von Stephan Illes in Jerusalem.* Wien, [1874?].

Irby, C.L. and Mangles, J., *Travels through... Palestine... in 1817-1818.* London, 1823.

Isaacs, A.A.	*The Dead Sea... during a Journey to Palestine in 1856-1857.* London, 1857.
——	*A Pictorial Tour in the Holy Land.* London, 1862.
Ish-Shalom, M.	*Christian Travels in the Holy Land, Descriptions and Sources on the History of the Jews in Palestine.* Tel Aviv, 1965 (Hebrew).

Jessup, H.H.	*Fifty-Three Years in Syria.* New York, *c.* 1910.
Joliffe, T.R.	*Letters from Palestine, Descriptive of a Tour through Galilee and Judaea with Some Account of the Dead Sea.* London, 1819.
Jones, Yolande.	"British Military Surveys of Palestine and Syria 1840-1 (Jerusalem Map Scale 1:4,800)," *Cartographic Journal of the British Cartographic Society*, X (1973), pp. 29-41.
Jowett, M.	*Christian Researches in the Holy Land in 1823-1824.* London, 1826.

Kamieniec, Menaḥem Mendel of, *Korot Ha'itim....* Jerusalem, 1975 (Hebrew). (First published in Vilna, 1839 [Hebrew].)

Kaniel, Y.	"Les problèmes de l'éducation à Jérusalem au XIXe siècle," in *Zakhor Le-Abraham—Mélanges Abraham Elmaleh.* Edited by H.Z. Hirschberg. Jerusalem, 1972, pp. 140-168 (Hebrew).
——	"Social Relations between Sephardim and Ashkenazim in the... Nineteenth Century," *Vatiqin* (1975), pp. 47-65 (Hebrew).

411

Katzburg, N.   "Features of the Development of Jerusalem outside the City Walls," in *Yad Yoseph Rivlin*, pp. 37-46 (Hebrew).

——   "Documents of the History of the Ottoman Law concerning the Acquisition of Property by Foreign Nationals," in *Yad Yoseph Rivlin*, pp. 151-159 (Hebrew).

——   "Cultural Conflicts in the Jewish World, and the 'Old Yishuv' in Jerusalem in the Nineteenth Century," *Chapters*, I (1973), pp. 301-309 (Hebrew).

Kean, J.   *Among the Holy Places*. London, 1894.

Keep ye Justice and do Righteousness (*Shimru Mishpat va-'asu Tzedaka*; pamphlet). Jerusalem, 1903 (Hebrew).

Kellner, J.   *For Zion's Sake: World Jewry's Efforts to Relieve Distress in the Yishuv 1869-1882*. Jerusalem, 1976 (Hebrew).

Kelly, W.K.   *Syria and the Holy Land*. London, 1844.

Kelman, J.   *The Holy Land*. London, 1912.

Kenth, S.H.   *Gath to the Cedars: Travels in the Holy Land and Palmyra during 1872*. London, 1874.

Kingslake, A.W.   *"Eothen" or Traces of Travel*. New York, 1854.

Klausner, J.   *The Zionist Movement in Russia*, vol. I: *The Awakening of a People* (Jerusalem, 1962); vols. II-III: *From Kattowitz to Basel* (Jerusalem, 1965) (Hebrew).

Kollat, I.   "Organization of the Yishuv and Crystallization of its Political Stance until World War I," *Keshet*, IV (1970), pp. 17-28 (Hebrew).

Kümmel, A.   *Karte der Materialien zur Topographie des alten Jerusalem (Scale 1:2,800)*. Leipzig, 1904.

Lagerlöf, Selma.   *Jerusalem* (Translated by J. Bröchner). London, 1903.

Lamartine, A.   *Souvenirs, Impressions....* Paris, 1835.

Leven, N.   *Cinquante Ans d'Histoire L'Alliance Israélite Universelle (1860-1910)*. Paris, 1911.

Levontin, Z.D.   *To the Land of Our Forefathers*, vol. I: *The History of Hovevei Zion, 1882-1889*; vol. II: *The History of the Zionist Movement, 1901-1914*. Tel Aviv, 1924 (Hebrew).

Lewis, B.   *The Middle East and the West*. London, 1964.

——   *The Emergence of Modern Turkey*. London, 1968.

Liebtrut, F.   *Reise nach dem Morgenland... Jerusalem, und das heilige Land*. Hamburg, 1854.

Liévin de Hamme, Le Frère, *Guide-Indicateur des Sanctuaires et Lieux historiques de la Terre-Sainte*. Jerusalem, 1869.

——   *Guide to the Holy Places and Historical Sites in the Holy Land*. Belgium, 1875.

Light, H.   *Travels in Egypt, Nubia, the Holy Land, Mount Lebanon and Cyprus*. London, 1818.

Lindsay, A.W.C.   *Letters on Egypt, Edom and the Holy Land*. London, 1839.

Lortet, D.   *La Syrie d'aujourd'hui. Voyages dans la Phénicie, le Liban et la Judée*. Paris, 1884.

Luke, H.C. and Keith-Roach, E., *The Handbook of Palestine*. London, 1922.

Luncz, A.M.	*Ways of Zion and Jerusalem*. Jerusalem, 1876 (Hebrew).
——	*Jahrbuch*. Wien, 1882.
——	*Guide to Eretz-Israel and Syria*. Jerusalem, 1891 (Hebrew).
——	*Jerusalem Yearbook for the Diffusion of an Accurate Knowledge of Ancient and Modern Palestine*. 13 vols.: Jerusalem, I (1882); II (1887); III (1889); IV (1892); V (1898-1901); VI (1902-1904); VII (1907); VIII (1909); IX (1911); X (1914); XI-XII (1917); XIII (1919) (Hebrew).
——	*Litterarischer Palästina Almanach*. 21 vols., 1896-1916 (Hebrew).
——	*Selected Essays: Ways of Zion and Jerusalem*. Arranged and edited by G. Kressel. Jerusalem, 1970 (Hebrew).
de Luynes, A.M., le Duc, *Voyage d'Exploration à la Mer Morte....* Paris, 1874.	
Lynch, W.F.	*Narrative of the United States Expedition to the River Jordan and the Dead Sea*. Philadelphia, 1849.
Macalister, R.A.S. and Masterman, E.W.G., "Occasional Papers on the Modern Inhabitants of Palestine," *PEF QSt,* 1905, pp. 48-60; 343-356; 1906, pp. 33-49; 110-114; 221-223; 286-291.	
MacGregor, J.	*The Rob Roy on the Jordan*. London, 1886.
Macleod, N.	*Half Hours in the Holy Land....* London, 1884.
Madden, R.R.	*Travels in Turkey, Egypt, Nubia and Palestine in 1824-1827.* London, 1829.
Madox, J.	*Excursions in the Holy Land....* London, 1834.
Malachi, A.R.	*Studies in the History of the Old Yishuv*. Tel Aviv, 1971 (Hebrew).
Manning, S.	*Those Holy Fields....* London, 1874.
Ma'oz, M.	*Ottoman Reforms in Syria and Palestine 1840-1861....* Oxford, 1968.
——	"Jerusalem in the Last Hundred Years of Turkish Ottoman Rule," *Chapters,* I (1973), pp. 260-272 (Hebrew).
——	"Changes in the Position of the Jewish Communities of Palestine and Syria in the Mid-Nineteenth Century," in *Studies on Palestine during the Ottoman Period*. Edited by M. Ma'oz. Jerusalem, 1975, pp. 142-163.
Margoliouth, M.	*A Pilgrimage to the Land of My Fathers*. London, 1850.
Marston, T.E.	*Britain's Imperial Role in the Red Sea Area 1800-1878.* Hamden, Connecticut, 1961.
Martineau, H.	*Eastern Life....* London, 1850.
Maschopoulous, Nicephore, *La Terre Sainte: Essai sur l'histoire politique et diplomatique des Lieux Saints de Chrétienté*. Athens, 1957.	
Masterman, E.W.G.	*Hygiene and Diseases in Palestine in Modern and Biblical Times.* London, n.d.
——	"Palestine, its Resources and Suitability for Colonization," *Geographical Journal,* L (1917), pp. 12-32.
Medebielle, P.	*The Diocese of the Latin Patriarchate of Jerusalem*. Jerusalem, 1963.

413

Meisel, J.   *History of the Sir Moses Montefiore Testimonial Fund.* Jerusalem, 1939 (Hebrew).

——   "The Jewish Settlement in Eretz-Israel in 1839," *Sefunot*, VI (1962), pp. 425-479 (Hebrew).

Merrill, S.   *East of the Jordan: A Record of Travel and Observation in the Country of Moab, Gilead and Bashan during the Years 1875-7.* New York, 1883.

Mertens, P.A.   "Centenaire d'un livre: le 'Guide de T.S.' du fr. Liévin de Hamme," in *La Terre Sainte*, Jerusalem, 1969, pp. 322-329.

Meyer, H.M.Z.   *Jerusalem—Maps and Views.* Jerusalem, 1971.

Michlin, H.M.   *In the Mirror of the Ages.* Tel Aviv, 1950 (Hebrew).

Millard, D.   *A Journal of Travels in... the Holy Land.* Rochester, England, 1843.

Monro, V.   *Summer Rambles in Syria....* London, 1835.

Montagu, S. and Asher, A., *Report to the Committee of the Sir Moses Montefiore Testimonial Fund.* London, 1875.

Montefiore, [Lady] Judith, *Private Journal of a Visit to Egypt and Palestine (1827).* Jerusalem, 1975. (First published in London, 1836; only pp. 128-234 reproduced.)

——   *Notes from a Private Journal of a Visit to Egypt and Palestine (1839).* London, 1844.

Montefiore, [Sir] M. and Montefiore, Lady J., *Diaries of Sir Moses and Lady Montefiore.* Edited by L. Loewe. Chicago, 1895.

Mott, M.   *Stones of Palestine.* London, 1865.

Munk, S.   *Palästina....* Edited by M.A. Levy. Breslau, 1871.

Murray, J.   *Handbook for Travellers in Syria and Palestine.* London, 1875.

Nahon, S.U.   *Sir Moses Montefiore: A Life in the Service of Jewry.* Jerusalem, 1965.

Neil, J.   *Palestine Re-Peopled.* London, 1883.

Neumann, B.   *Die heilige Stadt und deren Bewohner.* Hamburg, 1877.

Norov, A.S.   *Reise nach dem heiligen Lande im Jahre 1835.* St. Petersburg, 1838.

Nugent, [Lord].   *Lands, Classical and Sacred.* London, 1845.

Olin, S.   *Travels in Egypt... and the Holy Land.* New York, 1843.

Oliphant, L.   *The Land of Gilead.* London, 1880.

——   *Haifa, or Life in Modern Palestine.* London, 1887.

Orelli, G.   *Durch's heilige Land.* Basel, 1878.

Osborn, H.S.   *Palestine Past and Present.* Philadelphia, 1859.

Our Spiritual Possessions in Jerusalem: This is the Law of the House (Rekhushenu ha-Ruhani bi-Yrushalayim: Zot Torat ha-Bayit; Book of regulations of the Hayyei Olam yeshiva). Jerusalem, 1929.

Paleolog, F.   *Imperatorskoe pravoslavnoe Palestinskoe Obshchestvo; Ocherk ego deiatel'nost' za 1882-1890 gg.* St. Petersburg, 1891.

Palestine Office of the Zionist Organization, *Censi of Jews of Palestine*, vol. I: *Judaea.* Jaffa, 1918 (Hebrew).

Pardieu, C.   *Excursion en orient... la Palestine...* Paris, 1851.

Parkes, J.W.   *A History of Palestine from 135 A.D. to Modern Times.* New York, 1949.

Patterson, J.L.   *Journal of a Tour in Egypt, Palestine....* London, 1852.

Paxton, J.D.   *Letters from Palestine....* London, 1839.

Petermann, H.   *Reisen im Orient.* Leipzig, 1860-1861.

Petrozzi, M.T.   "The Franciscan Printing Press," *Christian News from Israel,* XXII, no. 2[6] (1971), pp. 64-69.

Pfeiffer, I.   *Visit to the Holy Land....* London, 1852.

Pierotti, E.   *Jerusalem Explored....* London, 1864.

——   *Customs and Traditions in Palestine....* London, 1864.

——   *Plan de Jérusalem ancienne et moderne. Topographie ancienne et moderne de Jérusalem.* Lausanne, 1870.

Pollack, A.N.   *The History of the Arabs from Their Beginnings until Today.* Jerusalem, 1946 (Hebrew).

Porath, Y.   *The Emergence of the Palestinian-Arab National Movement, 1918-1929.* Tel Aviv, 1974.

——   "The Political Awakening of the Palestinian Arabs...," in *Studies on Palestine during the Ottoman Period.* Edited by M. Ma'oz. Jerusalem, 1975, pp. 351-381.

Porter, J.I.   *The Giant Cities of Bashan and Syria's Holy Places.* London, 1869.

——   *Jerusalem, Bethany and Bethlehem.* London, 1887.

Porush, M.M.   *Fifty Years within the Walls: Essays.* Jerusalem, 1978 (Hebrew).

Press, J.   *Eretz-Israel and South-Syrian Travel Handbook.* Jerusalem, 1921 (Hebrew).

——   *History of the Laemel School in Jerusalem.* Jerusalem, 1936 (Hebrew).

——   *Studies in the Geography of Eretz-Israel and Biblical Topography.* Jerusalem, 1961 (Hebrew).

——   *A Hundred Years of Jerusalem: Memoirs of Two Generations.* Jerusalem, 1964 (Hebrew).

Prokesch, A.   *Reise ins heilige Land im Jahre 1829.* Wien, 1831.

Reicher, M.   *The Gates of Jerusalem.* Lemberg, 1870 (Hebrew).

Richardson, R.   *Travels along the Mediterranean....* London, 1822.

Richter, O.F.   *Wallfahrten im Morgenland....* Berlin, 1822.

Ritchie, W.   *Azuba or the Forsaken Land.* Edinburgh, 1856.

Ritter, C.   *The Comparative Geography of Palestine and the Sinaitic Peninsula.* Translated and adapted by W.L. Gage. Edinburgh, 1866.

Rivlin, A.B.   *The History of Jewish Settlement in the Nineteenth Century.* Tel Aviv, 1966 (Hebrew).

——   "Craftsmanship and Commerce in the Jewish Community of Jerusalem in the Last Century," *Sinai,* LXI (1967), pp. 185-190 (Hebrew).

Roberts, D.   *The Holy Land....* London, 1842-1849.

Robinson, E. and Smith, E., *Biblical Researches in Palestine*.... London, 1841.

—— *Later Biblical Researches*. London, 1856.

Rogers, M.E.   *Domestic Life in Palestine*. London, 1862.

Röhricht, R.   *Bibliotheca Geographica Palestinae von 333 bis 1878*. Berlin, 1890.

Rosen, F.   *Oriental Memoirs of a German Diplomat*. London, 1930.

Rosenan, M.J. and Wilinsky, C.F., "Public Health" (Report of experts submitted to *The Joint Palestine Survey Commission*). Boston, 1928, pp. 95-104.

Roser, J.   *Tagebuch meiner Reise nach... Syrien im Jahre 1834 bis 1835*. Mergentheim, 1836.

Rothschild, M.M.   *The "Halukka" as an Expression of the Attitude of Diaspora Jewry to the Jewish Community in Eretz-Israel, 1810-1860*. Jerusalem, 1969 (Hebrew).

Ruppin, A.   *Der Ausbau des Landes Israel*. Berlin, 1919.

——   *Soziologie der Juden*. Berlin, 1931.

Sabry, M.   *L'Empire Egyptien sous Mohamed-Ali et la question d'Orient (1811-1849)*. Paris, 1930.

Salomon, Yoel Moshe, *Yehuda vi-Yrushalayim: Yoel Moshe Salomon's Newspaper, 1877-1878*. Edited by G. Kressel. Jerusalem, 1956 (Hebrew).

Samuel Gobat, Bishop of Jerusalem, His Life and Work. London, 1884 (author not specified).

Sanjian, A.K.   *The Armenian Communities in Syria under Ottoman Dominion*. Cambridge, Mass., 1965.

Schattner, I.   *The Map of Eretz-Israel and Its History*. Jerusalem, 1951 (Hebrew).

Scherer, H.   *Eine Oster-Reise ins heilige Land in Briefen an Freunde*. Frankfurt, 1860.

Schick, C.   "Die Baugeschichte der Stadt Jerusalem," *ZDPV*, XVII (1894-95), pp. 261-276; "Karte der näheren Umgebung von Jerusalem, Masstab 1:10,000," *ibid*. XVIII, Tafel 4 (1894-95).

——   "The Quarter Bab-Hytta, Jerusalem," *PEF QSt* (1896), pp. 122-133.

——   "Preparations made for the Visit of the German Emperor," *PEF QSt* (1899), pp. 116-117.

Schirion, I.   *Memoirs*. Jerusalem, 1943 (Hebrew).

Schmelz, M.O.   "Some Demographic Peculiarities of the Jews of Jerusalem in the Nineteenth Century," in *Studies on Palestine during the Ottoman Period*. Edited by M. Ma'oz. Jerusalem, 1975, pp. 119-142.

Schneller, L.   *Vader Schneller, ein Patriarch der Evangelischen zending in het Heiligen Land*. Rotterdam, 1908.

Scholz, J.M.A.   *Reise in die Gegend zwischen... Ägypten, Palästina und Syrien in den Jahren 1820 und 1821*. Leipzig, 1822.

Schubert, G.H.   *Reise in das Morgenland in den Jahren 1836 und 1837*. Erlangen, 1838-1839.

Schultz, E.G.   *Jerusalem, eine Vorlesung*. Berlin, 1845.

416

Schulz, E.W.   *Reise in das gelobte Land.* Muellheim, 1852.

Schwarz, J.   *The Produce of the Land,* Jerusalem, 1845; third edition, revised and enlarged, published by A.M. Luncz, Jerusalem, 1900 (Hebrew; English translation by Isaac Leeser: *Descriptive Geography and Brief Historical Sketch of Palestine,* Philadelphia 1850).

——   *The Gates of Jerusalem — Documents for the History of Jerusalem and its Inhabitants (The Letters of Rabbi Joseph Schwarz).* Edited by B. Landau. Jerusalem, 1969 (Hebrew).

Seetzen, U.J.   *Reisen durch Syrien, Palästina....* Berlin, 1854-1859.

Sepp, J.N.   *Jerusalem und das heilige Land.* Hunter, 1863.

Shapira, I.   *Jerusalem — the Old City: Its History and Way of Life.* Jerusalem, 1945.

Sieber, F.W.   *Reise von Cairo nach Jerusalem....* Leipzig, 1823.

Skinner, T.   *Adventures during a Journey... and the Holy Land.* London, 1836.

Smith, G.A.   *Jerusalem: The Topography, Economics and History....* London, 1877.

Sokhovolsky, A.   "The Ottoman Land Law," *Keshet,* IV (1970), pp. 72-90 (Hebrew).

Sokolov, N.   *Eretz Ḥemda.* Warsaw, 1885 (Hebrew).

Solomon, M.   *Three Generations in the Yishuv, 1812-1913,* vol. II. Jerusalem, 1951 (Hebrew).

Spafford Vester, Bertha, *Our Jerusalem: an American Family in the Holy City 1881-1949.* London, 1951.

Spencer, J.A.   *The East: Sketches of Travels in Egypt and the Holy Land.* London, 1850.

Spyridon, S.N.   "Annals of Palestine 1821-1841," *Journal of the Palestine Oriental Society,* XVIII, nos. 1-2 (1938), pp. 63-132.

Stanley, A.P.   *Sermons preached before His Royal Highness, the Prince of Wales....* London, 1863.

——   *Sinai and Palestine.* London, 1864.

Stebbing, H.   *The Christians in Palestine or Scenes of Sacred History Illustrated from Sketches Taken on the Spot by W.H. Bartlett.* London, 1847.

Stephens, J.L.   *Incidents of Travel in Egypt, Arabia Petraea and the Holy Land.* New York, 1837.

Stewart, R.W.   *The Tent and the Khan: a Journey in Sinai and Palestine.* London, 1857.

Strauss, F.A.   *Sinai und Golgotha: Reise in das Morgenland.* Berlin, 1847.

Swift, J.F.   *Going to Jericho....* New York, 1868.

Taylor, B. and Reybaud, L., *La Syrie, l'Égypte, la Palestine....* Paris, 1839.

Taylor, I.J.S.   *La Syrie, la Palestine et la Judée.* Paris, 1855.

Temperly, H.   *England and the Near East: The Crimea.* London, 1936.

Thackeray, W.M.   *The Irish Sketch-book; and Notes of a Journey from Cornhill to Grand Cairo.* London, 1869.

Thomas, Margaret.   *Two Years in Palestine and Syria.* London, 1900.

Thomson, W.M.   *The Land and the Book....* New York, 1859.

Tibawi, A.L.   *British Interests in Palestine 1800-1901.* Oxford, 1961.

———   *American Interests in Syria 1800-1901.* Oxford, 1967.

———   *A Modern History of Syria including Lebanon and Palestine.* Edinburgh, 1969.

———   *Islamic Education, its Traditions and Modernizations in the Arab National System.* London, 1972.

Tobler, T.   *Lustreise ins Morgenland.* Zurich, 1839.

———   *Reise von Jerusalem... im Jahre 1846.* Ausland, 1846.

———   *Denkblätter aus Jerusalem.* Constance, 1853.

———   *Topographie von Jerusalem.* Berlin, 1853-1854.

———   *Dritte Wanderung nach Palästina im Jahre 1857.* Gotha, 1859.

———   *Planographie von Jerusalem (Memoir to the Plan of the Town and Environs of Jerusalem...,* by C.W.M. Van de Velde). Gotha, 1857.

———   *Nazareth in Palästina nebst Anhang d. vierten Wanderung.* Berlin, 1868.

Tokachinsky, I.M.   "The Court of Rabbi Yehuda the Ḥassid," in A.M. Luncz, *Almanac,* IX (1904), pp. 121-167 (Hebrew).

———   *The Holy City and its Inhabitants.* Jerusalem, 1969-1970 (Hebrew).

Trietsch, D.   *Palästina Handbuch.* Berlin, 1922.

Tristram, H.B.   *The Land of Israel....* London, 1866.

Triwaks, I. (ed.).   *The Trial of the Wall,* Tel Aviv, 1931 (Hebrew).

Triwaks, I. and Steinman, E., *Book of a Hundred Years.* Tel Aviv, 1938 (Hebrew).

Turner, W.   *Journal of a Tour in the Levant.* London, 1820.

Twain, Mark.   *The Innocents Abroad.* London and Glasgow, 1869.

Ussishkin, M.   *Seventieth Anniversary Volume.* Edited by R. Benjamin. Jerusalem, 1934 (Hebrew).

Van de Velde, C.W.M.   *Narrative of a Journey through Syria and Palestine in 1851.* London, 1854.

———   *Le Pays d'Israel. Collection de cent vues prises d'après nature dans la Syrie et la Palestine.* Paris, 1857.

Vereté, M.   "Why was a British Consulate Established in Jerusalem?" *English Historical Review,* LXXXV (1970), pp. 316-345.

Verney, N. and Dambmann, G., *Les puissances étrangères dans le Levant, en Syrie et en Palestine.* Paris, 1900.

Vilnay, Z.   *Jerusalem the Capital of Israel: The Old City and the New City,* vols. I, II. Jerusalem, various editions (Hebrew).

———   *The Holy Land in Old Prints and Maps.* Jerusalem, 1965.

Vincent, J.H., Lee, J.W., and Bain, R.E.M., *Earthly Footsteps of the Man of Galilee....* New York, 1894.

Vincent, L.H.   *Jérusalem: Recherches de Topographie, d'Archéologie et d'Histoire.* Paris, 1912.

Visino, J.N.   *Meine Wanderung nach Palästina.* Passeau, 1840.

Wallace, A.   *The Desert of the Holy Land.* Edinburgh, 1867.

Warburton, B.G.   *The Crescent and the Cross....* London, 1844.

Warren, C.   *Underground Jerusalem....* London, 1876.

Warren, C. and Conder, C.R., *Survey of Western Palestine: Jerusalem.* London, 1884.

Wartensleben-Schwissen, A.G., *Jerusalem.* Berlin, 1870.

Watson, C.M.   *The Story of Jerusalem.* London, 1918.

Weill, R.   *La Cité de David.* Paris, 1920.

Weinstein, M.   "The Religious and Social Life of Jerusalem in the Eighteenth Century," *Chapters,* I, pp. 178-188 (Hebrew).

Weiss, J.A.   *At Your Gates, Jerusalem — Reminiscences and Impressions.* Jerusalem, 1969 (Hebrew).

Whaley, Buck.   *Buck Whaley's Memoirs, including his Journey to Jerusalem...* (written 1797). Edited by E. Sullivan. London, 1906.

Wilde, W.R.   *Narrative of a Voyage to... Palestine.* Dublin, 1844.

Williams, G.   *The Holy City....* 1st edition, London, 1841; 2nd edition, London, 1849.

Wilson, C.W.   *Ordnance Survey of Jerusalem made in the years 1864 to 1865.* Southampton, 1866.

Wilson, C.W. (ed.).   *Picturesque Palestine, Sinai and Egypt.* London, 1880.

Wilson, C.W. and Warren, E., *The Recovery of Jerusalem....* Jerusalem, 1871.

Wilson, E.L.   *In Scripture Lands.* London, 1891.

Wilson, J.   *The Lands of the Bible Visited and Described....* London, 1847.

Wilson, W.R.   *Travels in the Holy Land....* London, 1822.

Wittman, W.   *Travels in Turkey, Asia Minor and across the Desert into Egypt, during the Years 1799, 1800 and 1801....* London, 1803.

Wolff, P.   "Zur neueren Geschichte Jerusalem von 1843-1884," *ZDPV,* VIII (1885), pp. 1-15.

Woodcook, W.J.   *Scripture Lands....* London, 1849.

Wortabet, G.M.   *Bayroot, Syria and the Syrians....* London, 1856.

Ya'ari, A.   "The Suffering of Ashkenazi Jews in Jerusalem at the Beginning of the Nineteenth Century," *Sinai,* V (1939-1940), pp. 270-278 (Hebrew).

——   *Travels in Eretz-Israel.* Tel Aviv, 1946 (Hebrew).

——   *Eretz-Israel Emissaries.* Jerusalem, 1951 (Hebrew).

——   *Letters from the Land of Israel.* 2nd edition. Ramat Gan, 1971 (Hebrew).

——   *Memoirs of Eretz-Israel.* 2nd edition. Ramat Gan, 1974 (Hebrew).

Ya'ari-Polskin, Y.   *Baron Edmond Rothschild (The Famous Benefactor),* vol. I. Tel Aviv, 1930 (Hebrew).

Yardeni, Galia.   *The Hebrew Press in Eretz-Israel 1863-1904.* Tel Aviv, 1969 (Hebrew).

Yehoshua, J.   *Childhood in the Old City of Jerusalem,* vol. II: *At Home and in the Street,* Jerusalem, 1966; vol. III: *Sages of Old Jerusalem,* Jerusalem, 1968 (Hebrew).

Yehuda, I.Y.	"The Wailing Wall," *Zion*, III (1929), pp. 95-163 (Hebrew).
Yellin, D.	"Ancient Jerusalem," in *In Jerusalem*, vol. I. Jaffa, 1913 (Hebrew).
____	*The Writings of David Yellin*, vol. I: *The Jerusalem of Yesterday (Letters from Jerusalem to "Hamelitz," 1869-1904)*. Jerusalem, 1972 (Hebrew).
____	*The Writings of David Yellin*, vol. II: *From Dan to Beersheba, Walks and Trips*. Jerusalem, 1973 (Hebrew).
Yellin, J.I.	*Our Forefathers: Chapters in History and Local Culture, Personalities and Stories*. Jerusalem, 1966 (Hebrew).
Yellin, Y.	*Memoirs of a Native of Jerusalem, 1830-1918*. Jerusalem, 1928 (Hebrew).
Zander, W.	*Israel and the Holy Places of Christendom*. London, 1971.
Zimmerman, K.I.	*Karten und Pläne zur Topographie des alten Jerusalem*. Basel, 1876.
Zimpel, E.	*Die Israeliten in Jerusalem*. Stuttgart, 1852.

Zuta, H.A. and Sukenik, L., *Our Country: Guide to Eretz-Israel and the Neighboring Countries*, vol. I: *Jerusalem and its Environs*. Jerusalem, 1920 (Hebrew).

List of Illustrations and Maps

422

Index of Persons

Index of Place Names

433

Index of Selected Subjects

437